DEATH NOTE

Black Edition
V

Story by Tsugumi Ohba   Art by Takeshi Obata

D1247585

Original Graphic Novel Edition
Volume 9

Original Graphic Novel Edition
Volume 10

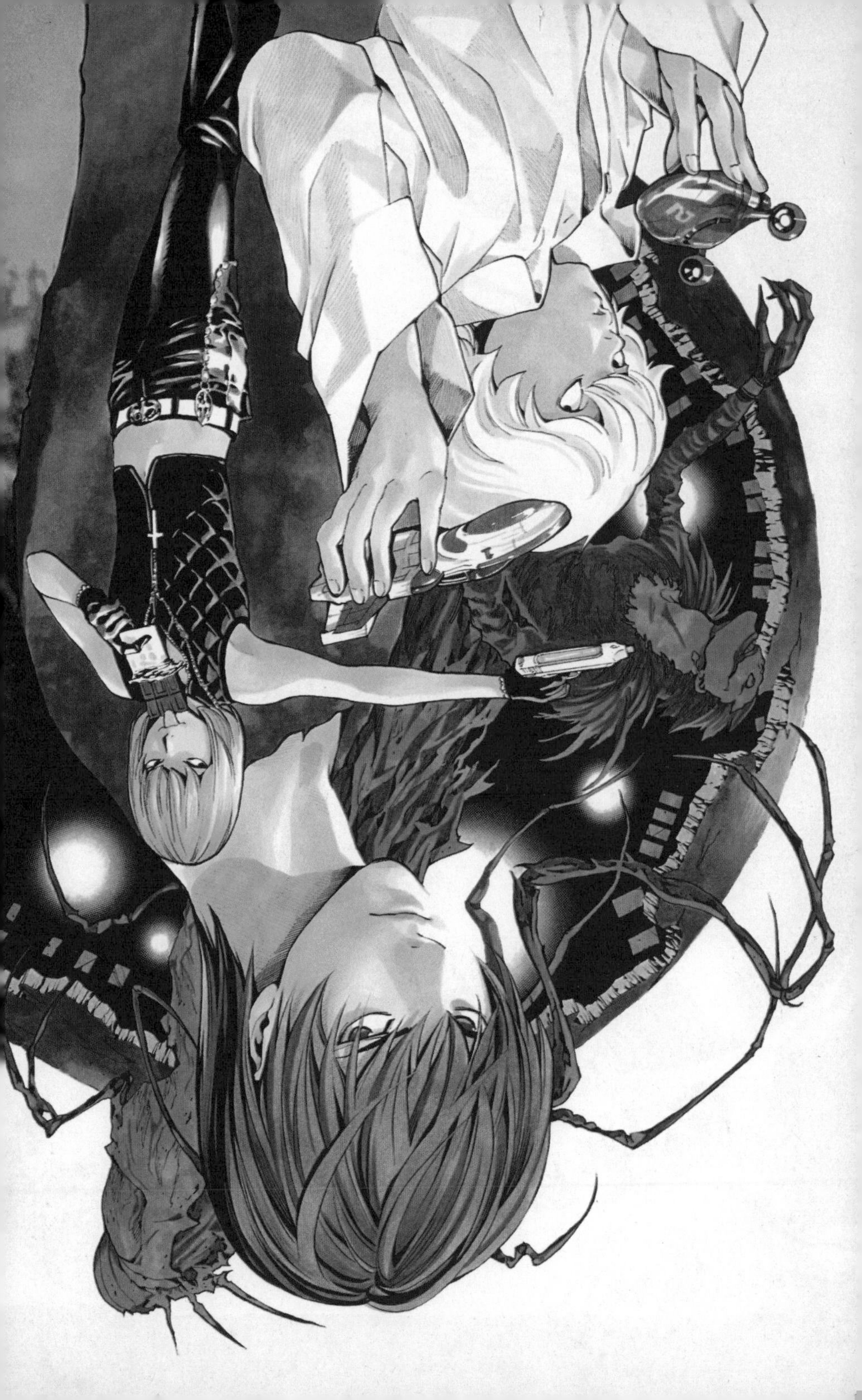

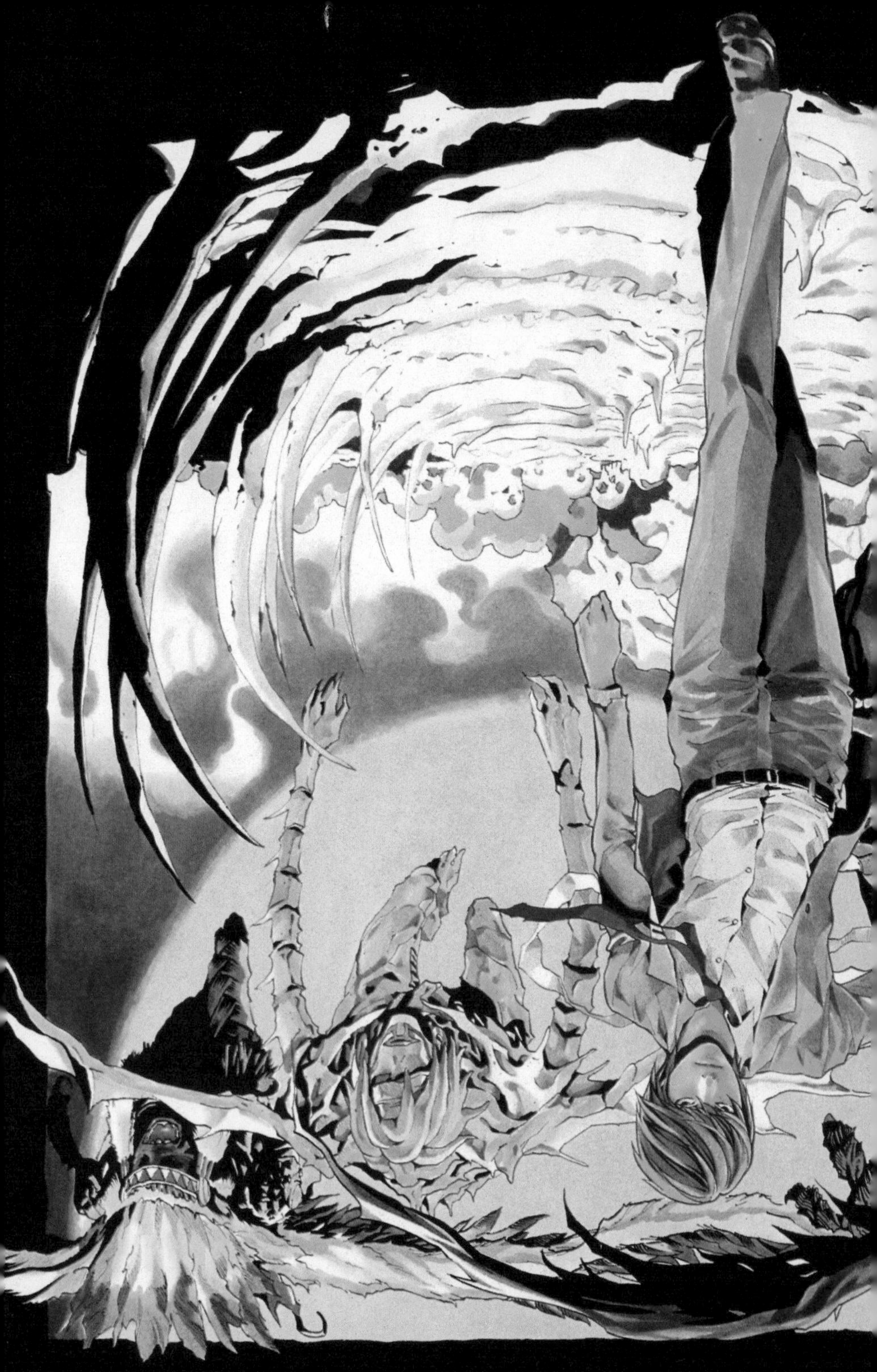

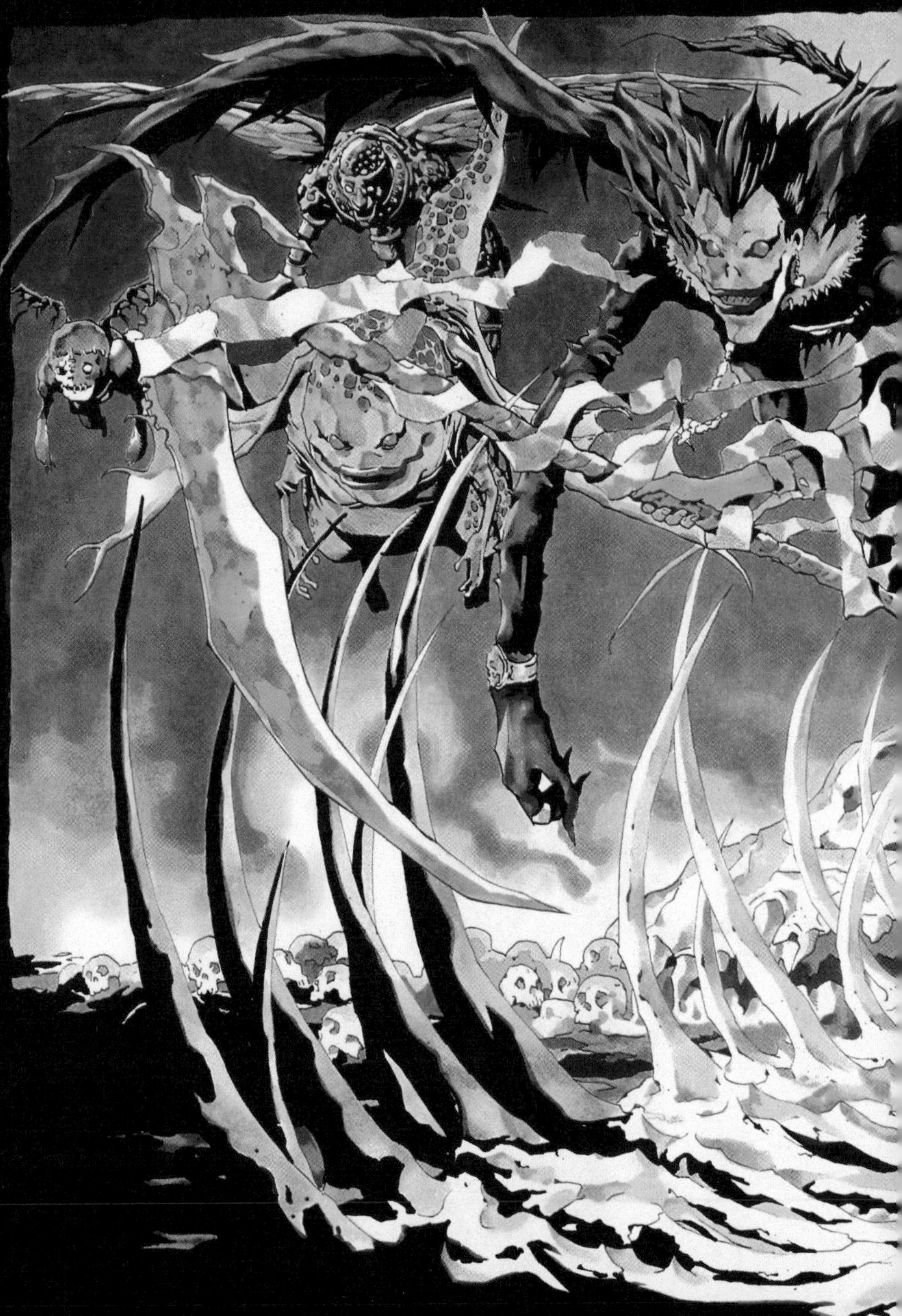

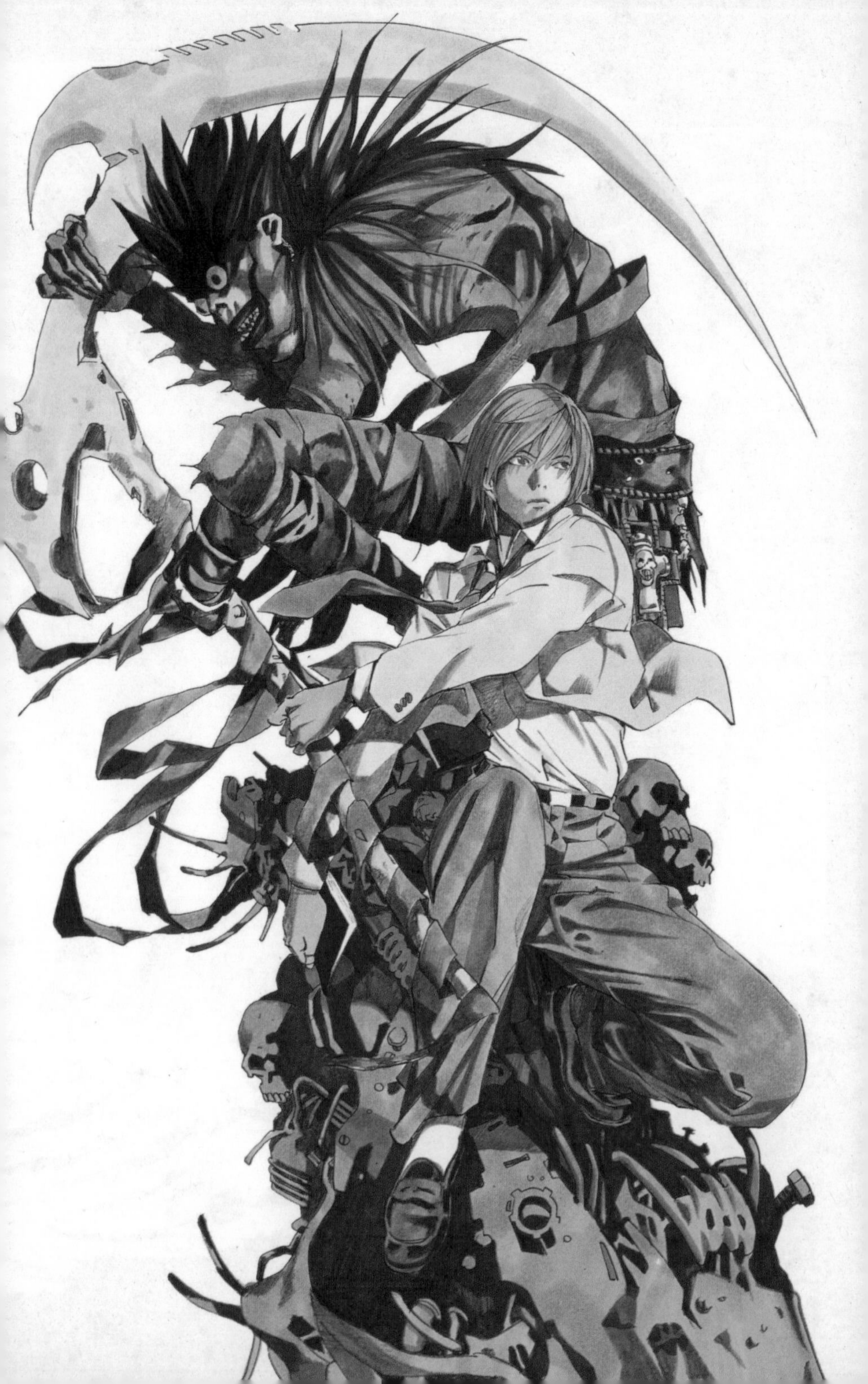

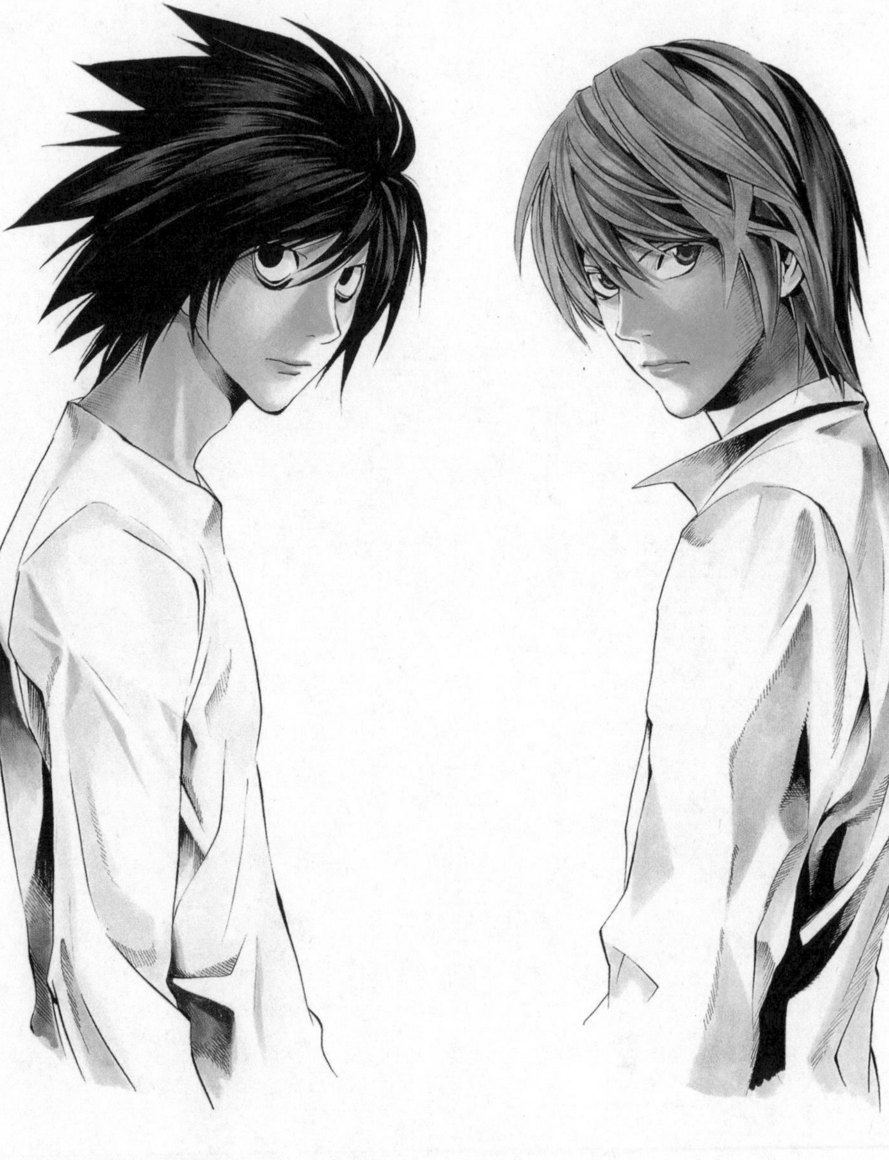

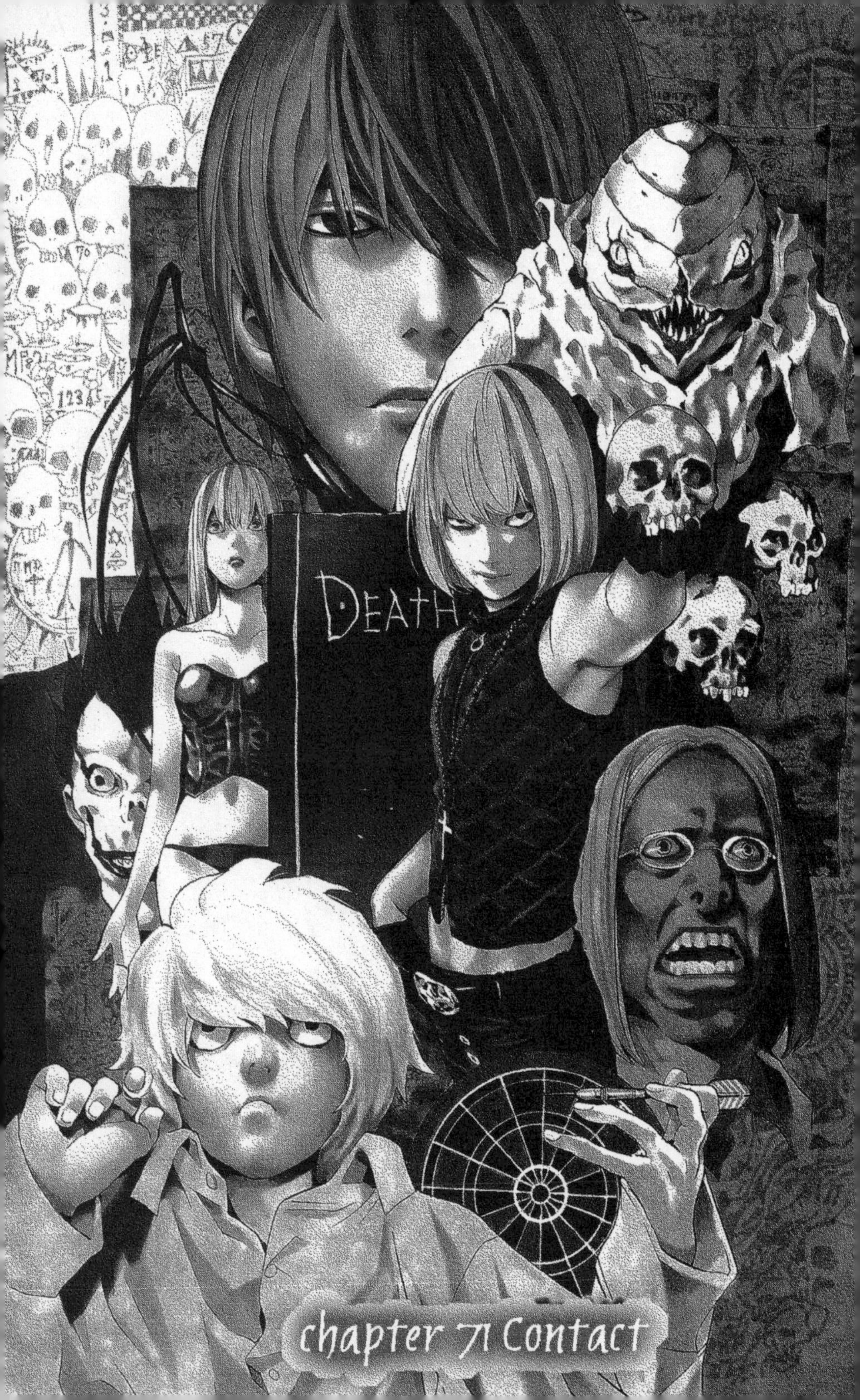
DEATH
chapter 71 Contact

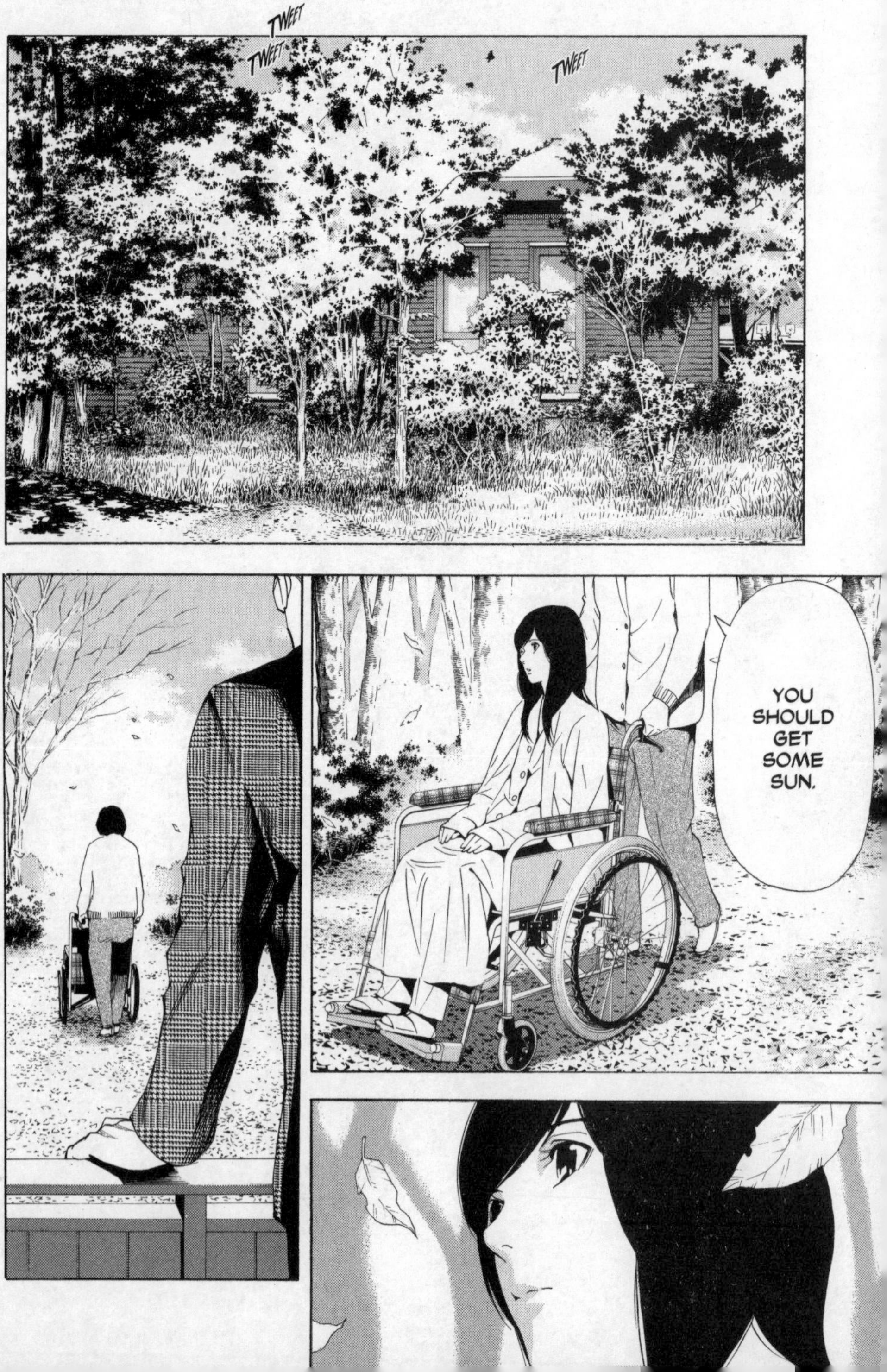
TWEET
TWEET
TWEET
YOU SHOULD GET SOME SUN.

READ THIS WAY

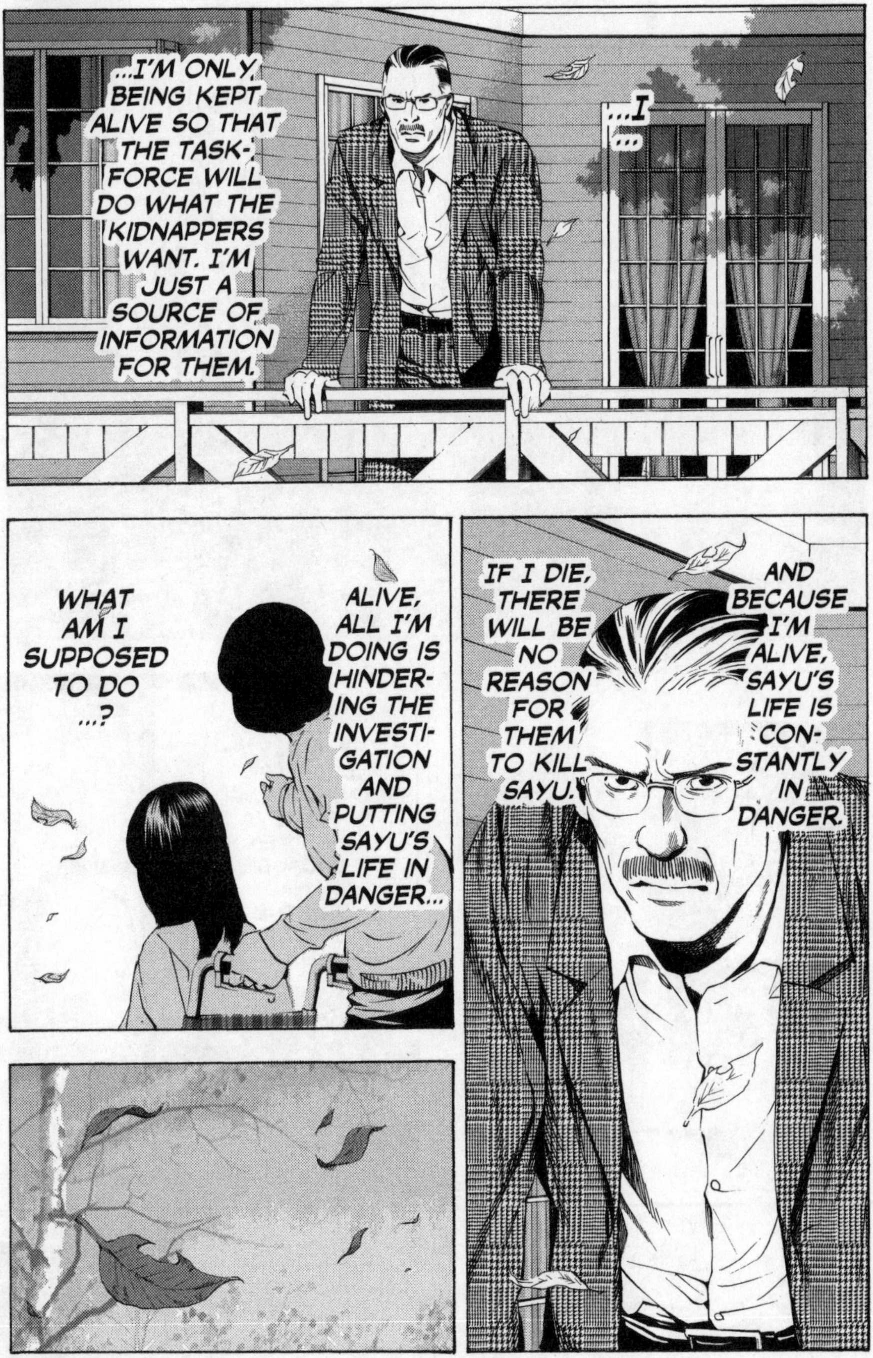
...I
...
...I'M ONLY BEING KEPT ALIVE SO THAT THE TASK-FORCE WILL DO WHAT THE KIDNAPPERS WANT. I'M JUST A SOURCE OF INFORMATION FOR THEM.
AND BECAUSE I'M ALIVE, SAYU'S LIFE IS CON-STANTLY IN DANGER.
IF I DIE, THERE WILL BE NO REASON FOR THEM TO KILL SAYU.
ALIVE, ALL I'M DOING IS HINDER-ING THE INVESTI-GATION AND PUTTING SAYU'S LIFE IN DANGER...
WHAT AM I SUPPOSED TO DO ...?

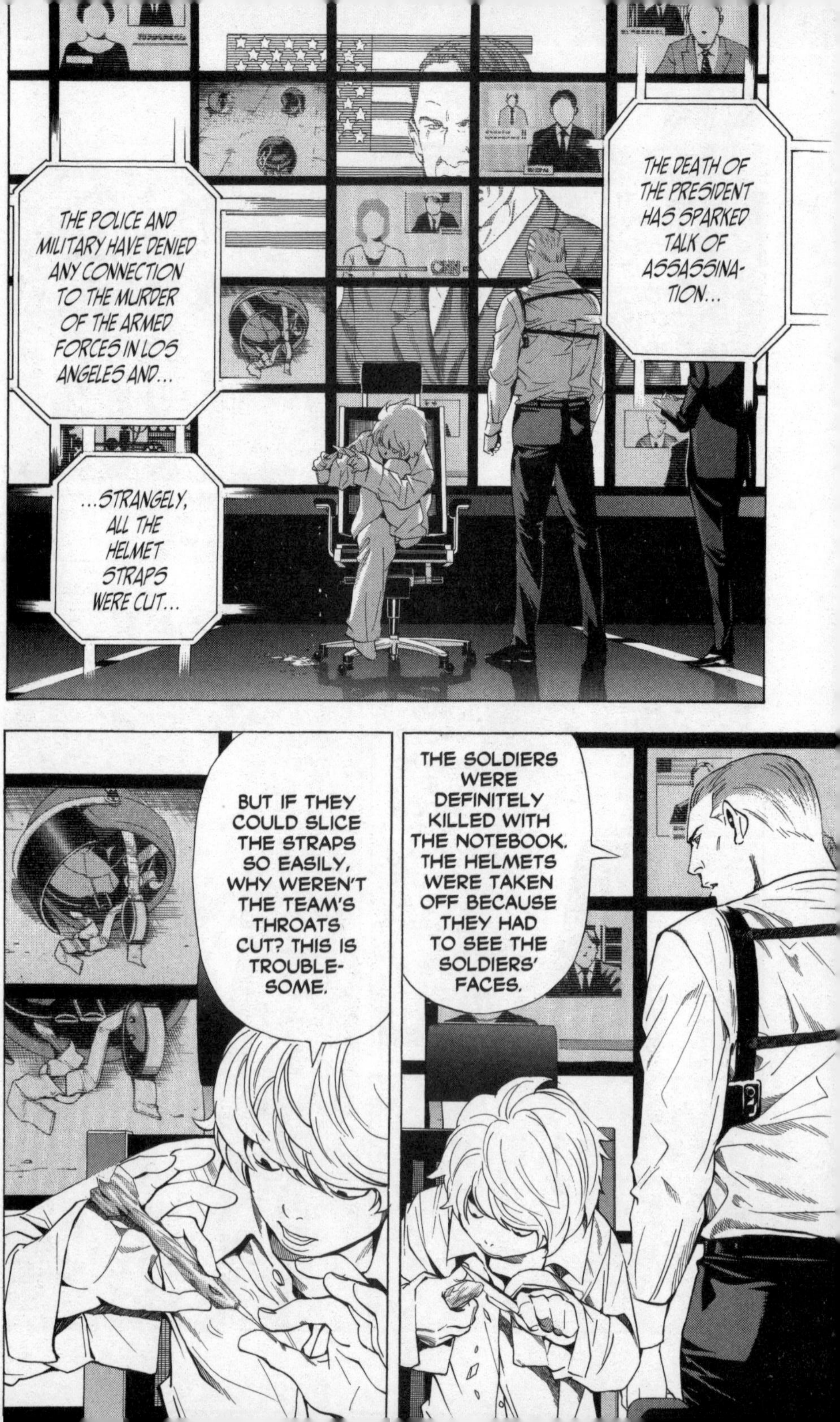
THE DEATH OF THE PRESIDENT HAS SPARKED TALK OF ASSASSINA-TION...
THE POLICE AND MILITARY HAVE DENIED ANY CONNECTION TO THE MURDER OF THE ARMED FORCES IN LOS ANGELES AND...
...STRANGELY, ALL THE HELMET STRAPS WERE CUT...
THE SOLDIERS WERE DEFINITELY KILLED WITH THE NOTEBOOK. THE HELMETS WERE TAKEN OFF BECAUSE THEY HAD TO SEE THE SOLDIERS' FACES.
BUT IF THEY COULD SLICE THE STRAPS SO EASILY, WHY WEREN'T THE TEAM'S THROATS CUT? THIS IS TROUBLE-SOME.

READ THIS WAY

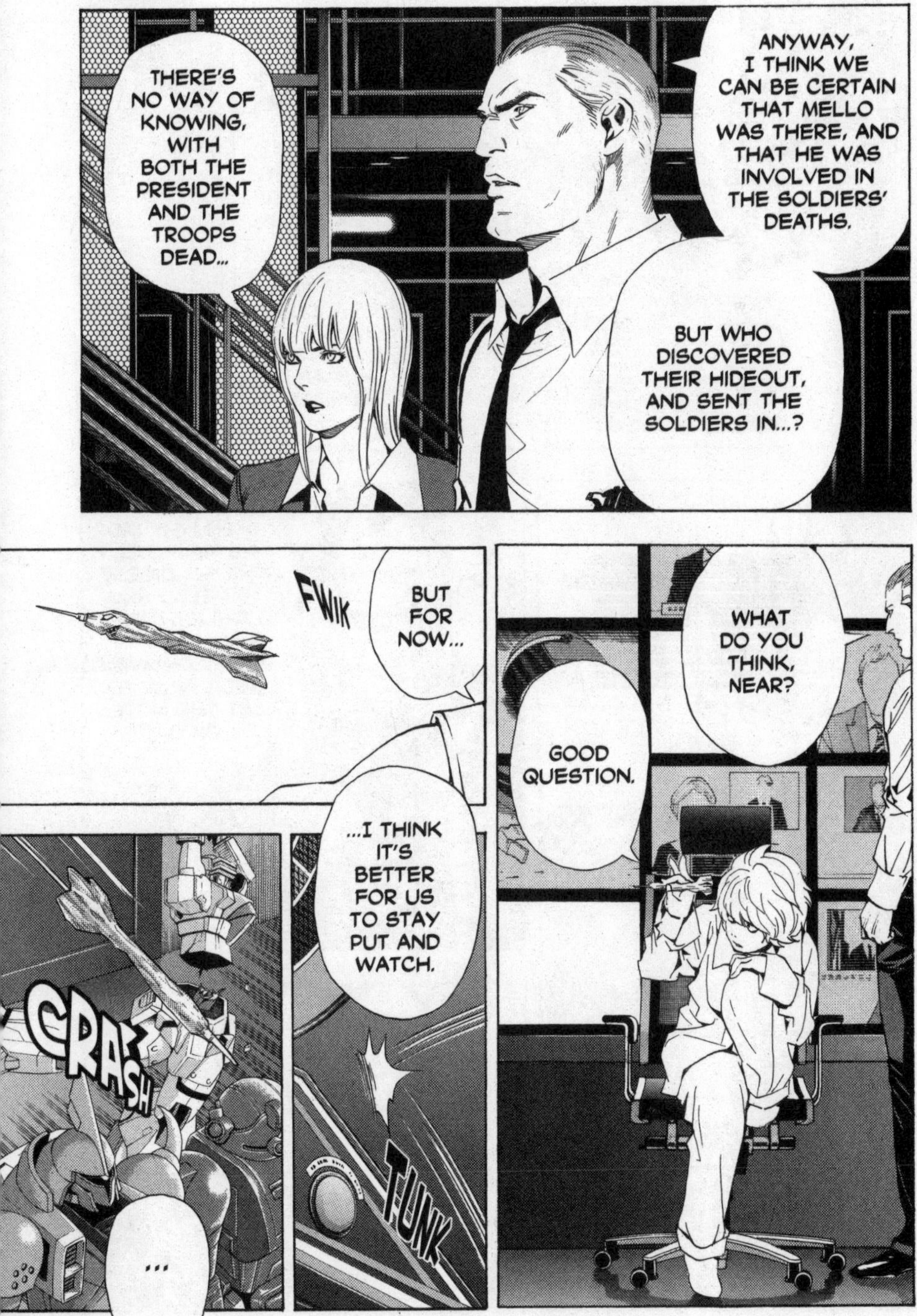
ANYWAY, I THINK WE CAN BE CERTAIN THAT MELLO WAS THERE, AND THAT HE WAS INVOLVED IN THE SOLDIERS' DEATHS.
THERE'S NO WAY OF KNOWING, WITH BOTH THE PRESIDENT AND THE TROOPS DEAD...
BUT WHO DISCOVERED THEIR HIDEOUT, AND SENT THE SOLDIERS IN...?
WHAT DO YOU THINK, NEAR?
GOOD QUESTION.
FWIK
BUT FOR NOW...
...I THINK IT'S BETTER FOR US TO STAY PUT AND WATCH.
TUNK
CRASH
...

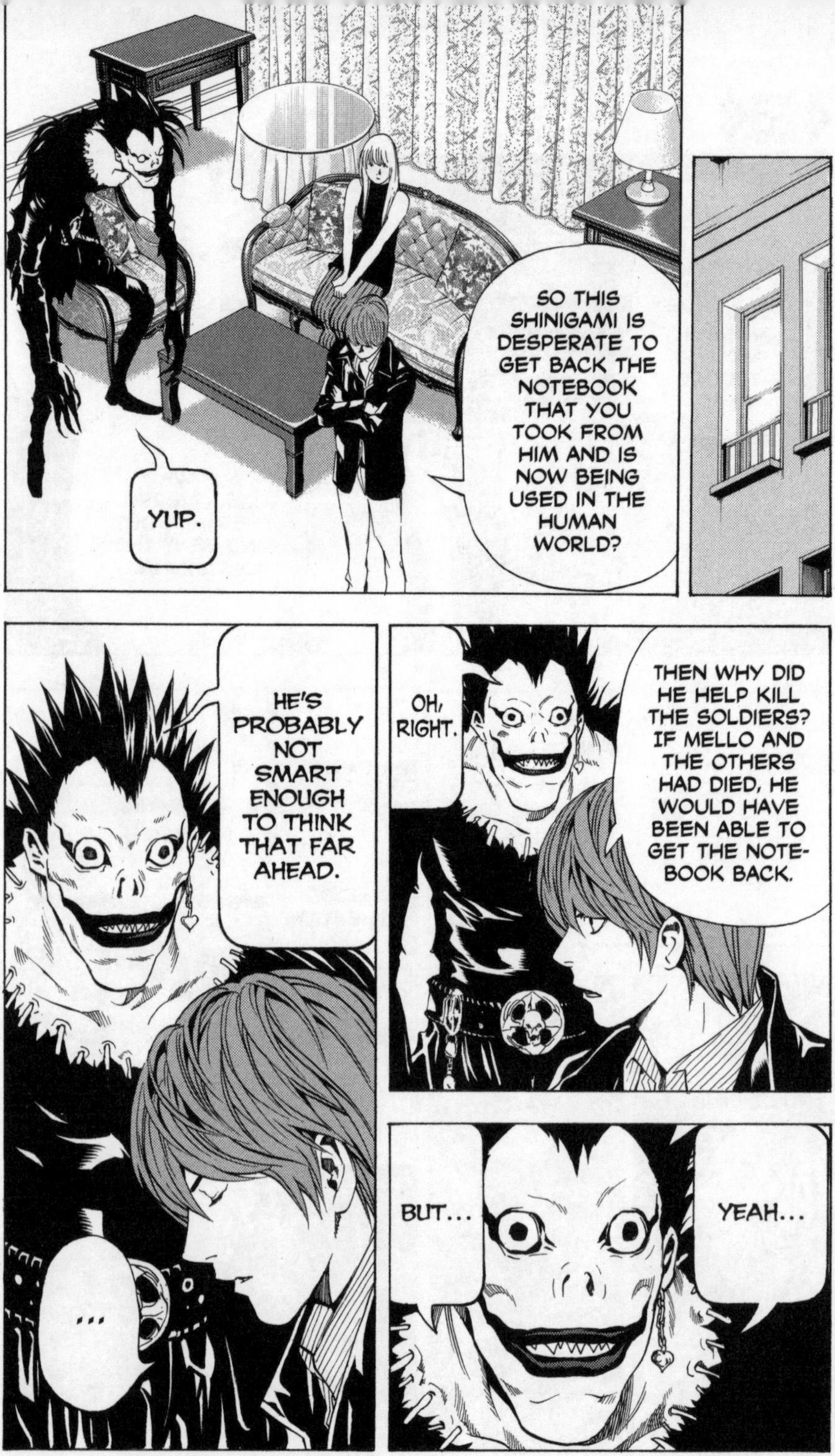
SO THIS SHINIGAMI IS DESPERATE TO GET BACK THE NOTEBOOK THAT YOU TOOK FROM HIM AND IS NOW BEING USED IN THE HUMAN WORLD?
YUP.
THEN WHY DID HE HELP KILL THE SOLDIERS? IF MELLO AND THE OTHERS HAD DIED, HE WOULD HAVE BEEN ABLE TO GET THE NOTE-BOOK BACK.
OH, RIGHT.
YEAH...
BUT...
HE'S PROBABLY NOT SMART ENOUGH TO THINK THAT FAR AHEAD.
...

READ THIS WAY

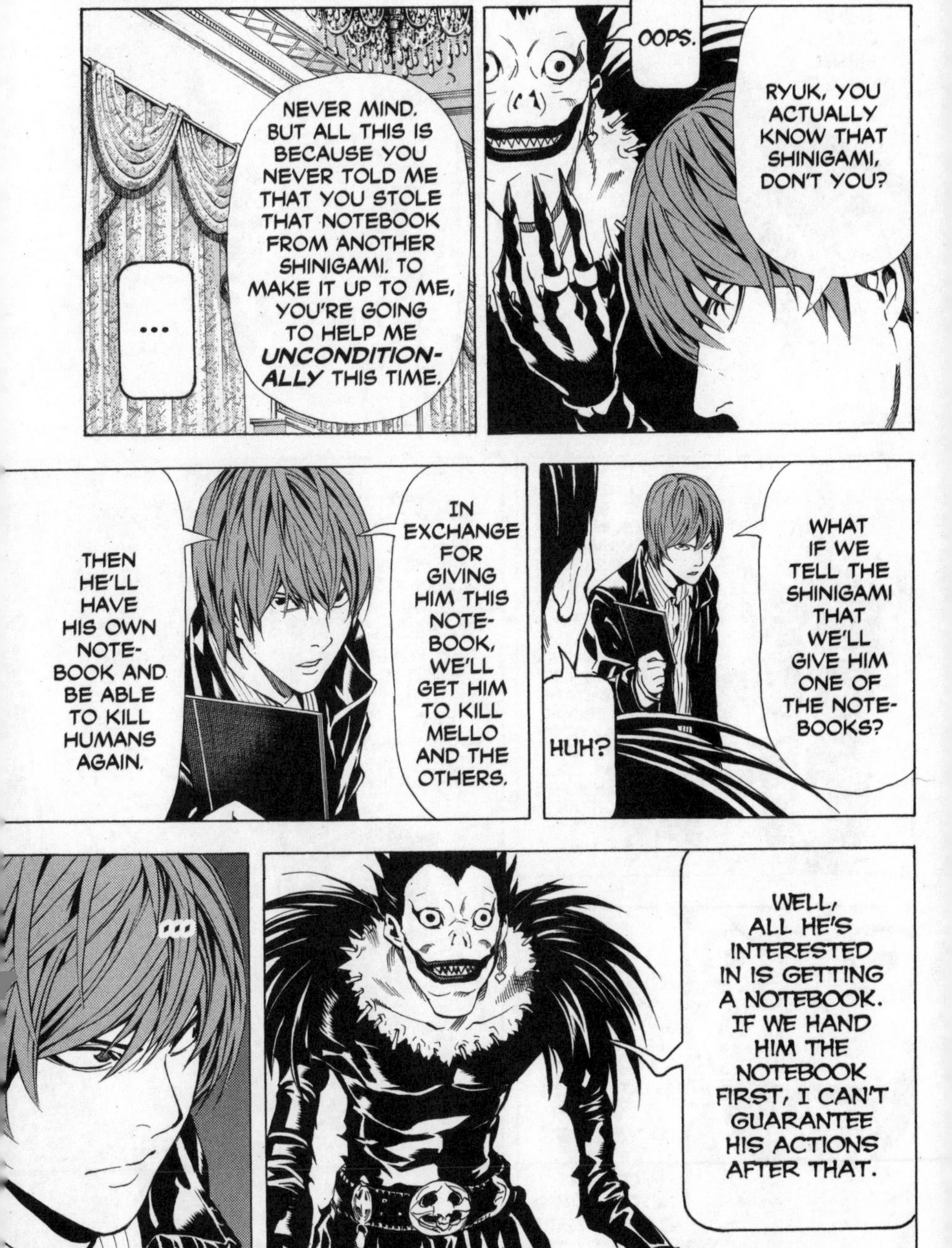
RYUK, YOU ACTUALLY KNOW THAT SHINIGAMI, DON'T YOU?
OOPS.
NEVER MIND. BUT ALL THIS IS BECAUSE YOU NEVER TOLD ME THAT YOU STOLE THAT NOTEBOOK FROM ANOTHER SHINIGAMI. TO MAKE IT UP TO ME, YOU'RE GOING TO HELP ME *UNCONDITION-ALLY* THIS TIME.
...
WHAT IF WE TELL THE SHINIGAMI THAT WE'LL GIVE HIM ONE OF THE NOTE-BOOKS?
HUH?
IN EXCHANGE FOR GIVING HIM THIS NOTE-BOOK, WE'LL GET HIM TO KILL MELLO AND THE OTHERS.
THEN HE'LL HAVE HIS OWN NOTE-BOOK AND BE ABLE TO KILL HUMANS AGAIN.
WELL, ALL HE'S INTERESTED IN IS GETTING A NOTEBOOK. IF WE HAND HIM THE NOTEBOOK FIRST, I CAN'T GUARANTEE HIS ACTIONS AFTER THAT.
...

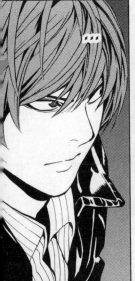

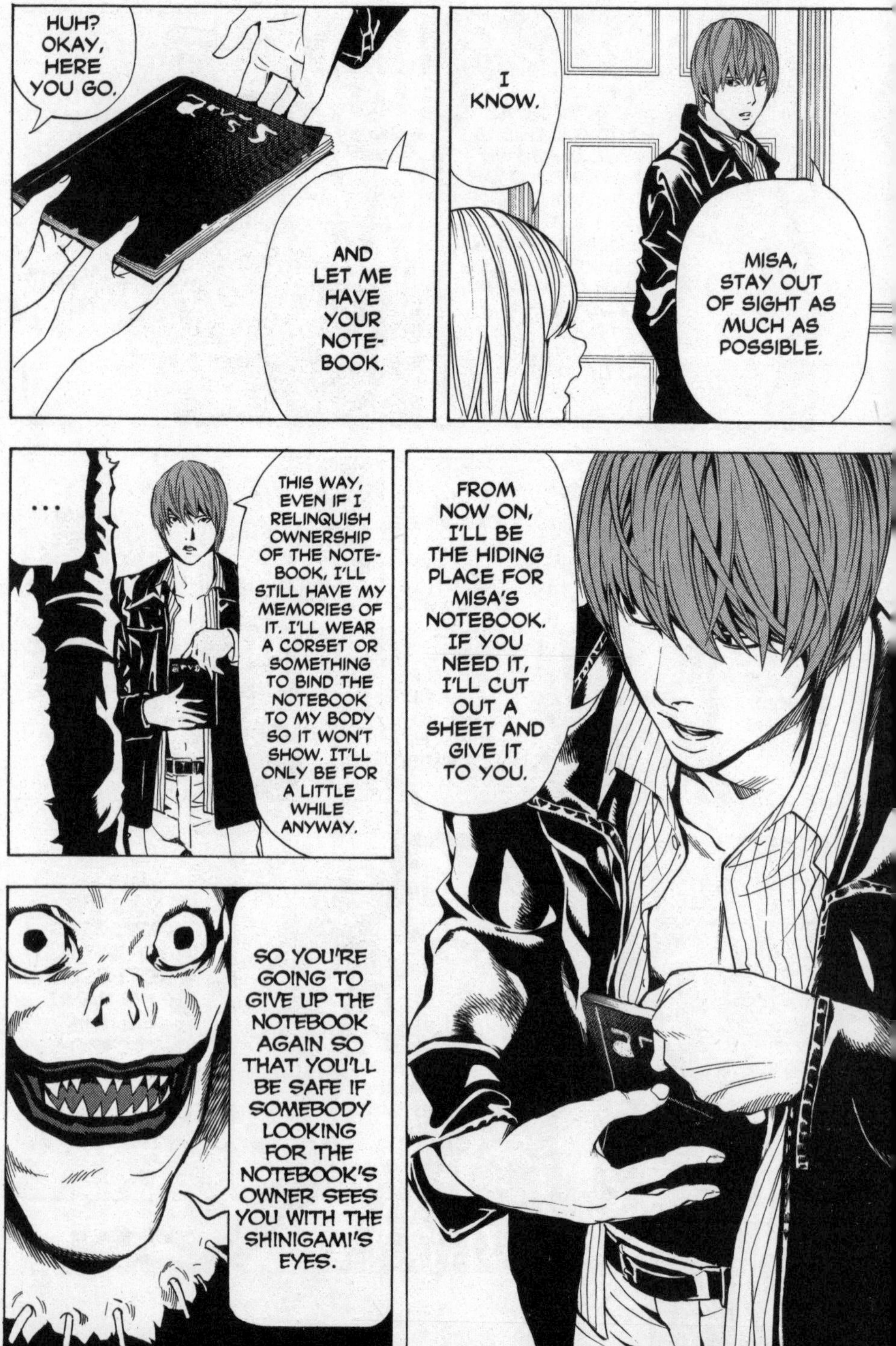
MISA, STAY OUT OF SIGHT AS MUCH AS POSSIBLE.
I KNOW.
AND LET ME HAVE YOUR NOTE-BOOK.
HUH? OKAY, HERE YOU GO.
FROM NOW ON, I'LL BE THE HIDING PLACE FOR MISA'S NOTEBOOK. IF YOU NEED IT, I'LL CUT OUT A SHEET AND GIVE IT TO YOU.
THIS WAY, EVEN IF I RELINQUISH OWNERSHIP OF THE NOTE-BOOK, I'LL STILL HAVE MY MEMORIES OF IT. I'LL WEAR A CORSET OR SOMETHING TO BIND THE NOTEBOOK TO MY BODY SO IT WON'T SHOW. IT'LL ONLY BE FOR A LITTLE WHILE ANYWAY.
...
SO YOU'RE GOING TO GIVE UP THE NOTEBOOK AGAIN SO THAT YOU'LL BE SAFE IF SOMEBODY LOOKING FOR THE NOTEBOOK'S OWNER SEES YOU WITH THE SHINIGAMI'S EYES.

READ THIS WAY

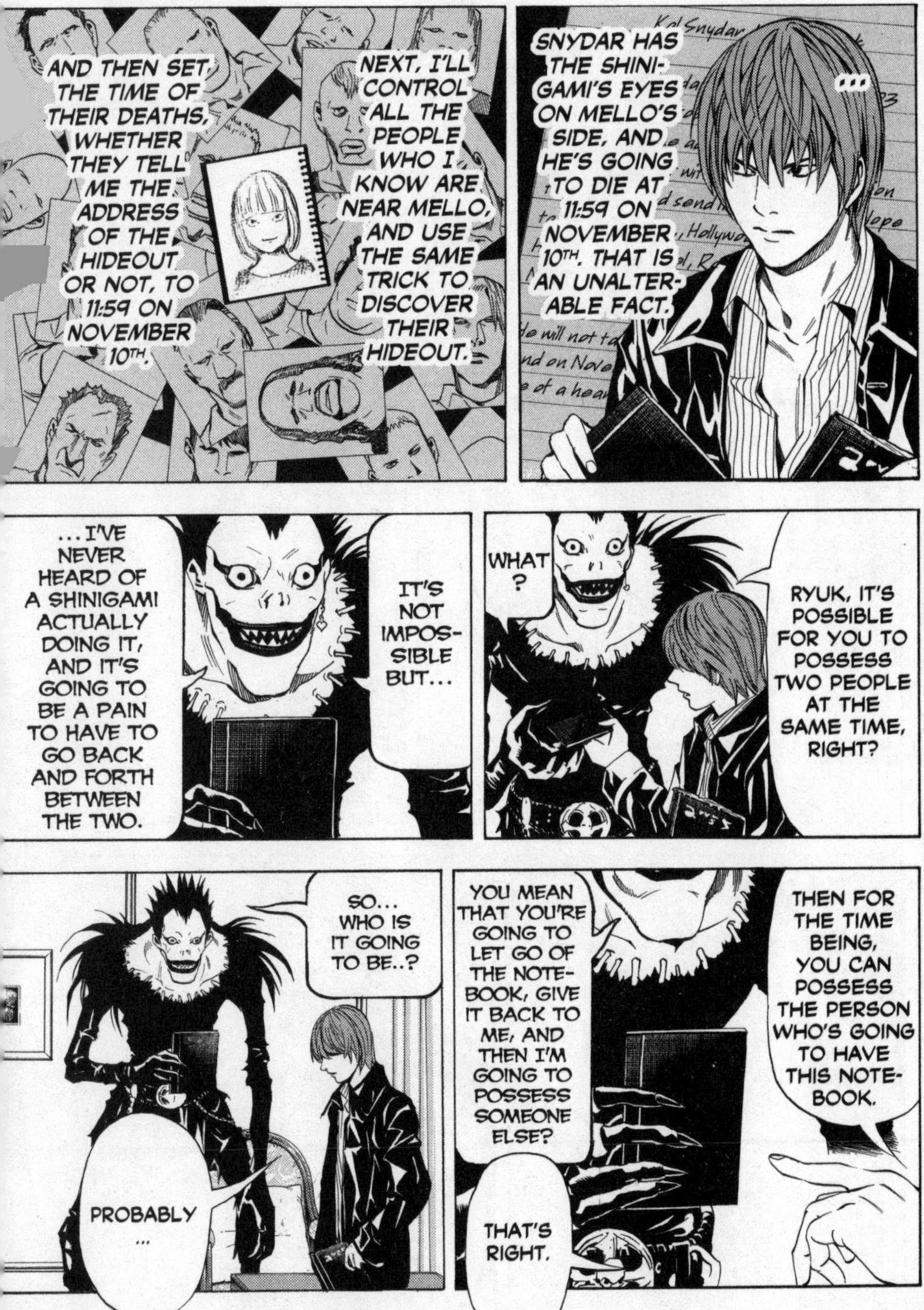

...
SNYDAR HAS THE SHINIGAMI'S EYES ON MELLO'S SIDE, AND HE'S GOING TO DIE AT 11:59 ON NOVEMBER 10TH. THAT IS AN UNALTERABLE FACT.
NEXT, I'LL CONTROL ALL THE PEOPLE WHO I KNOW ARE NEAR MELLO, AND USE THE SAME TRICK TO DISCOVER THEIR HIDEOUT.
AND THEN SET THE TIME OF THEIR DEATHS, WHETHER THEY TELL ME THE ADDRESS OF THE HIDEOUT OR NOT, TO 11:59 ON NOVEMBER 10TH.
RYUK, IT'S POSSIBLE FOR YOU TO POSSESS TWO PEOPLE AT THE SAME TIME, RIGHT?
WHAT?
IT'S NOT IMPOSSIBLE BUT...
...I'VE NEVER HEARD OF A SHINIGAMI ACTUALLY DOING IT, AND IT'S GOING TO BE A PAIN TO HAVE TO GO BACK AND FORTH BETWEEN THE TWO.
THEN FOR THE TIME BEING, YOU CAN POSSESS THE PERSON WHO'S GOING TO HAVE THIS NOTEBOOK.
YOU MEAN THAT YOU'RE GOING TO LET GO OF THE NOTEBOOK, GIVE IT BACK TO ME, AND THEN I'M GOING TO POSSESS SOMEONE ELSE?
THAT'S RIGHT.
SO... WHO IS IT GOING TO BE..?
PROBABLY ...

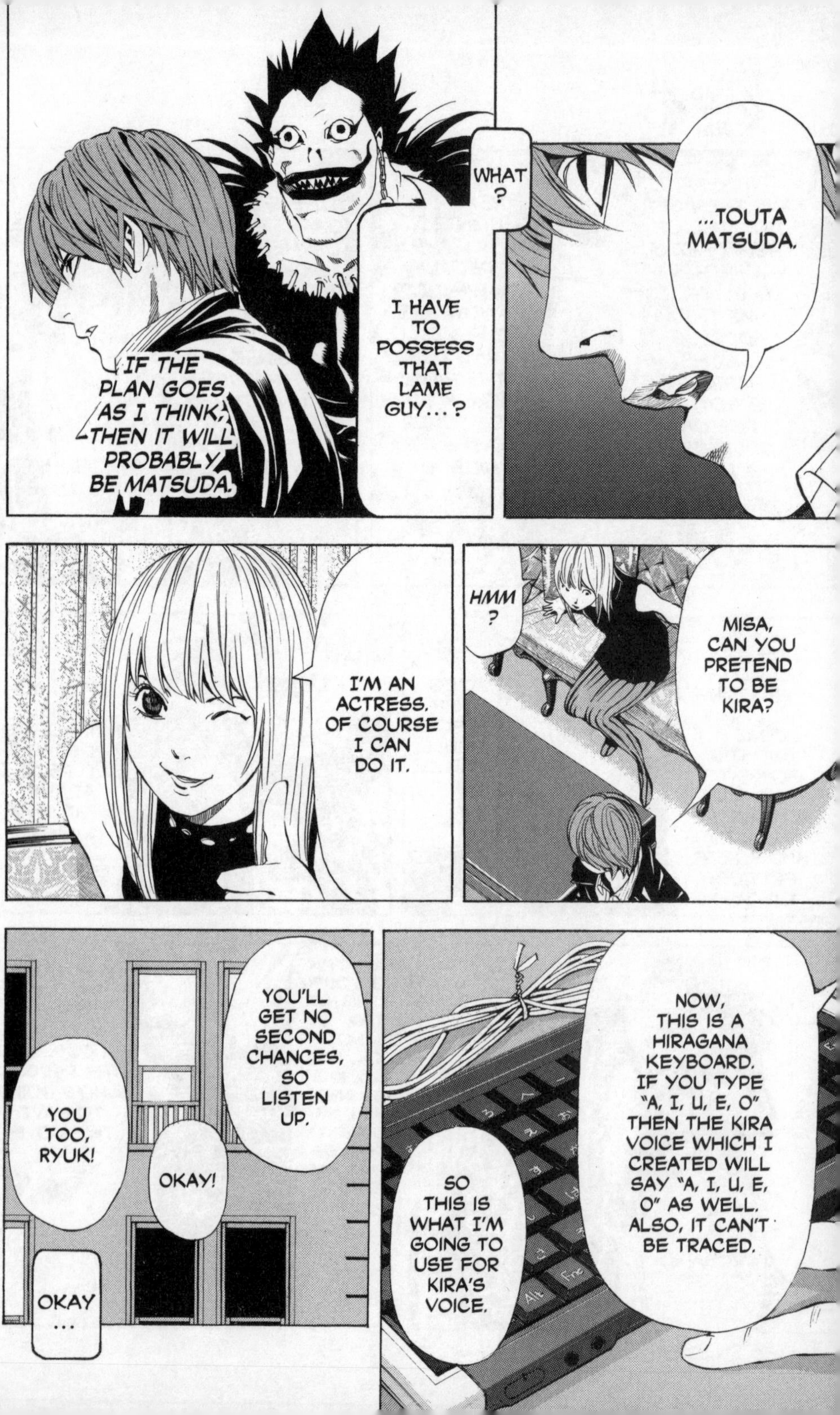
...TOUTA MATSUDA.
WHAT?
I HAVE TO POSSESS THAT LAME GUY...?
IF THE PLAN GOES AS I THINK, THEN IT WILL PROBABLY BE MATSUDA.
MISA, CAN YOU PRETEND TO BE KIRA?
HMM?
I'M AN ACTRESS. OF COURSE I CAN DO IT.
NOW, THIS IS A HIRAGANA KEYBOARD. IF YOU TYPE "A, I, U, E, O" THEN THE KIRA VOICE WHICH I CREATED WILL SAY "A, I, U, E, O" AS WELL. ALSO, IT CAN'T BE TRACED.
SO THIS IS WHAT I'M GOING TO USE FOR KIRA'S VOICE.
YOU'LL GET NO SECOND CHANCES, SO LISTEN UP.
OKAY!
YOU TOO, RYUK!
OKAY...

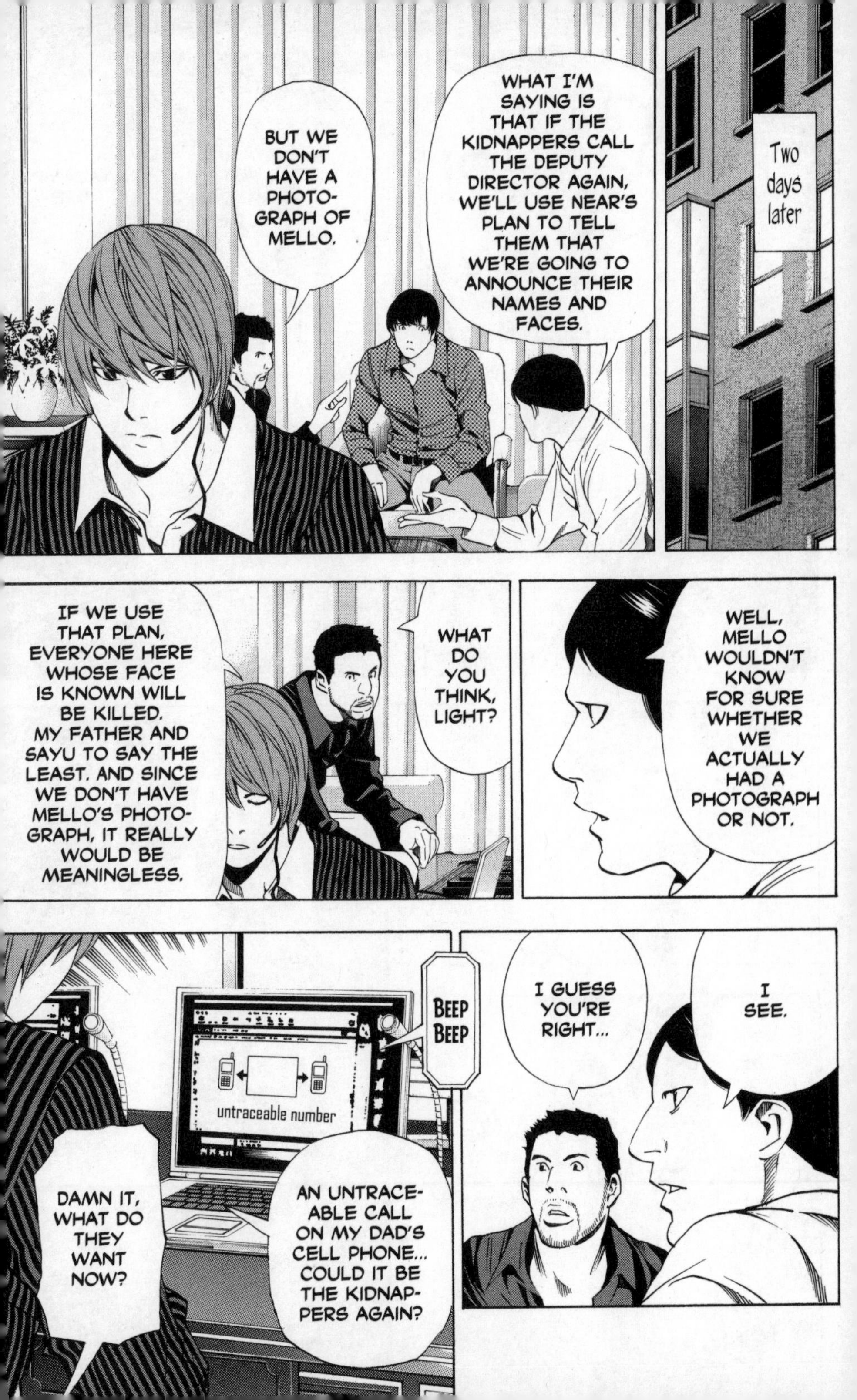
Two days later
WHAT I'M SAYING IS THAT IF THE KIDNAPPERS CALL THE DEPUTY DIRECTOR AGAIN, WE'LL USE NEAR'S PLAN TO TELL THEM THAT WE'RE GOING TO ANNOUNCE THEIR NAMES AND FACES.
BUT WE DON'T HAVE A PHOTOGRAPH OF MELLO.
WELL, MELLO WOULDN'T KNOW FOR SURE WHETHER WE ACTUALLY HAD A PHOTOGRAPH OR NOT.
WHAT DO YOU THINK, LIGHT?
IF WE USE THAT PLAN, EVERYONE HERE WHOSE FACE IS KNOWN WILL BE KILLED. MY FATHER AND SAYU TO SAY THE LEAST. AND SINCE WE DON'T HAVE MELLO'S PHOTOGRAPH, IT REALLY WOULD BE MEANINGLESS.
I SEE.
I GUESS YOU'RE RIGHT...
BEEP BEEP
untraceable number
AN UNTRACEABLE CALL ON MY DAD'S CELL PHONE... COULD IT BE THE KIDNAPPERS AGAIN?
DAMN IT, WHAT DO THEY WANT NOW?

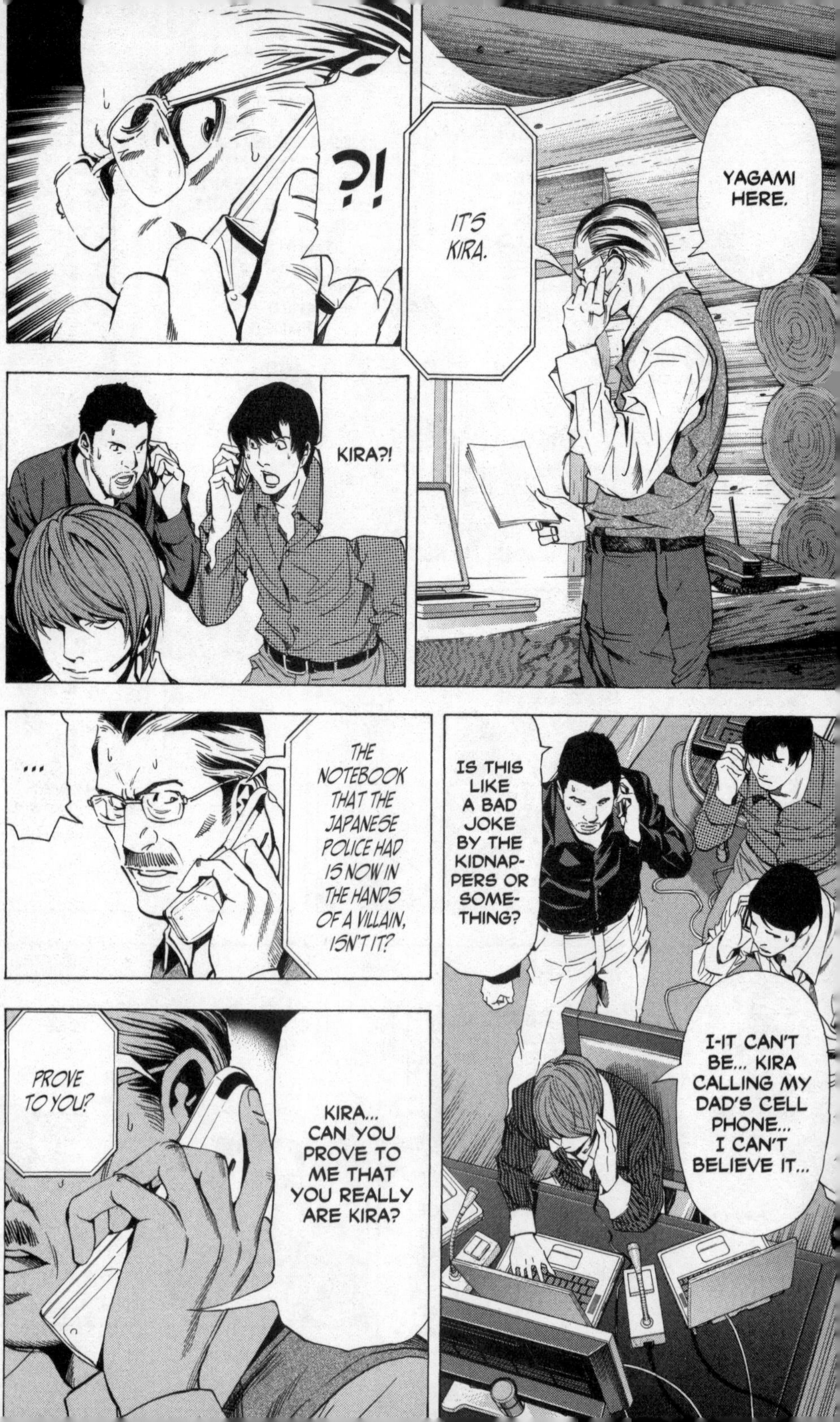
YAGAMI HERE.
IT'S KIRA.
?!
KIRA?!
IS THIS LIKE A BAD JOKE BY THE KIDNAPPERS OR SOMETHING?
I-IT CAN'T BE... KIRA CALLING MY DAD'S CELL PHONE... I CAN'T BELIEVE IT...
THE NOTEBOOK THAT THE JAPANESE POLICE HAD IS NOW IN THE HANDS OF A VILLAIN, ISN'T IT?
...
KIRA... CAN YOU PROVE TO ME THAT YOU REALLY ARE KIRA?
PROVE TO YOU?

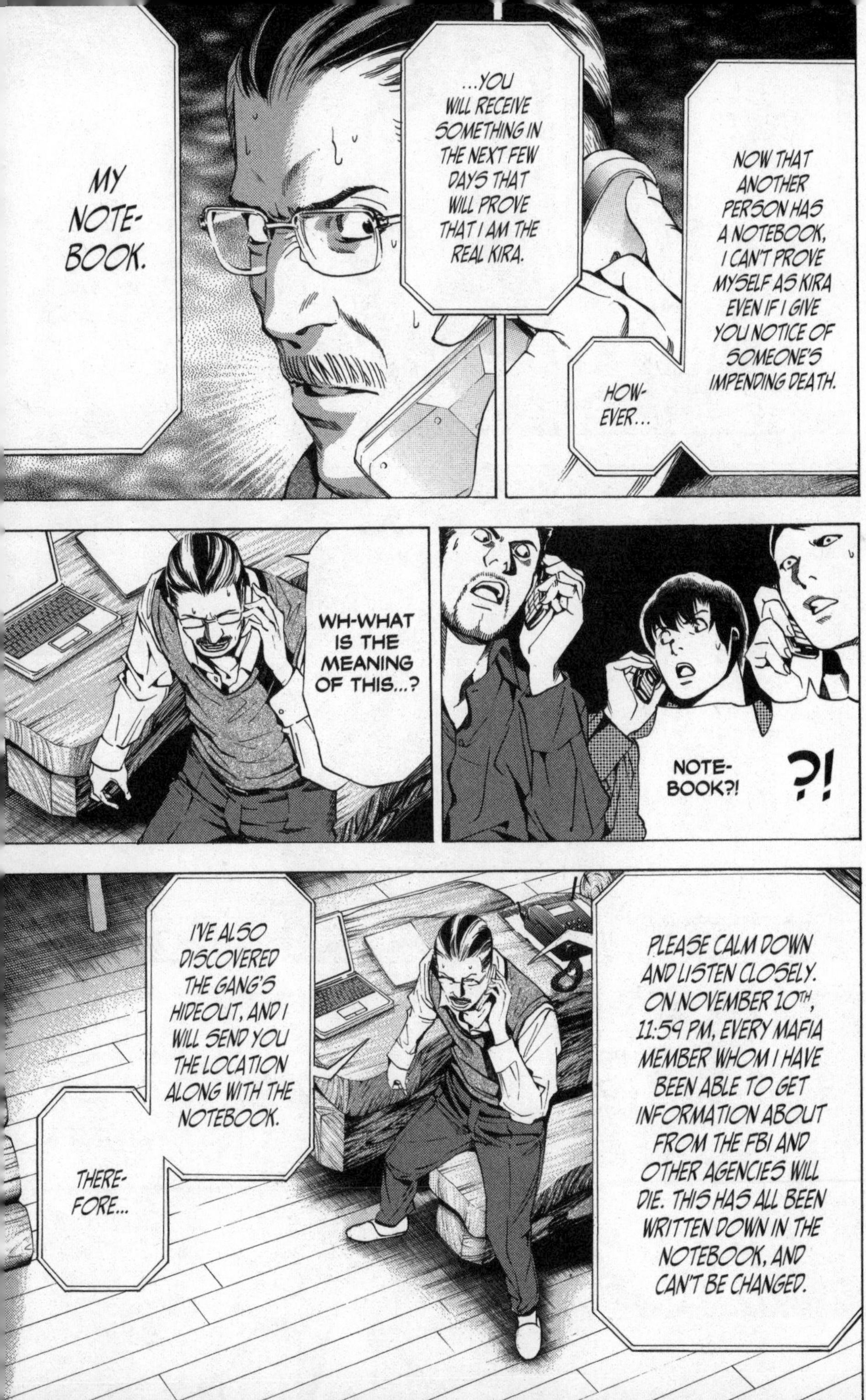
NOW THAT ANOTHER PERSON HAS A NOTEBOOK, I CAN'T PROVE MYSELF AS KIRA EVEN IF I GIVE YOU NOTICE OF SOMEONE'S IMPENDING DEATH.
HOW-EVER...
...YOU WILL RECEIVE SOMETHING IN THE NEXT FEW DAYS THAT WILL PROVE THAT I AM THE REAL KIRA.
MY NOTE-BOOK.
?!
NOTE-BOOK?!
WH-WHAT IS THE MEANING OF THIS...?
PLEASE CALM DOWN AND LISTEN CLOSELY. ON NOVEMBER 10TH, 11:59 PM, EVERY MAFIA MEMBER WHOM I HAVE BEEN ABLE TO GET INFORMATION ABOUT FROM THE FBI AND OTHER AGENCIES WILL DIE. THIS HAS ALL BEEN WRITTEN DOWN IN THE NOTEBOOK, AND CAN'T BE CHANGED.
I'VE ALSO DISCOVERED THE GANG'S HIDEOUT, AND I WILL SEND YOU THE LOCATION ALONG WITH THE NOTEBOOK.
THERE-FORE...

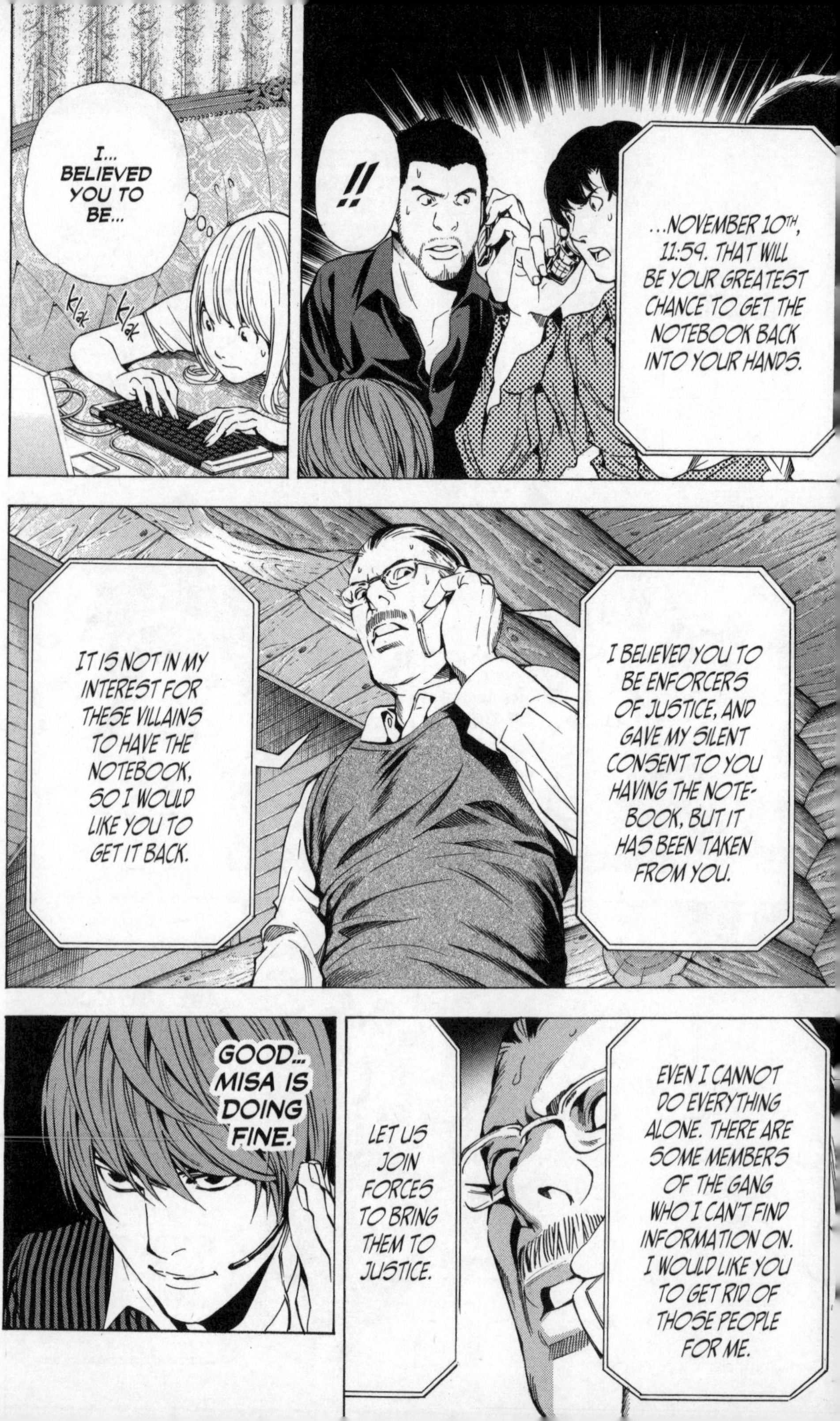
...NOVEMBER 10TH, 11:59. THAT WILL BE YOUR GREATEST CHANCE TO GET THE NOTEBOOK BACK INTO YOUR HANDS.
!!
I... BELIEVED YOU TO BE...
klak
klak
I BELIEVED YOU TO BE ENFORCERS OF JUSTICE, AND GAVE MY SILENT CONSENT TO YOU HAVING THE NOTE-BOOK, BUT IT HAS BEEN TAKEN FROM YOU.
IT IS NOT IN MY INTEREST FOR THESE VILLAINS TO HAVE THE NOTEBOOK, SO I WOULD LIKE YOU TO GET IT BACK.
EVEN I CANNOT DO EVERYTHING ALONE. THERE ARE SOME MEMBERS OF THE GANG WHO I CAN'T FIND INFORMATION ON. I WOULD LIKE YOU TO GET RID OF THOSE PEOPLE FOR ME.
LET US JOIN FORCES TO BRING THEM TO JUSTICE.
GOOD... MISA IS DOING FINE.

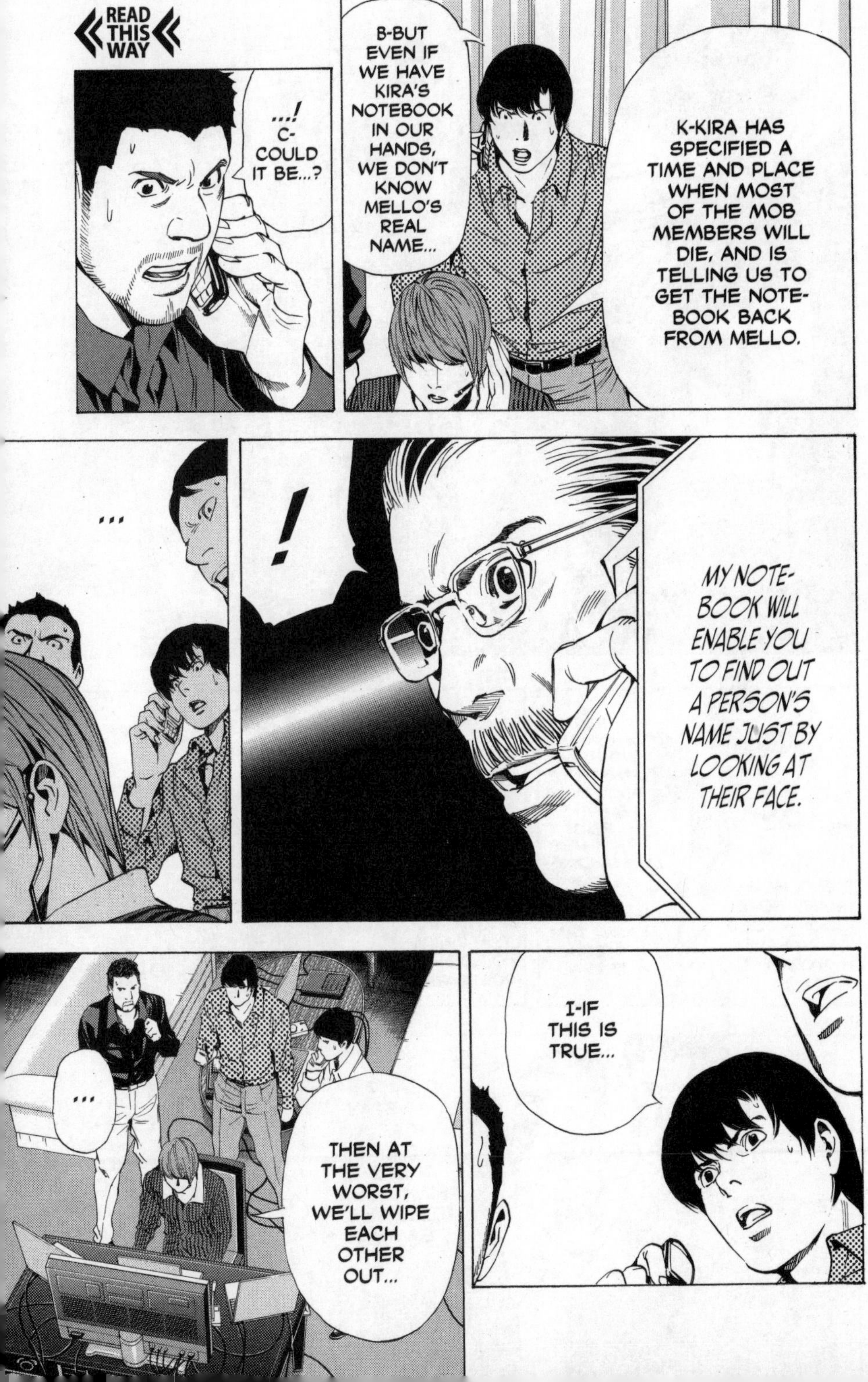
READ THIS WAY
K-KIRA HAS SPECIFIED A TIME AND PLACE WHEN MOST OF THE MOB MEMBERS WILL DIE, AND IS TELLING US TO GET THE NOTE-BOOK BACK FROM MELLO.
B-BUT EVEN IF WE HAVE KIRA'S NOTEBOOK IN OUR HANDS, WE DON'T KNOW MELLO'S REAL NAME...
...! C-COULD IT BE...?
MY NOTE-BOOK WILL ENABLE YOU TO FIND OUT A PERSON'S NAME JUST BY LOOKING AT THEIR FACE.
!
...
I-IF THIS IS TRUE...
THEN AT THE VERY WORST, WE'LL WIPE EACH OTHER OUT...
...

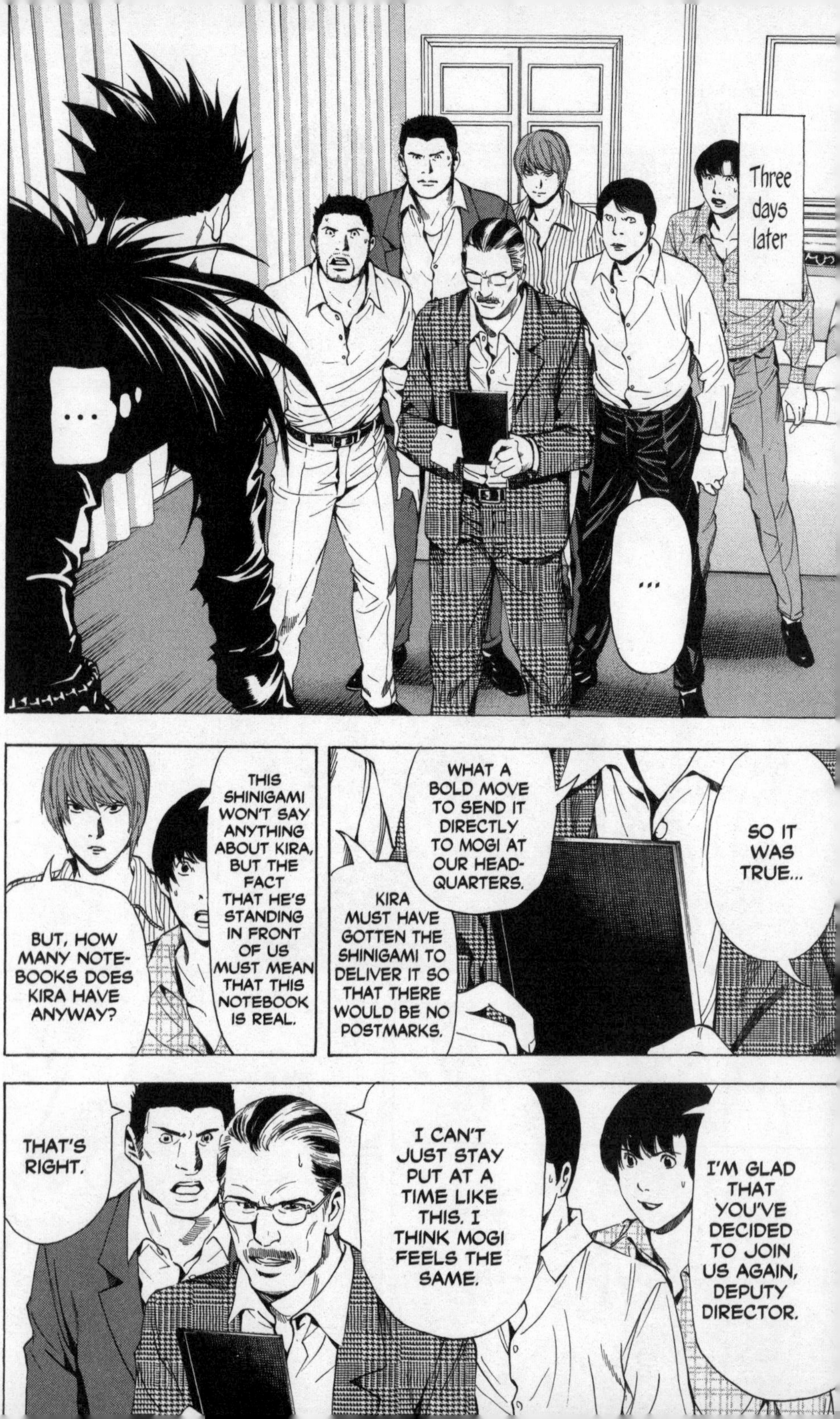
Three days later
...
...
SO IT WAS TRUE...
WHAT A BOLD MOVE TO SEND IT DIRECTLY TO MOGI AT OUR HEAD-QUARTERS.
KIRA MUST HAVE GOTTEN THE SHINIGAMI TO DELIVER IT SO THAT THERE WOULD BE NO POSTMARKS.
THIS SHINIGAMI WON'T SAY ANYTHING ABOUT KIRA, BUT THE FACT THAT HE'S STANDING IN FRONT OF US MUST MEAN THAT THIS NOTEBOOK IS REAL.
BUT, HOW MANY NOTE-BOOKS DOES KIRA HAVE ANYWAY?
I'M GLAD THAT YOU'VE DECIDED TO JOIN US AGAIN, DEPUTY DIRECTOR.
I CAN'T JUST STAY PUT AT A TIME LIKE THIS. I THINK MOGI FEELS THE SAME.
THAT'S RIGHT.

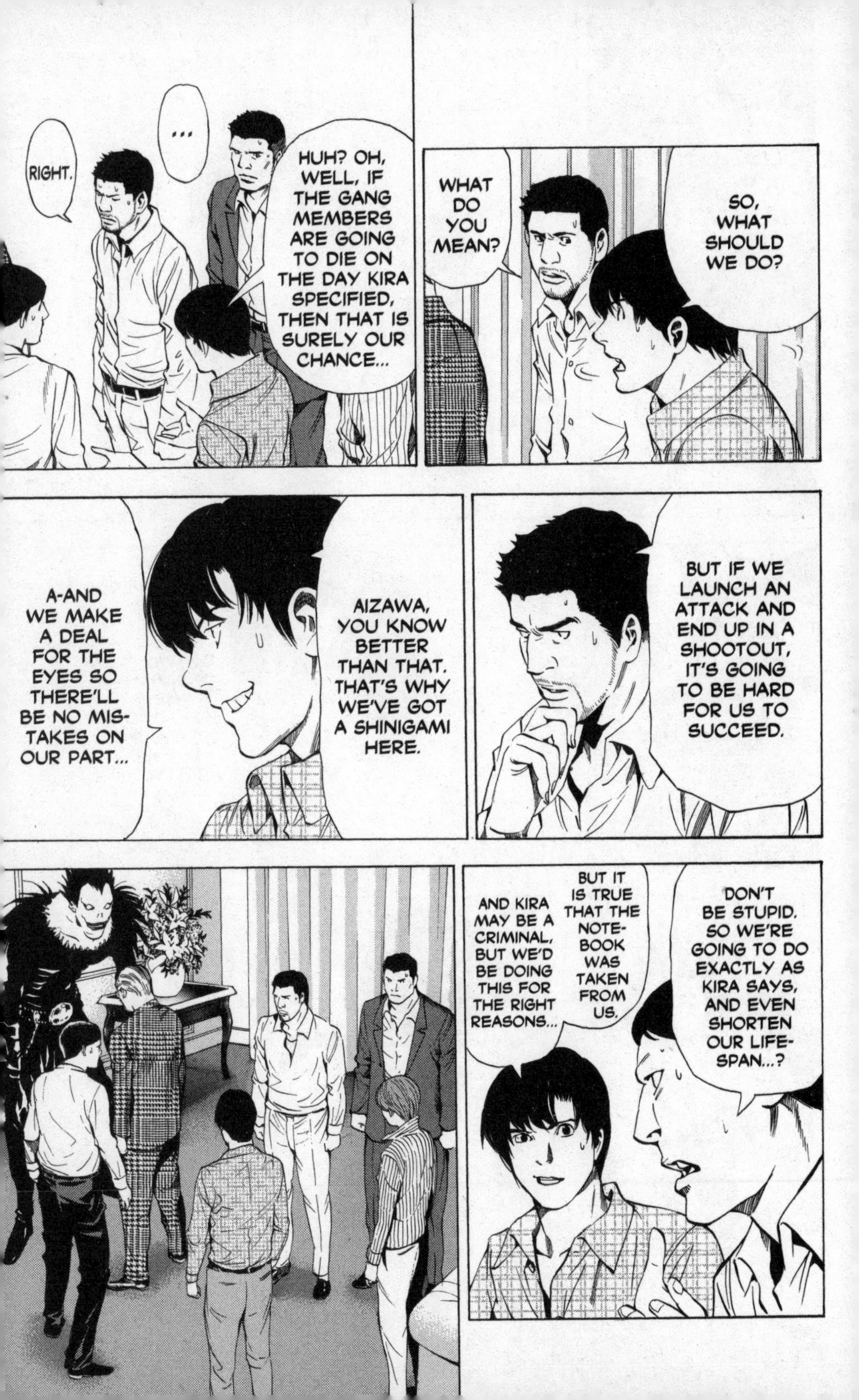
SO, WHAT SHOULD WE DO?
WHAT DO YOU MEAN?
HUH? OH, WELL, IF THE GANG MEMBERS ARE GOING TO DIE ON THE DAY KIRA SPECIFIED, THEN THAT IS SURELY OUR CHANCE...
...
RIGHT.
BUT IF WE LAUNCH AN ATTACK AND END UP IN A SHOOTOUT, IT'S GOING TO BE HARD FOR US TO SUCCEED.
AIZAWA, YOU KNOW BETTER THAN THAT. THAT'S WHY WE'VE GOT A SHINIGAMI HERE.
A-AND WE MAKE A DEAL FOR THE EYES SO THERE'LL BE NO MIS-TAKES ON OUR PART...
DON'T BE STUPID. SO WE'RE GOING TO DO EXACTLY AS KIRA SAYS, AND EVEN SHORTEN OUR LIFE-SPAN...?
BUT IT IS TRUE THAT THE NOTE-BOOK WAS TAKEN FROM US.
AND KIRA MAY BE A CRIMINAL, BUT WE'D BE DOING THIS FOR THE RIGHT REASONS...

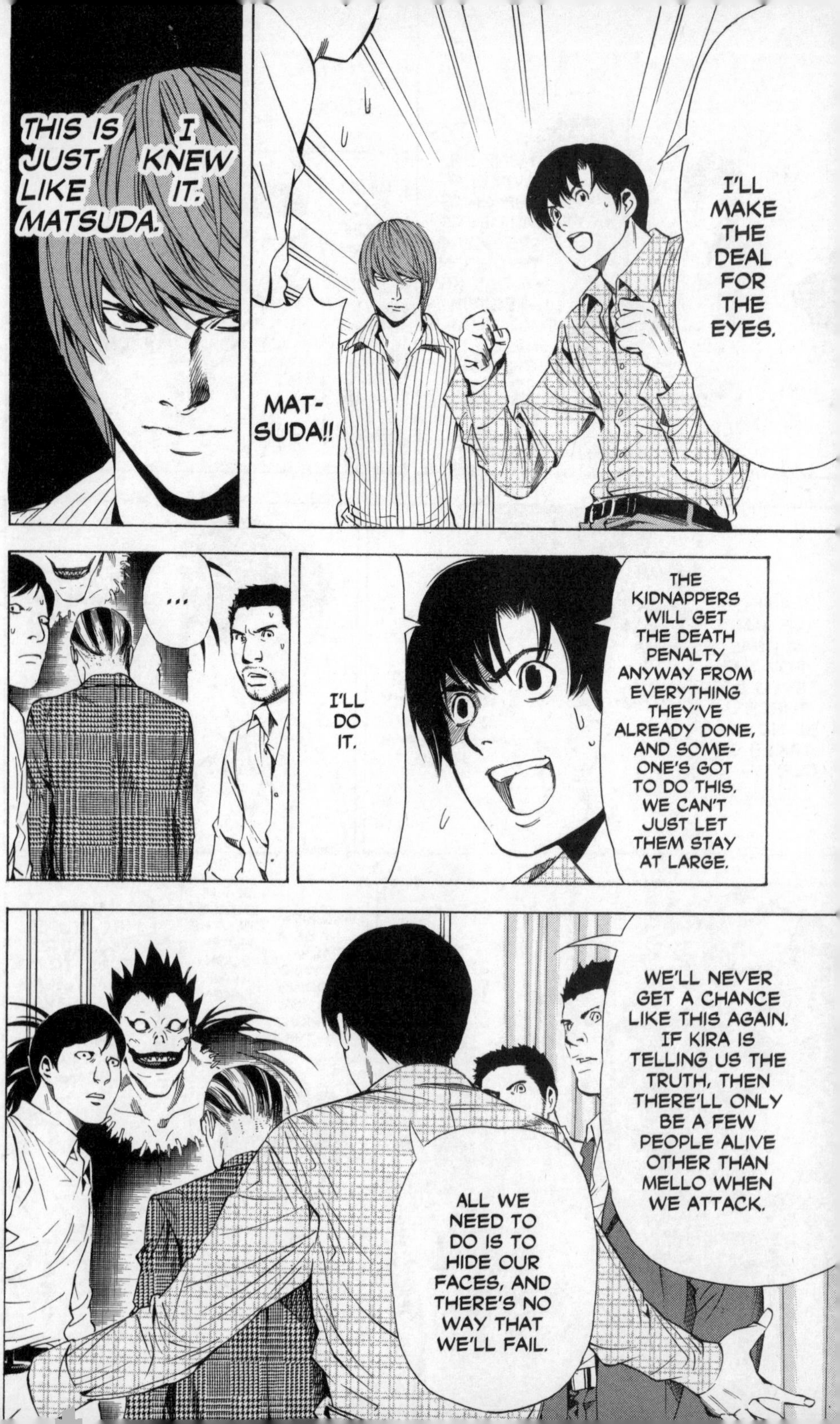
I'LL MAKE THE DEAL FOR THE EYES.
MAT-SUDA!!
I KNEW IT.
THIS IS JUST LIKE MATSUDA.
THE KIDNAPPERS WILL GET THE DEATH PENALTY ANYWAY FROM EVERYTHING THEY'VE ALREADY DONE, AND SOME-ONE'S GOT TO DO THIS. WE CAN'T JUST LET THEM STAY AT LARGE.
I'LL DO IT.
...
WE'LL NEVER GET A CHANCE LIKE THIS AGAIN. IF KIRA IS TELLING US THE TRUTH, THEN THERE'LL ONLY BE A FEW PEOPLE ALIVE OTHER THAN MELLO WHEN WE ATTACK.
ALL WE NEED TO DO IS TO HIDE OUR FACES, AND THERE'S NO WAY THAT WE'LL FAIL.

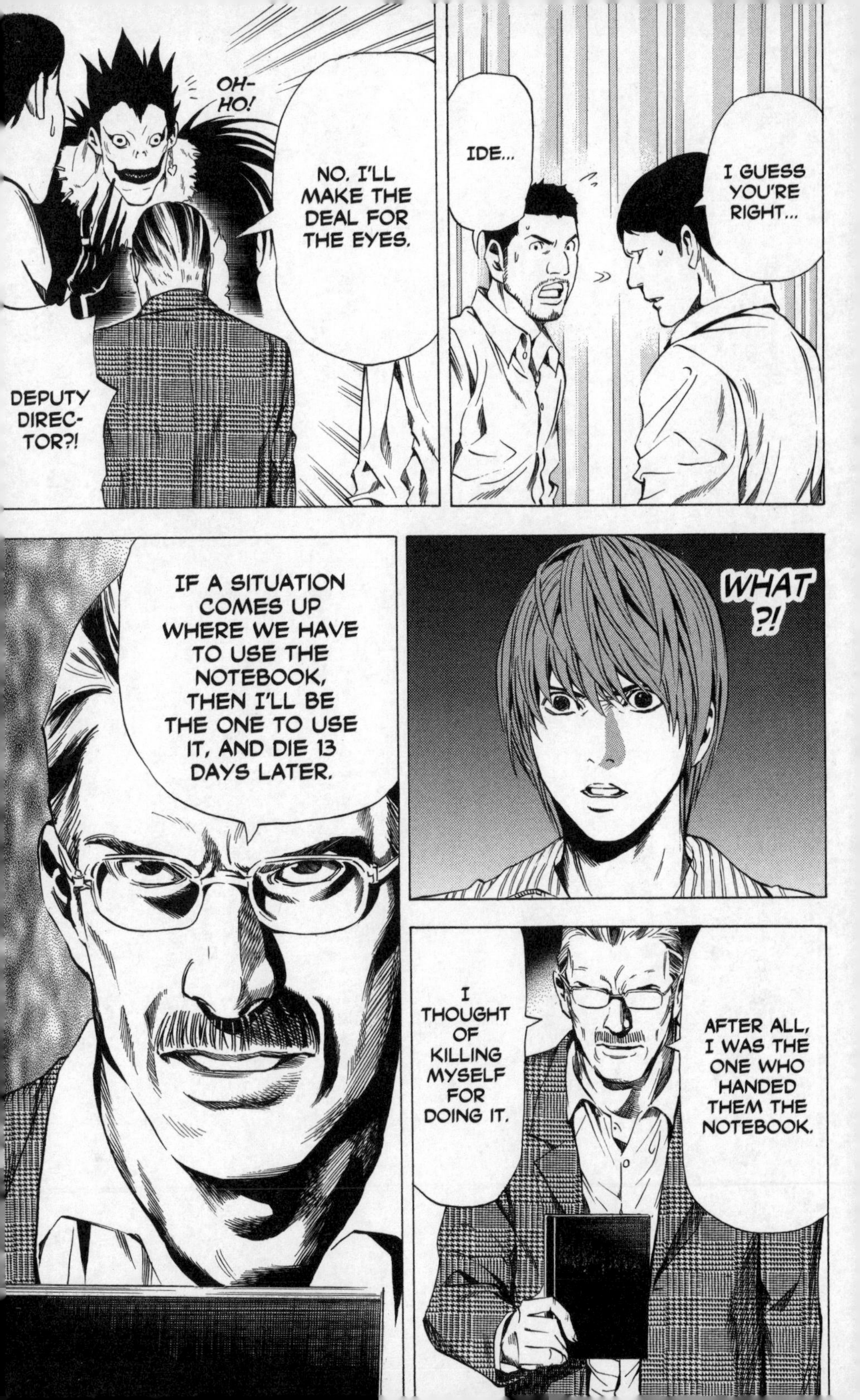
I GUESS YOU'RE RIGHT...
IDE...
NO. I'LL MAKE THE DEAL FOR THE EYES.
OH-HO!
DEPUTY DIRECTOR?!
WHAT?!
AFTER ALL, I WAS THE ONE WHO HANDED THEM THE NOTEBOOK.
I THOUGHT OF KILLING MYSELF FOR DOING IT.
IF A SITUATION COMES UP WHERE WE HAVE TO USE THE NOTEBOOK, THEN I'LL BE THE ONE TO USE IT, AND DIE 13 DAYS LATER.

DEATH NOTE
How to use it
XLVII

- Losing memory of the DEATH NOTE by passing on the ownership to another, or by abandoning its ownership will only occur when someone is actually killed using that DEATH NOTE. You will not lose memory of the DEATH NOTE, for example, if you merely owned it and had not written anyone's name.

In this case, you will not be able to hear the voice or see the figure of the god of death anymore. You will also lose the eye power of the god of death you traded with.

デスノートの所有権を、他の人間に移したり放棄したりする事で
そのノートに関する記憶等がなくなるのは、実際にノートに名前を書き込み
人間を殺した場合であり、所有しただけで名前を書き込んでいない場合は
そのノートに関する記憶は消えない。
しかし、所有した事で認知できていた死神の姿や声は認知できなくなるし、
取引をした死神の目も失われる。

chapter 72 Verification

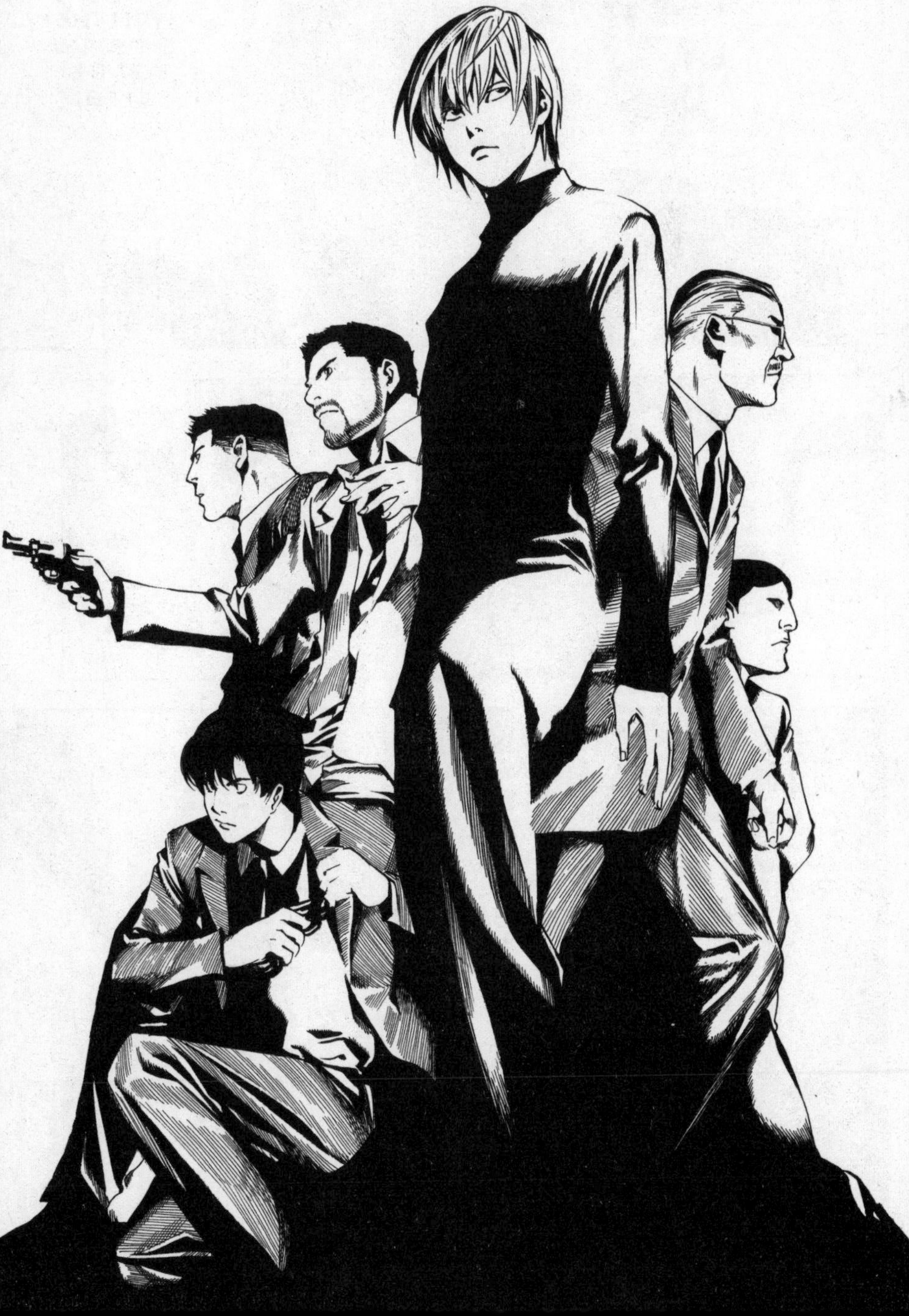

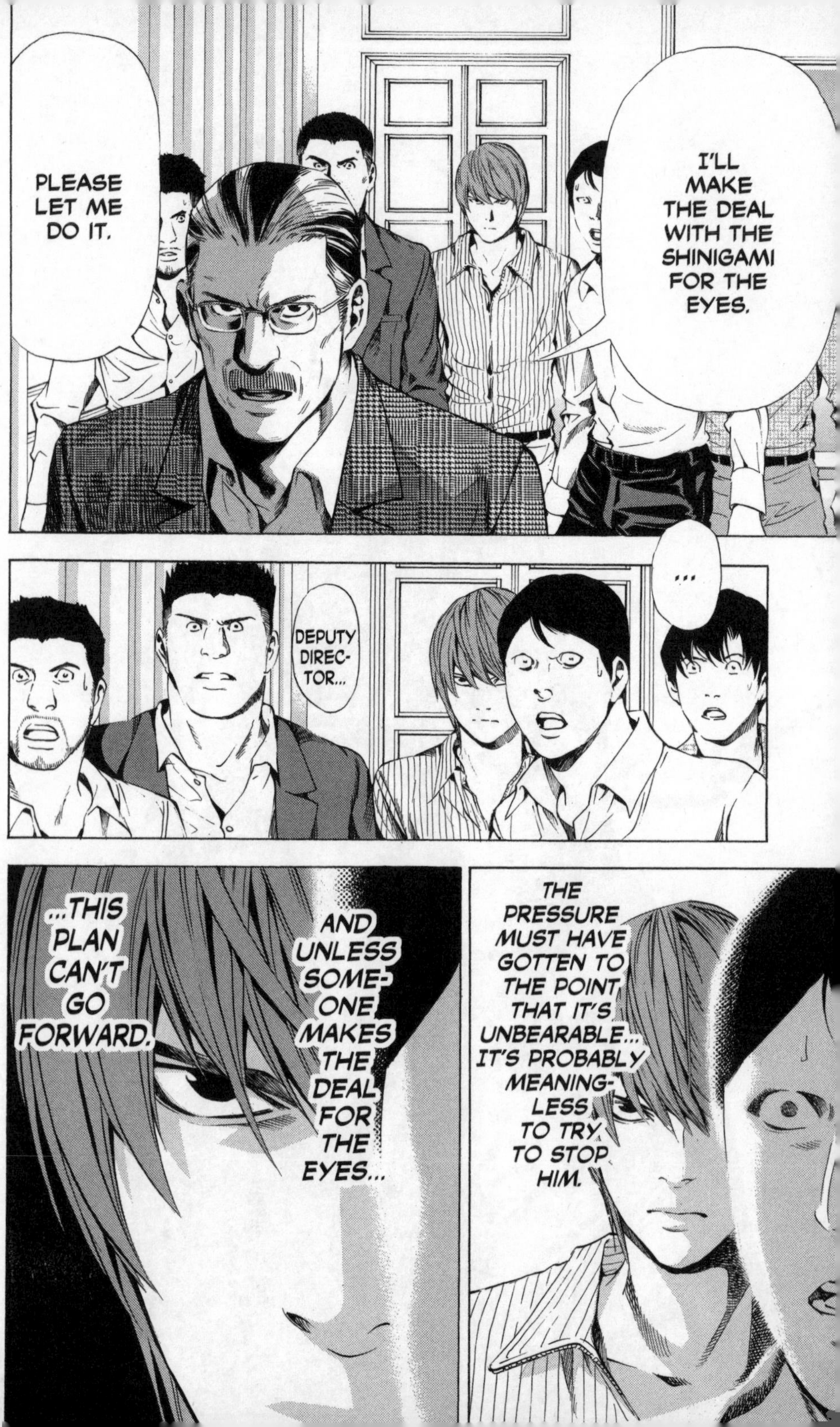
I'LL MAKE THE DEAL WITH THE SHINIGAMI FOR THE EYES.
PLEASE LET ME DO IT.
...
DEPUTY DIRECTOR...
THE PRESSURE MUST HAVE GOTTEN TO THE POINT THAT IT'S UNBEARABLE... IT'S PROBABLY MEANINGLESS TO TRY TO STOP HIM.
AND UNLESS SOMEONE MAKES THE DEAL FOR THE EYES...
...THIS PLAN CAN'T GO FORWARD.

READ THIS WAY

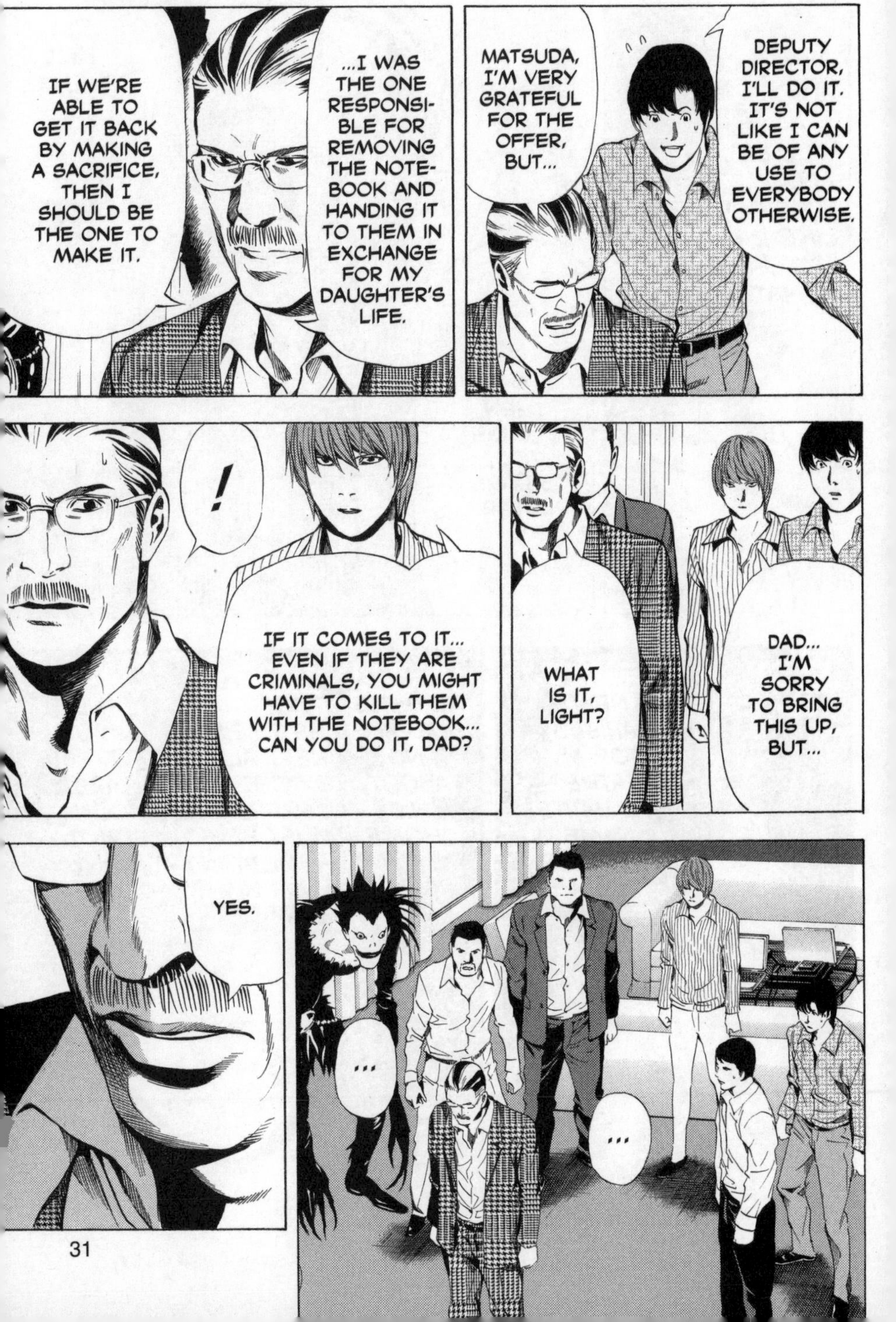
DEPUTY DIRECTOR, I'LL DO IT. IT'S NOT LIKE I CAN BE OF ANY USE TO EVERYBODY OTHERWISE.
MATSUDA, I'M VERY GRATEFUL FOR THE OFFER, BUT...
...I WAS THE ONE RESPONSIBLE FOR REMOVING THE NOTEBOOK AND HANDING IT TO THEM IN EXCHANGE FOR MY DAUGHTER'S LIFE.
IF WE'RE ABLE TO GET IT BACK BY MAKING A SACRIFICE, THEN I SHOULD BE THE ONE TO MAKE IT.
DAD... I'M SORRY TO BRING THIS UP, BUT...
WHAT IS IT, LIGHT?
IF IT COMES TO IT... EVEN IF THEY ARE CRIMINALS, YOU MIGHT HAVE TO KILL THEM WITH THE NOTEBOOK... CAN YOU DO IT, DAD?
!
...
...
YES.

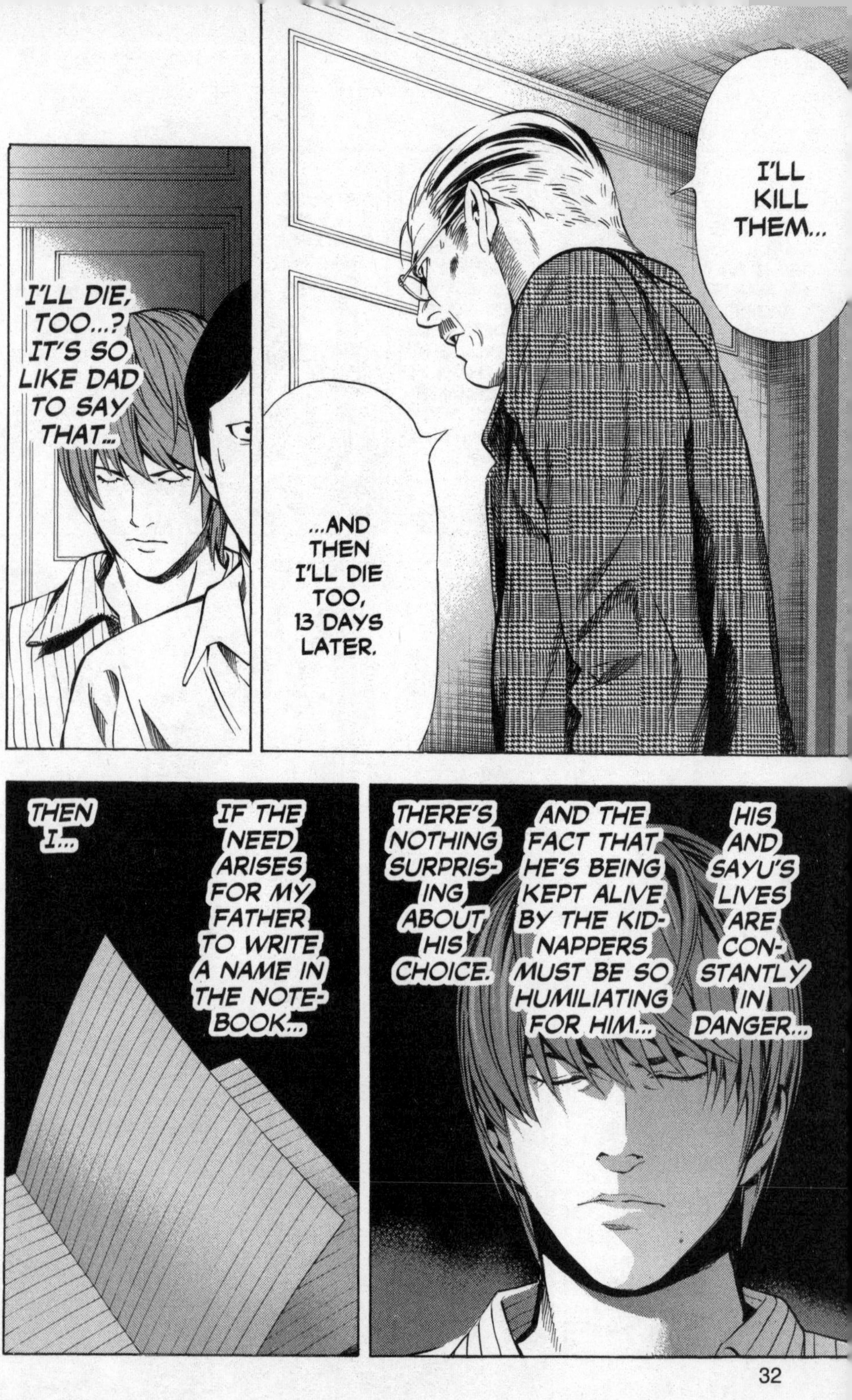
I'LL KILL THEM...
...AND THEN I'LL DIE TOO, 13 DAYS LATER.
I'LL DIE, TOO...? IT'S SO LIKE DAD TO SAY THAT...
HIS AND SAYU'S LIVES ARE CONSTANTLY IN DANGER...
AND THE FACT THAT HE'S BEING KEPT ALIVE BY THE KIDNAPPERS MUST BE SO HUMILIATING FOR HIM...
THERE'S NOTHING SURPRISING ABOUT HIS CHOICE.
IF THE NEED ARISES FOR MY FATHER TO WRITE A NAME IN THE NOTEBOOK...
THEN I...

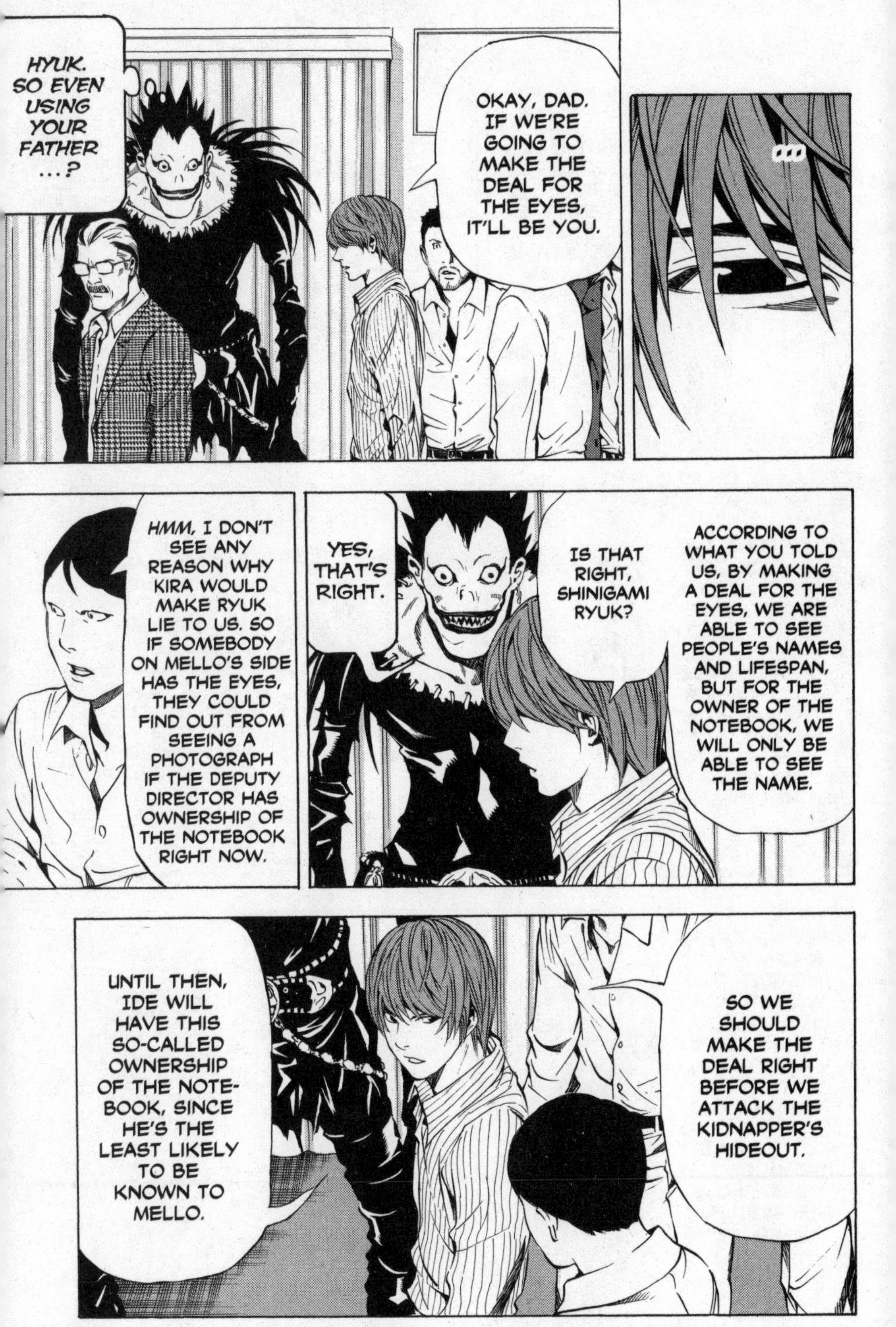
...
OKAY, DAD. IF WE'RE GOING TO MAKE THE DEAL FOR THE EYES, IT'LL BE YOU.
HYUK. SO EVEN USING YOUR FATHER ...?
ACCORDING TO WHAT YOU TOLD US, BY MAKING A DEAL FOR THE EYES, WE ARE ABLE TO SEE PEOPLE'S NAMES AND LIFESPAN, BUT FOR THE OWNER OF THE NOTEBOOK, WE WILL ONLY BE ABLE TO SEE THE NAME.
IS THAT RIGHT, SHINIGAMI RYUK?
YES, THAT'S RIGHT.
HMM, I DON'T SEE ANY REASON WHY KIRA WOULD MAKE RYUK LIE TO US. SO IF SOMEBODY ON MELLO'S SIDE HAS THE EYES, THEY COULD FIND OUT FROM SEEING A PHOTOGRAPH IF THE DEPUTY DIRECTOR HAS OWNERSHIP OF THE NOTEBOOK RIGHT NOW.
SO WE SHOULD MAKE THE DEAL RIGHT BEFORE WE ATTACK THE KIDNAPPER'S HIDEOUT.
UNTIL THEN, IDE WILL HAVE THIS SO-CALLED OWNERSHIP OF THE NOTE-BOOK, SINCE HE'S THE LEAST LIKELY TO BE KNOWN TO MELLO.

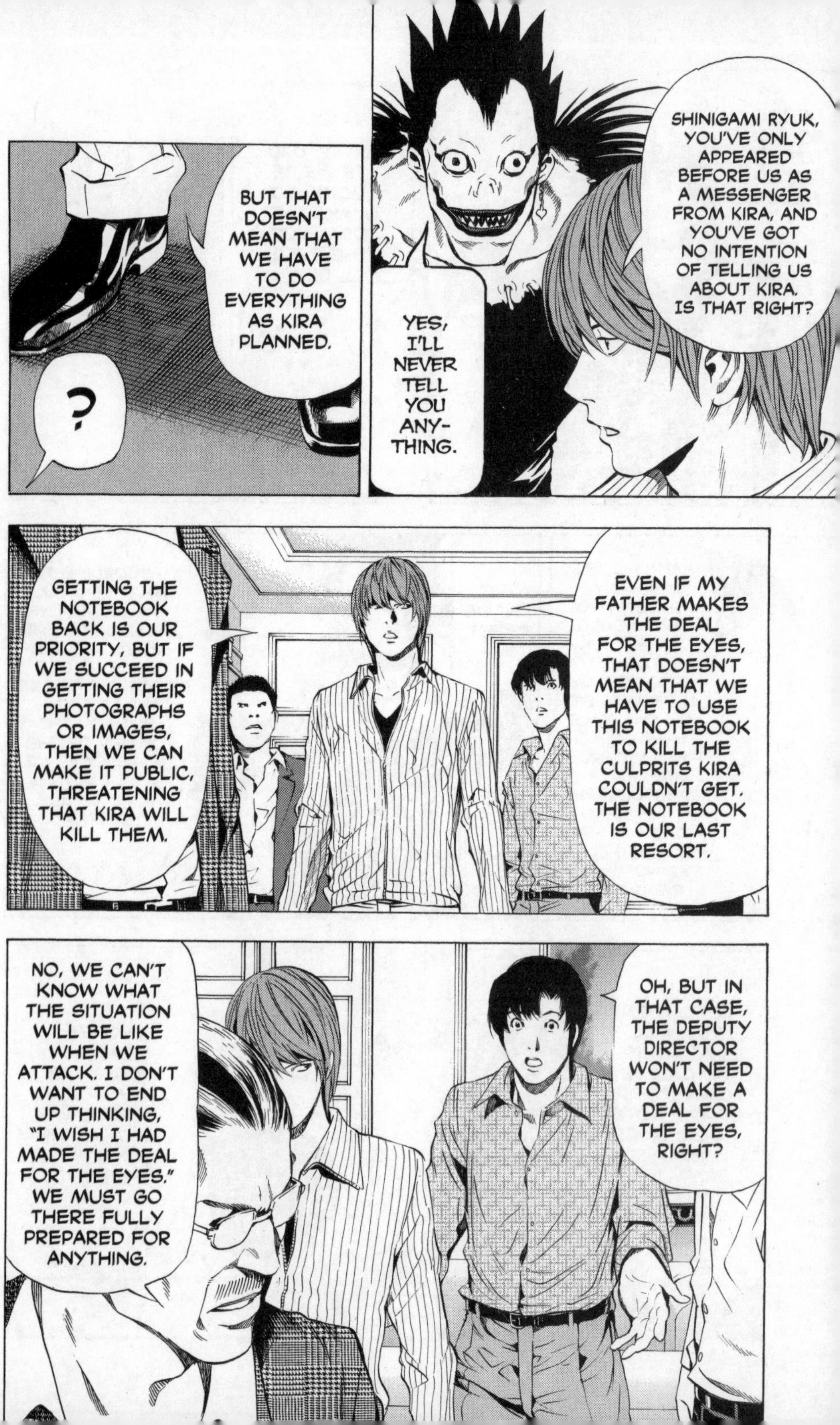
SHINIGAMI RYUK, YOU'VE ONLY APPEARED BEFORE US AS A MESSENGER FROM KIRA, AND YOU'VE GOT NO INTENTION OF TELLING US ABOUT KIRA. IS THAT RIGHT?
YES, I'LL NEVER TELL YOU ANY-THING.
BUT THAT DOESN'T MEAN THAT WE HAVE TO DO EVERYTHING AS KIRA PLANNED.
?
EVEN IF MY FATHER MAKES THE DEAL FOR THE EYES, THAT DOESN'T MEAN THAT WE HAVE TO USE THIS NOTEBOOK TO KILL THE CULPRITS KIRA COULDN'T GET. THE NOTEBOOK IS OUR LAST RESORT.
GETTING THE NOTEBOOK BACK IS OUR PRIORITY, BUT IF WE SUCCEED IN GETTING THEIR PHOTOGRAPHS OR IMAGES, THEN WE CAN MAKE IT PUBLIC, THREATENING THAT KIRA WILL KILL THEM.
OH, BUT IN THAT CASE, THE DEPUTY DIRECTOR WON'T NEED TO MAKE A DEAL FOR THE EYES, RIGHT?
NO, WE CAN'T KNOW WHAT THE SITUATION WILL BE LIKE WHEN WE ATTACK. I DON'T WANT TO END UP THINKING, "I WISH I HAD MADE THE DEAL FOR THE EYES." WE MUST GO THERE FULLY PREPARED FOR ANYTHING.

READ THIS WAY

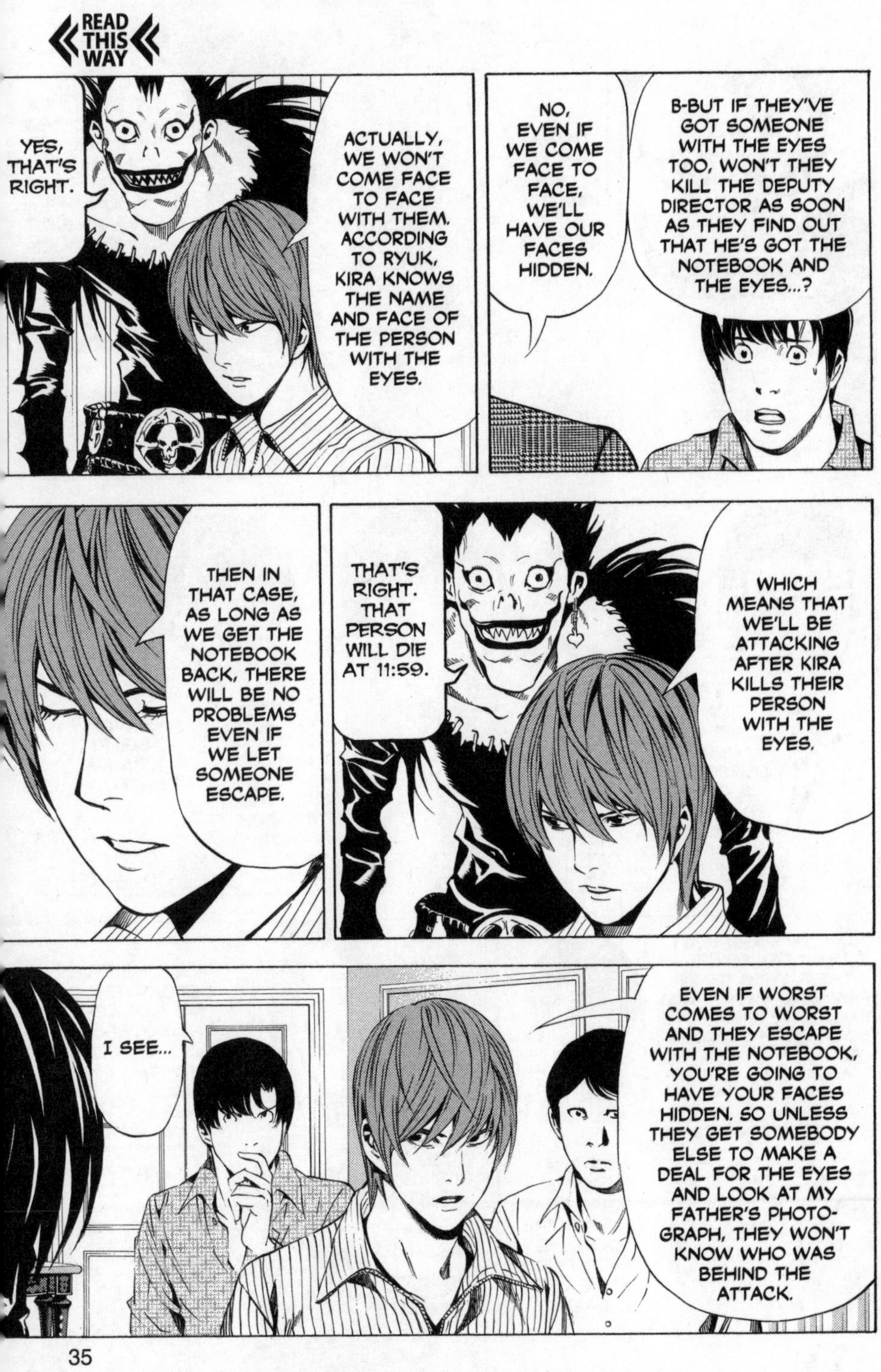
B-BUT IF THEY'VE GOT SOMEONE WITH THE EYES TOO, WON'T THEY KILL THE DEPUTY DIRECTOR AS SOON AS THEY FIND OUT THAT HE'S GOT THE NOTEBOOK AND THE EYES...?
NO, EVEN IF WE COME FACE TO FACE, WE'LL HAVE OUR FACES HIDDEN.
ACTUALLY, WE WON'T COME FACE TO FACE WITH THEM. ACCORDING TO RYUK, KIRA KNOWS THE NAME AND FACE OF THE PERSON WITH THE EYES.
YES, THAT'S RIGHT.
WHICH MEANS THAT WE'LL BE ATTACKING AFTER KIRA KILLS THEIR PERSON WITH THE EYES.
THAT'S RIGHT. THAT PERSON WILL DIE AT 11:59.
THEN IN THAT CASE, AS LONG AS WE GET THE NOTEBOOK BACK, THERE WILL BE NO PROBLEMS EVEN IF WE LET SOMEONE ESCAPE.
EVEN IF WORST COMES TO WORST AND THEY ESCAPE WITH THE NOTEBOOK, YOU'RE GOING TO HAVE YOUR FACES HIDDEN. SO UNLESS THEY GET SOMEBODY ELSE TO MAKE A DEAL FOR THE EYES AND LOOK AT MY FATHER'S PHOTOGRAPH, THEY WON'T KNOW WHO WAS BEHIND THE ATTACK.
I SEE...

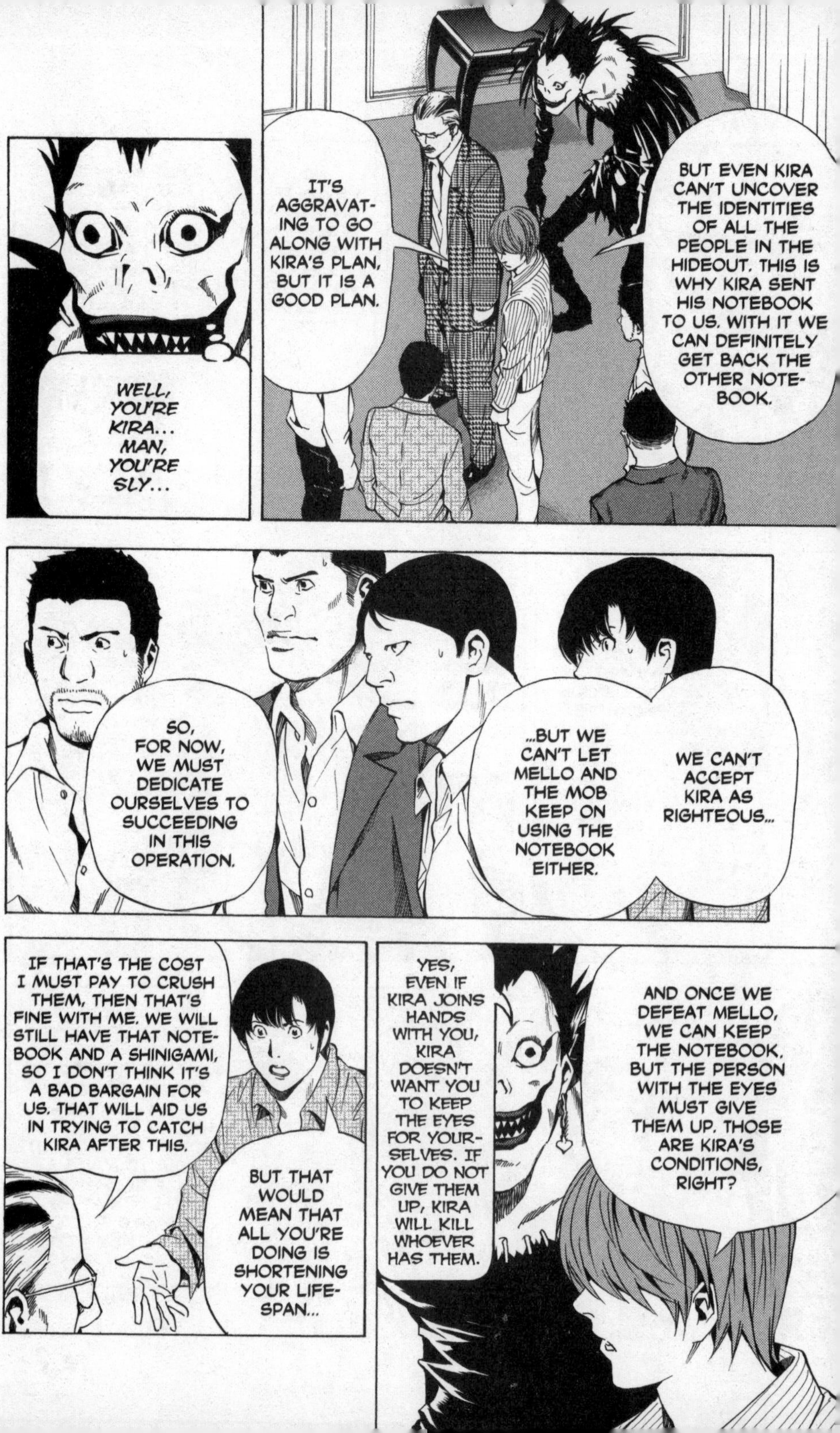
BUT EVEN KIRA CAN'T UNCOVER THE IDENTITIES OF ALL THE PEOPLE IN THE HIDEOUT. THIS IS WHY KIRA SENT HIS NOTEBOOK TO US. WITH IT WE CAN DEFINITELY GET BACK THE OTHER NOTE-BOOK.
IT'S AGGRAVAT-ING TO GO ALONG WITH KIRA'S PLAN, BUT IT IS A GOOD PLAN.
WELL, YOU'RE KIRA... MAN, YOU'RE SLY...
WE CAN'T ACCEPT KIRA AS RIGHTEOUS...
...BUT WE CAN'T LET MELLO AND THE MOB KEEP ON USING THE NOTEBOOK EITHER.
SO, FOR NOW, WE MUST DEDICATE OURSELVES TO SUCCEEDING IN THIS OPERATION.
AND ONCE WE DEFEAT MELLO, WE CAN KEEP THE NOTEBOOK, BUT THE PERSON WITH THE EYES MUST GIVE THEM UP. THOSE ARE KIRA'S CONDITIONS, RIGHT?
YES, EVEN IF KIRA JOINS HANDS WITH YOU, KIRA DOESN'T WANT YOU TO KEEP THE EYES FOR YOUR-SELVES. IF YOU DO NOT GIVE THEM UP, KIRA WILL KILL WHOEVER HAS THEM.
IF THAT'S THE COST I MUST PAY TO CRUSH THEM, THEN THAT'S FINE WITH ME. WE WILL STILL HAVE THAT NOTE-BOOK AND A SHINIGAMI, SO I DON'T THINK IT'S A BAD BARGAIN FOR US. THAT WILL AID US IN TRYING TO CATCH KIRA AFTER THIS.
BUT THAT WOULD MEAN THAT ALL YOU'RE DOING IS SHORTENING YOUR LIFE-SPAN...

READ THIS WAY

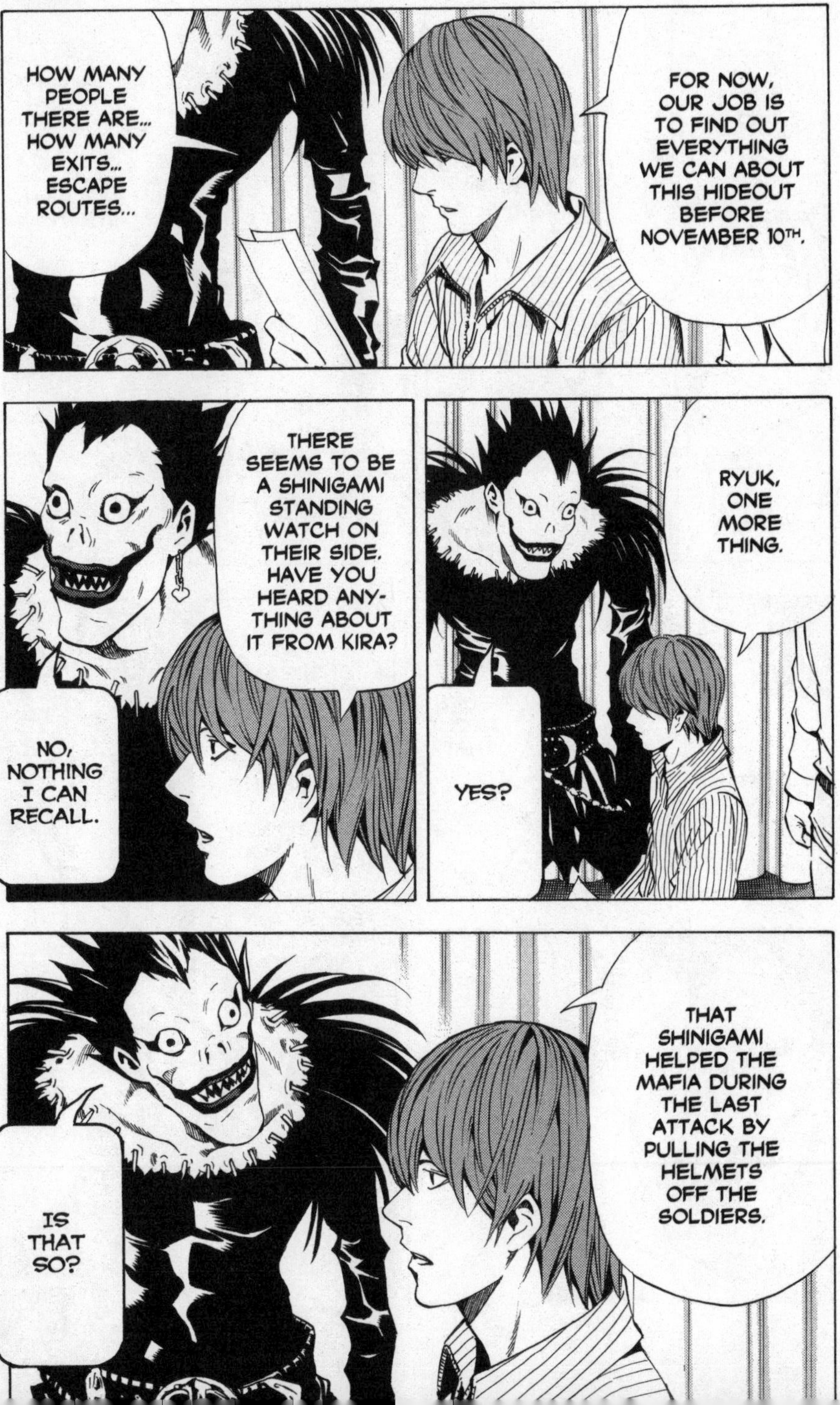
FOR NOW, OUR JOB IS TO FIND OUT EVERYTHING WE CAN ABOUT THIS HIDEOUT BEFORE NOVEMBER 10TH.
HOW MANY PEOPLE THERE ARE... HOW MANY EXITS... ESCAPE ROUTES...
RYUK, ONE MORE THING.
YES?
THERE SEEMS TO BE A SHINIGAMI STANDING WATCH ON THEIR SIDE. HAVE YOU HEARD ANYTHING ABOUT IT FROM KIRA?
NO, NOTHING I CAN RECALL.
THAT SHINIGAMI HELPED THE MAFIA DURING THE LAST ATTACK BY PULLING THE HELMETS OFF THE SOLDIERS.
IS THAT SO?

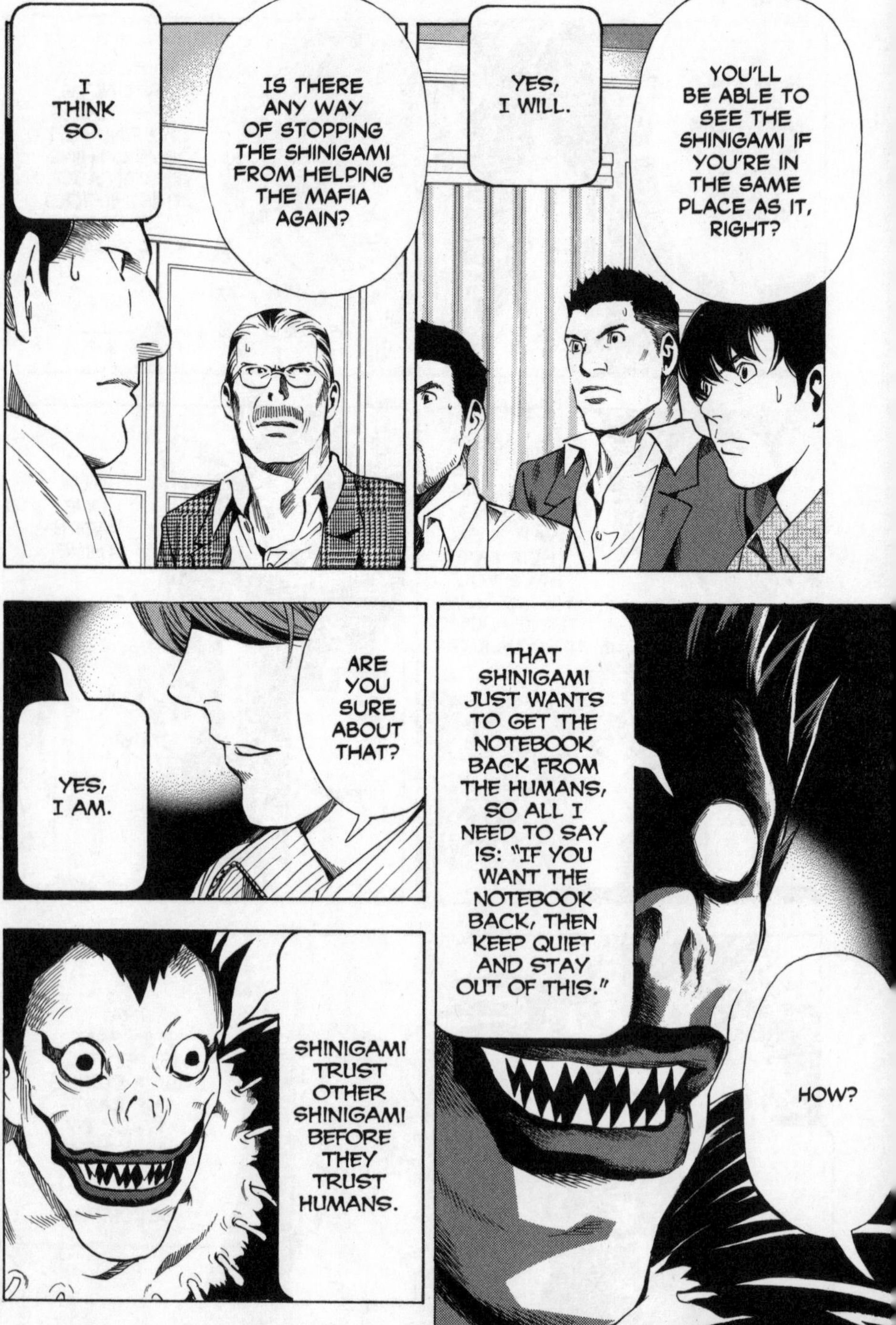
YOU'LL BE ABLE TO SEE THE SHINIGAMI IF YOU'RE IN THE SAME PLACE AS IT, RIGHT?
YES, I WILL.
IS THERE ANY WAY OF STOPPING THE SHINIGAMI FROM HELPING THE MAFIA AGAIN?
I THINK SO.
THAT SHINIGAMI JUST WANTS TO GET THE NOTEBOOK BACK FROM THE HUMANS, SO ALL I NEED TO SAY IS: "IF YOU WANT THE NOTEBOOK BACK, THEN KEEP QUIET AND STAY OUT OF THIS."
HOW?
ARE YOU SURE ABOUT THAT?
YES, I AM.
SHINIGAMI TRUST OTHER SHINIGAMI BEFORE THEY TRUST HUMANS.

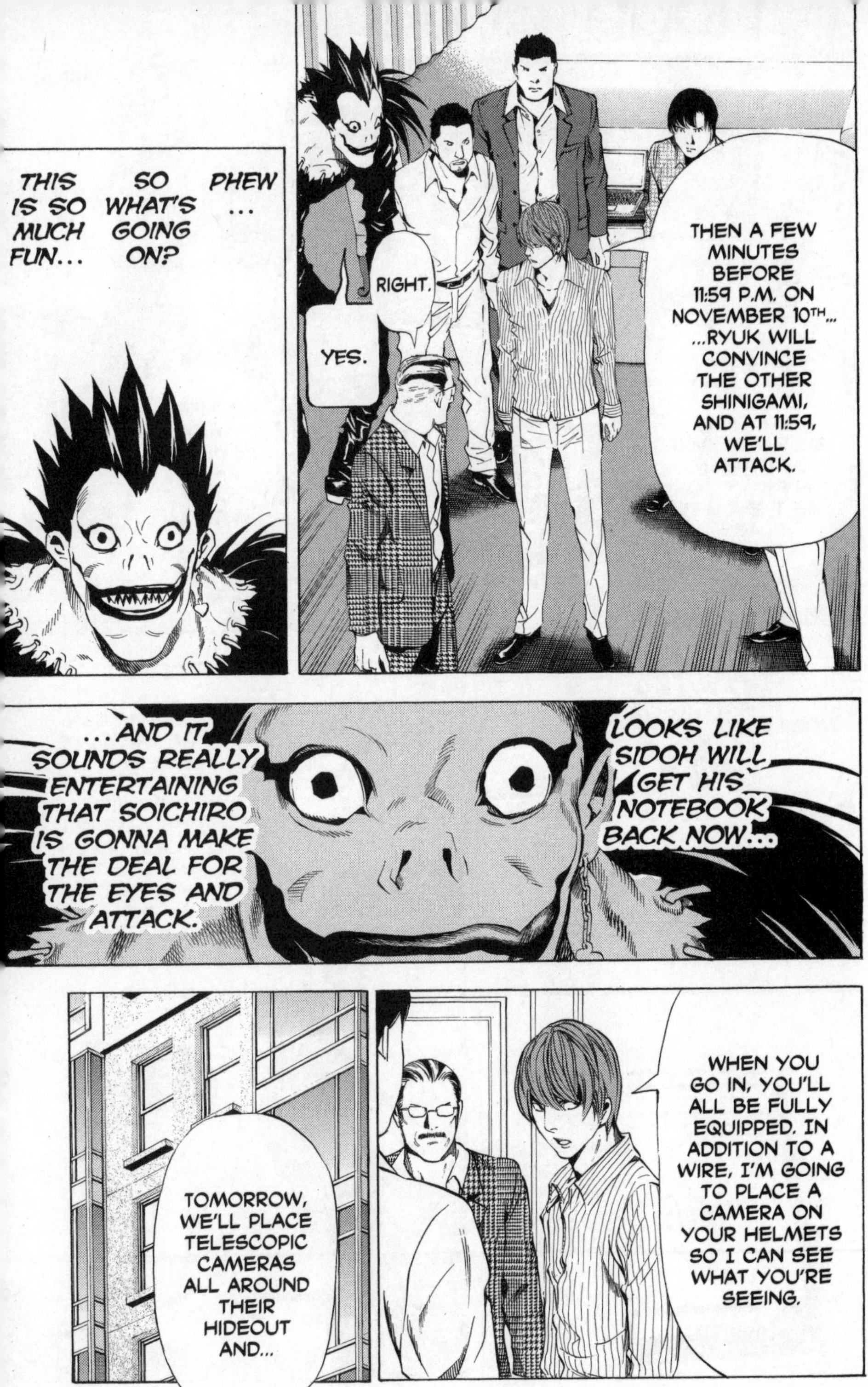
THEN A FEW MINUTES BEFORE 11:59 P.M. ON NOVEMBER 10TH... ...RYUK WILL CONVINCE THE OTHER SHINIGAMI, AND AT 11:59, WE'LL ATTACK.
RIGHT.
YES.
PHEW...
SO WHAT'S GOING ON?
THIS IS SO MUCH FUN...
LOOKS LIKE SIDOH WILL GET HIS NOTEBOOK BACK NOW...
...AND IT SOUNDS REALLY ENTERTAINING THAT SOICHIRO IS GONNA MAKE THE DEAL FOR THE EYES AND ATTACK.
WHEN YOU GO IN, YOU'LL ALL BE FULLY EQUIPPED. IN ADDITION TO A WIRE, I'M GOING TO PLACE A CAMERA ON YOUR HELMETS SO I CAN SEE WHAT YOU'RE SEEING.
TOMORROW, WE'LL PLACE TELESCOPIC CAMERAS ALL AROUND THEIR HIDEOUT AND...

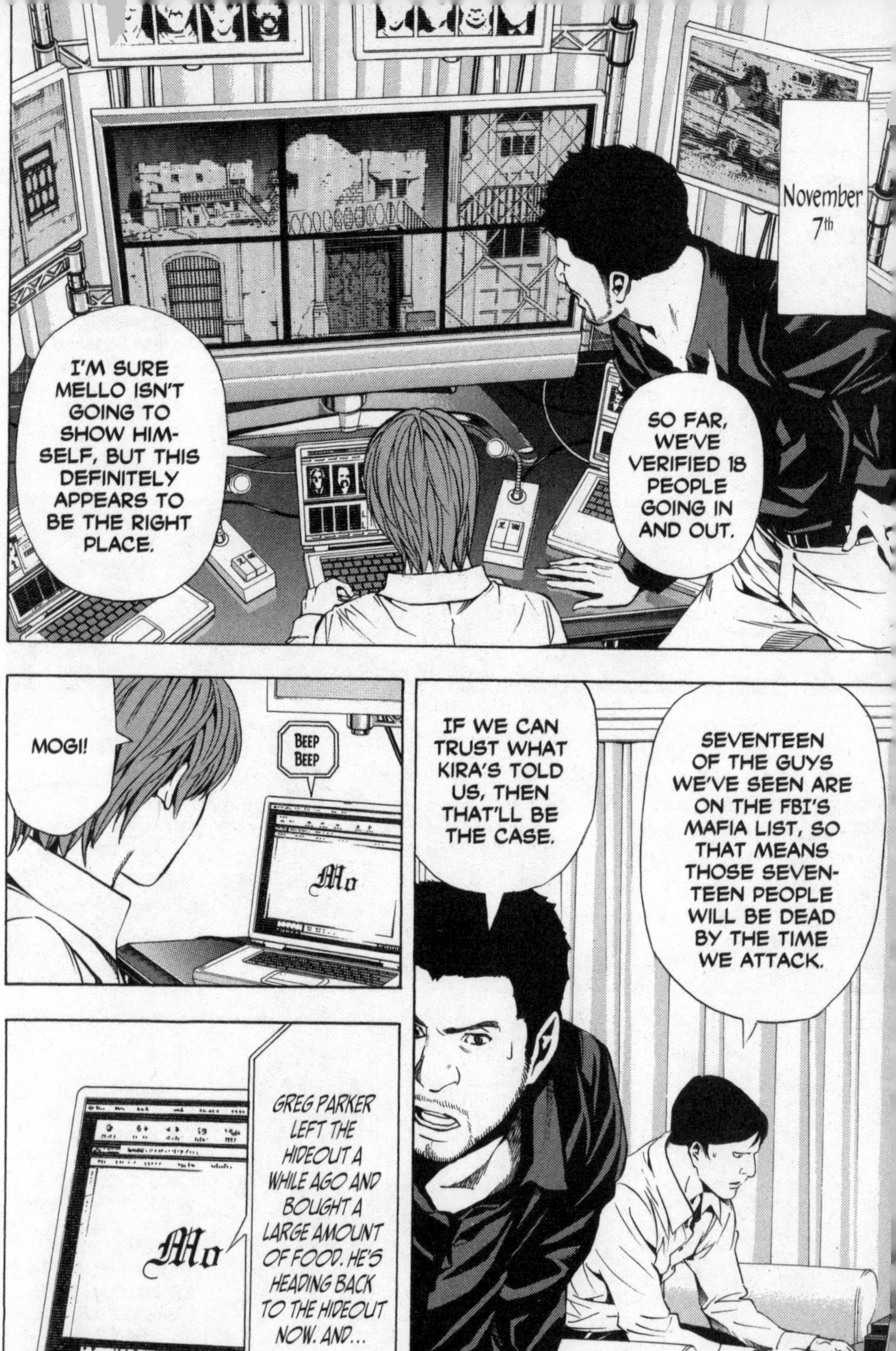

November 7th
SO FAR, WE'VE VERIFIED 18 PEOPLE GOING IN AND OUT.
I'M SURE MELLO ISN'T GOING TO SHOW HIMSELF, BUT THIS DEFINITELY APPEARS TO BE THE RIGHT PLACE.
SEVENTEEN OF THE GUYS WE'VE SEEN ARE ON THE FBI'S MAFIA LIST, SO THAT MEANS THOSE SEVENTEEN PEOPLE WILL BE DEAD BY THE TIME WE ATTACK.
IF WE CAN TRUST WHAT KIRA'S TOLD US, THEN THAT'LL BE THE CASE.
BEEP BEEP
Mo
MOGI!
GREG PARKER LEFT THE HIDEOUT A WHILE AGO AND BOUGHT A LARGE AMOUNT OF FOOD. HE'S HEADING BACK TO THE HIDEOUT NOW. AND...
Mo

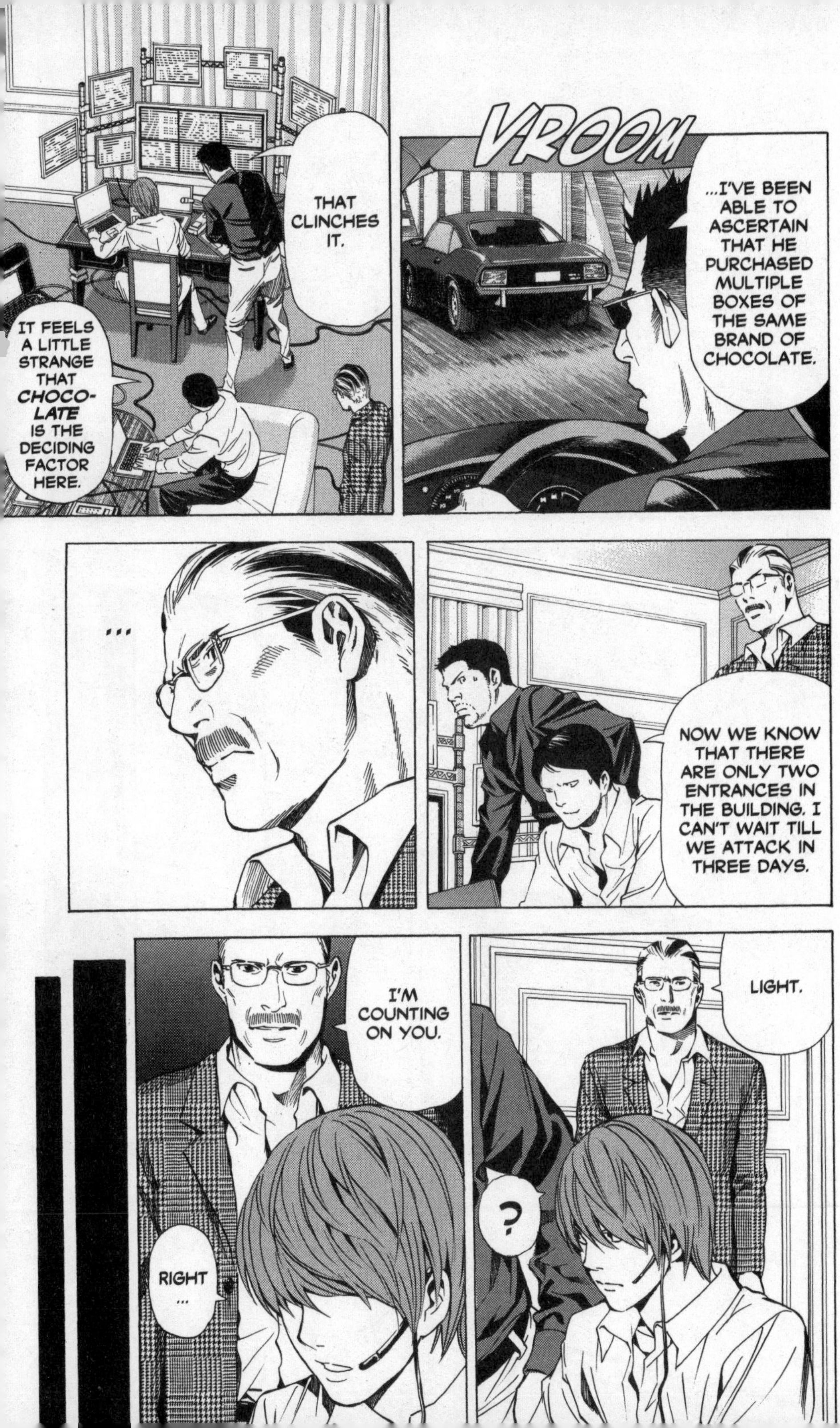
VROOM
...I'VE BEEN ABLE TO ASCERTAIN THAT HE PURCHASED MULTIPLE BOXES OF THE SAME BRAND OF CHOCOLATE.
THAT CLINCHES IT.
IT FEELS A LITTLE STRANGE THAT *CHOCOLATE* IS THE DECIDING FACTOR HERE.
NOW WE KNOW THAT THERE ARE ONLY TWO ENTRANCES IN THE BUILDING. I CAN'T WAIT TILL WE ATTACK IN THREE DAYS.
...
LIGHT.
?
I'M COUNTING ON YOU.
RIGHT ...

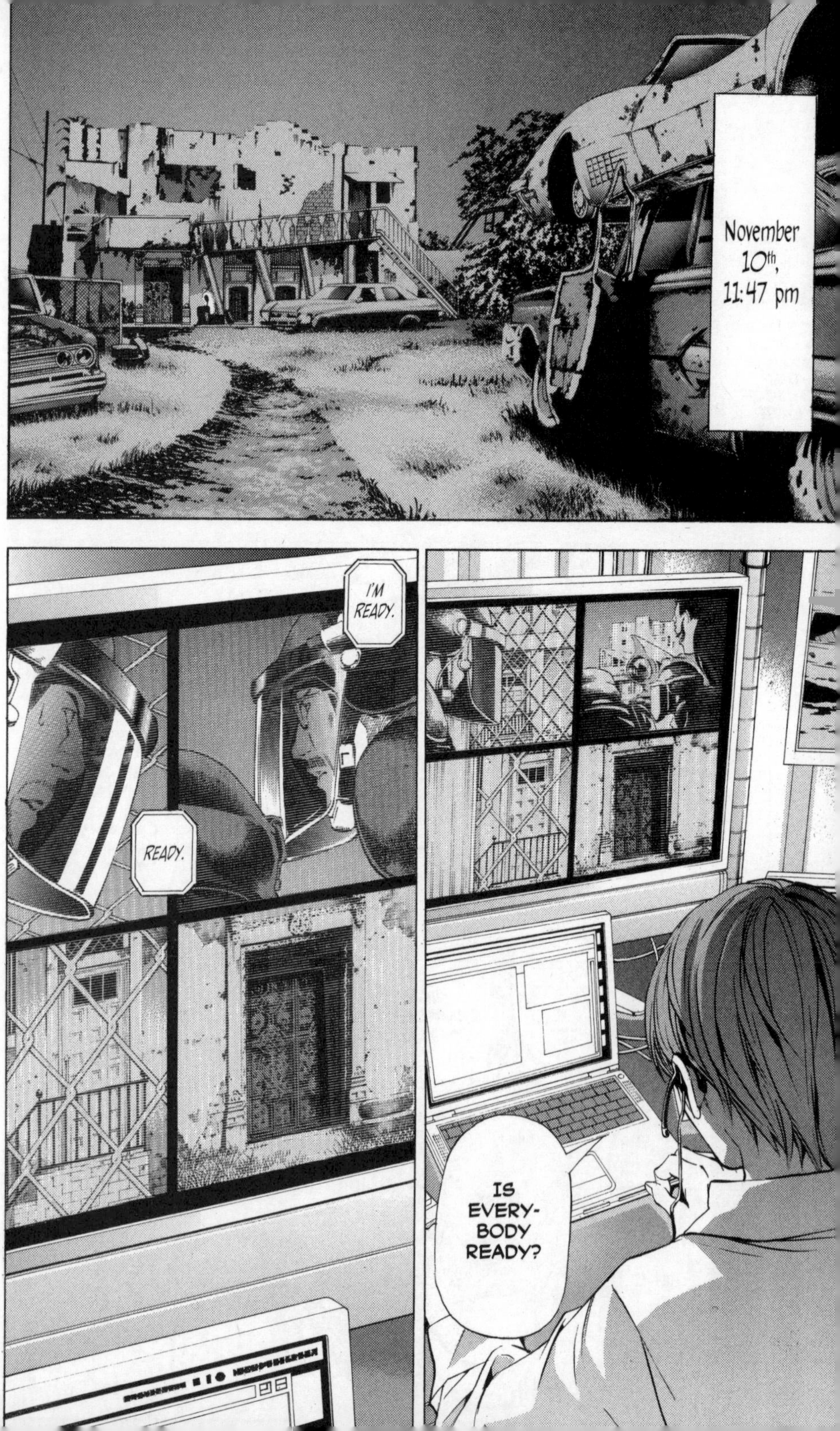
November 10th, 11:47 pm
IS EVERY-BODY READY?
I'M READY.
READY.

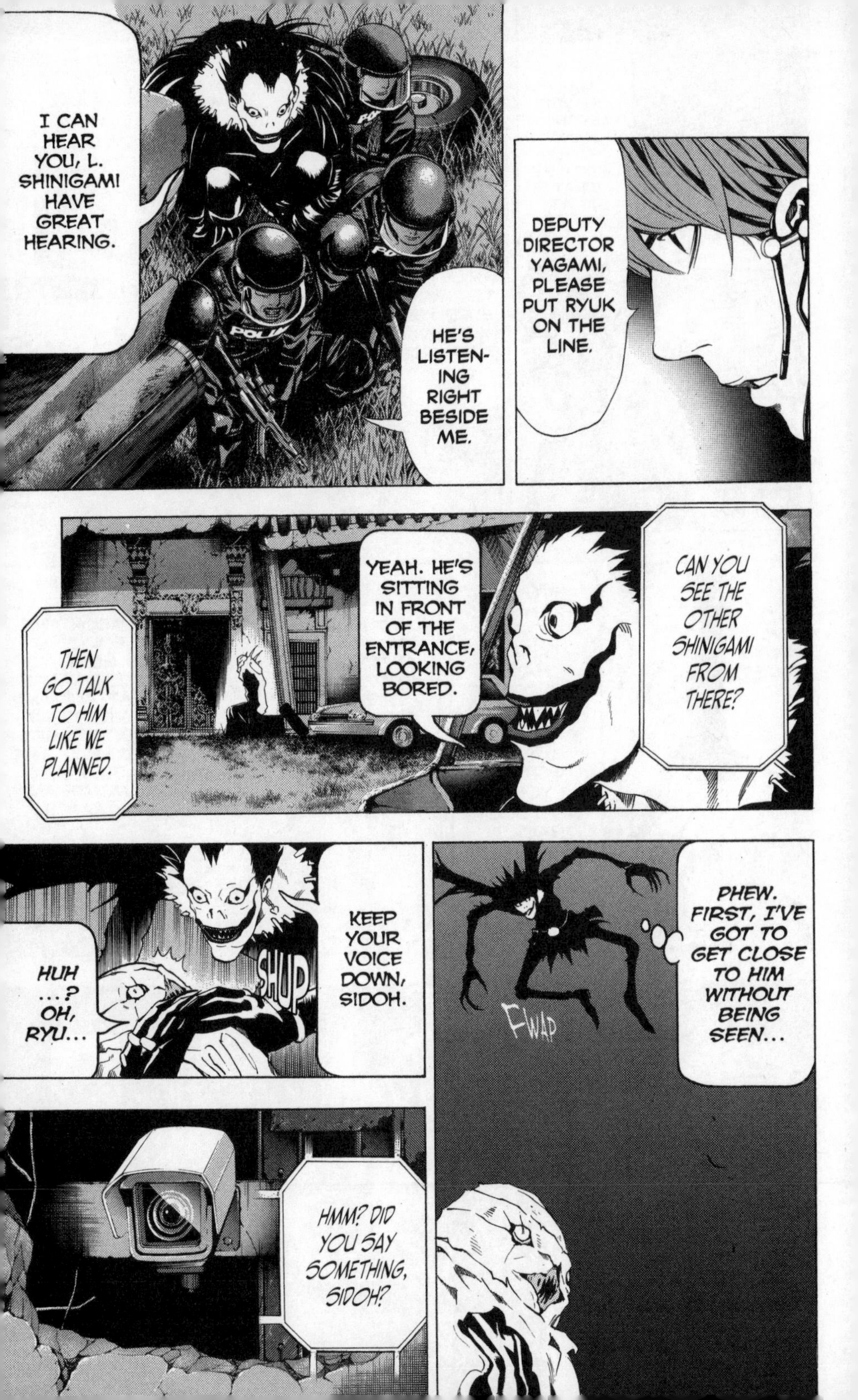
DEPUTY DIRECTOR YAGAMI, PLEASE PUT RYUK ON THE LINE.
HE'S LISTEN-ING RIGHT BESIDE ME.
I CAN HEAR YOU, L. SHINIGAMI HAVE GREAT HEARING.
CAN YOU SEE THE OTHER SHINIGAMI FROM THERE?
YEAH. HE'S SITTING IN FRONT OF THE ENTRANCE, LOOKING BORED.
THEN GO TALK TO HIM LIKE WE PLANNED.
PHEW. FIRST, I'VE GOT TO GET CLOSE TO HIM WITHOUT BEING SEEN...
FWAP
KEEP YOUR VOICE DOWN, SIDOH.
SHUP
HUH ...? OH, RYU...
HMM? DID YOU SAY SOMETHING, SIDOH?

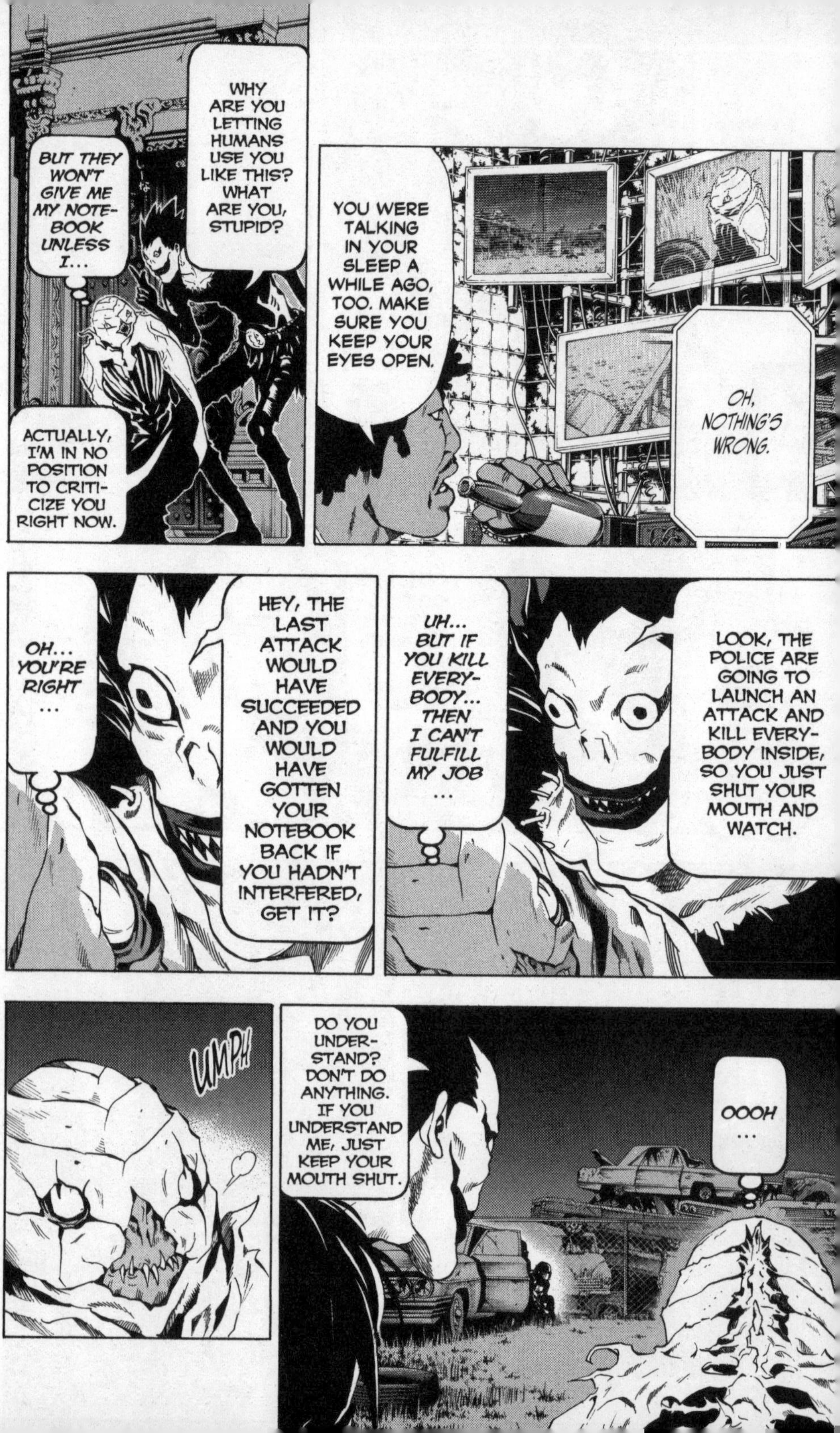
OH, NOTHING'S WRONG.
YOU WERE TALKING IN YOUR SLEEP A WHILE AGO, TOO. MAKE SURE YOU KEEP YOUR EYES OPEN.
WHY ARE YOU LETTING HUMANS USE YOU LIKE THIS? WHAT ARE YOU, STUPID?
BUT THEY WON'T GIVE ME MY NOTE-BOOK UNLESS I...
ACTUALLY, I'M IN NO POSITION TO CRITI-CIZE YOU RIGHT NOW.
LOOK, THE POLICE ARE GOING TO LAUNCH AN ATTACK AND KILL EVERY-BODY INSIDE, SO YOU JUST SHUT YOUR MOUTH AND WATCH.
UH... BUT IF YOU KILL EVERY-BODY... THEN I CAN'T FULFILL MY JOB ...
HEY, THE LAST ATTACK WOULD HAVE SUCCEEDED AND YOU WOULD HAVE GOTTEN YOUR NOTEBOOK BACK IF YOU HADN'T INTERFERED, GET IT?
OH... YOU'RE RIGHT ...
DO YOU UNDER-STAND? DON'T DO ANYTHING. IF YOU UNDERSTAND ME, JUST KEEP YOUR MOUTH SHUT.
OOOH ...
UMPH

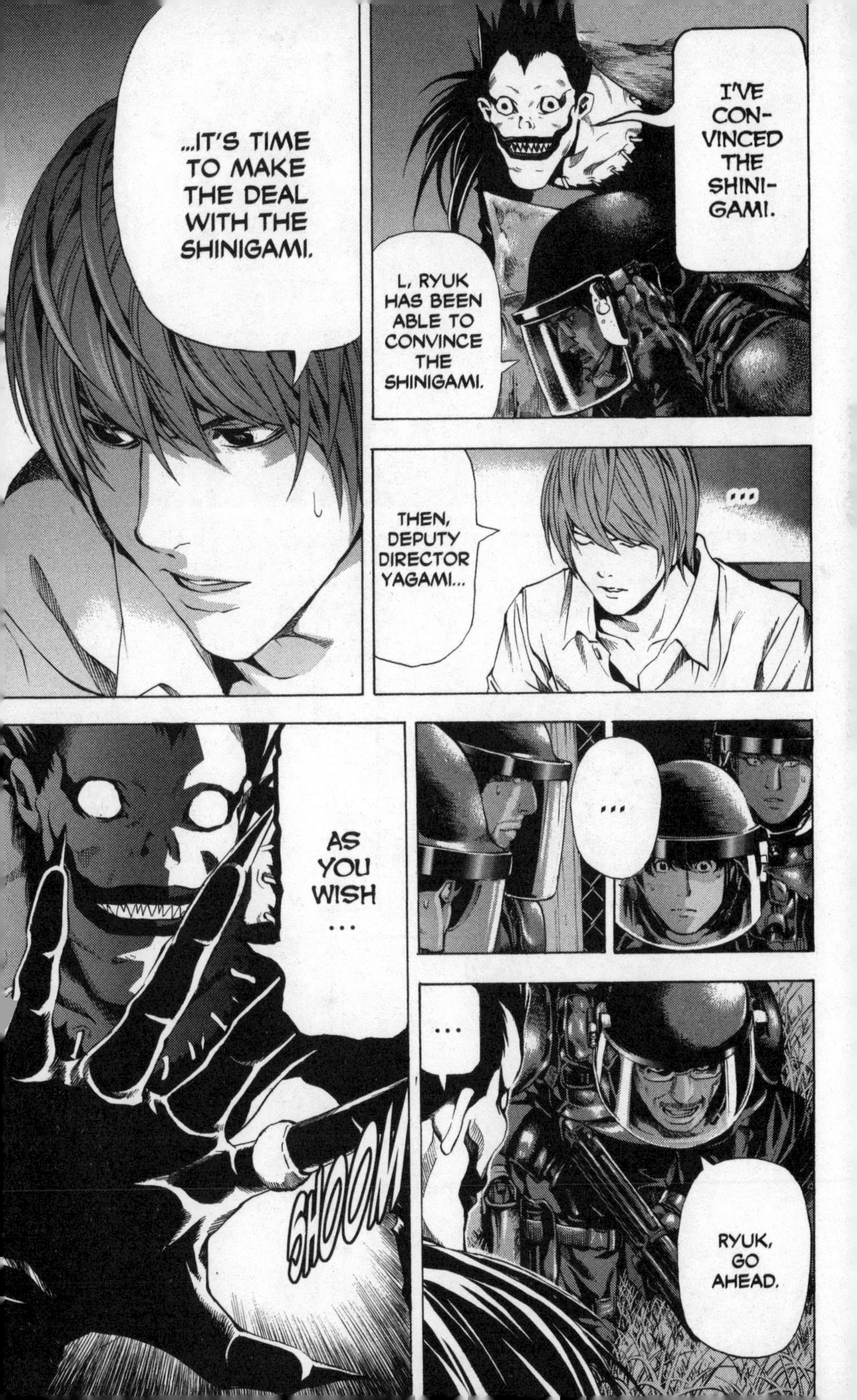
I'VE CONVINCED THE SHINIGAMI.
L, RYUK HAS BEEN ABLE TO CONVINCE THE SHINIGAMI.
...
THEN, DEPUTY DIRECTOR YAGAMI...
...IT'S TIME TO MAKE THE DEAL WITH THE SHINIGAMI.
...
...
RYUK, GO AHEAD.
AS YOU WISH...
SHOOM

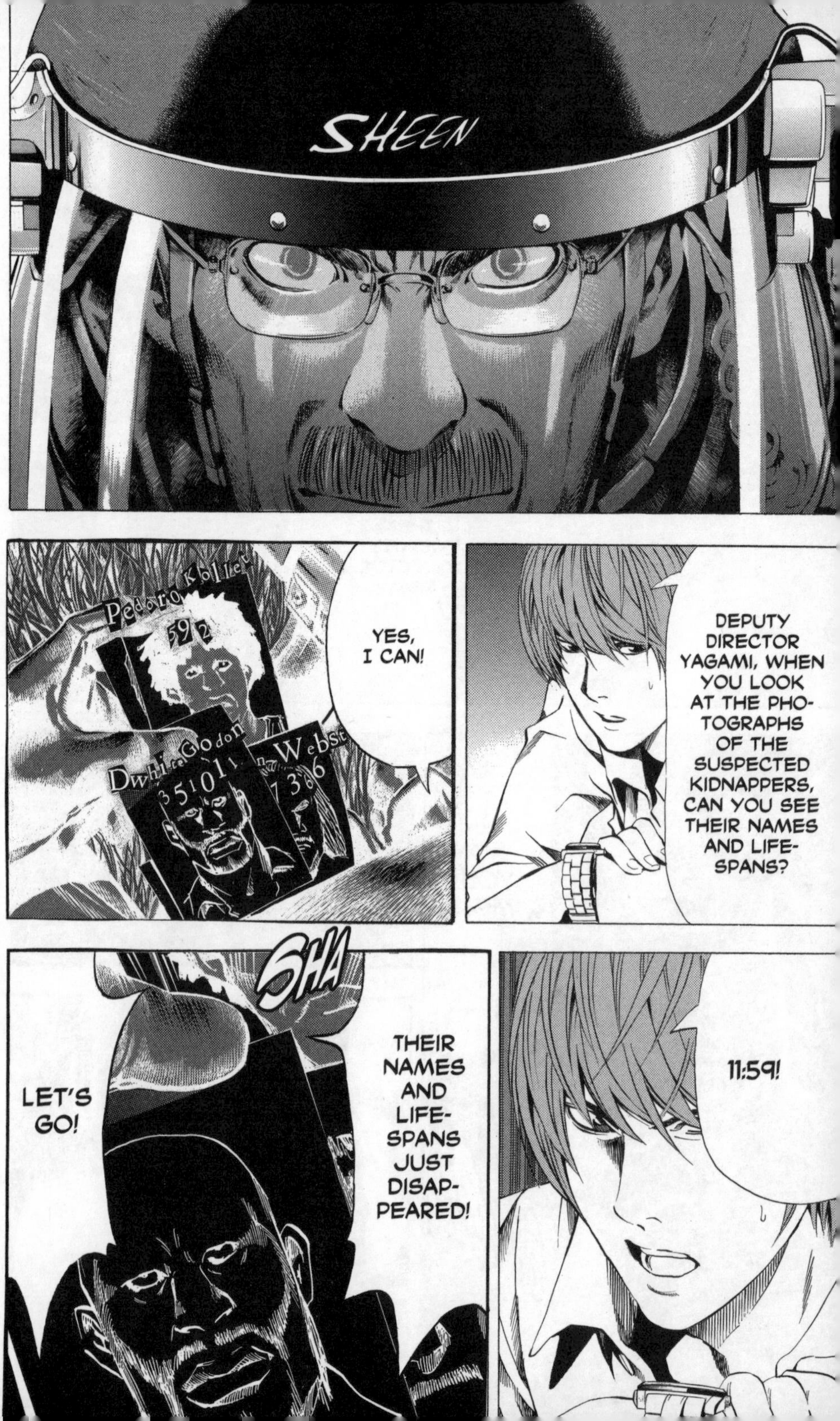
SHEEN
DEPUTY DIRECTOR YAGAMI, WHEN YOU LOOK AT THE PHOTOGRAPHS OF THE SUSPECTED KIDNAPPERS, CAN YOU SEE THEIR NAMES AND LIFESPANS?
YES, I CAN!
11:59!
SHA
THEIR NAMES AND LIFESPANS JUST DISAPPEARED!
LET'S GO!

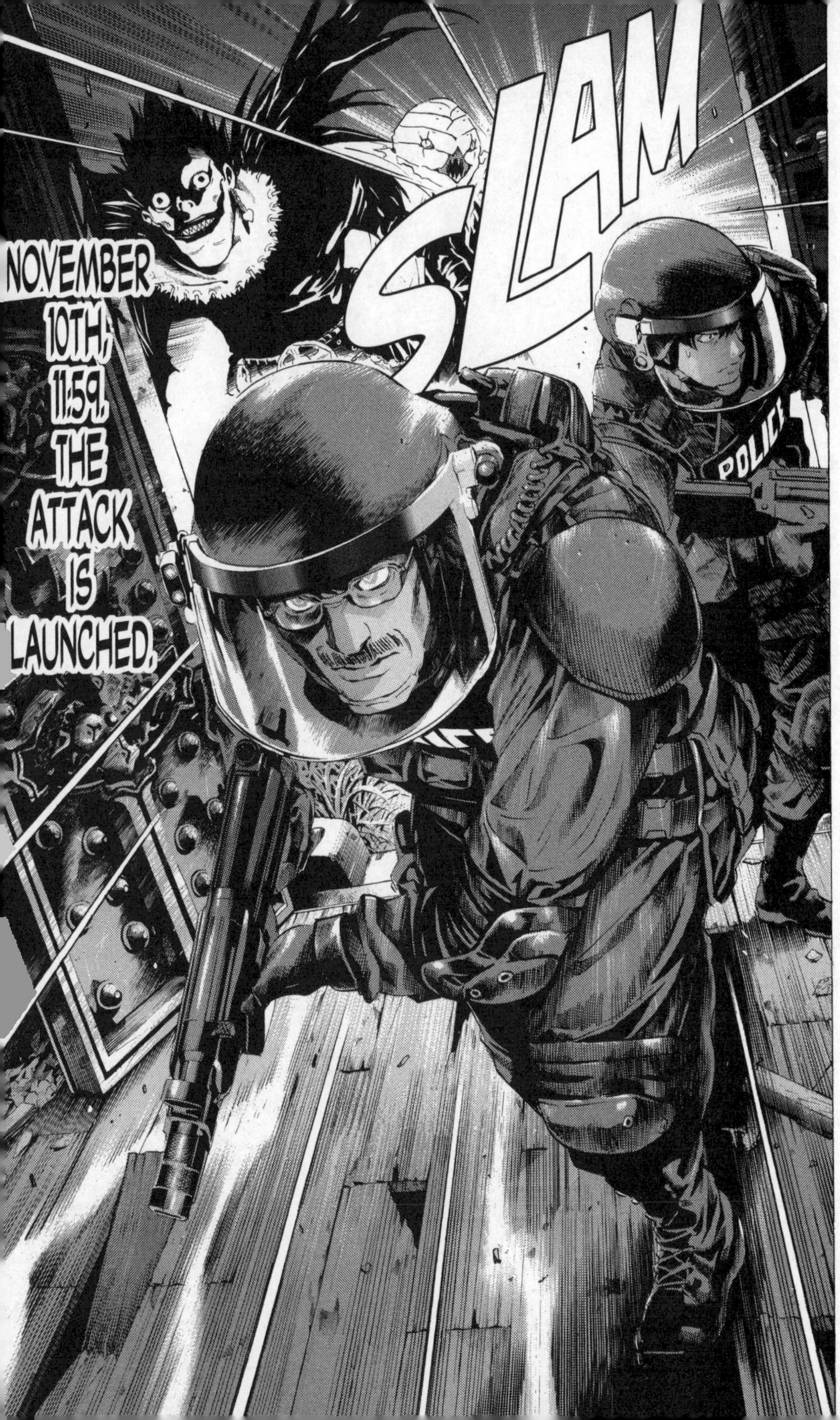

SLAM
NOVEMBER 10TH, 11:59. THE ATTACK IS LAUNCHED.
POLICE

DEATH NOTE
How to use it
XLVIII

- The god of death will not die from lack of sleep. Moreover, gods of death do not really need sleep. The meaning of sleep for gods of death is essentially different from humans and is merely laziness.

死神は寝なくとも死なないし、本来睡眠をとる必要はない。
死神の睡眠は、人間の睡眠とは明らかに異なり、それは単なる怠けである。

- Especially gods of death living in the human world that have passed on their DEATH NOTE shouldn't be lazy, as they are required to see the death of the human, but it is not that they are not allowed to sleep.

特に人間にノートを譲渡し人間界にいる死神は、
そのノートや使った人間の最期を見届けるという理由から
怠けるべきではないが掟ではない。

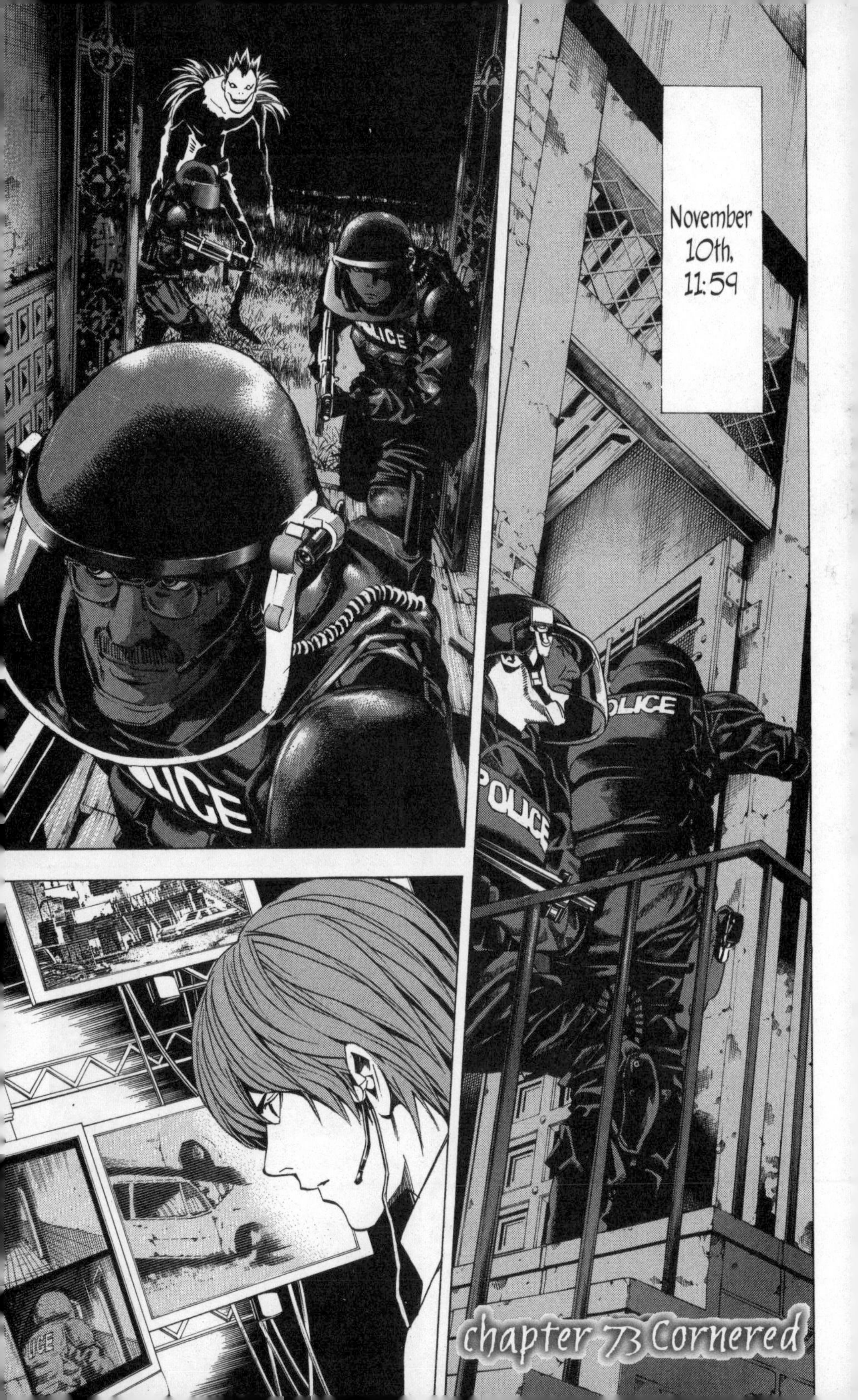
November 10th, 11:59
chapter 73 Cornered

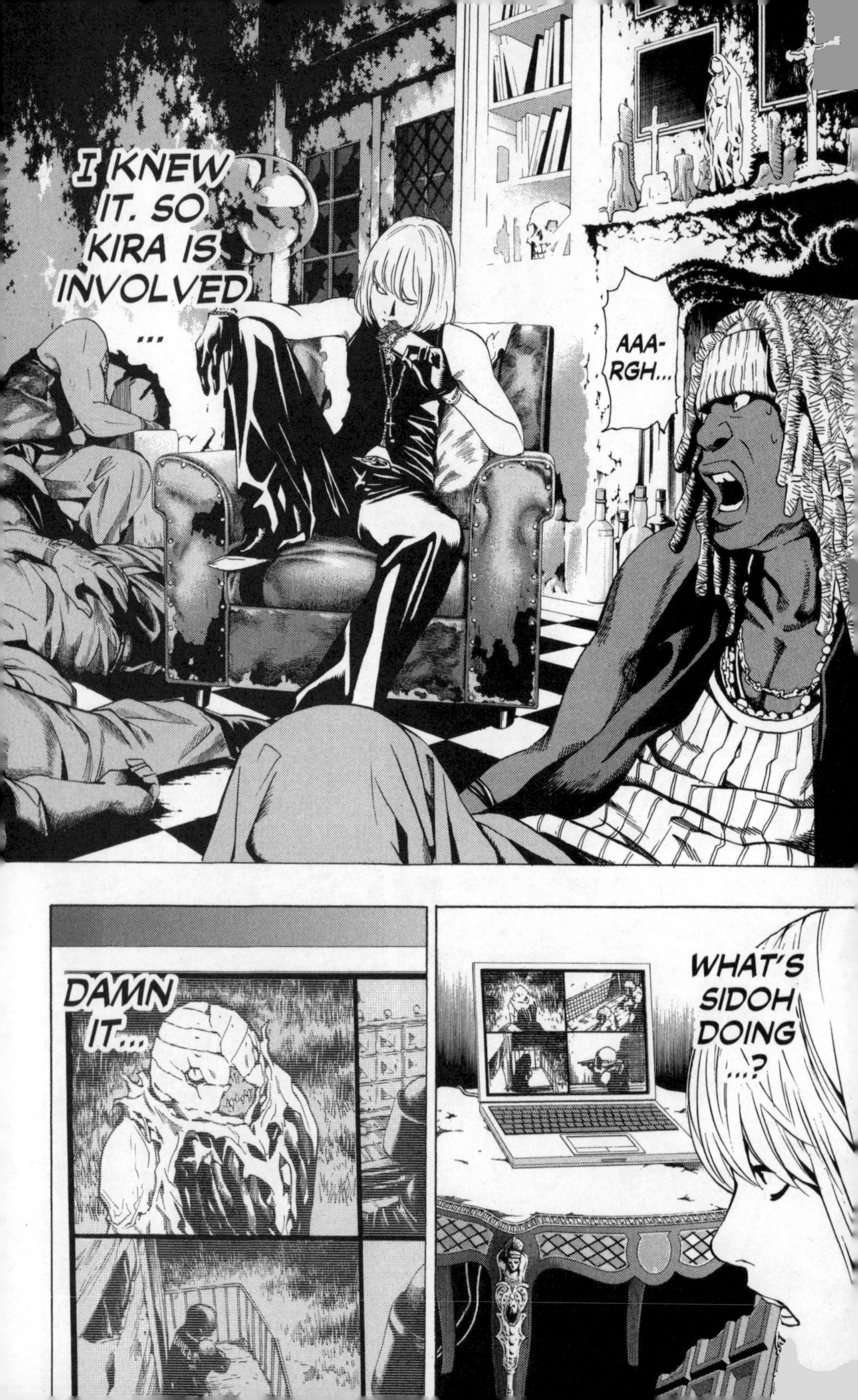
AAA-RGH...
I KNEW IT. SO KIRA IS INVOLVED...
WHAT'S SIDOH DOING...?
DAMN IT...

THEY'RE WELL PREPARED. I'M NOT READY FOR THEM YET...

...

KLATTER

CAMERAS... I CAN'T LET THEM SEE MY FACE.

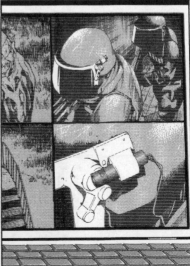

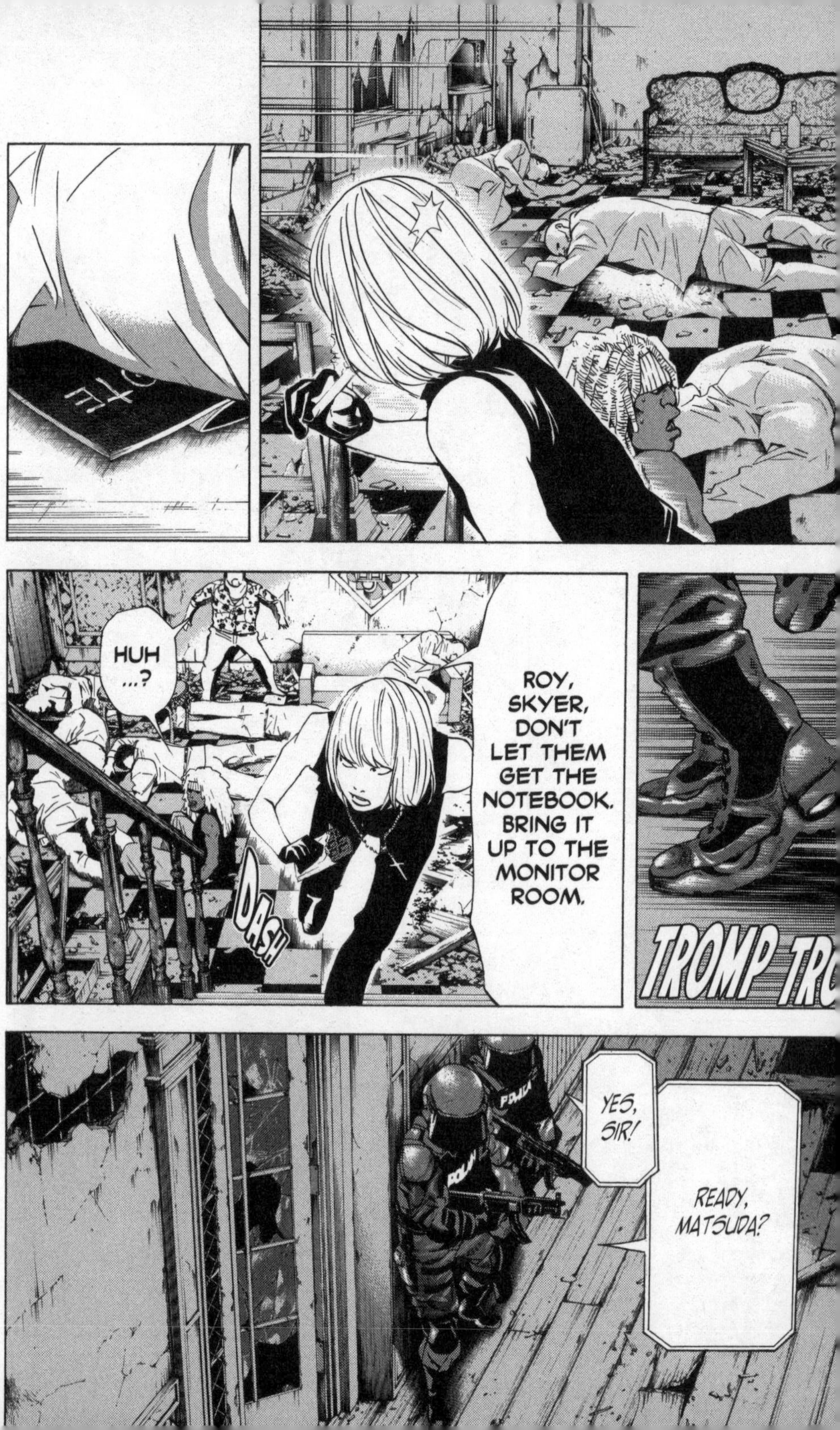
TROMP TRO
ROY, SKYER, DON'T LET THEM GET THE NOTEBOOK. BRING IT UP TO THE MONITOR ROOM.
HUH ...?
DASH
READY, MATSUDA?
YES, SIR!

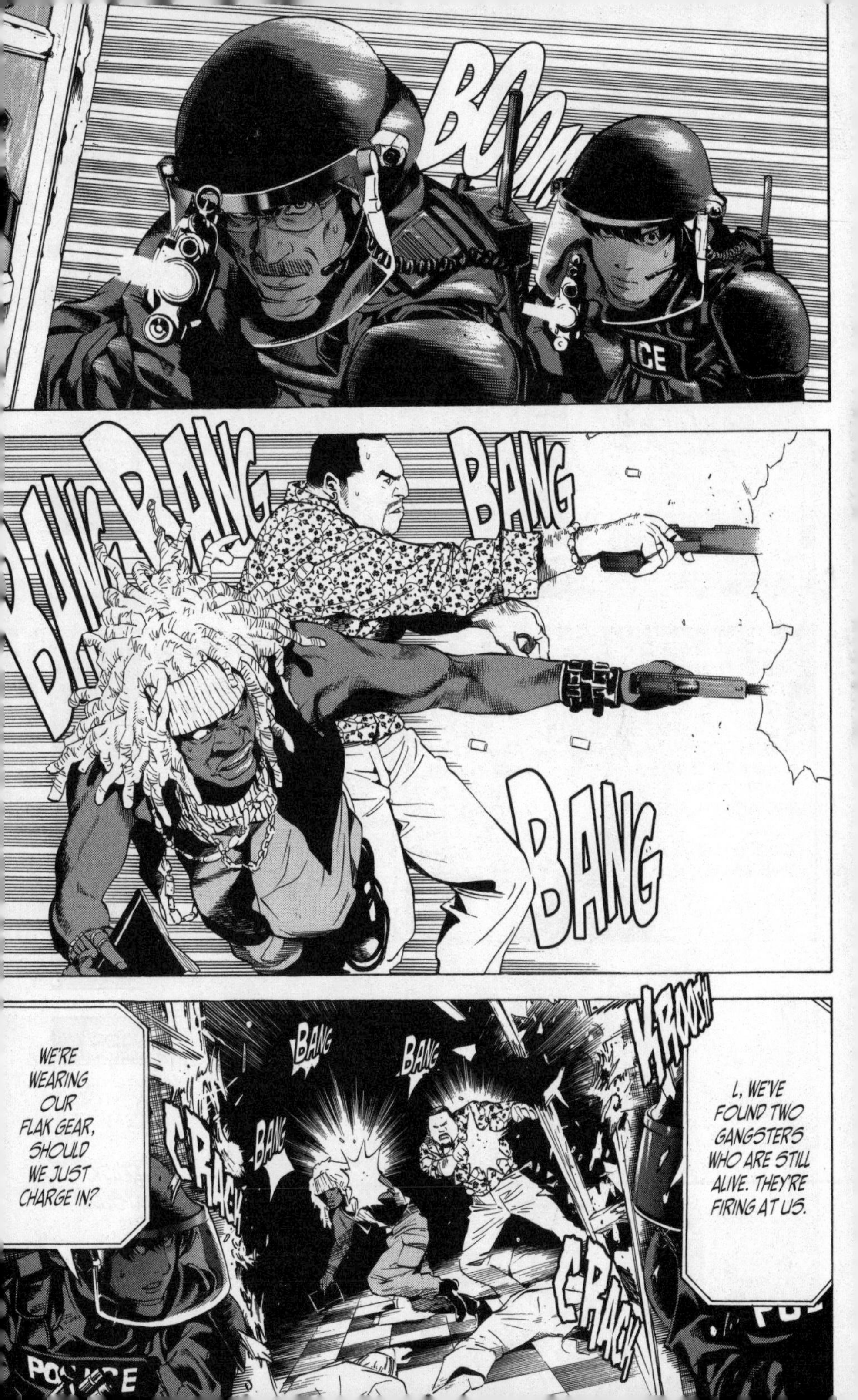
BOOM
ICE
BANG
BANG
BANG BANG
KROOSH
L, WE'VE FOUND TWO GANGSTERS WHO ARE STILL ALIVE. THEY'RE FIRING AT US.
BANG
BANG
BANG
CRACK
WE'RE WEARING OUR FLAK GEAR, SHOULD WE JUST CHARGE IN?
CRACK
POLICE

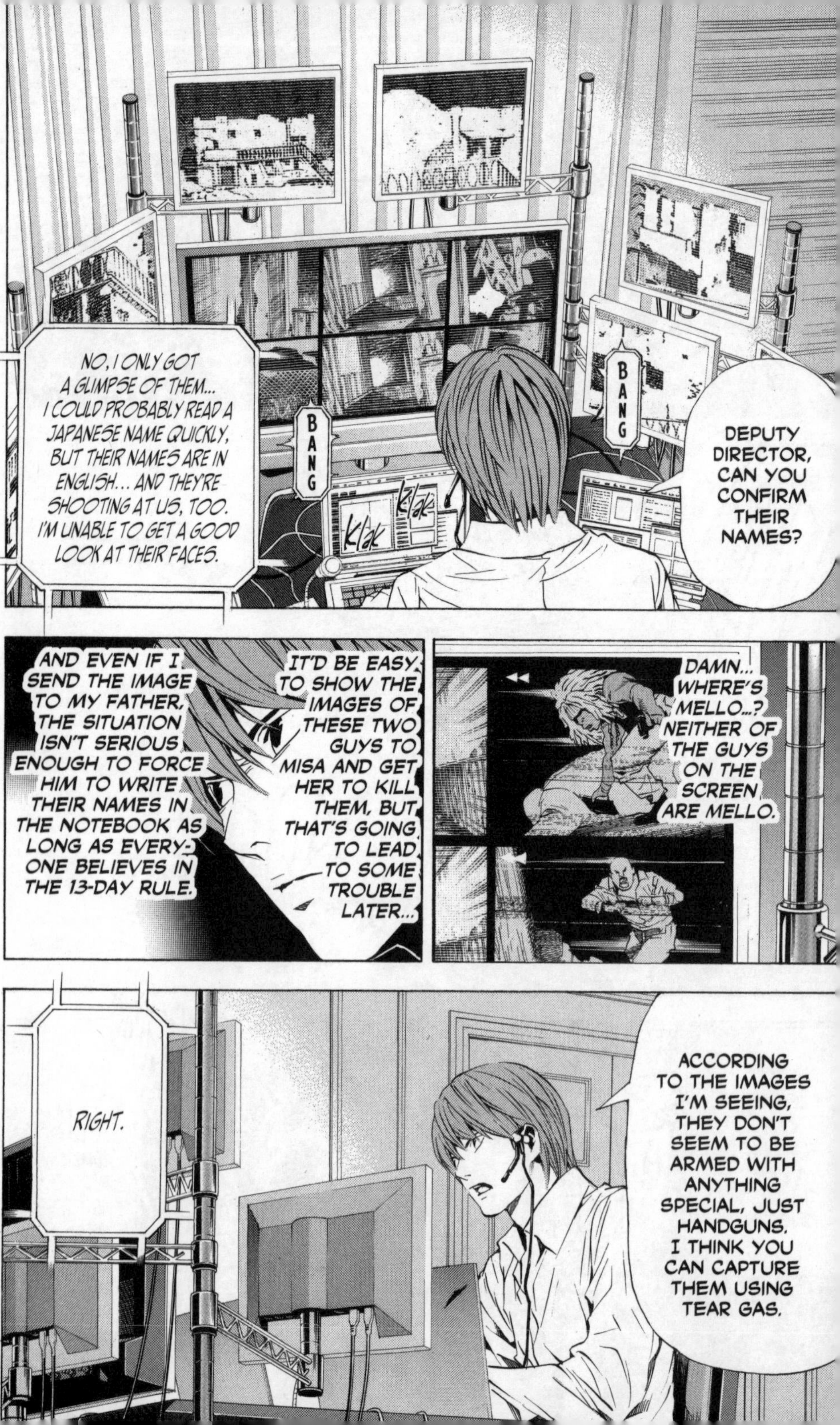
DEPUTY DIRECTOR, CAN YOU CONFIRM THEIR NAMES?
BANG
BANG
NO, I ONLY GOT A GLIMPSE OF THEM... I COULD PROBABLY READ A JAPANESE NAME QUICKLY, BUT THEIR NAMES ARE IN ENGLISH... AND THEY'RE SHOOTING AT US, TOO. I'M UNABLE TO GET A GOOD LOOK AT THEIR FACES.
KLAK
KLAK
DAMN... WHERE'S MELLO...? NEITHER OF THE GUYS ON THE SCREEN ARE MELLO.
IT'D BE EASY TO SHOW THE IMAGES OF THESE TWO GUYS TO MISA AND GET HER TO KILL THEM, BUT THAT'S GOING TO LEAD TO SOME TROUBLE LATER...
AND EVEN IF I SEND THE IMAGE TO MY FATHER, THE SITUATION ISN'T SERIOUS ENOUGH TO FORCE HIM TO WRITE THEIR NAMES IN THE NOTEBOOK AS LONG AS EVERY-ONE BELIEVES IN THE 13-DAY RULE.
ACCORDING TO THE IMAGES I'M SEEING, THEY DON'T SEEM TO BE ARMED WITH ANYTHING SPECIAL, JUST HANDGUNS. I THINK YOU CAN CAPTURE THEM USING TEAR GAS.
RIGHT.

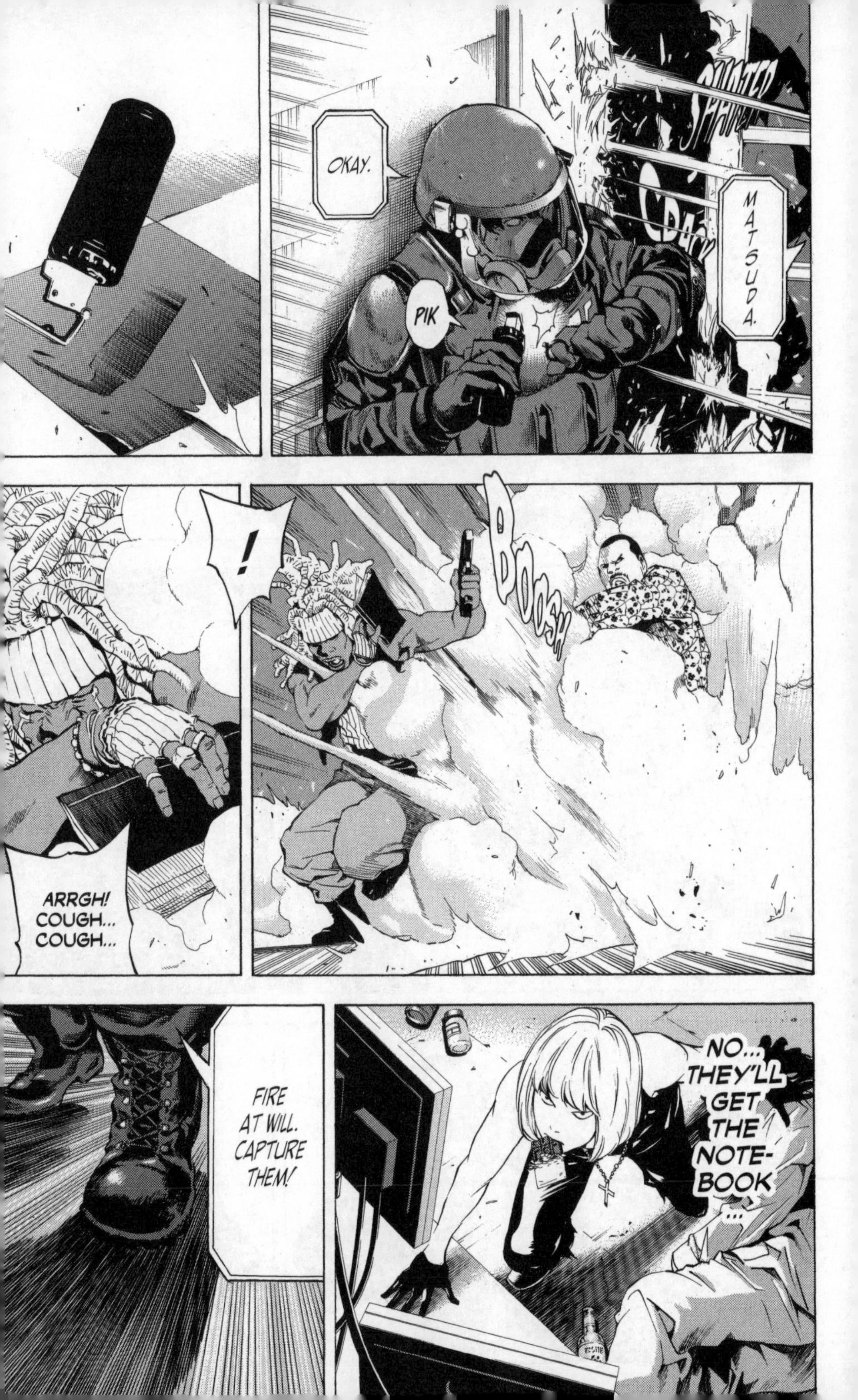
MATSUDA.
OKAY.
PIK
BOOSH
!
ARRGH! COUGH... COUGH...
NO... THEY'LL GET THE NOTE-BOOK...
FIRE AT WILL. CAPTURE THEM!

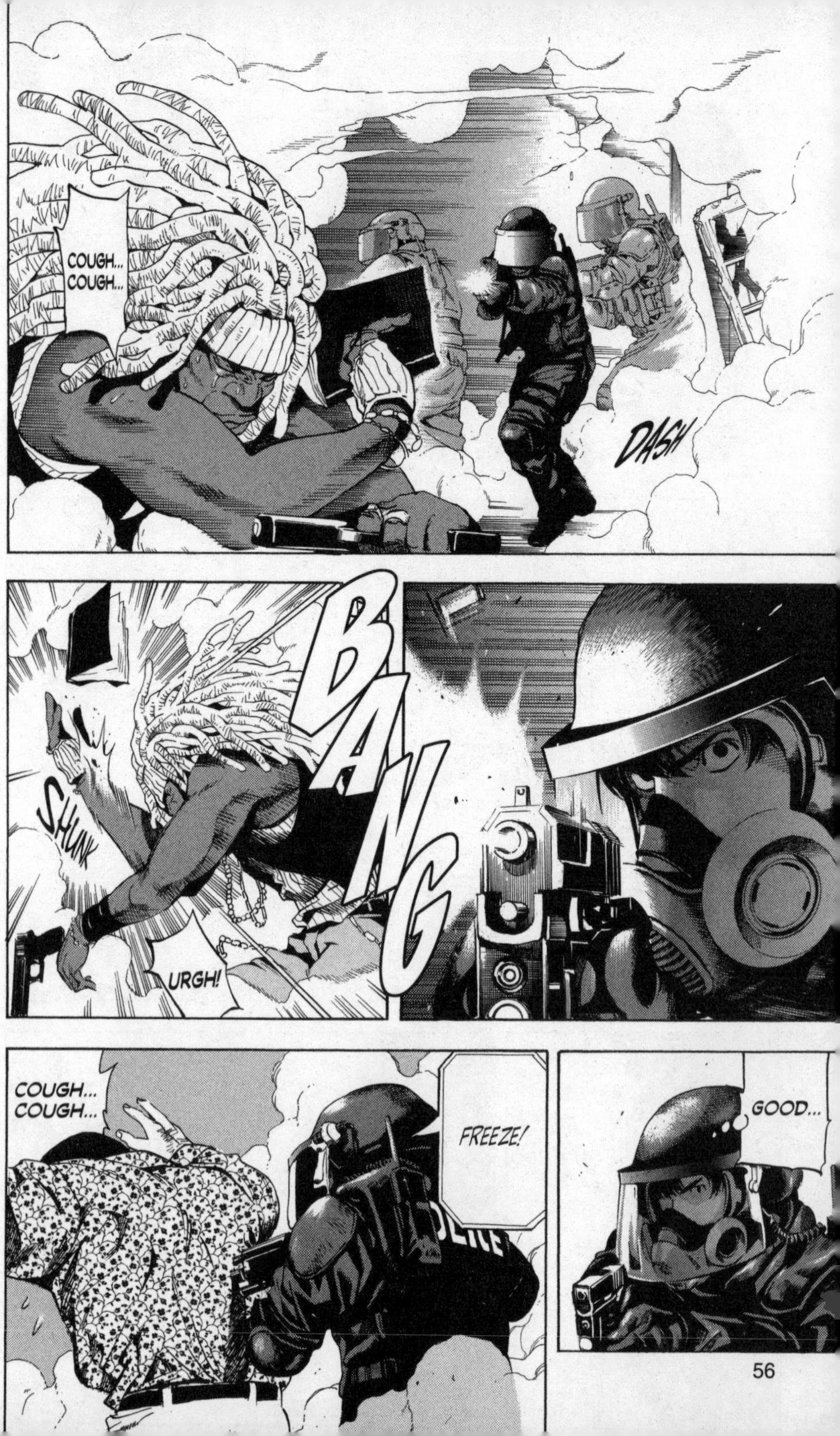
COUGH... COUGH...
DASH
BANG
SHUNK
URGH!
GOOD...
FREEZE!
COUGH... COUGH...

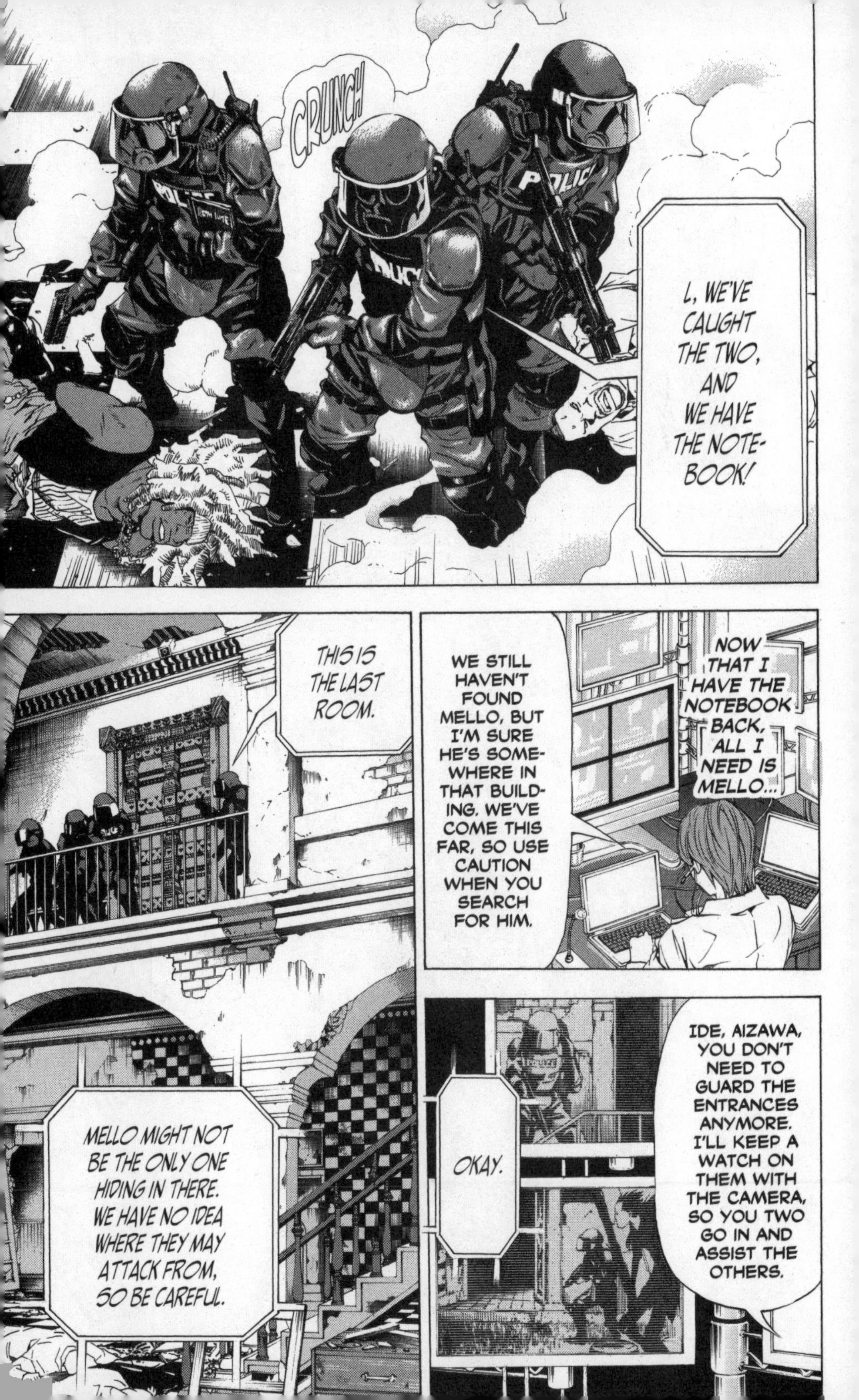
CRUNCH
L, WE'VE CAUGHT THE TWO, AND WE HAVE THE NOTEBOOK!
NOW THAT I HAVE THE NOTEBOOK BACK, ALL I NEED IS MELLO...
WE STILL HAVEN'T FOUND MELLO, BUT I'M SURE HE'S SOMEWHERE IN THAT BUILDING. WE'VE COME THIS FAR, SO USE CAUTION WHEN YOU SEARCH FOR HIM.
IDE, AIZAWA, YOU DON'T NEED TO GUARD THE ENTRANCES ANYMORE. I'LL KEEP A WATCH ON THEM WITH THE CAMERA, SO YOU TWO GO IN AND ASSIST THE OTHERS.
OKAY.
THIS IS THE LAST ROOM.
MELLO MIGHT NOT BE THE ONLY ONE HIDING IN THERE. WE HAVE NO IDEA WHERE THEY MAY ATTACK FROM, SO BE CAREFUL.

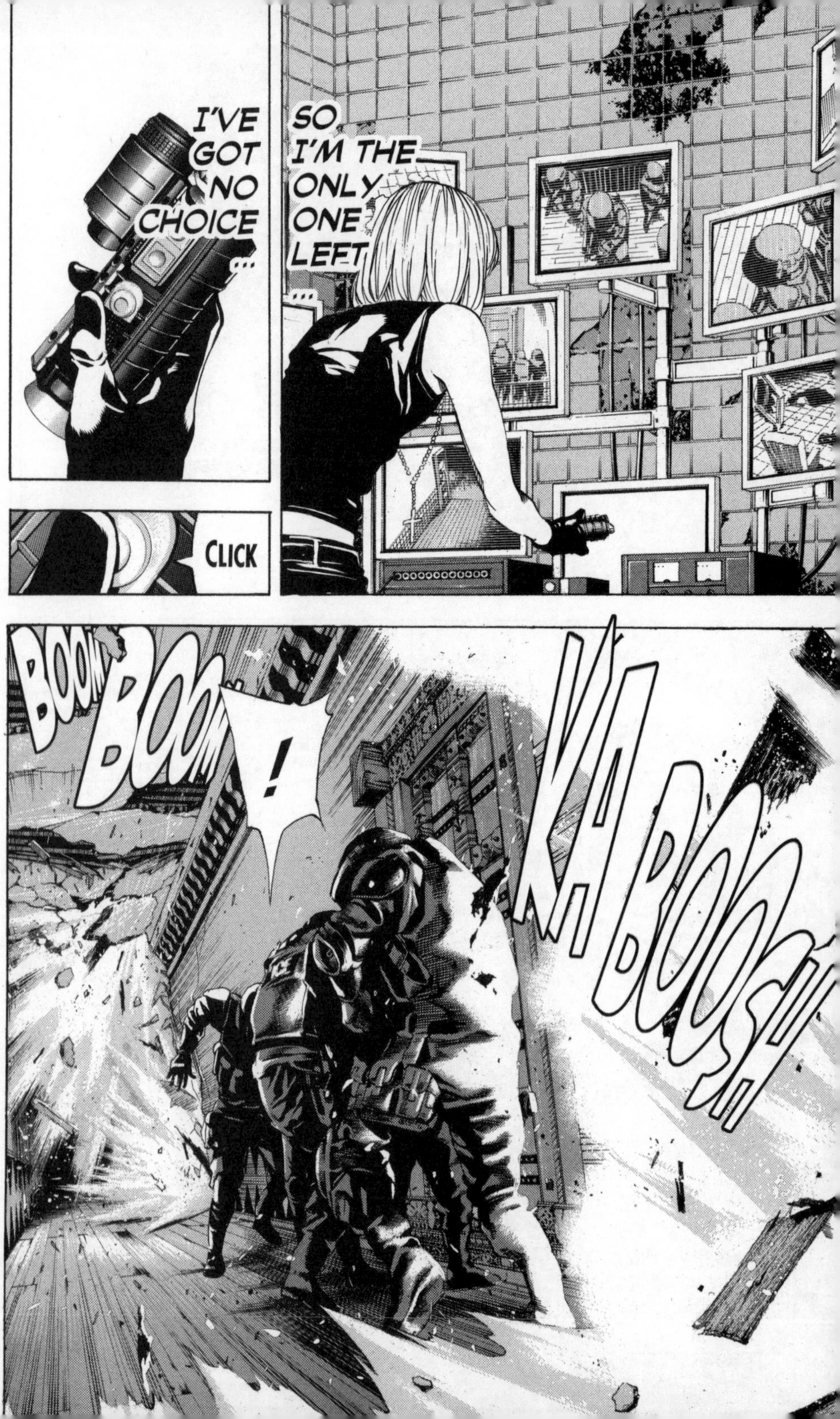

SO, I'M THE ONLY ONE LEFT...
I'VE GOT NO CHOICE...
CLICK
KA-BOOSH
!
BOOM
BOOM

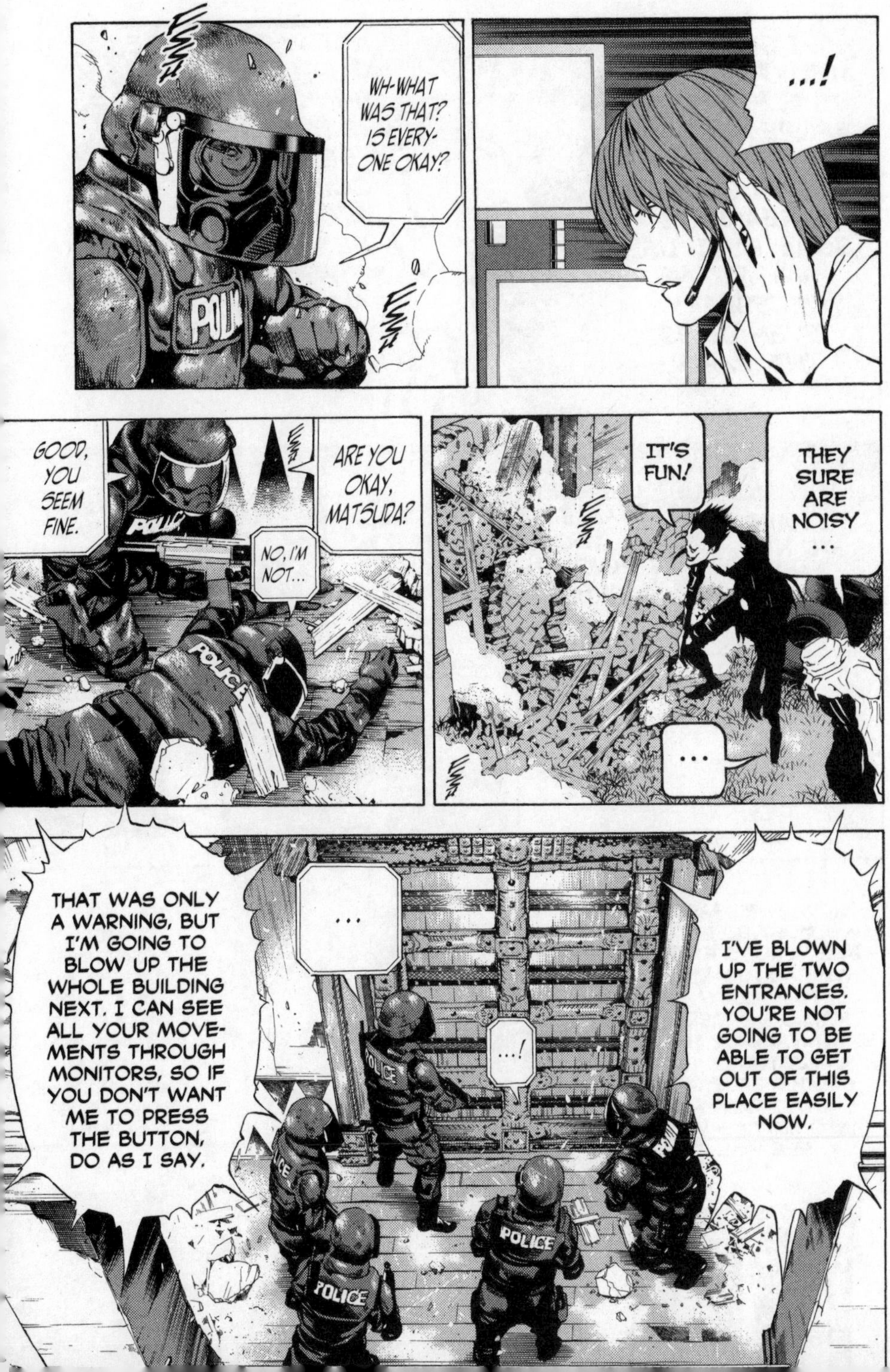
...!
WH-WHAT WAS THAT? IS EVERY-ONE OKAY?
THEY SURE ARE NOISY ...
IT'S FUN!
...
ARE YOU OKAY, MATSUDA?
NO, I'M NOT...
GOOD, YOU SEEM FINE.
I'VE BLOWN UP THE TWO ENTRANCES. YOU'RE NOT GOING TO BE ABLE TO GET OUT OF THIS PLACE EASILY NOW.
...!
...
THAT WAS ONLY A WARNING, BUT I'M GOING TO BLOW UP THE WHOLE BUILDING NEXT. I CAN SEE ALL YOUR MOVE-MENTS THROUGH MONITORS, SO IF YOU DON'T WANT ME TO PRESS THE BUTTON, DO AS I SAY.

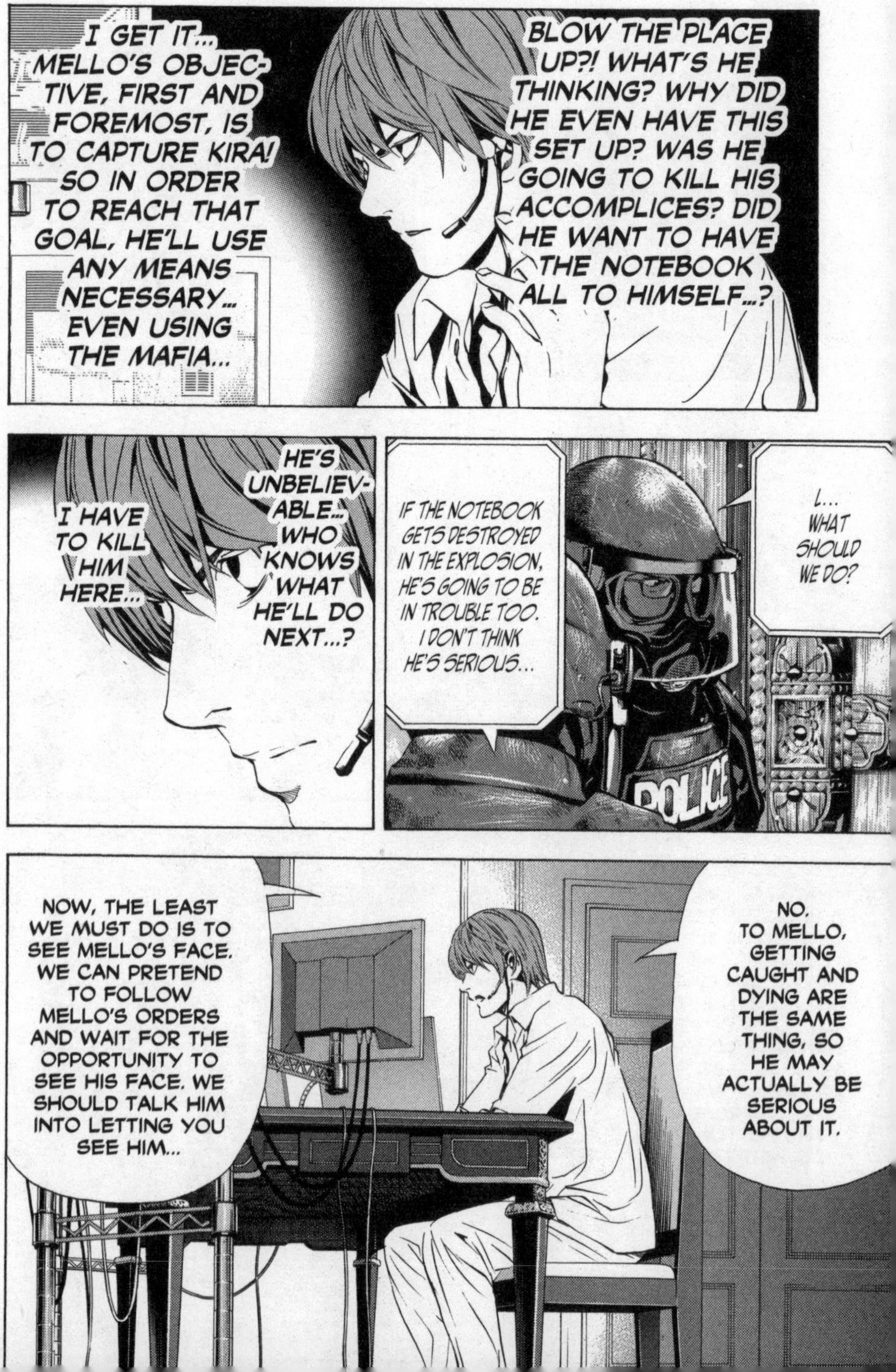
BLOW THE PLACE UP?! WHAT'S HE THINKING? WHY DID HE EVEN HAVE THIS SET UP? WAS HE GOING TO KILL HIS ACCOMPLICES? DID HE WANT TO HAVE THE NOTEBOOK ALL TO HIMSELF...?
I GET IT... MELLO'S OBJECTIVE, FIRST AND FOREMOST, IS TO CAPTURE KIRA! SO IN ORDER TO REACH THAT GOAL, HE'LL USE ANY MEANS NECESSARY... EVEN USING THE MAFIA...
L... WHAT SHOULD WE DO?
IF THE NOTEBOOK GETS DESTROYED IN THE EXPLOSION, HE'S GOING TO BE IN TROUBLE TOO. I DON'T THINK HE'S SERIOUS...
POLICE
HE'S UNBELIEVABLE... WHO KNOWS WHAT HE'LL DO NEXT...?
I HAVE TO KILL HIM HERE...
NO. TO MELLO, GETTING CAUGHT AND DYING ARE THE SAME THING, SO HE MAY ACTUALLY BE SERIOUS ABOUT IT.
NOW, THE LEAST WE MUST DO IS TO SEE MELLO'S FACE. WE CAN PRETEND TO FOLLOW MELLO'S ORDERS AND WAIT FOR THE OPPORTUNITY TO SEE HIS FACE. WE SHOULD TALK HIM INTO LETTING YOU SEE HIM...

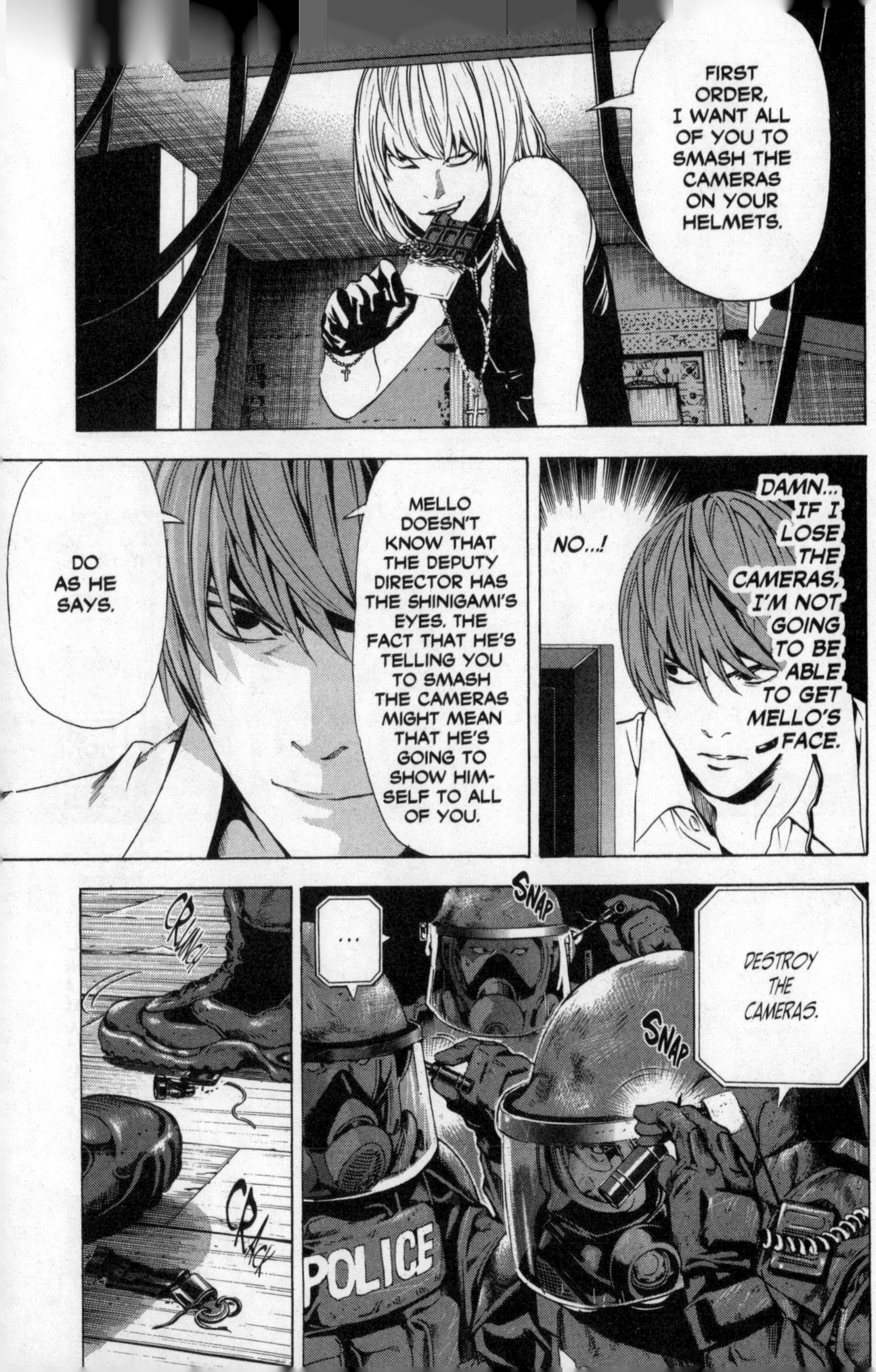
FIRST ORDER, I WANT ALL OF YOU TO SMASH THE CAMERAS ON YOUR HELMETS.
DAMN... IF I LOSE THE CAMERAS, I'M NOT GOING TO BE ABLE TO GET MELLO'S FACE.
NO...!
MELLO DOESN'T KNOW THAT THE DEPUTY DIRECTOR HAS THE SHINIGAMI'S EYES. THE FACT THAT HE'S TELLING YOU TO SMASH THE CAMERAS MIGHT MEAN THAT HE'S GOING TO SHOW HIM-SELF TO ALL OF YOU.
DO AS HE SAYS.
SNAP
DESTROY THE CAMERAS.
SNAP
...
POLICE
CRUNCH
CRACK

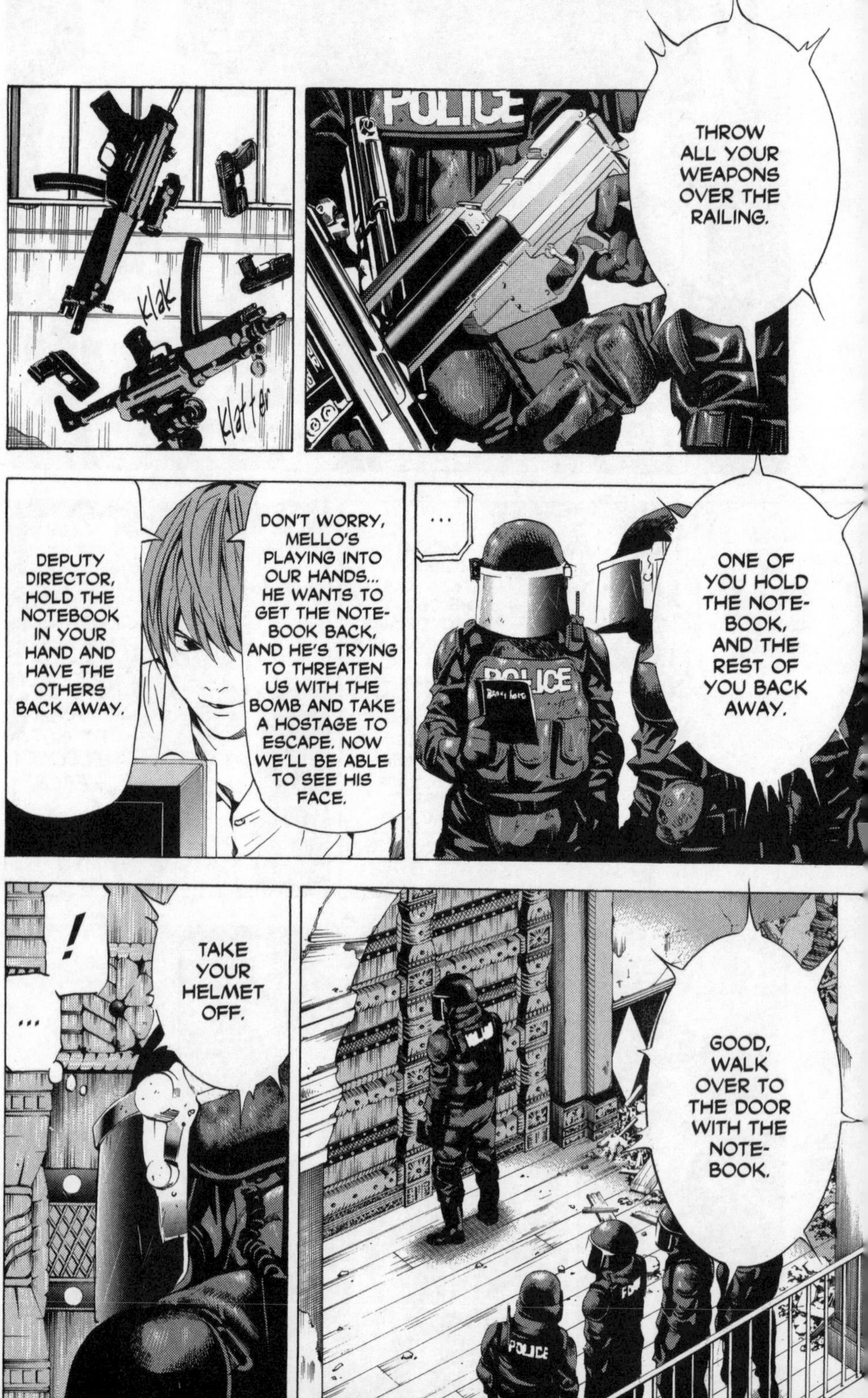
THROW ALL YOUR WEAPONS OVER THE RAILING.
KLAK
KLATTER
ONE OF YOU HOLD THE NOTE-BOOK, AND THE REST OF YOU BACK AWAY.
...
DON'T WORRY, MELLO'S PLAYING INTO OUR HANDS... HE WANTS TO GET THE NOTE-BOOK BACK, AND HE'S TRYING TO THREATEN US WITH THE BOMB AND TAKE A HOSTAGE TO ESCAPE. NOW WE'LL BE ABLE TO SEE HIS FACE.
DEPUTY DIRECTOR, HOLD THE NOTEBOOK IN YOUR HAND AND HAVE THE OTHERS BACK AWAY.
GOOD, WALK OVER TO THE DOOR WITH THE NOTE-BOOK.
TAKE YOUR HELMET OFF.
!
...

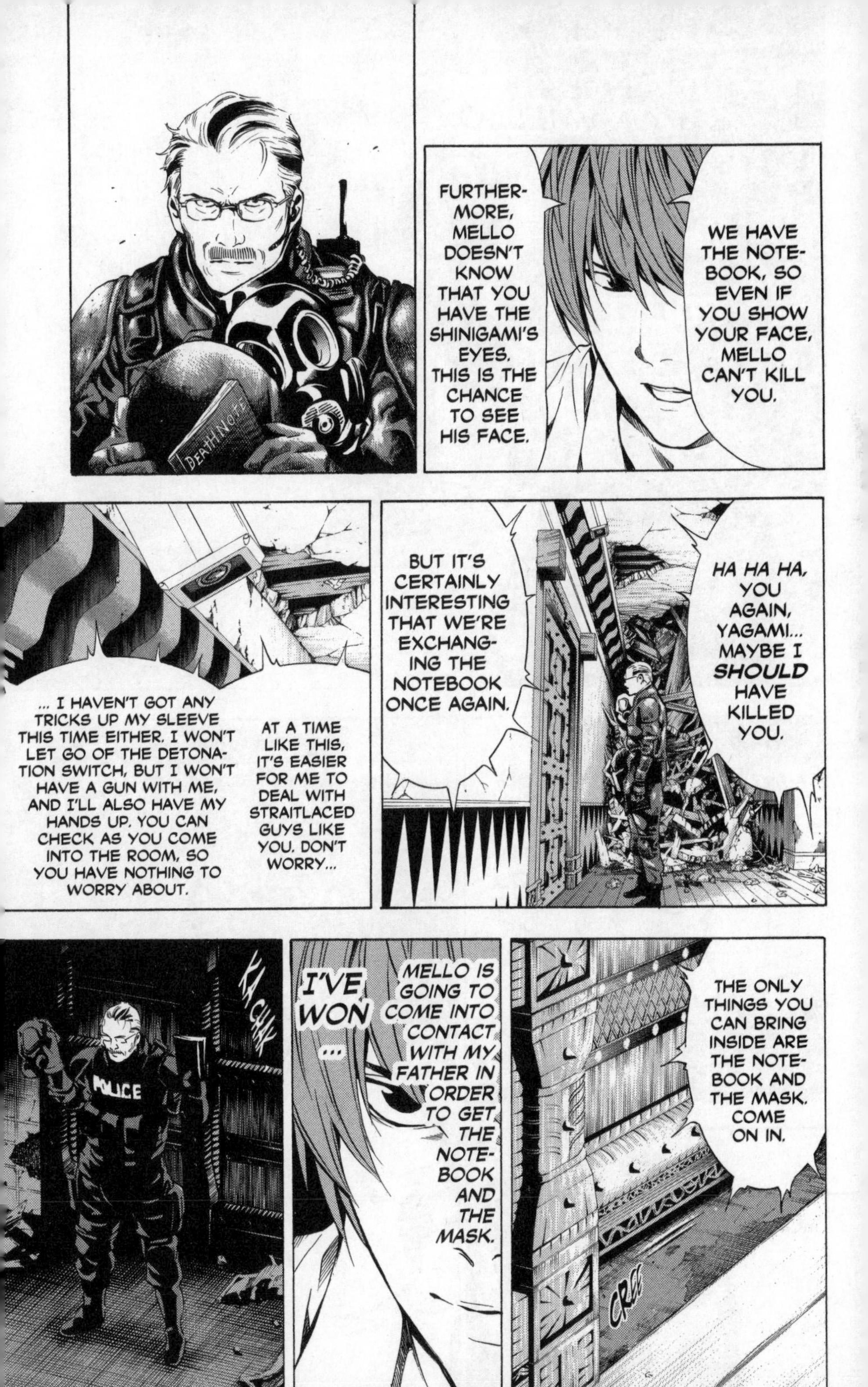
WE HAVE THE NOTE-BOOK, SO EVEN IF YOU SHOW YOUR FACE, MELLO CAN'T KILL YOU.
FURTHER-MORE, MELLO DOESN'T KNOW THAT YOU HAVE THE SHINIGAMI'S EYES. THIS IS THE CHANCE TO SEE HIS FACE.
DEATH NOTE
*HA HA HA, YOU AGAIN, YAGAMI... MAYBE I **SHOULD** HAVE KILLED YOU.*
BUT IT'S CERTAINLY INTERESTING THAT WE'RE EXCHANG-ING THE NOTEBOOK ONCE AGAIN.
AT A TIME LIKE THIS, IT'S EASIER FOR ME TO DEAL WITH STRAITLACED GUYS LIKE YOU. DON'T WORRY...
... I HAVEN'T GOT ANY TRICKS UP MY SLEEVE THIS TIME EITHER. I WON'T LET GO OF THE DETONA-TION SWITCH, BUT I WON'T HAVE A GUN WITH ME, AND I'LL ALSO HAVE MY HANDS UP. YOU CAN CHECK AS YOU COME INTO THE ROOM, SO YOU HAVE NOTHING TO WORRY ABOUT.
THE ONLY THINGS YOU CAN BRING INSIDE ARE THE NOTE-BOOK AND THE MASK. COME ON IN.
CREE
MELLO IS GOING TO COME INTO CONTACT WITH MY FATHER IN ORDER TO GET THE NOTE-BOOK AND THE MASK.
I'VE WON ...
KA CHAK
POLICE

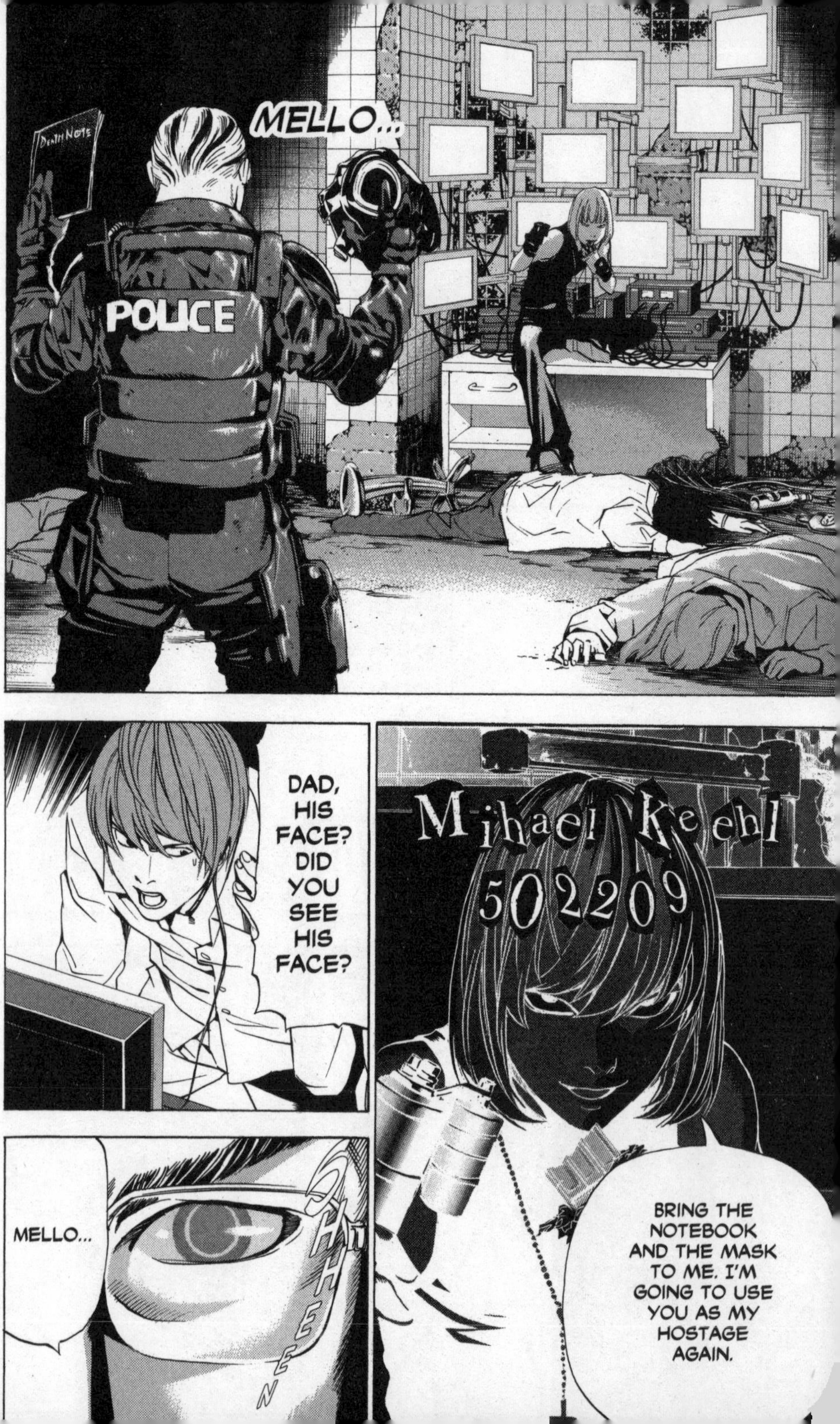
DEATH NOTE
MELLO...
POLICE
Mihael Keehl
502209
BRING THE NOTEBOOK AND THE MASK TO ME. I'M GOING TO USE YOU AS MY HOSTAGE AGAIN.
DAD, HIS FACE? DID YOU SEE HIS FACE?
SHHEEN
MELLO...

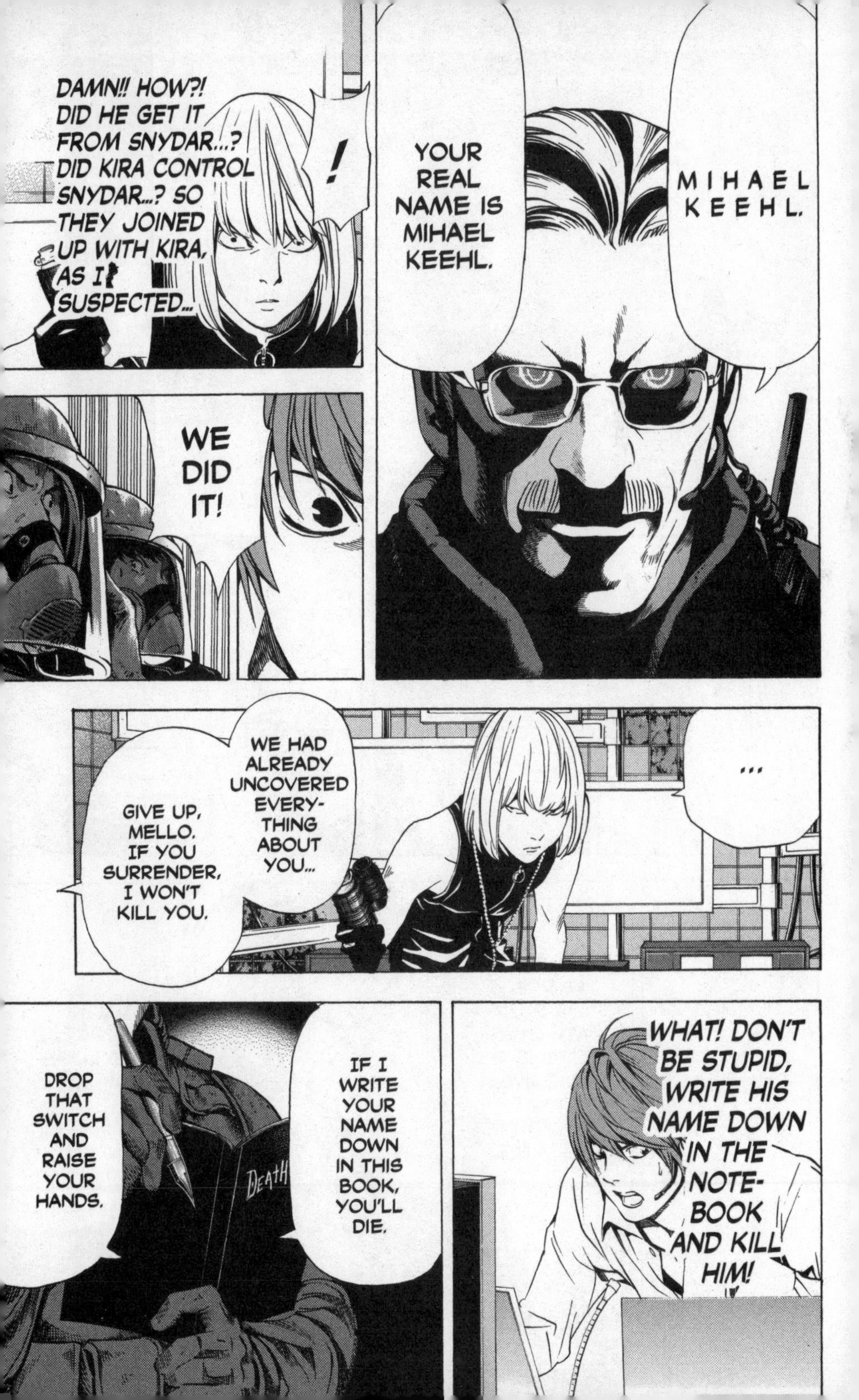
M I H A E L K E E H L.
YOUR REAL NAME IS MIHAEL KEEHL.
!
DAMN!! HOW?! DID HE GET IT FROM SNYDAR...? DID KIRA CONTROL SNYDAR...? SO THEY JOINED UP WITH KIRA, AS I SUSPECTED...
WE DID IT!
...
WE HAD ALREADY UNCOVERED EVERY-THING ABOUT YOU...
GIVE UP, MELLO. IF YOU SURRENDER, I WON'T KILL YOU.
WHAT! DON'T BE STUPID, WRITE HIS NAME DOWN IN THE NOTE-BOOK AND KILL HIM!
IF I WRITE YOUR NAME DOWN IN THIS BOOK, YOU'LL DIE.
DEATH
DROP THAT SWITCH AND RAISE YOUR HANDS.

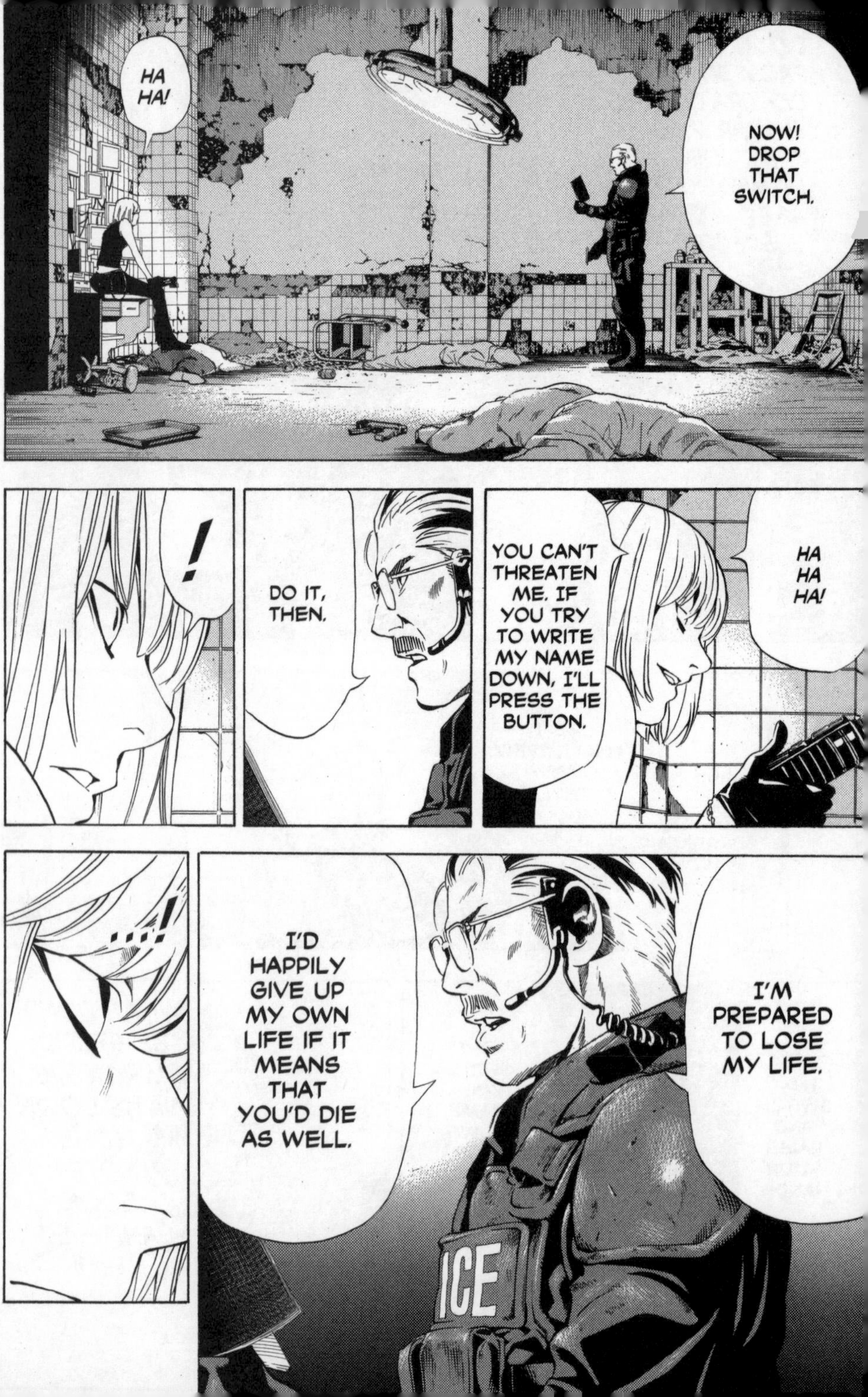
NOW! DROP THAT SWITCH.
HA HA!
HA HA HA!
YOU CAN'T THREATEN ME. IF YOU TRY TO WRITE MY NAME DOWN, I'LL PRESS THE BUTTON.
DO IT, THEN.
!
I'M PREPARED TO LOSE MY LIFE.
I'D HAPPILY GIVE UP MY OWN LIFE IF IT MEANS THAT YOU'D DIE AS WELL.
ICE
...!

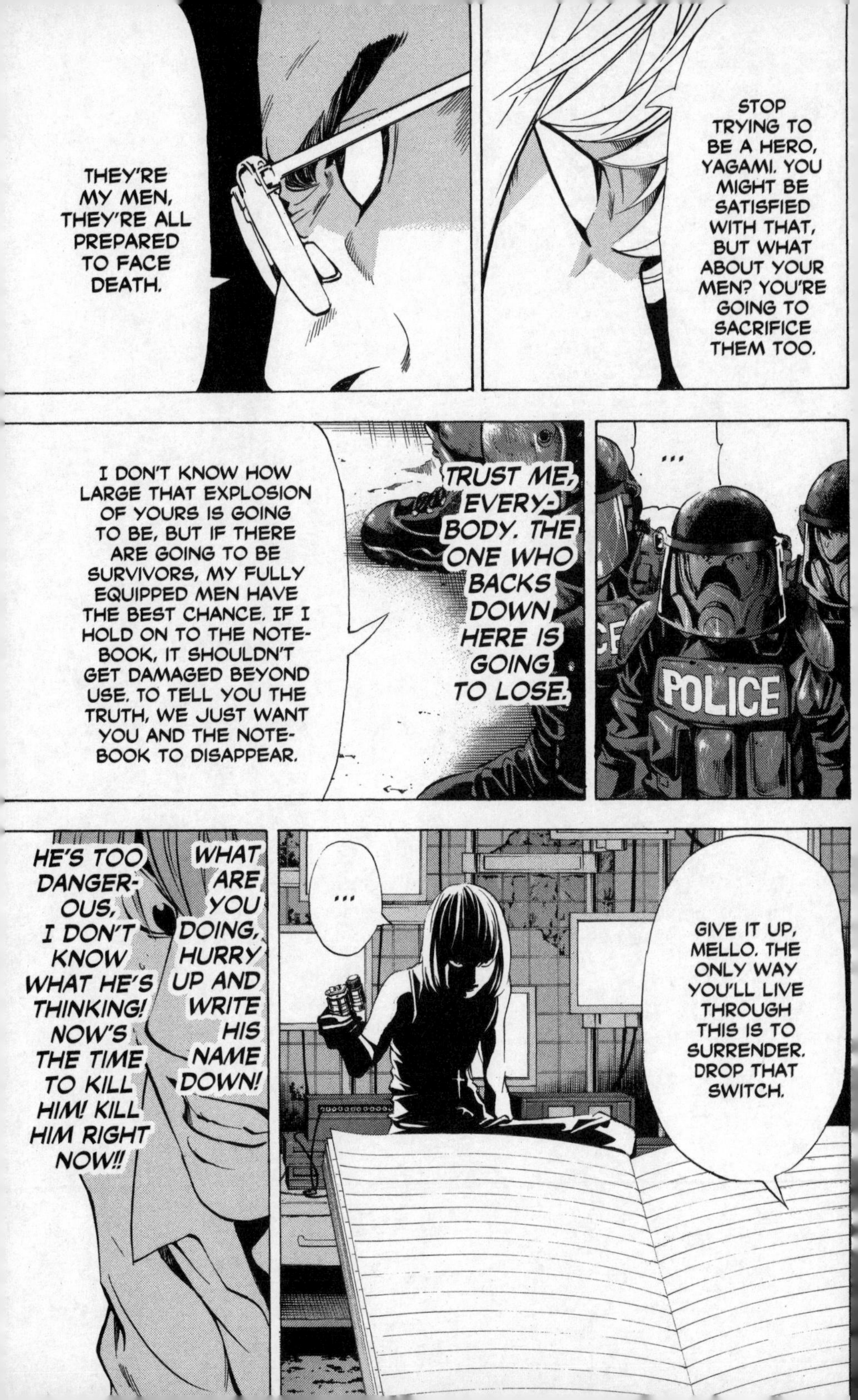
STOP TRYING TO BE A HERO, YAGAMI. YOU MIGHT BE SATISFIED WITH THAT, BUT WHAT ABOUT YOUR MEN? YOU'RE GOING TO SACRIFICE THEM TOO.
THEY'RE MY MEN, THEY'RE ALL PREPARED TO FACE DEATH.
...
TRUST ME, EVERY-BODY. THE ONE WHO BACKS DOWN HERE IS GOING TO LOSE.
POLICE
I DON'T KNOW HOW LARGE THAT EXPLOSION OF YOURS IS GOING TO BE, BUT IF THERE ARE GOING TO BE SURVIVORS, MY FULLY EQUIPPED MEN HAVE THE BEST CHANCE. IF I HOLD ON TO THE NOTE-BOOK, IT SHOULDN'T GET DAMAGED BEYOND USE. TO TELL YOU THE TRUTH, WE JUST WANT YOU AND THE NOTE-BOOK TO DISAPPEAR.
GIVE IT UP, MELLO. THE ONLY WAY YOU'LL LIVE THROUGH THIS IS TO SURRENDER. DROP THAT SWITCH.
...
WHAT ARE YOU DOING, HURRY UP AND WRITE HIS NAME DOWN!
HE'S TOO DANGER-OUS, I DON'T KNOW WHAT HE'S THINKING! NOW'S THE TIME TO KILL HIM! KILL HIM RIGHT NOW!!

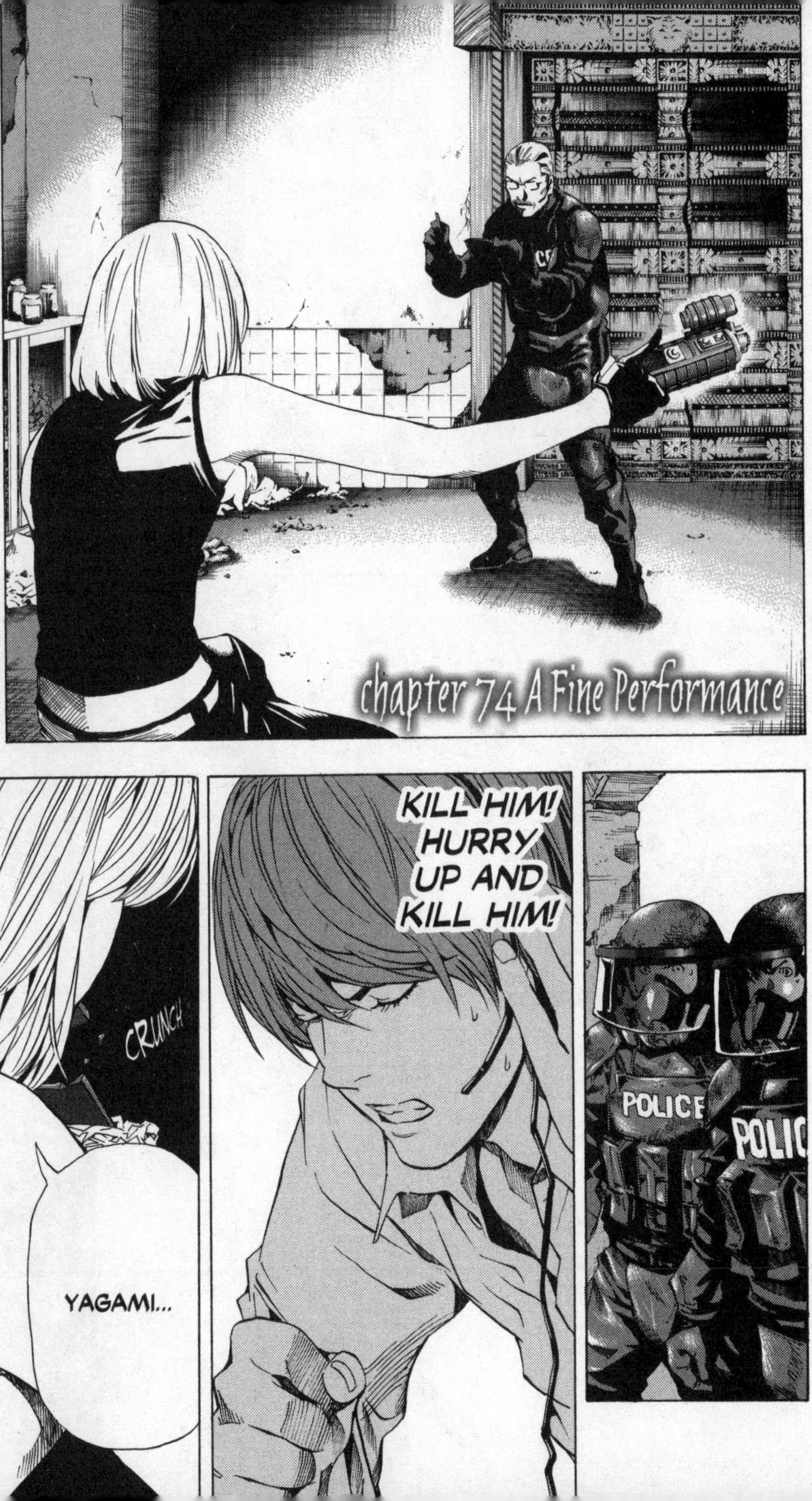
chapter 74 A Fine Performance
POLICE
POLIC
KILL HIM! HURRY UP AND KILL HIM!
CRUNCH
YAGAMI...

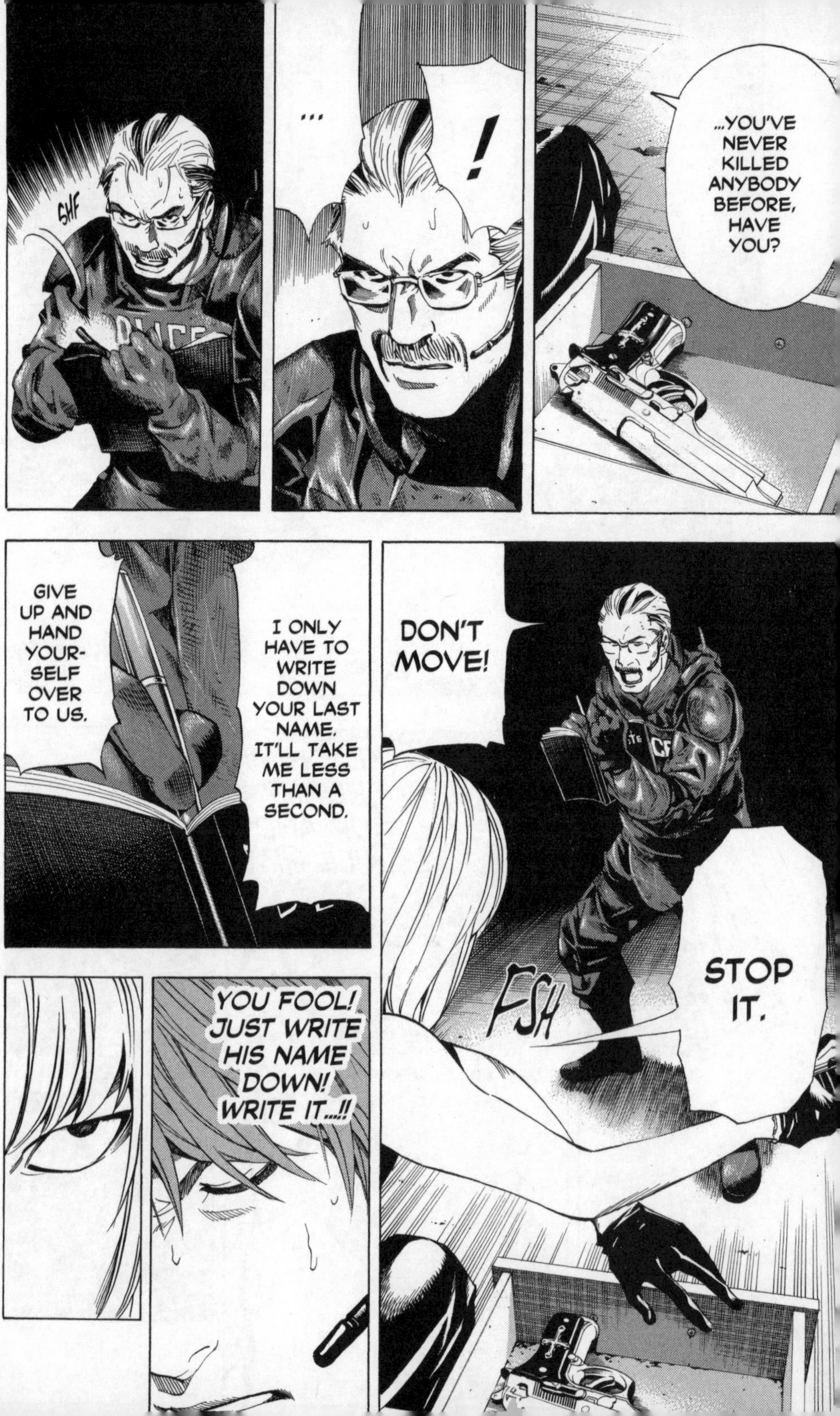
...YOU'VE NEVER KILLED ANYBODY BEFORE, HAVE YOU?
...
!
SHF
DON'T MOVE!
STOP IT.
FSH
I ONLY HAVE TO WRITE DOWN YOUR LAST NAME. IT'LL TAKE ME LESS THAN A SECOND.
GIVE UP AND HAND YOUR-SELF OVER TO US.
YOU FOOL! JUST WRITE HIS NAME DOWN! WRITE IT...!!

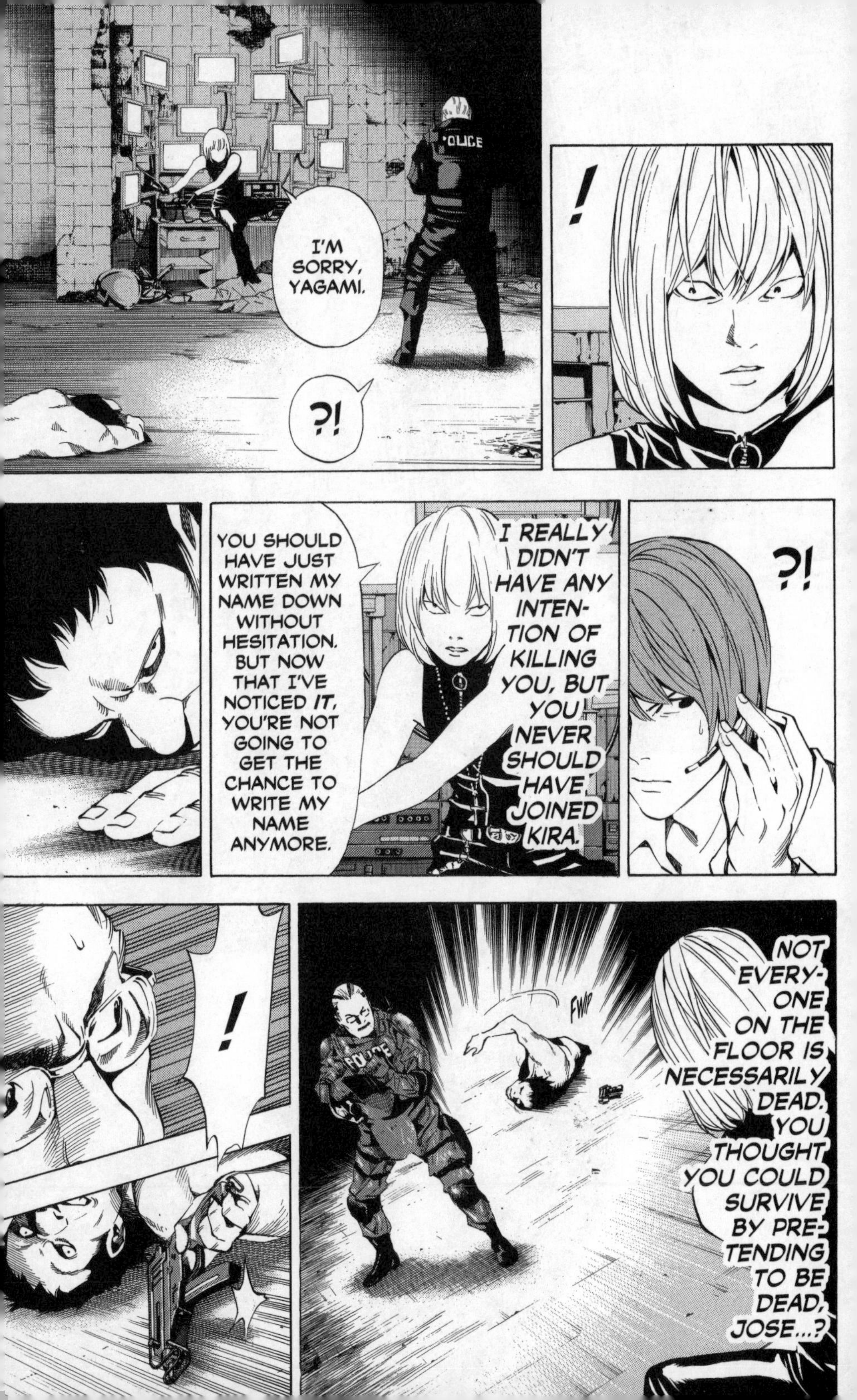
!
I'M SORRY, YAGAMI.
?!
?!
I REALLY DIDN'T HAVE ANY INTENTION OF KILLING YOU, BUT YOU NEVER SHOULD HAVE JOINED KIRA.
YOU SHOULD HAVE JUST WRITTEN MY NAME DOWN WITHOUT HESITATION. BUT NOW THAT I'VE NOTICED *IT*, YOU'RE NOT GOING TO GET THE CHANCE TO WRITE MY NAME ANYMORE.
NOT EVERYONE ON THE FLOOR IS NECESSARILY DEAD. YOU THOUGHT YOU COULD SURVIVE BY PRETENDING TO BE DEAD, JOSE...?
FWIP
!

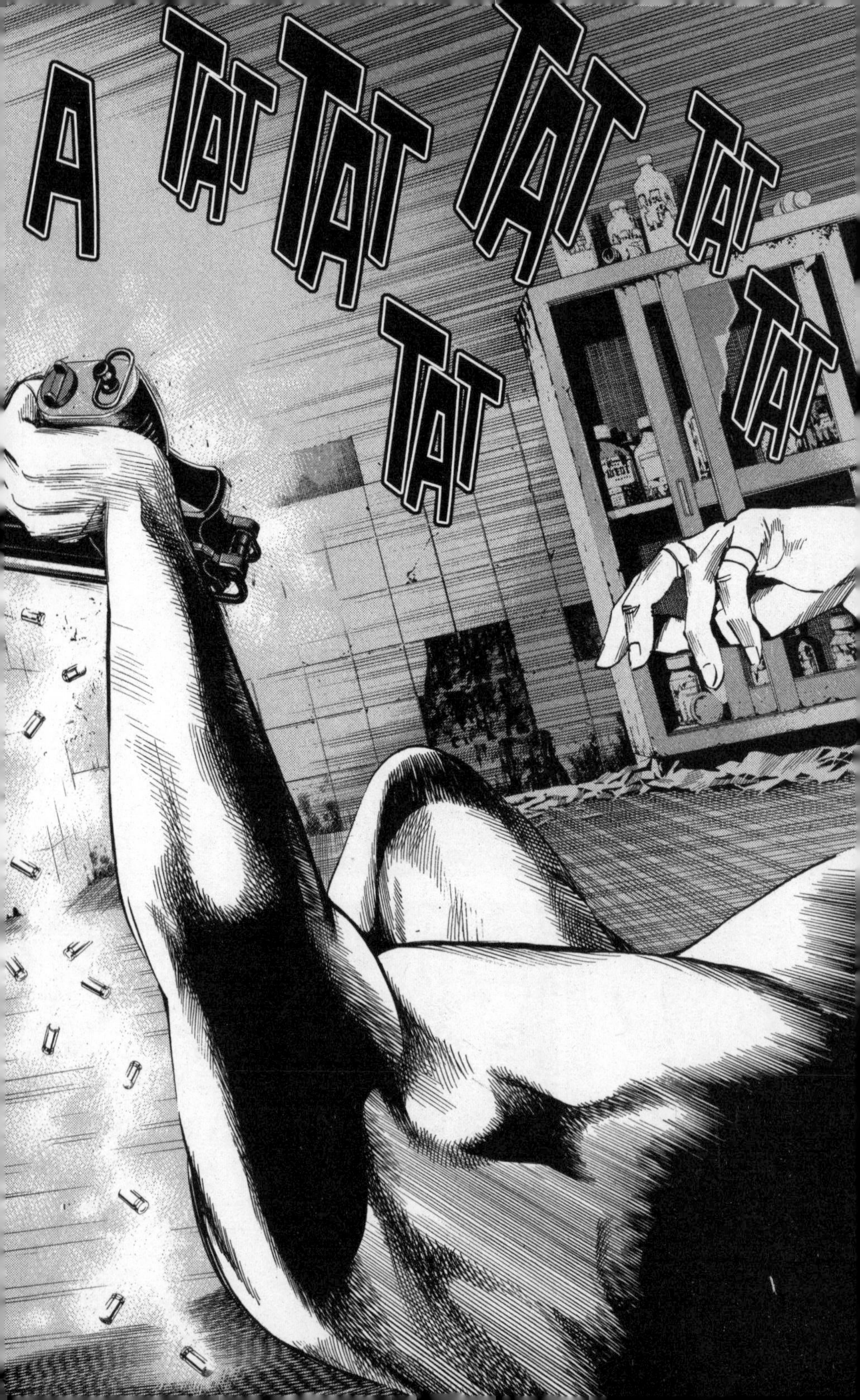
A TAT TAT TAT TAT TAT TAT

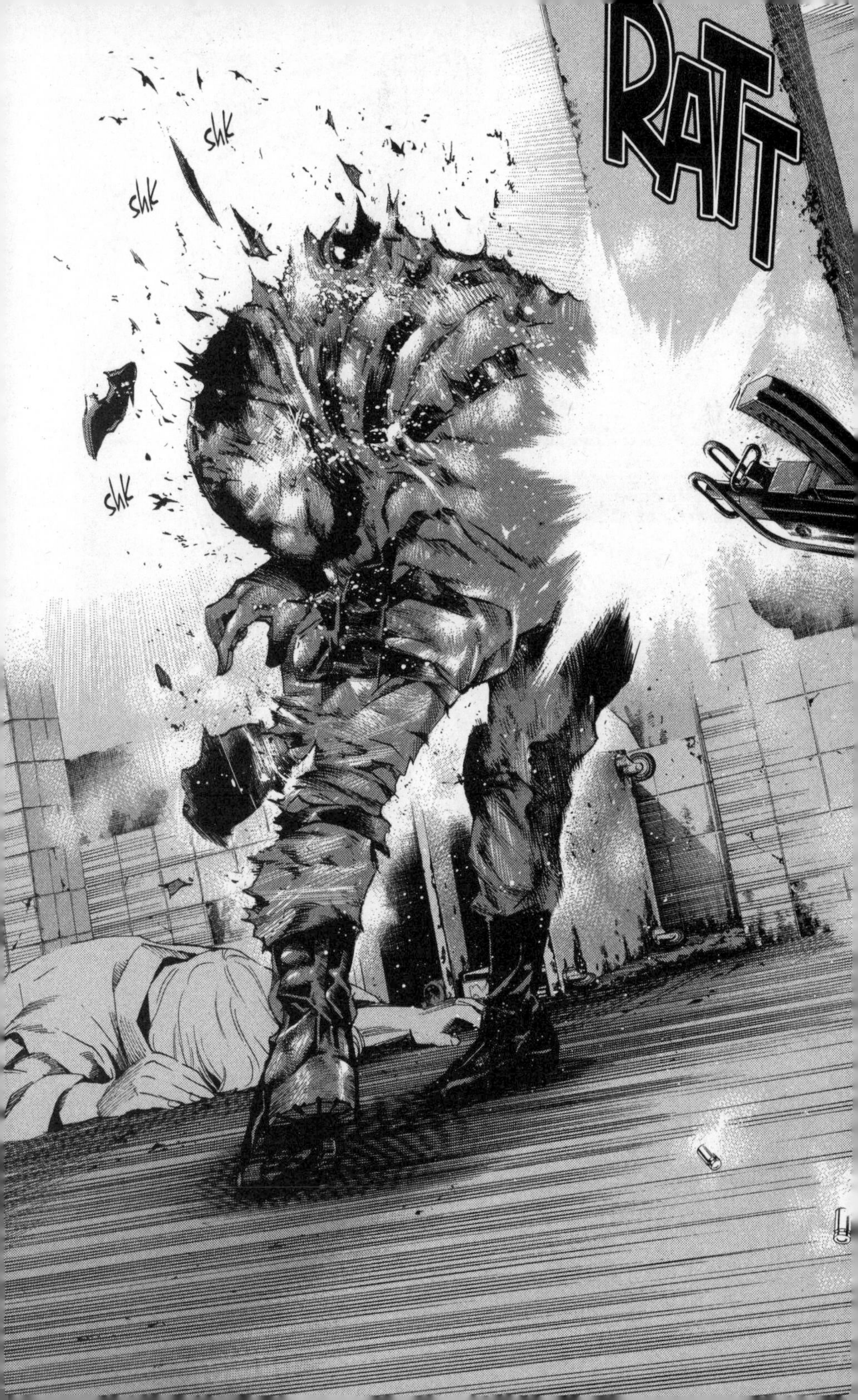
RATT
shk
shk
shk

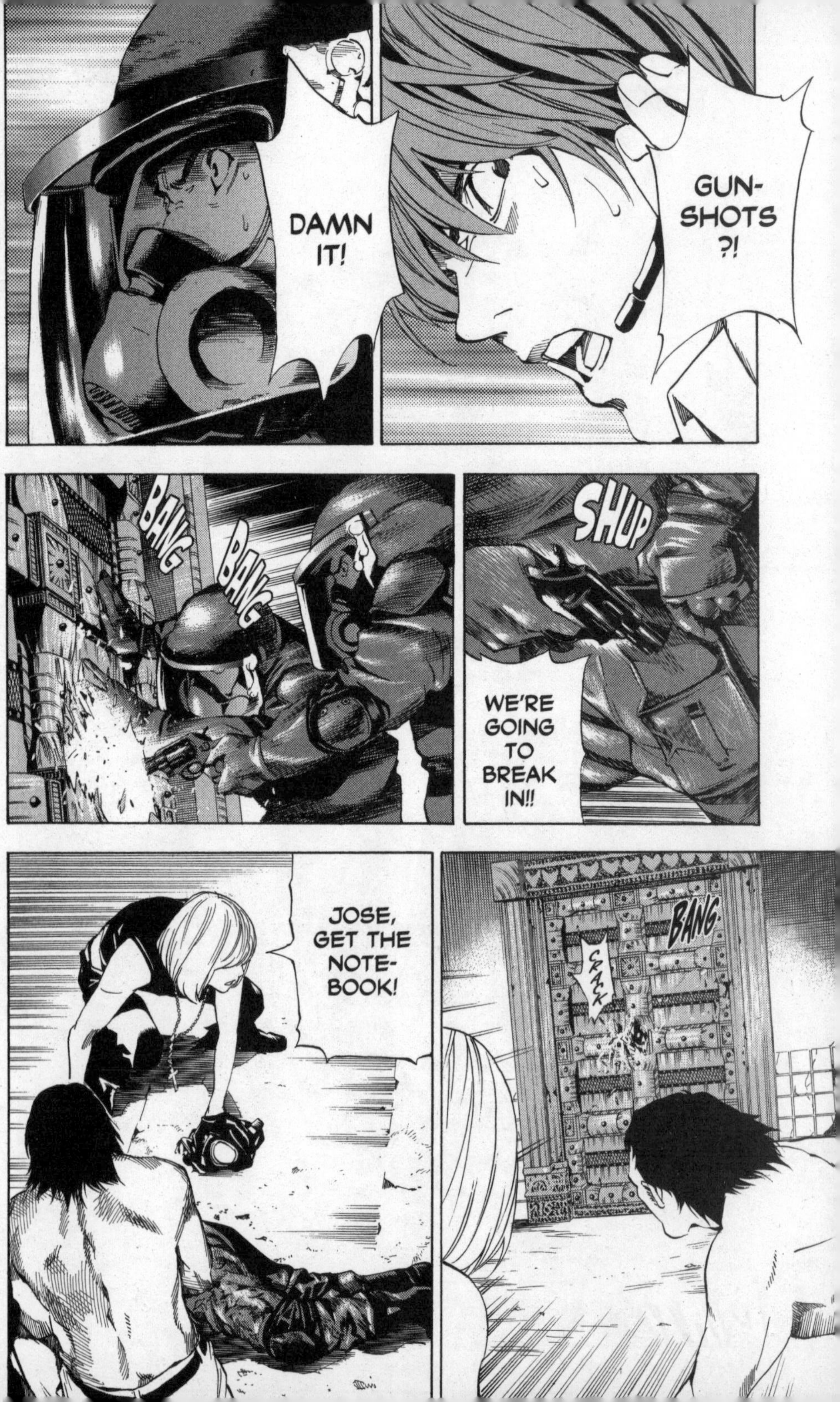
GUN-SHOTS?!
DAMN IT!
SHUP
WE'RE GOING TO BREAK IN!!
BANG
BANG
BANG
CRACK
JOSE, GET THE NOTE-BOOK!

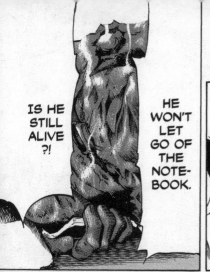

EVEN IF YAGAMI'S DEAD, I CAN'T LET THE OTHERS SEE MY FACE.
I-IT'S NO USE...
HE WON'T LET GO OF THE NOTE-BOOK.
IS HE STILL ALIVE ?!
chak
BOOM
DAMN!
RATTATAT
ATAT
BANG
BANG

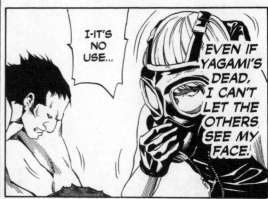

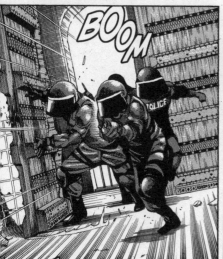

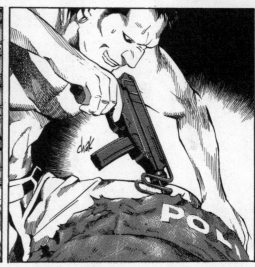

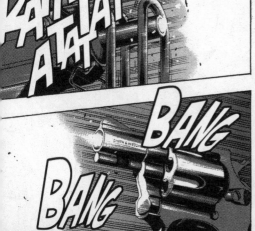

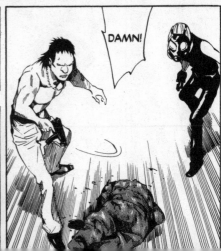

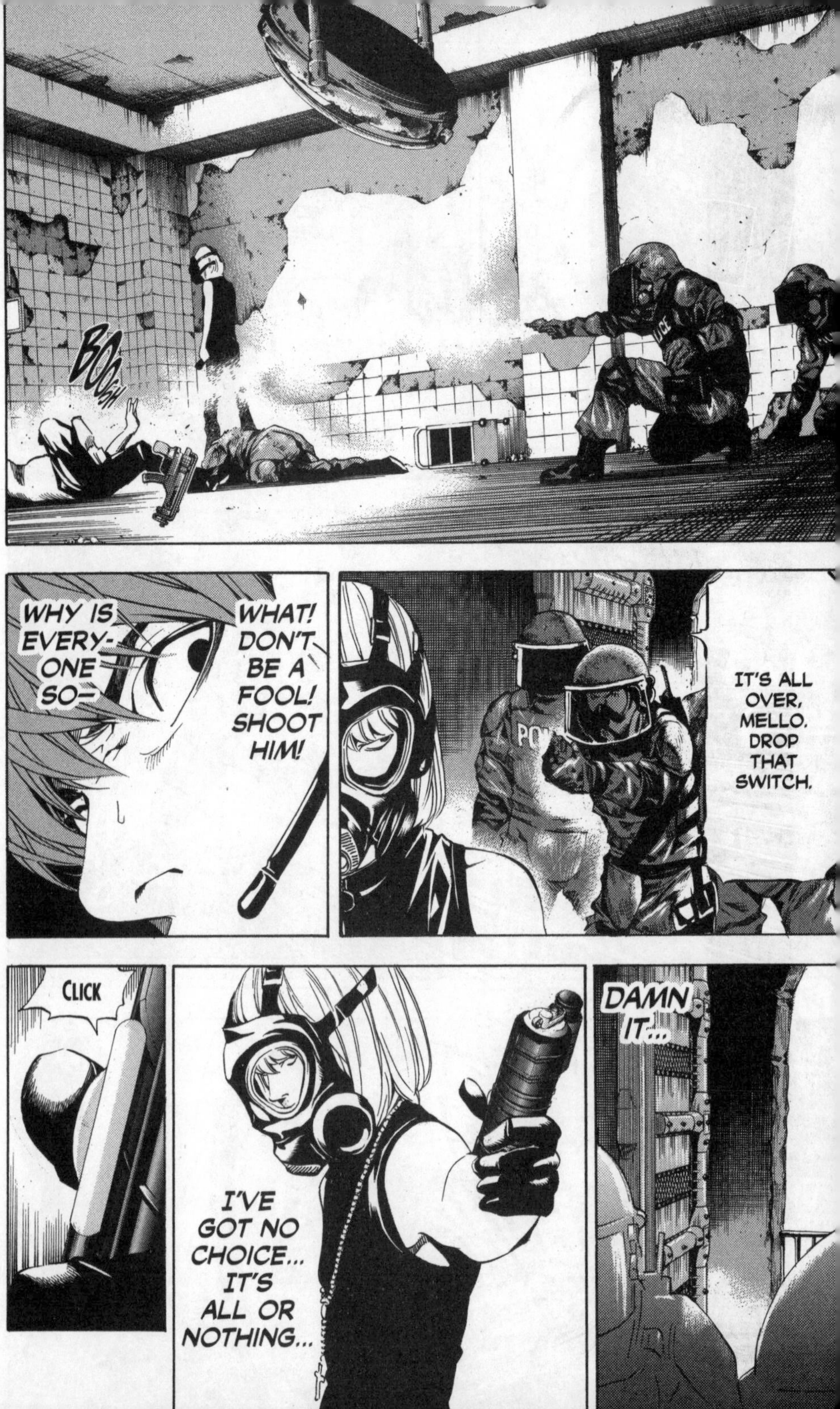
BOOSH
IT'S ALL OVER, MELLO. DROP THAT SWITCH.
WHAT! DON'T BE A FOOL! SHOOT HIM!
WHY IS EVERYONE SO—
DAMN IT...
I'VE GOT NO CHOICE... IT'S ALL OR NOTHING...
CLICK

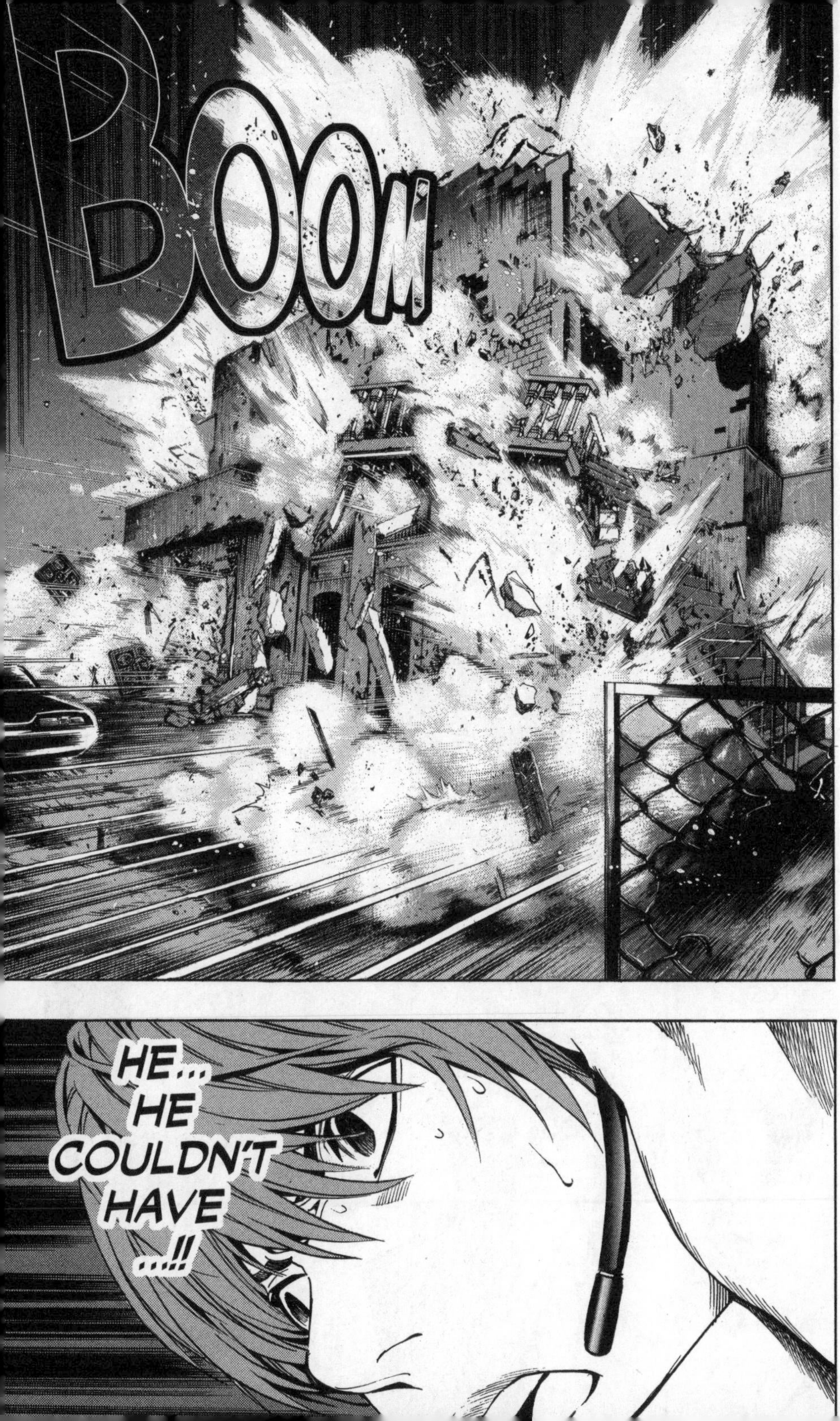
BOOM
HE... HE COULDN'T HAVE ...!!

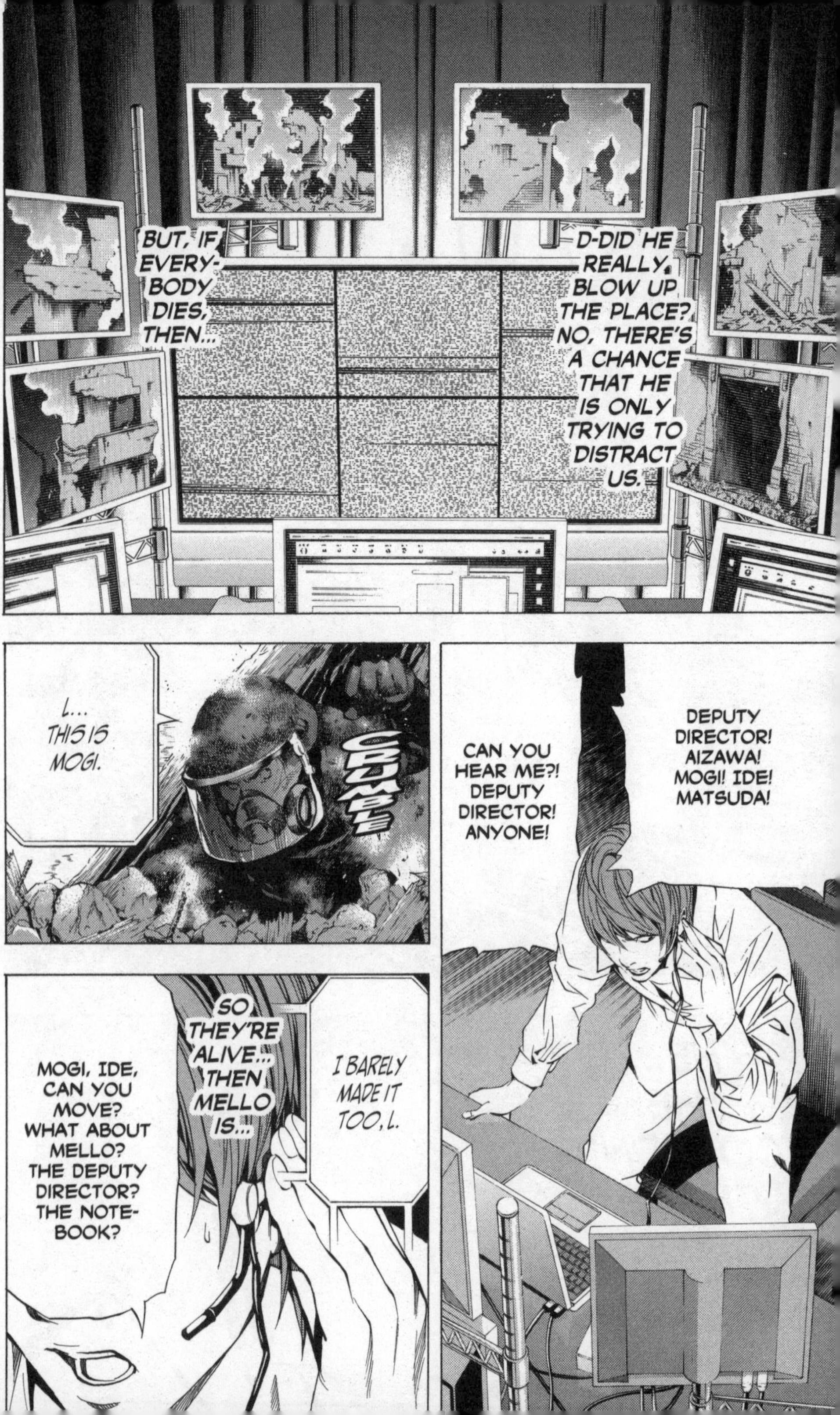
D-DID HE REALLY BLOW UP THE PLACE? NO, THERE'S A CHANCE THAT HE IS ONLY TRYING TO DISTRACT US.
BUT, IF EVERY-BODY DIES, THEN...
DEPUTY DIRECTOR! AIZAWA! MOGI! IDE! MATSUDA!
CAN YOU HEAR ME?! DEPUTY DIRECTOR! ANYONE!
L... THIS IS MOGI.
CRUMBLE
I BARELY MADE IT TOO, L.
SO THEY'RE ALIVE... THEN MELLO IS...
MOGI, IDE, CAN YOU MOVE? WHAT ABOUT MELLO? THE DEPUTY DIRECTOR? THE NOTE-BOOK?

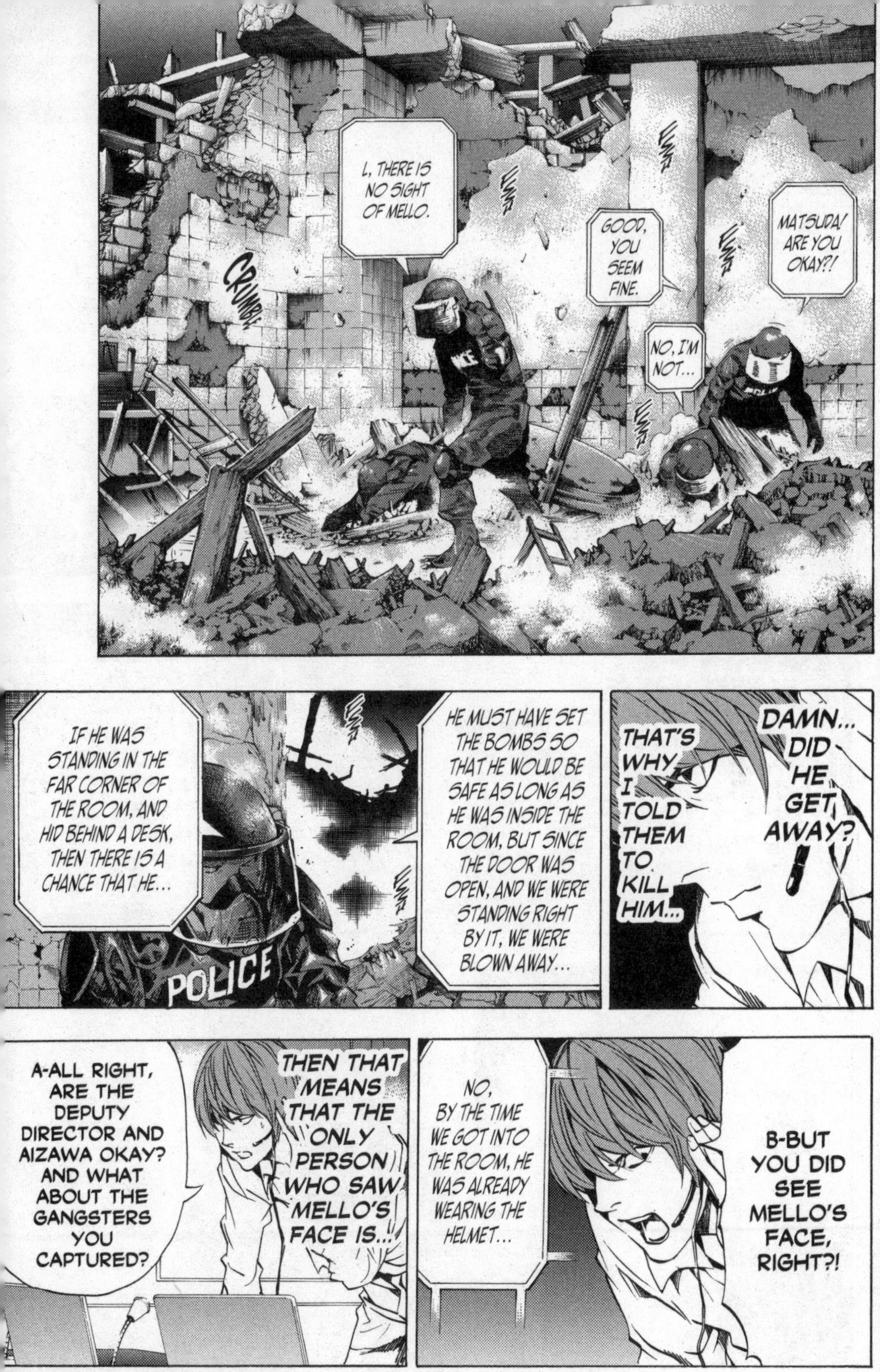
MATSUDA! ARE YOU OKAY?!
GOOD, YOU SEEM FINE.
NO, I'M NOT...
L, THERE IS NO SIGHT OF MELLO.
DAMN... DID HE GET AWAY?
THAT'S WHY I TOLD THEM TO KILL HIM...
HE MUST HAVE SET THE BOMBS SO THAT HE WOULD BE SAFE AS LONG AS HE WAS INSIDE THE ROOM, BUT SINCE THE DOOR WAS OPEN, AND WE WERE STANDING RIGHT BY IT, WE WERE BLOWN AWAY...
IF HE WAS STANDING IN THE FAR CORNER OF THE ROOM, AND HID BEHIND A DESK, THEN THERE IS A CHANCE THAT HE...
POLICE
B-BUT YOU DID SEE MELLO'S FACE, RIGHT?!
NO, BY THE TIME WE GOT INTO THE ROOM, HE WAS ALREADY WEARING THE HELMET...
THEN THAT MEANS THAT THE ONLY PERSON WHO SAW MELLO'S FACE IS...
A-ALL RIGHT, ARE THE DEPUTY DIRECTOR AND AIZAWA OKAY? AND WHAT ABOUT THE GANGSTERS YOU CAPTURED?

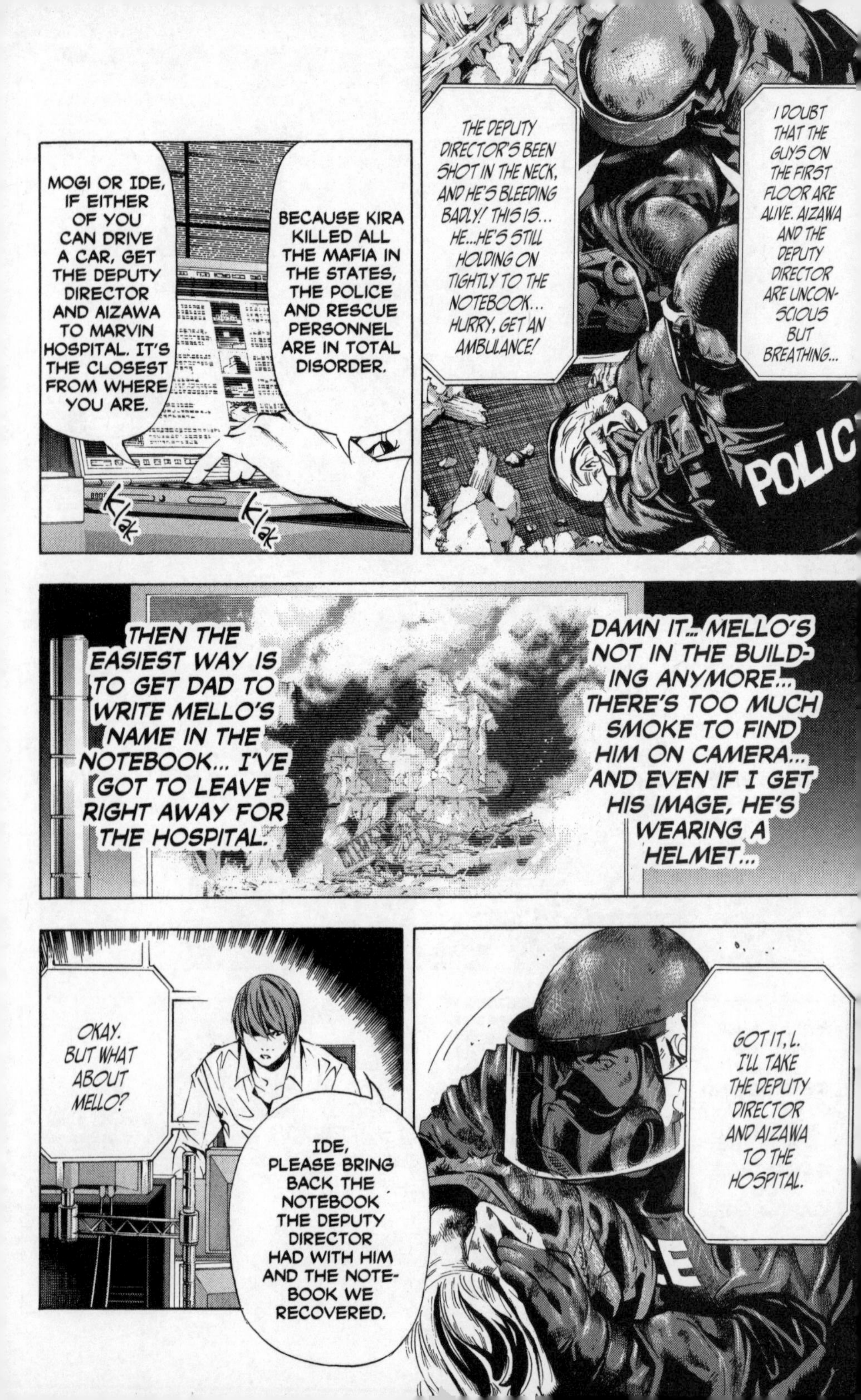
I DOUBT THAT THE GUYS ON THE FIRST FLOOR ARE ALIVE. AIZAWA AND THE DEPUTY DIRECTOR ARE UNCONSCIOUS BUT BREATHING...
THE DEPUTY DIRECTOR'S BEEN SHOT IN THE NECK, AND HE'S BLEEDING BADLY! THIS IS... HE...HE'S STILL HOLDING ON TIGHTLY TO THE NOTEBOOK... HURRY, GET AN AMBULANCE!
POLIC
BECAUSE KIRA KILLED ALL THE MAFIA IN THE STATES, THE POLICE AND RESCUE PERSONNEL ARE IN TOTAL DISORDER.
MOGI OR IDE, IF EITHER OF YOU CAN DRIVE A CAR, GET THE DEPUTY DIRECTOR AND AIZAWA TO MARVIN HOSPITAL. IT'S THE CLOSEST FROM WHERE YOU ARE.
Klak
Klak
DAMN IT... MELLO'S NOT IN THE BUILDING ANYMORE... THERE'S TOO MUCH SMOKE TO FIND HIM ON CAMERA... AND EVEN IF I GET HIS IMAGE, HE'S WEARING A HELMET...
THEN THE EASIEST WAY IS TO GET DAD TO WRITE MELLO'S NAME IN THE NOTEBOOK... I'VE GOT TO LEAVE RIGHT AWAY FOR THE HOSPITAL.
GOT IT, L. I'LL TAKE THE DEPUTY DIRECTOR AND AIZAWA TO THE HOSPITAL.
OKAY. BUT WHAT ABOUT MELLO?
IDE, PLEASE BRING BACK THE NOTEBOOK THE DEPUTY DIRECTOR HAD WITH HIM AND THE NOTEBOOK WE RECOVERED.

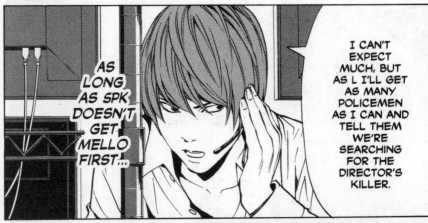

READ THIS WAY
I CAN'T EXPECT MUCH, BUT AS L I'LL GET AS MANY POLICEMEN AS I CAN AND TELL THEM WE'RE SEARCHING FOR THE DIRECTOR'S KILLER.
AS LONG AS SPK DOESN'T GET MELLO FIRST...
THE PROBLEM IS HOW MUCH MELLO KNOWS... ESPECIALLY ABOUT THE FAKE RULES...
IF HE HASN'T FOUND OUT ABOUT THE FAKE RULES, THEN I DON'T HAVE TO BOTHER WITH HIM. NO, FROM WHAT RYUK SAID, THAT OTHER SHINIGAMI DOESN'T SEEM VERY SMART. SO, I SHOULD ASSUME THAT MELLO ALREADY KNOWS. MELLO ALSO KNOWS ABOUT THE NOTEBOOK, AND IT'S OBVIOUS THAT HE'S OUT TO GET KIRA.
MELLO'S VERY EXISTENCE IS A DANGER TO ME. I'VE GOT TO KILL HIM, ANY WAY I CAN. ONCE MY FATHER REGAINS CONSCIOUSNESS, I'LL FORCE HIM TO WRITE MELLO'S NAME IN THE NOTEBOOK IF I HAVE TO...
HEY, THAT OLD MAN TOOK THE NOTEBOOK WITH HIM, SO NOW I CAN'T GET IT. WHERE ARE THEY TAKING THE NOTEBOOK TO THIS TIME?
YOU JUST STOOD OUTSIDE AND DID NOTHING. YOU SHOULD HAVE TAKEN THE NOTEBOOK BACK WHEN ITS OWNER DIED...
RYUK, YOU'RE THE ONE WHO TOLD ME TO SHUT UP AND JUST WATCH.

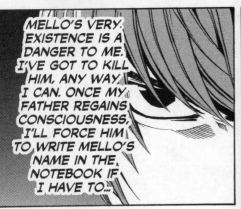

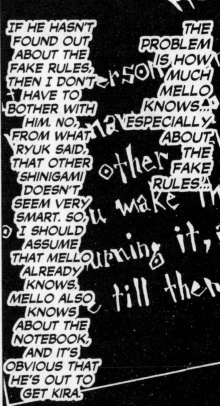

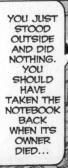

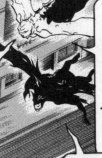

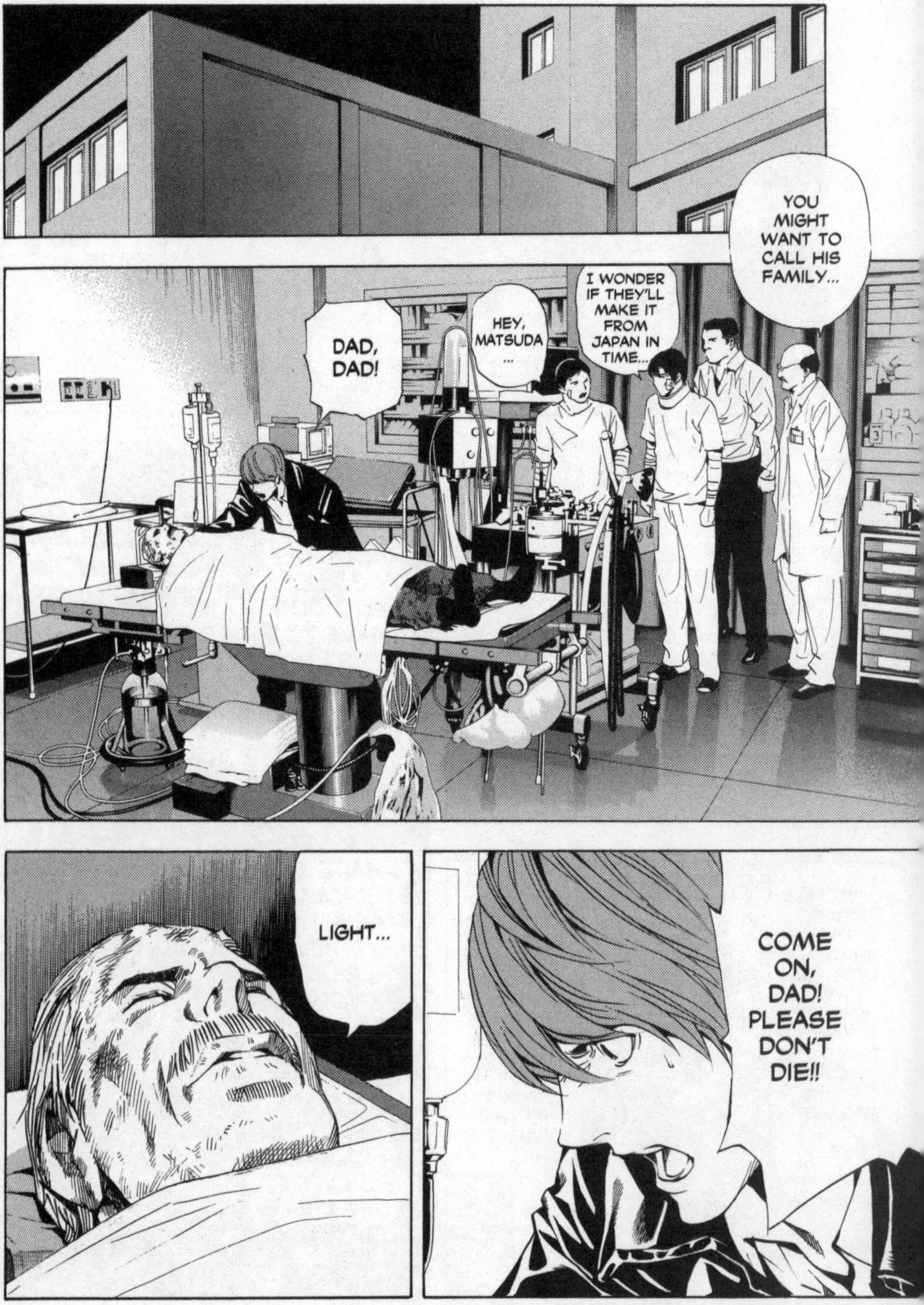
YOU MIGHT WANT TO CALL HIS FAMILY...
I WONDER IF THEY'LL MAKE IT FROM JAPAN IN TIME...
HEY, MATSUDA ...
DAD, DAD!
COME ON, DAD! PLEASE DON'T DIE!!
LIGHT...

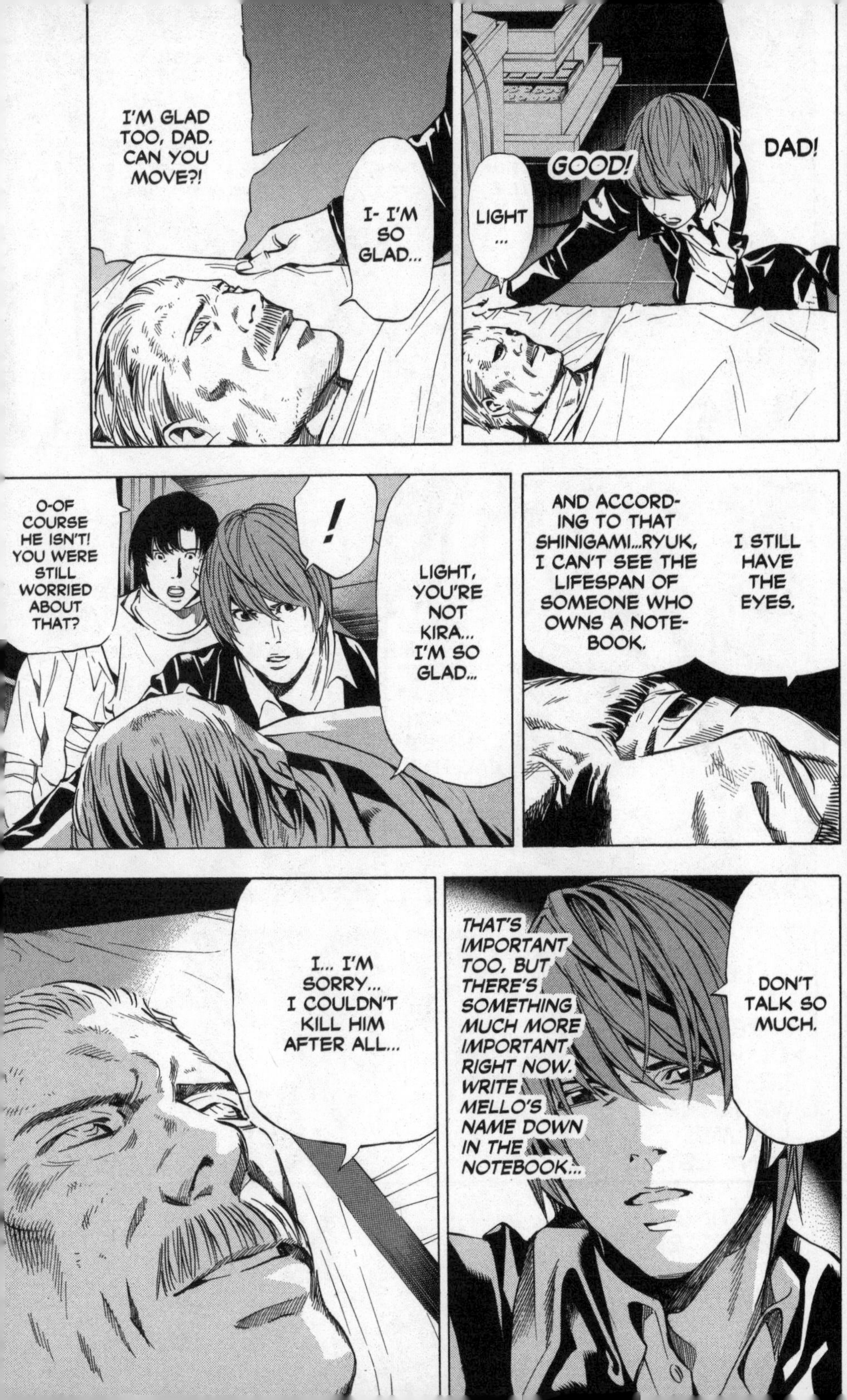
DAD!
GOOD!
LIGHT ...
I- I'M SO GLAD...
I'M GLAD TOO, DAD. CAN YOU MOVE?!
I STILL HAVE THE EYES.
AND ACCORDING TO THAT SHINIGAMI...RYUK, I CAN'T SEE THE LIFESPAN OF SOMEONE WHO OWNS A NOTE-BOOK.
!
LIGHT, YOU'RE NOT KIRA... I'M SO GLAD...
O-OF COURSE HE ISN'T! YOU WERE STILL WORRIED ABOUT THAT?
DON'T TALK SO MUCH.
THAT'S IMPORTANT TOO, BUT THERE'S SOMETHING MUCH MORE IMPORTANT RIGHT NOW. WRITE MELLO'S NAME DOWN IN THE NOTEBOOK...
I... I'M SORRY... I COULDN'T KILL HIM AFTER ALL...

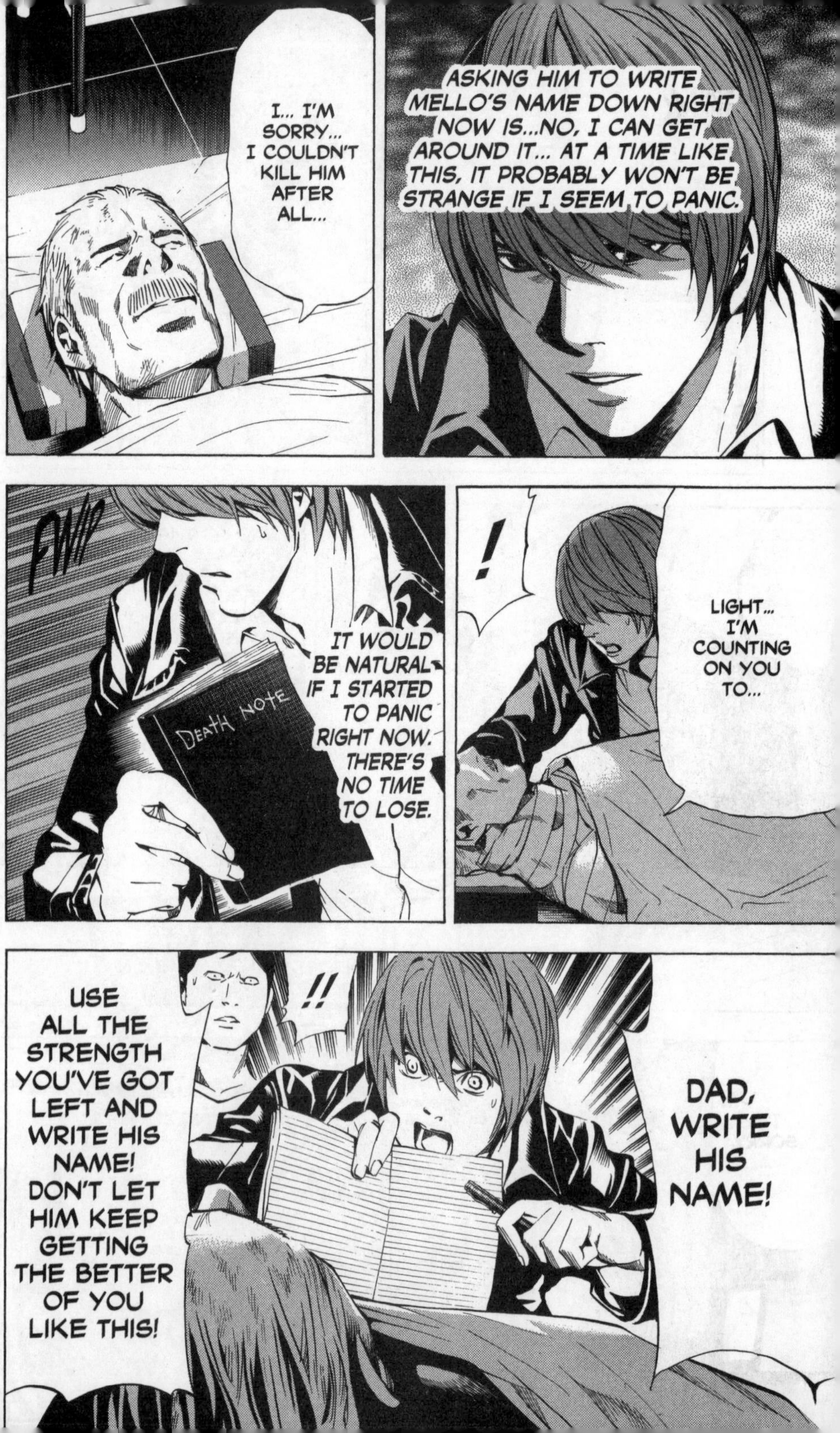
ASKING HIM TO WRITE MELLO'S NAME DOWN RIGHT NOW IS...NO, I CAN GET AROUND IT... AT A TIME LIKE THIS, IT PROBABLY WON'T BE STRANGE IF I SEEM TO PANIC.
I... I'M SORRY... I COULDN'T KILL HIM AFTER ALL...
!
LIGHT... I'M COUNTING ON YOU TO...
FWIP
IT WOULD BE NATURAL IF I STARTED TO PANIC RIGHT NOW. THERE'S NO TIME TO LOSE.
DEATH NOTE
!!
DAD, WRITE HIS NAME!
USE ALL THE STRENGTH YOU'VE GOT LEFT AND WRITE HIS NAME! DON'T LET HIM KEEP GETTING THE BETTER OF YOU LIKE THIS!

WRITE IT, DAD! HURRY UP AND REMEMBER HIS FACE!

IDE...

COME ON DAD, DO YOU WANT TO DIE IN VAIN?

L-LIGHT...

DAD!

BEEEEEEEEEEP

I'M SORRY...

Life Scope

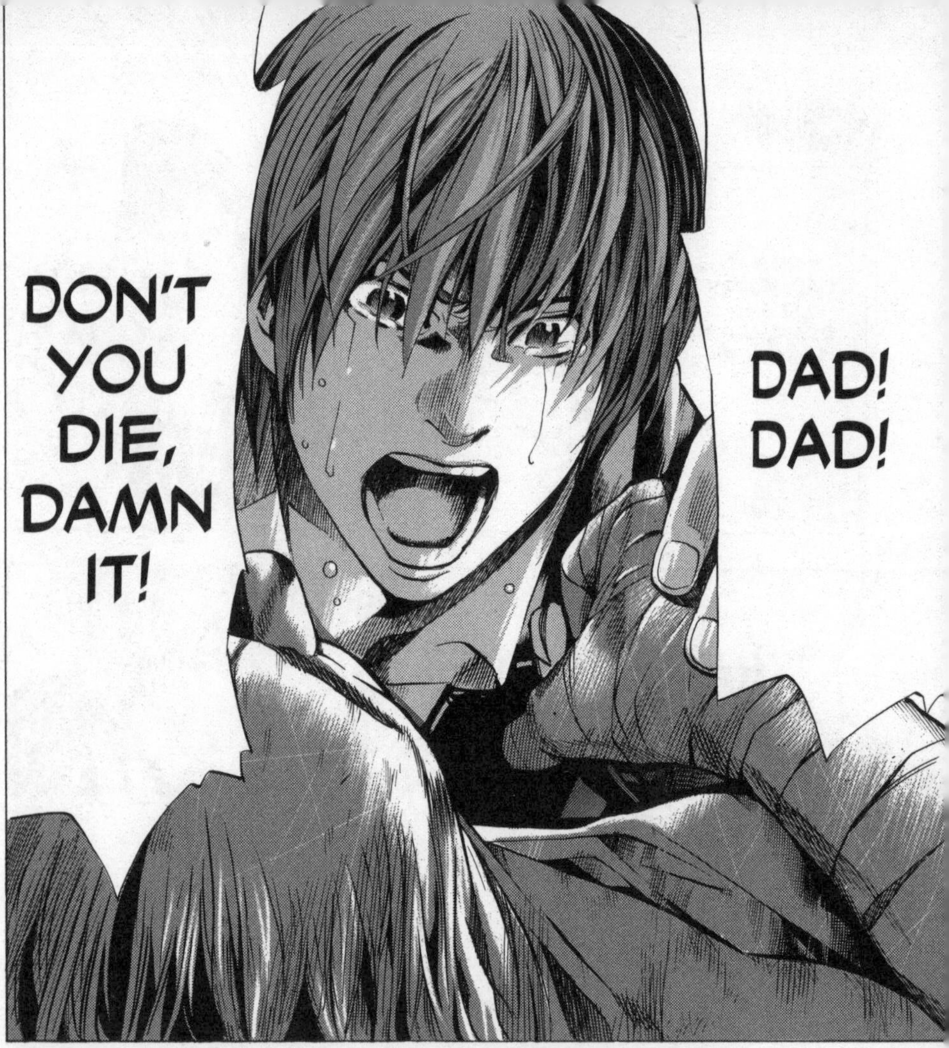
DAD! DAD!
DON'T YOU DIE, DAMN IT!

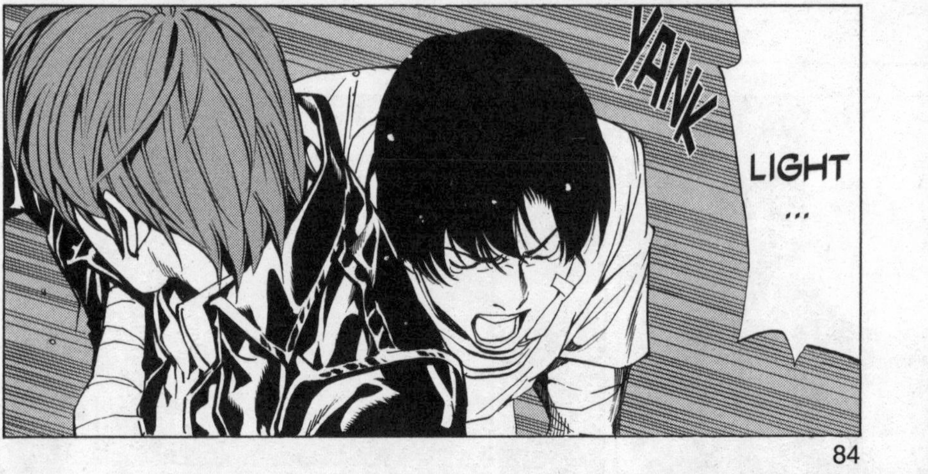
YANK
LIGHT ...

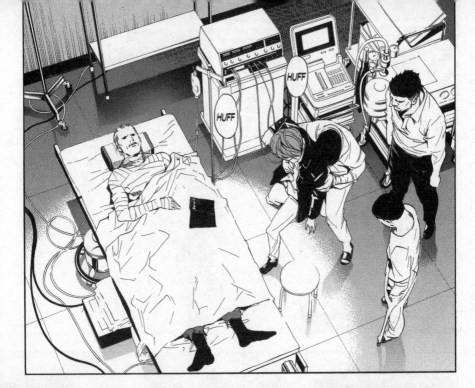

? EVERYONE, PLEASE COME OUTSIDE.

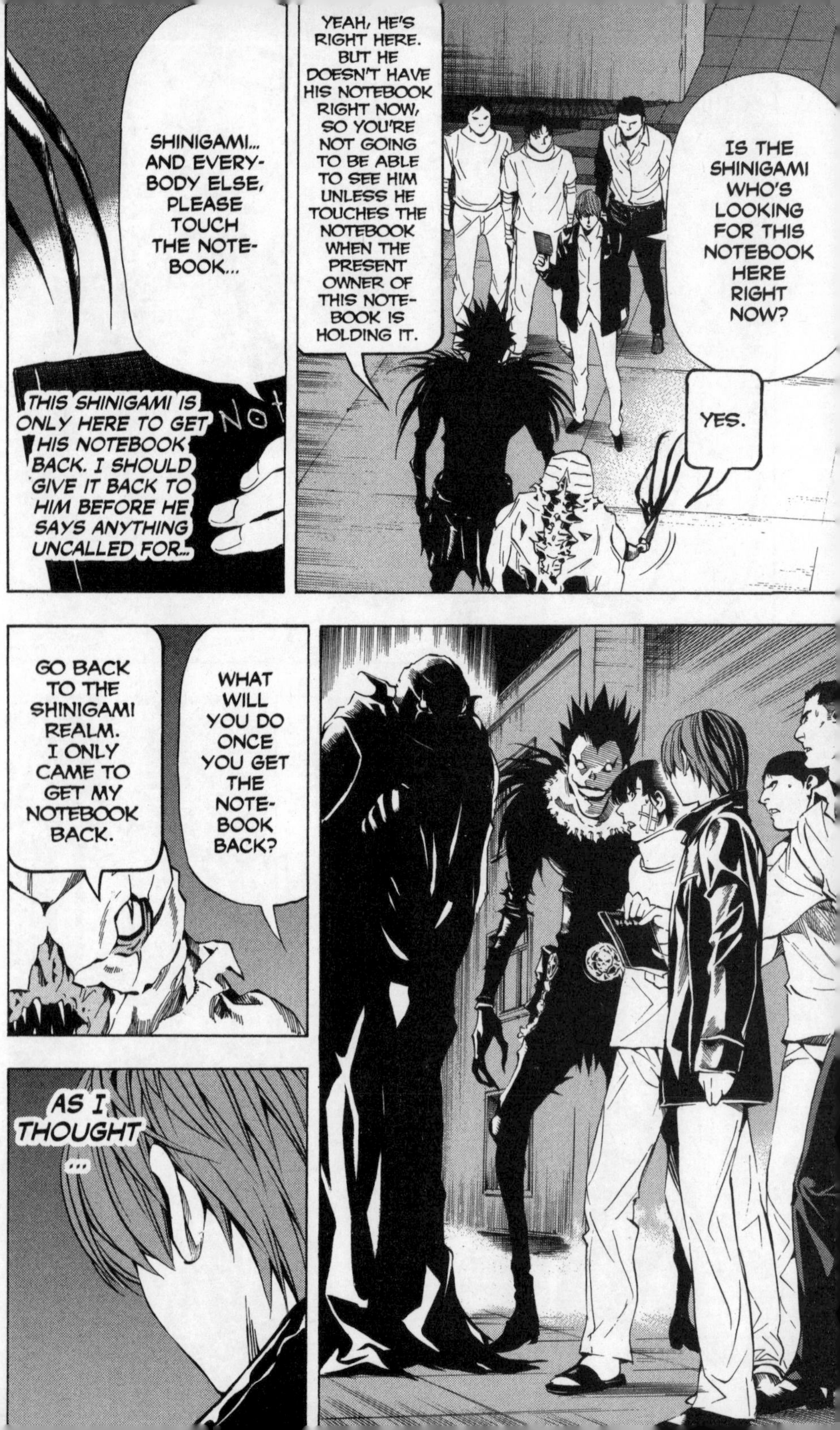
IS THE SHINIGAMI WHO'S LOOKING FOR THIS NOTEBOOK HERE RIGHT NOW?
YES.
YEAH, HE'S RIGHT HERE. BUT HE DOESN'T HAVE HIS NOTEBOOK RIGHT NOW, SO YOU'RE NOT GOING TO BE ABLE TO SEE HIM UNLESS HE TOUCHES THE NOTEBOOK WHEN THE PRESENT OWNER OF THIS NOTEBOOK IS HOLDING IT.
SHINIGAMI... AND EVERYBODY ELSE, PLEASE TOUCH THE NOTEBOOK...
THIS SHINIGAMI IS ONLY HERE TO GET HIS NOTEBOOK BACK. I SHOULD GIVE IT BACK TO HIM BEFORE HE SAYS ANYTHING UNCALLED FOR...
WHAT WILL YOU DO ONCE YOU GET THE NOTEBOOK BACK?
GO BACK TO THE SHINIGAMI REALM. I ONLY CAME TO GET MY NOTEBOOK BACK.
AS I THOUGHT...

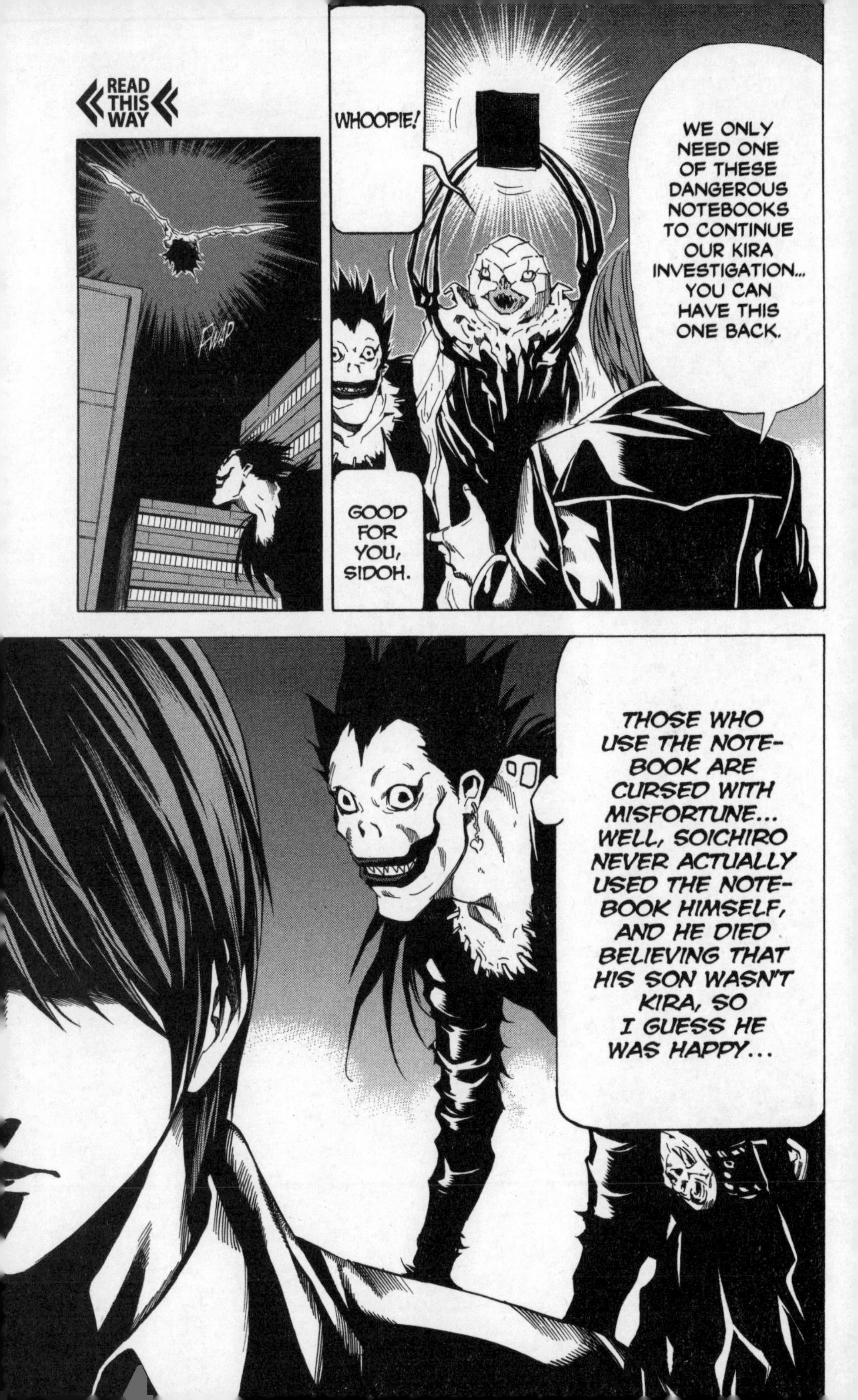
READ THIS WAY
WE ONLY NEED ONE OF THESE DANGEROUS NOTEBOOKS TO CONTINUE OUR KIRA INVESTIGATION... YOU CAN HAVE THIS ONE BACK.
WHOOPIE!
GOOD FOR YOU, SIDOH.
FWAP
THOSE WHO USE THE NOTE-BOOK ARE CURSED WITH MISFORTUNE... WELL, SOICHIRO NEVER ACTUALLY USED THE NOTE-BOOK HIMSELF, AND HE DIED BELIEVING THAT HIS SON WASN'T KIRA, SO I GUESS HE WAS HAPPY...

DEATH NOTE
How to use it

XLIX

- Only 6 DEATH NOTEs are allowed to exist at a time in the human world. Of course, the DEATH NOTE that the god of death owns does not count. This means only 6 gods of death that have passed on their DEATH NOTE to humans can stay in the human world.

人間界で同時に存在していいデスノートは6冊まで。
もちろん死神自身が所有するノートはその数に入らない。
よって、人間にノートを所有させる事で人間界にいていい死神も6匹まで。

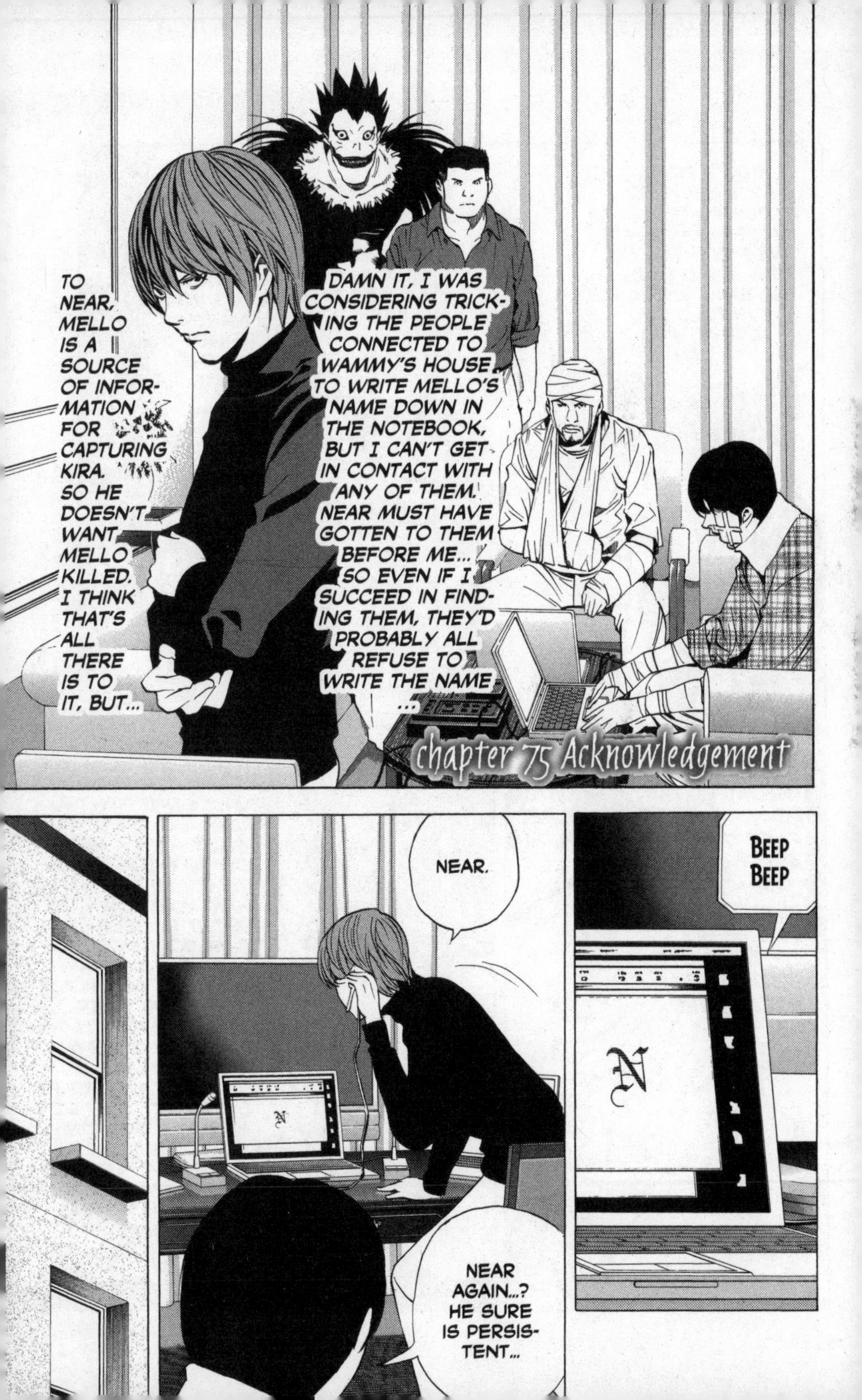
DAMN IT, I WAS CONSIDERING TRICKING THE PEOPLE CONNECTED TO WAMMY'S HOUSE TO WRITE MELLO'S NAME DOWN IN THE NOTEBOOK, BUT I CAN'T GET IN CONTACT WITH ANY OF THEM. NEAR MUST HAVE GOTTEN TO THEM BEFORE ME... SO EVEN IF I SUCCEED IN FINDING THEM, THEY'D PROBABLY ALL REFUSE TO WRITE THE NAME...
TO NEAR, MELLO IS A SOURCE OF INFORMATION FOR CAPTURING KIRA. SO HE DOESN'T WANT MELLO KILLED. I THINK THAT'S ALL THERE IS TO IT, BUT...
chapter 75 Acknowledgement
BEEP BEEP
NEAR.
NEAR AGAIN...? HE SURE IS PERSISTENT...

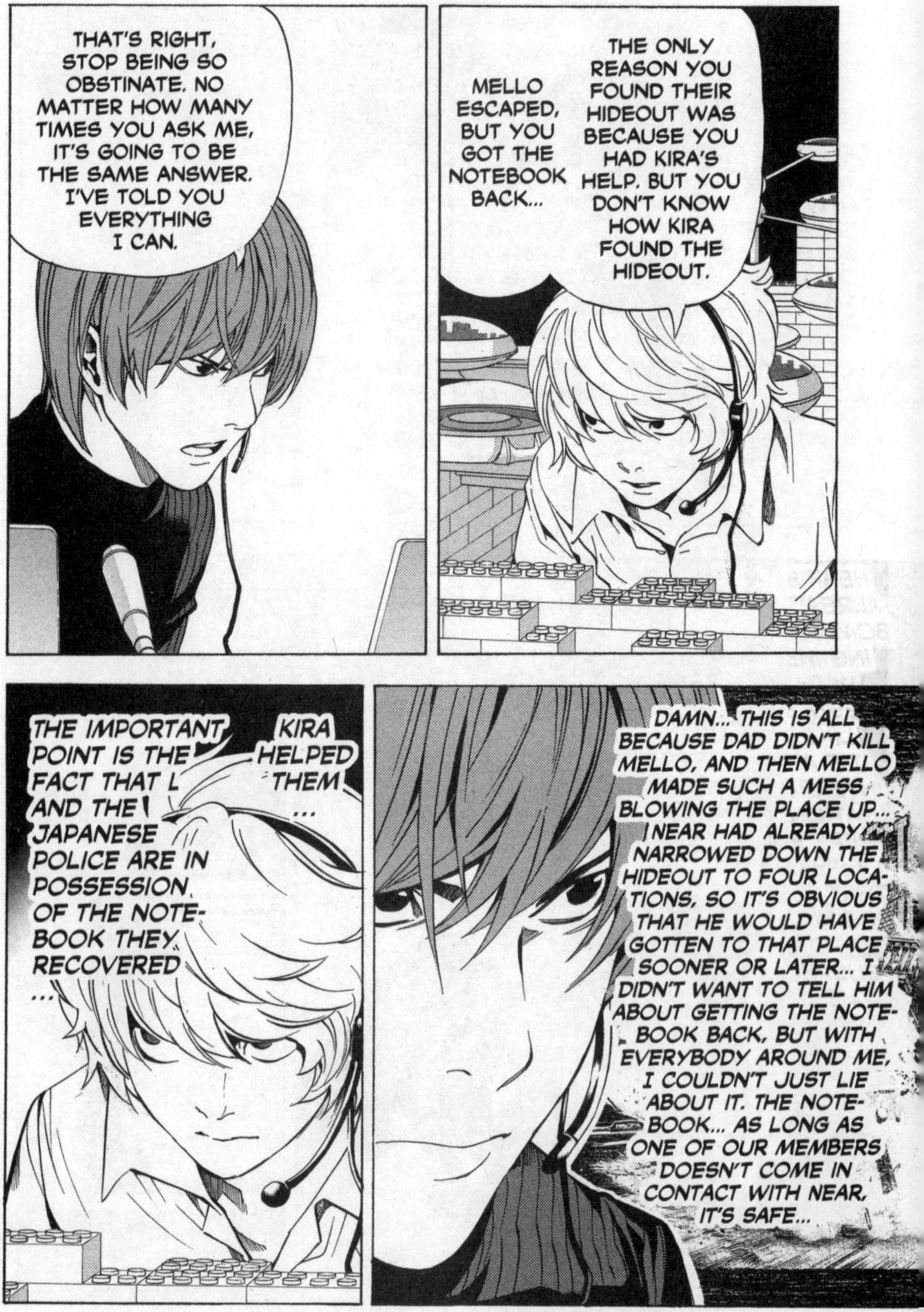
THE ONLY REASON YOU FOUND THEIR HIDEOUT WAS BECAUSE YOU HAD KIRA'S HELP. BUT YOU DON'T KNOW HOW KIRA FOUND THE HIDEOUT.
MELLO ESCAPED, BUT YOU GOT THE NOTEBOOK BACK...
THAT'S RIGHT, STOP BEING SO OBSTINATE. NO MATTER HOW MANY TIMES YOU ASK ME, IT'S GOING TO BE THE SAME ANSWER. I'VE TOLD YOU EVERYTHING I CAN.
DAMN... THIS IS ALL BECAUSE DAD DIDN'T KILL MELLO, AND THEN MELLO MADE SUCH A MESS BLOWING THE PLACE UP... NEAR HAD ALREADY NARROWED DOWN THE HIDEOUT TO FOUR LOCATIONS, SO IT'S OBVIOUS THAT HE WOULD HAVE GOTTEN TO THAT PLACE SOONER OR LATER... I DIDN'T WANT TO TELL HIM ABOUT GETTING THE NOTEBOOK BACK, BUT WITH EVERYBODY AROUND ME, I COULDN'T JUST LIE ABOUT IT. THE NOTEBOOK... AS LONG AS ONE OF OUR MEMBERS DOESN'T COME IN CONTACT WITH NEAR, IT'S SAFE...
KIRA HELPED THEM...
THE IMPORTANT POINT IS THE FACT THAT L AND THE JAPANESE POLICE ARE IN POSSESSION OF THE NOTEBOOK THEY RECOVERED...

READ THIS WAY

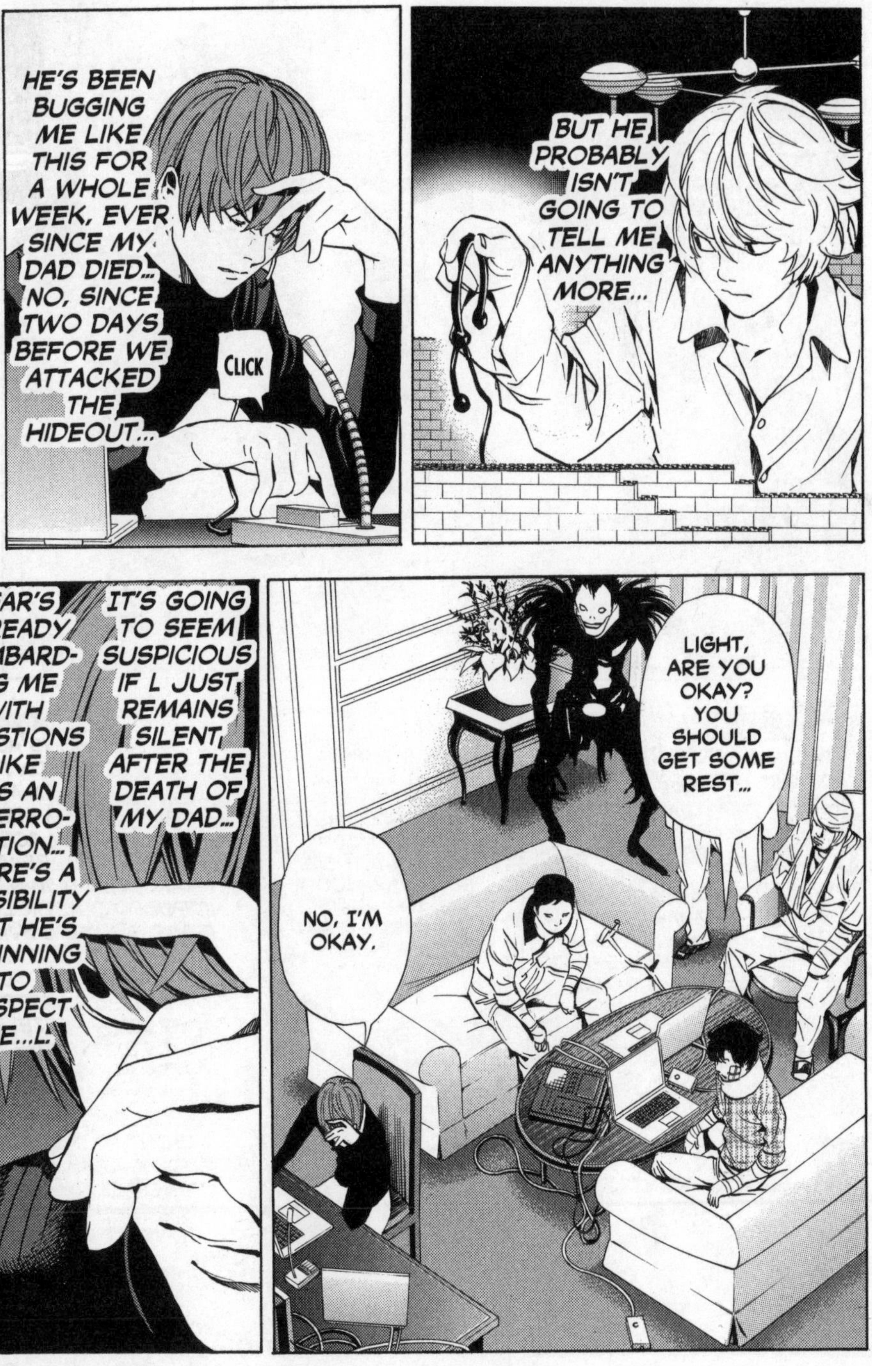
BUT HE PROBABLY ISN'T GOING TO TELL ME ANYTHING MORE...
HE'S BEEN BUGGING ME LIKE THIS FOR A WHOLE WEEK, EVER SINCE MY DAD DIED... NO, SINCE TWO DAYS BEFORE WE ATTACKED THE HIDEOUT...
CLICK
LIGHT, ARE YOU OKAY? YOU SHOULD GET SOME REST...
NO, I'M OKAY.
IT'S GOING TO SEEM SUSPICIOUS IF L JUST REMAINS SILENT, AFTER THE DEATH OF MY DAD...
NEAR'S ALREADY BOMBARDING ME WITH QUESTIONS LIKE IT'S AN INTERROGATION... THERE'S A POSSIBILITY THAT HE'S BEGINNING TO SUSPECT ME...L.

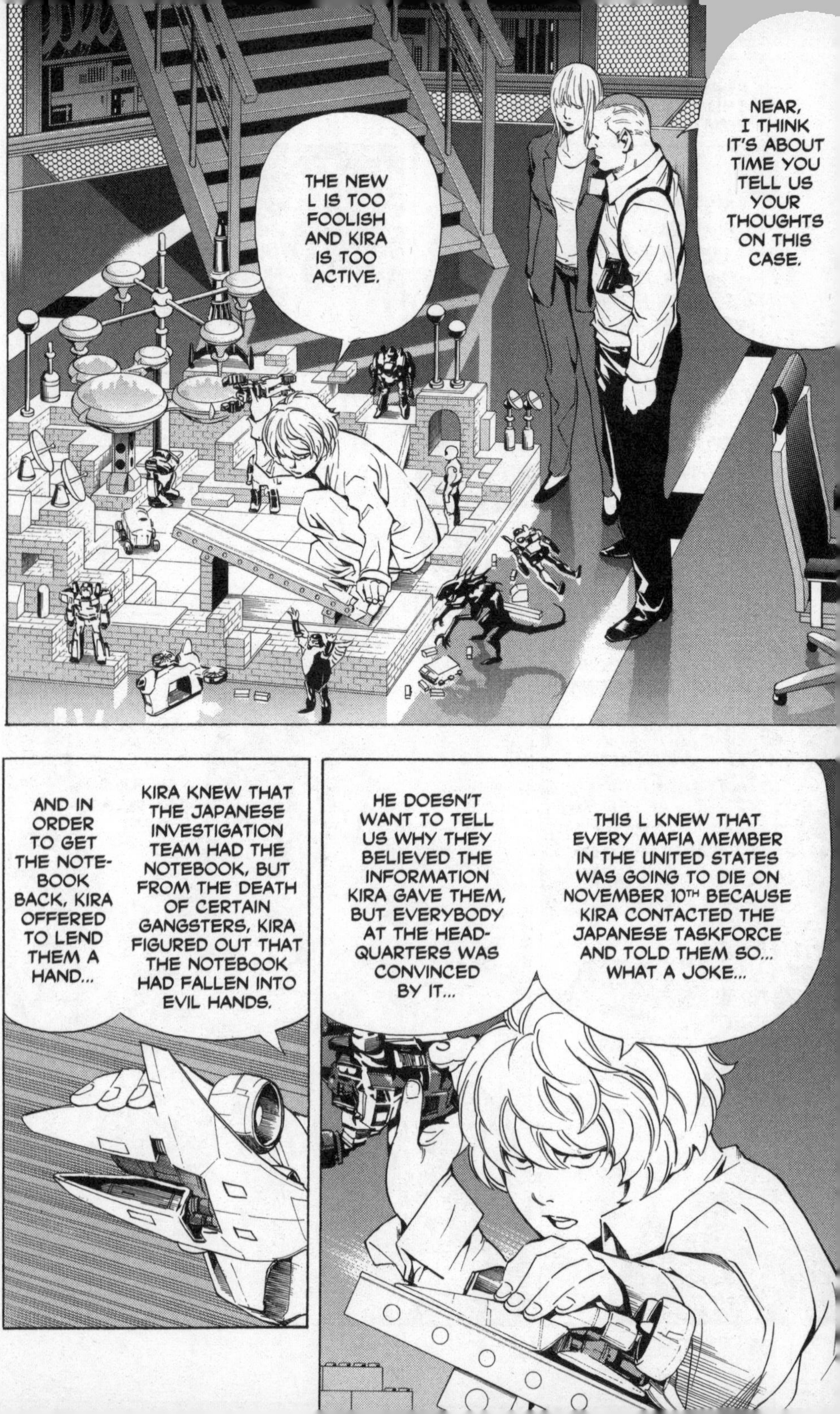
NEAR, I THINK IT'S ABOUT TIME YOU TELL US YOUR THOUGHTS ON THIS CASE.
THE NEW L IS TOO FOOLISH AND KIRA IS TOO ACTIVE.
THIS L KNEW THAT EVERY MAFIA MEMBER IN THE UNITED STATES WAS GOING TO DIE ON NOVEMBER 10TH BECAUSE KIRA CONTACTED THE JAPANESE TASKFORCE AND TOLD THEM SO... WHAT A JOKE...
HE DOESN'T WANT TO TELL US WHY THEY BELIEVED THE INFORMATION KIRA GAVE THEM, BUT EVERYBODY AT THE HEAD-QUARTERS WAS CONVINCED BY IT...
KIRA KNEW THAT THE JAPANESE INVESTIGATION TEAM HAD THE NOTEBOOK, BUT FROM THE DEATH OF CERTAIN GANGSTERS, KIRA FIGURED OUT THAT THE NOTEBOOK HAD FALLEN INTO EVIL HANDS.
AND IN ORDER TO GET THE NOTE-BOOK BACK, KIRA OFFERED TO LEND THEM A HAND...

READ THIS WAY

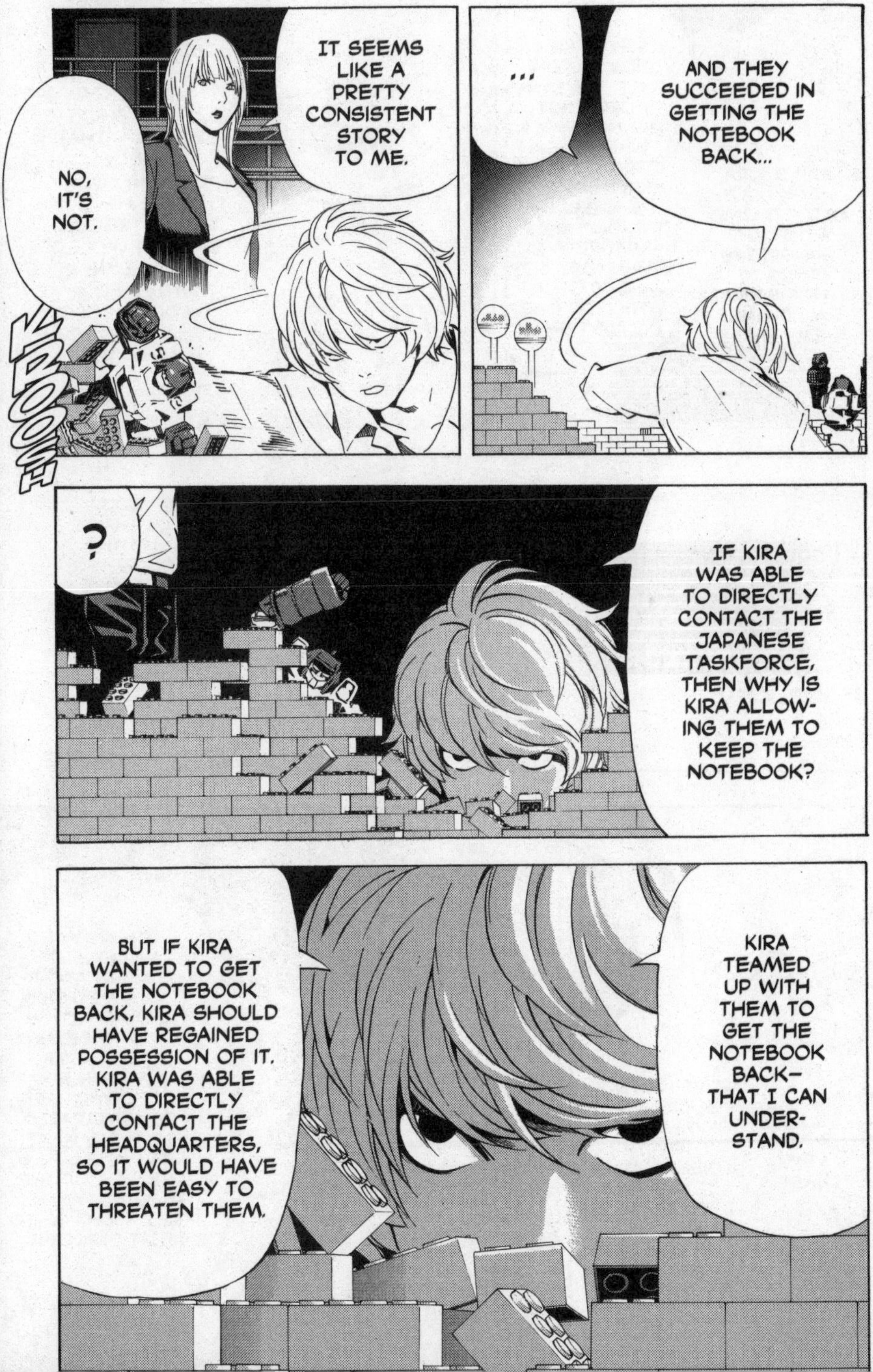
AND THEY SUCCEEDED IN GETTING THE NOTEBOOK BACK...
...
IT SEEMS LIKE A PRETTY CONSISTENT STORY TO ME.
NO, IT'S NOT.
IF KIRA WAS ABLE TO DIRECTLY CONTACT THE JAPANESE TASKFORCE, THEN WHY IS KIRA ALLOWING THEM TO KEEP THE NOTEBOOK?
?
KIRA TEAMED UP WITH THEM TO GET THE NOTEBOOK BACK— THAT I CAN UNDER-STAND.
BUT IF KIRA WANTED TO GET THE NOTEBOOK BACK, KIRA SHOULD HAVE REGAINED POSSESSION OF IT. KIRA WAS ABLE TO DIRECTLY CONTACT THE HEADQUARTERS, SO IT WOULD HAVE BEEN EASY TO THREATEN THEM.

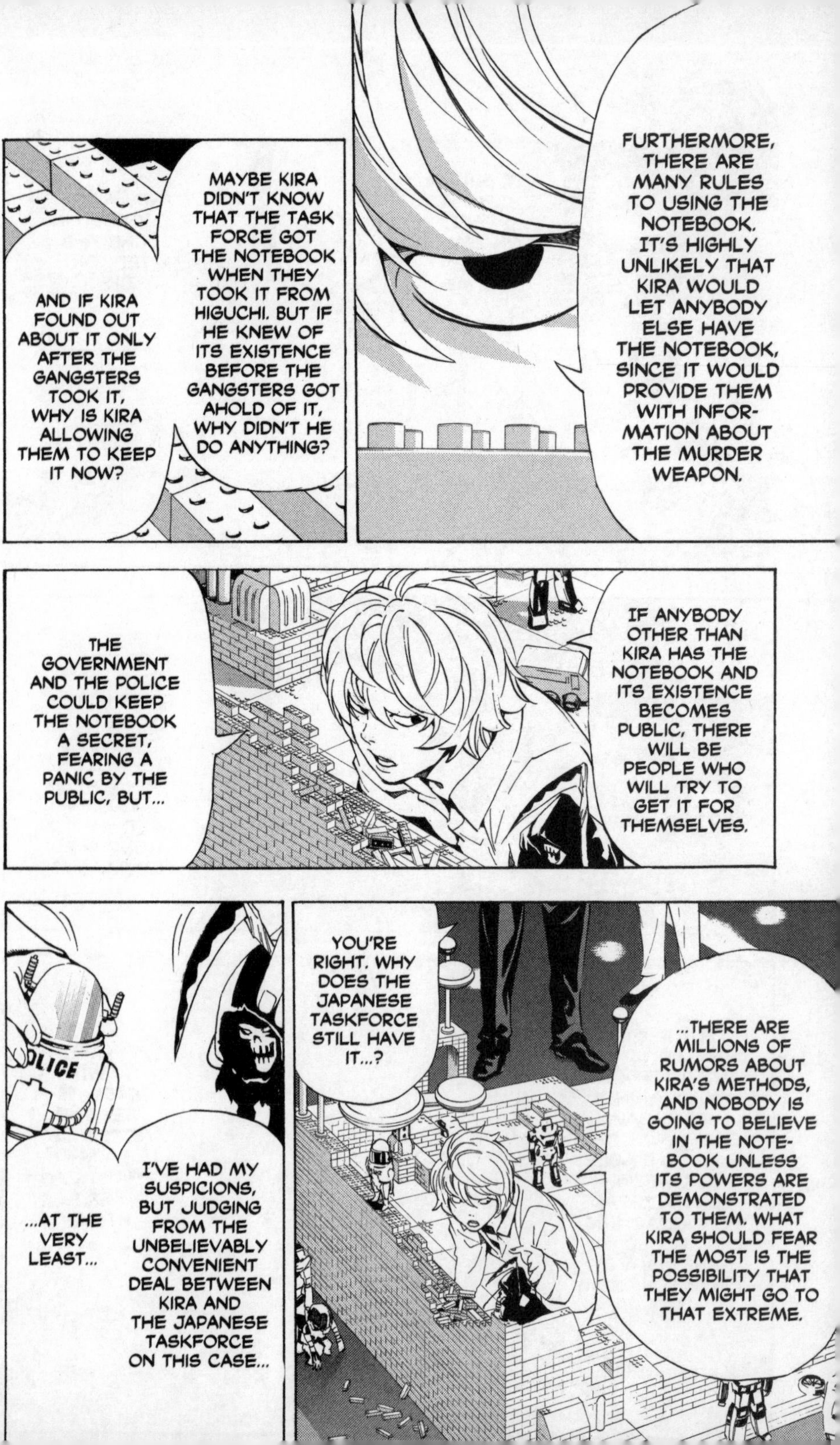
FURTHERMORE, THERE ARE MANY RULES TO USING THE NOTEBOOK. IT'S HIGHLY UNLIKELY THAT KIRA WOULD LET ANYBODY ELSE HAVE THE NOTEBOOK, SINCE IT WOULD PROVIDE THEM WITH INFORMATION ABOUT THE MURDER WEAPON.
MAYBE KIRA DIDN'T KNOW THAT THE TASK FORCE GOT THE NOTEBOOK WHEN THEY TOOK IT FROM HIGUCHI. BUT IF HE KNEW OF ITS EXISTENCE BEFORE THE GANGSTERS GOT AHOLD OF IT, WHY DIDN'T HE DO ANYTHING?
AND IF KIRA FOUND OUT ABOUT IT ONLY AFTER THE GANGSTERS TOOK IT, WHY IS KIRA ALLOWING THEM TO KEEP IT NOW?
IF ANYBODY OTHER THAN KIRA HAS THE NOTEBOOK AND ITS EXISTENCE BECOMES PUBLIC, THERE WILL BE PEOPLE WHO WILL TRY TO GET IT FOR THEMSELVES.
THE GOVERNMENT AND THE POLICE COULD KEEP THE NOTEBOOK A SECRET, FEARING A PANIC BY THE PUBLIC, BUT...
...THERE ARE MILLIONS OF RUMORS ABOUT KIRA'S METHODS, AND NOBODY IS GOING TO BELIEVE IN THE NOTEBOOK UNLESS ITS POWERS ARE DEMONSTRATED TO THEM. WHAT KIRA SHOULD FEAR THE MOST IS THE POSSIBILITY THAT THEY MIGHT GO TO THAT EXTREME.
YOU'RE RIGHT. WHY DOES THE JAPANESE TASKFORCE STILL HAVE IT...?
I'VE HAD MY SUSPICIONS, BUT JUDGING FROM THE UNBELIEVABLY CONVENIENT DEAL BETWEEN KIRA AND THE JAPANESE TASKFORCE ON THIS CASE...
...AT THE VERY LEAST...
POLICE

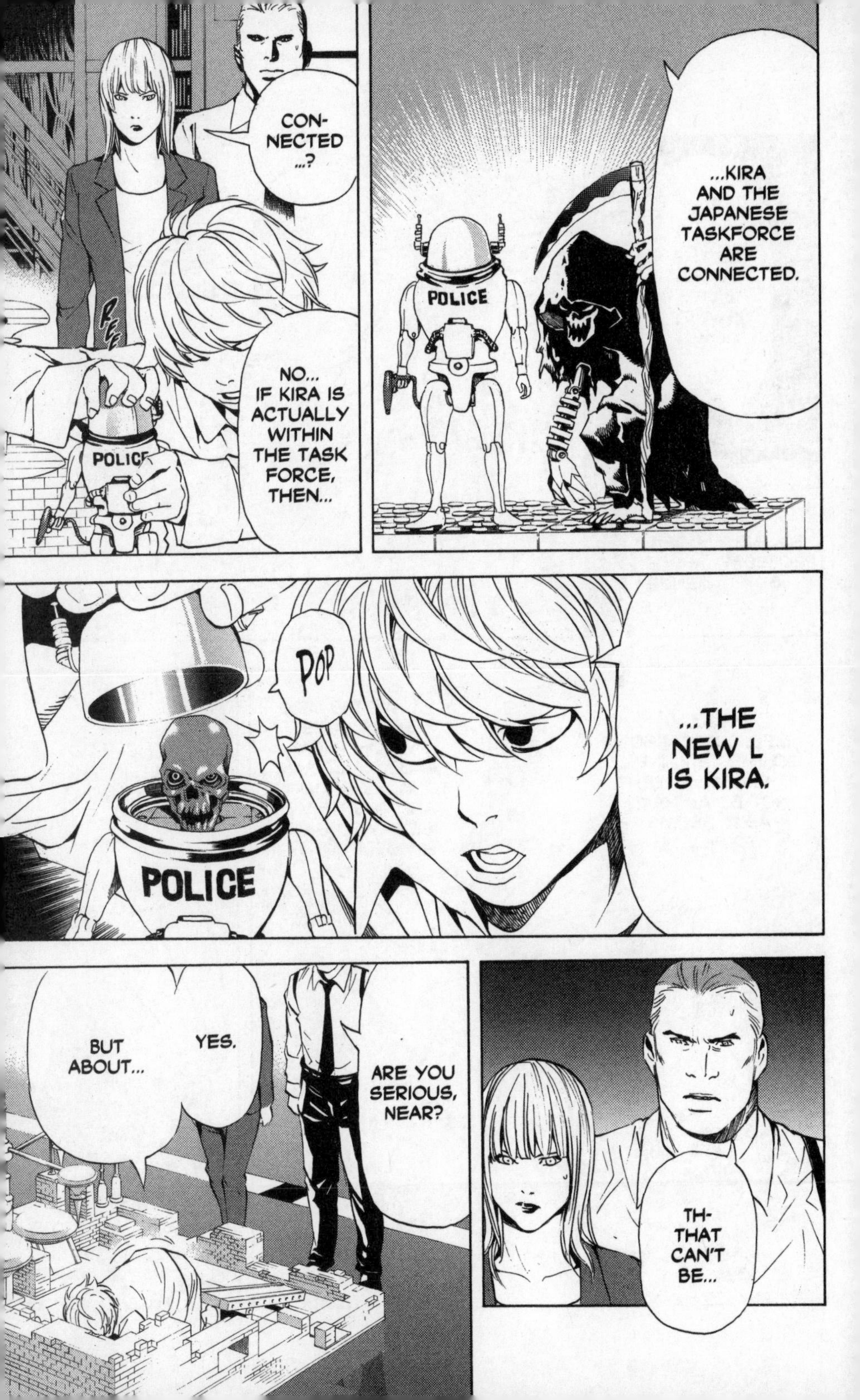
...KIRA AND THE JAPANESE TASKFORCE ARE CONNECTED.
CON-NECTED ...?
NO... IF KIRA IS ACTUALLY WITHIN THE TASK FORCE, THEN...
POLICE
...THE NEW L IS KIRA.
POP
POLICE
TH-THAT CAN'T BE...
ARE YOU SERIOUS, NEAR?
YES.
BUT ABOUT...

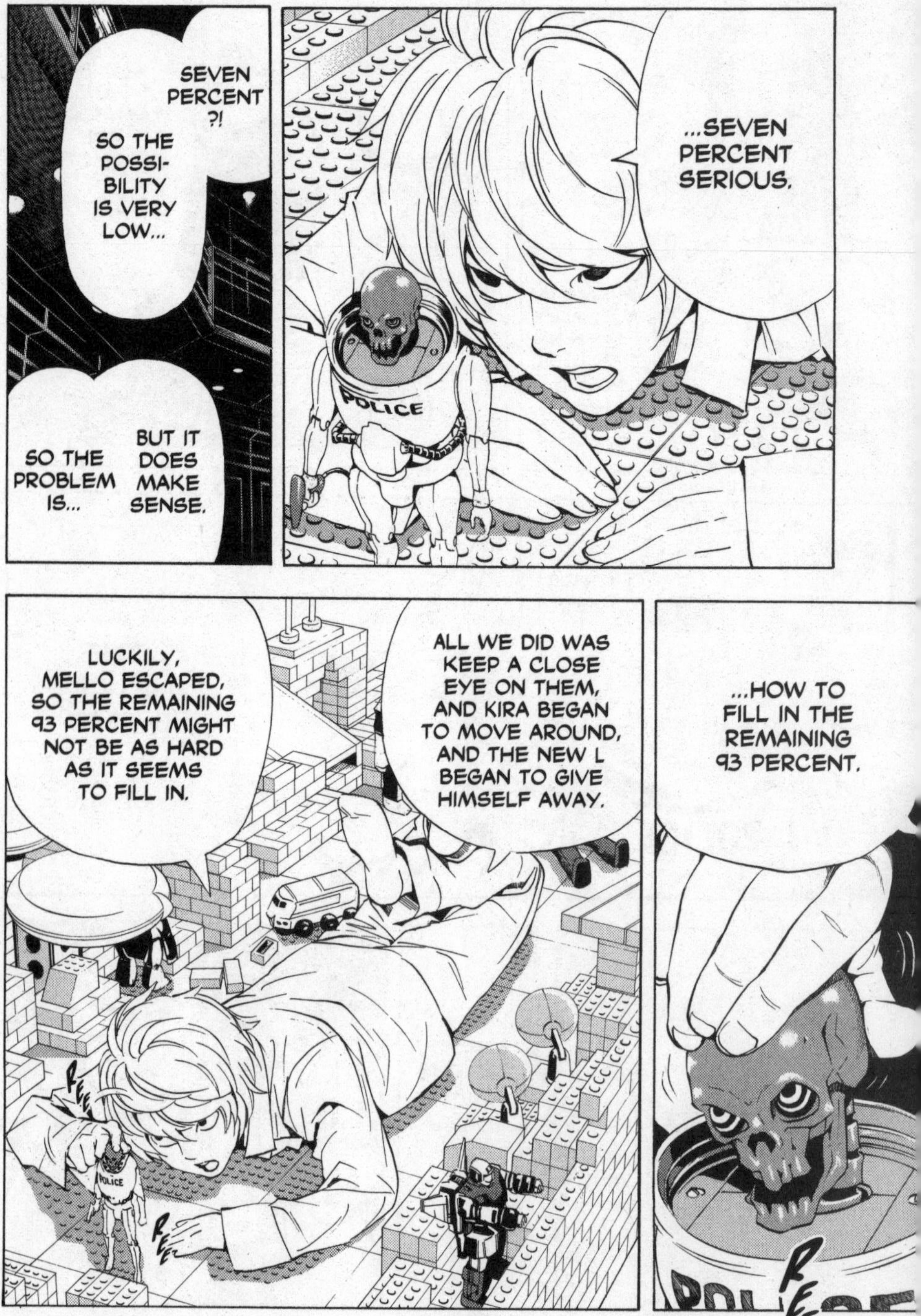
...SEVEN PERCENT SERIOUS.
SEVEN PERCENT ?!
SO THE POSSI-BILITY IS VERY LOW...
BUT IT DOES MAKE SENSE.
SO THE PROBLEM IS...
...HOW TO FILL IN THE REMAINING 93 PERCENT.
REE
ALL WE DID WAS KEEP A CLOSE EYE ON THEM, AND KIRA BEGAN TO MOVE AROUND, AND THE NEW L BEGAN TO GIVE HIMSELF AWAY.
LUCKILY, MELLO ESCAPED, SO THE REMAINING 93 PERCENT MIGHT NOT BE AS HARD AS IT SEEMS TO FILL IN.
REE
REE

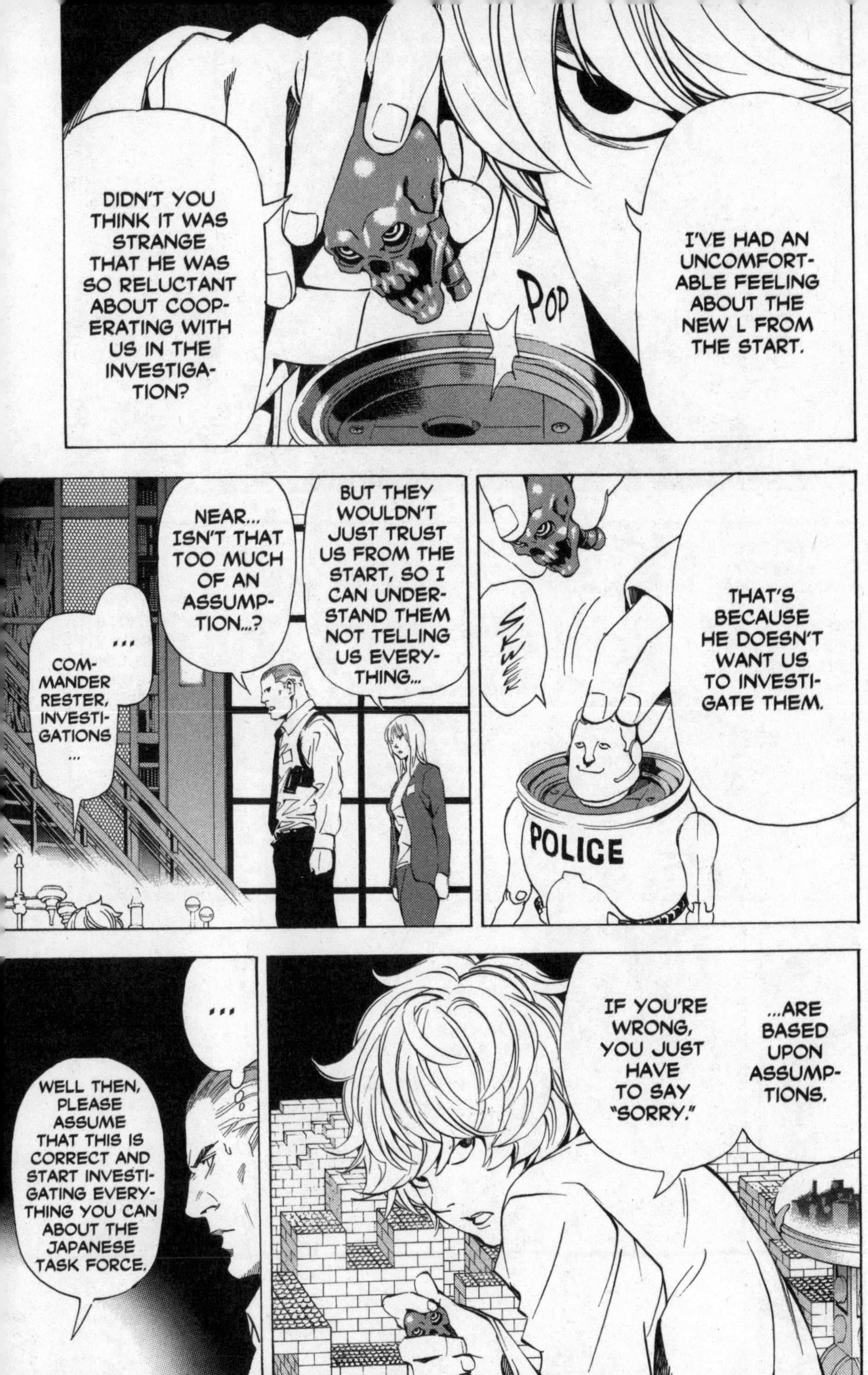
I'VE HAD AN UNCOMFORTABLE FEELING ABOUT THE NEW L FROM THE START.
POP
DIDN'T YOU THINK IT WAS STRANGE THAT HE WAS SO RELUCTANT ABOUT COOPERATING WITH US IN THE INVESTIGATION?
THAT'S BECAUSE HE DOESN'T WANT US TO INVESTIGATE THEM.
POLICE
BUT THEY WOULDN'T JUST TRUST US FROM THE START, SO I CAN UNDERSTAND THEM NOT TELLING US EVERYTHING...
NEAR... ISN'T THAT TOO MUCH OF AN ASSUMPTION...?
... COMMANDER RESTER, INVESTIGATIONS ...
...ARE BASED UPON ASSUMPTIONS.
IF YOU'RE WRONG, YOU JUST HAVE TO SAY "SORRY."
...
WELL THEN, PLEASE ASSUME THAT THIS IS CORRECT AND START INVESTIGATING EVERYTHING YOU CAN ABOUT THE JAPANESE TASK FORCE.

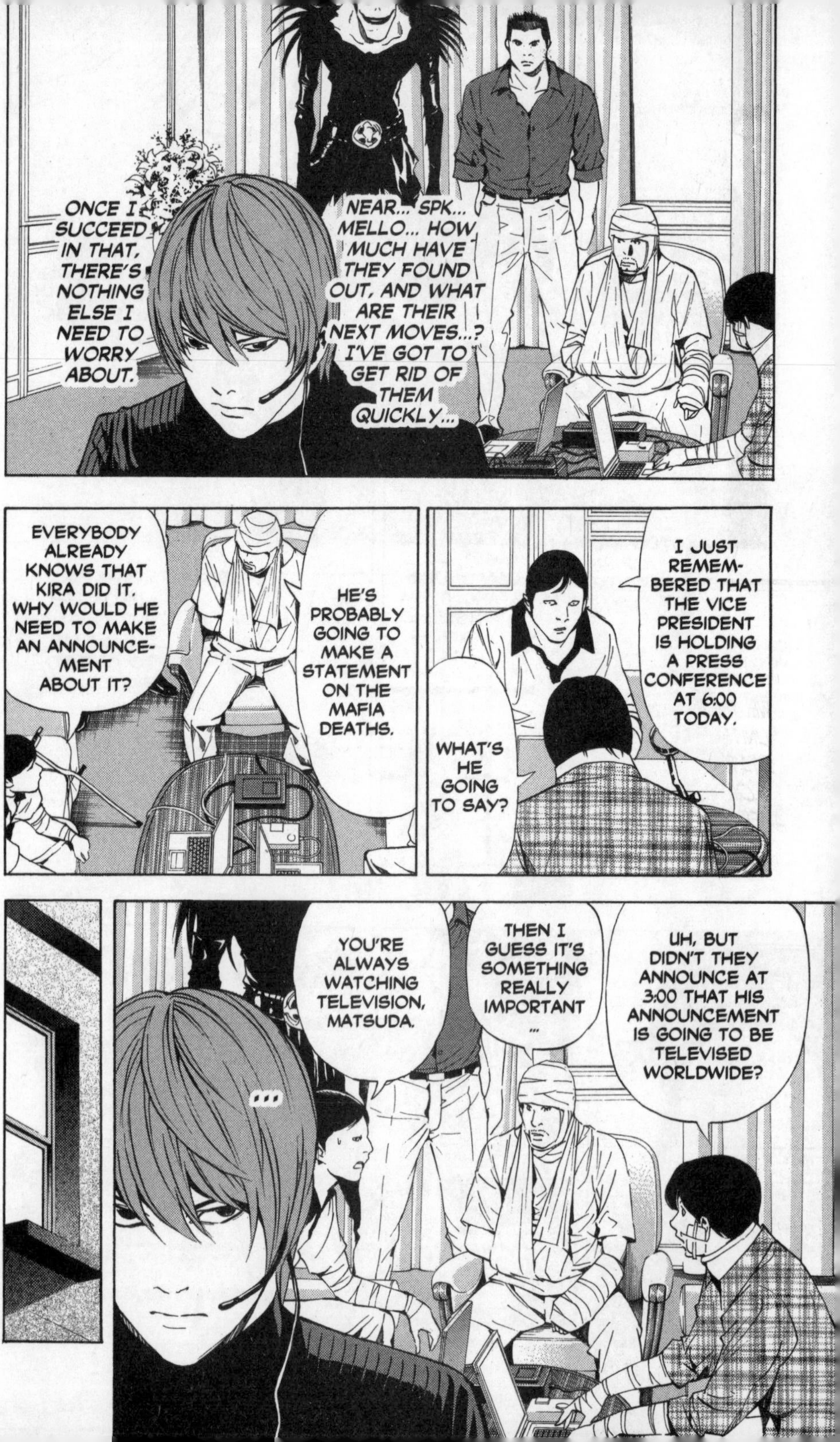
NEAR... SPK... MELLO... HOW MUCH HAVE THEY FOUND OUT, AND WHAT ARE THEIR NEXT MOVES...? I'VE GOT TO GET RID OF THEM QUICKLY...
ONCE I SUCCEED IN THAT, THERE'S NOTHING ELSE I NEED TO WORRY ABOUT.
I JUST REMEMBERED THAT THE VICE PRESIDENT IS HOLDING A PRESS CONFERENCE AT 6:00 TODAY.
WHAT'S HE GOING TO SAY?
HE'S PROBABLY GOING TO MAKE A STATEMENT ON THE MAFIA DEATHS.
EVERYBODY ALREADY KNOWS THAT KIRA DID IT. WHY WOULD HE NEED TO MAKE AN ANNOUNCEMENT ABOUT IT?
UH, BUT DIDN'T THEY ANNOUNCE AT 3:00 THAT HIS ANNOUNCEMENT IS GOING TO BE TELEVISED WORLDWIDE?
THEN I GUESS IT'S SOMETHING REALLY IMPORTANT ...
YOU'RE ALWAYS WATCHING TELEVISION, MATSUDA.
...

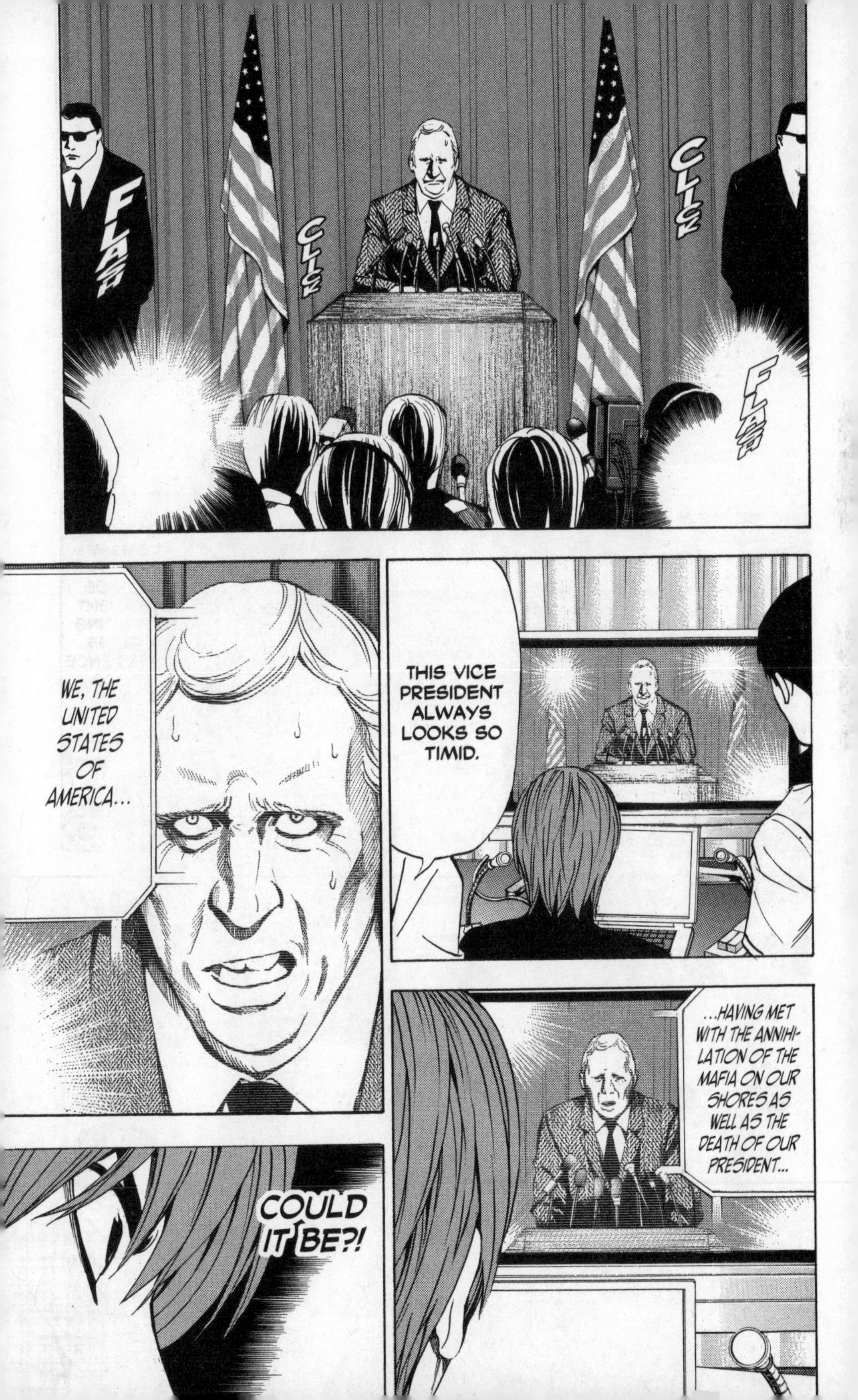
CLICK
FLASH
CLICK
FLASH
THIS VICE PRESIDENT ALWAYS LOOKS SO TIMID.
WE, THE UNITED STATES OF AMERICA...
...HAVING MET WITH THE ANNIHI-LATION OF THE MAFIA ON OUR SHORES AS WELL AS THE DEATH OF OUR PRESIDENT...
COULD IT BE?!

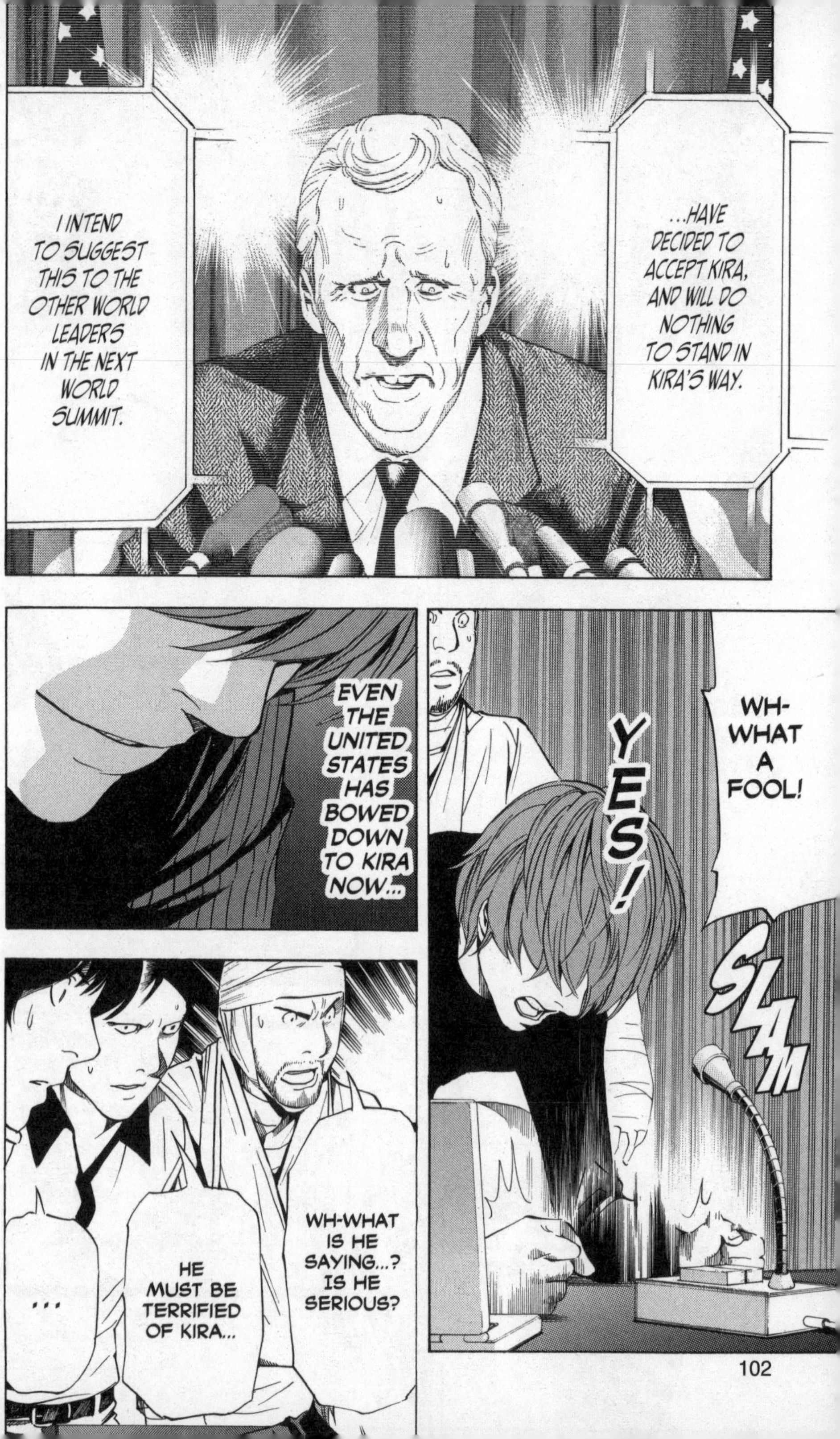

...HAVE DECIDED TO ACCEPT KIRA, AND WILL DO NOTHING TO STAND IN KIRA'S WAY.
I INTEND TO SUGGEST THIS TO THE OTHER WORLD LEADERS IN THE NEXT WORLD SUMMIT.
WH-WHAT A FOOL!
YES!
SLAM
EVEN THE UNITED STATES HAS BOWED DOWN TO KIRA NOW...
WH-WHAT IS HE SAYING...? IS HE SERIOUS?
HE MUST BE TERRIFIED OF KIRA...
...

READ THIS WAY

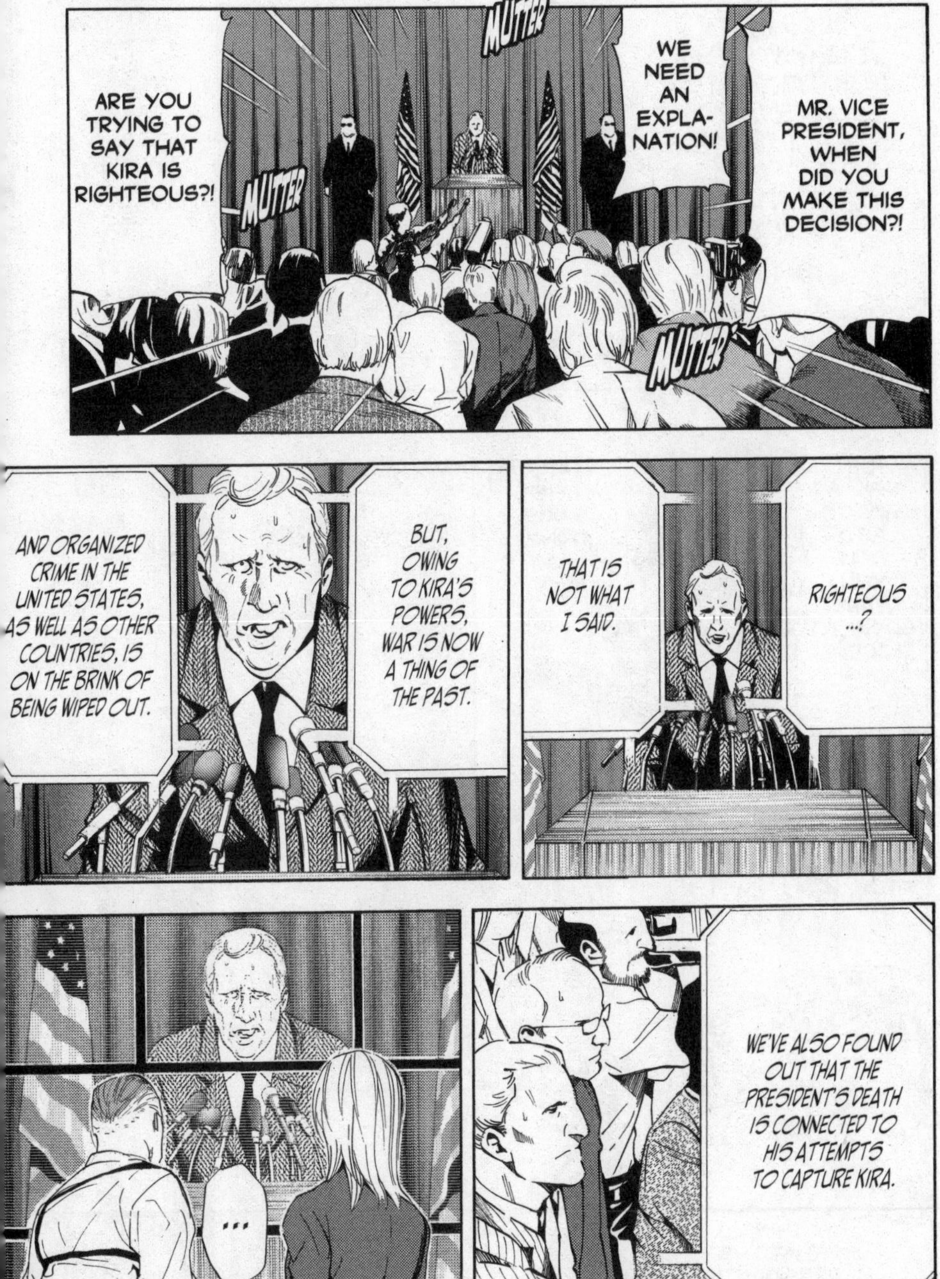

MR. VICE PRESIDENT, WHEN DID YOU MAKE THIS DECISION?!
WE NEED AN EXPLANATION!
MUTTER
ARE YOU TRYING TO SAY THAT KIRA IS RIGHTEOUS?!
MUTTER
MUTTER
RIGHTEOUS ...?
THAT IS NOT WHAT I SAID.
BUT, OWING TO KIRA'S POWERS, WAR IS NOW A THING OF THE PAST.
AND ORGANIZED CRIME IN THE UNITED STATES, AS WELL AS OTHER COUNTRIES, IS ON THE BRINK OF BEING WIPED OUT.
WE'VE ALSO FOUND OUT THAT THE PRESIDENT'S DEATH IS CONNECTED TO HIS ATTEMPTS TO CAPTURE KIRA.
...

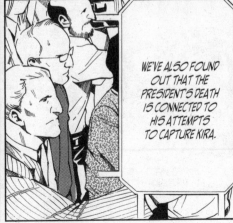

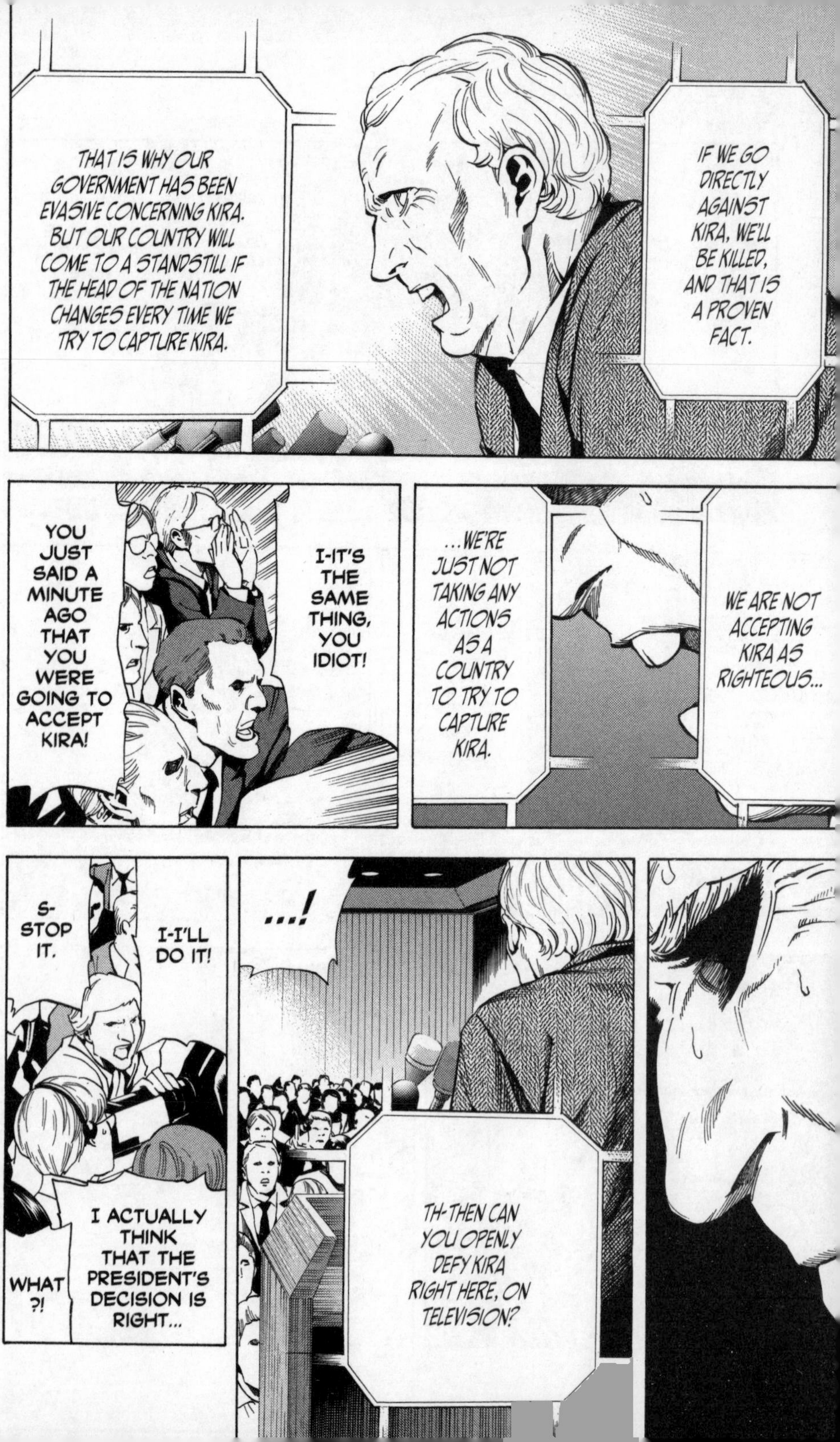
IF WE GO DIRECTLY AGAINST KIRA, WE'LL BE KILLED, AND THAT IS A PROVEN FACT.
THAT IS WHY OUR GOVERNMENT HAS BEEN EVASIVE CONCERNING KIRA. BUT OUR COUNTRY WILL COME TO A STANDSTILL IF THE HEAD OF THE NATION CHANGES EVERY TIME WE TRY TO CAPTURE KIRA.
WE ARE NOT ACCEPTING KIRA AS RIGHTEOUS...
...WE'RE JUST NOT TAKING ANY ACTIONS AS A COUNTRY TO TRY TO CAPTURE KIRA.
I-IT'S THE SAME THING, YOU IDIOT!
YOU JUST SAID A MINUTE AGO THAT YOU WERE GOING TO ACCEPT KIRA!
...!
TH-THEN CAN YOU OPENLY DEFY KIRA RIGHT HERE, ON TELEVISION?
I-I'LL DO IT!
S-STOP IT.
I ACTUALLY THINK THAT THE PRESIDENT'S DECISION IS RIGHT...
WHAT?!

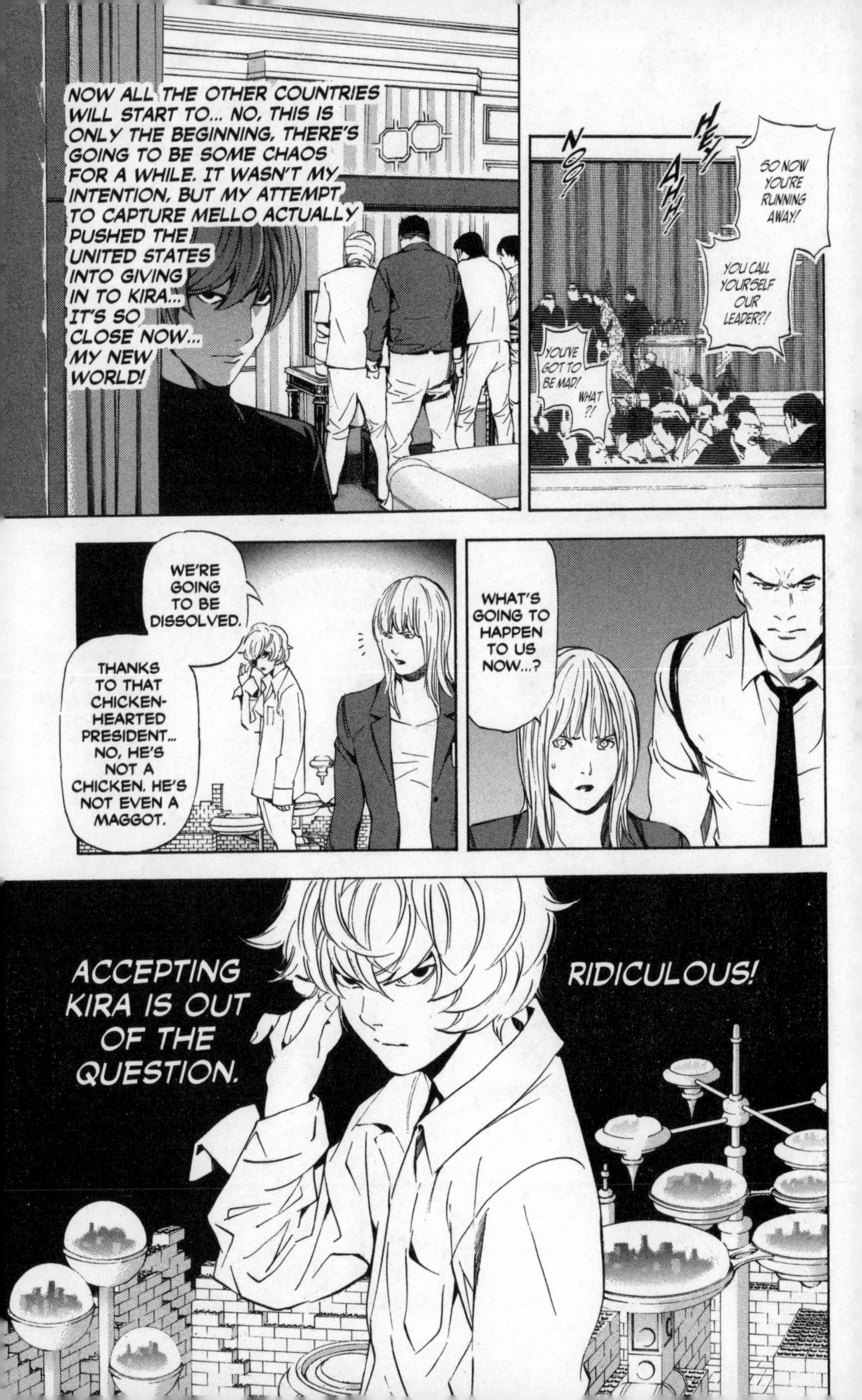
HEY!
AHH!
NOO!
SO NOW YOU'RE RUNNING AWAY!
YOU CALL YOURSELF OUR LEADER?!
YOU'VE GOT TO BE MAD!
WHAT?!
NOW ALL THE OTHER COUNTRIES WILL START TO... NO, THIS IS ONLY THE BEGINNING, THERE'S GOING TO BE SOME CHAOS FOR A WHILE. IT WASN'T MY INTENTION, BUT MY ATTEMPT TO CAPTURE MELLO ACTUALLY PUSHED THE UNITED STATES INTO GIVING IN TO KIRA... IT'S SO CLOSE NOW... MY NEW WORLD!
WHAT'S GOING TO HAPPEN TO US NOW...?
WE'RE GOING TO BE DISSOLVED.
THANKS TO THAT CHICKEN-HEARTED PRESIDENT... NO, HE'S NOT A CHICKEN. HE'S NOT EVEN A MAGGOT.
RIDICULOUS!
ACCEPTING KIRA IS OUT OF THE QUESTION.

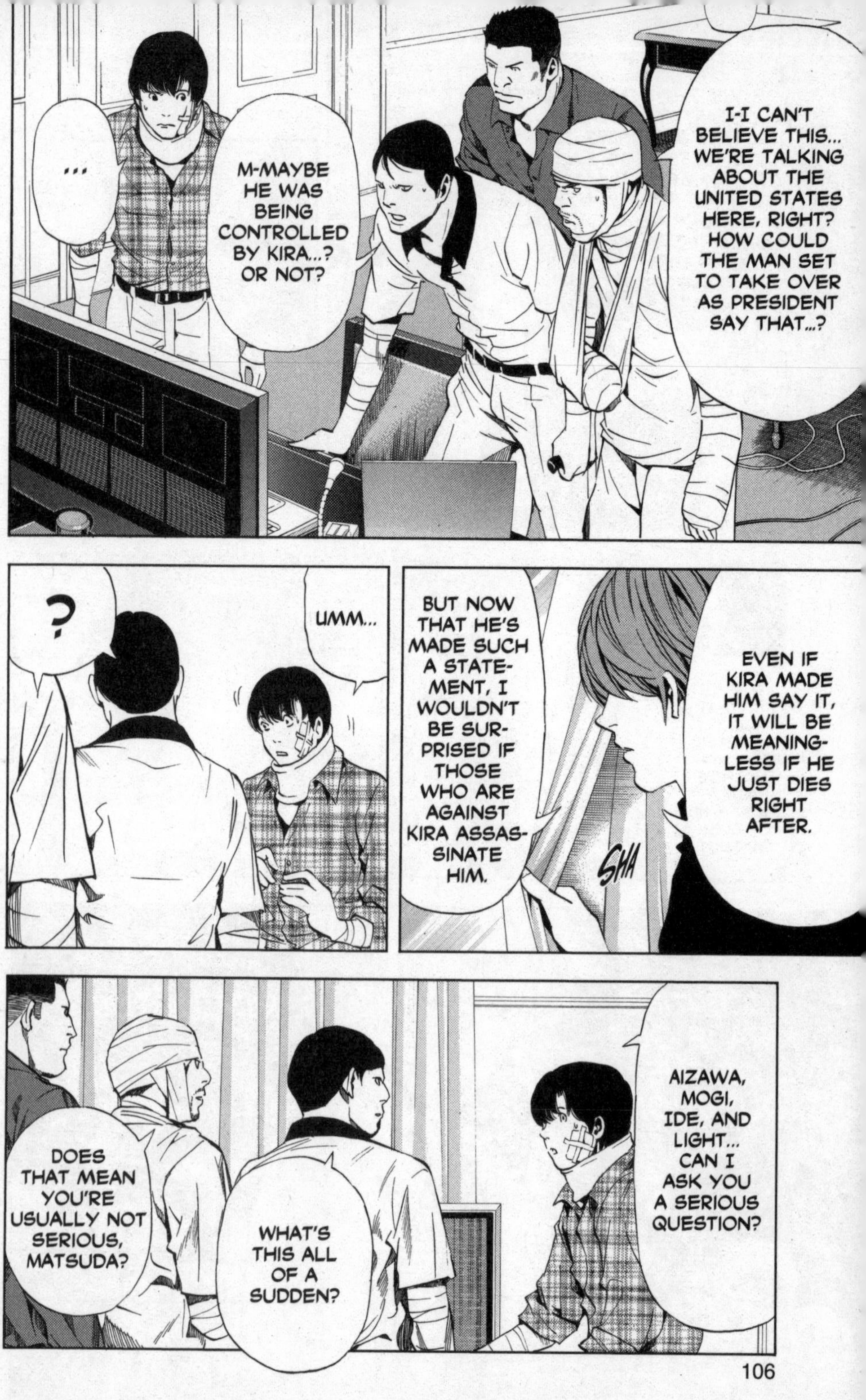
I-I CAN'T BELIEVE THIS... WE'RE TALKING ABOUT THE UNITED STATES HERE, RIGHT? HOW COULD THE MAN SET TO TAKE OVER AS PRESIDENT SAY THAT...?
M-MAYBE HE WAS BEING CONTROLLED BY KIRA...? OR NOT?
...
EVEN IF KIRA MADE HIM SAY IT, IT WILL BE MEANING-LESS IF HE JUST DIES RIGHT AFTER.
SHA
BUT NOW THAT HE'S MADE SUCH A STATE-MENT, I WOULDN'T BE SUR-PRISED IF THOSE WHO ARE AGAINST KIRA ASSAS-SINATE HIM.
UMM...
?
AIZAWA, MOGI, IDE, AND LIGHT... CAN I ASK YOU A SERIOUS QUESTION?
WHAT'S THIS ALL OF A SUDDEN?
DOES THAT MEAN YOU'RE USUALLY NOT SERIOUS, MATSUDA?

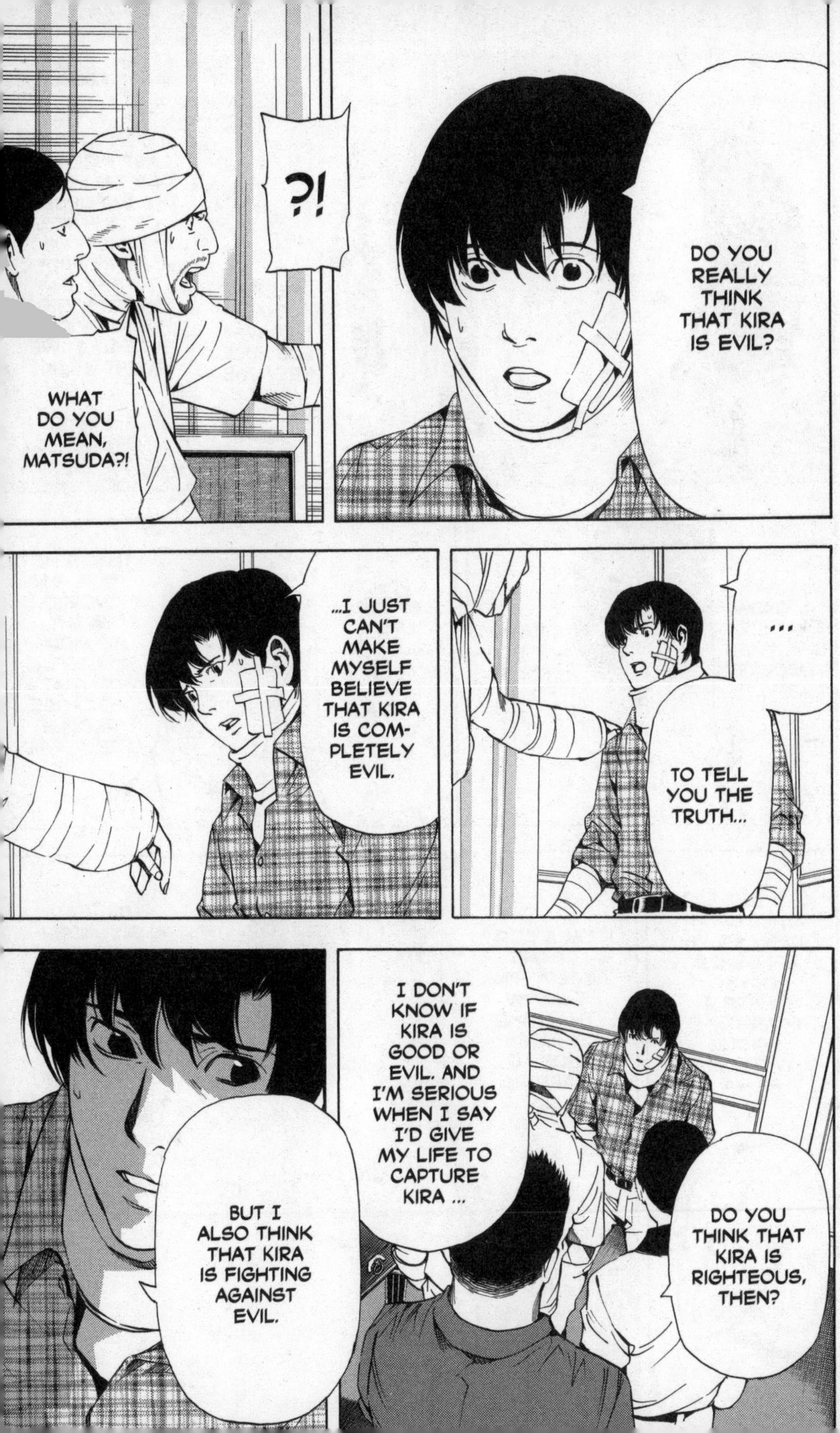

DO YOU REALLY THINK THAT KIRA IS EVIL?
?!
WHAT DO YOU MEAN, MATSUDA?!
...
TO TELL YOU THE TRUTH...
...I JUST CAN'T MAKE MYSELF BELIEVE THAT KIRA IS COM-PLETELY EVIL.
DO YOU THINK THAT KIRA IS RIGHTEOUS, THEN?
I DON'T KNOW IF KIRA IS GOOD OR EVIL. AND I'M SERIOUS WHEN I SAY I'D GIVE MY LIFE TO CAPTURE KIRA ...
BUT I ALSO THINK THAT KIRA IS FIGHTING AGAINST EVIL.

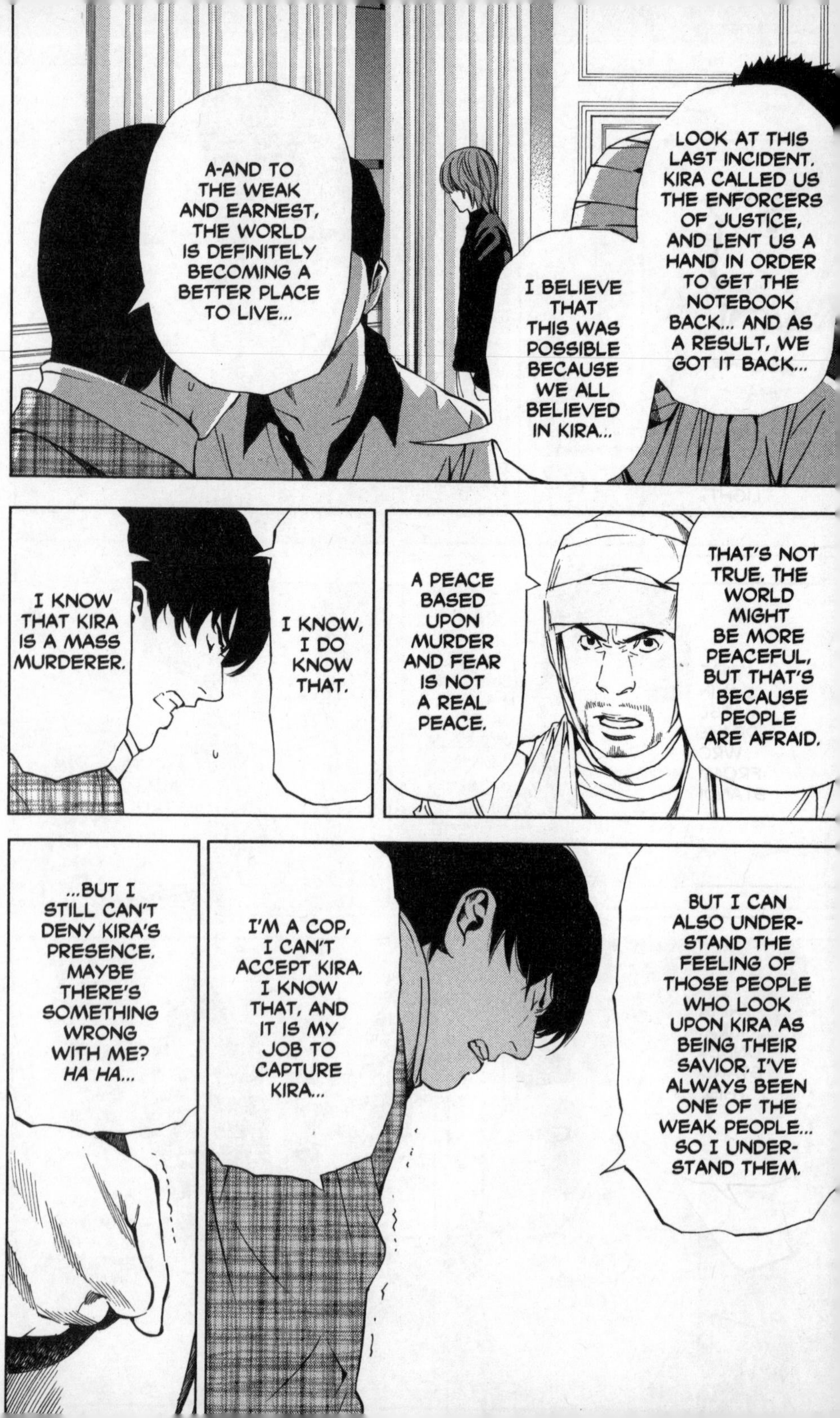
LOOK AT THIS LAST INCIDENT. KIRA CALLED US THE ENFORCERS OF JUSTICE, AND LENT US A HAND IN ORDER TO GET THE NOTEBOOK BACK... AND AS A RESULT, WE GOT IT BACK...
I BELIEVE THAT THIS WAS POSSIBLE BECAUSE WE ALL BELIEVED IN KIRA...
A-AND TO THE WEAK AND EARNEST, THE WORLD IS DEFINITELY BECOMING A BETTER PLACE TO LIVE...
THAT'S NOT TRUE. THE WORLD MIGHT BE MORE PEACEFUL, BUT THAT'S BECAUSE PEOPLE ARE AFRAID.
A PEACE BASED UPON MURDER AND FEAR IS NOT A REAL PEACE.
I KNOW, I DO KNOW THAT.
I KNOW THAT KIRA IS A MASS MURDERER.
BUT I CAN ALSO UNDERSTAND THE FEELING OF THOSE PEOPLE WHO LOOK UPON KIRA AS BEING THEIR SAVIOR. I'VE ALWAYS BEEN ONE OF THE WEAK PEOPLE... SO I UNDERSTAND THEM.
I'M A COP, I CAN'T ACCEPT KIRA. I KNOW THAT, AND IT IS MY JOB TO CAPTURE KIRA...
...BUT I STILL CAN'T DENY KIRA'S PRESENCE. MAYBE THERE'S SOMETHING WRONG WITH ME? *HA HA...*

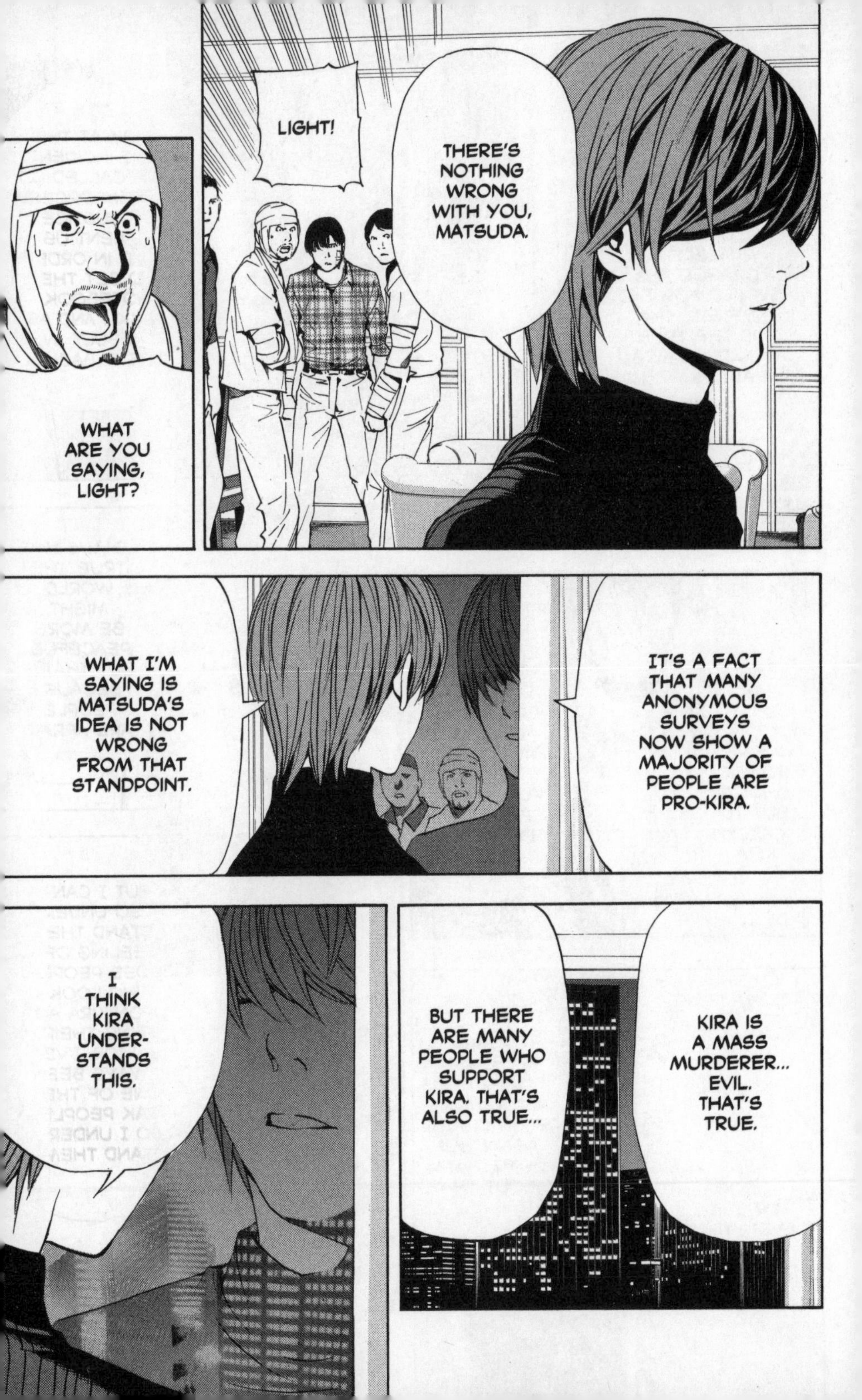
THERE'S NOTHING WRONG WITH YOU, MATSUDA.
LIGHT!
WHAT ARE YOU SAYING, LIGHT?
IT'S A FACT THAT MANY ANONYMOUS SURVEYS NOW SHOW A MAJORITY OF PEOPLE ARE PRO-KIRA.
WHAT I'M SAYING IS MATSUDA'S IDEA IS NOT WRONG FROM THAT STANDPOINT.
KIRA IS A MASS MURDERER... EVIL. THAT'S TRUE.
BUT THERE ARE MANY PEOPLE WHO SUPPORT KIRA. THAT'S ALSO TRUE...
I THINK KIRA UNDER-STANDS THIS.

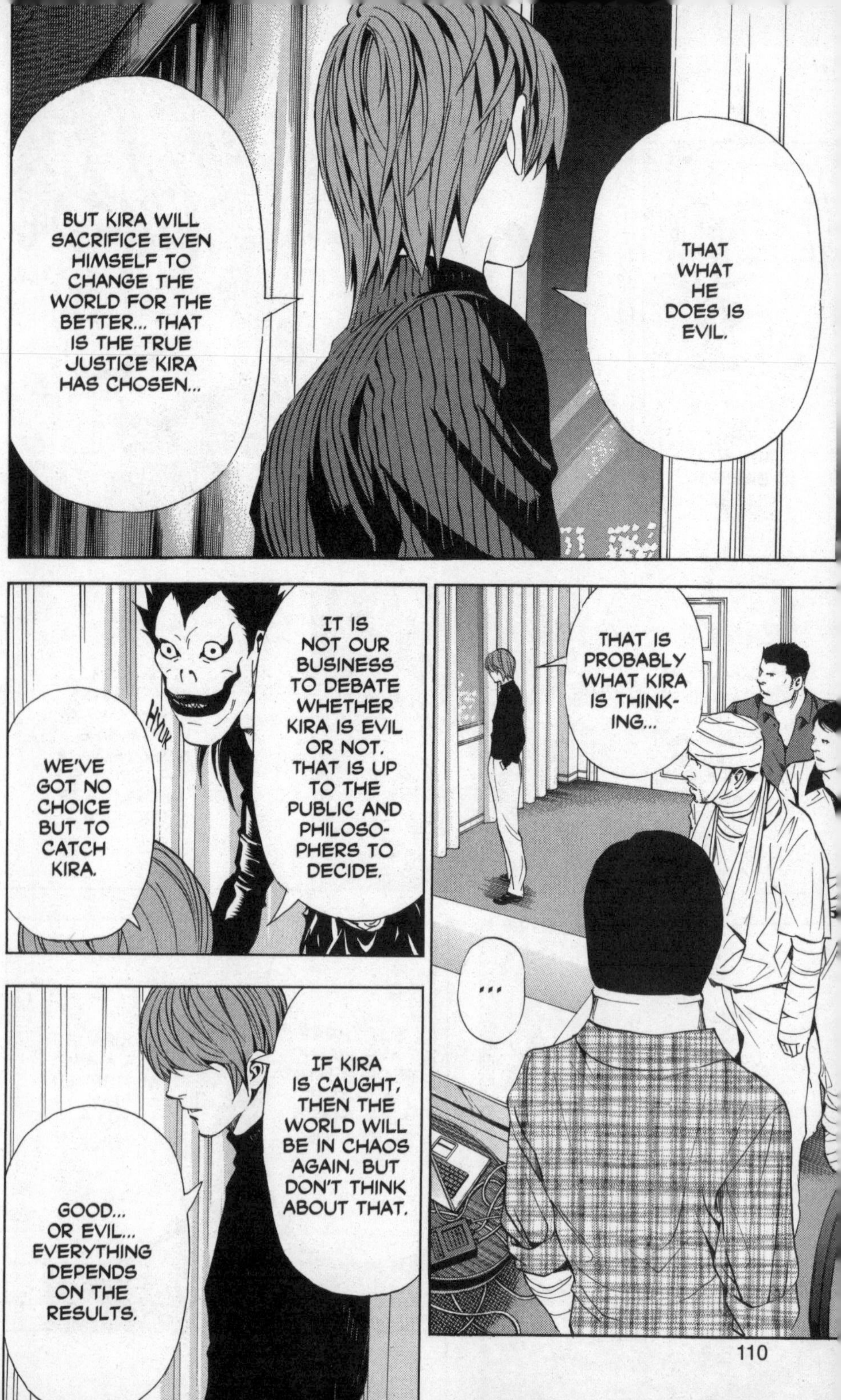
THAT WHAT HE DOES IS EVIL.
BUT KIRA WILL SACRIFICE EVEN HIMSELF TO CHANGE THE WORLD FOR THE BETTER... THAT IS THE TRUE JUSTICE KIRA HAS CHOSEN...
THAT IS PROBABLY WHAT KIRA IS THINK-ING...
...
IT IS NOT OUR BUSINESS TO DEBATE WHETHER KIRA IS EVIL OR NOT. THAT IS UP TO THE PUBLIC AND PHILOSO-PHERS TO DECIDE.
HYUK
WE'VE GOT NO CHOICE BUT TO CATCH KIRA.
IF KIRA IS CAUGHT, THEN THE WORLD WILL BE IN CHAOS AGAIN, BUT DON'T THINK ABOUT THAT.
GOOD... OR EVIL... EVERYTHING DEPENDS ON THE RESULTS.

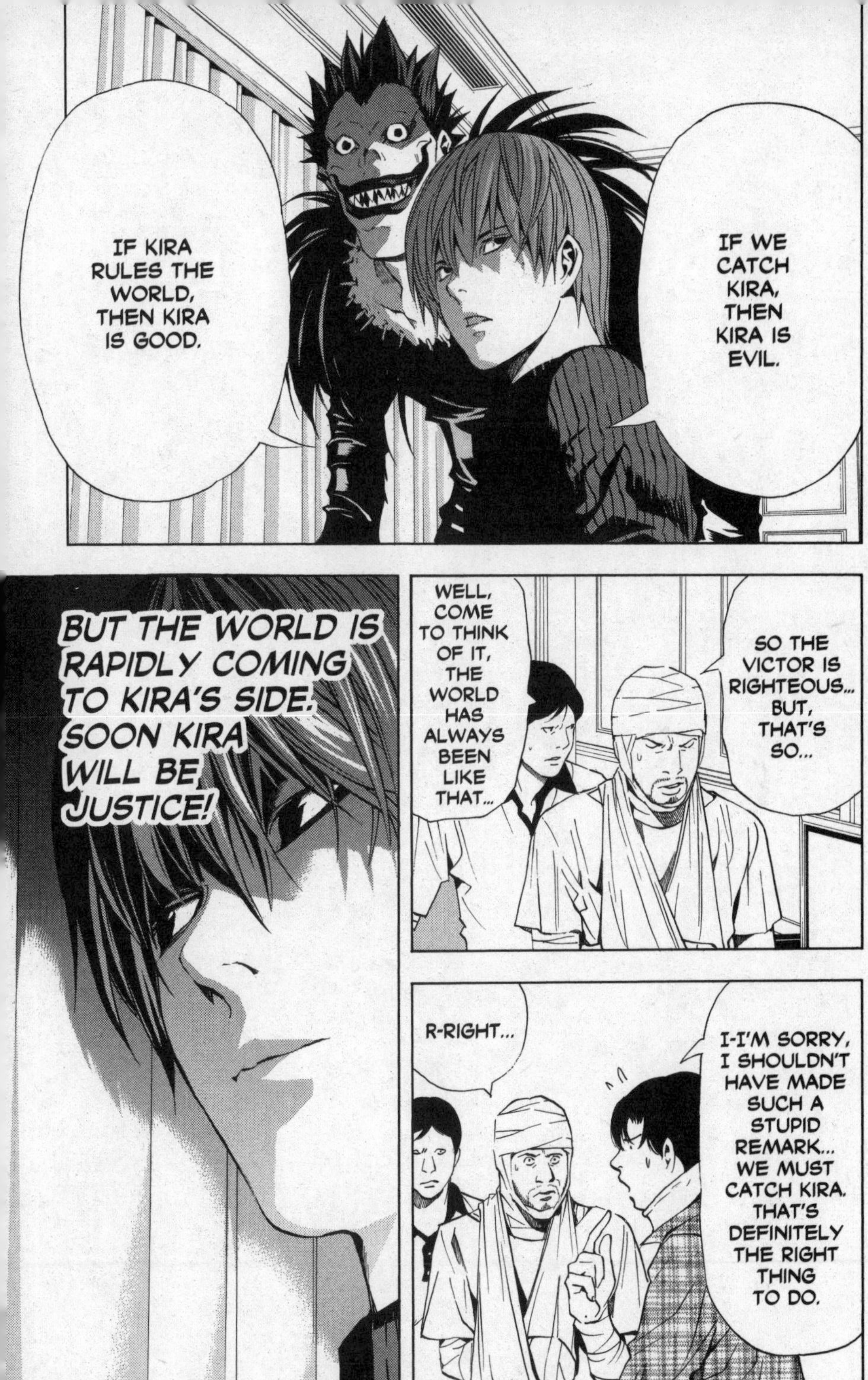
IF WE CATCH KIRA, THEN KIRA IS EVIL.
IF KIRA RULES THE WORLD, THEN KIRA IS GOOD.
SO THE VICTOR IS RIGHTEOUS... BUT, THAT'S SO...
WELL, COME TO THINK OF IT, THE WORLD HAS ALWAYS BEEN LIKE THAT...
I-I'M SORRY, I SHOULDN'T HAVE MADE SUCH A STUPID REMARK... WE MUST CATCH KIRA. THAT'S DEFINITELY THE RIGHT THING TO DO.
R-RIGHT...
BUT THE WORLD IS RAPIDLY COMING TO KIRA'S SIDE. SOON KIRA WILL BE JUSTICE!

DEATH NOTE
HOW to USE it
L

○ One god of death is allowed to pass on DEATH NOTES to only 3 humans at a time.

<ruby>一<rt>いっ</rt>匹<rt>ぴき</rt></ruby>の<ruby>死神<rt>しにがみ</rt></ruby>が、<ruby>同時<rt>どうじ</rt></ruby>に<ruby>異<rt>こと</rt></ruby>なる<ruby>人間<rt>にんげん</rt></ruby>にデスノートを<ruby>渡<rt>わた</rt></ruby>していいのは<ruby>三人<rt>さんにん</rt></ruby>まで。

○ It is possible for a single god of death to hand out up to 6 DEATH NOTES, for example, by handing 3 humans 2 DEATH NOTES each.

デスノートを<ruby>渡<rt>わた</rt></ruby>す<ruby>人間<rt>にんげん</rt></ruby>が<ruby>三人<rt>さんにん</rt></ruby>までであれば、
たとえば2<ruby>冊<rt>さつ</rt></ruby>ずつ<ruby>三人<rt>さんにん</rt></ruby>に<ruby>渡<rt>わた</rt></ruby>すという<ruby>様<rt>よう</rt></ruby>に、<ruby>一<rt>いっ</rt>匹<rt>ぴき</rt></ruby>の<ruby>死神<rt>しにがみ</rt></ruby>が6<ruby>冊<rt>さつ</rt></ruby>まで
ノートを<ruby>人間<rt>にんげん</rt></ruby>に<ruby>持<rt>も</rt></ruby>たせることは<ruby>可能<rt>かのう</rt></ruby>である。

○ In other words, one human could own all 6 DEATH NOTE.

よって、<ruby>一人<rt>ひとり</rt></ruby>の<ruby>人間<rt>にんげん</rt></ruby>が6<ruby>冊<rt>さつ</rt></ruby>のノートを<ruby>使用<rt>しよう</rt></ruby>する<ruby>事<rt>こと</rt></ruby>も<ruby>可能<rt>かのう</rt></ruby>である。

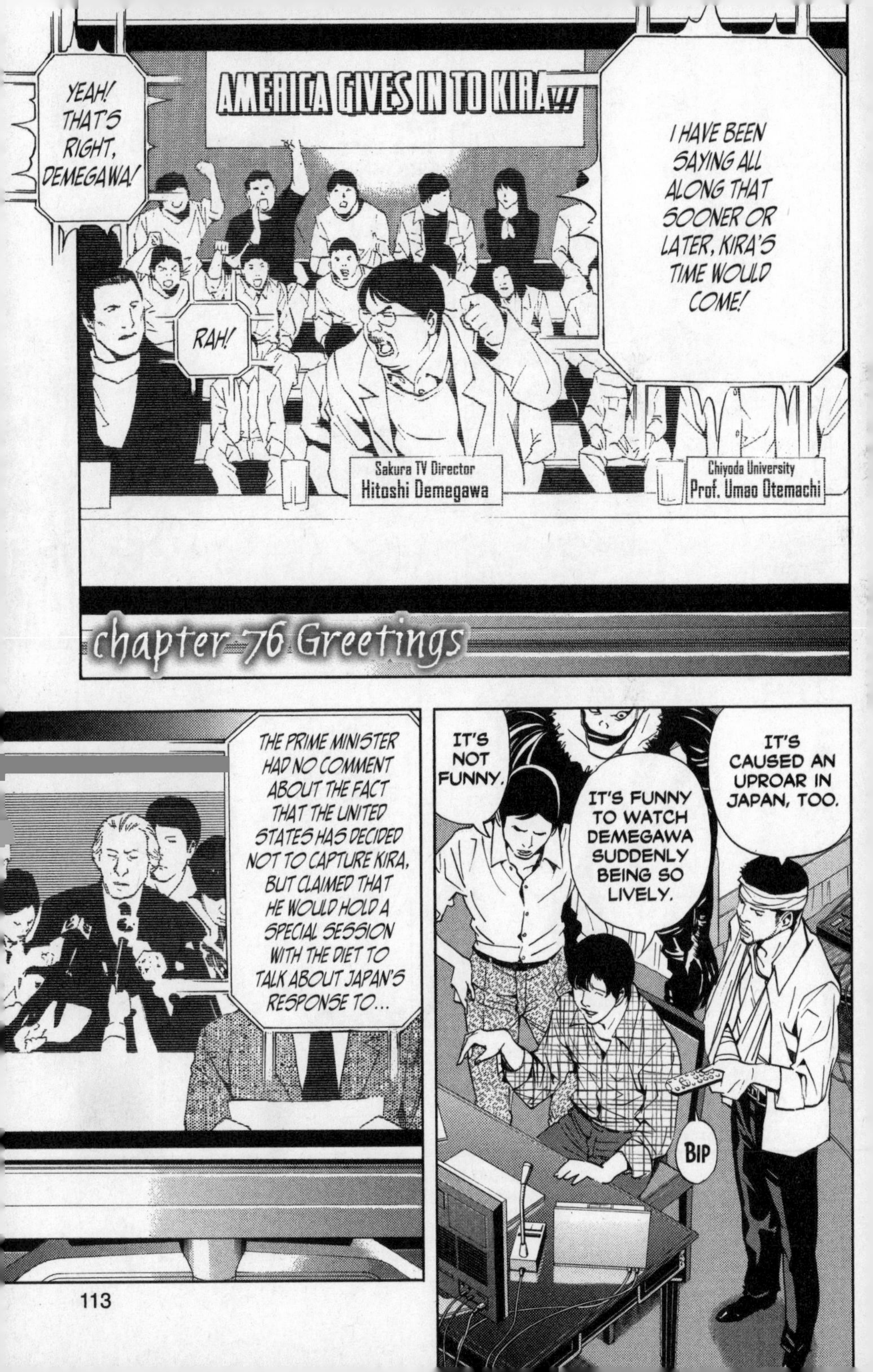
AMERICA GIVES IN TO KIRA!!
I HAVE BEEN SAYING ALL ALONG THAT SOONER OR LATER, KIRA'S TIME WOULD COME!
YEAH! THAT'S RIGHT, DEMEGAWA!
RAH!
Chiyoda University Prof. Umao Otemachi
Sakura TV Director Hitoshi Demegawa
chapter 76 Greetings
IT'S CAUSED AN UPROAR IN JAPAN, TOO.
IT'S FUNNY TO WATCH DEMEGAWA SUDDENLY BEING SO LIVELY.
IT'S NOT FUNNY.
BIP
THE PRIME MINISTER HAD NO COMMENT ABOUT THE FACT THAT THE UNITED STATES HAS DECIDED NOT TO CAPTURE KIRA, BUT CLAIMED THAT HE WOULD HOLD A SPECIAL SESSION WITH THE DIET TO TALK ABOUT JAPAN'S RESPONSE TO...

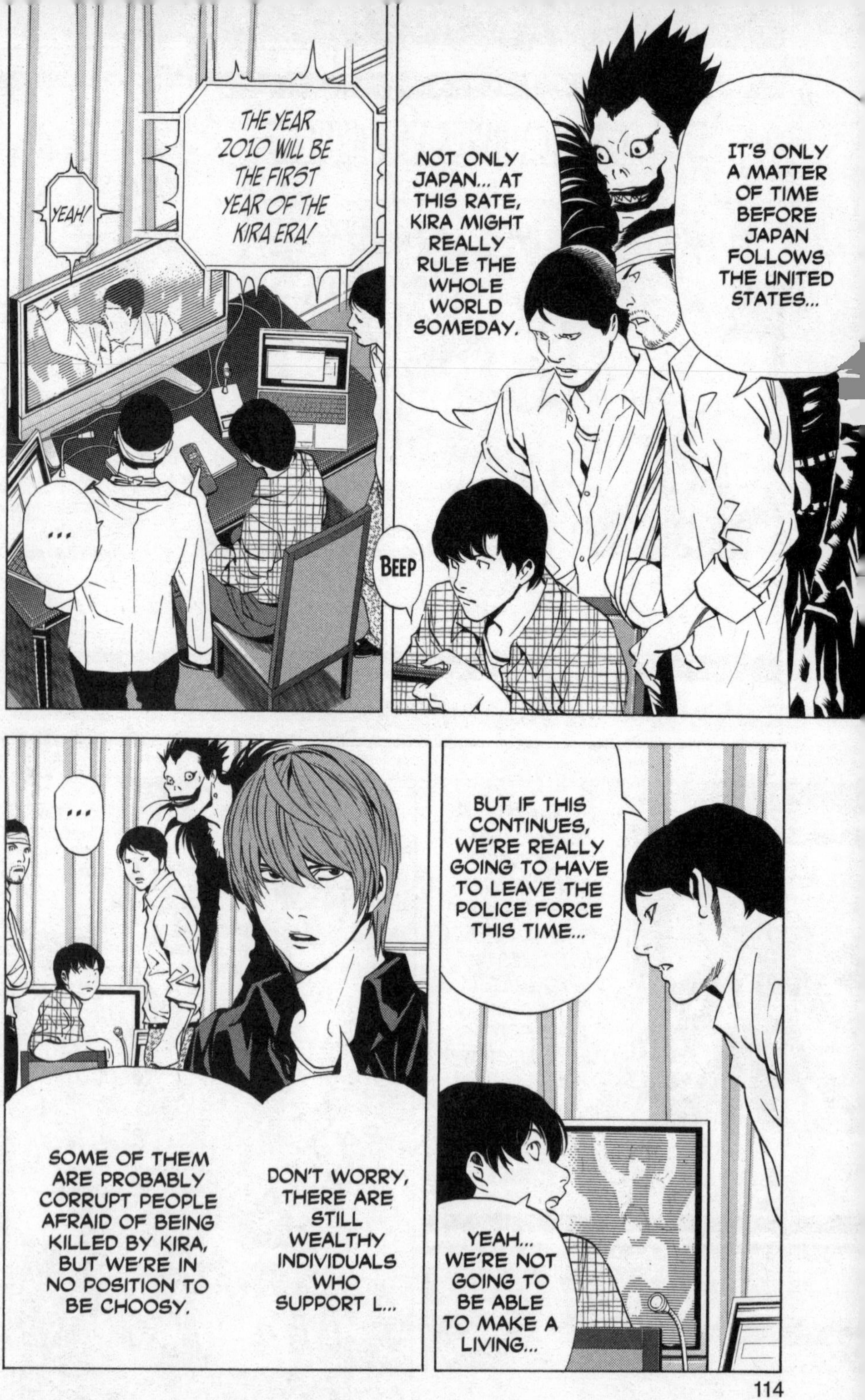

IT'S ONLY A MATTER OF TIME BEFORE JAPAN FOLLOWS THE UNITED STATES...
NOT ONLY JAPAN... AT THIS RATE, KIRA MIGHT REALLY RULE THE WHOLE WORLD SOMEDAY.
BEEP
THE YEAR 2010 WILL BE THE FIRST YEAR OF THE KIRA ERA!
YEAH!
...
BUT IF THIS CONTINUES, WE'RE REALLY GOING TO HAVE TO LEAVE THE POLICE FORCE THIS TIME...
YEAH... WE'RE NOT GOING TO BE ABLE TO MAKE A LIVING...
...
DON'T WORRY, THERE ARE STILL WEALTHY INDIVIDUALS WHO SUPPORT L...
SOME OF THEM ARE PROBABLY CORRUPT PEOPLE AFRAID OF BEING KILLED BY KIRA, BUT WE'RE IN NO POSITION TO BE CHOOSY.

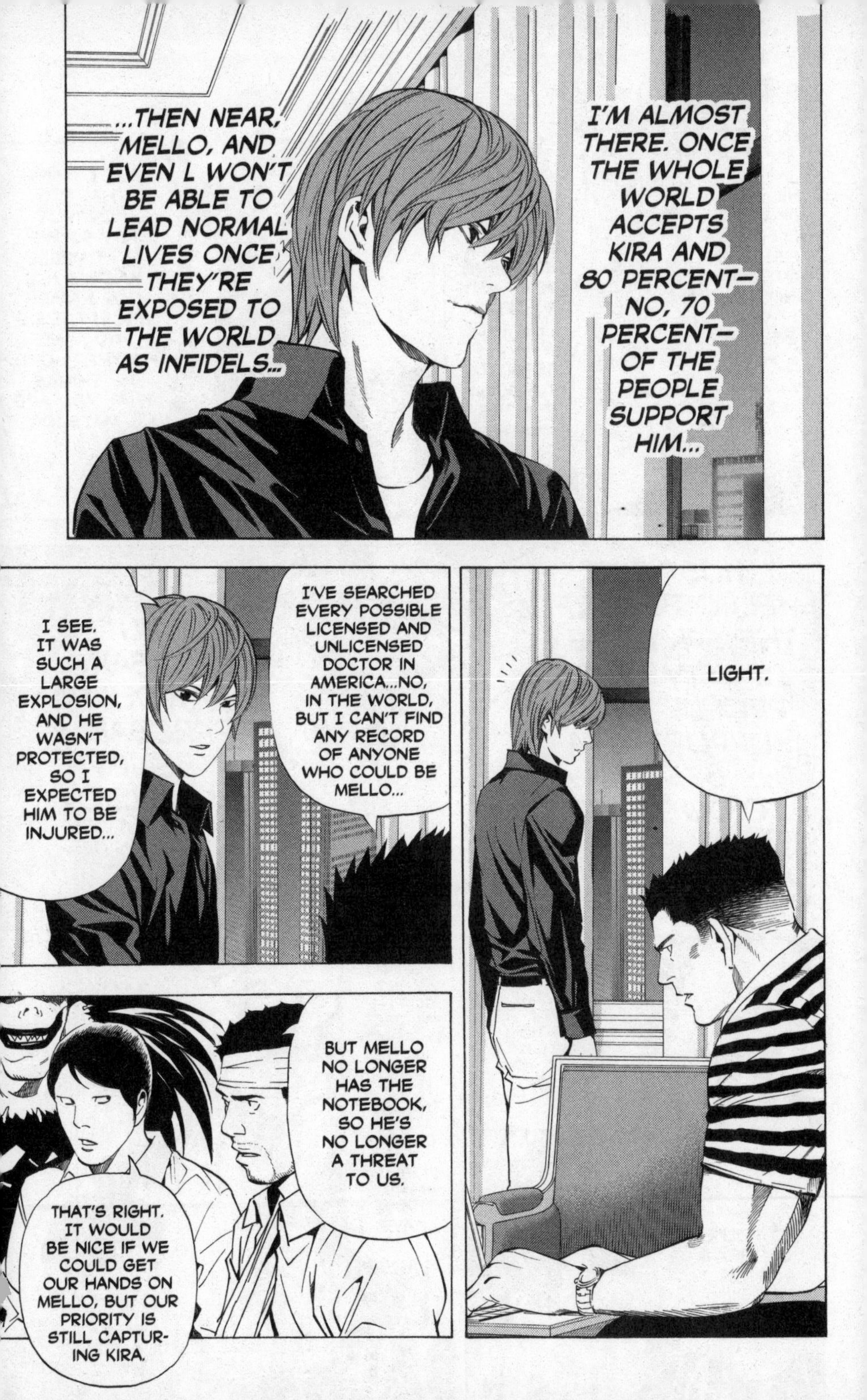
I'M ALMOST THERE. ONCE THE WHOLE WORLD ACCEPTS KIRA AND 80 PERCENT– NO, 70 PERCENT– OF THE PEOPLE SUPPORT HIM...
...THEN NEAR, MELLO, AND EVEN L WON'T BE ABLE TO LEAD NORMAL LIVES ONCE THEY'RE EXPOSED TO THE WORLD AS INFIDELS...
LIGHT.
I'VE SEARCHED EVERY POSSIBLE LICENSED AND UNLICENSED DOCTOR IN AMERICA...NO, IN THE WORLD, BUT I CAN'T FIND ANY RECORD OF ANYONE WHO COULD BE MELLO...
I SEE. IT WAS SUCH A LARGE EXPLOSION, AND HE WASN'T PROTECTED, SO I EXPECTED HIM TO BE INJURED...
BUT MELLO NO LONGER HAS THE NOTEBOOK, SO HE'S NO LONGER A THREAT TO US.
THAT'S RIGHT. IT WOULD BE NICE IF WE COULD GET OUR HANDS ON MELLO, BUT OUR PRIORITY IS STILL CAPTURING KIRA.

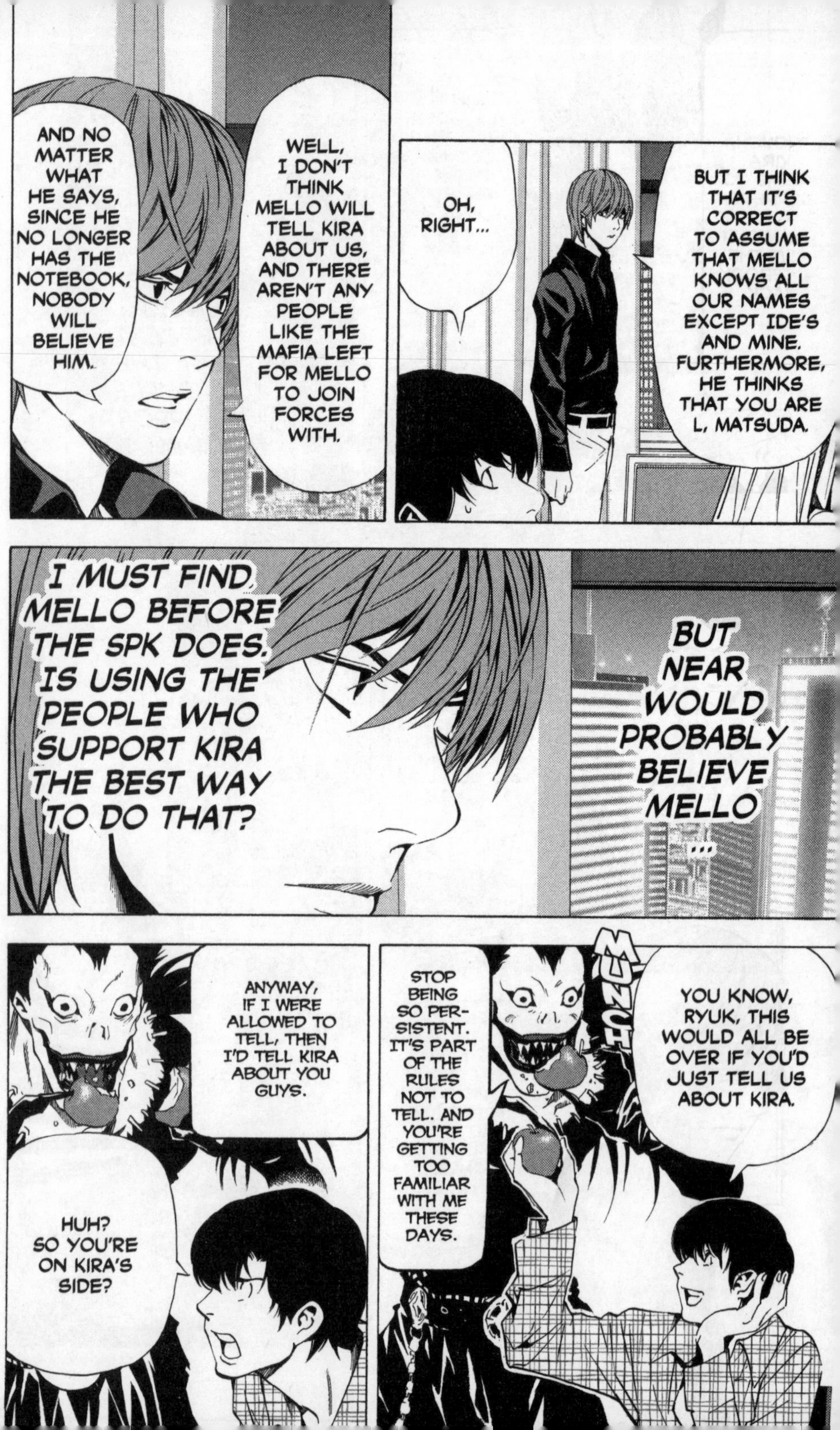
BUT I THINK THAT IT'S CORRECT TO ASSUME THAT MELLO KNOWS ALL OUR NAMES EXCEPT IDE'S AND MINE. FURTHERMORE, HE THINKS THAT YOU ARE L, MATSUDA.
OH, RIGHT...
WELL, I DON'T THINK MELLO WILL TELL KIRA ABOUT US, AND THERE AREN'T ANY PEOPLE LIKE THE MAFIA LEFT FOR MELLO TO JOIN FORCES WITH.
AND NO MATTER WHAT HE SAYS, SINCE HE NO LONGER HAS THE NOTEBOOK, NOBODY WILL BELIEVE HIM.
BUT NEAR WOULD PROBABLY BELIEVE MELLO ...
I MUST FIND MELLO BEFORE THE SPK DOES. IS USING THE PEOPLE WHO SUPPORT KIRA THE BEST WAY TO DO THAT?
MUNCH
YOU KNOW, RYUK, THIS WOULD ALL BE OVER IF YOU'D JUST TELL US ABOUT KIRA.
STOP BEING SO PER-SISTENT. IT'S PART OF THE RULES NOT TO TELL. AND YOU'RE GETTING TOO FAMILIAR WITH ME THESE DAYS.
ANYWAY, IF I WERE ALLOWED TO TELL, THEN I'D TELL KIRA ABOUT YOU GUYS.
HUH? SO YOU'RE ON KIRA'S SIDE?

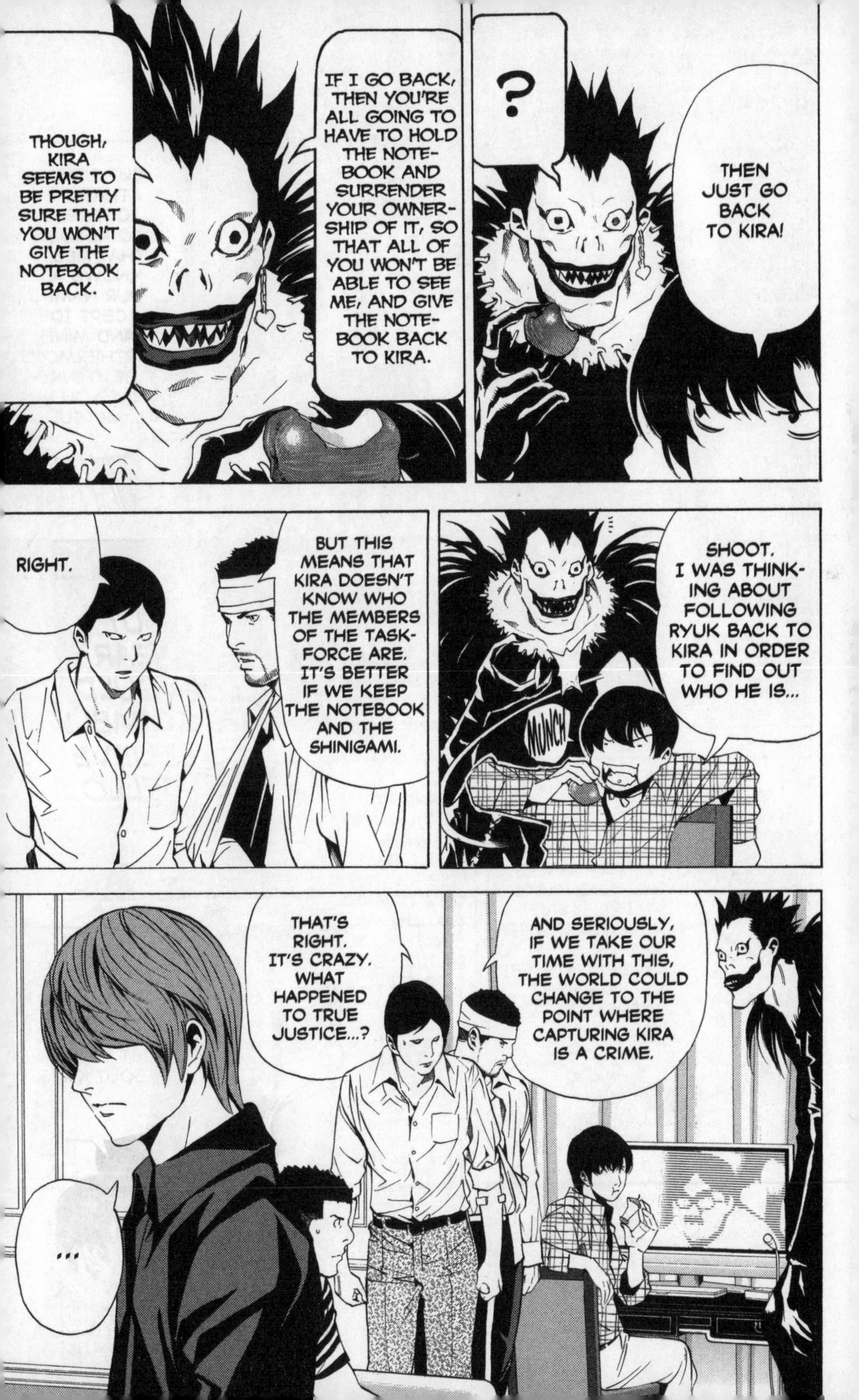
THEN JUST GO BACK TO KIRA!
?
IF I GO BACK, THEN YOU'RE ALL GOING TO HAVE TO HOLD THE NOTE-BOOK AND SURRENDER YOUR OWNER-SHIP OF IT, SO THAT ALL OF YOU WON'T BE ABLE TO SEE ME, AND GIVE THE NOTE-BOOK BACK TO KIRA.
THOUGH, KIRA SEEMS TO BE PRETTY SURE THAT YOU WON'T GIVE THE NOTEBOOK BACK.
SHOOT. I WAS THINK-ING ABOUT FOLLOWING RYUK BACK TO KIRA IN ORDER TO FIND OUT WHO HE IS...
MUNCH
BUT THIS MEANS THAT KIRA DOESN'T KNOW WHO THE MEMBERS OF THE TASK-FORCE ARE. IT'S BETTER IF WE KEEP THE NOTEBOOK AND THE SHINIGAMI.
RIGHT.
AND SERIOUSLY, IF WE TAKE OUR TIME WITH THIS, THE WORLD COULD CHANGE TO THE POINT WHERE CAPTURING KIRA IS A CRIME.
THAT'S RIGHT. IT'S CRAZY. WHAT HAPPENED TO TRUE JUSTICE...?
...

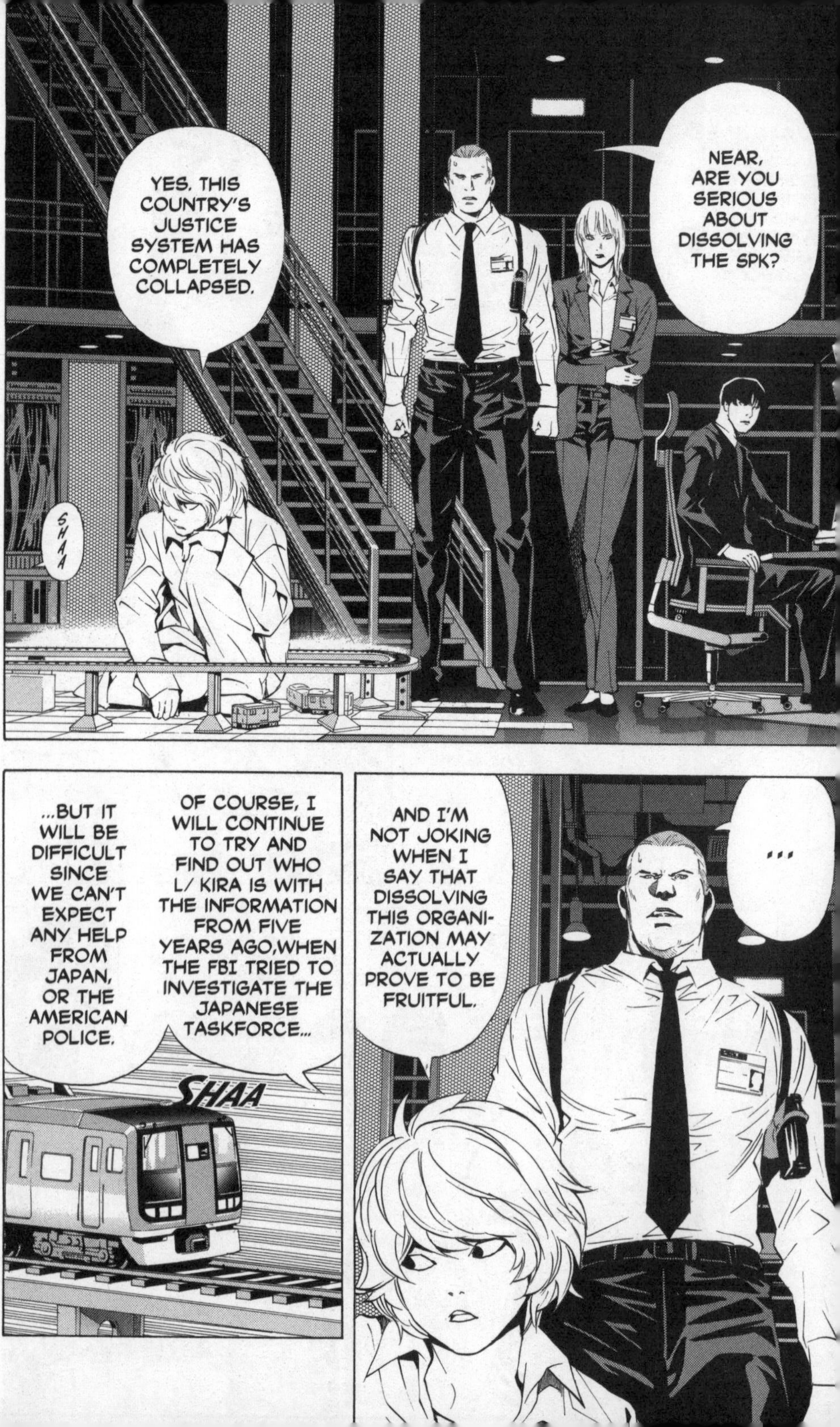
NEAR, ARE YOU SERIOUS ABOUT DISSOLVING THE SPK?
YES. THIS COUNTRY'S JUSTICE SYSTEM HAS COMPLETELY COLLAPSED.
SHAA
...
AND I'M NOT JOKING WHEN I SAY THAT DISSOLVING THIS ORGANIZATION MAY ACTUALLY PROVE TO BE FRUITFUL.
OF COURSE, I WILL CONTINUE TO TRY AND FIND OUT WHO L/ KIRA IS WITH THE INFORMATION FROM FIVE YEARS AGO, WHEN THE FBI TRIED TO INVESTIGATE THE JAPANESE TASKFORCE...
...BUT IT WILL BE DIFFICULT SINCE WE CAN'T EXPECT ANY HELP FROM JAPAN, OR THE AMERICAN POLICE.
SHAA

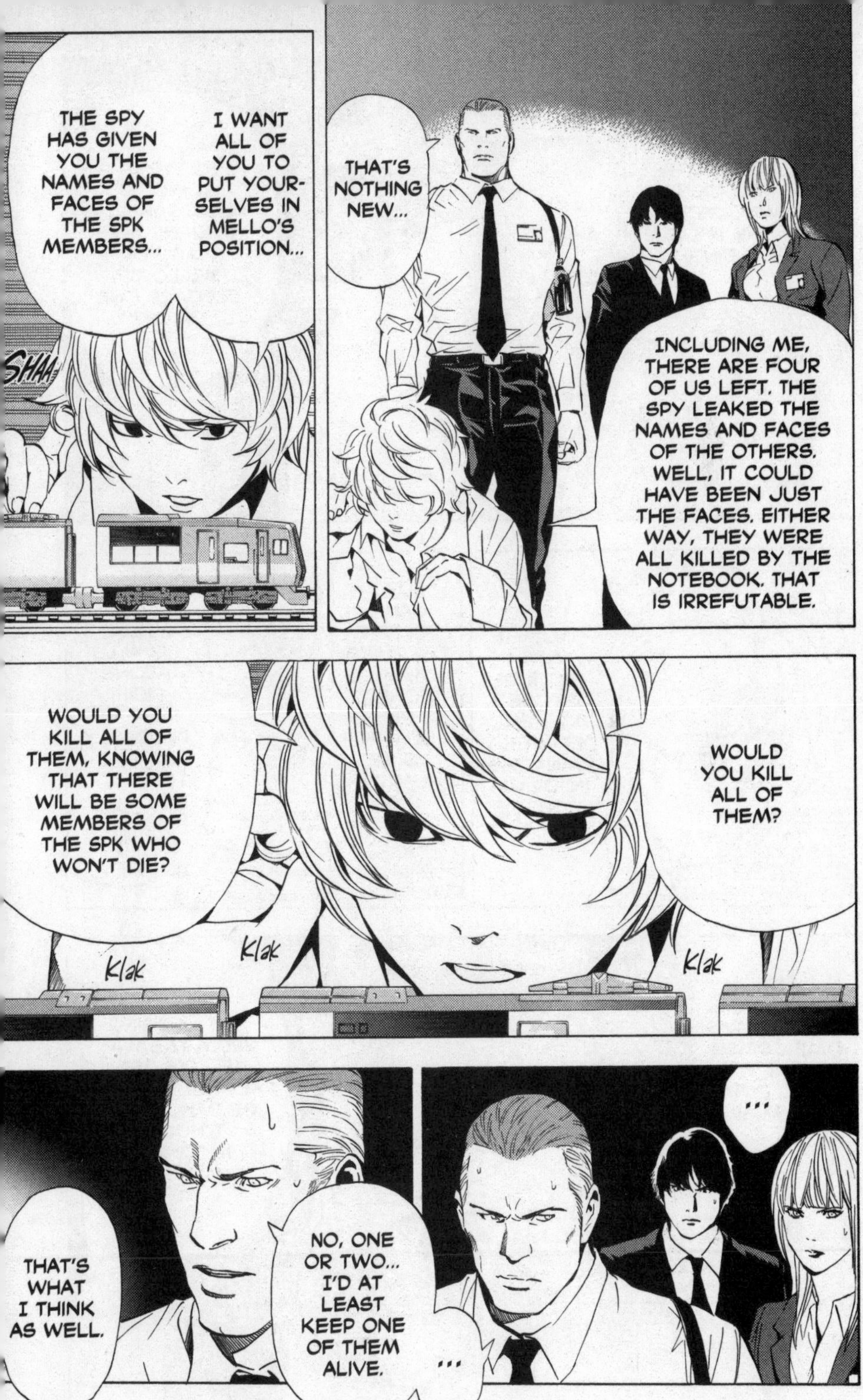
THAT'S NOTHING NEW...
INCLUDING ME, THERE ARE FOUR OF US LEFT. THE SPY LEAKED THE NAMES AND FACES OF THE OTHERS. WELL, IT COULD HAVE BEEN JUST THE FACES. EITHER WAY, THEY WERE ALL KILLED BY THE NOTEBOOK. THAT IS IRREFUTABLE.
I WANT ALL OF YOU TO PUT YOURSELVES IN MELLO'S POSITION...
THE SPY HAS GIVEN YOU THE NAMES AND FACES OF THE SPK MEMBERS...
SHAA
WOULD YOU KILL ALL OF THEM?
Klak
WOULD YOU KILL ALL OF THEM, KNOWING THAT THERE WILL BE SOME MEMBERS OF THE SPK WHO WON'T DIE?
Klak
Klak
...
...
NO, ONE OR TWO... I'D AT LEAST KEEP ONE OF THEM ALIVE.
THAT'S WHAT I THINK AS WELL.

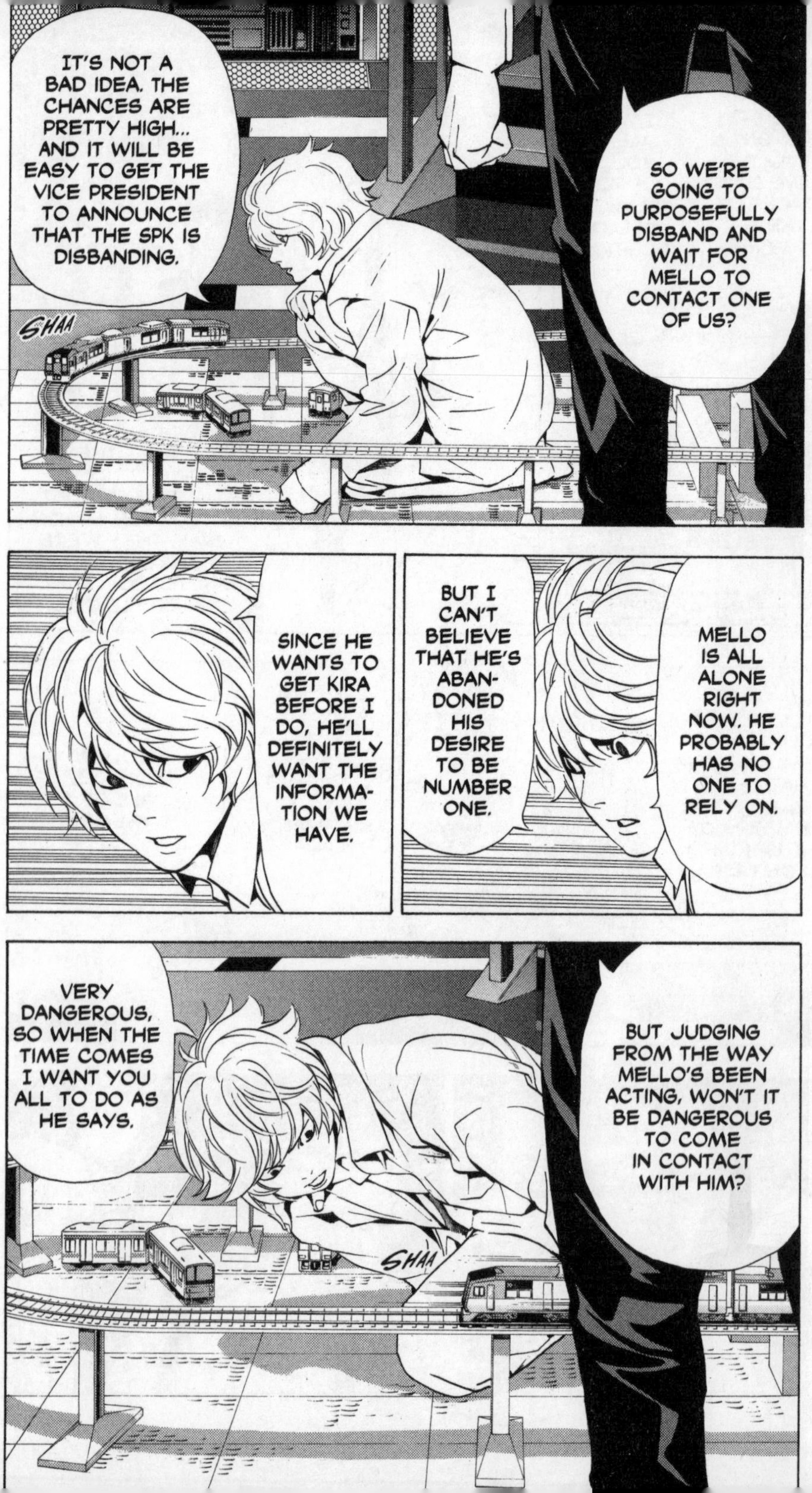
SO WE'RE GOING TO PURPOSEFULLY DISBAND AND WAIT FOR MELLO TO CONTACT ONE OF US?
IT'S NOT A BAD IDEA. THE CHANCES ARE PRETTY HIGH... AND IT WILL BE EASY TO GET THE VICE PRESIDENT TO ANNOUNCE THAT THE SPK IS DISBANDING.
SHAA
MELLO IS ALL ALONE RIGHT NOW. HE PROBABLY HAS NO ONE TO RELY ON.
BUT I CAN'T BELIEVE THAT HE'S ABANDONED HIS DESIRE TO BE NUMBER ONE.
SINCE HE WANTS TO GET KIRA BEFORE I DO, HE'LL DEFINITELY WANT THE INFORMATION WE HAVE.
BUT JUDGING FROM THE WAY MELLO'S BEEN ACTING, WON'T IT BE DANGEROUS TO COME IN CONTACT WITH HIM?
VERY DANGEROUS, SO WHEN THE TIME COMES I WANT YOU ALL TO DO AS HE SAYS.
SHAA

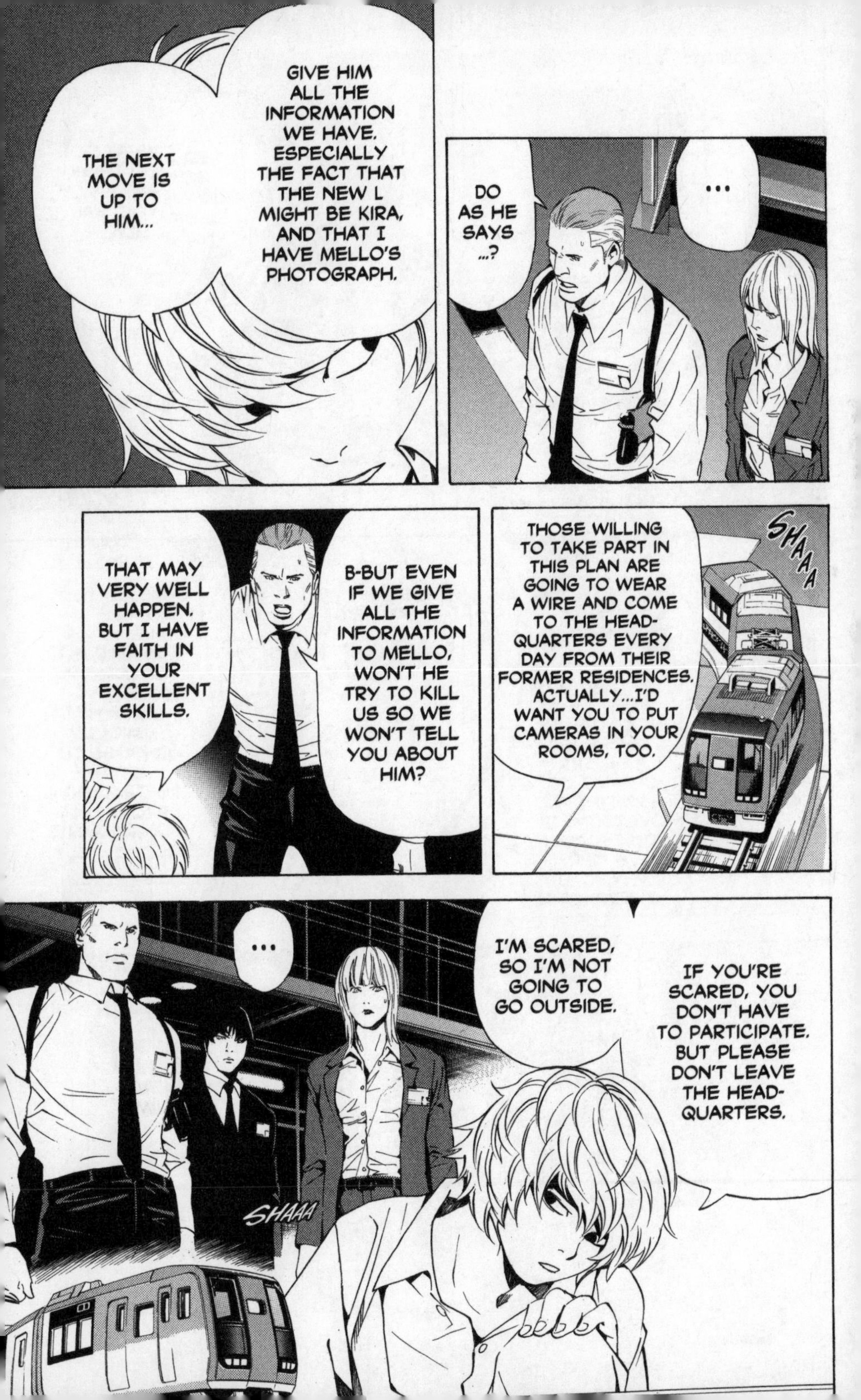
...
DO AS HE SAYS ...?
GIVE HIM ALL THE INFORMATION WE HAVE. ESPECIALLY THE FACT THAT THE NEW L MIGHT BE KIRA, AND THAT I HAVE MELLO'S PHOTOGRAPH.
THE NEXT MOVE IS UP TO HIM...
SHAAA
THOSE WILLING TO TAKE PART IN THIS PLAN ARE GOING TO WEAR A WIRE AND COME TO THE HEAD-QUARTERS EVERY DAY FROM THEIR FORMER RESIDENCES. ACTUALLY...I'D WANT YOU TO PUT CAMERAS IN YOUR ROOMS, TOO.
B-BUT EVEN IF WE GIVE ALL THE INFORMATION TO MELLO, WON'T HE TRY TO KILL US SO WE WON'T TELL YOU ABOUT HIM?
THAT MAY VERY WELL HAPPEN. BUT I HAVE FAITH IN YOUR EXCELLENT SKILLS.
I'M SCARED, SO I'M NOT GOING TO GO OUTSIDE.
IF YOU'RE SCARED, YOU DON'T HAVE TO PARTICIPATE. BUT PLEASE DON'T LEAVE THE HEAD-QUARTERS.
...
SHAAA

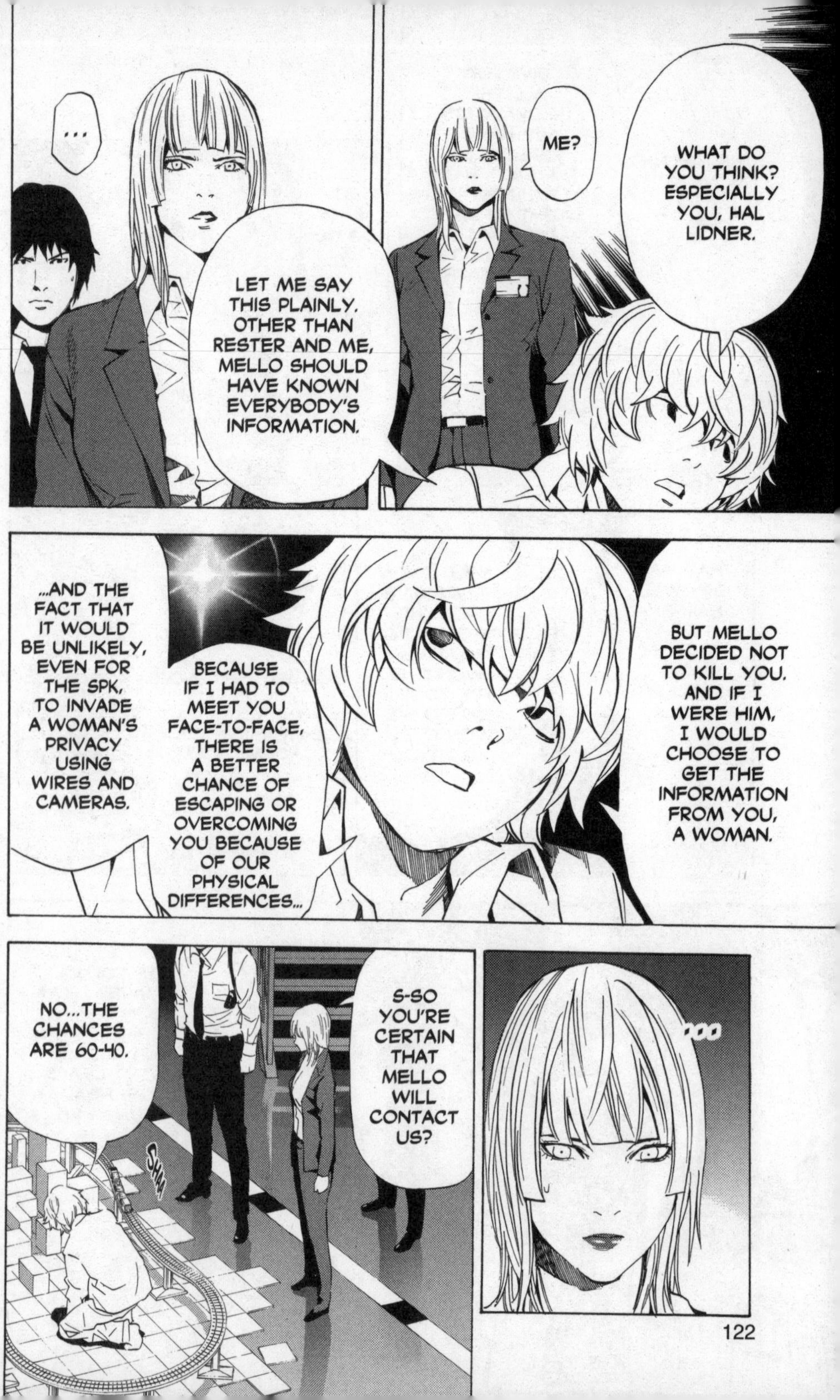
WHAT DO YOU THINK? ESPECIALLY YOU, HAL LIDNER.
ME?
LET ME SAY THIS PLAINLY. OTHER THAN RESTER AND ME, MELLO SHOULD HAVE KNOWN EVERYBODY'S INFORMATION.
...
BUT MELLO DECIDED NOT TO KILL YOU. AND IF I WERE HIM, I WOULD CHOOSE TO GET THE INFORMATION FROM YOU, A WOMAN.
BECAUSE IF I HAD TO MEET YOU FACE-TO-FACE, THERE IS A BETTER CHANCE OF ESCAPING OR OVERCOMING YOU BECAUSE OF OUR PHYSICAL DIFFERENCES...
...AND THE FACT THAT IT WOULD BE UNLIKELY, EVEN FOR THE SPK, TO INVADE A WOMAN'S PRIVACY USING WIRES AND CAMERAS.
S-SO YOU'RE CERTAIN THAT MELLO WILL CONTACT US?
NO...THE CHANCES ARE 60-40.

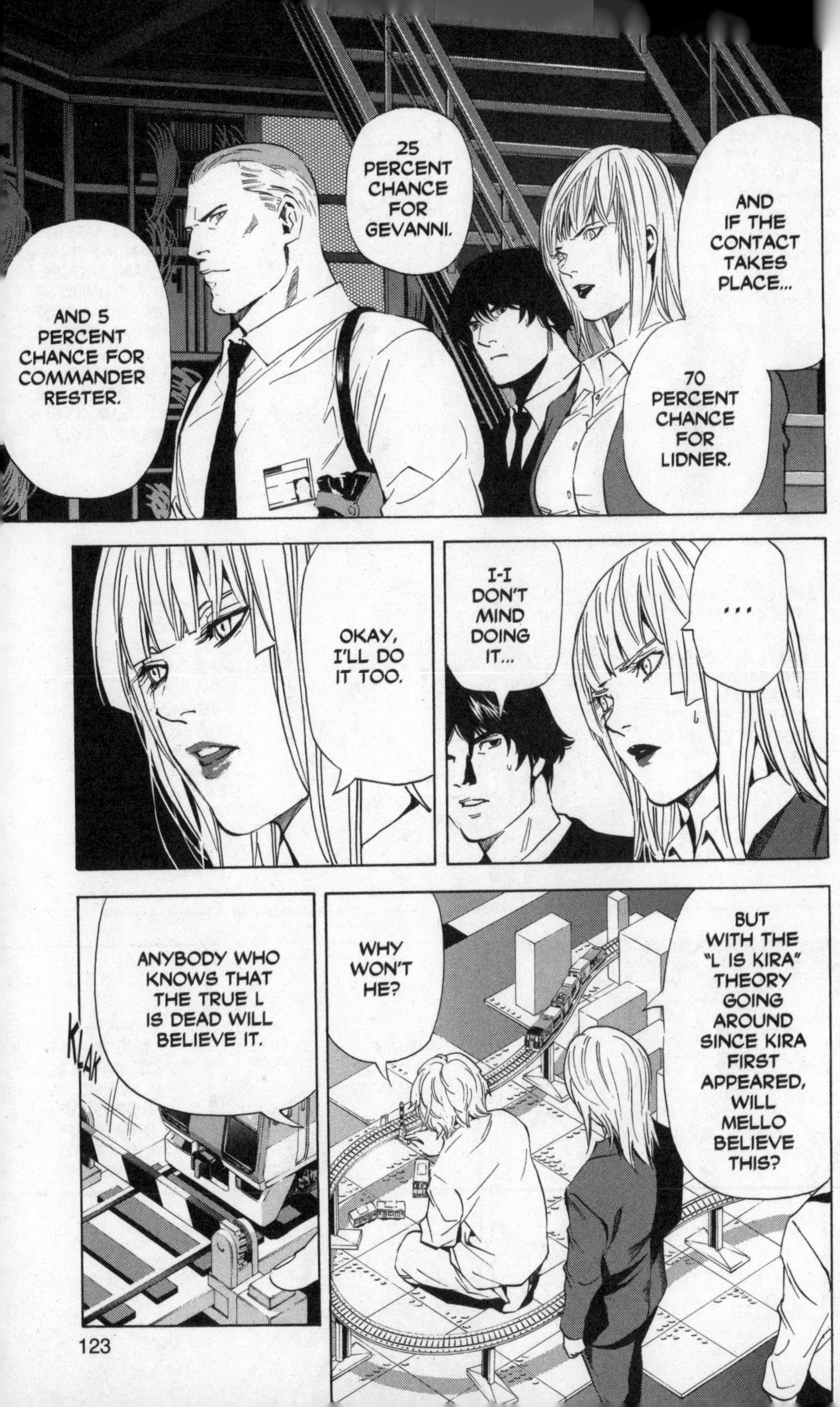
AND IF THE CONTACT TAKES PLACE...
70 PERCENT CHANCE FOR LIDNER.
25 PERCENT CHANCE FOR GEVANNI.
AND 5 PERCENT CHANCE FOR COMMANDER RESTER.
...
I-I DON'T MIND DOING IT...
OKAY, I'LL DO IT TOO.
BUT WITH THE "L IS KIRA" THEORY GOING AROUND SINCE KIRA FIRST APPEARED, WILL MELLO BELIEVE THIS?
WHY WON'T HE?
ANYBODY WHO KNOWS THAT THE TRUE L IS DEAD WILL BELIEVE IT.
KLAK

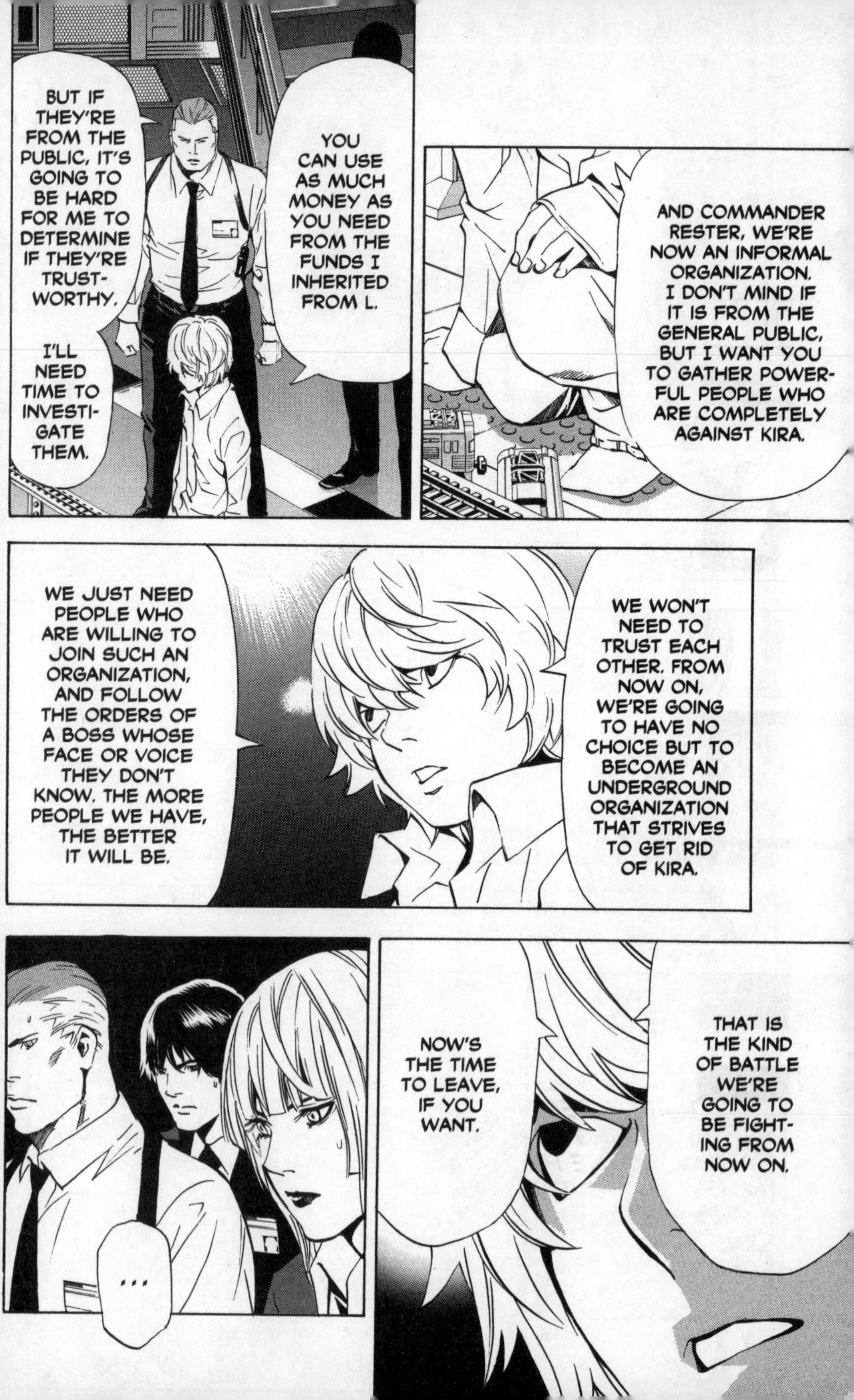
AND COMMANDER RESTER, WE'RE NOW AN INFORMAL ORGANIZATION. I DON'T MIND IF IT IS FROM THE GENERAL PUBLIC, BUT I WANT YOU TO GATHER POWERFUL PEOPLE WHO ARE COMPLETELY AGAINST KIRA.
YOU CAN USE AS MUCH MONEY AS YOU NEED FROM THE FUNDS I INHERITED FROM L.
BUT IF THEY'RE FROM THE PUBLIC, IT'S GOING TO BE HARD FOR ME TO DETERMINE IF THEY'RE TRUSTWORTHY.
I'LL NEED TIME TO INVESTIGATE THEM.
WE WON'T NEED TO TRUST EACH OTHER. FROM NOW ON, WE'RE GOING TO HAVE NO CHOICE BUT TO BECOME AN UNDERGROUND ORGANIZATION THAT STRIVES TO GET RID OF KIRA.
WE JUST NEED PEOPLE WHO ARE WILLING TO JOIN SUCH AN ORGANIZATION, AND FOLLOW THE ORDERS OF A BOSS WHOSE FACE OR VOICE THEY DON'T KNOW. THE MORE PEOPLE WE HAVE, THE BETTER IT WILL BE.
THAT IS THE KIND OF BATTLE WE'RE GOING TO BE FIGHTING FROM NOW ON.
NOW'S THE TIME TO LEAVE, IF YOU WANT.
...

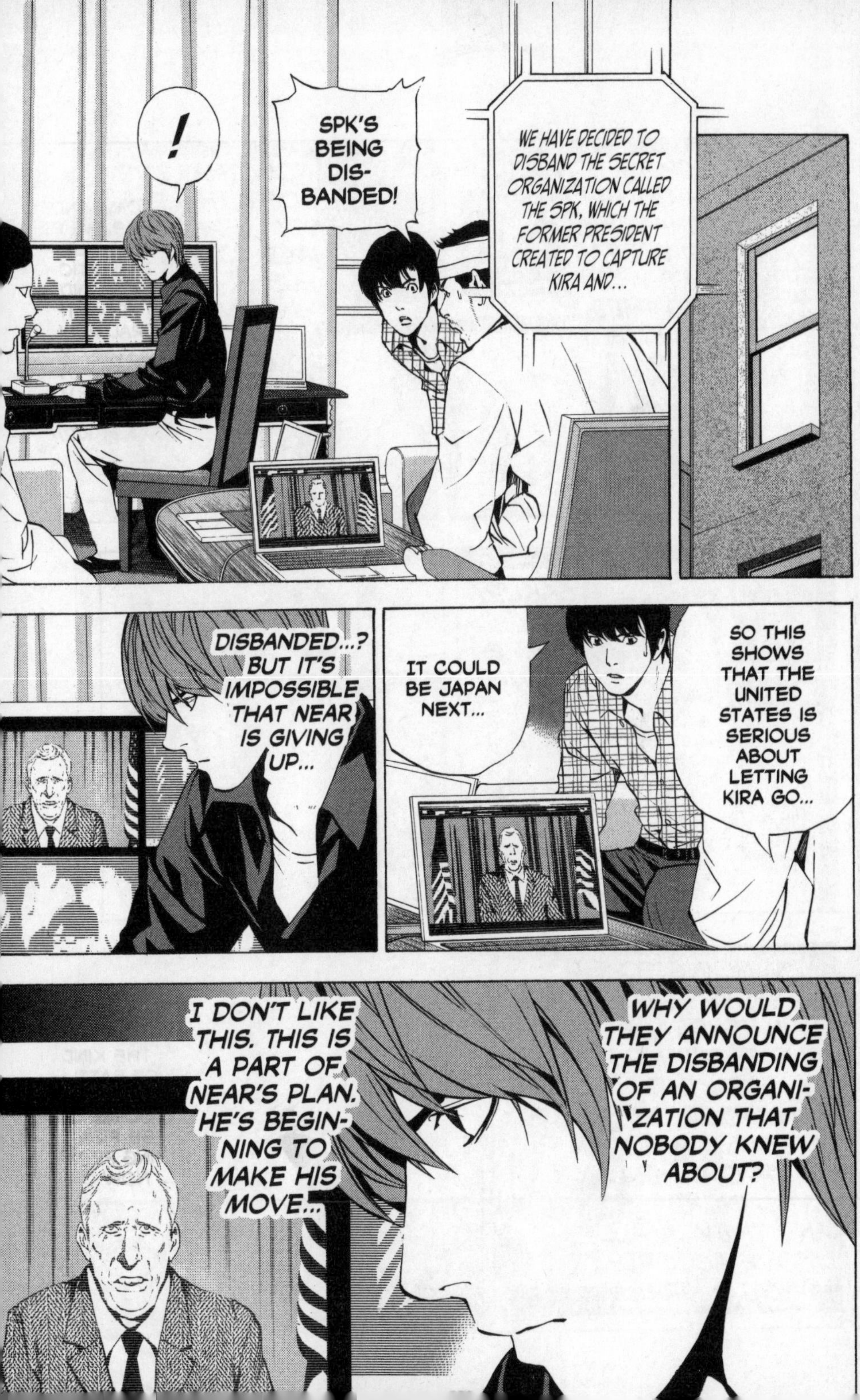
WE HAVE DECIDED TO DISBAND THE SECRET ORGANIZATION CALLED THE SPK, WHICH THE FORMER PRESIDENT CREATED TO CAPTURE KIRA AND...
SPK'S BEING DIS-BANDED!
!
SO THIS SHOWS THAT THE UNITED STATES IS SERIOUS ABOUT LETTING KIRA GO...
IT COULD BE JAPAN NEXT...
DISBANDED...? BUT IT'S IMPOSSIBLE THAT NEAR IS GIVING UP...
WHY WOULD THEY ANNOUNCE THE DISBANDING OF AN ORGANI-ZATION THAT NOBODY KNEW ABOUT?
I DON'T LIKE THIS. THIS IS A PART OF NEAR'S PLAN. HE'S BEGIN-NING TO MAKE HIS MOVE...

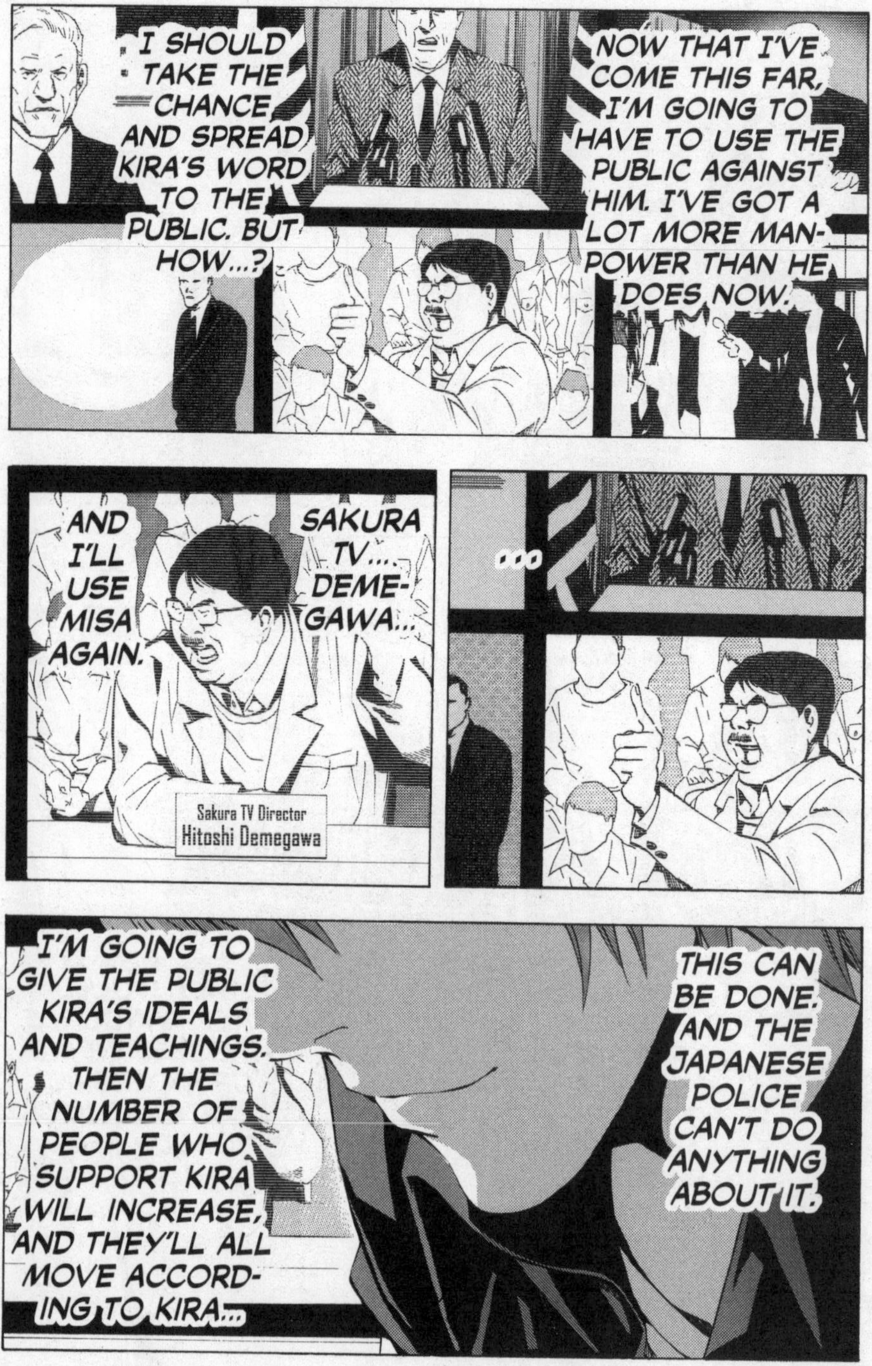
NOW THAT I'VE COME THIS FAR, I'M GOING TO HAVE TO USE THE PUBLIC AGAINST HIM. I'VE GOT A LOT MORE MAN-POWER THAN HE DOES NOW.
I SHOULD TAKE THE CHANCE, AND SPREAD KIRA'S WORD TO THE PUBLIC. BUT HOW...?
...
SAKURA TV.... DEME-GAWA...
AND I'LL USE MISA AGAIN.
Sakura TV Director Hitoshi Demegawa
I'M GOING TO GIVE THE PUBLIC KIRA'S IDEALS AND TEACHINGS. THEN THE NUMBER OF PEOPLE WHO SUPPORT KIRA WILL INCREASE, AND THEY'LL ALL MOVE ACCORD-ING TO KIRA...
THIS CAN BE DONE. AND THE JAPANESE POLICE CAN'T DO ANYTHING ABOUT IT.

READ THIS WAY

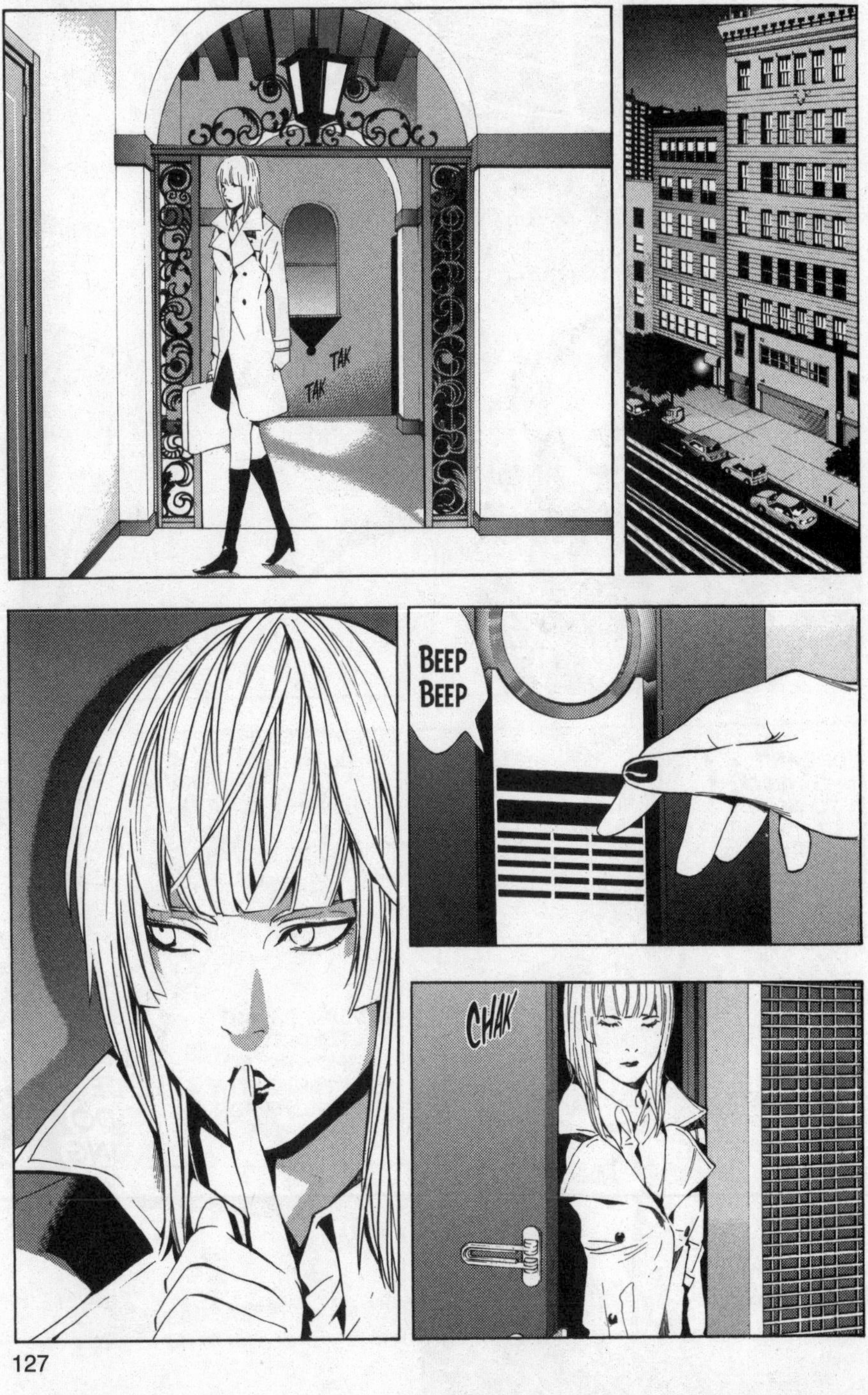
TAK
TAK
BEEP BEEP
CHAK

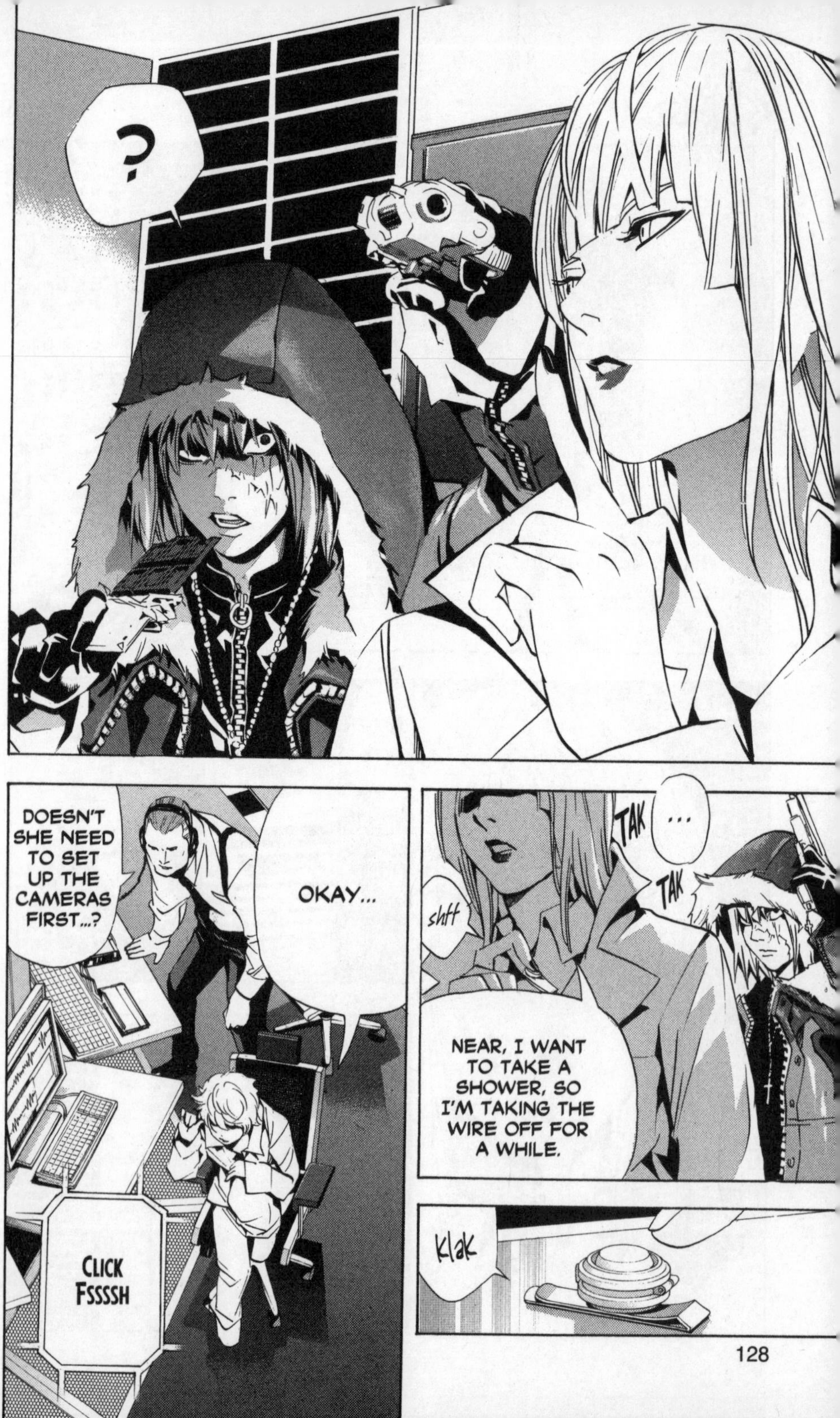
?
...
TAK
TAK
shff
NEAR, I WANT TO TAKE A SHOWER, SO I'M TAKING THE WIRE OFF FOR A WHILE.
klak
DOESN'T SHE NEED TO SET UP THE CAMERAS FIRST...?
OKAY...
CLICK FSSSSH

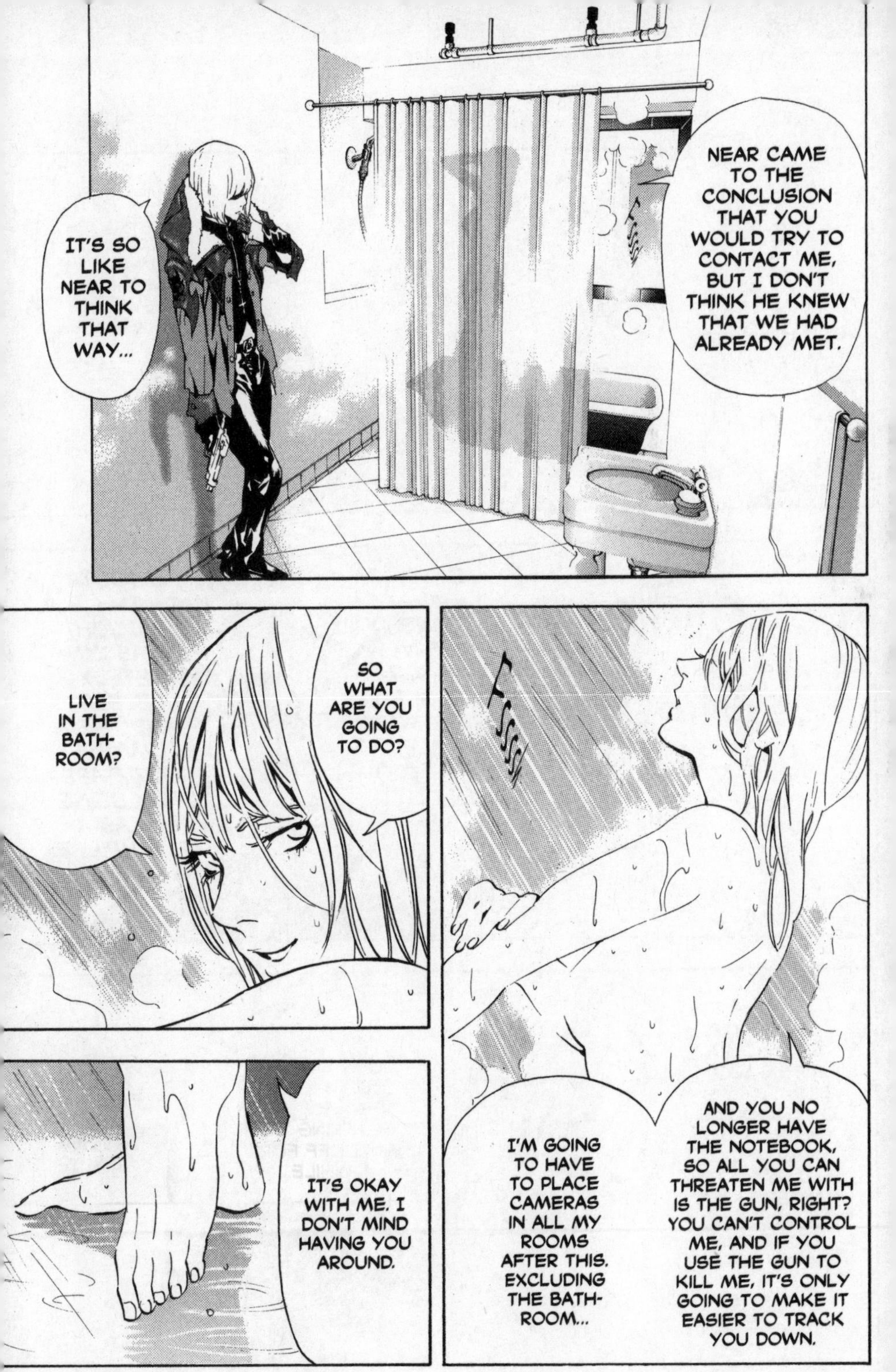
NEAR CAME TO THE CONCLUSION THAT YOU WOULD TRY TO CONTACT ME, BUT I DON'T THINK HE KNEW THAT WE HAD ALREADY MET.
IT'S SO LIKE NEAR TO THINK THAT WAY...
AND YOU NO LONGER HAVE THE NOTEBOOK, SO ALL YOU CAN THREATEN ME WITH IS THE GUN, RIGHT? YOU CAN'T CONTROL ME, AND IF YOU USE THE GUN TO KILL ME, IT'S ONLY GOING TO MAKE IT EASIER TO TRACK YOU DOWN.
I'M GOING TO HAVE TO PLACE CAMERAS IN ALL MY ROOMS AFTER THIS. EXCLUDING THE BATH-ROOM...
SO WHAT ARE YOU GOING TO DO?
LIVE IN THE BATH-ROOM?
IT'S OKAY WITH ME. I DON'T MIND HAVING YOU AROUND.

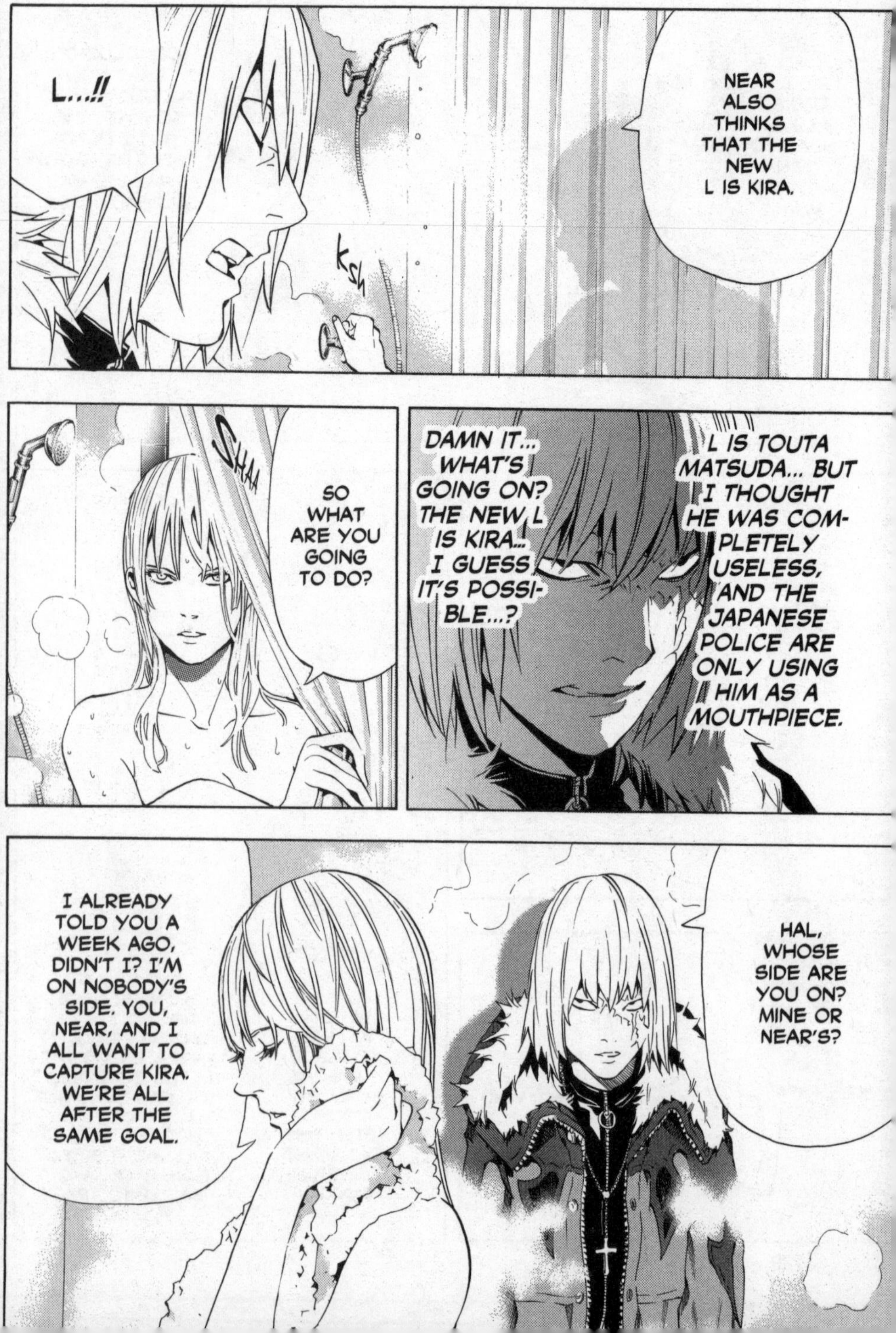
NEAR ALSO THINKS THAT THE NEW L IS KIRA.
L...!!
KSH
L IS TOUTA MATSUDA... BUT I THOUGHT HE WAS COM-PLETELY USELESS, AND THE JAPANESE POLICE ARE ONLY USING HIM AS A MOUTHPIECE.
DAMN IT... WHAT'S GOING ON? THE NEW L IS KIRA... I GUESS IT'S POSSI-BLE...?
SHAA
SO WHAT ARE YOU GOING TO DO?
HAL, WHOSE SIDE ARE YOU ON? MINE OR NEAR'S?
I ALREADY TOLD YOU A WEEK AGO, DIDN'T I? I'M ON NOBODY'S SIDE. YOU, NEAR, AND I ALL WANT TO CAPTURE KIRA. WE'RE ALL AFTER THE SAME GOAL.

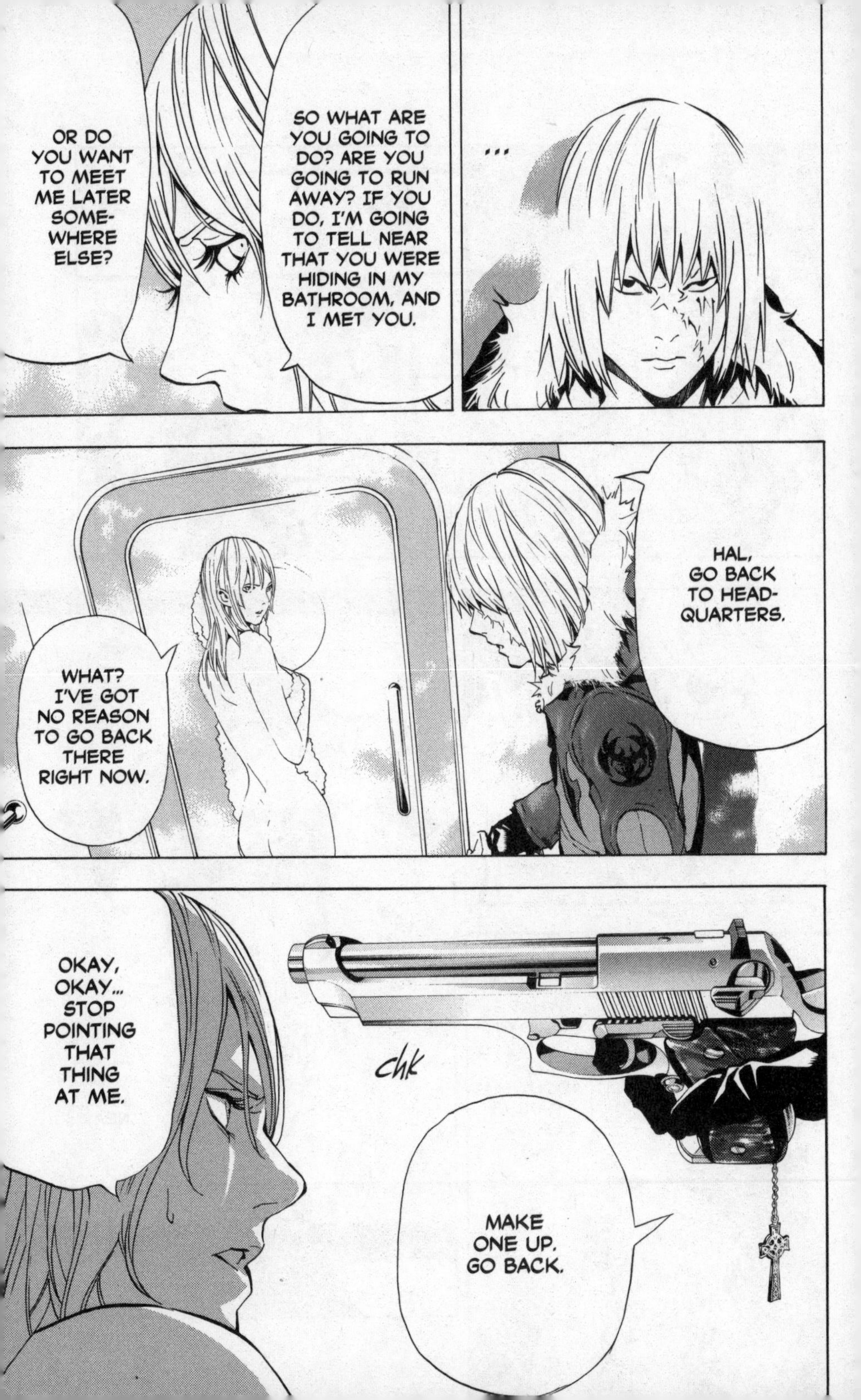
...
SO WHAT ARE YOU GOING TO DO? ARE YOU GOING TO RUN AWAY? IF YOU DO, I'M GOING TO TELL NEAR THAT YOU WERE HIDING IN MY BATHROOM, AND I MET YOU.
OR DO YOU WANT TO MEET ME LATER SOME-WHERE ELSE?
HAL, GO BACK TO HEAD-QUARTERS.
WHAT? I'VE GOT NO REASON TO GO BACK THERE RIGHT NOW.
OKAY, OKAY... STOP POINTING THAT THING AT ME.
chk
MAKE ONE UP. GO BACK.

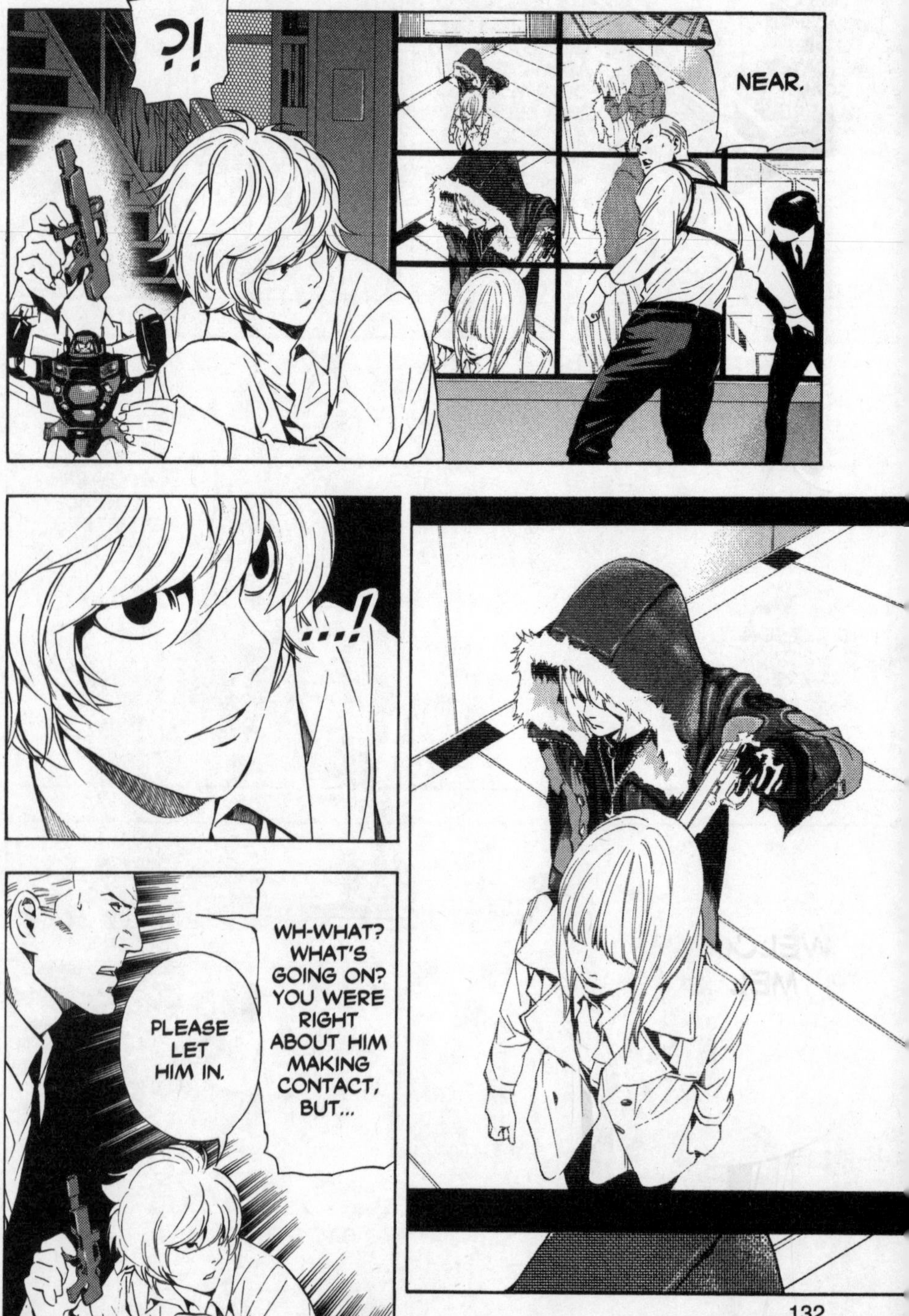
NEAR.
?!
...!
WH-WHAT? WHAT'S GOING ON? YOU WERE RIGHT ABOUT HIM MAKING CONTACT, BUT...
PLEASE LET HIM IN.

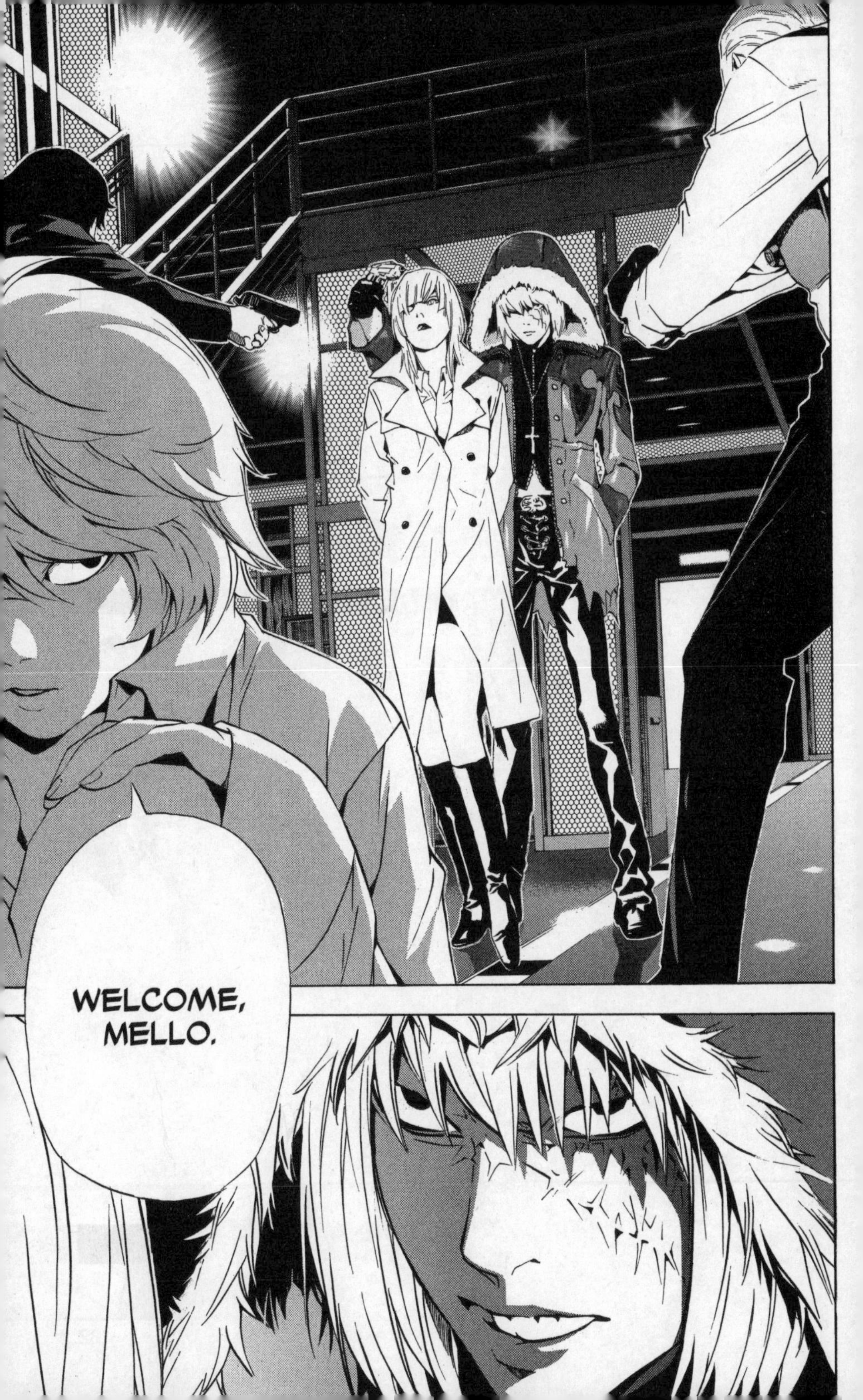
WELCOME, MELLO.

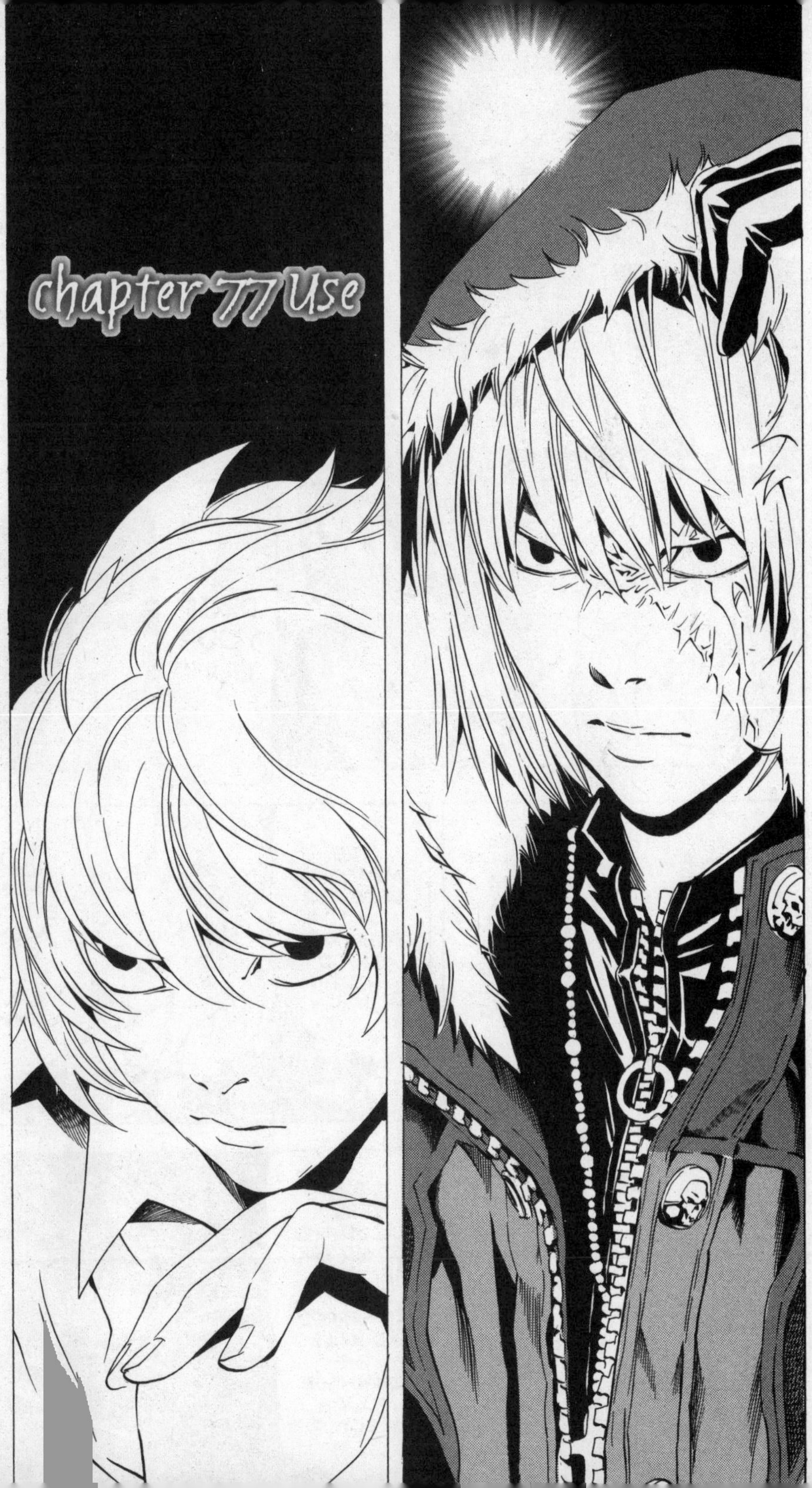
chapter 77 Use

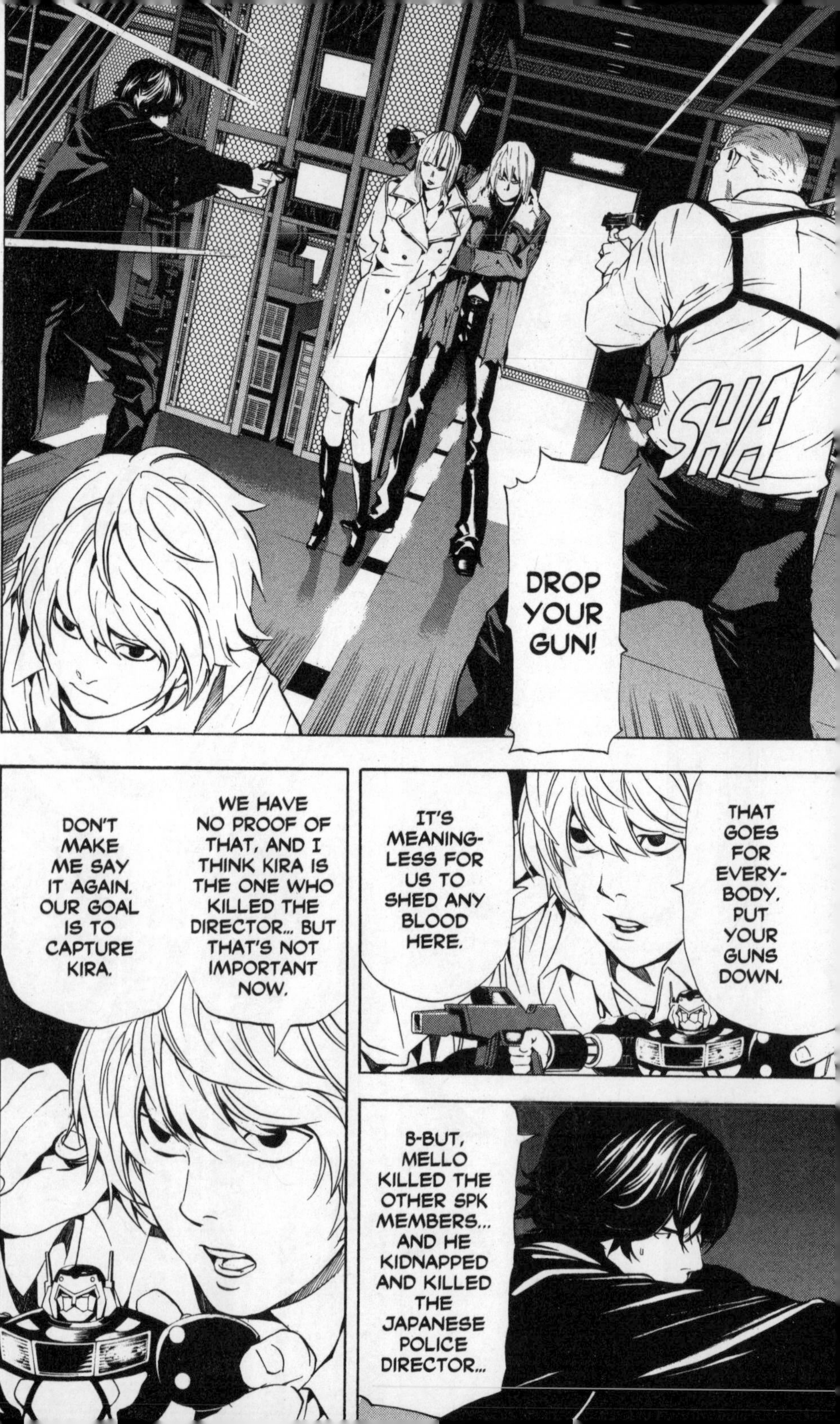
SHA
DROP YOUR GUN!
THAT GOES FOR EVERYBODY. PUT YOUR GUNS DOWN.
IT'S MEANINGLESS FOR US TO SHED ANY BLOOD HERE.
B-BUT, MELLO KILLED THE OTHER SPK MEMBERS... AND HE KIDNAPPED AND KILLED THE JAPANESE POLICE DIRECTOR...
WE HAVE NO PROOF OF THAT, AND I THINK KIRA IS THE ONE WHO KILLED THE DIRECTOR... BUT THAT'S NOT IMPORTANT NOW.
DON'T MAKE ME SAY IT AGAIN. OUR GOAL IS TO CAPTURE KIRA.

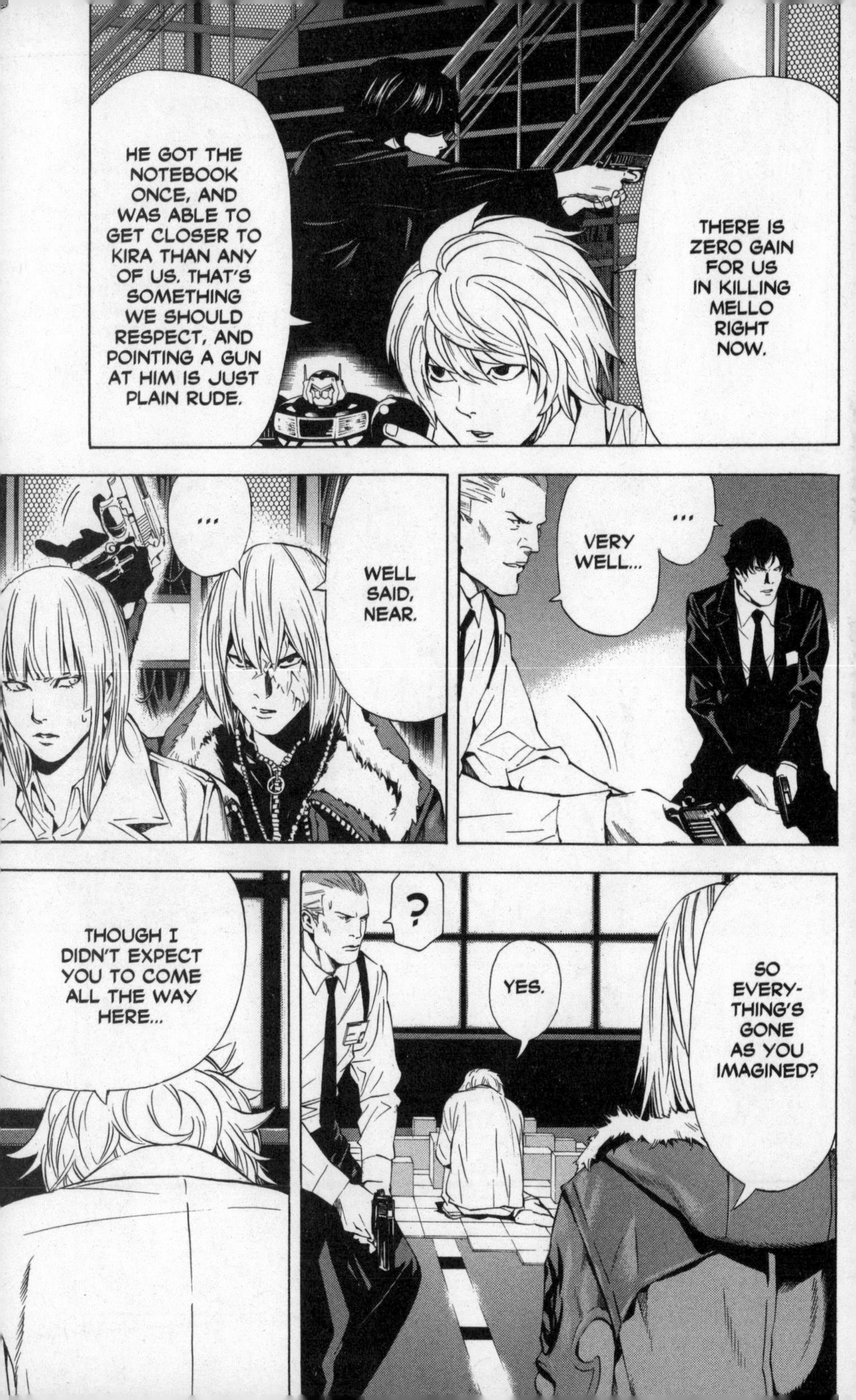
THERE IS ZERO GAIN FOR US IN KILLING MELLO RIGHT NOW.
HE GOT THE NOTEBOOK ONCE, AND WAS ABLE TO GET CLOSER TO KIRA THAN ANY OF US. THAT'S SOMETHING WE SHOULD RESPECT, AND POINTING A GUN AT HIM IS JUST PLAIN RUDE.
... VERY WELL...
WELL SAID, NEAR.
...
SO EVERY-THING'S GONE AS YOU IMAGINED?
?
YES.
THOUGH I DIDN'T EXPECT YOU TO COME ALL THE WAY HERE...

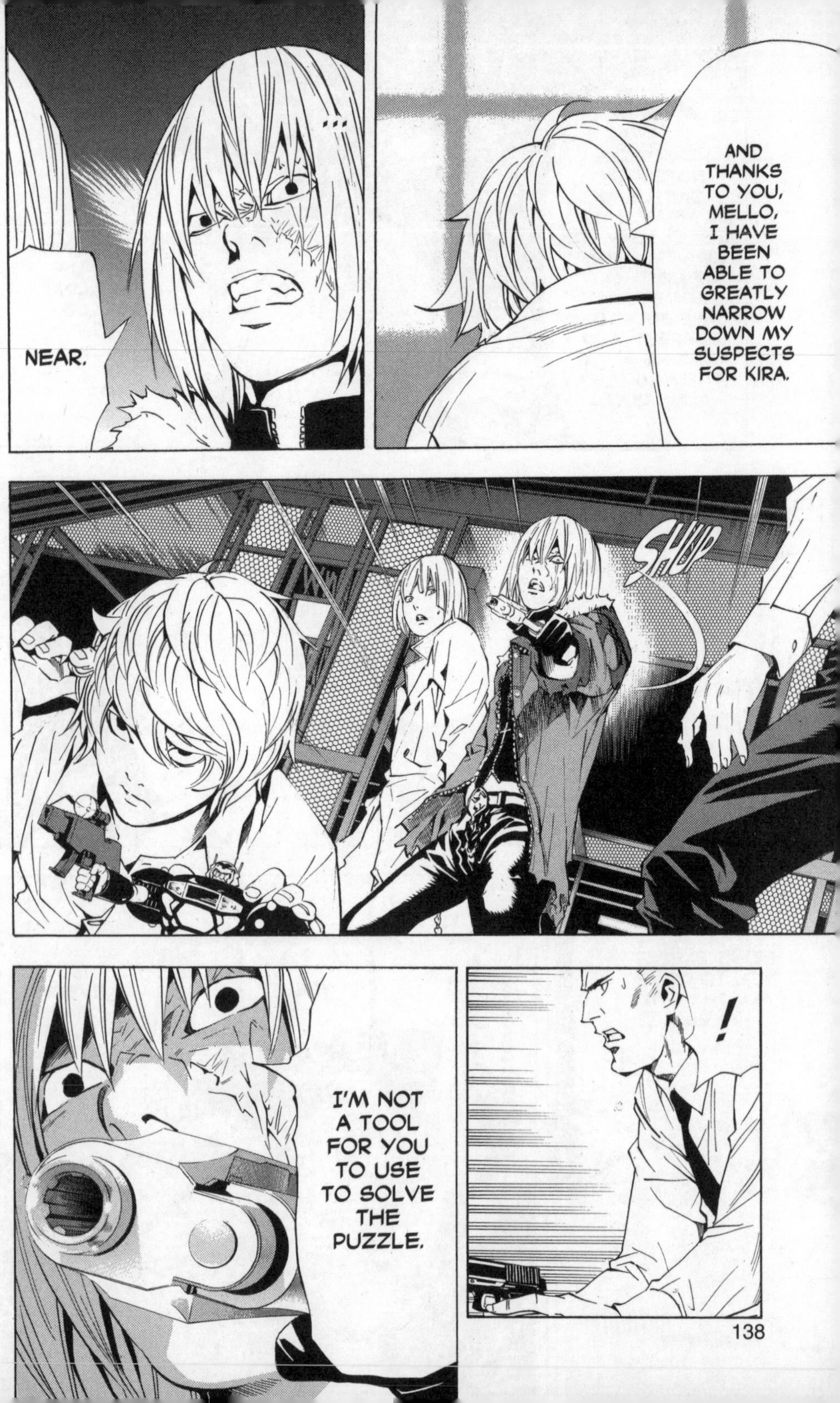
AND THANKS TO YOU, MELLO, I HAVE BEEN ABLE TO GREATLY NARROW DOWN MY SUSPECTS FOR KIRA.
...
NEAR.
SHUP
!
I'M NOT A TOOL FOR YOU TO USE TO SOLVE THE PUZZLE.

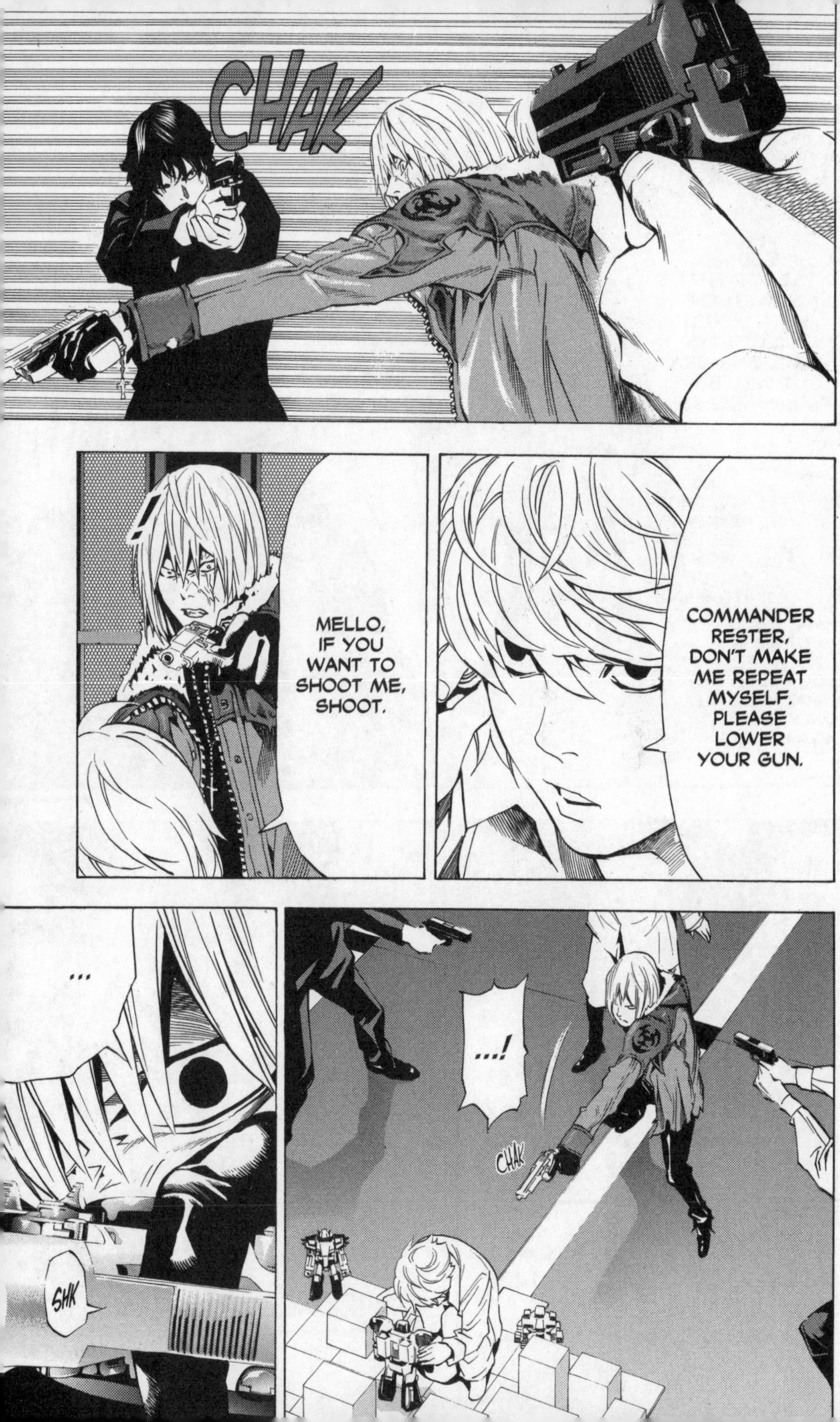
CHAK
COMMANDER RESTER, DON'T MAKE ME REPEAT MYSELF. PLEASE LOWER YOUR GUN.
MELLO, IF YOU WANT TO SHOOT ME, SHOOT.
...!
CHAK
...
SHK

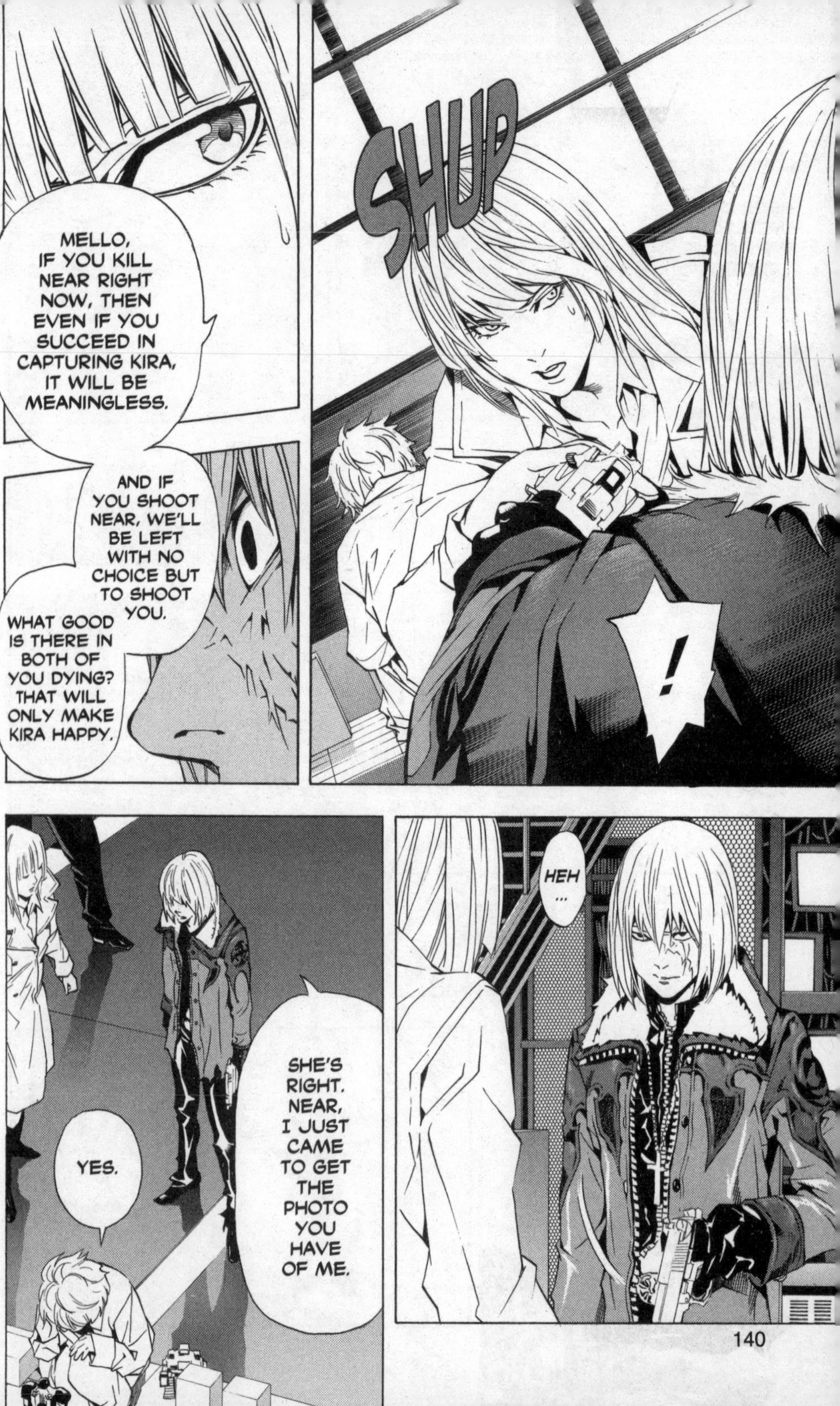
SHUP
!
MELLO, IF YOU KILL NEAR RIGHT NOW, THEN EVEN IF YOU SUCCEED IN CAPTURING KIRA, IT WILL BE MEANINGLESS.
AND IF YOU SHOOT NEAR, WE'LL BE LEFT WITH NO CHOICE BUT TO SHOOT YOU.
WHAT GOOD IS THERE IN BOTH OF YOU DYING? THAT WILL ONLY MAKE KIRA HAPPY.
HEH ...
SHE'S RIGHT. NEAR, I JUST CAME TO GET THE PHOTO YOU HAVE OF ME.
YES.

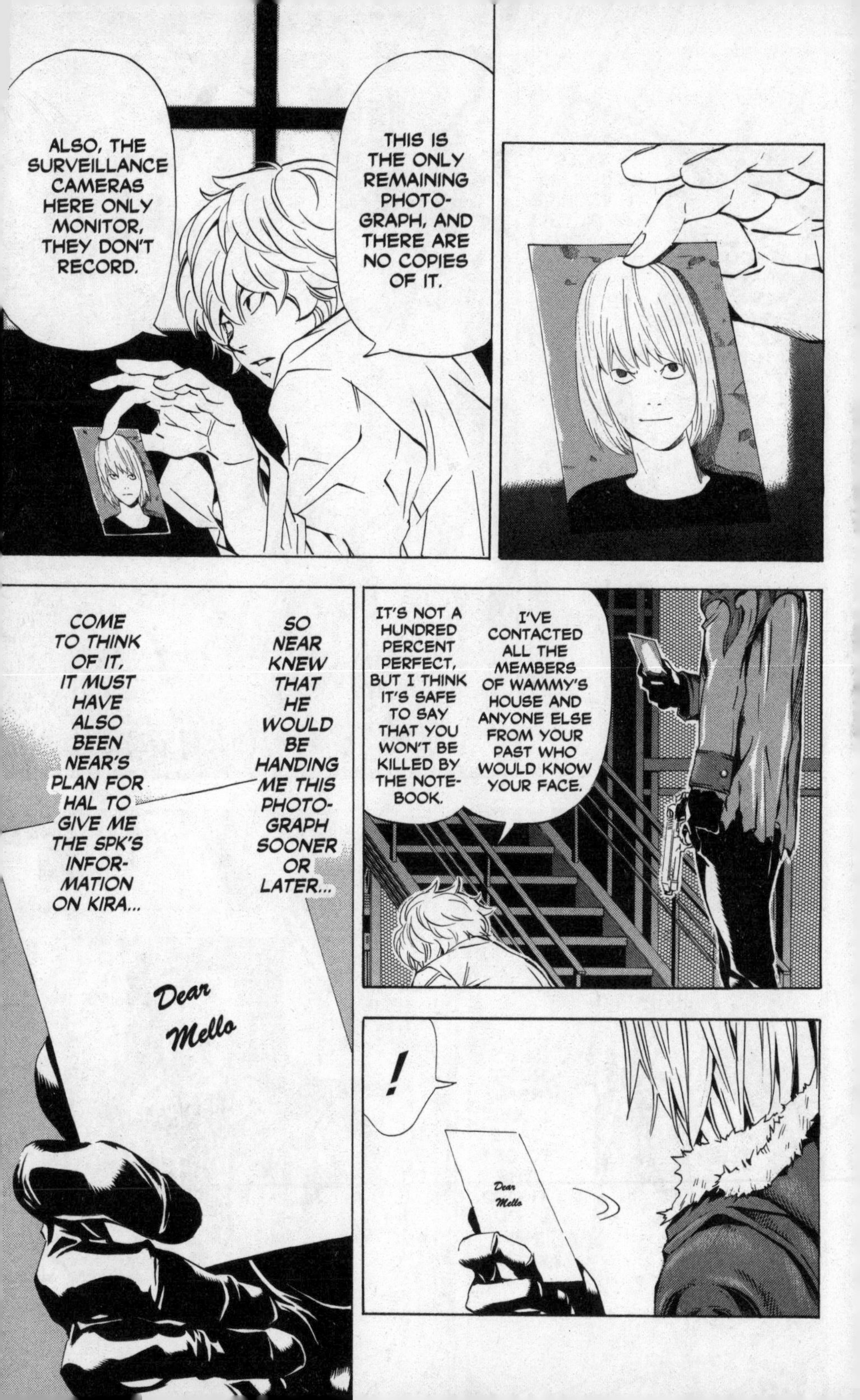
THIS IS THE ONLY REMAINING PHOTOGRAPH, AND THERE ARE NO COPIES OF IT.
ALSO, THE SURVEILLANCE CAMERAS HERE ONLY MONITOR, THEY DON'T RECORD.
I'VE CONTACTED ALL THE MEMBERS OF WAMMY'S HOUSE AND ANYONE ELSE FROM YOUR PAST WHO WOULD KNOW YOUR FACE.
IT'S NOT A HUNDRED PERCENT PERFECT, BUT I THINK IT'S SAFE TO SAY THAT YOU WON'T BE KILLED BY THE NOTEBOOK.
!
Dear Mello
SO NEAR KNEW THAT HE WOULD BE HANDING ME THIS PHOTOGRAPH SOONER OR LATER...
COME TO THINK OF IT, IT MUST HAVE ALSO BEEN NEAR'S PLAN FOR HAL TO GIVE ME THE SPK'S INFORMATION ON KIRA...
Dear Mello

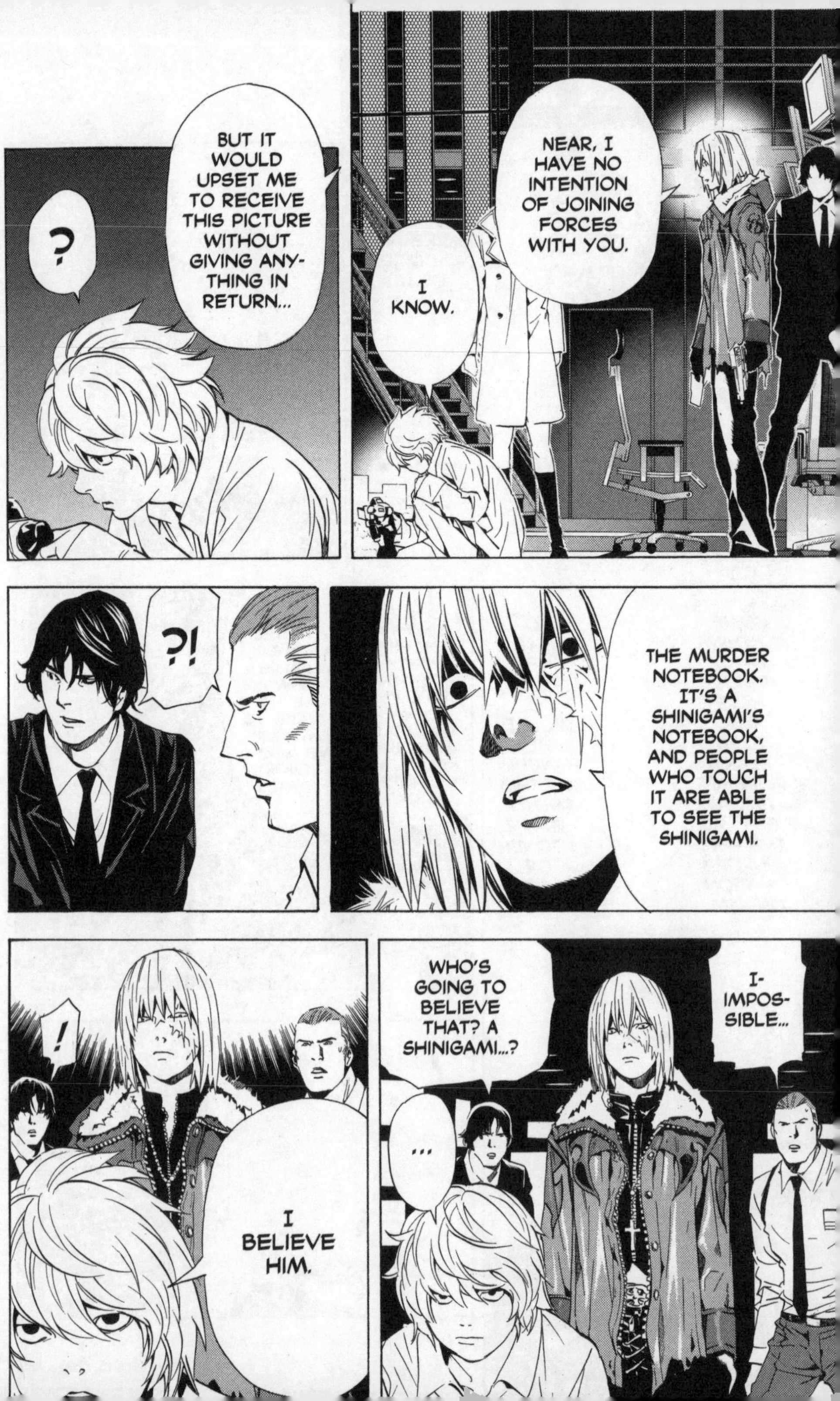
NEAR, I HAVE NO INTENTION OF JOINING FORCES WITH YOU.
I KNOW.
BUT IT WOULD UPSET ME TO RECEIVE THIS PICTURE WITHOUT GIVING ANY-THING IN RETURN...
?
THE MURDER NOTEBOOK. IT'S A SHINIGAMI'S NOTEBOOK, AND PEOPLE WHO TOUCH IT ARE ABLE TO SEE THE SHINIGAMI.
?!
I-IMPOS-SIBLE...
WHO'S GOING TO BELIEVE THAT? A SHINIGAMI...?
...
!
I BELIEVE HIM.

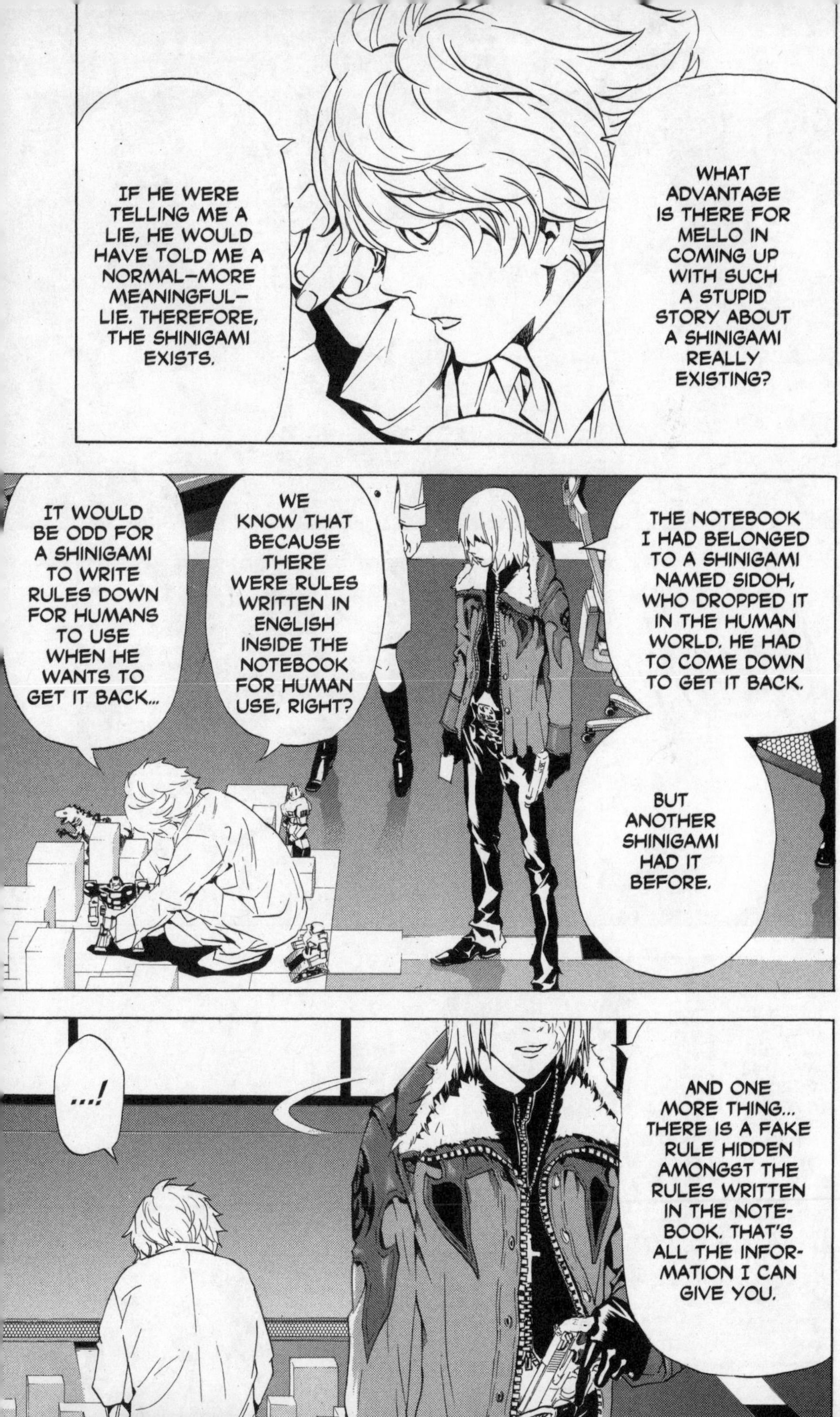
WHAT ADVANTAGE IS THERE FOR MELLO IN COMING UP WITH SUCH A STUPID STORY ABOUT A SHINIGAMI REALLY EXISTING?
IF HE WERE TELLING ME A LIE, HE WOULD HAVE TOLD ME A NORMAL—MORE MEANINGFUL—LIE. THEREFORE, THE SHINIGAMI EXISTS.
THE NOTEBOOK I HAD BELONGED TO A SHINIGAMI NAMED SIDOH, WHO DROPPED IT IN THE HUMAN WORLD. HE HAD TO COME DOWN TO GET IT BACK.
BUT ANOTHER SHINIGAMI HAD IT BEFORE.
WE KNOW THAT BECAUSE THERE WERE RULES WRITTEN IN ENGLISH INSIDE THE NOTEBOOK FOR HUMAN USE, RIGHT?
IT WOULD BE ODD FOR A SHINIGAMI TO WRITE RULES DOWN FOR HUMANS TO USE WHEN HE WANTS TO GET IT BACK...
AND ONE MORE THING... THERE IS A FAKE RULE HIDDEN AMONGST THE RULES WRITTEN IN THE NOTE-BOOK. THAT'S ALL THE INFOR-MATION I CAN GIVE YOU.
...!

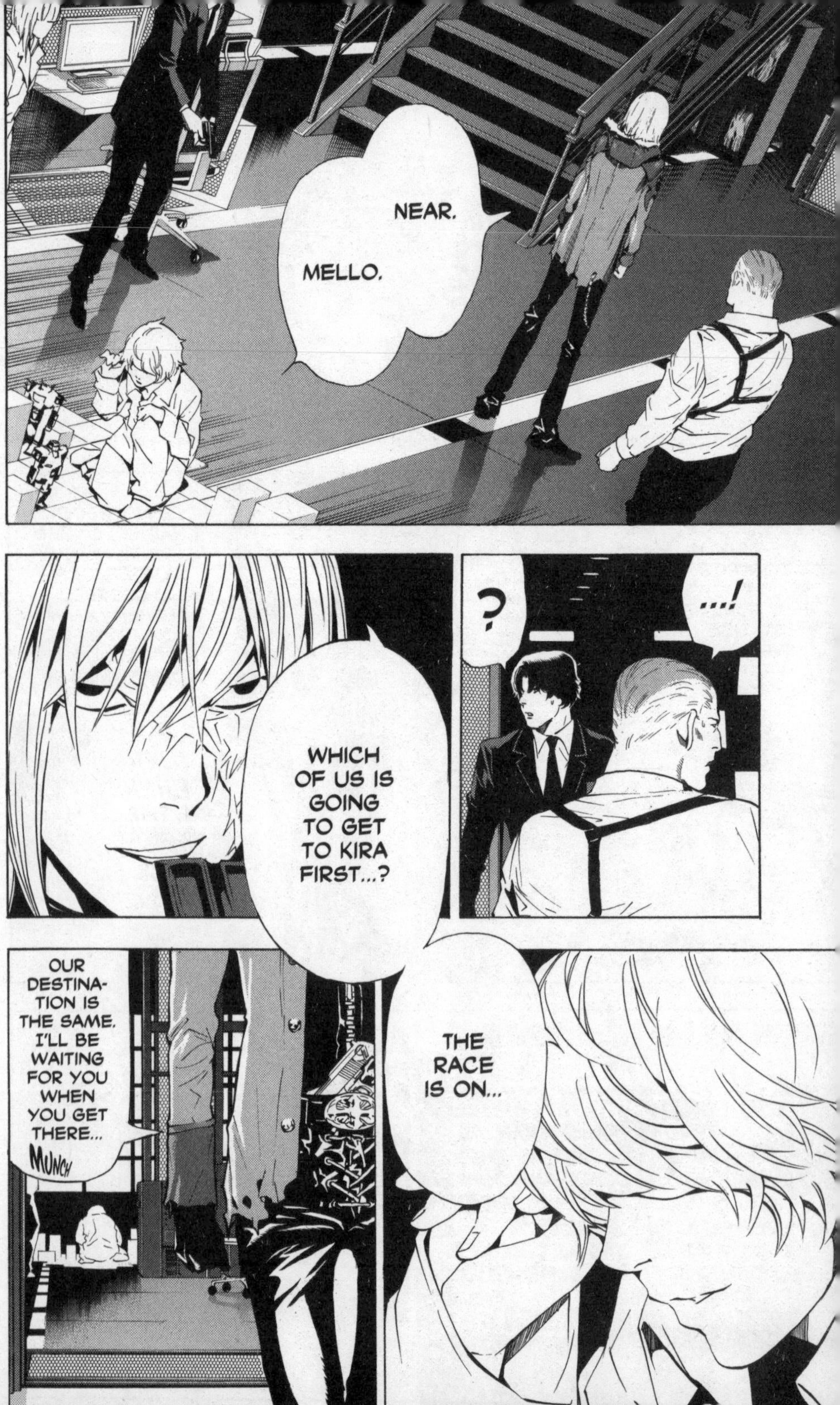
NEAR.
MELLO.
...!
?
WHICH OF US IS GOING TO GET TO KIRA FIRST...?
THE RACE IS ON...
OUR DESTINA-TION IS THE SAME. I'LL BE WAITING FOR YOU WHEN YOU GET THERE...
MUNCH

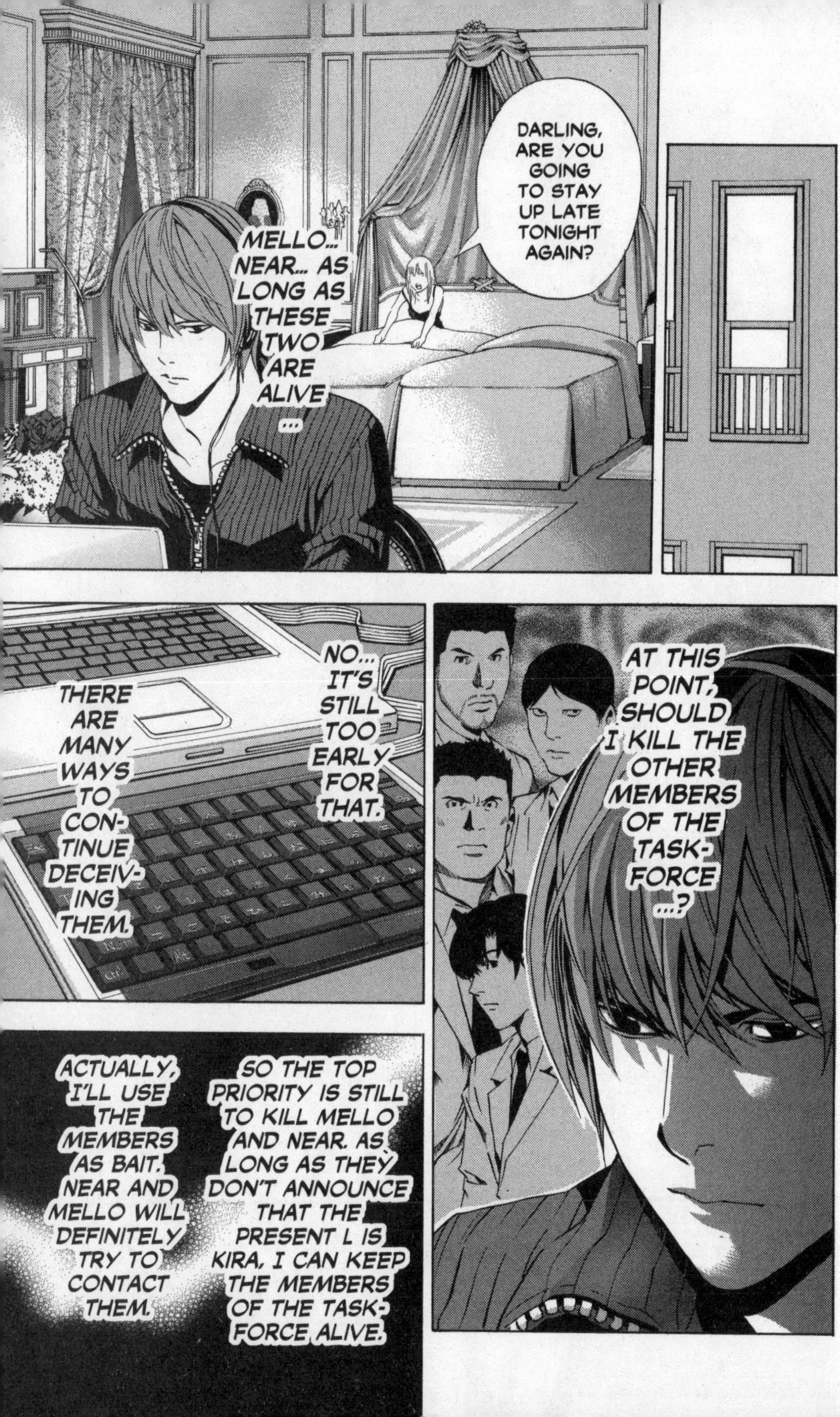
DARLING, ARE YOU GOING TO STAY UP LATE TONIGHT AGAIN?
MELLO... NEAR... AS LONG AS THESE TWO ARE ALIVE ...
AT THIS POINT, SHOULD I KILL THE OTHER MEMBERS OF THE TASK-FORCE ...?
NO... IT'S STILL TOO EARLY FOR THAT.
THERE ARE MANY WAYS TO CONTINUE DECEIVING THEM.
SO THE TOP PRIORITY IS STILL TO KILL MELLO AND NEAR. AS LONG AS THEY DON'T ANNOUNCE THAT THE PRESENT L IS KIRA, I CAN KEEP THE MEMBERS OF THE TASK-FORCE ALIVE.
ACTUALLY, I'LL USE THE MEMBERS AS BAIT. NEAR AND MELLO WILL DEFINITELY TRY TO CONTACT THEM.

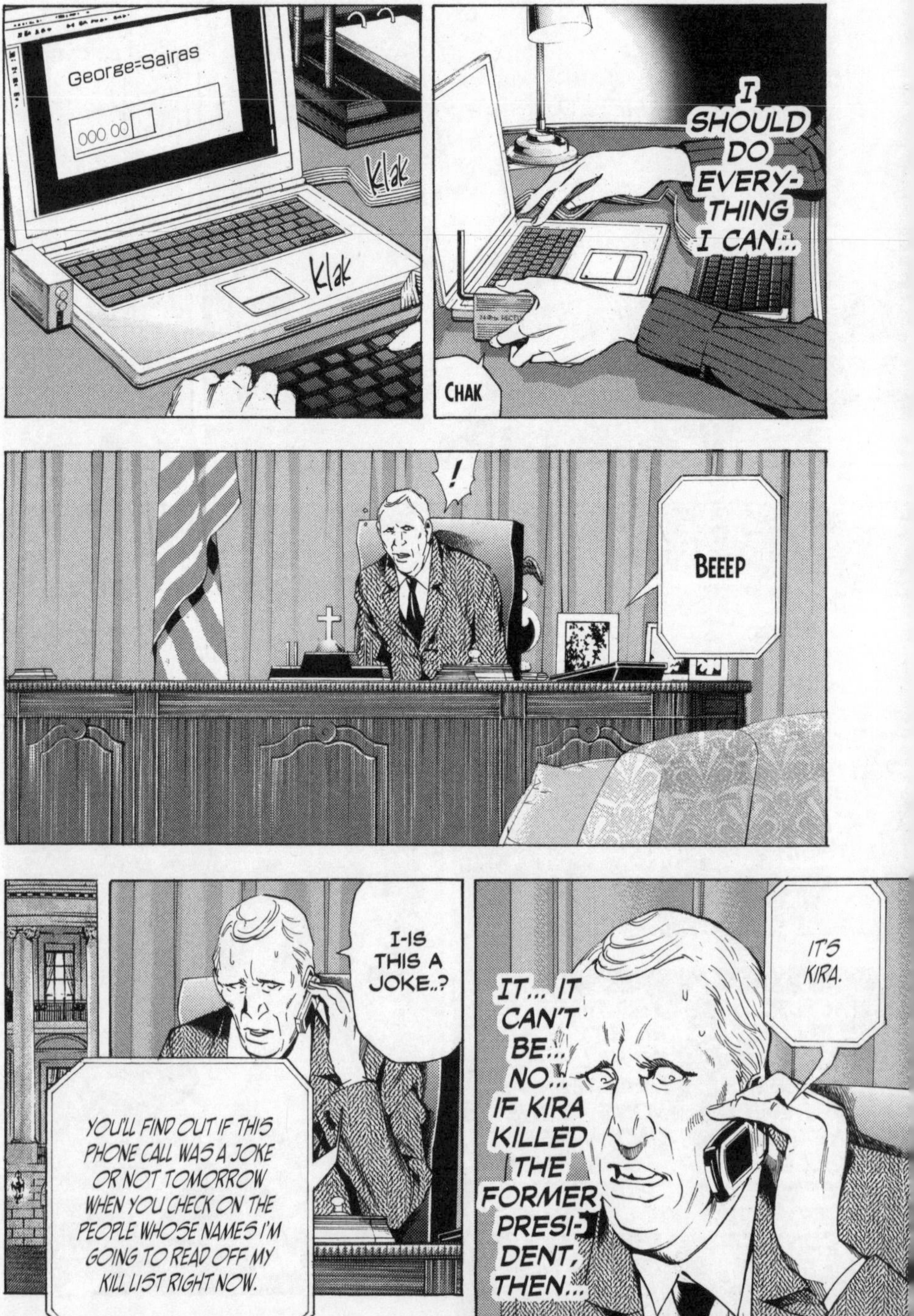
I SHOULD DO EVERY-THING I CAN...
CHAK
George=Sairas
000.00
Klak
Klak
!
BEEEP
IT'S KIRA.
IT... IT CAN'T BE... NO... IF KIRA KILLED THE FORMER PRESI-DENT, THEN...
I-IS THIS A JOKE..?
YOU'LL FIND OUT IF THIS PHONE CALL WAS A JOKE OR NOT TOMORROW WHEN YOU CHECK ON THE PEOPLE WHOSE NAMES I'M GOING TO READ OFF MY KILL LIST RIGHT NOW.

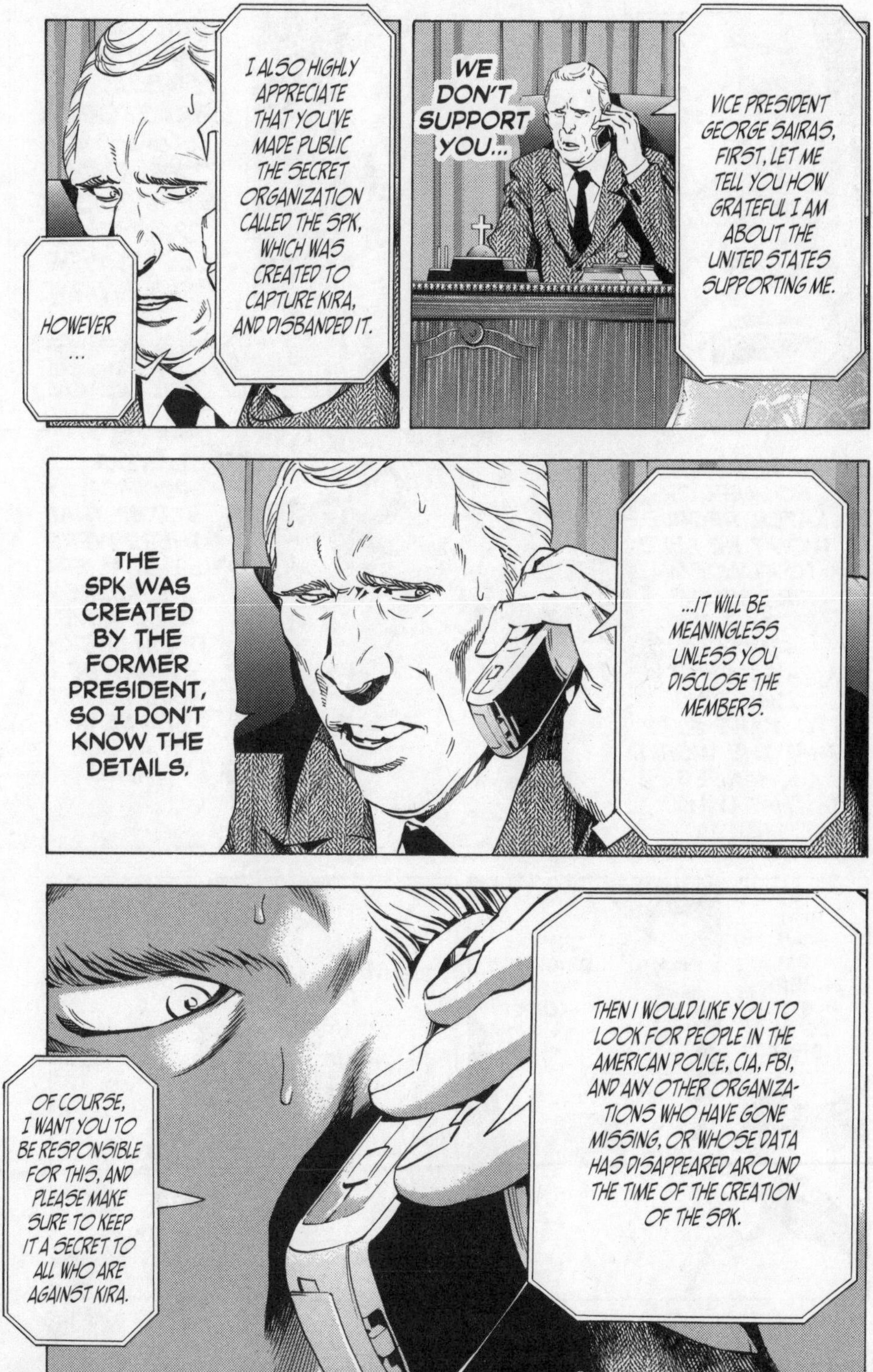
VICE PRESIDENT GEORGE SAIRAS, FIRST, LET ME TELL YOU HOW GRATEFUL I AM ABOUT THE UNITED STATES SUPPORTING ME.
WE DON'T SUPPORT YOU...
I ALSO HIGHLY APPRECIATE THAT YOU'VE MADE PUBLIC THE SECRET ORGANIZATION CALLED THE SPK, WHICH WAS CREATED TO CAPTURE KIRA, AND DISBANDED IT.
HOWEVER ...
...IT WILL BE MEANINGLESS UNLESS YOU DISCLOSE THE MEMBERS.
THE SPK WAS CREATED BY THE FORMER PRESIDENT, SO I DON'T KNOW THE DETAILS.
THEN I WOULD LIKE YOU TO LOOK FOR PEOPLE IN THE AMERICAN POLICE, CIA, FBI, AND ANY OTHER ORGANIZATIONS WHO HAVE GONE MISSING, OR WHOSE DATA HAS DISAPPEARED AROUND THE TIME OF THE CREATION OF THE SPK.
OF COURSE, I WANT YOU TO BE RESPONSIBLE FOR THIS, AND PLEASE MAKE SURE TO KEEP IT A SECRET TO ALL WHO ARE AGAINST KIRA.

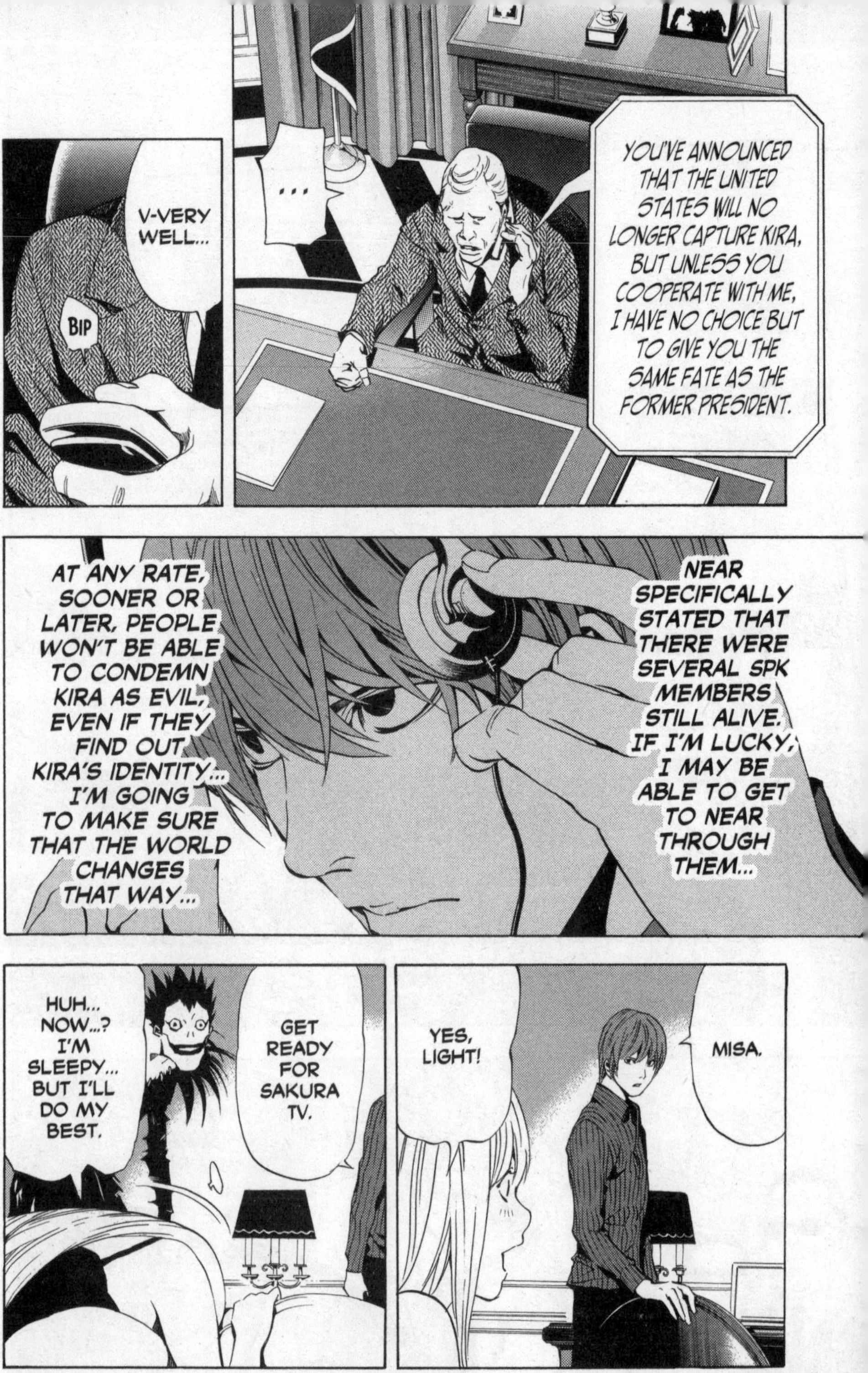
YOU'VE ANNOUNCED THAT THE UNITED STATES WILL NO LONGER CAPTURE KIRA, BUT UNLESS YOU COOPERATE WITH ME, I HAVE NO CHOICE BUT TO GIVE YOU THE SAME FATE AS THE FORMER PRESIDENT.
...
V-VERY WELL...
BIP
NEAR SPECIFICALLY STATED THAT THERE WERE SEVERAL SPK MEMBERS STILL ALIVE. IF I'M LUCKY, I MAY BE ABLE TO GET TO NEAR THROUGH THEM...
AT ANY RATE, SOONER OR LATER, PEOPLE WON'T BE ABLE TO CONDEMN KIRA AS EVIL, EVEN IF THEY FIND OUT KIRA'S IDENTITY... I'M GOING TO MAKE SURE THAT THE WORLD CHANGES THAT WAY...
MISA.
YES, LIGHT!
GET READY FOR SAKURA TV.
HUH... NOW...? I'M SLEEPY... BUT I'LL DO MY BEST.

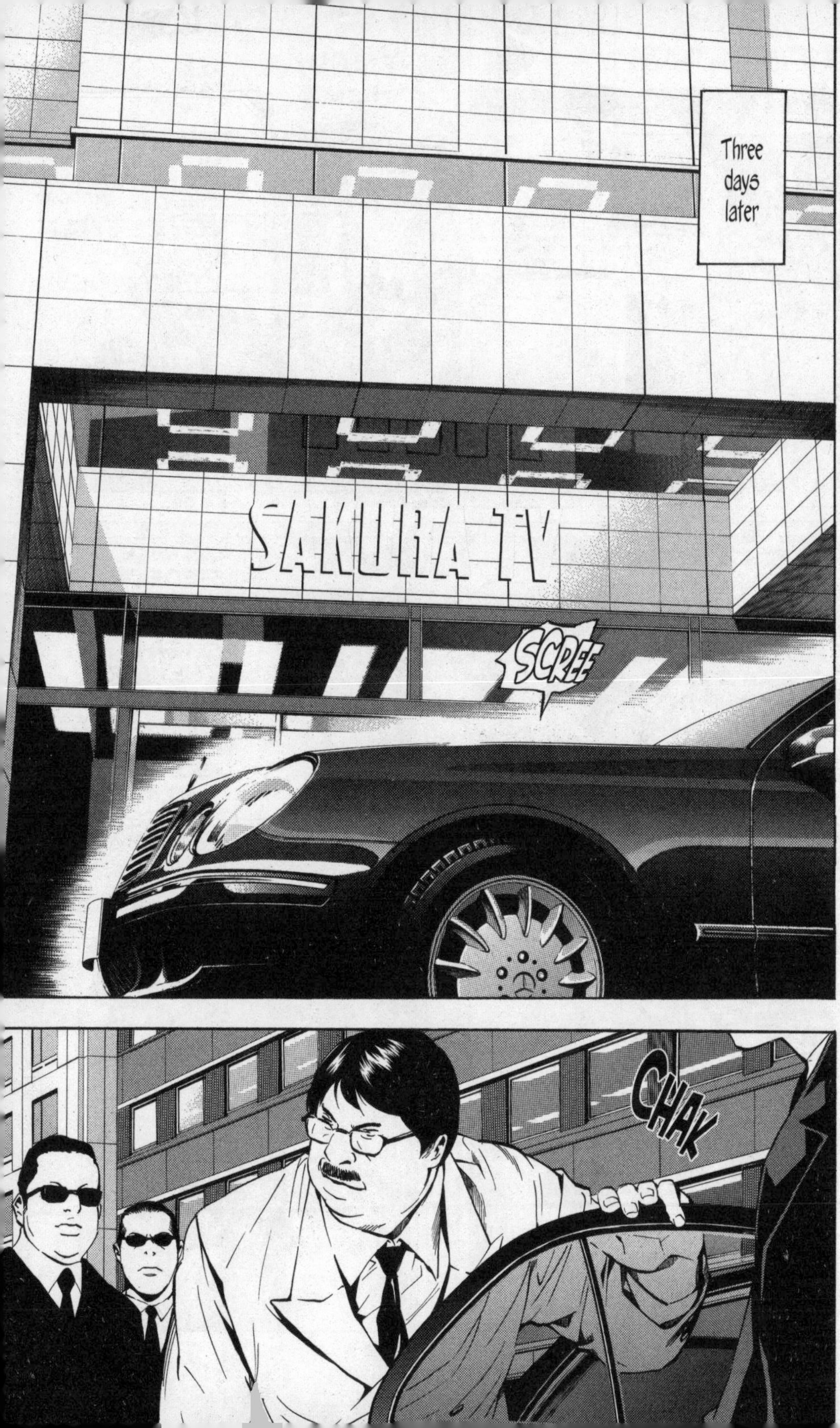
Three days later
SAKURA TV
SCREE
CHAK

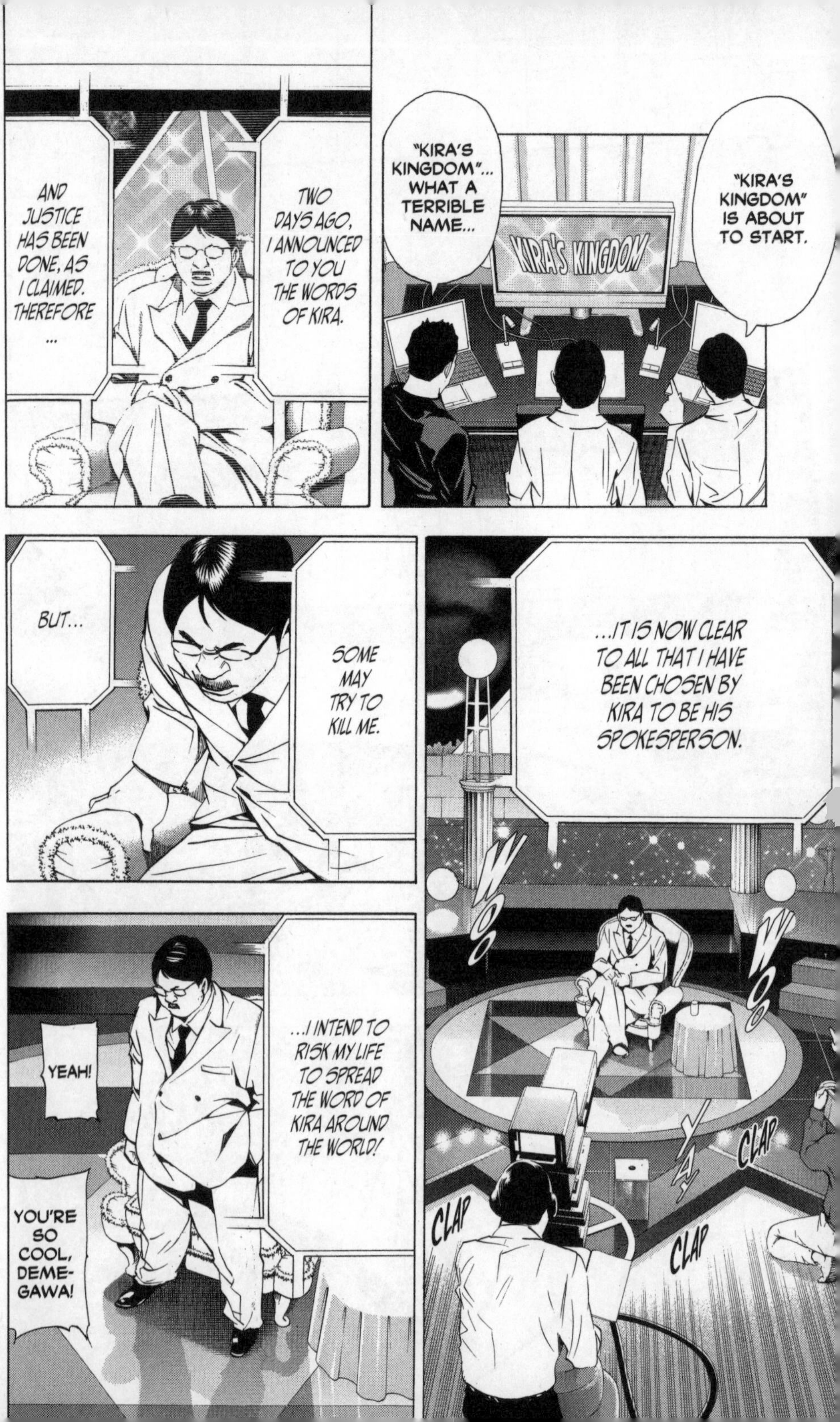
"KIRA'S KINGDOM" IS ABOUT TO START.
"KIRA'S KINGDOM"... WHAT A TERRIBLE NAME...
KIRA'S KINGDOM
TWO DAYS AGO, I ANNOUNCED TO YOU THE WORDS OF KIRA.
AND JUSTICE HAS BEEN DONE, AS I CLAIMED. THEREFORE...
...IT IS NOW CLEAR TO ALL THAT I HAVE BEEN CHOSEN BY KIRA TO BE HIS SPOKESPERSON.
WOO
WOO
YAY
CLAP
CLAP
CLAP
BUT...
SOME MAY TRY TO KILL ME.
...I INTEND TO RISK MY LIFE TO SPREAD THE WORD OF KIRA AROUND THE WORLD!
YEAH!
YOU'RE SO COOL, DEME-GAWA!

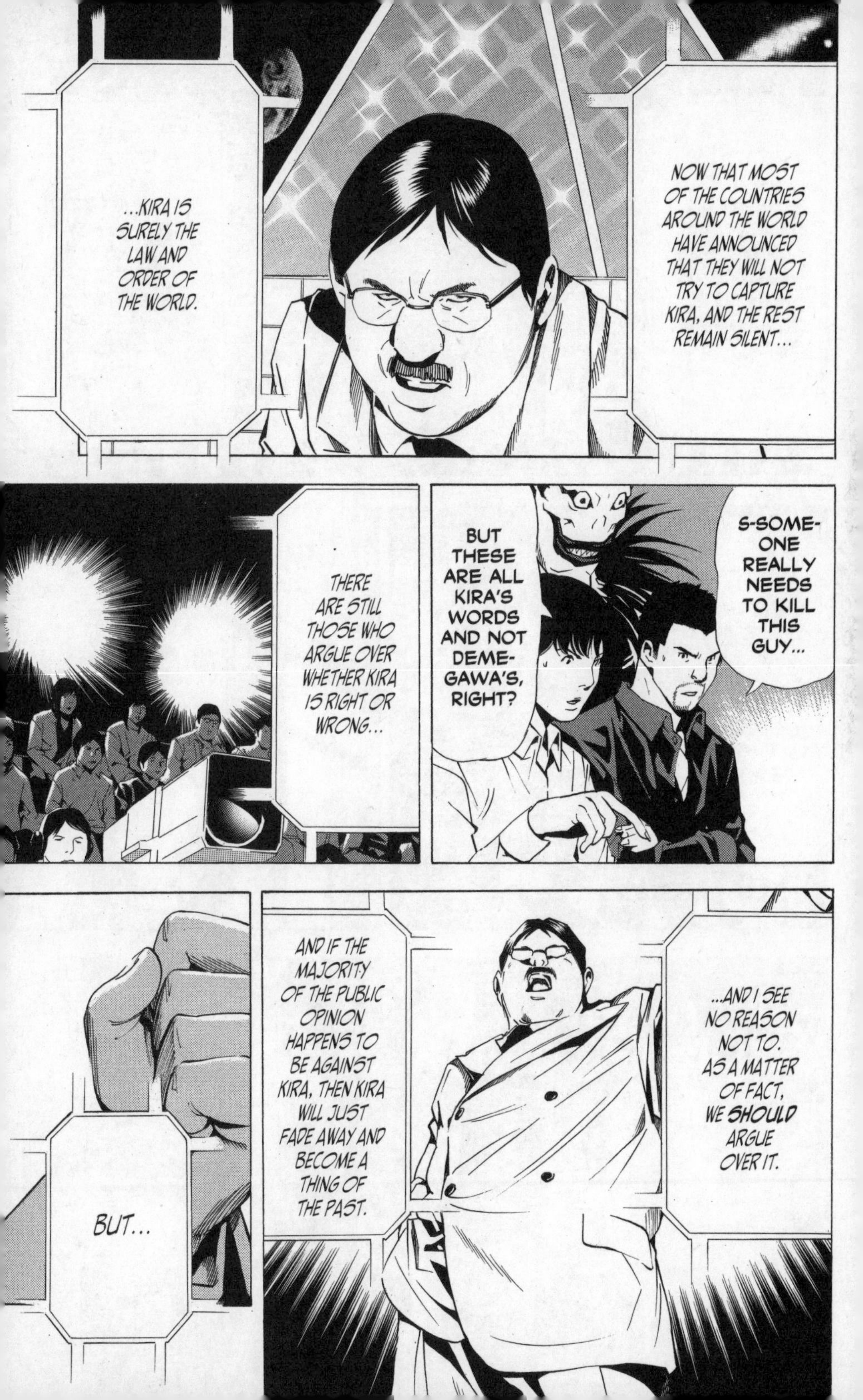
NOW THAT MOST OF THE COUNTRIES AROUND THE WORLD HAVE ANNOUNCED THAT THEY WILL NOT TRY TO CAPTURE KIRA, AND THE REST REMAIN SILENT...
...KIRA IS SURELY THE LAW AND ORDER OF THE WORLD.
S-SOMEONE REALLY NEEDS TO KILL THIS GUY...
BUT THESE ARE ALL KIRA'S WORDS AND NOT DEMEGAWA'S, RIGHT?
THERE ARE STILL THOSE WHO ARGUE OVER WHETHER KIRA IS RIGHT OR WRONG...
...AND I SEE NO REASON NOT TO. AS A MATTER OF FACT, WE **SHOULD** ARGUE OVER IT.
AND IF THE MAJORITY OF THE PUBLIC OPINION HAPPENS TO BE AGAINST KIRA, THEN KIRA WILL JUST FADE AWAY AND BECOME A THING OF THE PAST.
BUT...

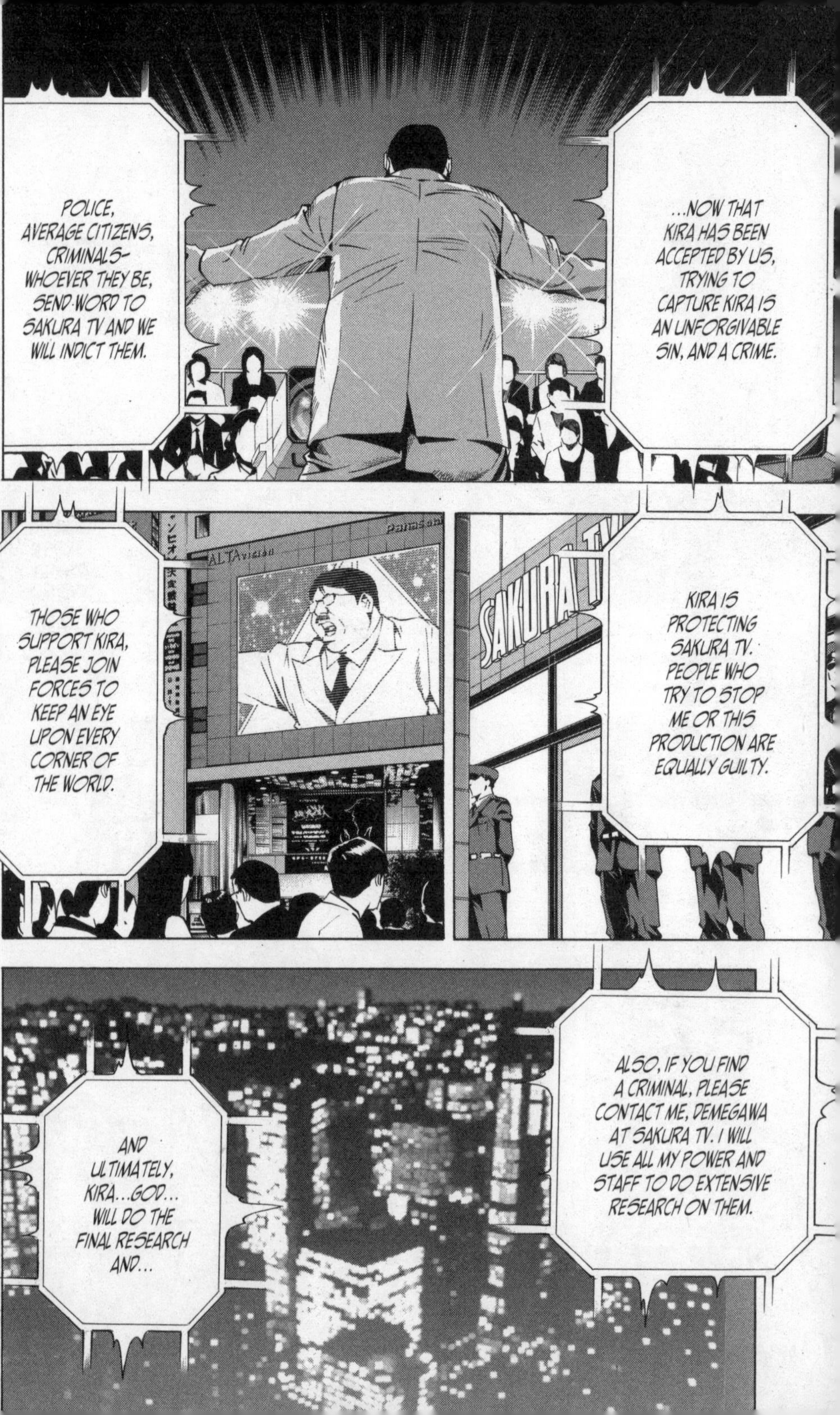
...NOW THAT KIRA HAS BEEN ACCEPTED BY US, TRYING TO CAPTURE KIRA IS AN UNFORGIVABLE SIN, AND A CRIME.
POLICE, AVERAGE CITIZENS, CRIMINALS- WHOEVER THEY BE, SEND WORD TO SAKURA TV AND WE WILL INDICT THEM.
KIRA IS PROTECTING SAKURA TV. PEOPLE WHO TRY TO STOP ME OR THIS PRODUCTION ARE EQUALLY GUILTY.
THOSE WHO SUPPORT KIRA, PLEASE JOIN FORCES TO KEEP AN EYE UPON EVERY CORNER OF THE WORLD.
ALSO, IF YOU FIND A CRIMINAL, PLEASE CONTACT ME, DEMEGAWA AT SAKURA TV. I WILL USE ALL MY POWER AND STAFF TO DO EXTENSIVE RESEARCH ON THEM.
AND ULTIMATELY, KIRA...GOD... WILL DO THE FINAL RESEARCH AND...

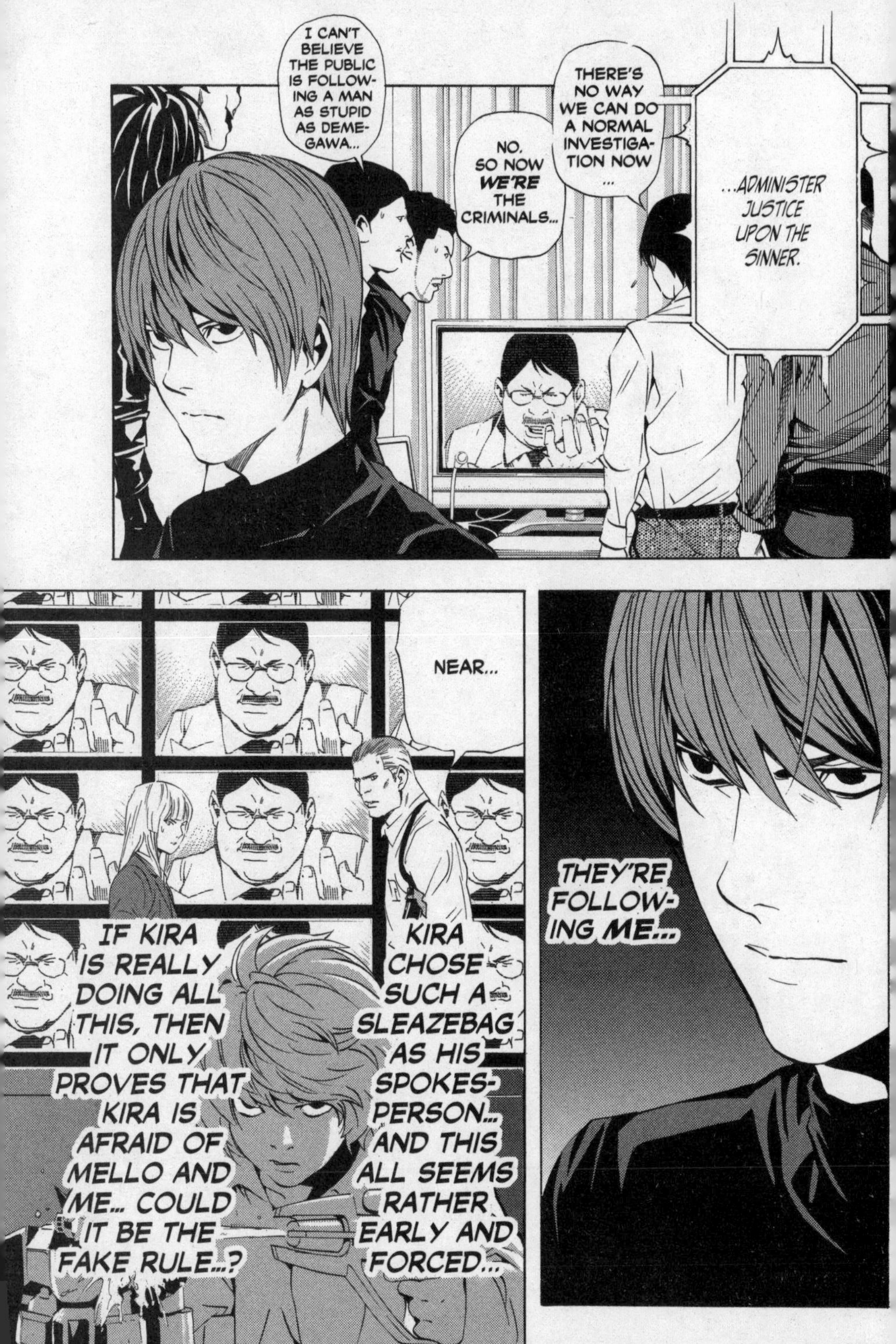
...ADMINISTER JUSTICE UPON THE SINNER.
THERE'S NO WAY WE CAN DO A NORMAL INVESTIGATION NOW ...
NO, SO NOW *WE'RE* THE CRIMINALS...
I CAN'T BELIEVE THE PUBLIC IS FOLLOWING A MAN AS STUPID AS DEMEGAWA...
THEY'RE FOLLOWING *ME*...
NEAR...
KIRA CHOSE SUCH A SLEAZEBAG AS HIS SPOKESPERSON... AND THIS ALL SEEMS RATHER EARLY AND FORCED...
IF KIRA IS REALLY DOING ALL THIS, THEN IT ONLY PROVES THAT KIRA IS AFRAID OF MELLO AND ME... COULD IT BE THE FAKE RULE...?

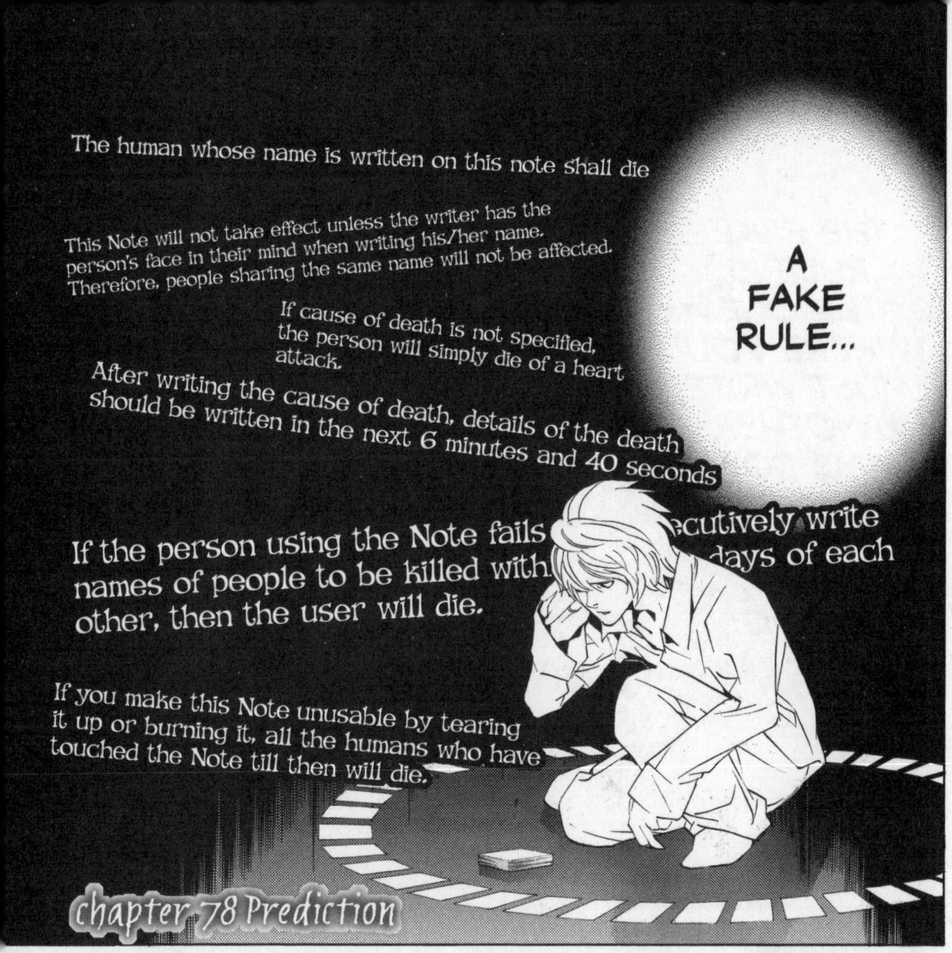
The human whose name is written on this note shall die
This Note will not take effect unless the writer has the person's face in their mind when writing his/her name. Therefore, people sharing the same name will not be affected.
A FAKE RULE...
If cause of death is not specified, the person will simply die of a heart attack.
After writing the cause of death, details of the death should be written in the next 6 minutes and 40 seconds
If the person using the Note fails
ecutively write
days of each
names of people to be killed with
other, then the user will die.
If you make this Note unusable by tearing it up or burning it, all the humans who have touched the Note till then will die.
chapter 78 Prediction

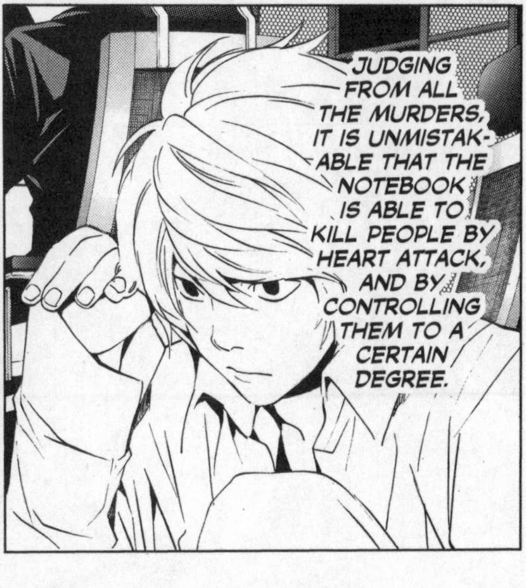
JUDGING FROM ALL THE MURDERS, IT IS UNMISTAKABLE THAT THE NOTEBOOK IS ABLE TO KILL PEOPLE BY HEART ATTACK, AND BY CONTROLLING THEM TO A CERTAIN DEGREE.

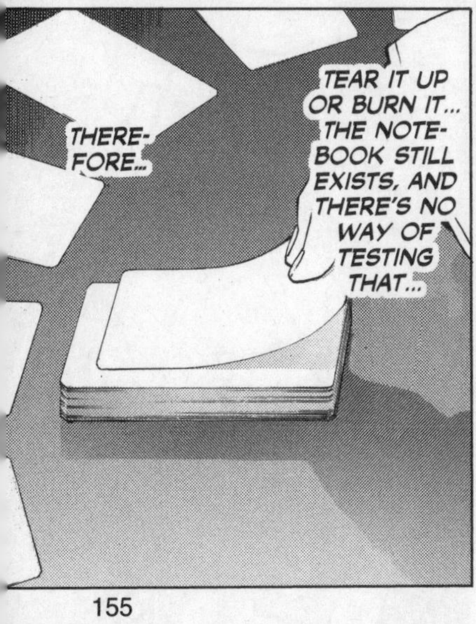
TEAR IT UP OR BURN IT... THE NOTEBOOK STILL EXISTS, AND THERE'S NO WAY OF TESTING THAT...
THEREFORE...

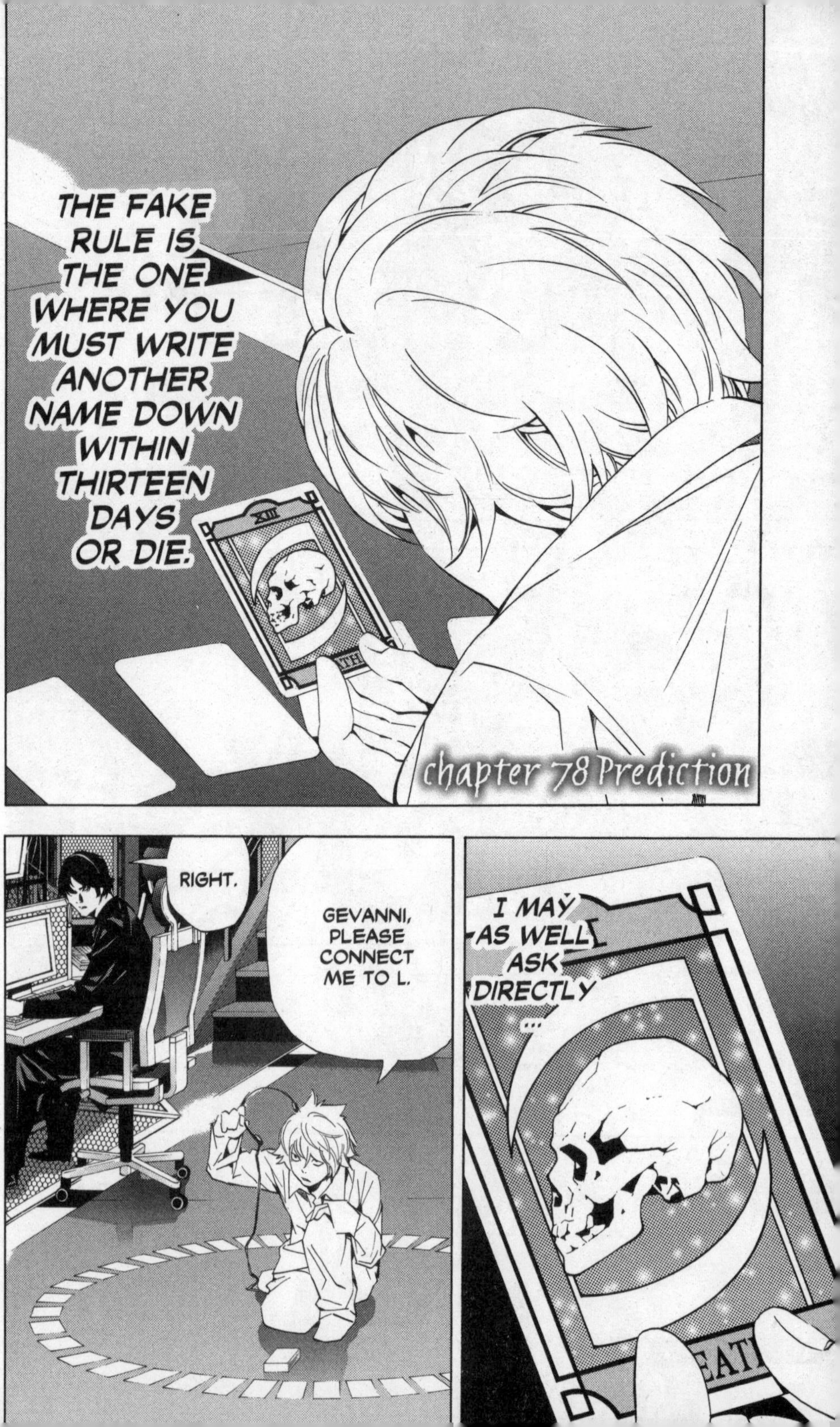
THE FAKE RULE IS THE ONE WHERE YOU MUST WRITE ANOTHER NAME DOWN WITHIN THIRTEEN DAYS OR DIE.
chapter 78 Prediction
I MAY AS WELL ASK DIRECTLY ...
GEVANNI, PLEASE CONNECT ME TO L.
RIGHT.

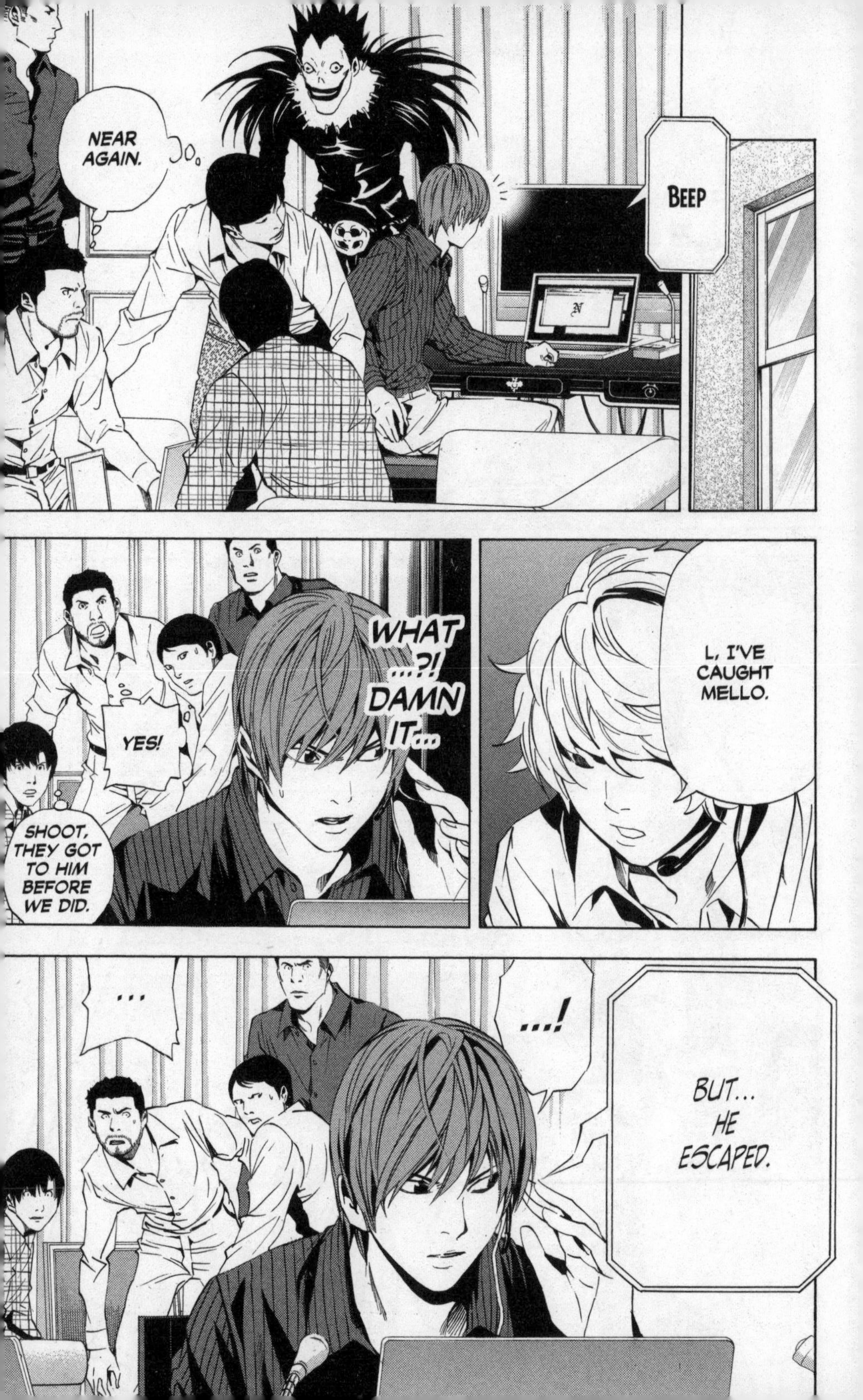
BEEP
NEAR AGAIN.
L, I'VE CAUGHT MELLO.
WHAT ...?! DAMN IT...
YES!
SHOOT, THEY GOT TO HIM BEFORE WE DID.
BUT... HE ESCAPED.
...!
...

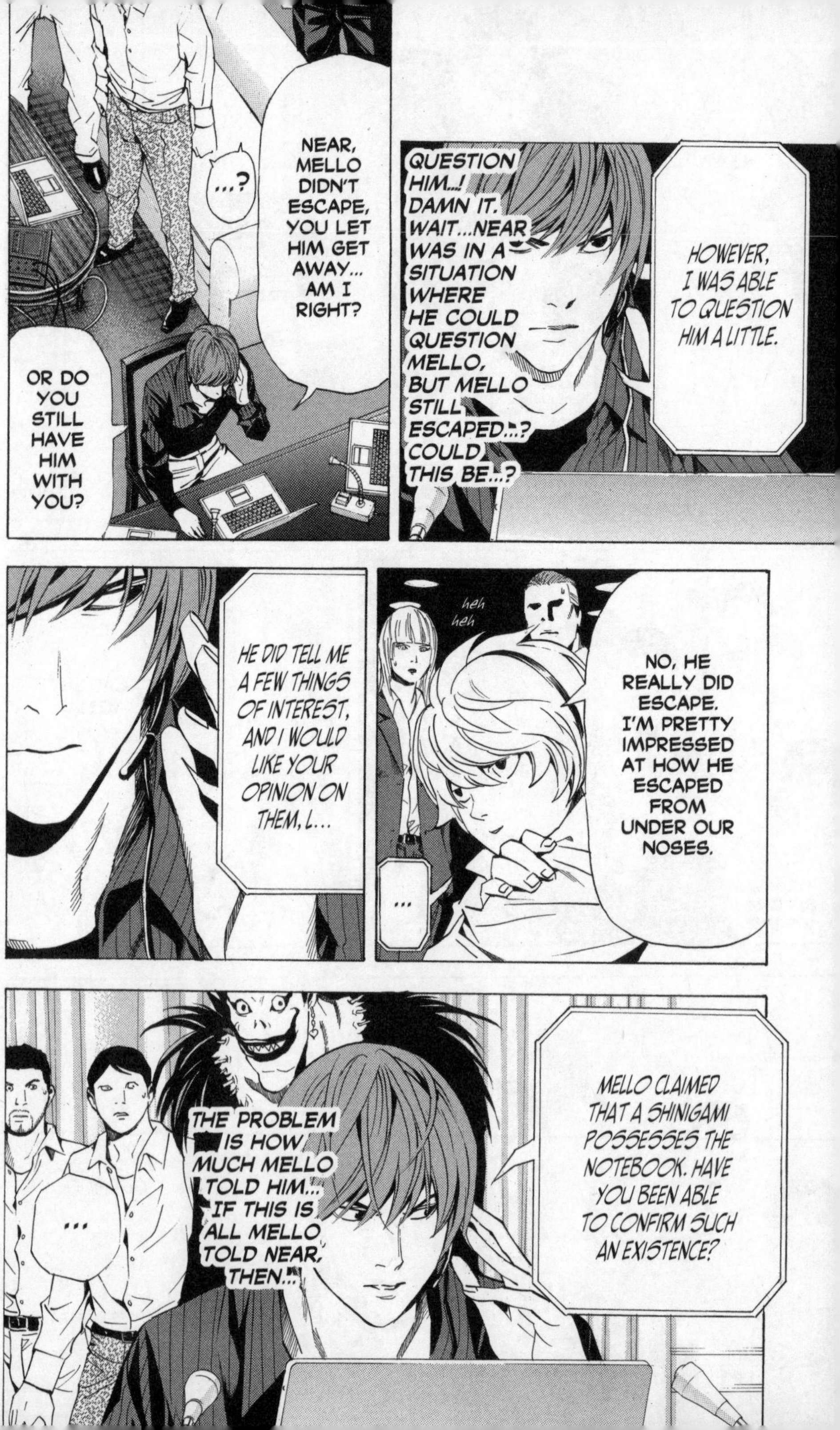
HOWEVER, I WAS ABLE TO QUESTION HIM A LITTLE.
QUESTION HIM...! DAMN IT. WAIT...NEAR WAS IN A SITUATION WHERE HE COULD QUESTION MELLO, BUT MELLO STILL ESCAPED...? COULD THIS BE...?
NEAR, MELLO DIDN'T ESCAPE, YOU LET HIM GET AWAY... AM I RIGHT?
...?
OR DO YOU STILL HAVE HIM WITH YOU?
NO, HE REALLY DID ESCAPE. I'M PRETTY IMPRESSED AT HOW HE ESCAPED FROM UNDER OUR NOSES.
heh heh
...
HE DID TELL ME A FEW THINGS OF INTEREST, AND I WOULD LIKE YOUR OPINION ON THEM, L...
MELLO CLAIMED THAT A SHINIGAMI POSSESSES THE NOTEBOOK. HAVE YOU BEEN ABLE TO CONFIRM SUCH AN EXISTENCE?
THE PROBLEM IS HOW MUCH MELLO TOLD HIM... IF THIS IS ALL MELLO TOLD NEAR, THEN...
...

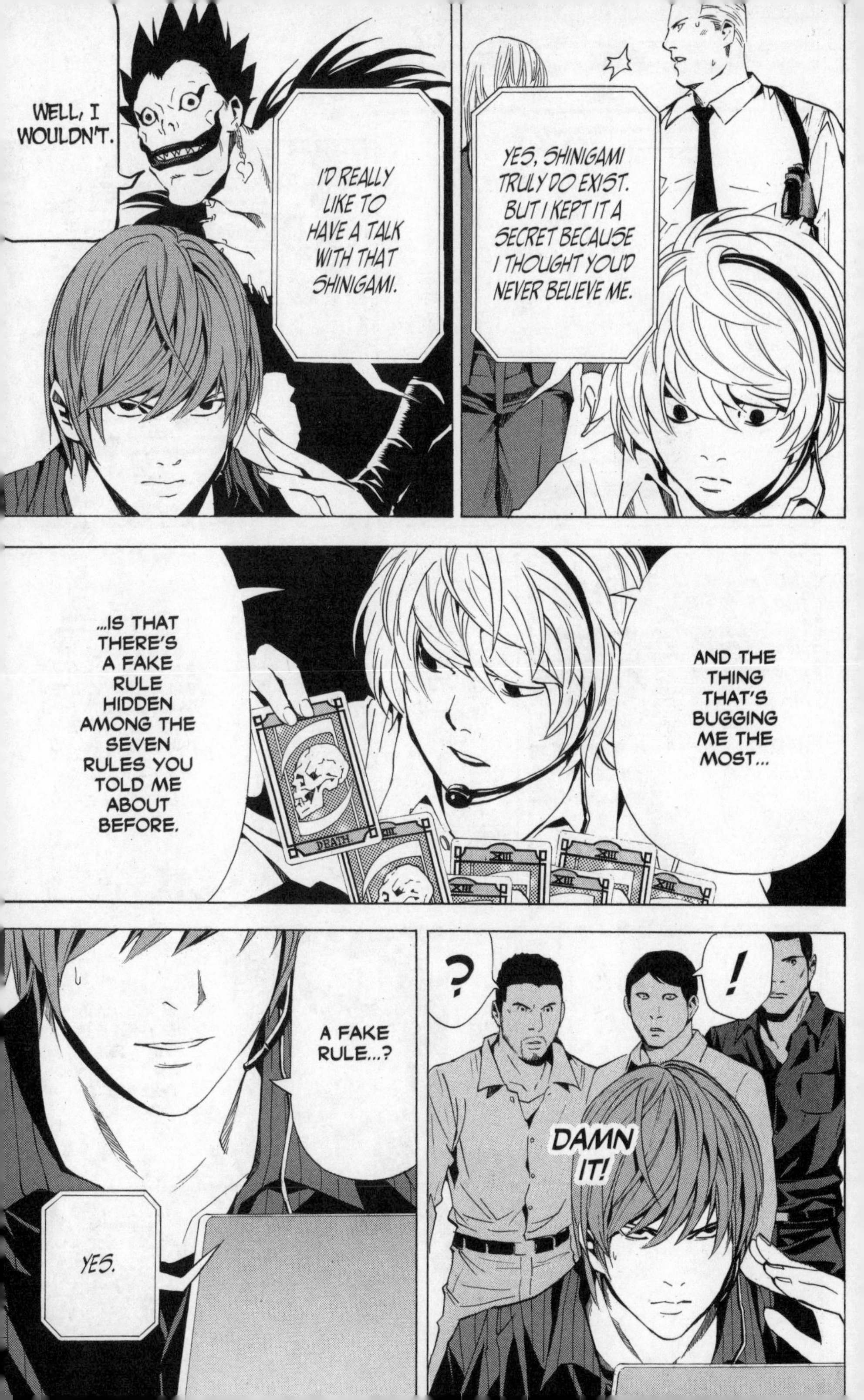
YES, SHINIGAMI TRULY DO EXIST. BUT I KEPT IT A SECRET BECAUSE I THOUGHT YOU'D NEVER BELIEVE ME.
I'D REALLY LIKE TO HAVE A TALK WITH THAT SHINIGAMI.
WELL, I WOULDN'T.
AND THE THING THAT'S BUGGING ME THE MOST...
...IS THAT THERE'S A FAKE RULE HIDDEN AMONG THE SEVEN RULES YOU TOLD ME ABOUT BEFORE.
!
?
DAMN IT!
A FAKE RULE...?
YES.

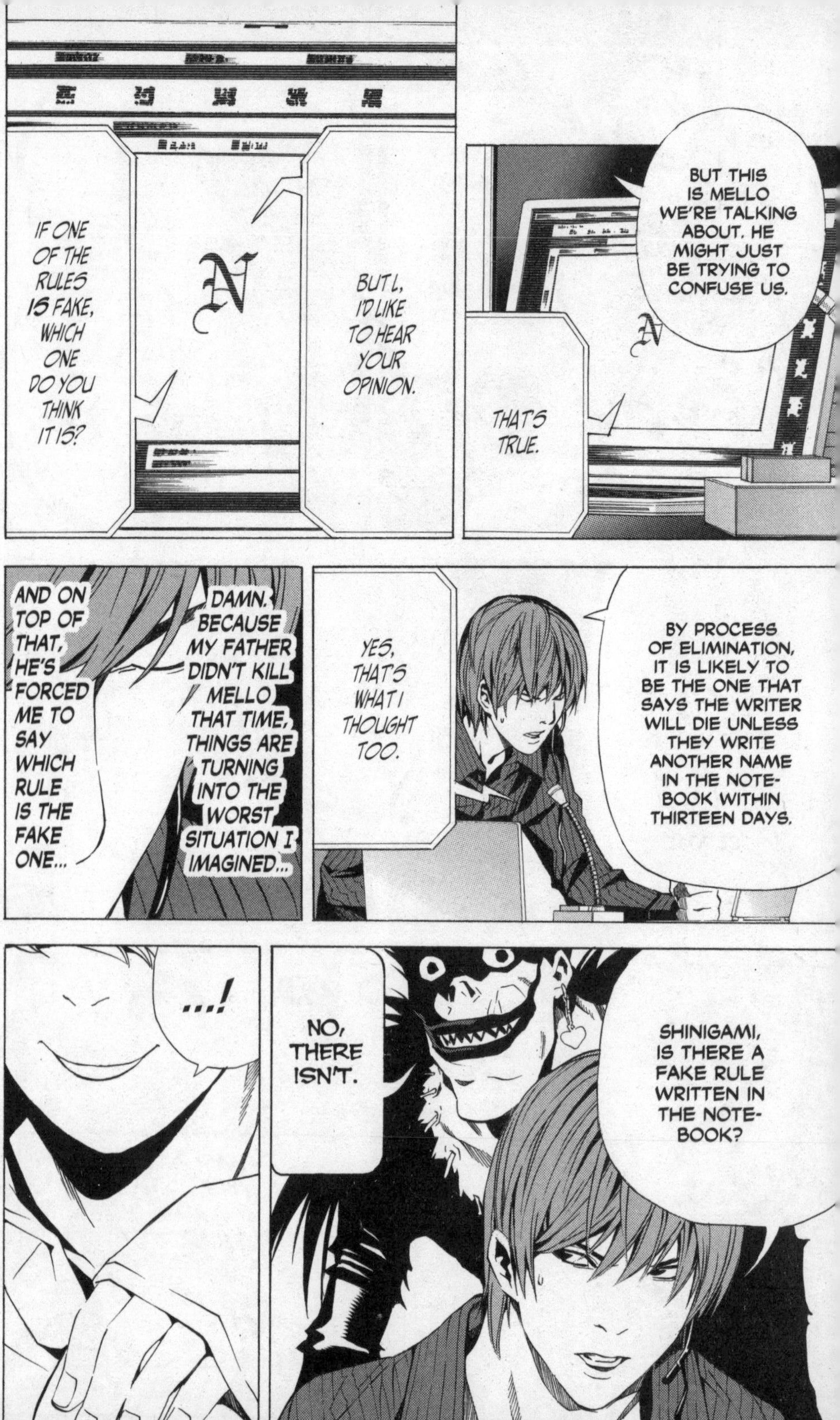

BUT THIS IS MELLO WE'RE TALKING ABOUT. HE MIGHT JUST BE TRYING TO CONFUSE US.
THAT'S TRUE.
BUT L, I'D LIKE TO HEAR YOUR OPINION.
IF ONE OF THE RULES IS FAKE, WHICH ONE DO YOU THINK IT IS?
BY PROCESS OF ELIMINATION, IT IS LIKELY TO BE THE ONE THAT SAYS THE WRITER WILL DIE UNLESS THEY WRITE ANOTHER NAME IN THE NOTE-BOOK WITHIN THIRTEEN DAYS.
YES, THAT'S WHAT I THOUGHT TOO.
DAMN. BECAUSE MY FATHER DIDN'T KILL MELLO THAT TIME, THINGS ARE TURNING INTO THE WORST SITUATION I IMAGINED...
AND ON TOP OF THAT, HE'S FORCED ME TO SAY WHICH RULE IS THE FAKE ONE...
SHINIGAMI, IS THERE A FAKE RULE WRITTEN IN THE NOTE-BOOK?
NO, THERE ISN'T.
...!

READ THIS WAY

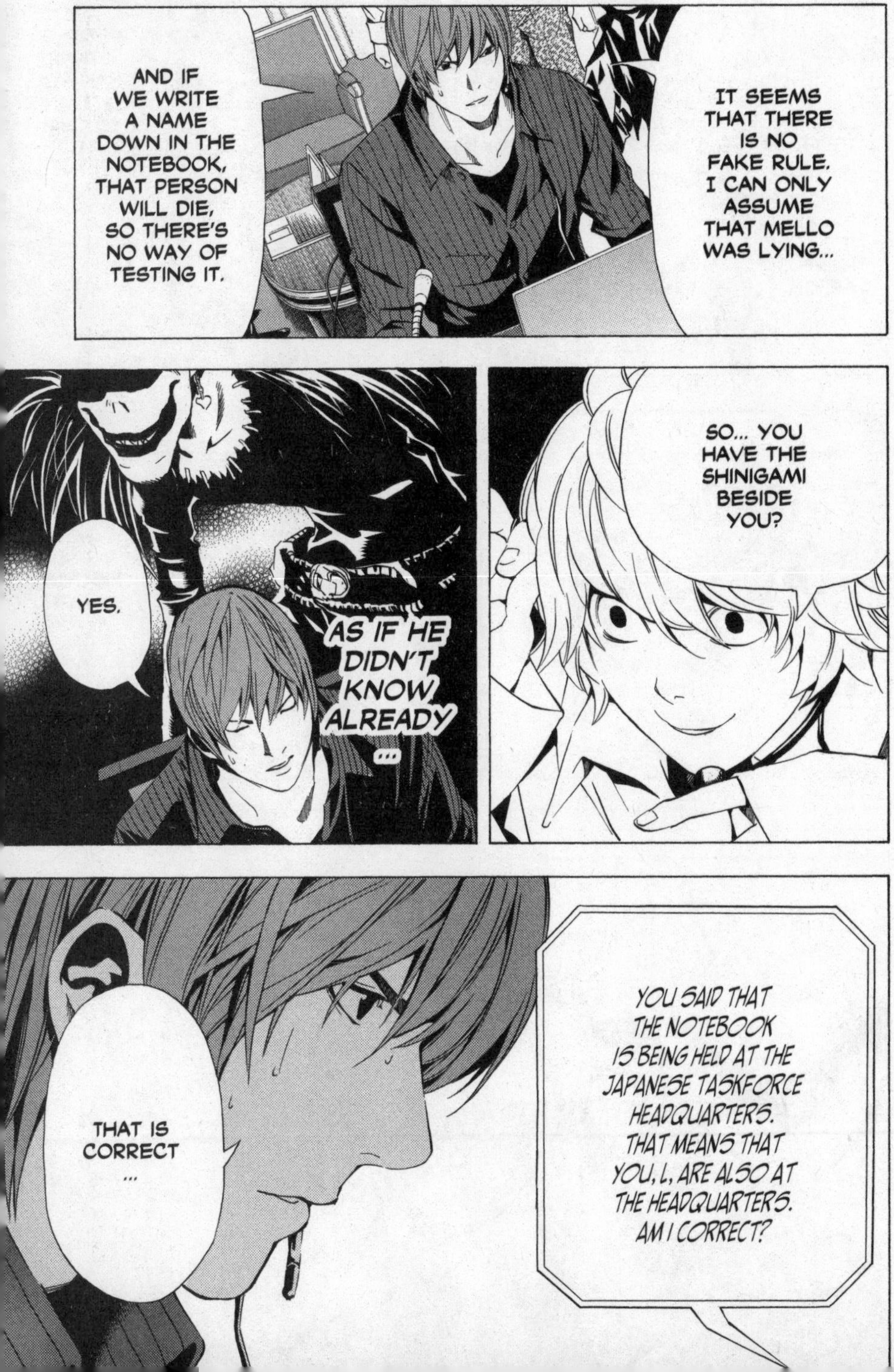
IT SEEMS THAT THERE IS NO FAKE RULE. I CAN ONLY ASSUME THAT MELLO WAS LYING...
AND IF WE WRITE A NAME DOWN IN THE NOTEBOOK, THAT PERSON WILL DIE, SO THERE'S NO WAY OF TESTING IT.
SO... YOU HAVE THE SHINIGAMI BESIDE YOU?
YES.
AS IF HE DIDN'T KNOW ALREADY ...
YOU SAID THAT THE NOTEBOOK IS BEING HELD AT THE JAPANESE TASKFORCE HEADQUARTERS. THAT MEANS THAT YOU, L, ARE ALSO AT THE HEADQUARTERS. AM I CORRECT?
THAT IS CORRECT ...

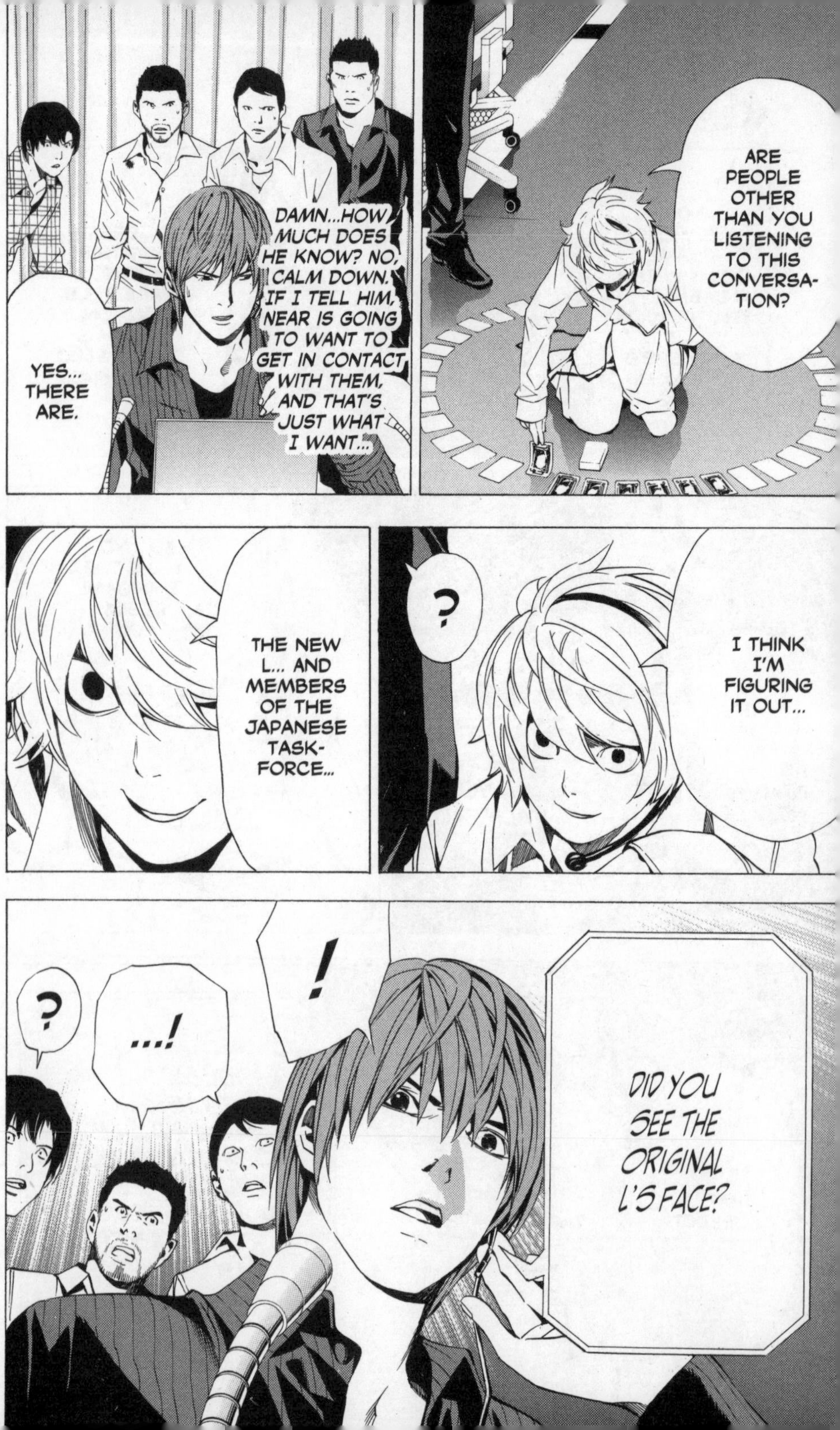
ARE PEOPLE OTHER THAN YOU LISTENING TO THIS CONVERSATION?
DAMN...HOW MUCH DOES HE KNOW? NO, CALM DOWN. IF I TELL HIM, NEAR IS GOING TO WANT TO GET IN CONTACT WITH THEM, AND THAT'S JUST WHAT I WANT...
YES... THERE ARE.
I THINK I'M FIGURING IT OUT...
?
THE NEW L... AND MEMBERS OF THE JAPANESE TASK-FORCE...
DID YOU SEE THE ORIGINAL L'S FACE?
!
...!
?

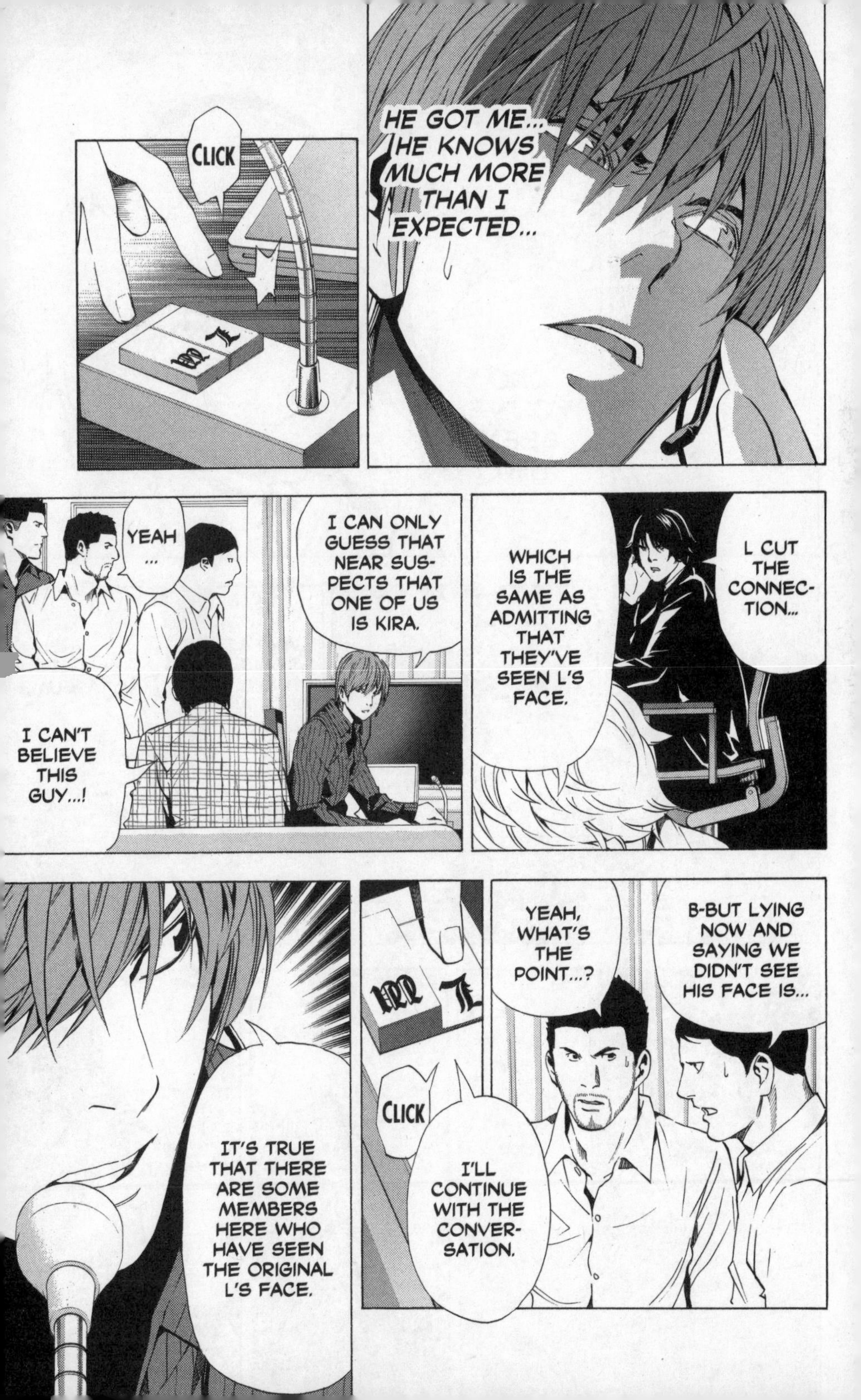
HE GOT ME... HE KNOWS MUCH MORE THAN I EXPECTED...
CLICK
L CUT THE CONNECTION...
WHICH IS THE SAME AS ADMITTING THAT THEY'VE SEEN L'S FACE.
I CAN ONLY GUESS THAT NEAR SUSPECTS THAT ONE OF US IS KIRA.
YEAH ...
I CAN'T BELIEVE THIS GUY...!
B-BUT LYING NOW AND SAYING WE DIDN'T SEE HIS FACE IS...
YEAH, WHAT'S THE POINT...?
CLICK
I'LL CONTINUE WITH THE CONVERSATION.
IT'S TRUE THAT THERE ARE SOME MEMBERS HERE WHO HAVE SEEN THE ORIGINAL L'S FACE.

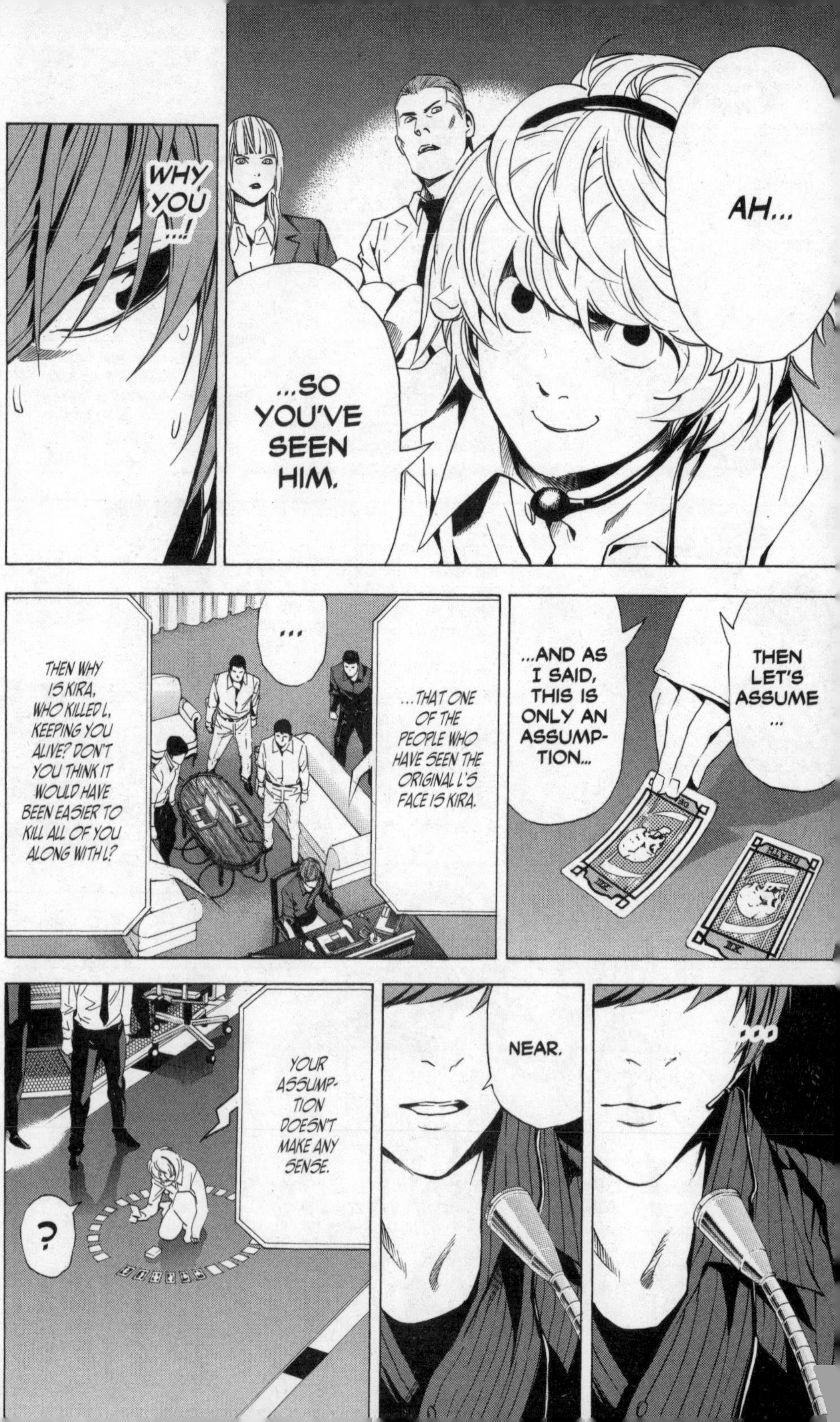
AH...
...SO YOU'VE SEEN HIM.
WHY YOU ...!
THEN LET'S ASSUME ...
...AND AS I SAID, THIS IS ONLY AN ASSUMPTION...
...
...THAT ONE OF THE PEOPLE WHO HAVE SEEN THE ORIGINAL L'S FACE IS KIRA.
THEN WHY IS KIRA, WHO KILLED L, KEEPING YOU ALIVE? DON'T YOU THINK IT WOULD HAVE BEEN EASIER TO KILL ALL OF YOU ALONG WITH L?
...
NEAR.
YOUR ASSUMPTION DOESN'T MAKE ANY SENSE.
?

READ THIS WAY

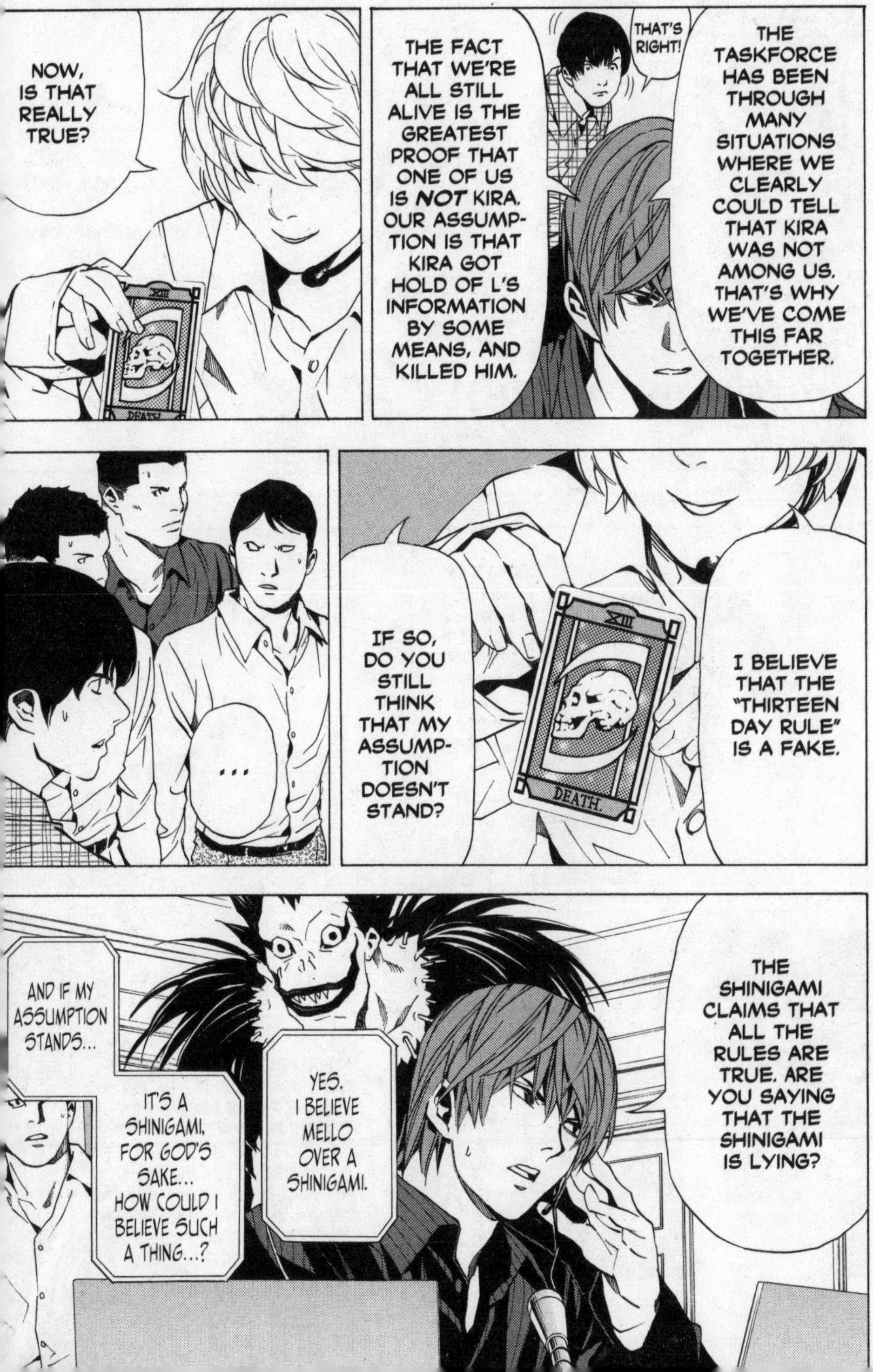
THE TASKFORCE HAS BEEN THROUGH MANY SITUATIONS WHERE WE CLEARLY COULD TELL THAT KIRA WAS NOT AMONG US. THAT'S WHY WE'VE COME THIS FAR TOGETHER.
THAT'S RIGHT!
THE FACT THAT WE'RE ALL STILL ALIVE IS THE GREATEST PROOF THAT ONE OF US IS *NOT* KIRA. OUR ASSUMPTION IS THAT KIRA GOT HOLD OF L'S INFORMATION BY SOME MEANS, AND KILLED HIM.
NOW, IS THAT REALLY TRUE?
I BELIEVE THAT THE "THIRTEEN DAY RULE" IS A FAKE.
IF SO, DO YOU STILL THINK THAT MY ASSUMPTION DOESN'T STAND?
...
THE SHINIGAMI CLAIMS THAT ALL THE RULES ARE TRUE. ARE YOU SAYING THAT THE SHINIGAMI IS LYING?
AND IF MY ASSUMPTION STANDS...
YES. I BELIEVE MELLO OVER A SHINIGAMI.
IT'S A SHINIGAMI, FOR GOD'S SAKE... HOW COULD I BELIEVE SUCH A THING...?

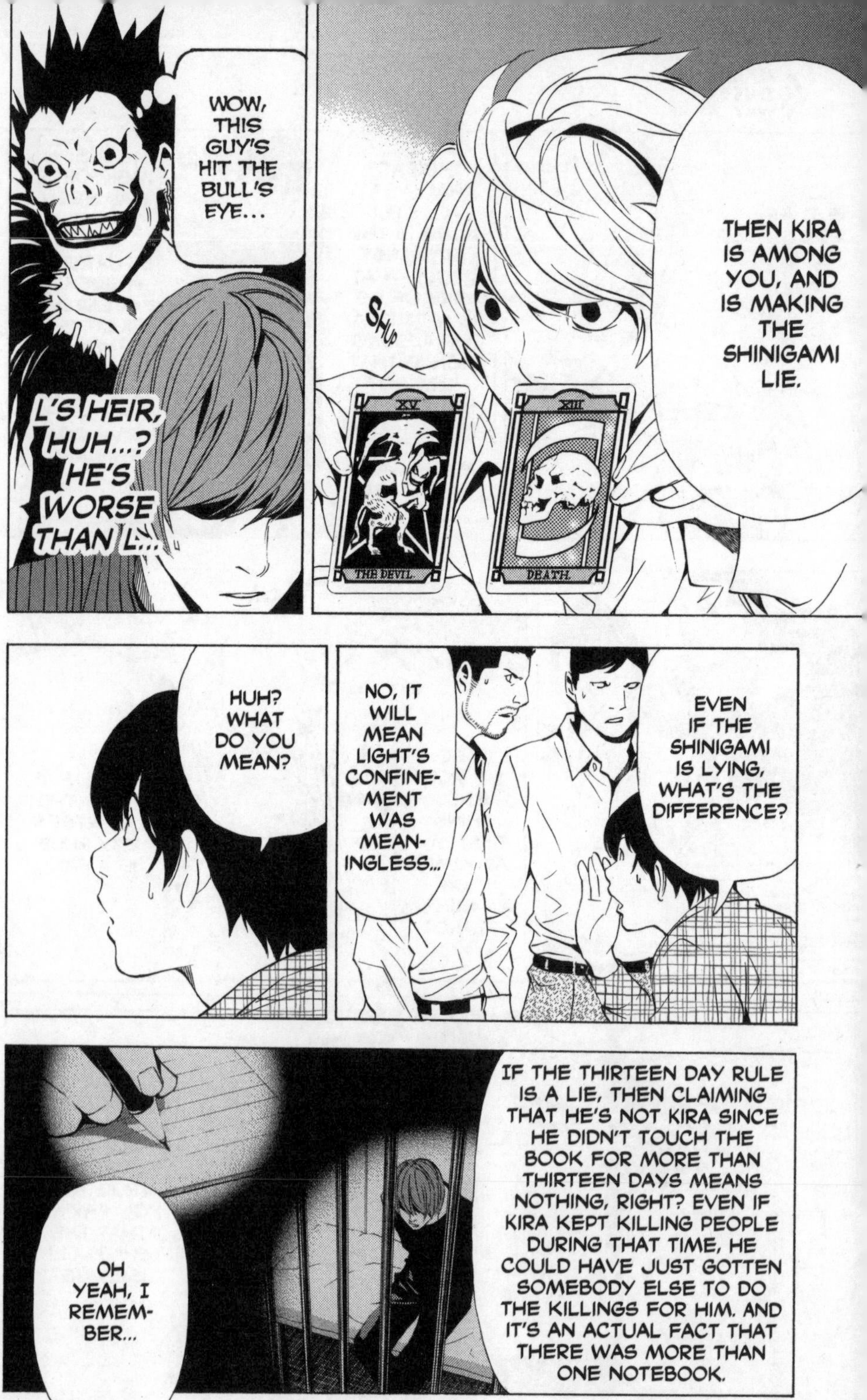
THEN KIRA IS AMONG YOU, AND IS MAKING THE SHINIGAMI LIE.
SHUP
XV
THE DEVIL
XIII
DEATH
WOW, THIS GUY'S HIT THE BULL'S EYE...
L'S HEIR, HUH...? HE'S WORSE THAN L...
EVEN IF THE SHINIGAMI IS LYING, WHAT'S THE DIFFERENCE?
NO, IT WILL MEAN LIGHT'S CONFINEMENT WAS MEANINGLESS...
HUH? WHAT DO YOU MEAN?
IF THE THIRTEEN DAY RULE IS A LIE, THEN CLAIMING THAT HE'S NOT KIRA SINCE HE DIDN'T TOUCH THE BOOK FOR MORE THAN THIRTEEN DAYS MEANS NOTHING, RIGHT? EVEN IF KIRA KEPT KILLING PEOPLE DURING THAT TIME, HE COULD HAVE JUST GOTTEN SOMEBODY ELSE TO DO THE KILLINGS FOR HIM. AND IT'S AN ACTUAL FACT THAT THERE WAS MORE THAN ONE NOTEBOOK.
OH YEAH, I REMEMBER...

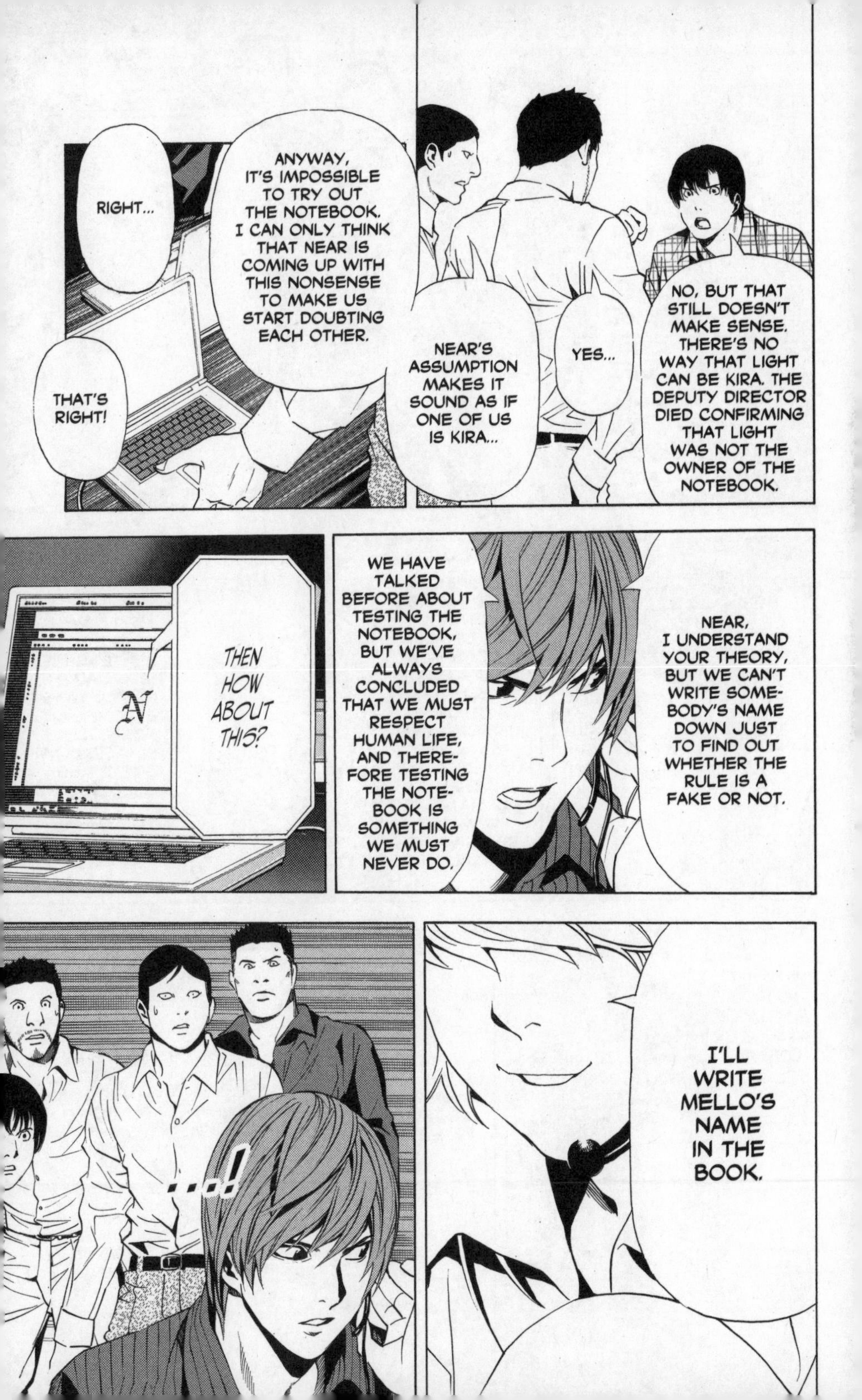
NO, BUT THAT STILL DOESN'T MAKE SENSE. THERE'S NO WAY THAT LIGHT CAN BE KIRA. THE DEPUTY DIRECTOR DIED CONFIRMING THAT LIGHT WAS NOT THE OWNER OF THE NOTEBOOK.
YES...
NEAR'S ASSUMPTION MAKES IT SOUND AS IF ONE OF US IS KIRA...
ANYWAY, IT'S IMPOSSIBLE TO TRY OUT THE NOTEBOOK. I CAN ONLY THINK THAT NEAR IS COMING UP WITH THIS NONSENSE TO MAKE US START DOUBTING EACH OTHER.
RIGHT...
THAT'S RIGHT!
NEAR, I UNDERSTAND YOUR THEORY, BUT WE CAN'T WRITE SOME-BODY'S NAME DOWN JUST TO FIND OUT WHETHER THE RULE IS A FAKE OR NOT.
WE HAVE TALKED BEFORE ABOUT TESTING THE NOTEBOOK, BUT WE'VE ALWAYS CONCLUDED THAT WE MUST RESPECT HUMAN LIFE, AND THERE-FORE TESTING THE NOTE-BOOK IS SOMETHING WE MUST NEVER DO.
N
THEN HOW ABOUT THIS?
I'LL WRITE MELLO'S NAME IN THE BOOK.
...!

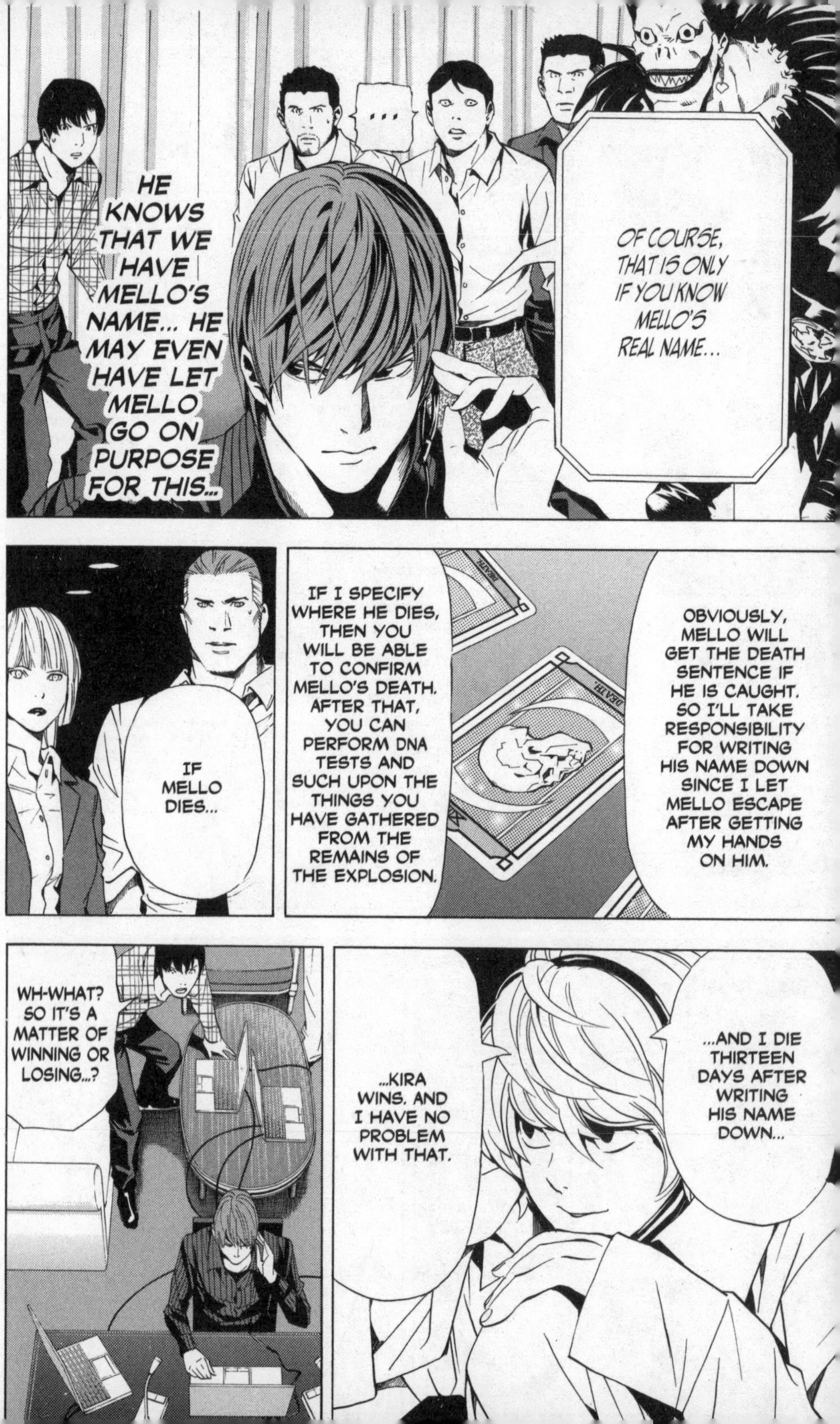
OF COURSE, THAT IS ONLY IF YOU KNOW MELLO'S REAL NAME...
....
HE KNOWS THAT WE HAVE MELLO'S NAME... HE MAY EVEN HAVE LET MELLO GO ON PURPOSE FOR THIS...
OBVIOUSLY, MELLO WILL GET THE DEATH SENTENCE IF HE IS CAUGHT. SO I'LL TAKE RESPONSIBILITY FOR WRITING HIS NAME DOWN SINCE I LET MELLO ESCAPE AFTER GETTING MY HANDS ON HIM.
IF I SPECIFY WHERE HE DIES, THEN YOU WILL BE ABLE TO CONFIRM MELLO'S DEATH. AFTER THAT, YOU CAN PERFORM DNA TESTS AND SUCH UPON THE THINGS YOU HAVE GATHERED FROM THE REMAINS OF THE EXPLOSION.
IF MELLO DIES...
...AND I DIE THIRTEEN DAYS AFTER WRITING HIS NAME DOWN...
...KIRA WINS. AND I HAVE NO PROBLEM WITH THAT.
WH-WHAT? SO IT'S A MATTER OF WINNING OR LOSING...?

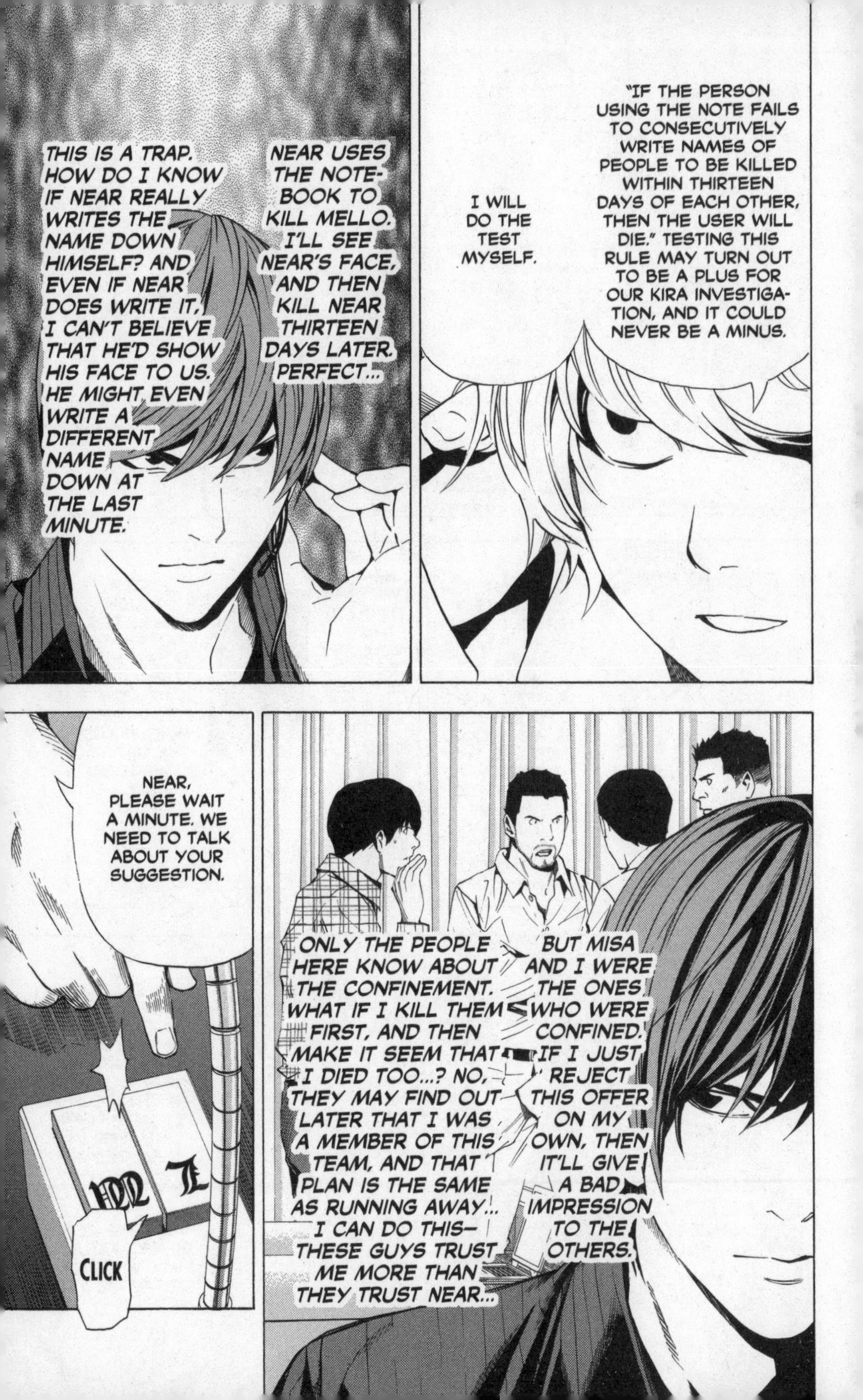
"IF THE PERSON USING THE NOTE FAILS TO CONSECUTIVELY WRITE NAMES OF PEOPLE TO BE KILLED WITHIN THIRTEEN DAYS OF EACH OTHER, THEN THE USER WILL DIE." TESTING THIS RULE MAY TURN OUT TO BE A PLUS FOR OUR KIRA INVESTIGATION, AND IT COULD NEVER BE A MINUS.
I WILL DO THE TEST MYSELF.
NEAR USES THE NOTEBOOK TO KILL MELLO. I'LL SEE NEAR'S FACE, AND THEN KILL NEAR THIRTEEN DAYS LATER. PERFECT...
THIS IS A TRAP. HOW DO I KNOW IF NEAR REALLY WRITES THE NAME DOWN HIMSELF? AND EVEN IF NEAR DOES WRITE IT, I CAN'T BELIEVE THAT HE'D SHOW HIS FACE TO US. HE MIGHT EVEN WRITE A DIFFERENT NAME DOWN AT THE LAST MINUTE.
BUT MISA AND I WERE THE ONES WHO WERE CONFINED. IF I JUST REJECT THIS OFFER ON MY OWN, THEN IT'LL GIVE A BAD IMPRESSION TO THE OTHERS.
ONLY THE PEOPLE HERE KNOW ABOUT THE CONFINEMENT. WHAT IF I KILL THEM FIRST, AND THEN MAKE IT SEEM THAT I DIED TOO...? NO, THEY MAY FIND OUT LATER THAT I WAS A MEMBER OF THIS TEAM, AND THAT PLAN IS THE SAME AS RUNNING AWAY... I CAN DO THIS— THESE GUYS TRUST ME MORE THAN THEY TRUST NEAR...
NEAR, PLEASE WAIT A MINUTE. WE NEED TO TALK ABOUT YOUR SUGGESTION.
CLICK

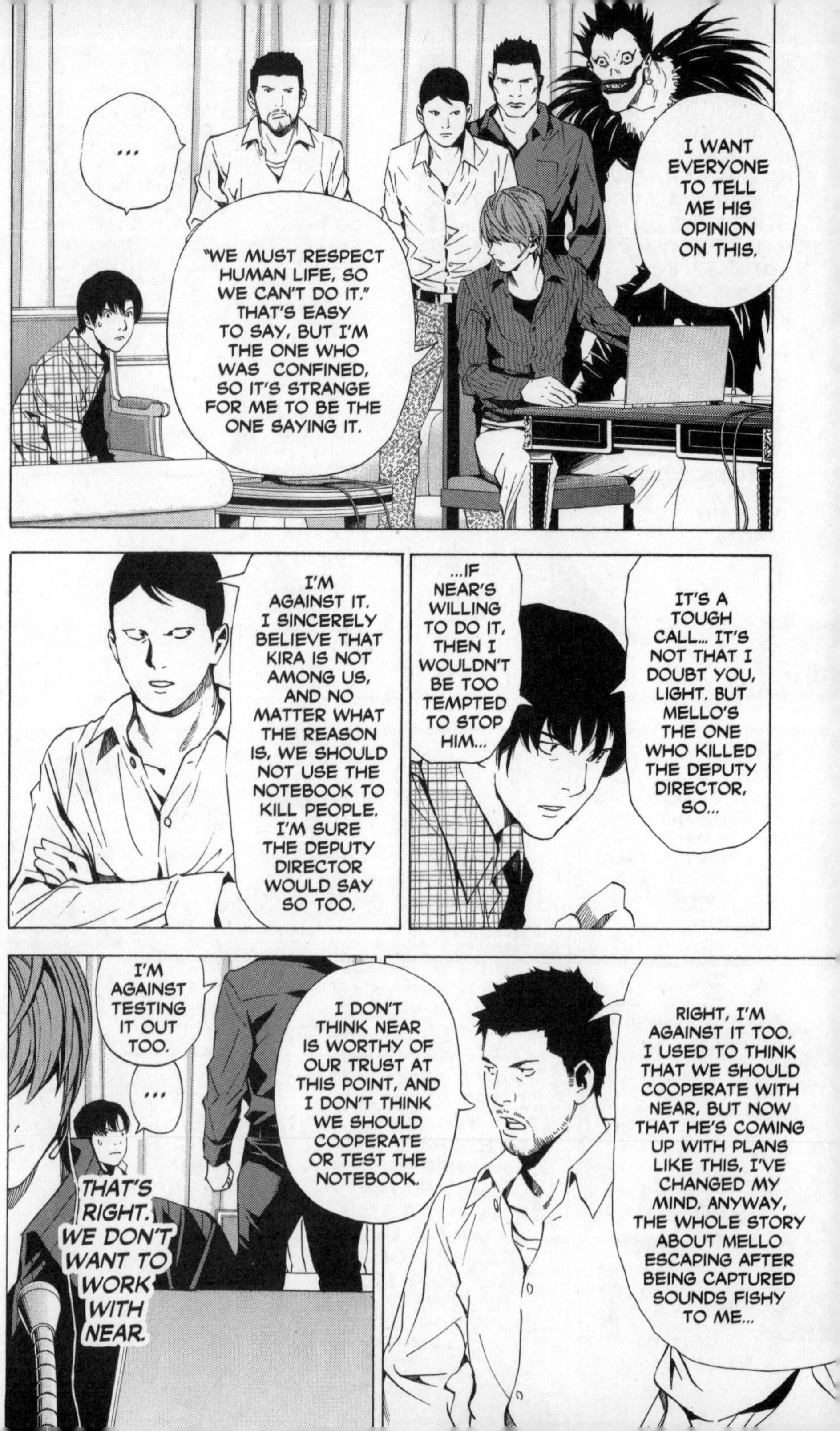
I WANT EVERYONE TO TELL ME HIS OPINION ON THIS.
...
"WE MUST RESPECT HUMAN LIFE, SO WE CAN'T DO IT." THAT'S EASY TO SAY, BUT I'M THE ONE WHO WAS CONFINED, SO IT'S STRANGE FOR ME TO BE THE ONE SAYING IT.
IT'S A TOUGH CALL... IT'S NOT THAT I DOUBT YOU, LIGHT. BUT MELLO'S THE ONE WHO KILLED THE DEPUTY DIRECTOR, SO...
...IF NEAR'S WILLING TO DO IT, THEN I WOULDN'T BE TOO TEMPTED TO STOP HIM...
I'M AGAINST IT. I SINCERELY BELIEVE THAT KIRA IS NOT AMONG US, AND NO MATTER WHAT THE REASON IS, WE SHOULD NOT USE THE NOTEBOOK TO KILL PEOPLE. I'M SURE THE DEPUTY DIRECTOR WOULD SAY SO TOO.
RIGHT, I'M AGAINST IT TOO. I USED TO THINK THAT WE SHOULD COOPERATE WITH NEAR, BUT NOW THAT HE'S COMING UP WITH PLANS LIKE THIS, I'VE CHANGED MY MIND. ANYWAY, THE WHOLE STORY ABOUT MELLO ESCAPING AFTER BEING CAPTURED SOUNDS FISHY TO ME...
I DON'T THINK NEAR IS WORTHY OF OUR TRUST AT THIS POINT, AND I DON'T THINK WE SHOULD COOPERATE OR TEST THE NOTEBOOK.
I'M AGAINST TESTING IT OUT TOO.
...
THAT'S RIGHT. WE DON'T WANT TO WORK WITH NEAR.

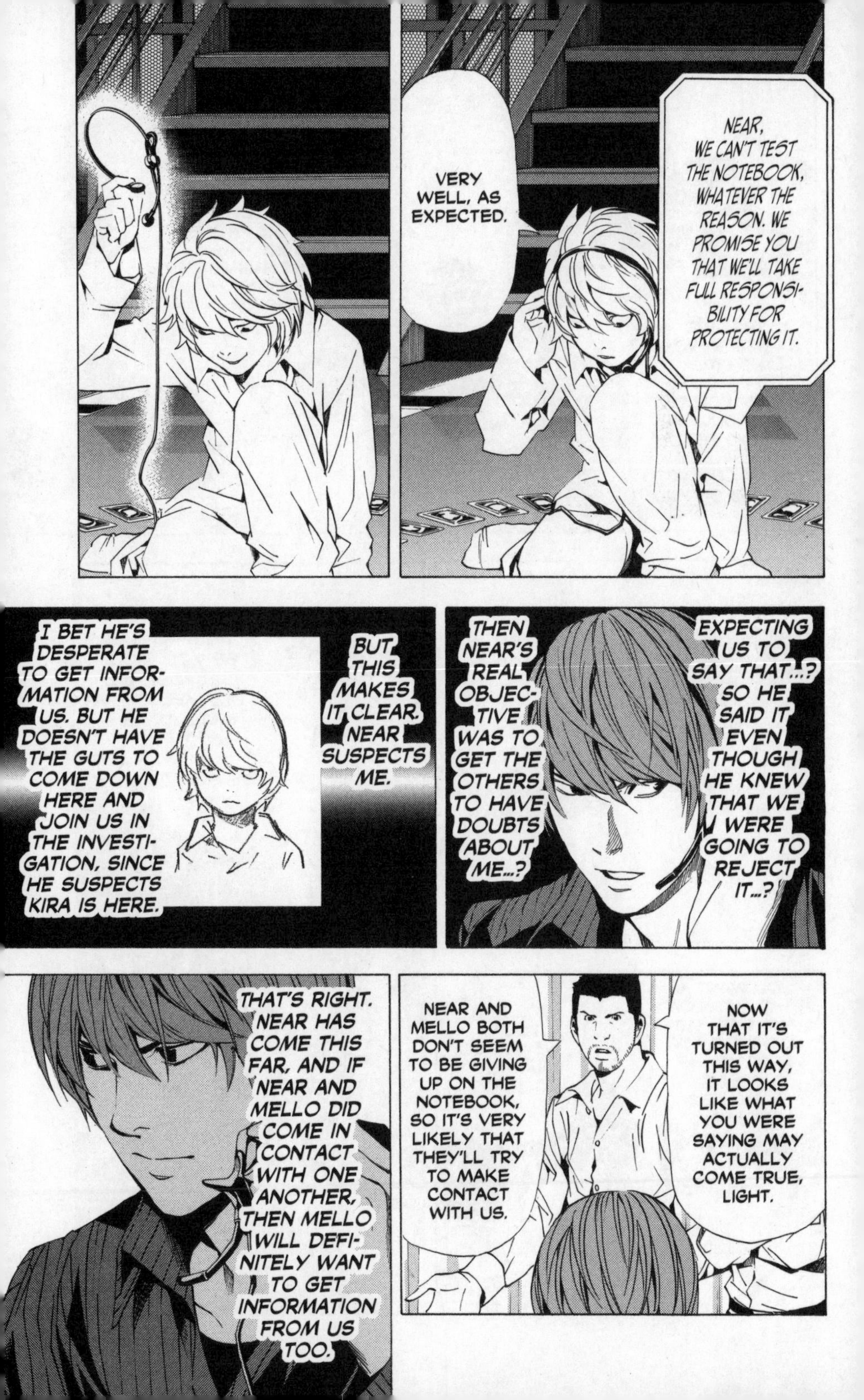
NEAR, WE CAN'T TEST THE NOTEBOOK, WHATEVER THE REASON. WE PROMISE YOU THAT WE'LL TAKE FULL RESPONSIBILITY FOR PROTECTING IT.
VERY WELL, AS EXPECTED.
EXPECTING US TO SAY THAT...? SO HE SAID IT EVEN THOUGH HE KNEW THAT WE WERE GOING TO REJECT IT...?
THEN NEAR'S REAL OBJECTIVE WAS TO GET THE OTHERS TO HAVE DOUBTS ABOUT ME...?
BUT THIS MAKES IT CLEAR. NEAR SUSPECTS ME.
I BET HE'S DESPERATE TO GET INFORMATION FROM US. BUT HE DOESN'T HAVE THE GUTS TO COME DOWN HERE AND JOIN US IN THE INVESTIGATION, SINCE HE SUSPECTS KIRA IS HERE.
NOW THAT IT'S TURNED OUT THIS WAY, IT LOOKS LIKE WHAT YOU WERE SAYING MAY ACTUALLY COME TRUE, LIGHT.
NEAR AND MELLO BOTH DON'T SEEM TO BE GIVING UP ON THE NOTEBOOK, SO IT'S VERY LIKELY THAT THEY'LL TRY TO MAKE CONTACT WITH US.
THAT'S RIGHT. NEAR HAS COME THIS FAR, AND IF NEAR AND MELLO DID COME IN CONTACT WITH ONE ANOTHER, THEN MELLO WILL DEFINITELY WANT TO GET INFORMATION FROM US TOO.

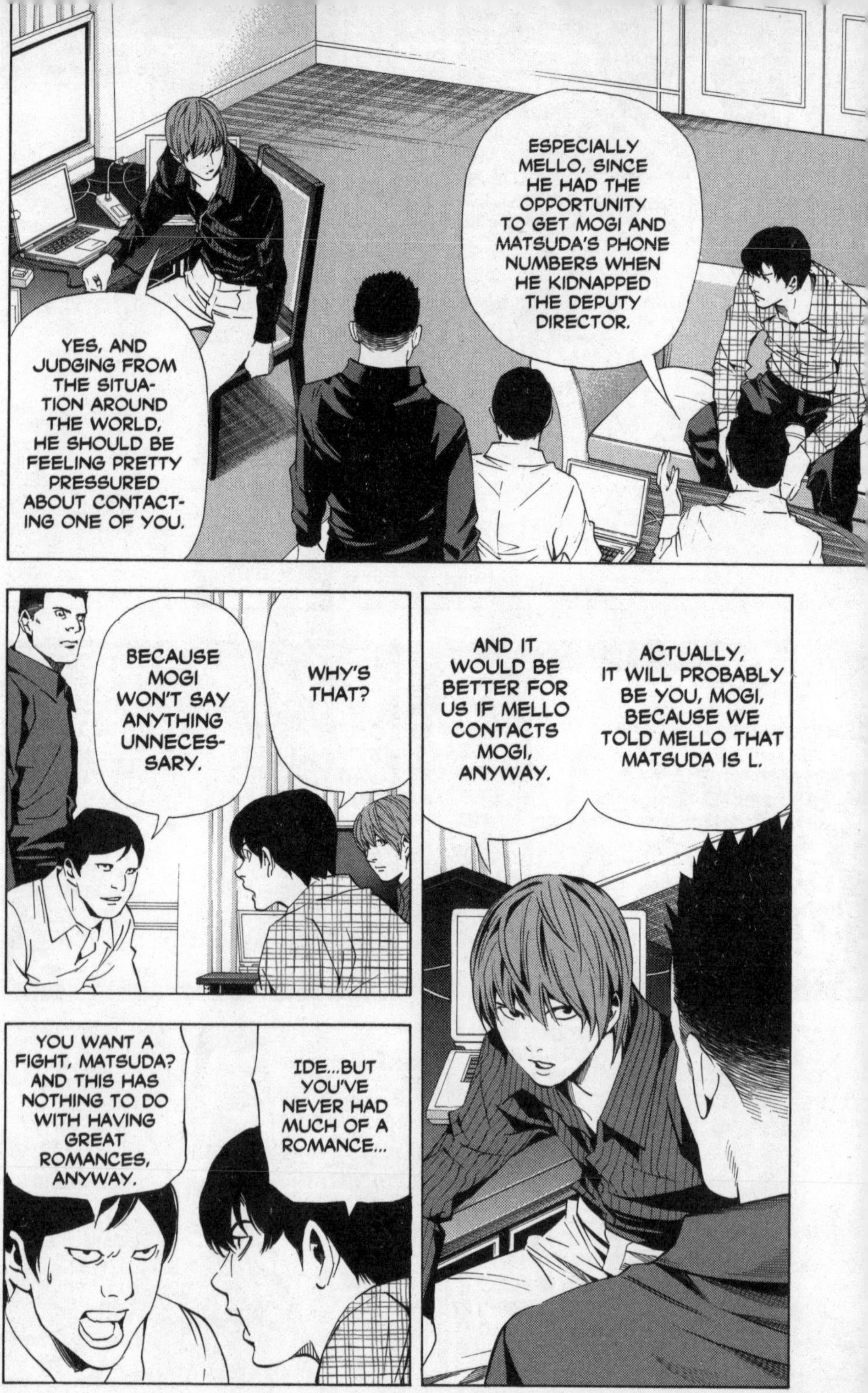
ESPECIALLY MELLO, SINCE HE HAD THE OPPORTUNITY TO GET MOGI AND MATSUDA'S PHONE NUMBERS WHEN HE KIDNAPPED THE DEPUTY DIRECTOR.
YES, AND JUDGING FROM THE SITUATION AROUND THE WORLD, HE SHOULD BE FEELING PRETTY PRESSURED ABOUT CONTACTING ONE OF YOU.
ACTUALLY, IT WILL PROBABLY BE YOU, MOGI, BECAUSE WE TOLD MELLO THAT MATSUDA IS L.
AND IT WOULD BE BETTER FOR US IF MELLO CONTACTS MOGI, ANYWAY.
WHY'S THAT?
BECAUSE MOGI WON'T SAY ANYTHING UNNECESSARY.
IDE...BUT YOU'VE NEVER HAD MUCH OF A ROMANCE...
YOU WANT A FIGHT, MATSUDA? AND THIS HAS NOTHING TO DO WITH HAVING GREAT ROMANCES, ANYWAY.

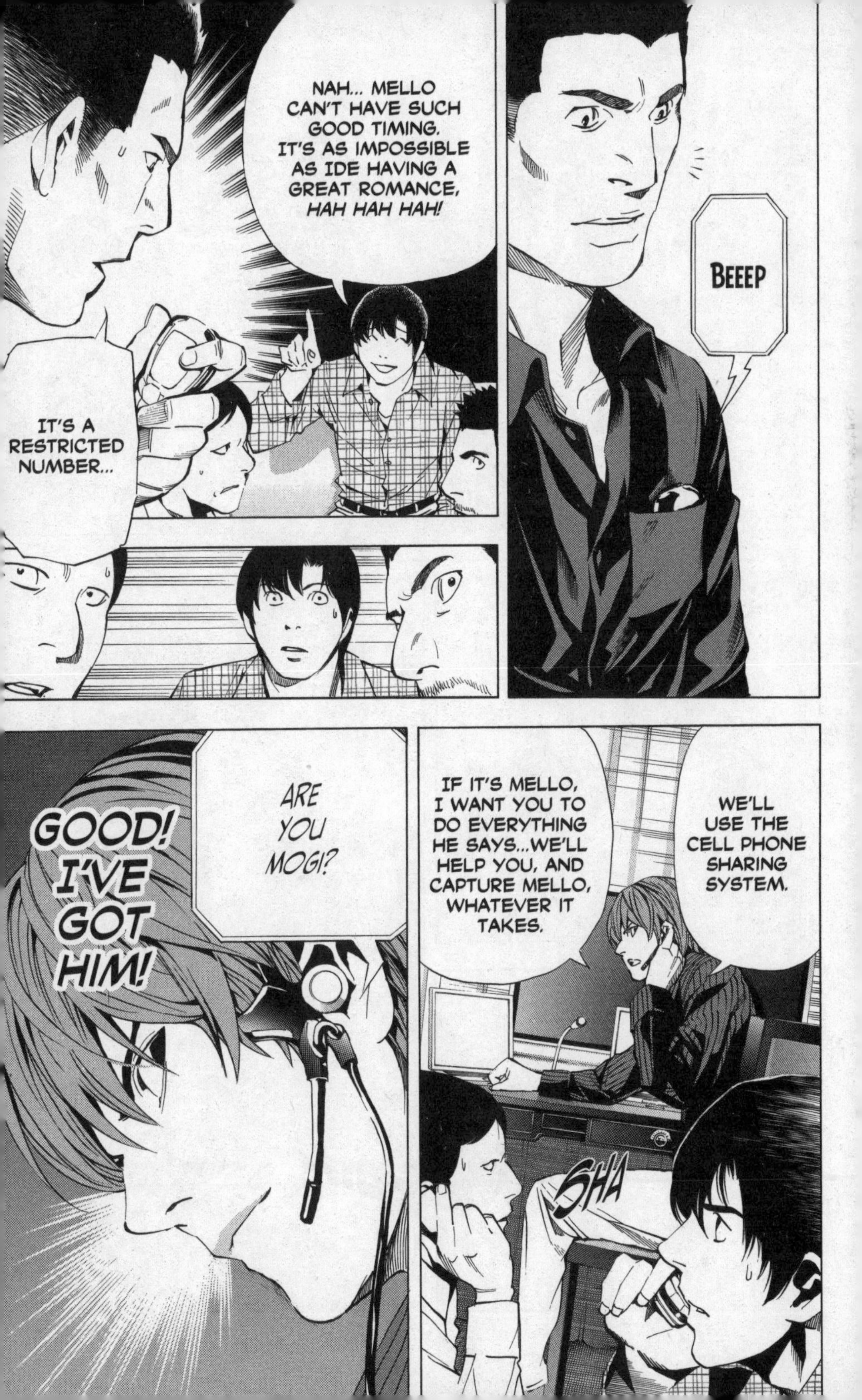
BEEEP
NAH... MELLO CAN'T HAVE SUCH GOOD TIMING. IT'S AS IMPOSSIBLE AS IDE HAVING A GREAT ROMANCE, *HAH HAH HAH!*
IT'S A RESTRICTED NUMBER...
WE'LL USE THE CELL PHONE SHARING SYSTEM.
IF IT'S MELLO, I WANT YOU TO DO EVERYTHING HE SAYS...WE'LL HELP YOU, AND CAPTURE MELLO, WHATEVER IT TAKES.
SHA
ARE YOU MOGI?
GOOD! I'VE GOT HIM!

DEATH NOTE
How to use it
LI

○ However, if a seventh DEATH NOTE is owned by a human in the
human world, nothing will happen even if used,.

仮に人間界に7冊目のデスノートが存在し人間が使ったとしても、
そのノートはなんの効力も持たない。

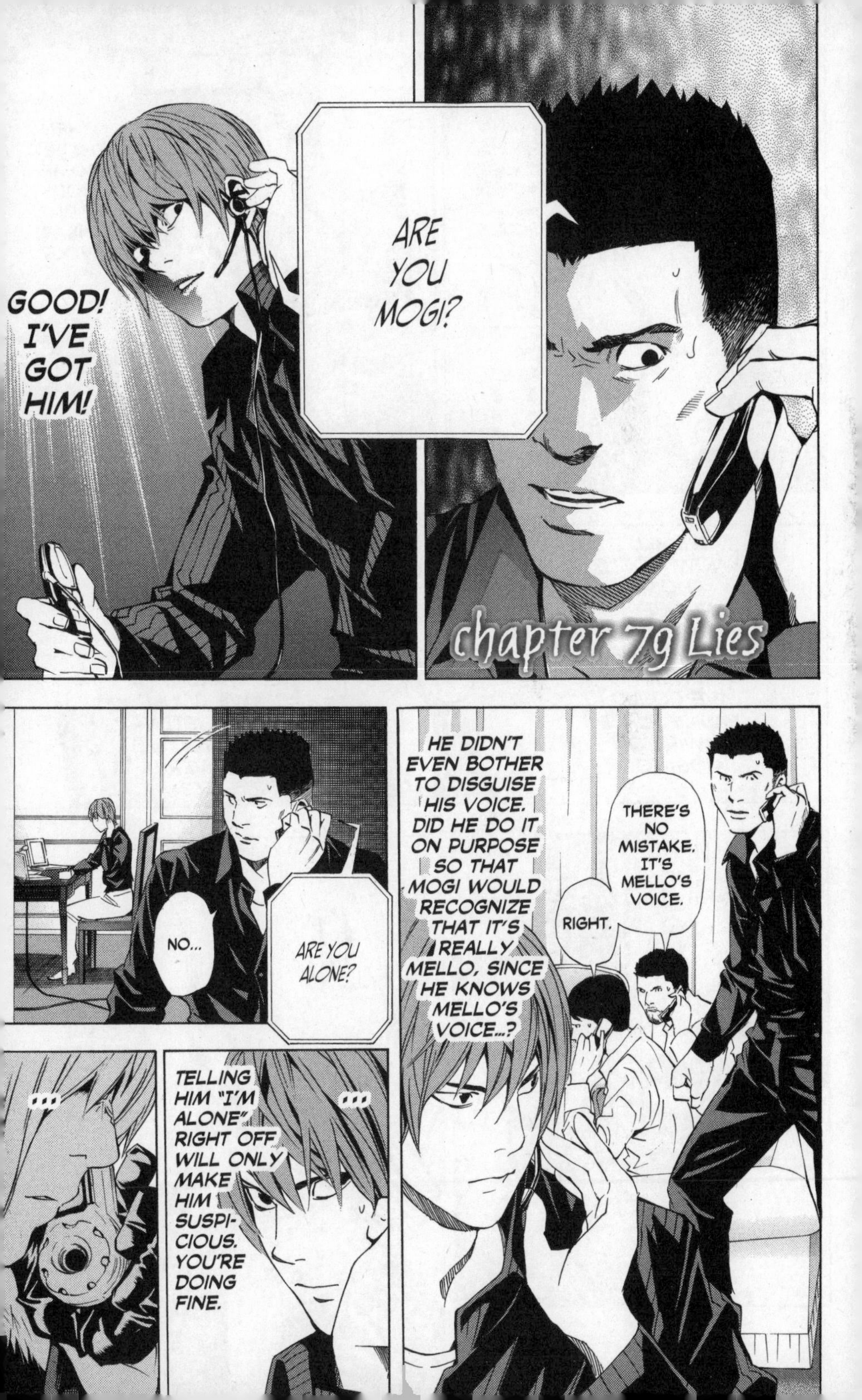
ARE YOU MOGI?
chapter 79 Lies
GOOD! I'VE GOT HIM!
THERE'S NO MISTAKE. IT'S MELLO'S VOICE.
RIGHT.
HE DIDN'T EVEN BOTHER TO DISGUISE HIS VOICE. DID HE DO IT ON PURPOSE SO THAT MOGI WOULD RECOGNIZE THAT IT'S REALLY MELLO, SINCE HE KNOWS MELLO'S VOICE...?
ARE YOU ALONE?
NO...
...
TELLING HIM "I'M ALONE" RIGHT OFF WILL ONLY MAKE HIM SUSPICIOUS. YOU'RE DOING FINE.
...

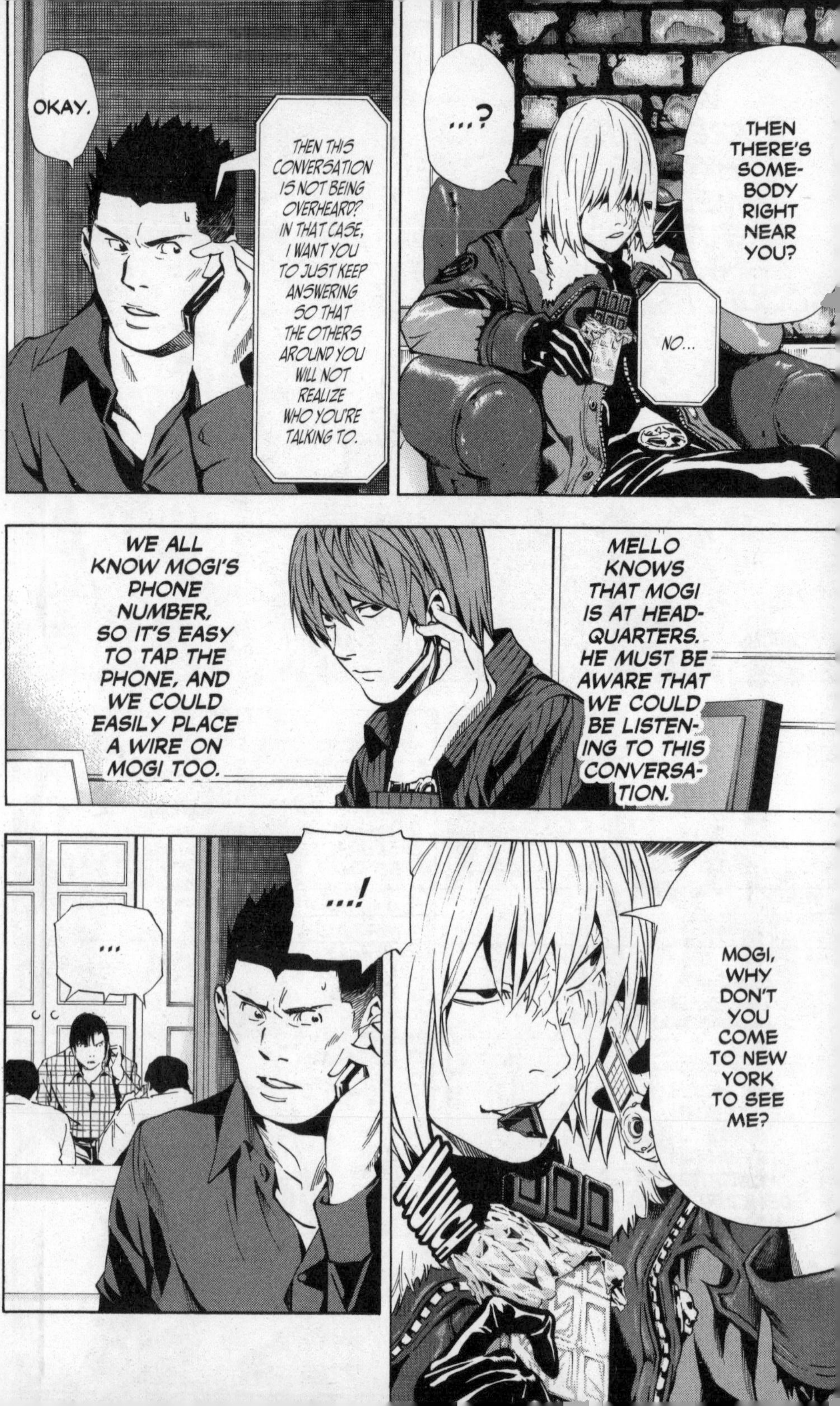
...?
THEN THERE'S SOMEBODY RIGHT NEAR YOU?
NO...
THEN THIS CONVERSATION IS NOT BEING OVERHEARD? IN THAT CASE, I WANT YOU TO JUST KEEP ANSWERING SO THAT THE OTHERS AROUND YOU WILL NOT REALIZE WHO YOU'RE TALKING TO.
OKAY.
MELLO KNOWS THAT MOGI IS AT HEAD-QUARTERS. HE MUST BE AWARE THAT WE COULD BE LISTEN-ING TO THIS CONVERSA-TION.
WE ALL KNOW MOGI'S PHONE NUMBER, SO IT'S EASY TO TAP THE PHONE, AND WE COULD EASILY PLACE A WIRE ON MOGI TOO.
MOGI, WHY DON'T YOU COME TO NEW YORK TO SEE ME?
MUNCH
...!
...

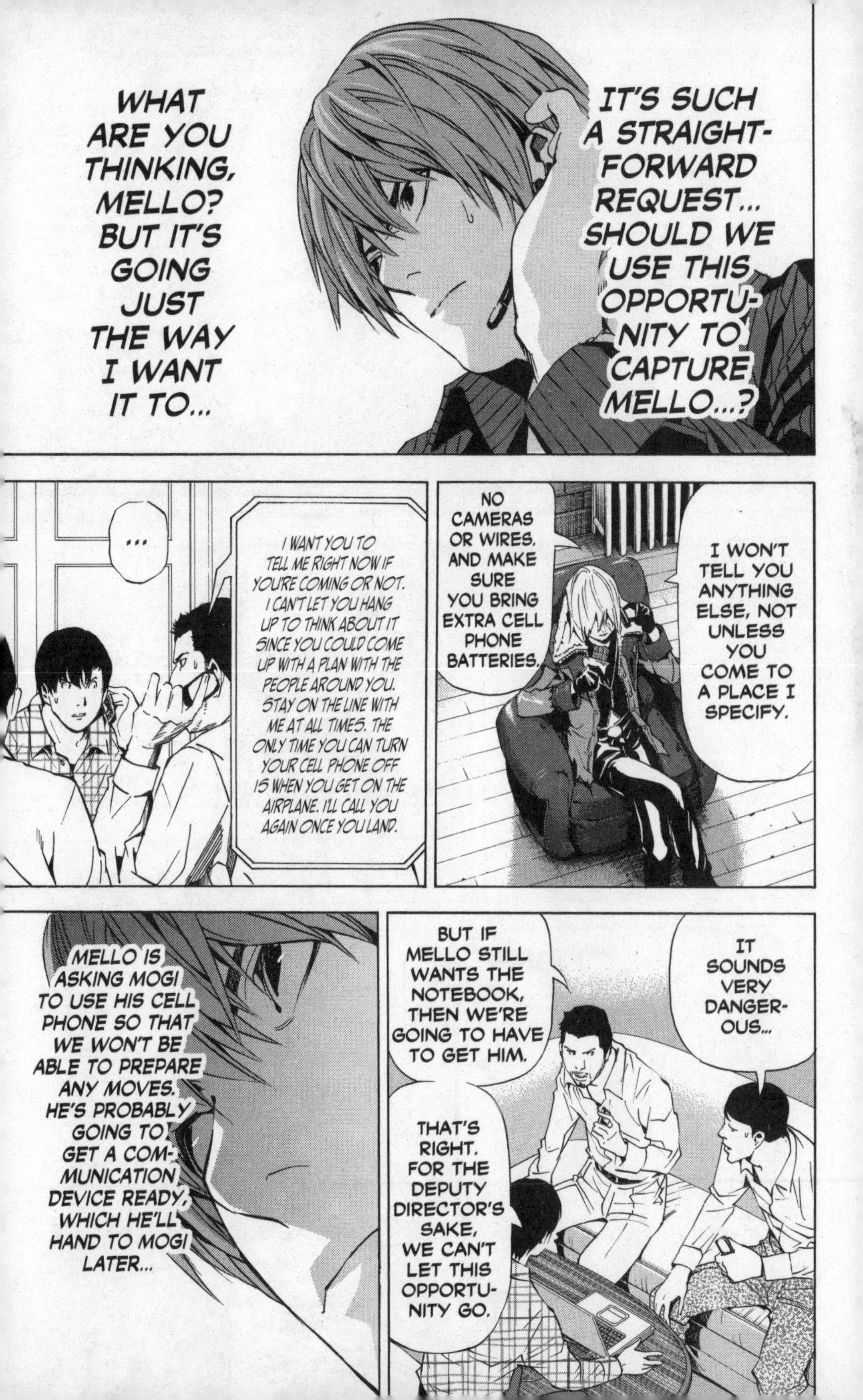
IT'S SUCH A STRAIGHT-FORWARD REQUEST... SHOULD WE USE THIS OPPORTU-NITY TO CAPTURE MELLO...?
WHAT ARE YOU THINKING, MELLO? BUT IT'S GOING JUST THE WAY I WANT IT TO...
I WON'T TELL YOU ANYTHING ELSE, NOT UNLESS YOU COME TO A PLACE I SPECIFY.
NO CAMERAS OR WIRES. AND MAKE SURE YOU BRING EXTRA CELL PHONE BATTERIES.
I WANT YOU TO TELL ME RIGHT NOW IF YOU'RE COMING OR NOT. I CAN'T LET YOU HANG UP TO THINK ABOUT IT SINCE YOU COULD COME UP WITH A PLAN WITH THE PEOPLE AROUND YOU. STAY ON THE LINE WITH ME AT ALL TIMES. THE ONLY TIME YOU CAN TURN YOUR CELL PHONE OFF IS WHEN YOU GET ON THE AIRPLANE. I'LL CALL YOU AGAIN ONCE YOU LAND.
...
IT SOUNDS VERY DANGER-OUS...
BUT IF MELLO STILL WANTS THE NOTEBOOK, THEN WE'RE GOING TO HAVE TO GET HIM.
THAT'S RIGHT. FOR THE DEPUTY DIRECTOR'S SAKE, WE CAN'T LET THIS OPPORTU-NITY GO.
MELLO IS ASKING MOGI TO USE HIS CELL PHONE SO THAT WE WON'T BE ABLE TO PREPARE ANY MOVES. HE'S PROBABLY GOING TO GET A COM-MUNICATION DEVICE READY, WHICH HE'LL HAND TO MOGI LATER...

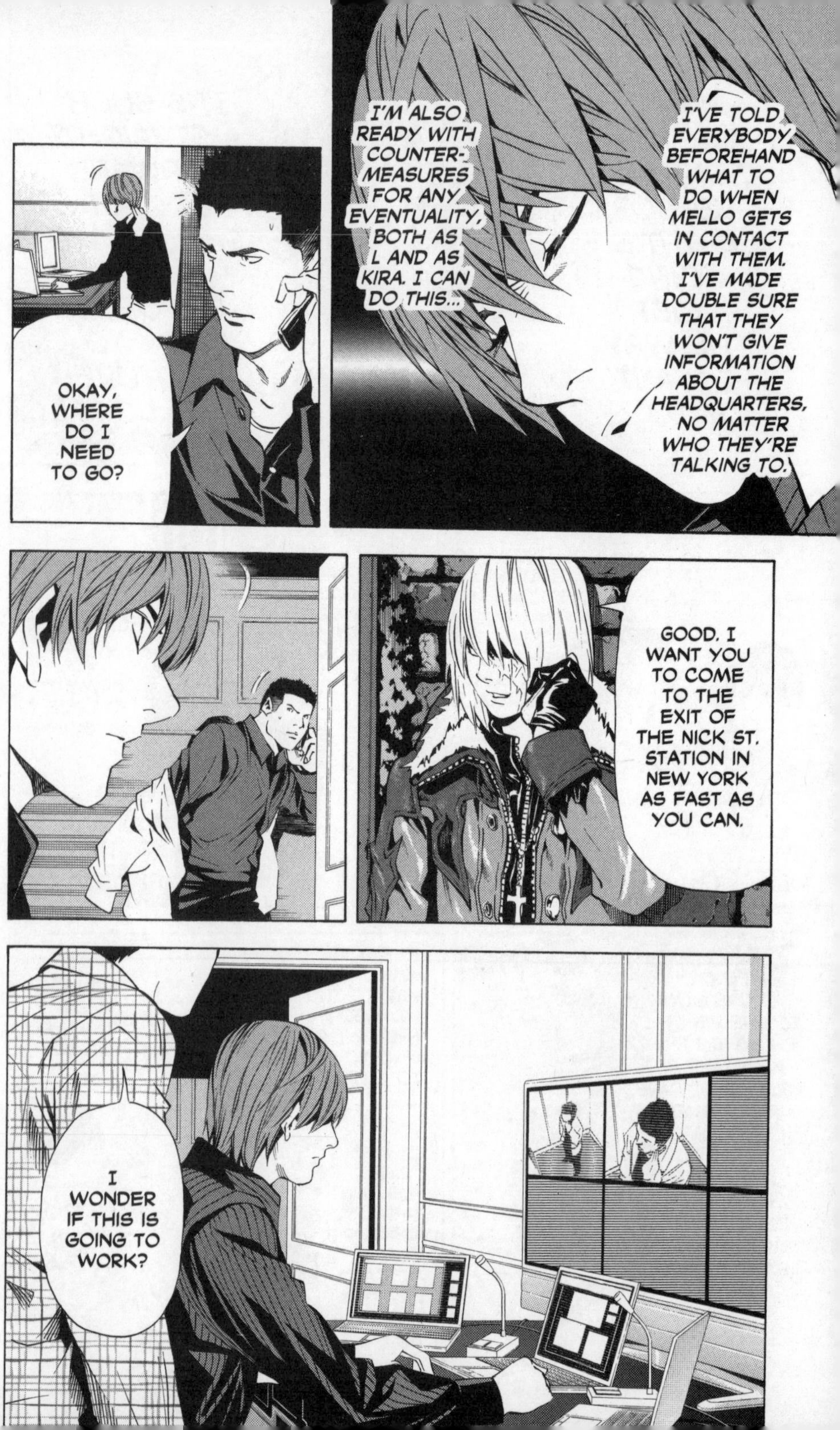
I'VE TOLD EVERYBODY BEFOREHAND WHAT TO DO WHEN MELLO GETS IN CONTACT WITH THEM. I'VE MADE DOUBLE SURE THAT THEY WON'T GIVE INFORMATION ABOUT THE HEADQUARTERS, NO MATTER WHO THEY'RE TALKING TO.
I'M ALSO READY WITH COUNTER-MEASURES FOR ANY EVENTUALITY, BOTH AS L AND AS KIRA. I CAN DO THIS...
OKAY, WHERE DO I NEED TO GO?
GOOD. I WANT YOU TO COME TO THE EXIT OF THE NICK ST. STATION IN NEW YORK AS FAST AS YOU CAN.
I WONDER IF THIS IS GOING TO WORK?

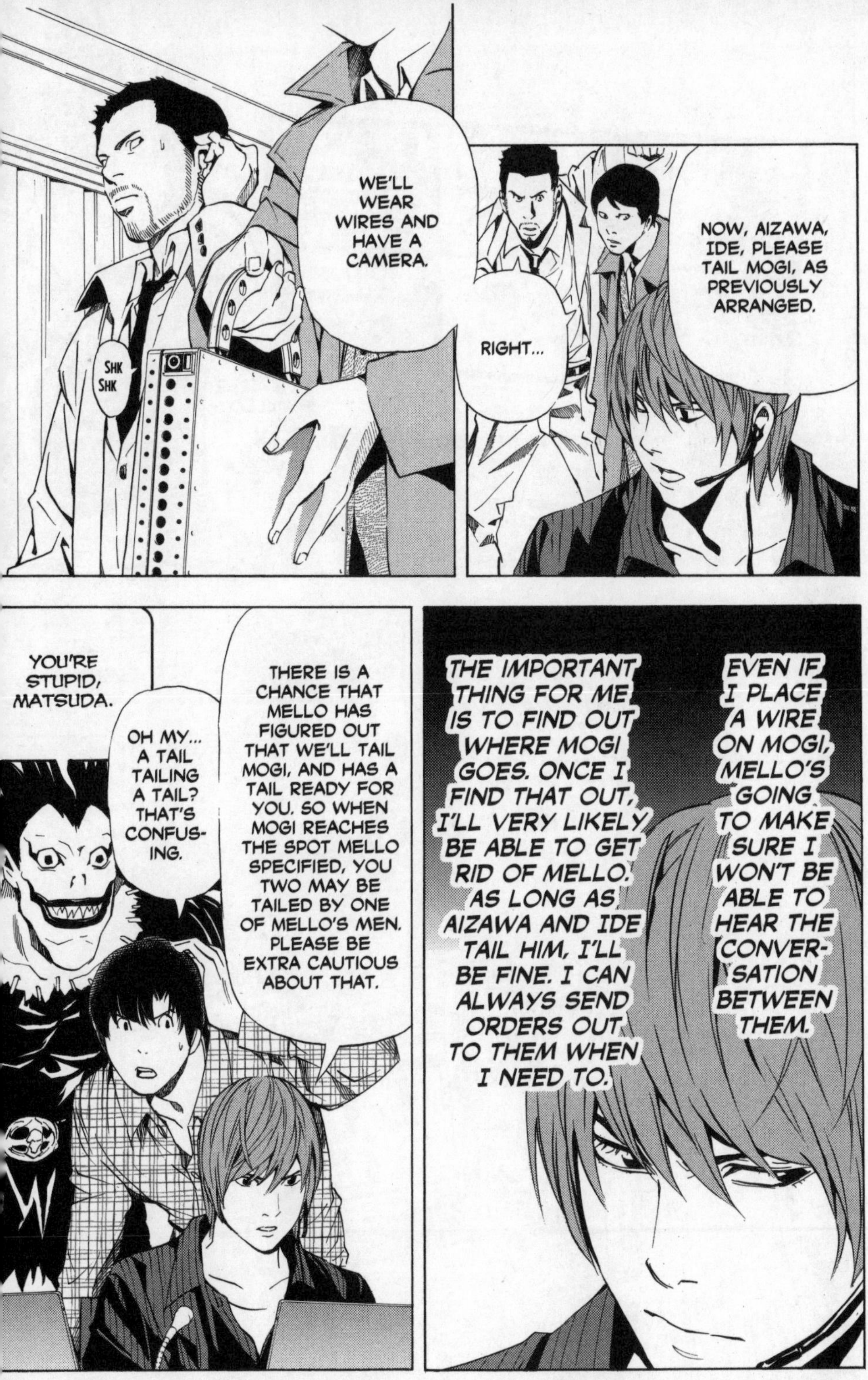
NOW, AIZAWA, IDE, PLEASE TAIL MOGI, AS PREVIOUSLY ARRANGED.
RIGHT...
WE'LL WEAR WIRES AND HAVE A CAMERA.
SHK SHK
EVEN IF I PLACE A WIRE ON MOGI, MELLO'S GOING TO MAKE SURE I WON'T BE ABLE TO HEAR THE CONVER-SATION BETWEEN THEM.
THE IMPORTANT THING FOR ME IS TO FIND OUT WHERE MOGI GOES. ONCE I FIND THAT OUT, I'LL VERY LIKELY BE ABLE TO GET RID OF MELLO. AS LONG AS AIZAWA AND IDE TAIL HIM, I'LL BE FINE. I CAN ALWAYS SEND ORDERS OUT TO THEM WHEN I NEED TO.
THERE IS A CHANCE THAT MELLO HAS FIGURED OUT THAT WE'LL TAIL MOGI, AND HAS A TAIL READY FOR YOU. SO WHEN MOGI REACHES THE SPOT MELLO SPECIFIED, YOU TWO MAY BE TAILED BY ONE OF MELLO'S MEN. PLEASE BE EXTRA CAUTIOUS ABOUT THAT.
OH MY... A TAIL TAILING A TAIL? THAT'S CONFUS-ING.
YOU'RE STUPID, MATSUDA.

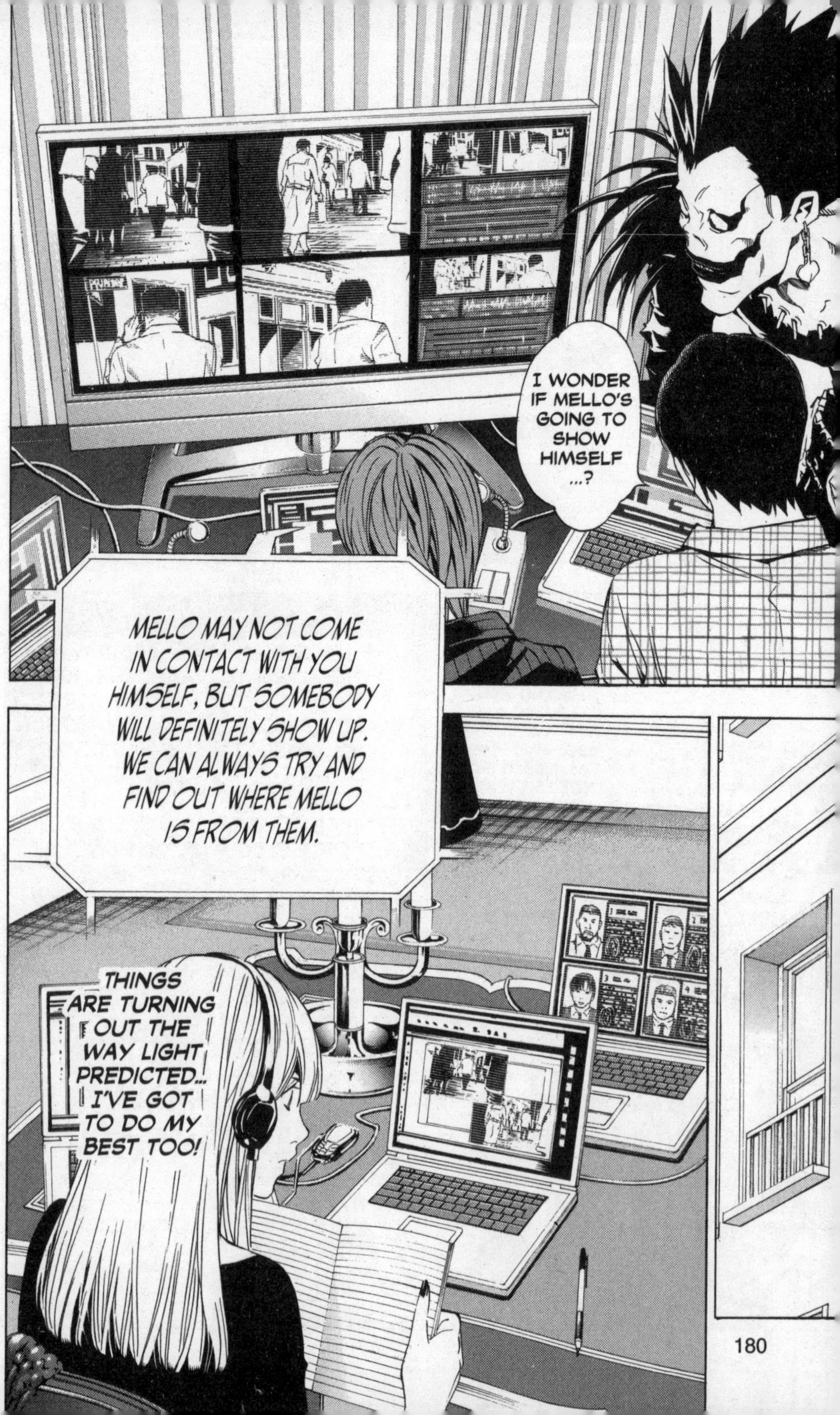
I WONDER IF MELLO'S GOING TO SHOW HIMSELF ...?
MELLO MAY NOT COME IN CONTACT WITH YOU HIMSELF, BUT SOMEBODY WILL DEFINITELY SHOW UP. WE CAN ALWAYS TRY AND FIND OUT WHERE MELLO IS FROM THEM.
THINGS ARE TURNING OUT THE WAY LIGHT PREDICTED... I'VE GOT TO DO MY BEST TOO!

READ THIS WAY

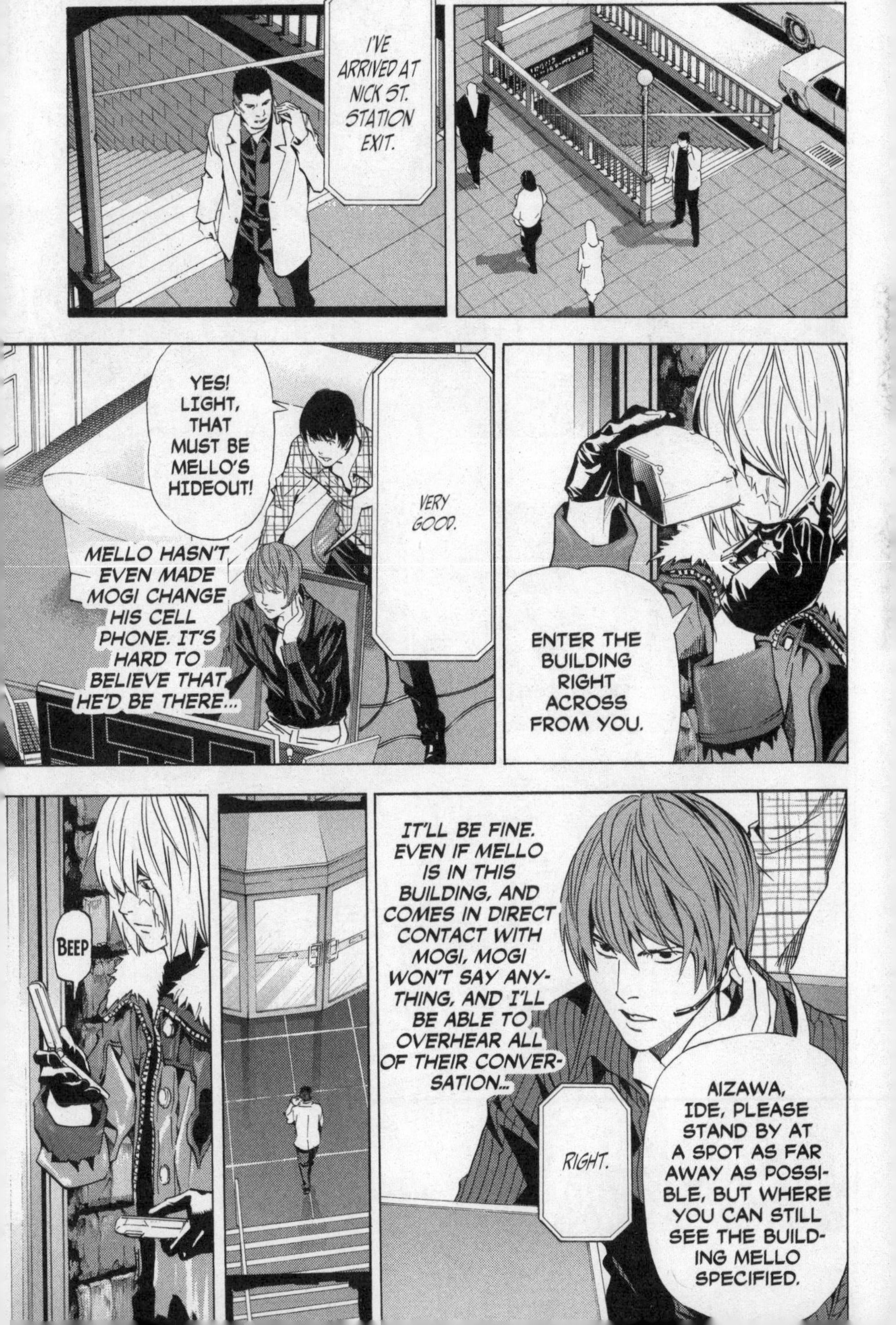

I'VE ARRIVED AT NICK ST. STATION EXIT.
ENTER THE BUILDING RIGHT ACROSS FROM YOU.
VERY GOOD.
YES! LIGHT, THAT MUST BE MELLO'S HIDEOUT!
MELLO HASN'T EVEN MADE MOGI CHANGE HIS CELL PHONE. IT'S HARD TO BELIEVE THAT HE'D BE THERE...
IT'LL BE FINE. EVEN IF MELLO IS IN THIS BUILDING, AND COMES IN DIRECT CONTACT WITH MOGI, MOGI WON'T SAY ANYTHING, AND I'LL BE ABLE TO OVERHEAR ALL OF THEIR CONVERSATION...
AIZAWA, IDE, PLEASE STAND BY AT A SPOT AS FAR AWAY AS POSSIBLE, BUT WHERE YOU CAN STILL SEE THE BUILDING MELLO SPECIFIED.
RIGHT.
BEEP

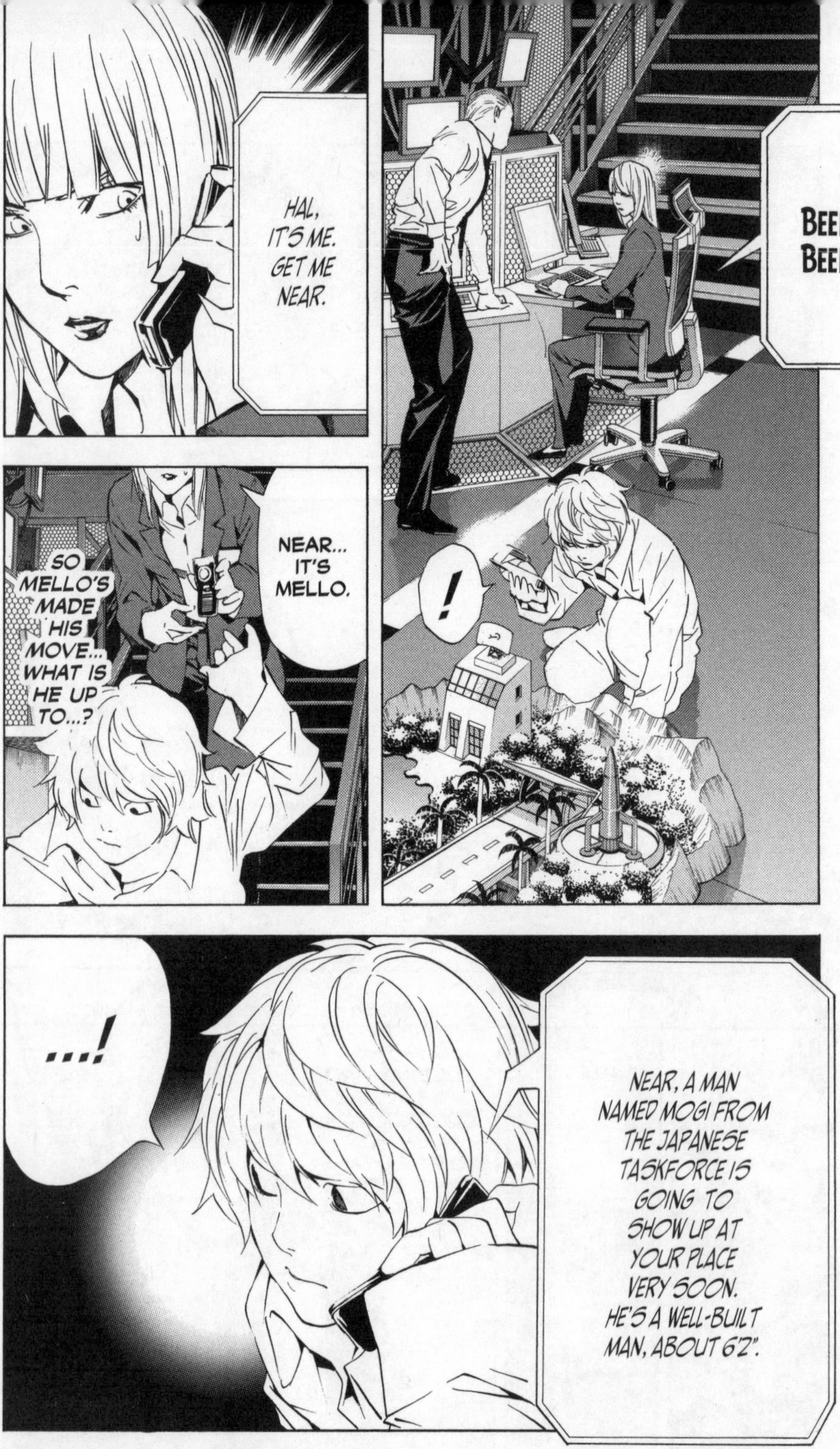
BEEP BEEP
!
HAL, IT'S ME. GET ME NEAR.
NEAR... IT'S MELLO.
SO MELLO'S MADE HIS MOVE... WHAT IS HE UP TO...?
NEAR, A MAN NAMED MOGI FROM THE JAPANESE TASKFORCE IS GOING TO SHOW UP AT YOUR PLACE VERY SOON. HE'S A WELL-BUILT MAN, ABOUT 6'2".
...!

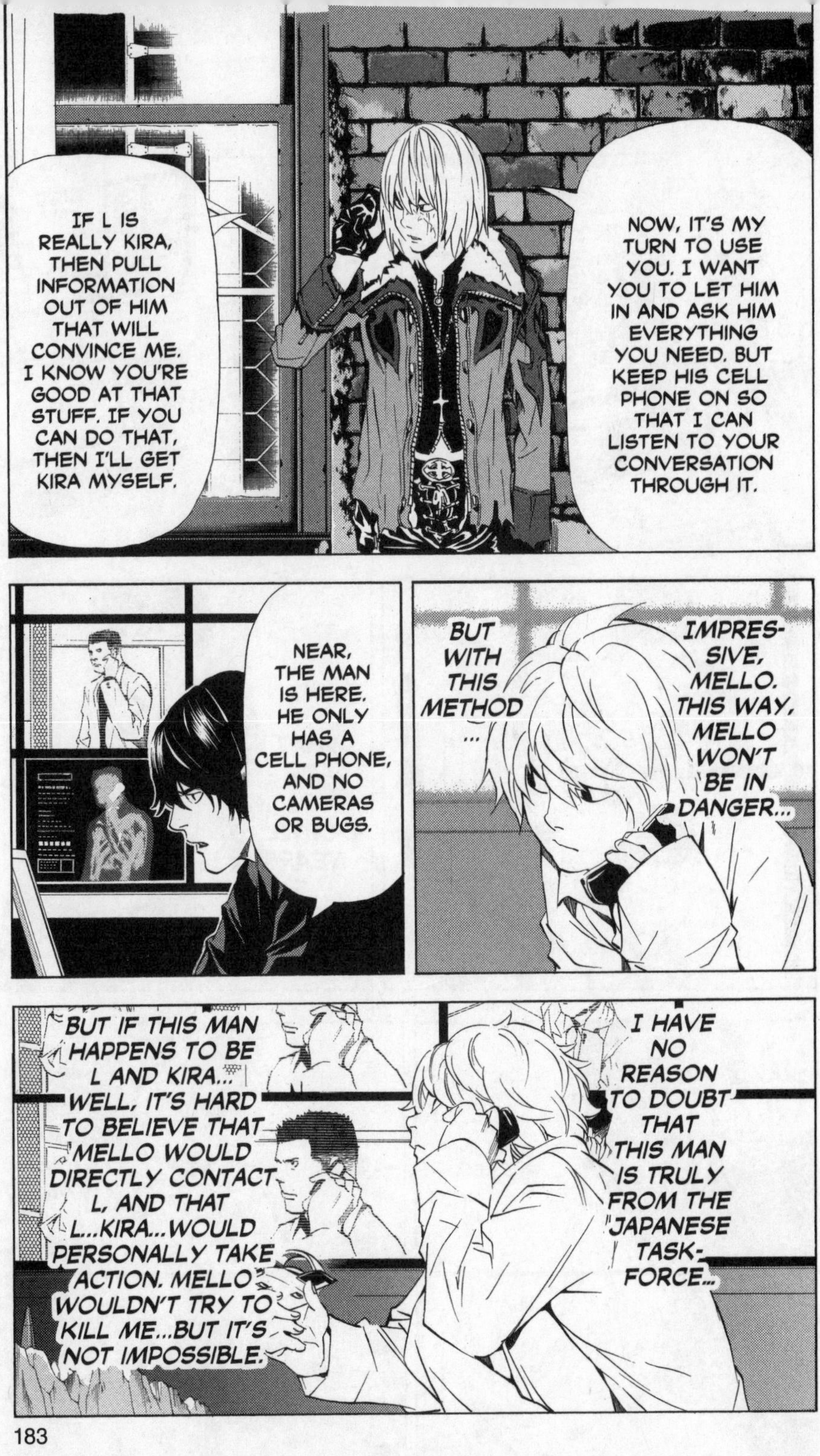
NOW, IT'S MY TURN TO USE YOU. I WANT YOU TO LET HIM IN AND ASK HIM EVERYTHING YOU NEED. BUT KEEP HIS CELL PHONE ON SO THAT I CAN LISTEN TO YOUR CONVERSATION THROUGH IT.
IF L IS REALLY KIRA, THEN PULL INFORMATION OUT OF HIM THAT WILL CONVINCE ME. I KNOW YOU'RE GOOD AT THAT STUFF. IF YOU CAN DO THAT, THEN I'LL GET KIRA MYSELF.
IMPRES-SIVE, MELLO. THIS WAY, MELLO WON'T BE IN DANGER...
BUT WITH THIS METHOD ...
NEAR, THE MAN IS HERE. HE ONLY HAS A CELL PHONE, AND NO CAMERAS OR BUGS.
I HAVE NO REASON TO DOUBT THAT THIS MAN IS TRULY FROM THE JAPANESE TASK-FORCE...
BUT IF THIS MAN HAPPENS TO BE L AND KIRA... WELL, IT'S HARD TO BELIEVE THAT MELLO WOULD DIRECTLY CONTACT L, AND THAT L...KIRA...WOULD PERSONALLY TAKE ACTION. MELLO WOULDN'T TRY TO KILL ME...BUT IT'S NOT IMPOSSIBLE.

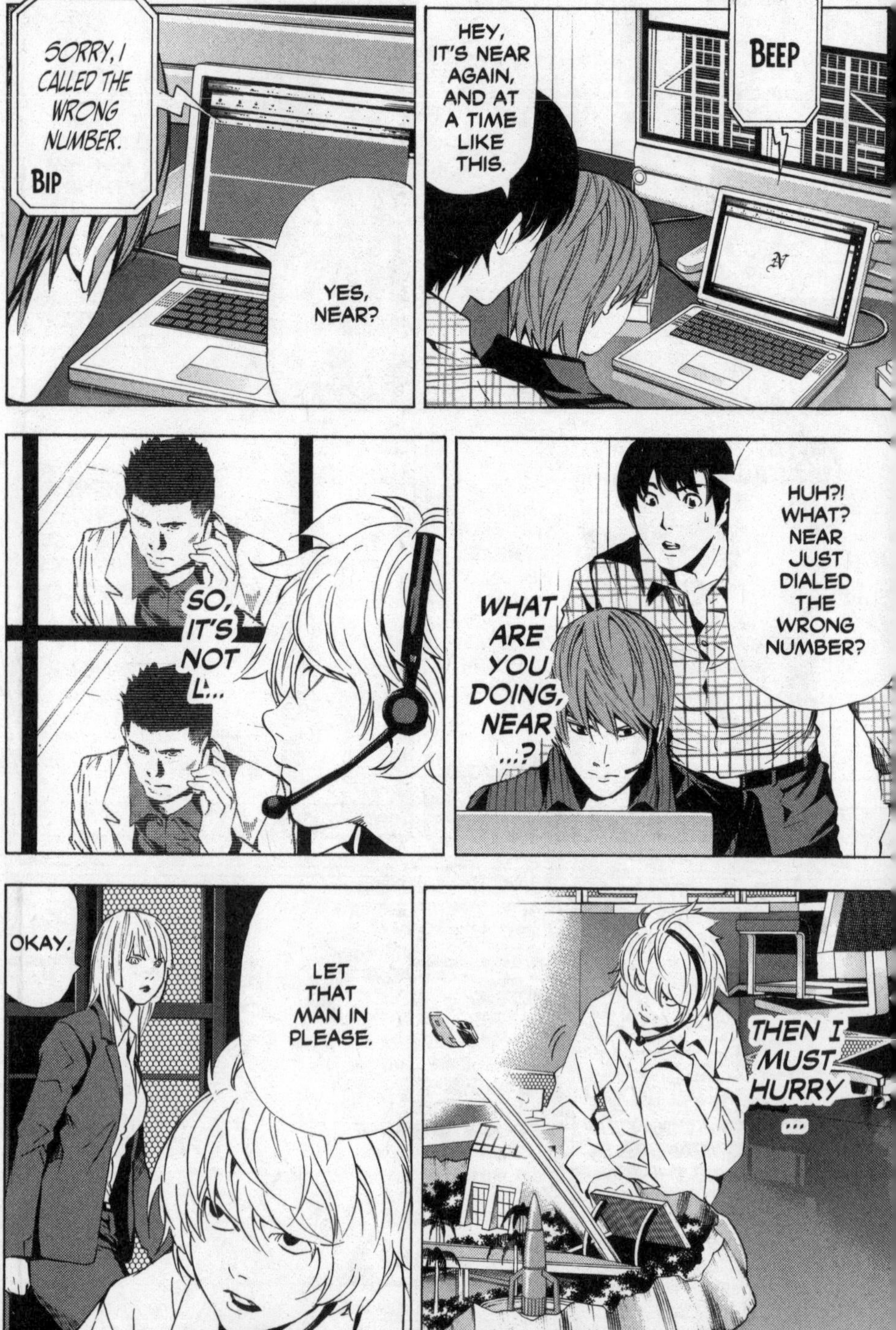
BEEP
HEY, IT'S NEAR AGAIN, AND AT A TIME LIKE THIS.
YES, NEAR?
SORRY, I CALLED THE WRONG NUMBER.
BIP
HUH?! WHAT? NEAR JUST DIALED THE WRONG NUMBER?
WHAT ARE YOU DOING, NEAR ...?
SO, IT'S NOT L...
THEN I MUST HURRY ...
LET THAT MAN IN PLEASE.
OKAY.

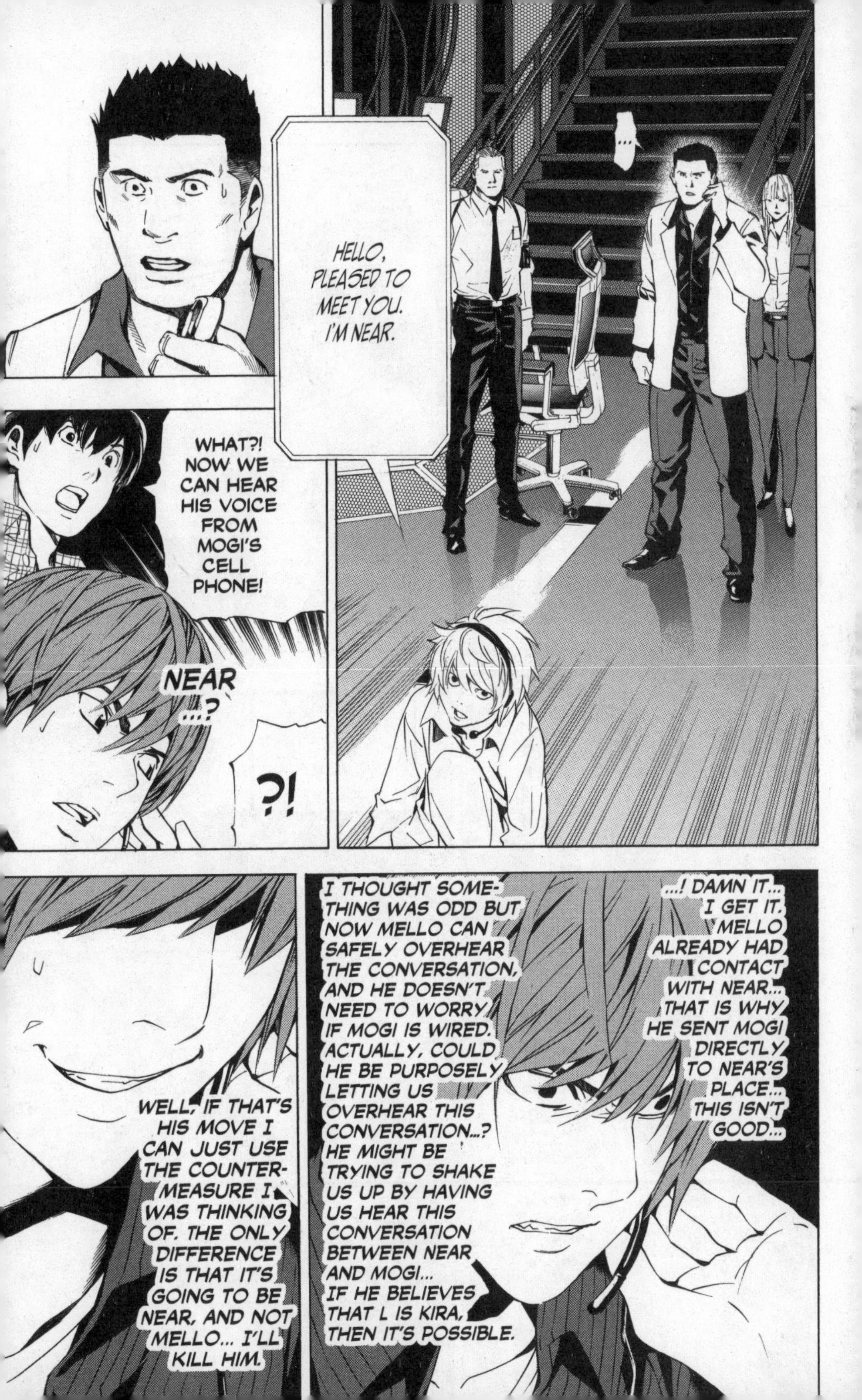
...
HELLO, PLEASED TO MEET YOU. I'M NEAR.
WHAT?! NOW WE CAN HEAR HIS VOICE FROM MOGI'S CELL PHONE!
NEAR ...?
?!
...! DAMN IT... I GET IT. MELLO ALREADY HAD CONTACT WITH NEAR... THAT IS WHY HE SENT MOGI DIRECTLY TO NEAR'S PLACE... THIS ISN'T GOOD...
I THOUGHT SOME-THING WAS ODD BUT NOW MELLO CAN SAFELY OVERHEAR THE CONVERSATION, AND HE DOESN'T NEED TO WORRY IF MOGI IS WIRED. ACTUALLY, COULD HE BE PURPOSELY LETTING US OVERHEAR THIS CONVERSATION...? HE MIGHT BE TRYING TO SHAKE US UP BY HAVING US HEAR THIS CONVERSATION BETWEEN NEAR AND MOGI... IF HE BELIEVES THAT L IS KIRA, THEN IT'S POSSIBLE.
WELL, IF THAT'S HIS MOVE I CAN JUST USE THE COUNTER-MEASURE I WAS THINKING OF. THE ONLY DIFFERENCE IS THAT IT'S GOING TO BE NEAR, AND NOT MELLO... I'LL KILL HIM.

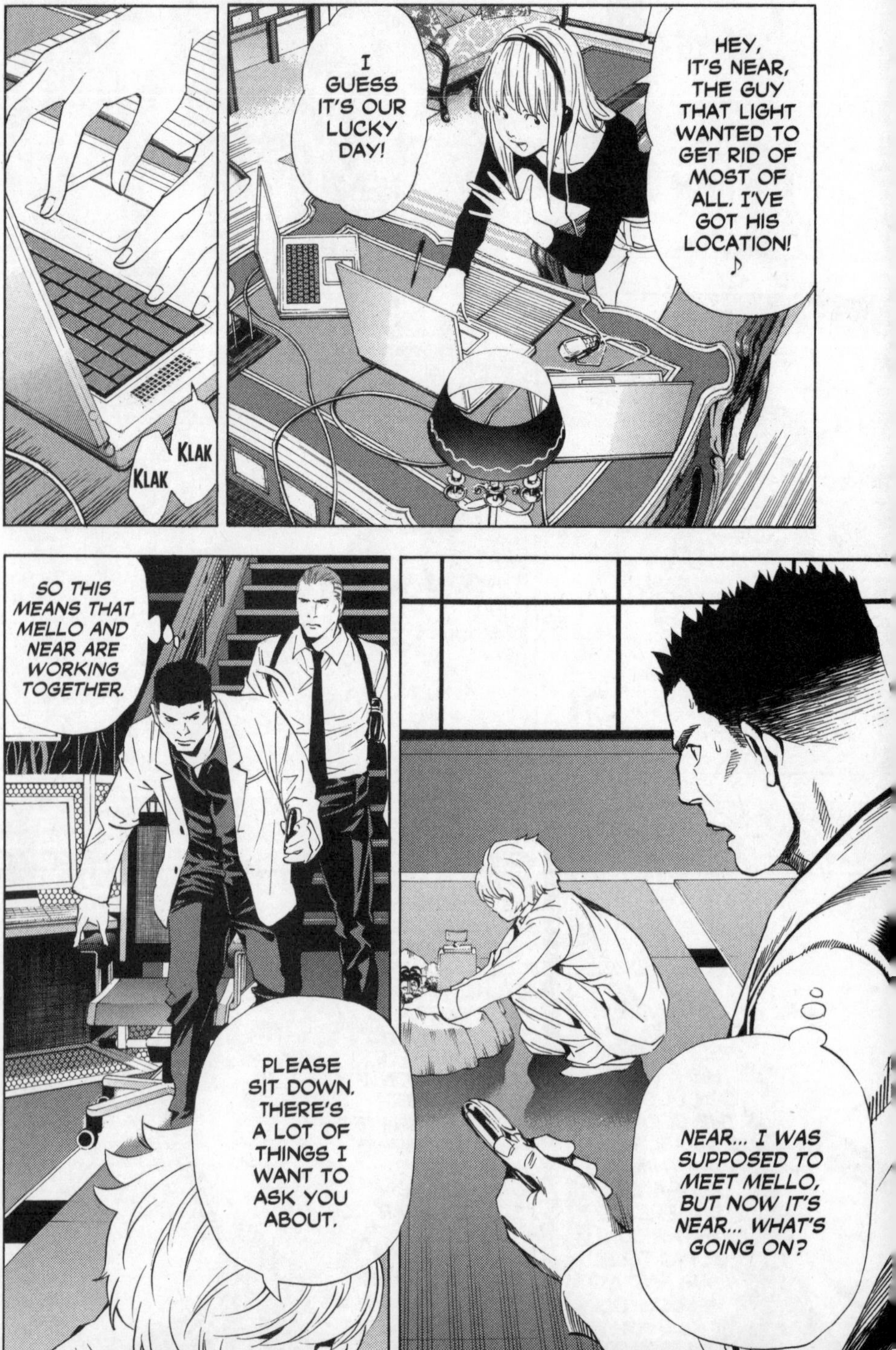
HEY, IT'S NEAR, THE GUY THAT LIGHT WANTED TO GET RID OF MOST OF ALL. I'VE GOT HIS LOCATION! ♪
I GUESS IT'S OUR LUCKY DAY!
KLAK
KLAK
NEAR... I WAS SUPPOSED TO MEET MELLO, BUT NOW IT'S NEAR... WHAT'S GOING ON?
PLEASE SIT DOWN. THERE'S A LOT OF THINGS I WANT TO ASK YOU ABOUT.
SO THIS MEANS THAT MELLO AND NEAR ARE WORKING TOGETHER.

READ THIS WAY

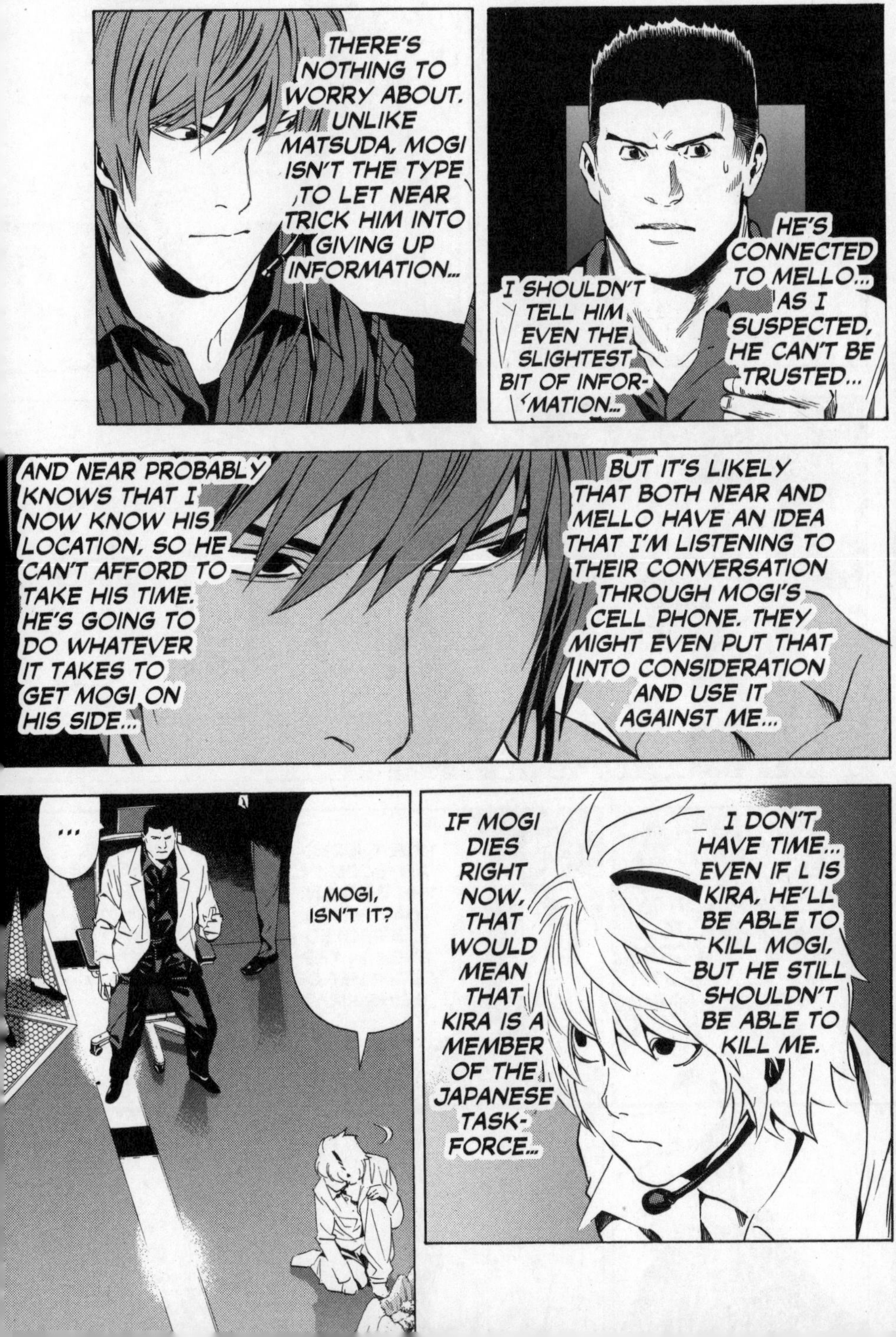

HE'S CONNECTED TO MELLO... AS I SUSPECTED, HE CAN'T BE TRUSTED...
I SHOULDN'T TELL HIM EVEN THE SLIGHTEST BIT OF INFOR-MATION...
THERE'S NOTHING TO WORRY ABOUT. UNLIKE MATSUDA, MOGI ISN'T THE TYPE TO LET NEAR TRICK HIM INTO GIVING UP INFORMATION...
BUT IT'S LIKELY THAT BOTH NEAR AND MELLO HAVE AN IDEA THAT I'M LISTENING TO THEIR CONVERSATION THROUGH MOGI'S CELL PHONE. THEY MIGHT EVEN PUT THAT INTO CONSIDERATION AND USE IT AGAINST ME...
AND NEAR PROBABLY KNOWS THAT I NOW KNOW HIS LOCATION, SO HE CAN'T AFFORD TO TAKE HIS TIME. HE'S GOING TO DO WHATEVER IT TAKES TO GET MOGI ON HIS SIDE...
I DON'T HAVE TIME... EVEN IF L IS KIRA, HE'LL BE ABLE TO KILL MOGI, BUT HE STILL SHOULDN'T BE ABLE TO KILL ME.
IF MOGI DIES RIGHT NOW, THAT WOULD MEAN THAT KIRA IS A MEMBER OF THE JAPANESE TASK-FORCE...
MOGI, ISN'T IT?
...

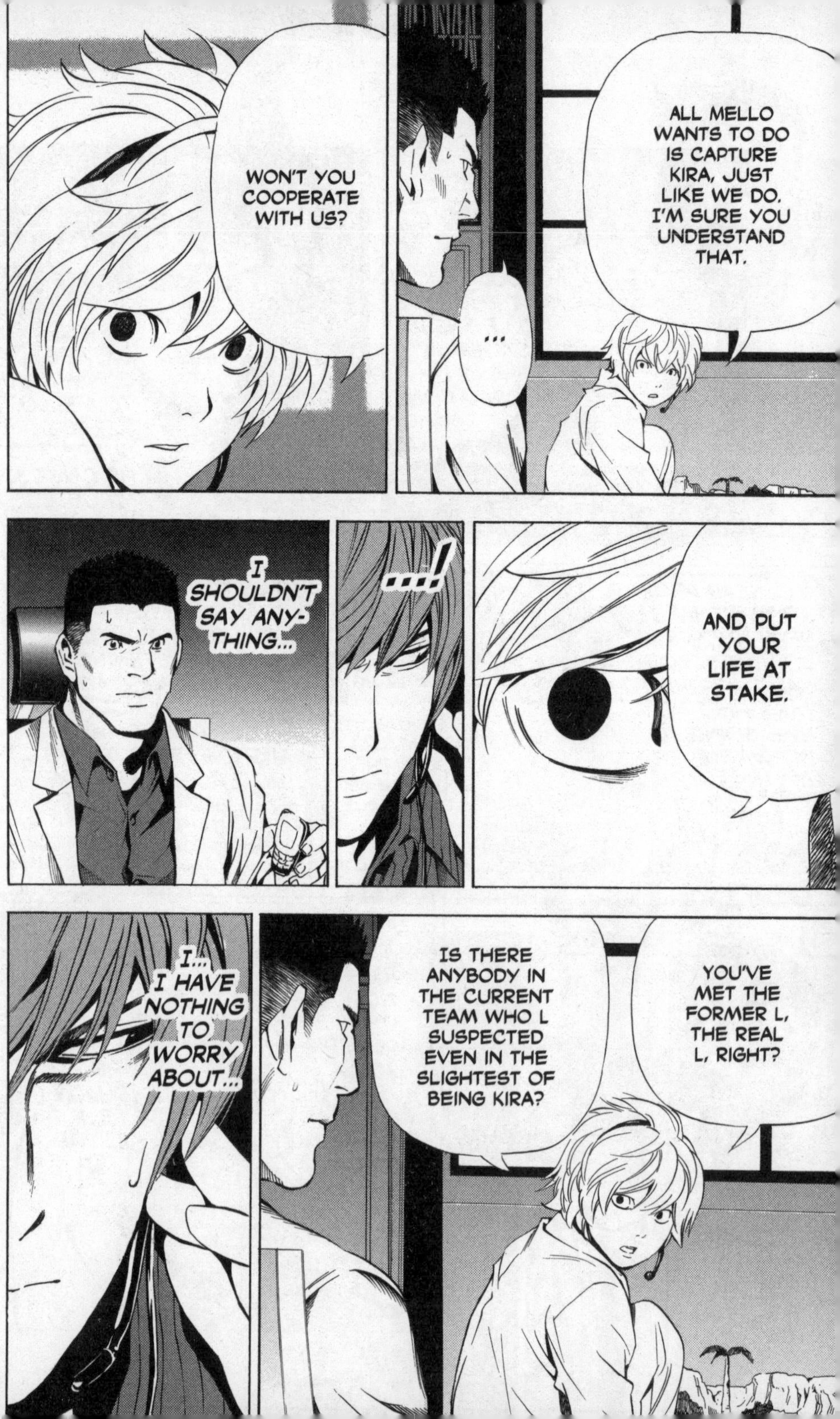
ALL MELLO WANTS TO DO IS CAPTURE KIRA, JUST LIKE WE DO. I'M SURE YOU UNDERSTAND THAT.
...
WON'T YOU COOPERATE WITH US?
AND PUT YOUR LIFE AT STAKE.
...!
I SHOULDN'T SAY ANY-THING...
YOU'VE MET THE FORMER L, THE REAL L, RIGHT?
IS THERE ANYBODY IN THE CURRENT TEAM WHO L SUSPECTED EVEN IN THE SLIGHTEST OF BEING KIRA?
I... I HAVE NOTHING TO WORRY ABOUT...

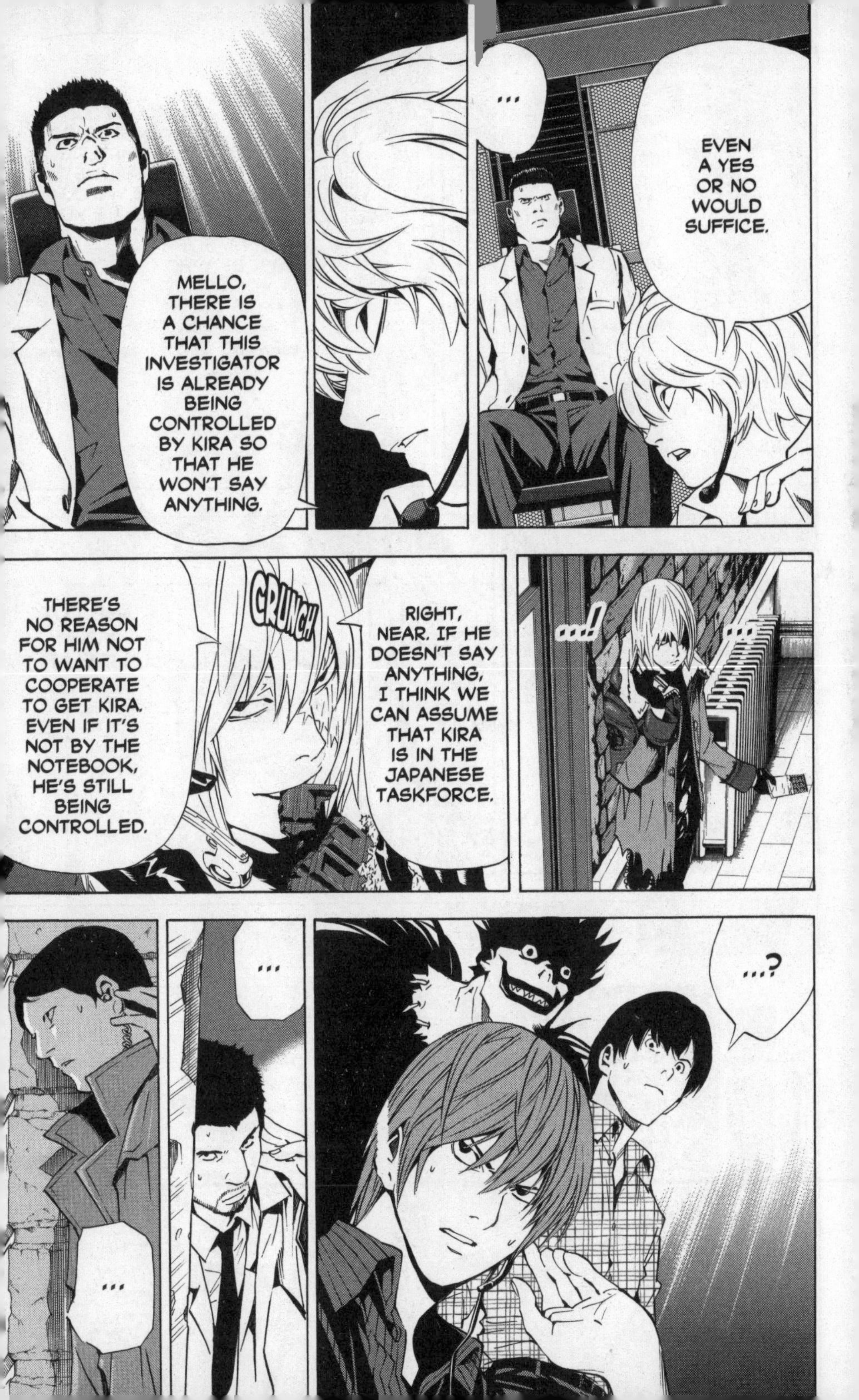
EVEN A YES OR NO WOULD SUFFICE.
...
MELLO, THERE IS A CHANCE THAT THIS INVESTIGATOR IS ALREADY BEING CONTROLLED BY KIRA SO THAT HE WON'T SAY ANYTHING.
...
...!
RIGHT, NEAR. IF HE DOESN'T SAY ANYTHING, I THINK WE CAN ASSUME THAT KIRA IS IN THE JAPANESE TASKFORCE.
CRUNCH
THERE'S NO REASON FOR HIM NOT TO WANT TO COOPERATE TO GET KIRA. EVEN IF IT'S NOT BY THE NOTEBOOK, HE'S STILL BEING CONTROLLED.
...?
...
...

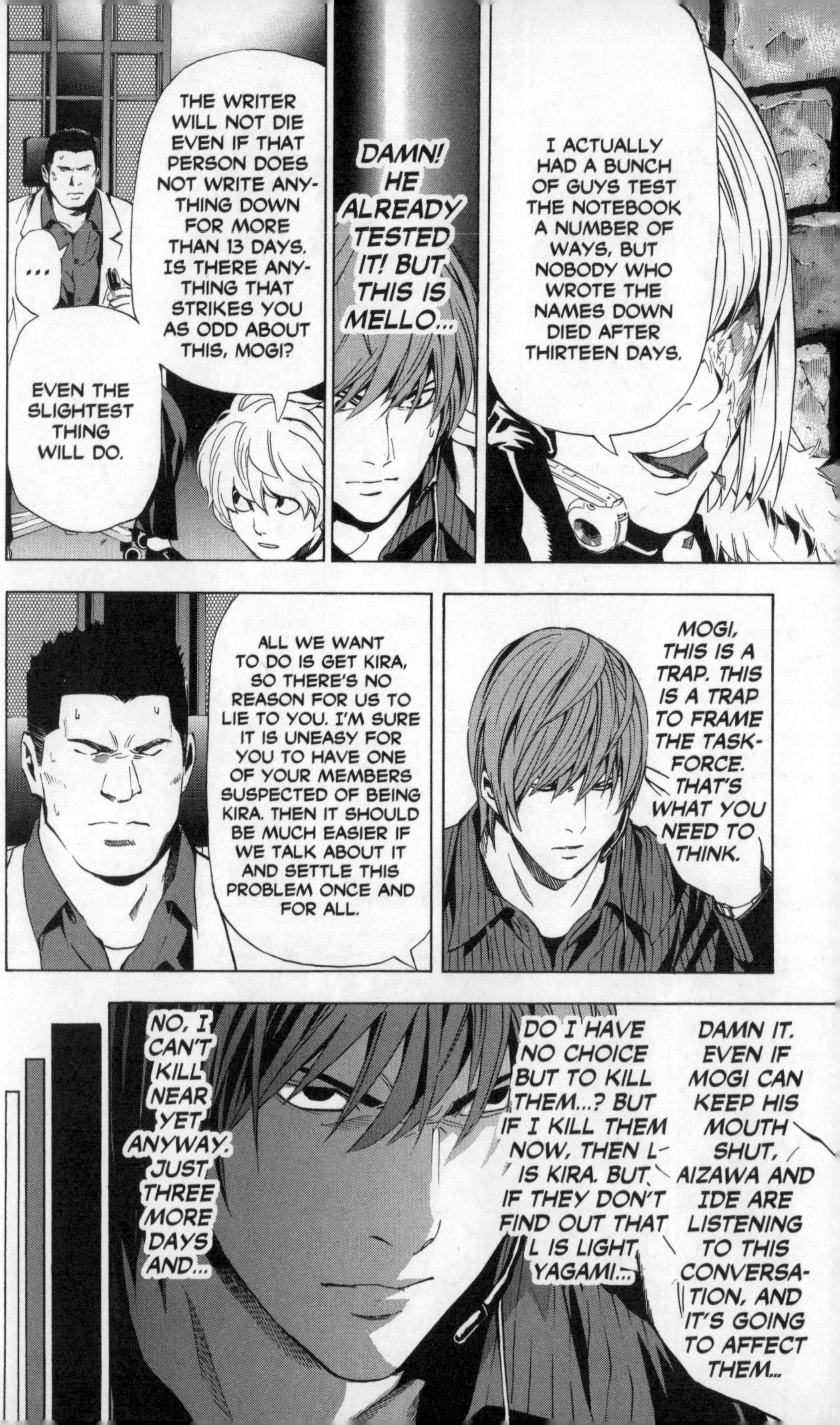
I ACTUALLY HAD A BUNCH OF GUYS TEST THE NOTEBOOK A NUMBER OF WAYS, BUT NOBODY WHO WROTE THE NAMES DOWN DIED AFTER THIRTEEN DAYS.
DAMN! HE ALREADY TESTED IT! BUT THIS IS MELLO...
THE WRITER WILL NOT DIE EVEN IF THAT PERSON DOES NOT WRITE ANYTHING DOWN FOR MORE THAN 13 DAYS. IS THERE ANYTHING THAT STRIKES YOU AS ODD ABOUT THIS, MOGI?
...
EVEN THE SLIGHTEST THING WILL DO.
MOGI, THIS IS A TRAP. THIS IS A TRAP TO FRAME THE TASK-FORCE. THAT'S WHAT YOU NEED TO THINK.
ALL WE WANT TO DO IS GET KIRA, SO THERE'S NO REASON FOR US TO LIE TO YOU. I'M SURE IT IS UNEASY FOR YOU TO HAVE ONE OF YOUR MEMBERS SUSPECTED OF BEING KIRA. THEN IT SHOULD BE MUCH EASIER IF WE TALK ABOUT IT AND SETTLE THIS PROBLEM ONCE AND FOR ALL.
DAMN IT. EVEN IF MOGI CAN KEEP HIS MOUTH SHUT, AIZAWA AND IDE ARE LISTENING TO THIS CONVERSATION, AND IT'S GOING TO AFFECT THEM...
DO I HAVE NO CHOICE BUT TO KILL THEM...? BUT IF I KILL THEM NOW, THEN L IS KIRA. BUT IF THEY DON'T FIND OUT THAT L IS LIGHT YAGAMI...
NO, I CAN'T KILL NEAR YET ANYWAY. JUST THREE MORE DAYS AND...

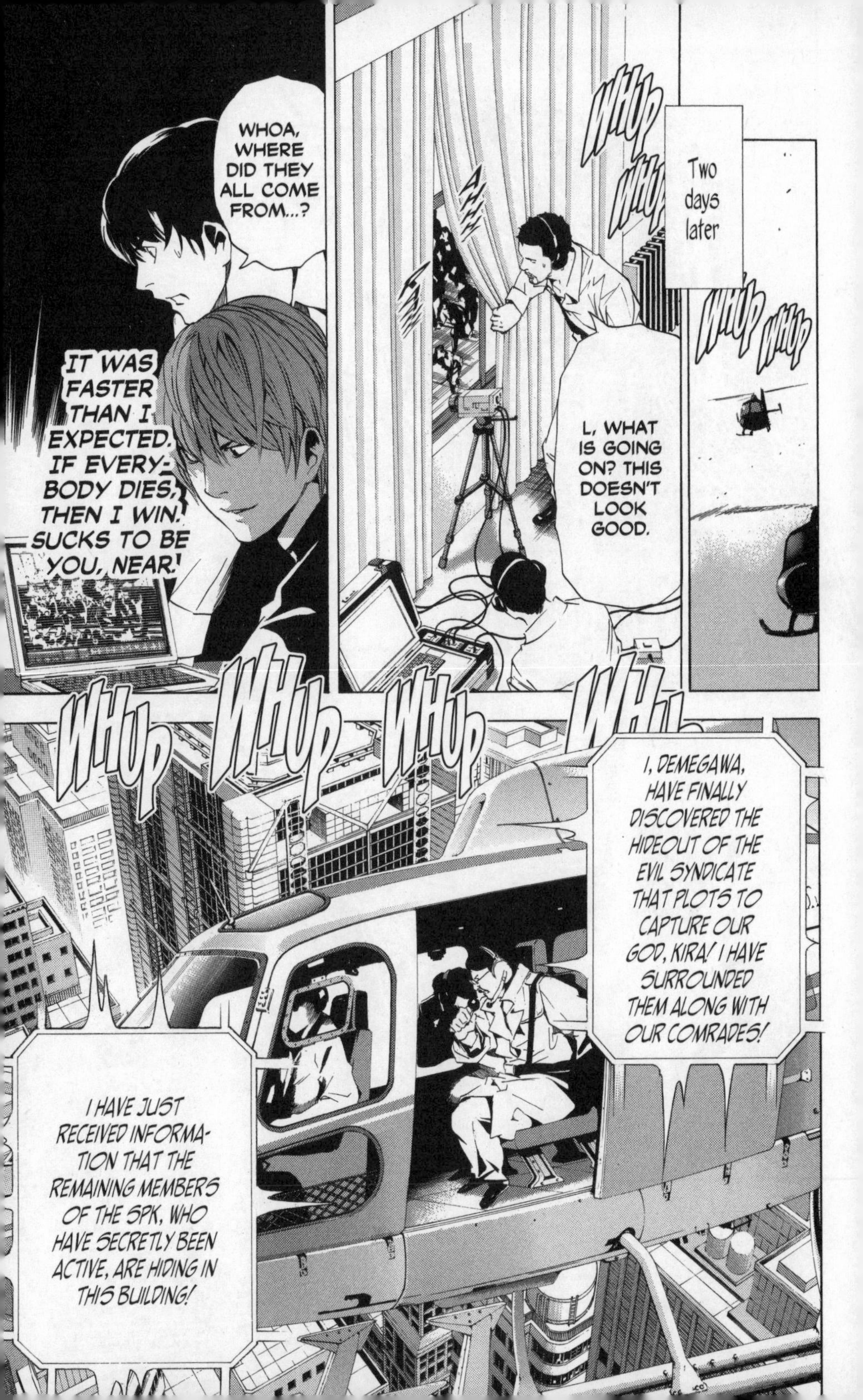
WHUP WHUP
Two days later
WHUP WHUP
L, WHAT IS GOING ON? THIS DOESN'T LOOK GOOD.
WHOA, WHERE DID THEY ALL COME FROM...?
IT WAS FASTER THAN I EXPECTED. IF EVERY-BODY DIES, THEN I WIN. SUCKS TO BE YOU, NEAR.
WHUP WHUP WHUP WHU
I, DEMEGAWA, HAVE FINALLY DISCOVERED THE HIDEOUT OF THE EVIL SYNDICATE THAT PLOTS TO CAPTURE OUR GOD, KIRA! I HAVE SURROUNDED THEM ALONG WITH OUR COMRADES!
I HAVE JUST RECEIVED INFORMA-TION THAT THE REMAINING MEMBERS OF THE SPK, WHO HAVE SECRETLY BEEN ACTIVE, ARE HIDING IN THIS BUILDING!

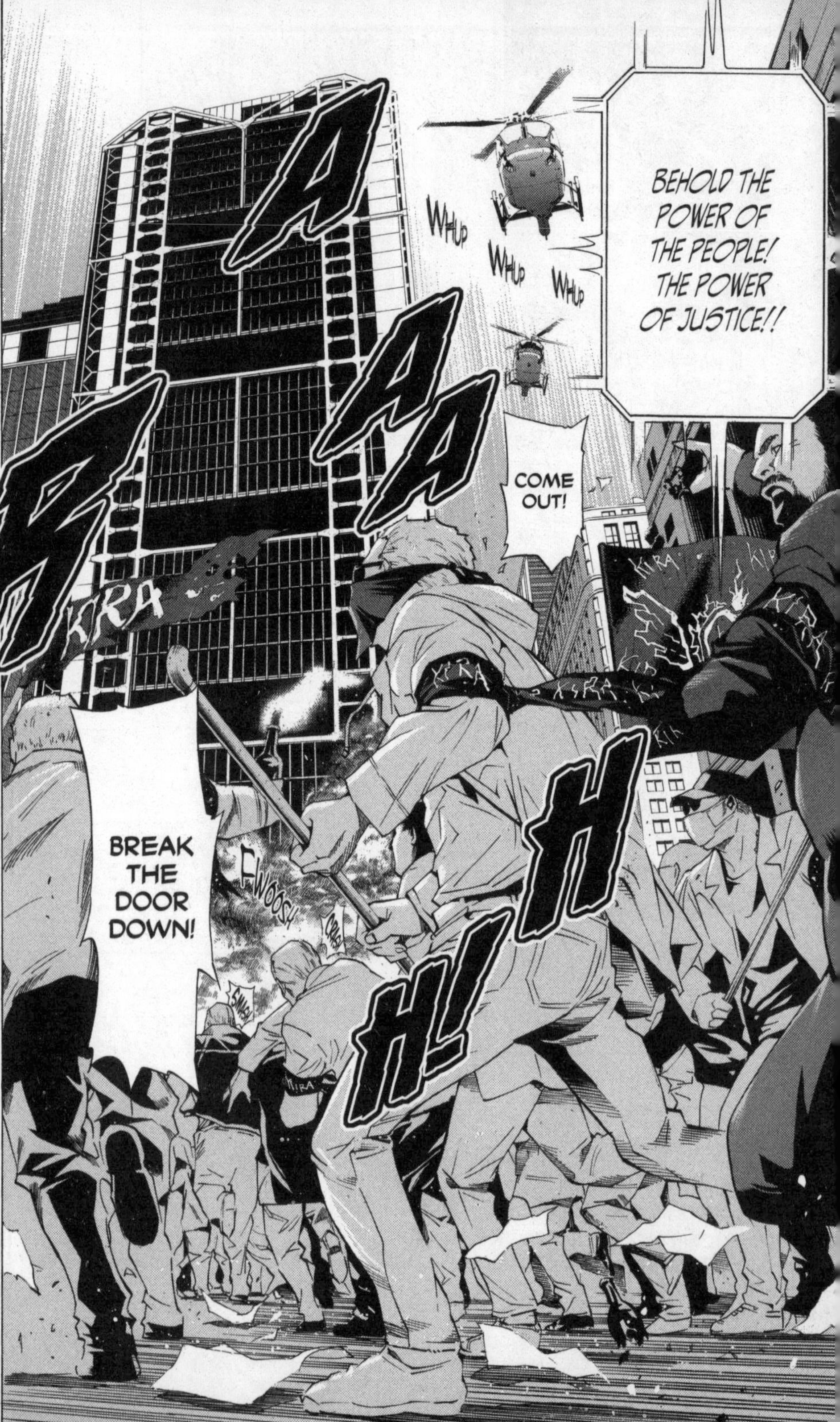
BEHOLD THE POWER OF THE PEOPLE! THE POWER OF JUSTICE!!
WHUP
WHUP
WHUP
RAAAHHH!
COME OUT!
KIRA
BREAK THE DOOR DOWN!
FWOOSH
CRASH
SMASH

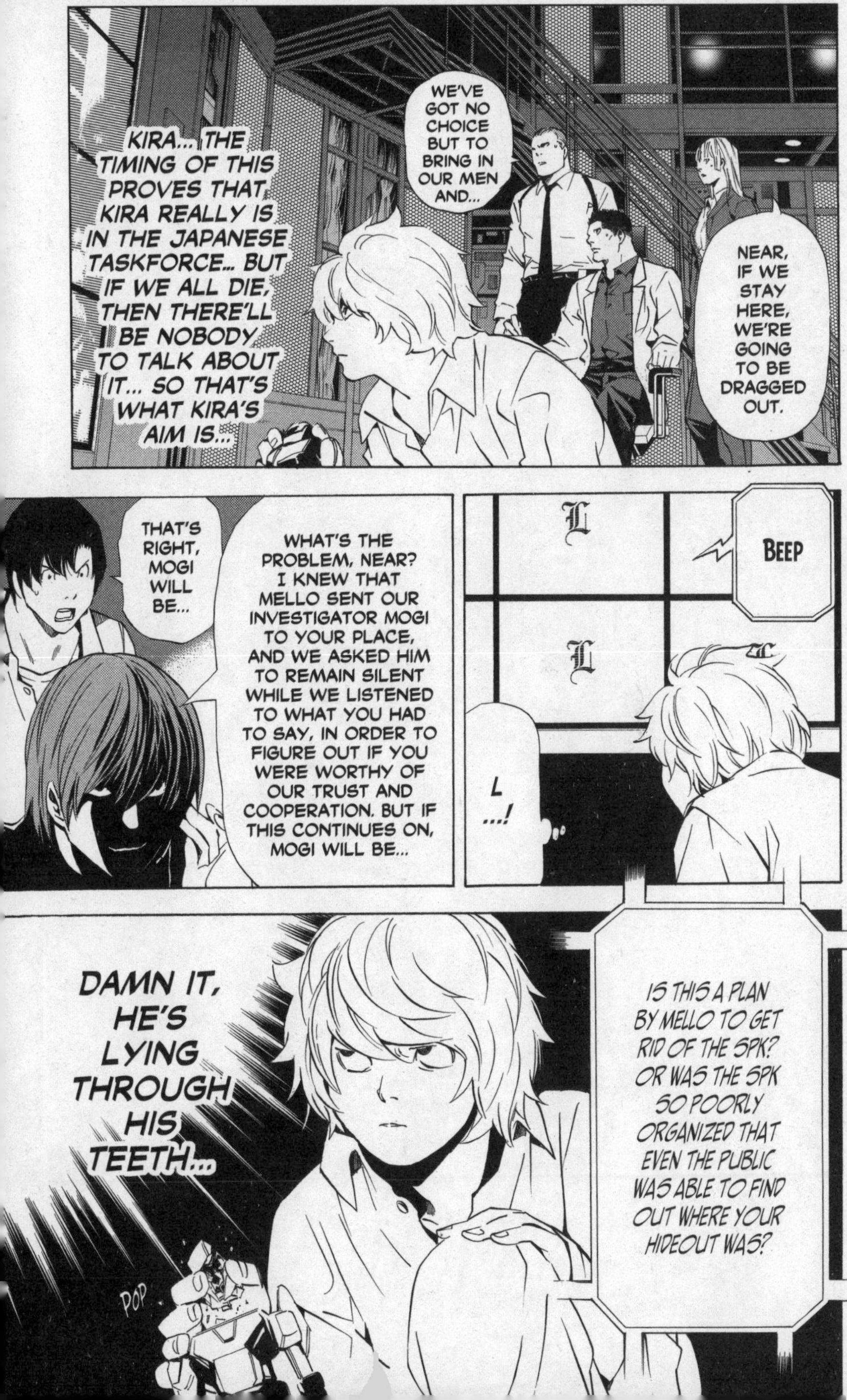
NEAR, IF WE STAY HERE, WE'RE GOING TO BE DRAGGED OUT.
WE'VE GOT NO CHOICE BUT TO BRING IN OUR MEN AND...
KIRA... THE TIMING OF THIS PROVES THAT KIRA REALLY IS IN THE JAPANESE TASKFORCE... BUT IF WE ALL DIE, THEN THERE'LL BE NOBODY TO TALK ABOUT IT... SO THAT'S WHAT KIRA'S AIM IS...
BEEP
L ...!
WHAT'S THE PROBLEM, NEAR? I KNEW THAT MELLO SENT OUR INVESTIGATOR MOGI TO YOUR PLACE, AND WE ASKED HIM TO REMAIN SILENT WHILE WE LISTENED TO WHAT YOU HAD TO SAY, IN ORDER TO FIGURE OUT IF YOU WERE WORTHY OF OUR TRUST AND COOPERATION. BUT IF THIS CONTINUES ON, MOGI WILL BE...
THAT'S RIGHT, MOGI WILL BE...
IS THIS A PLAN BY MELLO TO GET RID OF THE SPK? OR WAS THE SPK SO POORLY ORGANIZED THAT EVEN THE PUBLIC WAS ABLE TO FIND OUT WHERE YOUR HIDEOUT WAS?
DAMN IT, HE'S LYING THROUGH HIS TEETH...
POP

DEATH NOTE

How to use it

LII

° In the event that there are more than 6 DEATH NOTES in the human world, only the first 6 DEATH NOTES that have been delivered to humans will have effect.

　7冊以上のノートが人間界にある場合、その効力があるのは
人間の手に渡った順番が早い6冊である。

° The seventh DEATH NOTE will not become active until one of the other 6 DEATH NOTES is burned up, or a god of death takes one of them back to the world of gods of death.

　1冊が燃える等してノートの効力を失うか、
死神が所有したり死神界に持ち帰らなければ、7冊目に効力は生まれない。

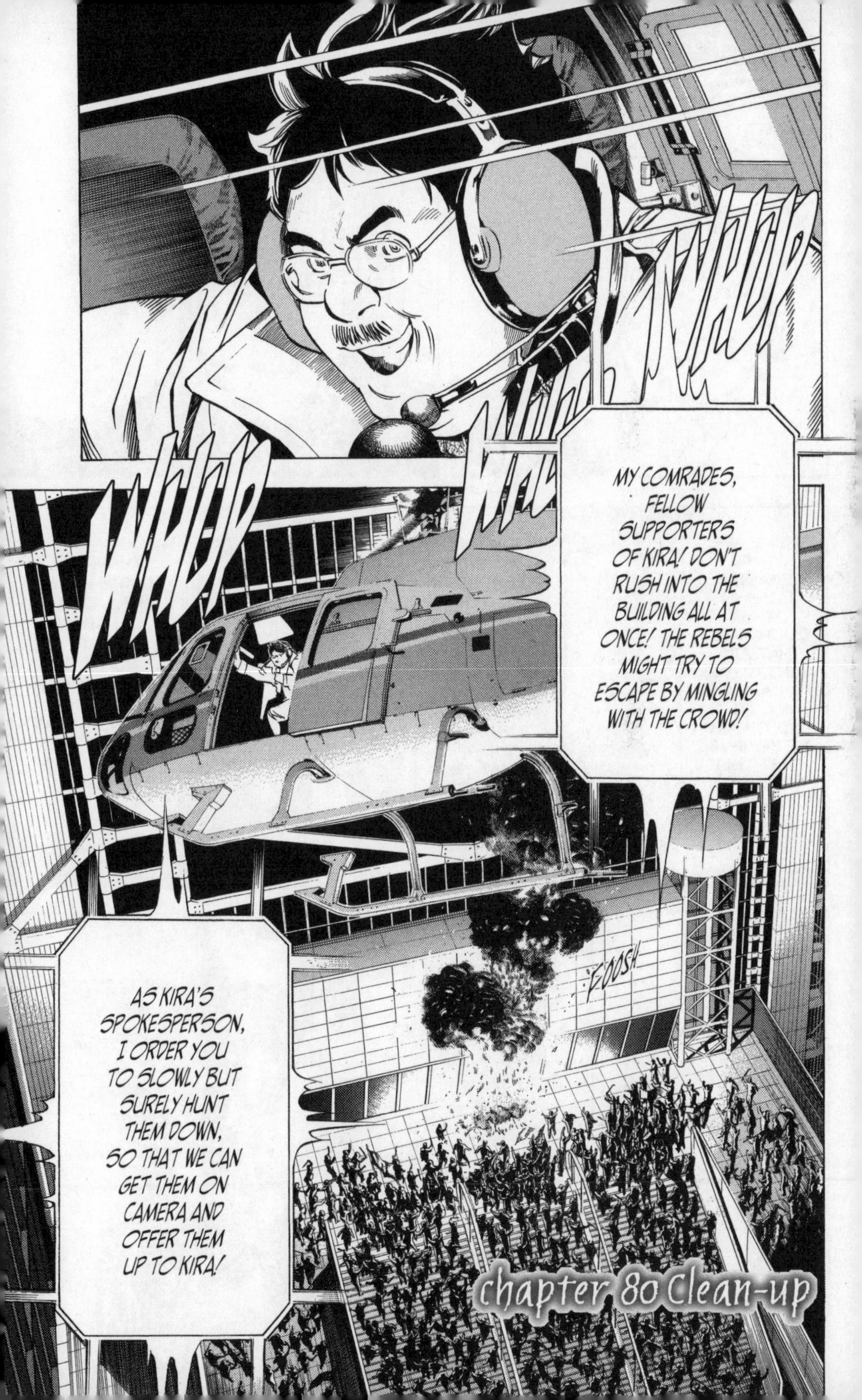
WHUP WHUP
WHUP
MY COMRADES, FELLOW SUPPORTERS OF KIRA! DON'T RUSH INTO THE BUILDING ALL AT ONCE! THE REBELS MIGHT TRY TO ESCAPE BY MINGLING WITH THE CROWD!
WHUP
FOOSH
AS KIRA'S SPOKESPERSON, I ORDER YOU TO SLOWLY BUT SURELY HUNT THEM DOWN, SO THAT WE CAN GET THEM ON CAMERA AND OFFER THEM UP TO KIRA!
chapter 80 Clean-up

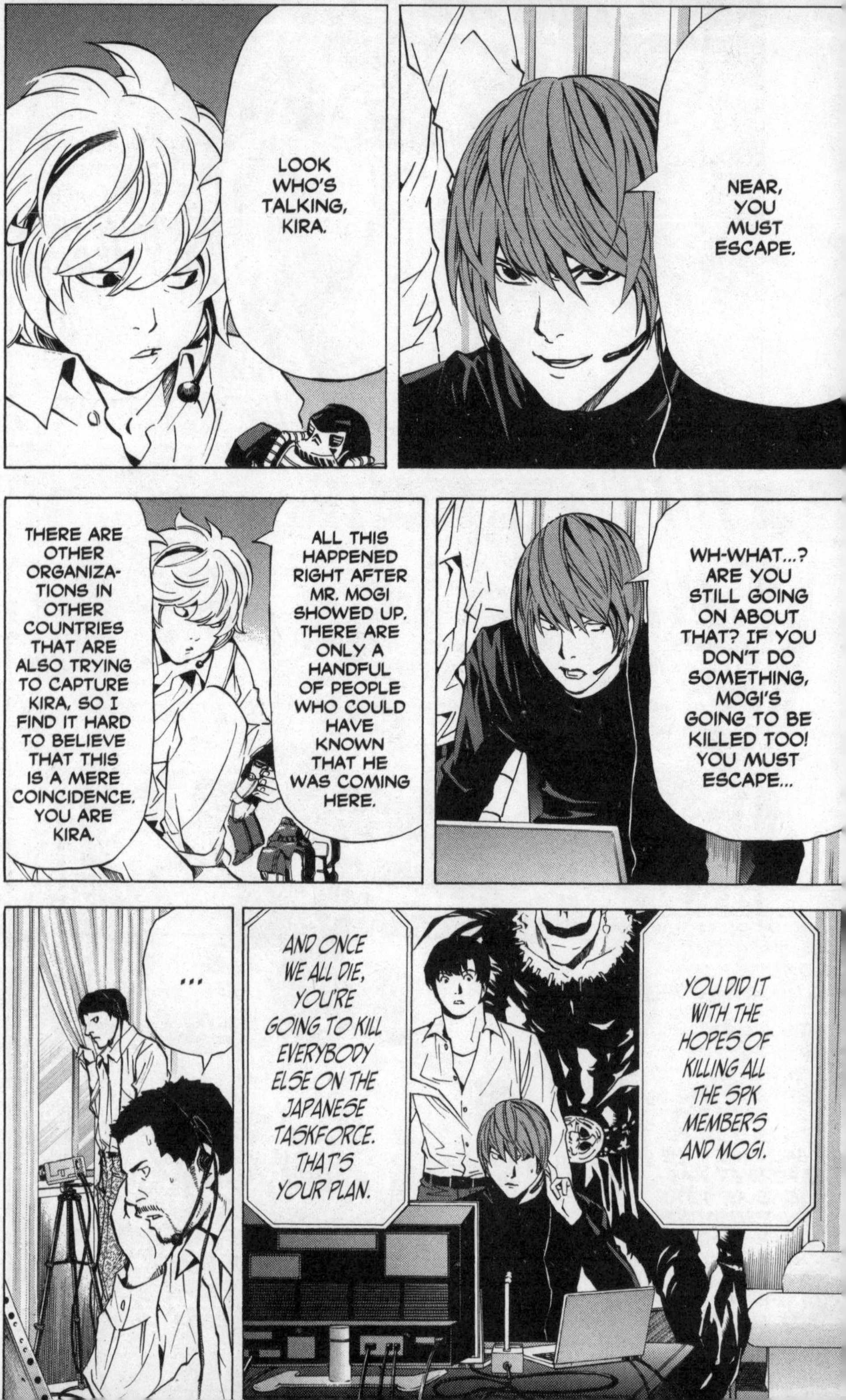
NEAR, YOU MUST ESCAPE.
LOOK WHO'S TALKING, KIRA.
WH-WHAT...? ARE YOU STILL GOING ON ABOUT THAT? IF YOU DON'T DO SOMETHING, MOGI'S GOING TO BE KILLED TOO! YOU MUST ESCAPE...
ALL THIS HAPPENED RIGHT AFTER MR. MOGI SHOWED UP. THERE ARE ONLY A HANDFUL OF PEOPLE WHO COULD HAVE KNOWN THAT HE WAS COMING HERE.
THERE ARE OTHER ORGANIZATIONS IN OTHER COUNTRIES THAT ARE ALSO TRYING TO CAPTURE KIRA, SO I FIND IT HARD TO BELIEVE THAT THIS IS A MERE COINCIDENCE. YOU ARE KIRA.
YOU DID IT WITH THE HOPES OF KILLING ALL THE SPK MEMBERS AND MOGI.
AND ONCE WE ALL DIE, YOU'RE GOING TO KILL EVERYBODY ELSE ON THE JAPANESE TASKFORCE. THAT'S YOUR PLAN.
...

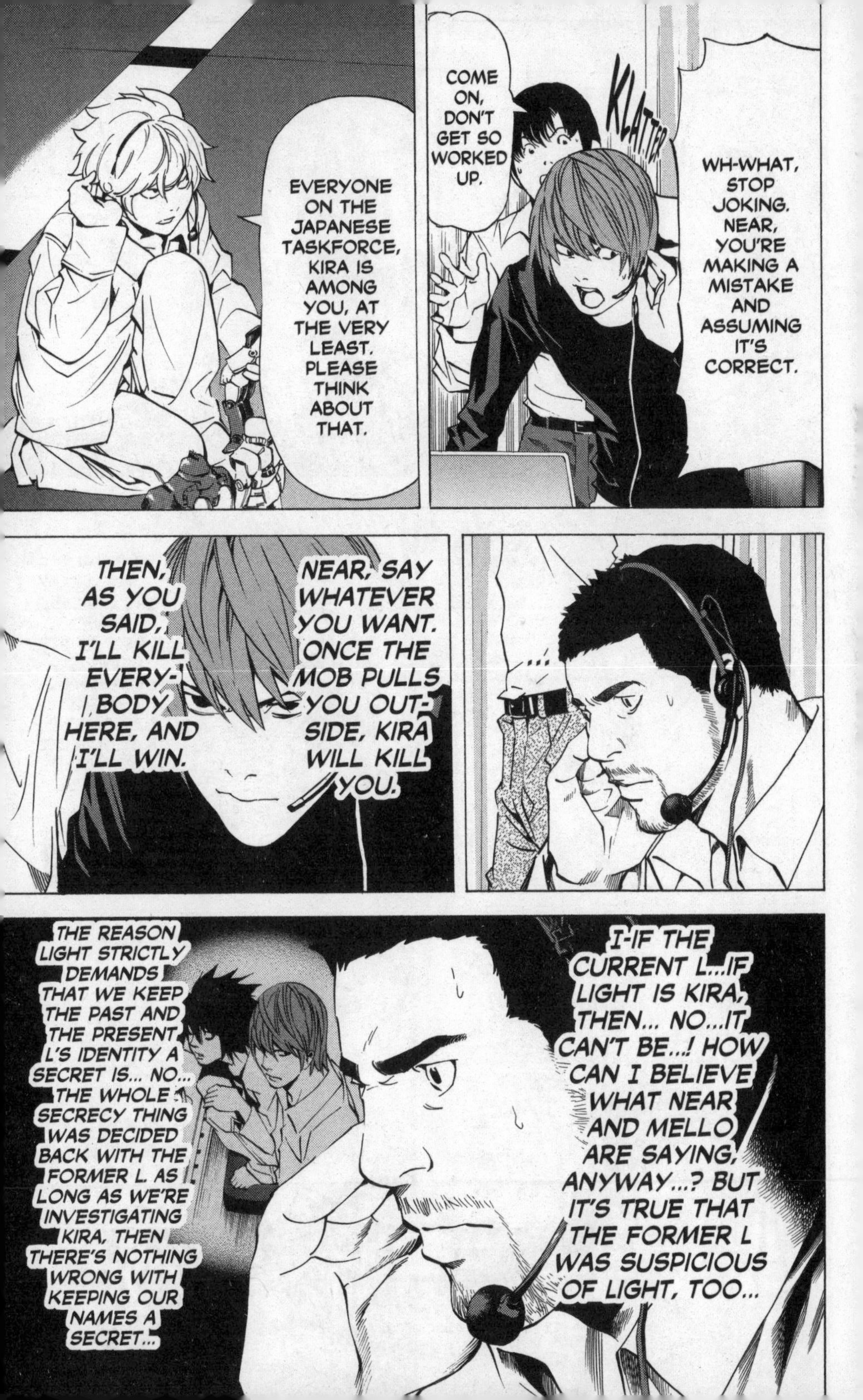
WH-WHAT, STOP JOKING. NEAR, YOU'RE MAKING A MISTAKE AND ASSUMING IT'S CORRECT.
KLATTER
COME ON, DON'T GET SO WORKED UP.
EVERYONE ON THE JAPANESE TASKFORCE, KIRA IS AMONG YOU, AT THE VERY LEAST. PLEASE THINK ABOUT THAT.
...
NEAR, SAY WHATEVER YOU WANT. ONCE THE MOB PULLS YOU OUTSIDE, KIRA WILL KILL YOU.
THEN, AS YOU SAID, I'LL KILL EVERYBODY HERE, AND I'LL WIN.
I-IF THE CURRENT L...IF LIGHT IS KIRA, THEN... NO...IT CAN'T BE...! HOW CAN I BELIEVE WHAT NEAR AND MELLO ARE SAYING, ANYWAY...? BUT IT'S TRUE THAT THE FORMER L WAS SUSPICIOUS OF LIGHT, TOO...
THE REASON LIGHT STRICTLY DEMANDS THAT WE KEEP THE PAST AND THE PRESENT L'S IDENTITY A SECRET IS... NO... THE WHOLE SECRECY THING WAS DECIDED BACK WITH THE FORMER L. AS LONG AS WE'RE INVESTIGATING KIRA, THEN THERE'S NOTHING WRONG WITH KEEPING OUR NAMES A SECRET...

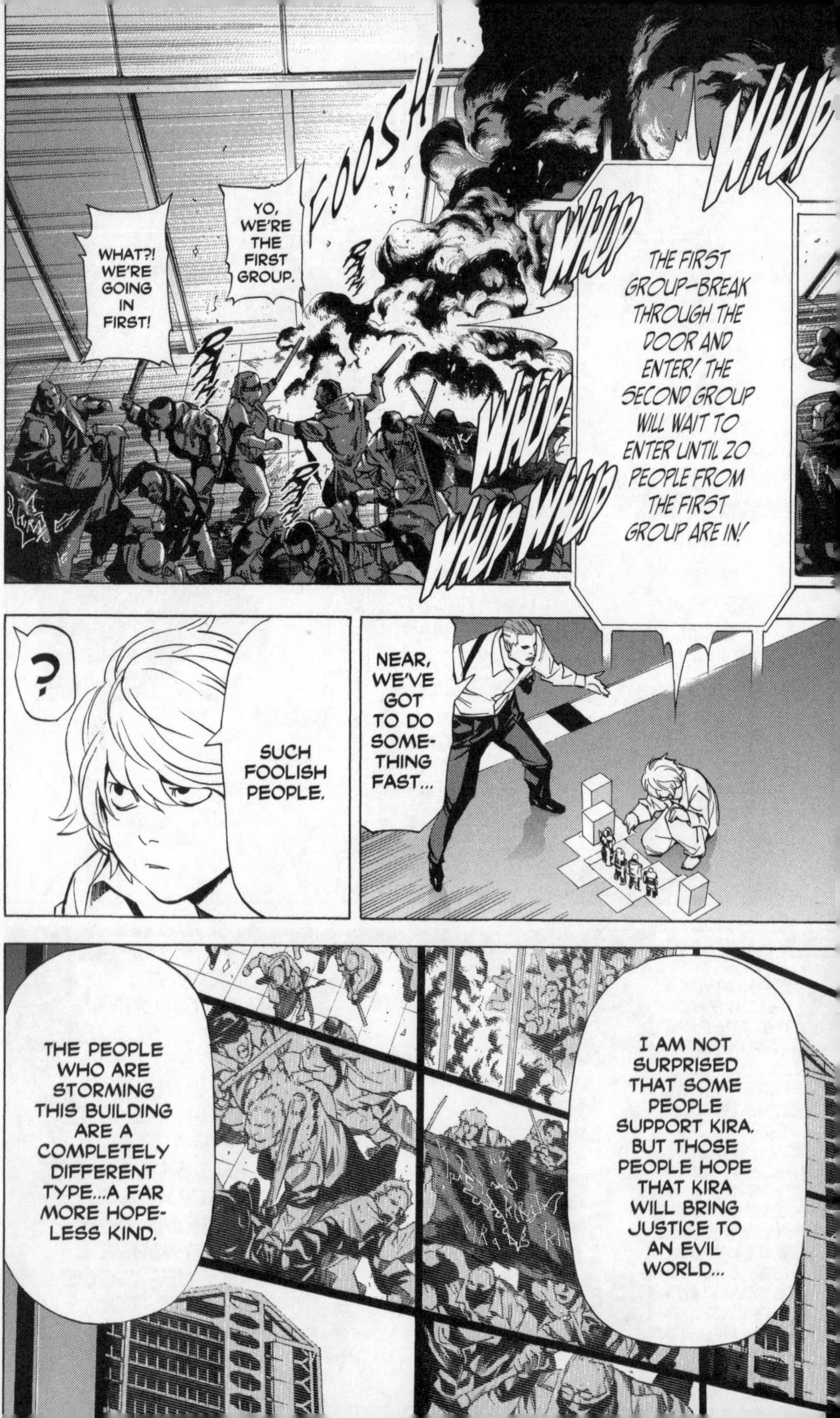
WHUP
WHUP
THE FIRST GROUP–BREAK THROUGH THE DOOR AND ENTER! THE SECOND GROUP WILL WAIT TO ENTER UNTIL 20 PEOPLE FROM THE FIRST GROUP ARE IN!
WHUP
WHUP WHUP
FOOSH
YO, WE'RE THE FIRST GROUP.
WHAT?! WE'RE GOING IN FIRST!
NEAR, WE'VE GOT TO DO SOME-THING FAST...
SUCH FOOLISH PEOPLE.
?
I AM NOT SURPRISED THAT SOME PEOPLE SUPPORT KIRA. BUT THOSE PEOPLE HOPE THAT KIRA WILL BRING JUSTICE TO AN EVIL WORLD...
THE PEOPLE WHO ARE STORMING THIS BUILDING ARE A COMPLETELY DIFFERENT TYPE...A FAR MORE HOPE-LESS KIND.

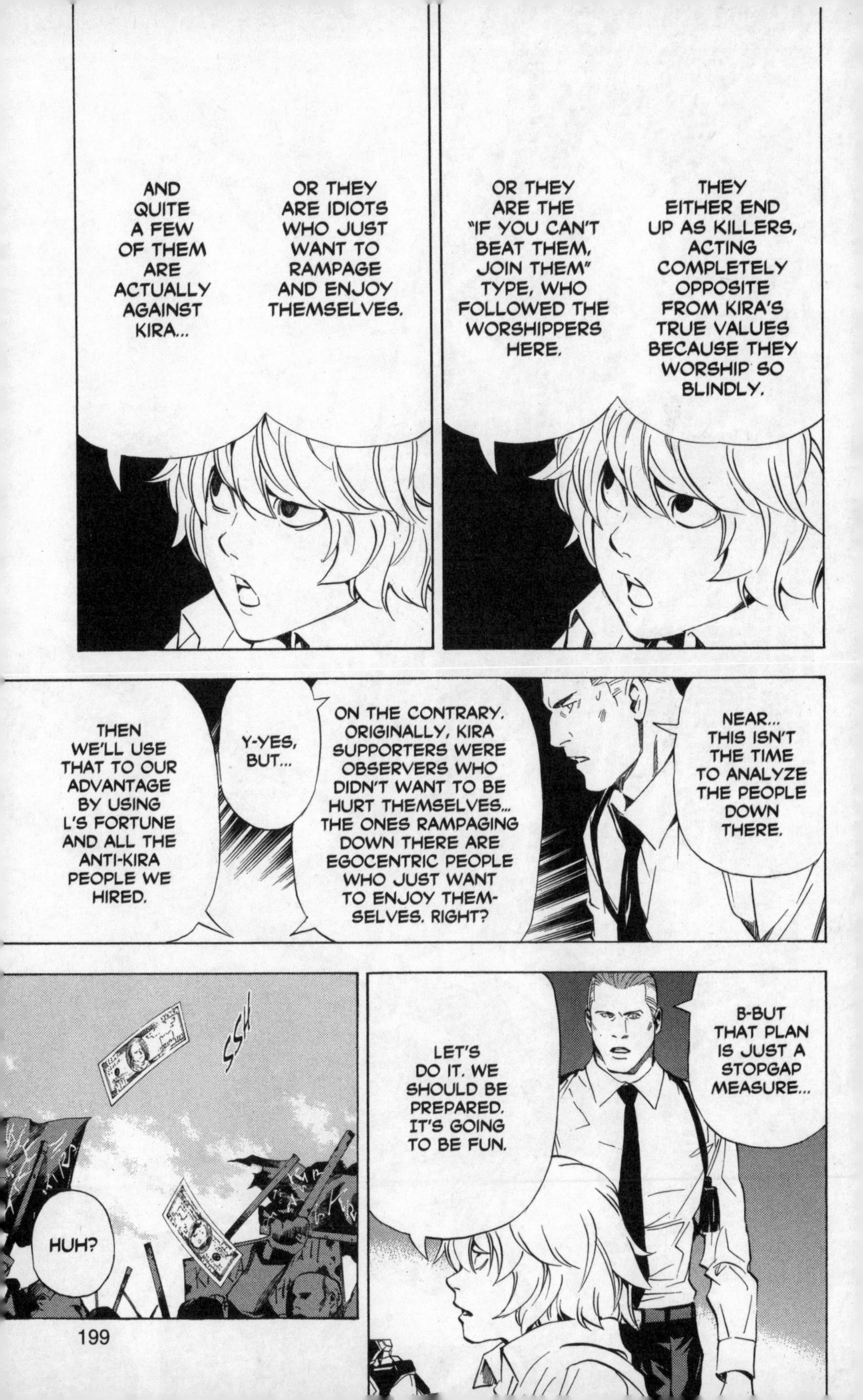
THEY EITHER END UP AS KILLERS, ACTING COMPLETELY OPPOSITE FROM KIRA'S TRUE VALUES BECAUSE THEY WORSHIP SO BLINDLY.
OR THEY ARE THE "IF YOU CAN'T BEAT THEM, JOIN THEM" TYPE, WHO FOLLOWED THE WORSHIPPERS HERE.
OR THEY ARE IDIOTS WHO JUST WANT TO RAMPAGE AND ENJOY THEMSELVES.
AND QUITE A FEW OF THEM ARE ACTUALLY AGAINST KIRA...
NEAR... THIS ISN'T THE TIME TO ANALYZE THE PEOPLE DOWN THERE.
ON THE CONTRARY. ORIGINALLY, KIRA SUPPORTERS WERE OBSERVERS WHO DIDN'T WANT TO BE HURT THEMSELVES... THE ONES RAMPAGING DOWN THERE ARE EGOCENTRIC PEOPLE WHO JUST WANT TO ENJOY THEM-SELVES. RIGHT?
Y-YES, BUT...
THEN WE'LL USE THAT TO OUR ADVANTAGE BY USING L'S FORTUNE AND ALL THE ANTI-KIRA PEOPLE WE HIRED.
B-BUT THAT PLAN IS JUST A STOPGAP MEASURE...
LET'S DO IT. WE SHOULD BE PREPARED. IT'S GOING TO BE FUN.
SSH
HUH?

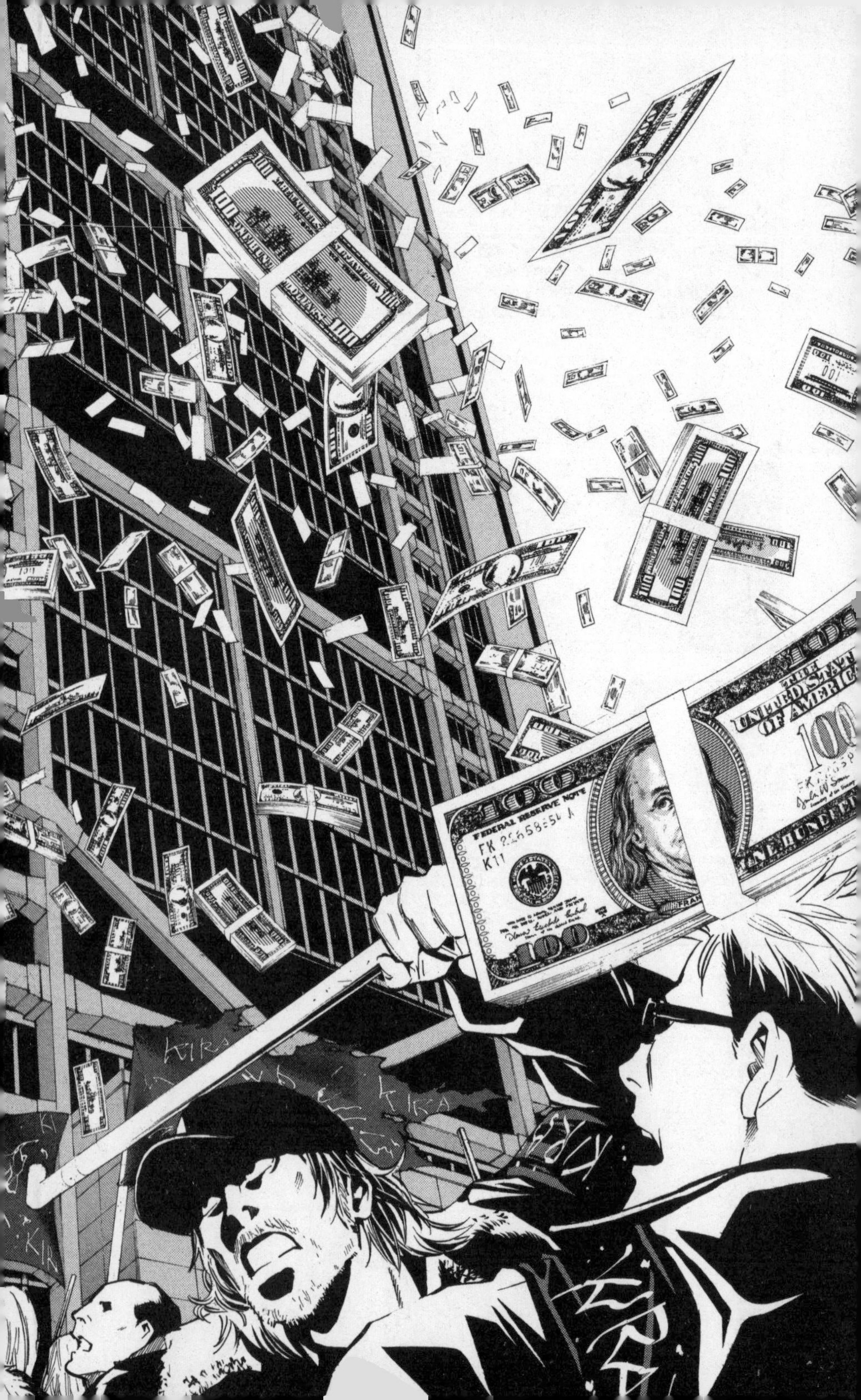
KIRA
FEDERAL RESERVE NOTE

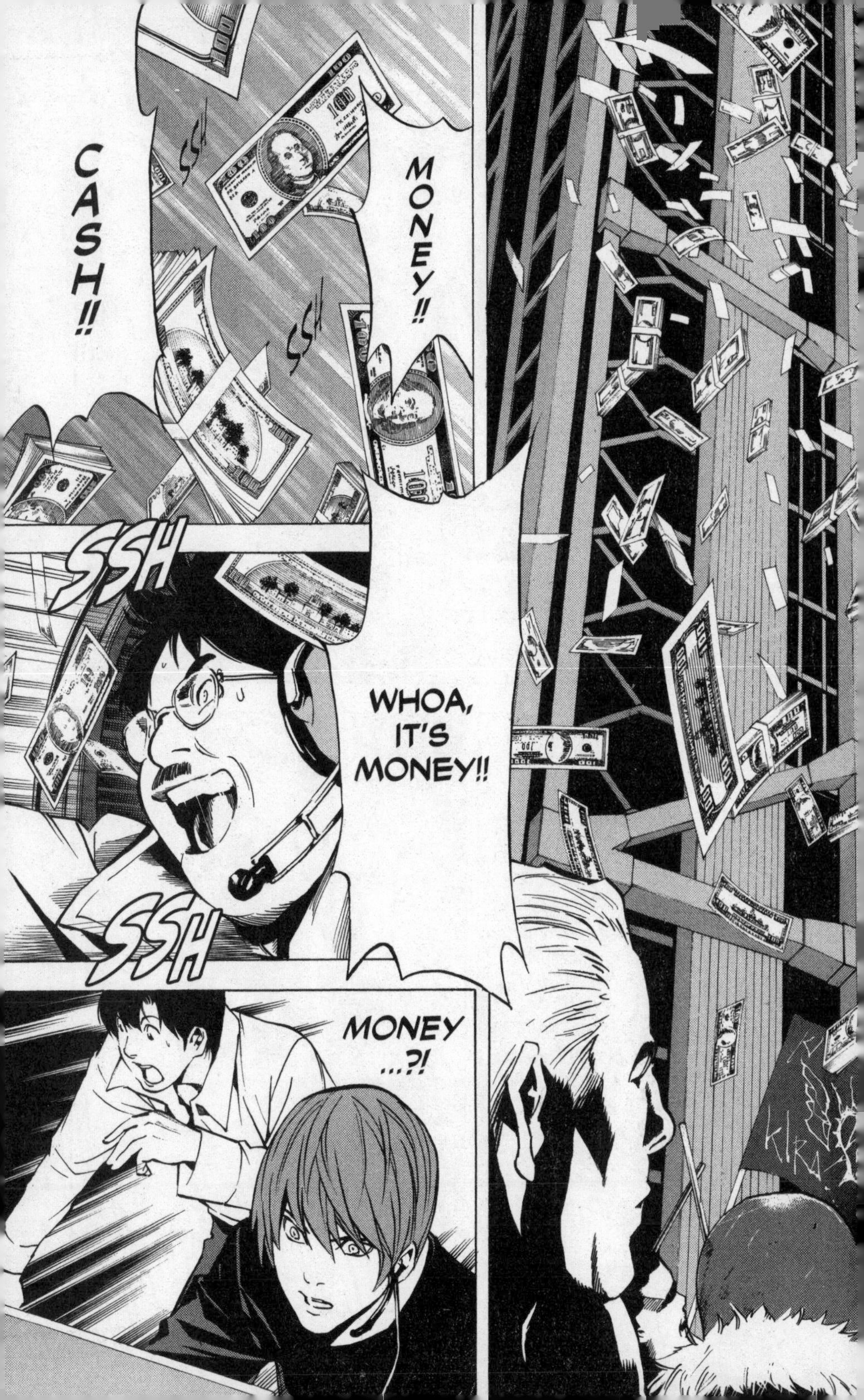
MONEY!!
CASH!!
WHOA, IT'S MONEY!!
SSH
SSH
MONEY ...?!

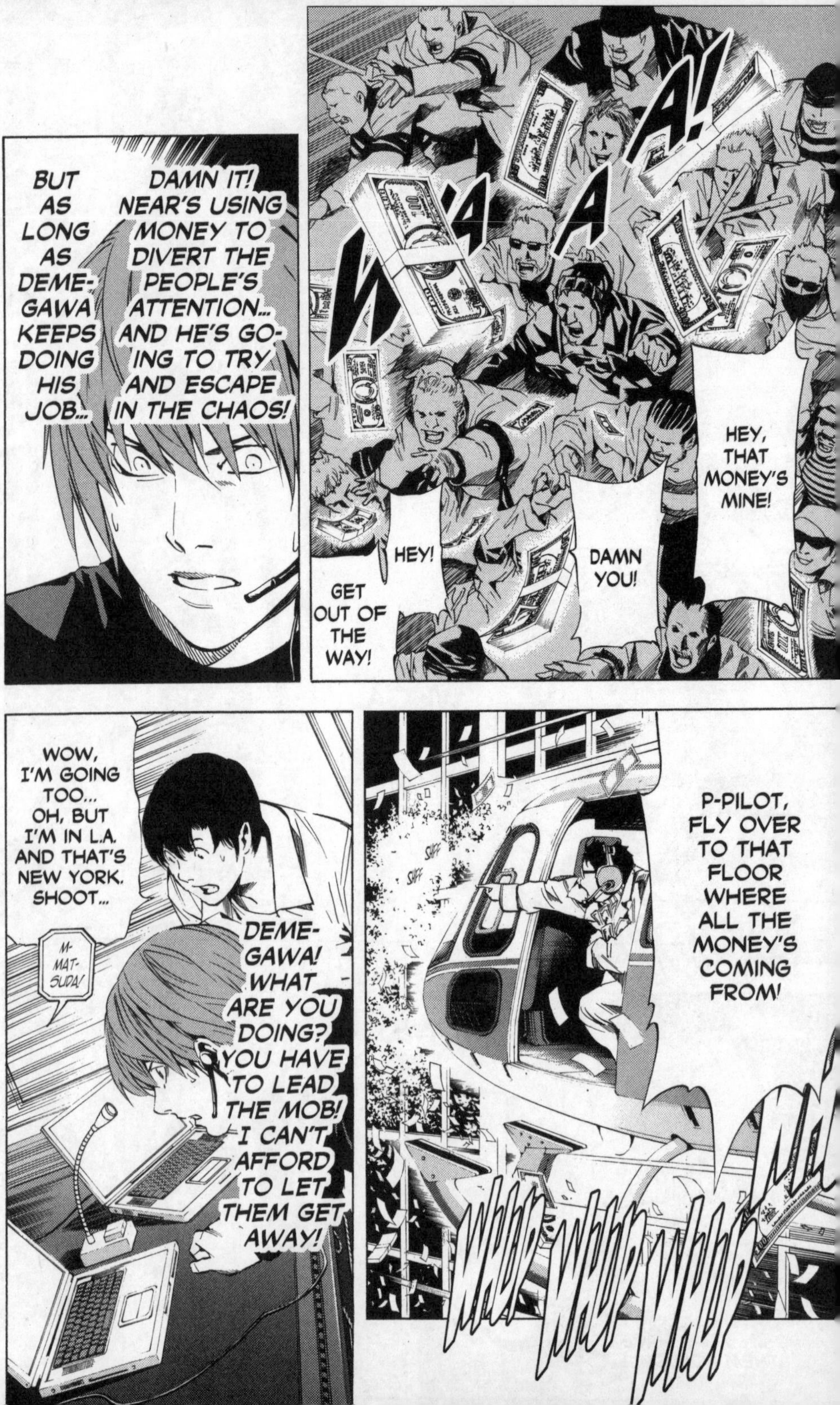
WAAA!
HEY, THAT MONEY'S MINE!
DAMN YOU!
HEY!
GET OUT OF THE WAY!
DAMN IT! NEAR'S USING MONEY TO DIVERT THE PEOPLE'S ATTENTION... AND HE'S GOING TO TRY AND ESCAPE IN THE CHAOS!
BUT AS LONG AS DEMEGAWA KEEPS DOING HIS JOB...
P-PILOT, FLY OVER TO THAT FLOOR WHERE ALL THE MONEY'S COMING FROM!
WOW, I'M GOING TOO... OH, BUT I'M IN L.A. AND THAT'S NEW YORK. SHOOT...
M-MATSUDA!
DEMEGAWA! WHAT ARE YOU DOING? YOU HAVE TO LEAD THE MOB! I CAN'T AFFORD TO LET THEM GET AWAY!

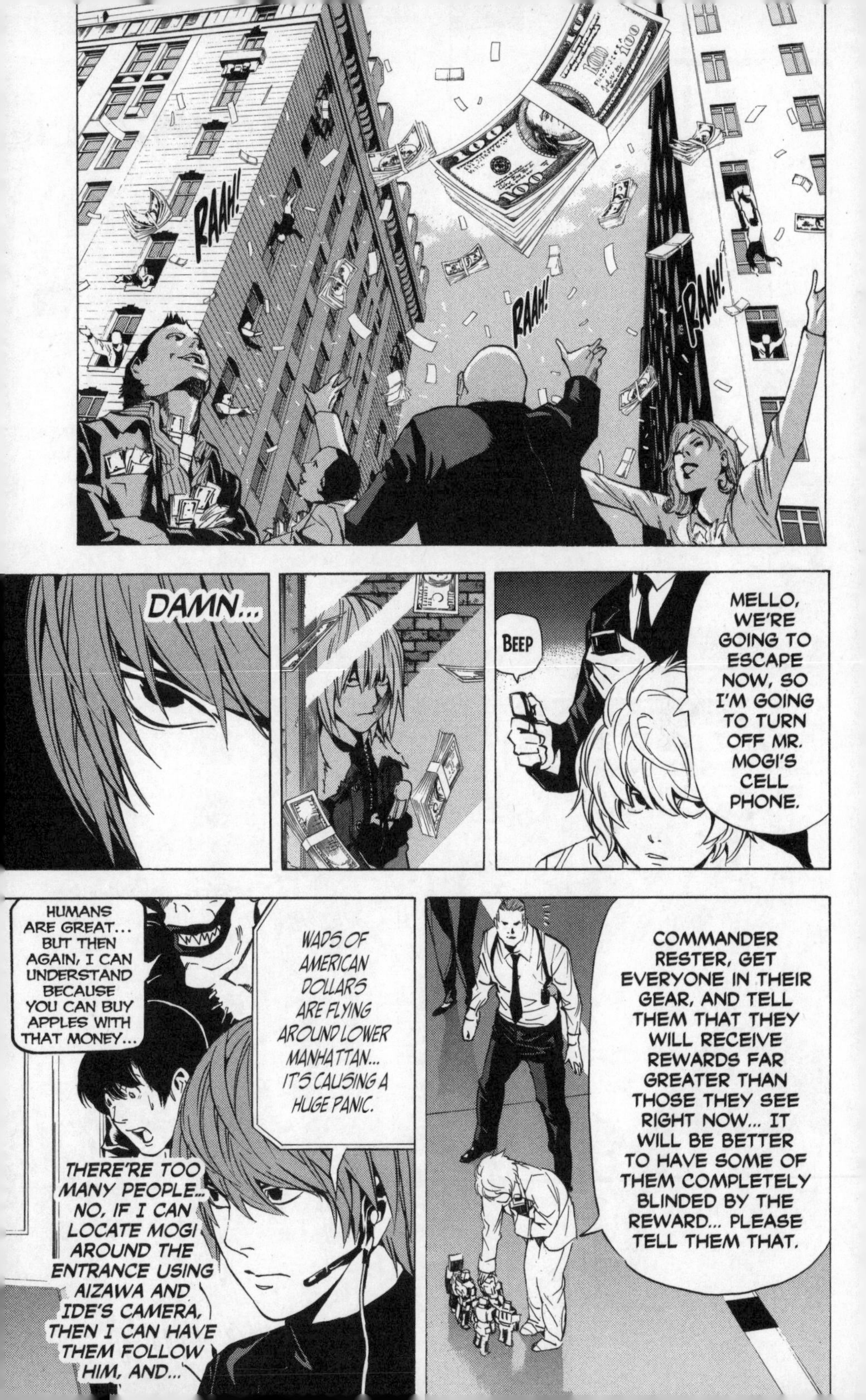
RAAH!
RAAH!
RAAH!
BEEP
MELLO, WE'RE GOING TO ESCAPE NOW, SO I'M GOING TO TURN OFF MR. MOGI'S CELL PHONE.
DAMN...
COMMANDER RESTER, GET EVERYONE IN THEIR GEAR, AND TELL THEM THAT THEY WILL RECEIVE REWARDS FAR GREATER THAN THOSE THEY SEE RIGHT NOW... IT WILL BE BETTER TO HAVE SOME OF THEM COMPLETELY BLINDED BY THE REWARD... PLEASE TELL THEM THAT.
WADS OF AMERICAN DOLLARS ARE FLYING AROUND LOWER MANHATTAN... IT'S CAUSING A HUGE PANIC.
HUMANS ARE GREAT... BUT THEN AGAIN, I CAN UNDERSTAND BECAUSE YOU CAN BUY APPLES WITH THAT MONEY...
THERE'RE TOO MANY PEOPLE... NO, IF I CAN LOCATE MOGI AROUND THE ENTRANCE USING AIZAWA AND IDE'S CAMERA, THEN I CAN HAVE THEM FOLLOW HIM, AND...

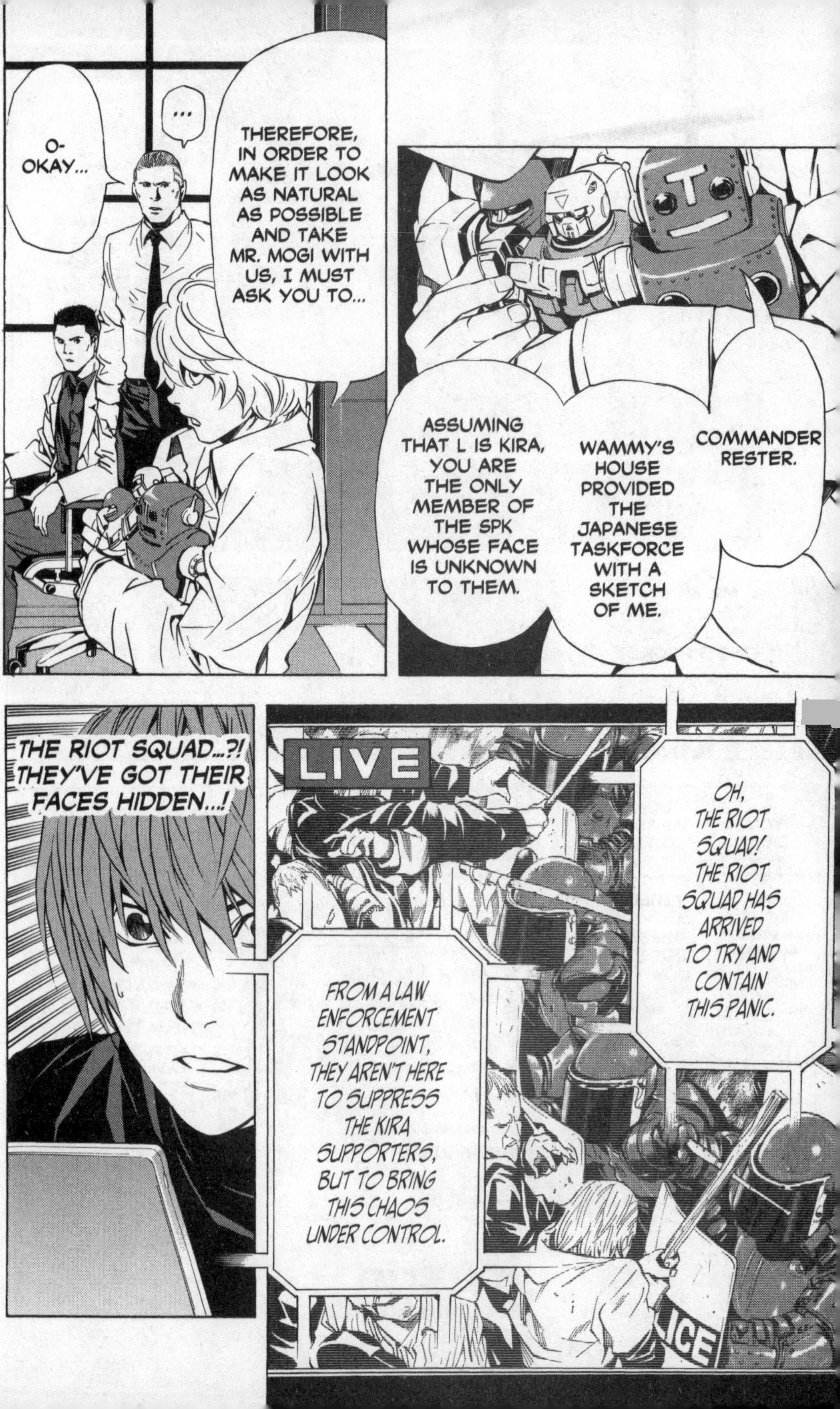

COMMANDER RESTER.
WAMMY'S HOUSE PROVIDED THE JAPANESE TASKFORCE WITH A SKETCH OF ME.
ASSUMING THAT L IS KIRA, YOU ARE THE ONLY MEMBER OF THE SPK WHOSE FACE IS UNKNOWN TO THEM.
THEREFORE, IN ORDER TO MAKE IT LOOK AS NATURAL AS POSSIBLE AND TAKE MR. MOGI WITH US, I MUST ASK YOU TO...
...
O-OKAY...
LIVE
OH, THE RIOT SQUAD! THE RIOT SQUAD HAS ARRIVED TO TRY AND CONTAIN THIS PANIC.
FROM A LAW ENFORCEMENT STANDPOINT, THEY AREN'T HERE TO SUPPRESS THE KIRA SUPPORTERS, BUT TO BRING THIS CHAOS UNDER CONTROL.
THE RIOT SQUAD...?! THEY'VE GOT THEIR FACES HIDDEN...!

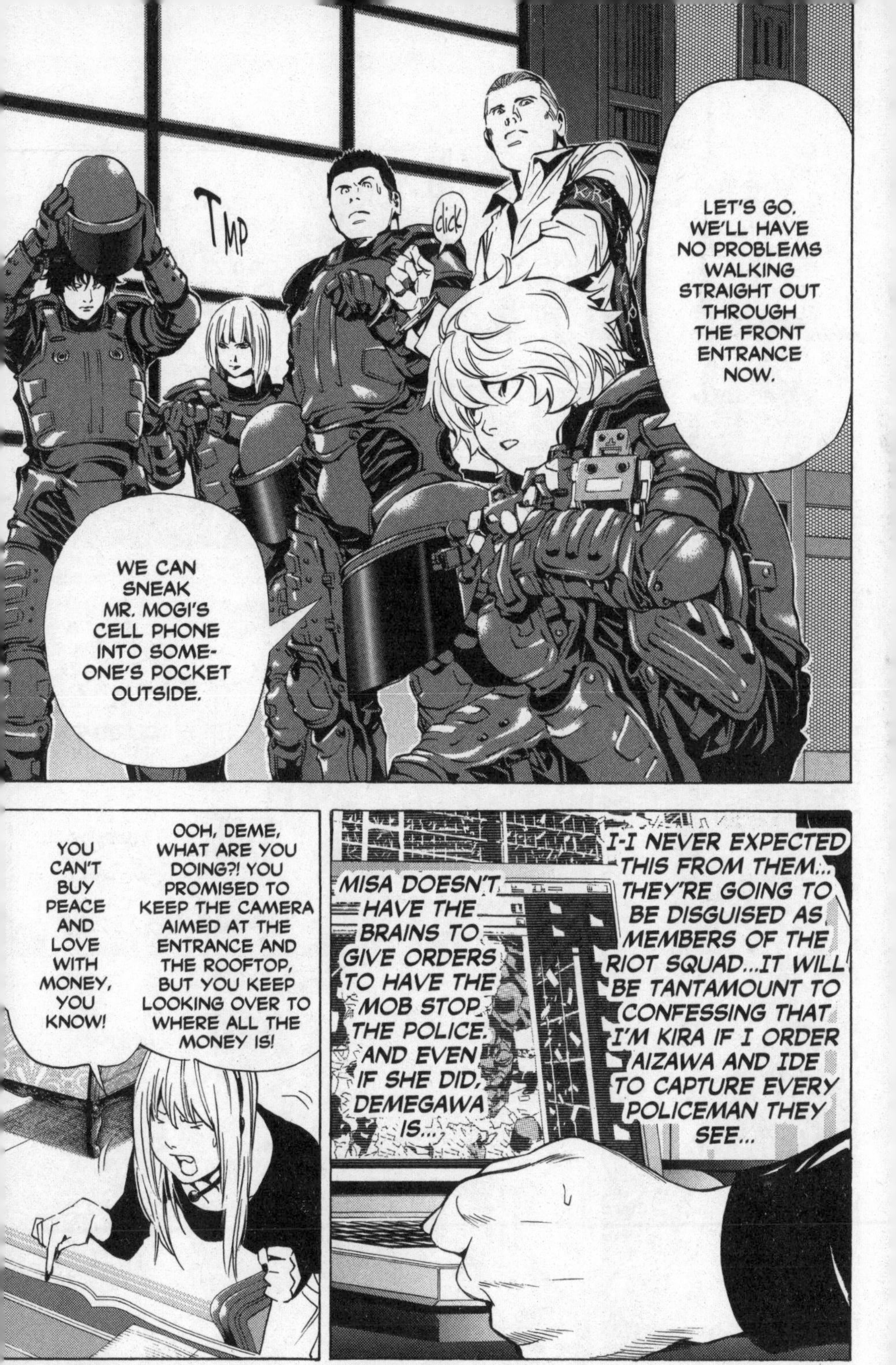
LET'S GO. WE'LL HAVE NO PROBLEMS WALKING STRAIGHT OUT THROUGH THE FRONT ENTRANCE NOW.
click
TMP
WE CAN SNEAK MR. MOGI'S CELL PHONE INTO SOME-ONE'S POCKET OUTSIDE.
I-I NEVER EXPECTED THIS FROM THEM... THEY'RE GOING TO BE DISGUISED AS MEMBERS OF THE RIOT SQUAD...IT WILL BE TANTAMOUNT TO CONFESSING THAT I'M KIRA IF I ORDER AIZAWA AND IDE TO CAPTURE EVERY POLICEMAN THEY SEE...
MISA DOESN'T HAVE THE BRAINS TO GIVE ORDERS TO HAVE THE MOB STOP THE POLICE. AND EVEN IF SHE DID, DEMEGAWA IS...
OOH, DEME, WHAT ARE YOU DOING?! YOU PROMISED TO KEEP THE CAMERA AIMED AT THE ENTRANCE AND THE ROOFTOP, BUT YOU KEEP LOOKING OVER TO WHERE ALL THE MONEY IS!
YOU CAN'T BUY PEACE AND LOVE WITH MONEY, YOU KNOW!

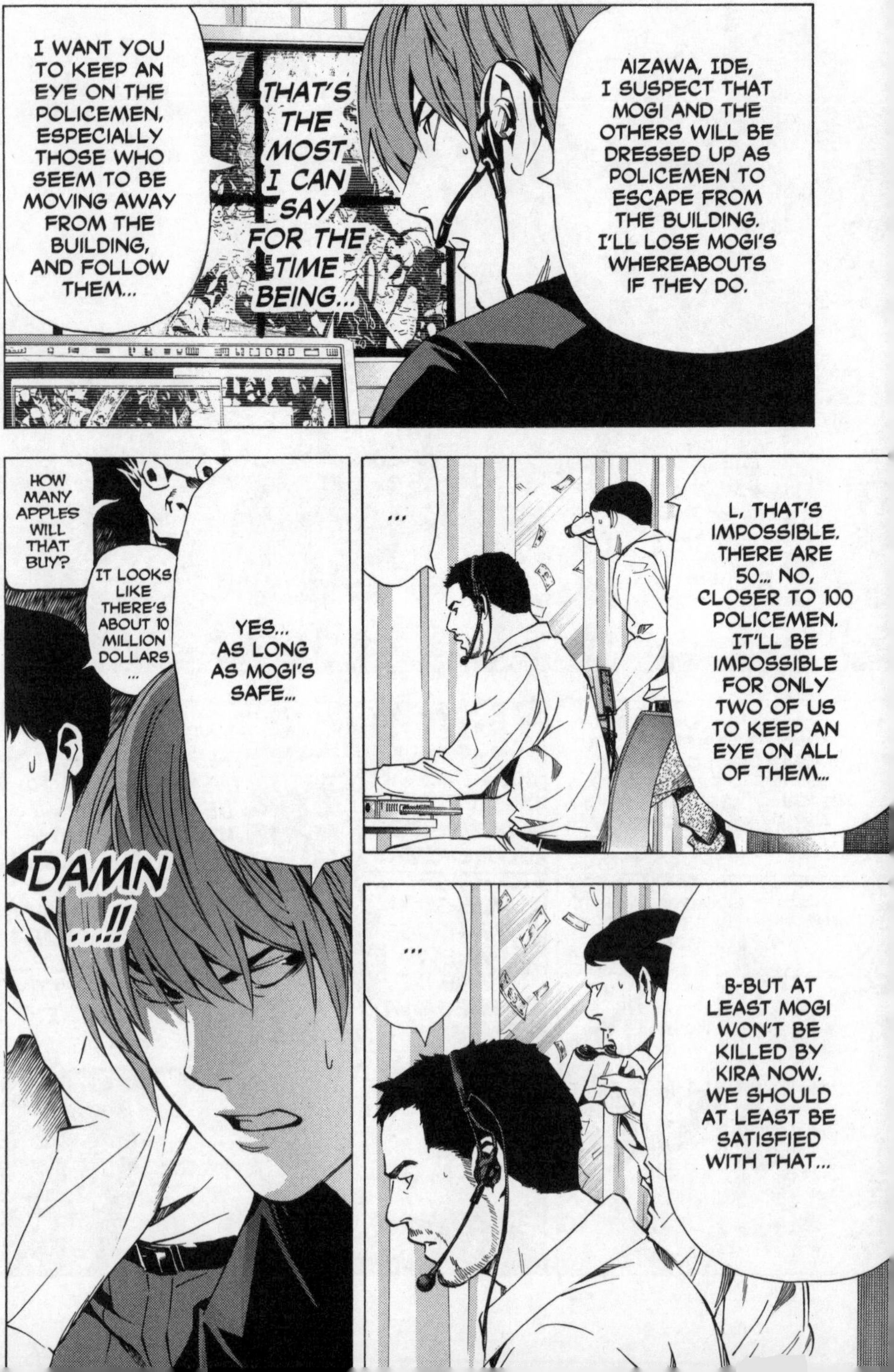
AIZAWA, IDE, I SUSPECT THAT MOGI AND THE OTHERS WILL BE DRESSED UP AS POLICEMEN TO ESCAPE FROM THE BUILDING. I'LL LOSE MOGI'S WHEREABOUTS IF THEY DO.
I WANT YOU TO KEEP AN EYE ON THE POLICEMEN, ESPECIALLY THOSE WHO SEEM TO BE MOVING AWAY FROM THE BUILDING, AND FOLLOW THEM...
THAT'S THE MOST I CAN SAY FOR THE TIME BEING...
L, THAT'S IMPOSSIBLE. THERE ARE 50... NO, CLOSER TO 100 POLICEMEN. IT'LL BE IMPOSSIBLE FOR ONLY TWO OF US TO KEEP AN EYE ON ALL OF THEM...
...
B-BUT AT LEAST MOGI WON'T BE KILLED BY KIRA NOW. WE SHOULD AT LEAST BE SATISFIED WITH THAT...
...
YES... AS LONG AS MOGI'S SAFE...
HOW MANY APPLES WILL THAT BUY?
IT LOOKS LIKE THERE'S ABOUT 10 MILLION DOLLARS ...
DAMN ...!!

READ THIS WAY

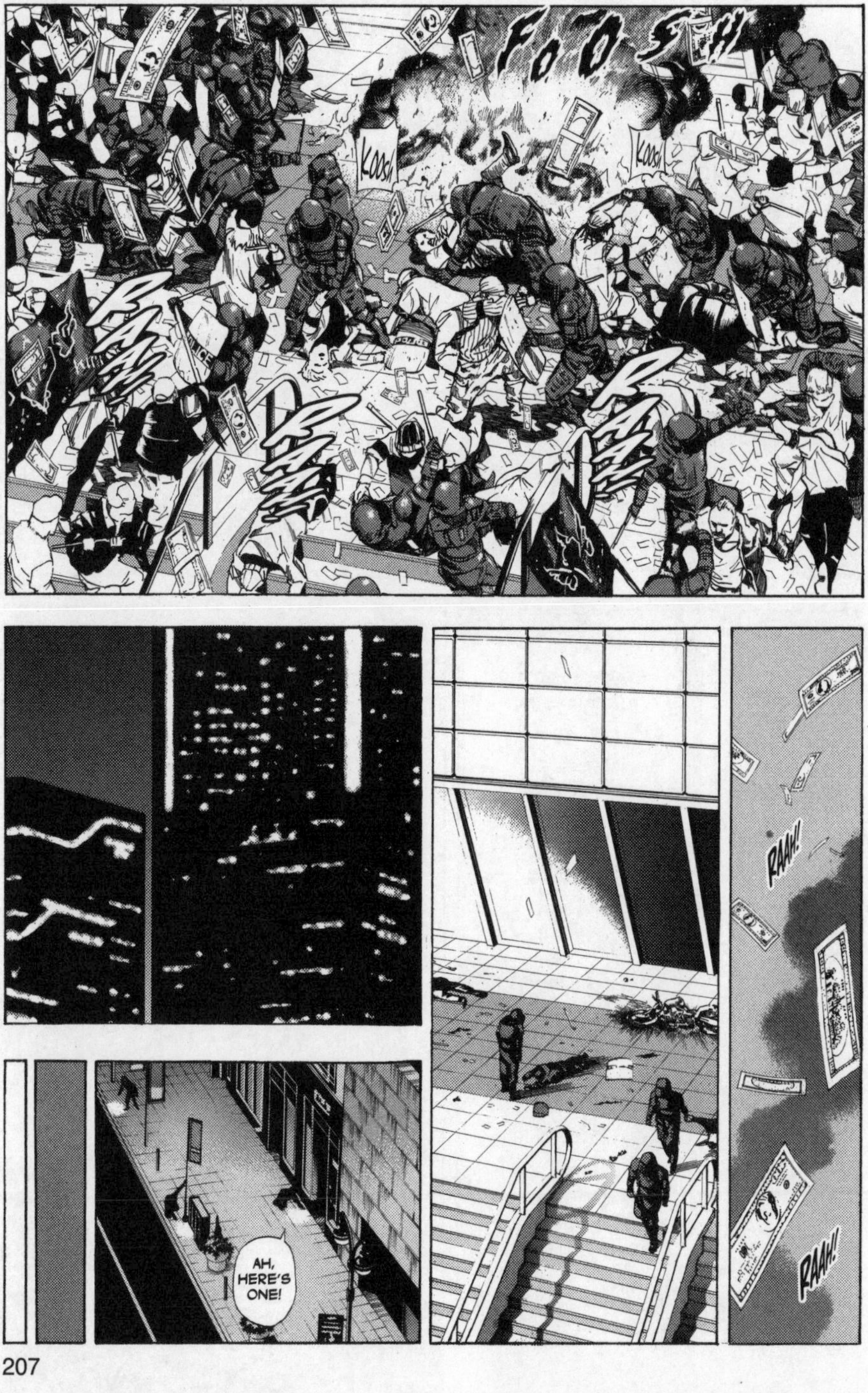
FOOSH
KOOSH
KOOSH
RAAH!
RAAH!
AH, HERE'S ONE!

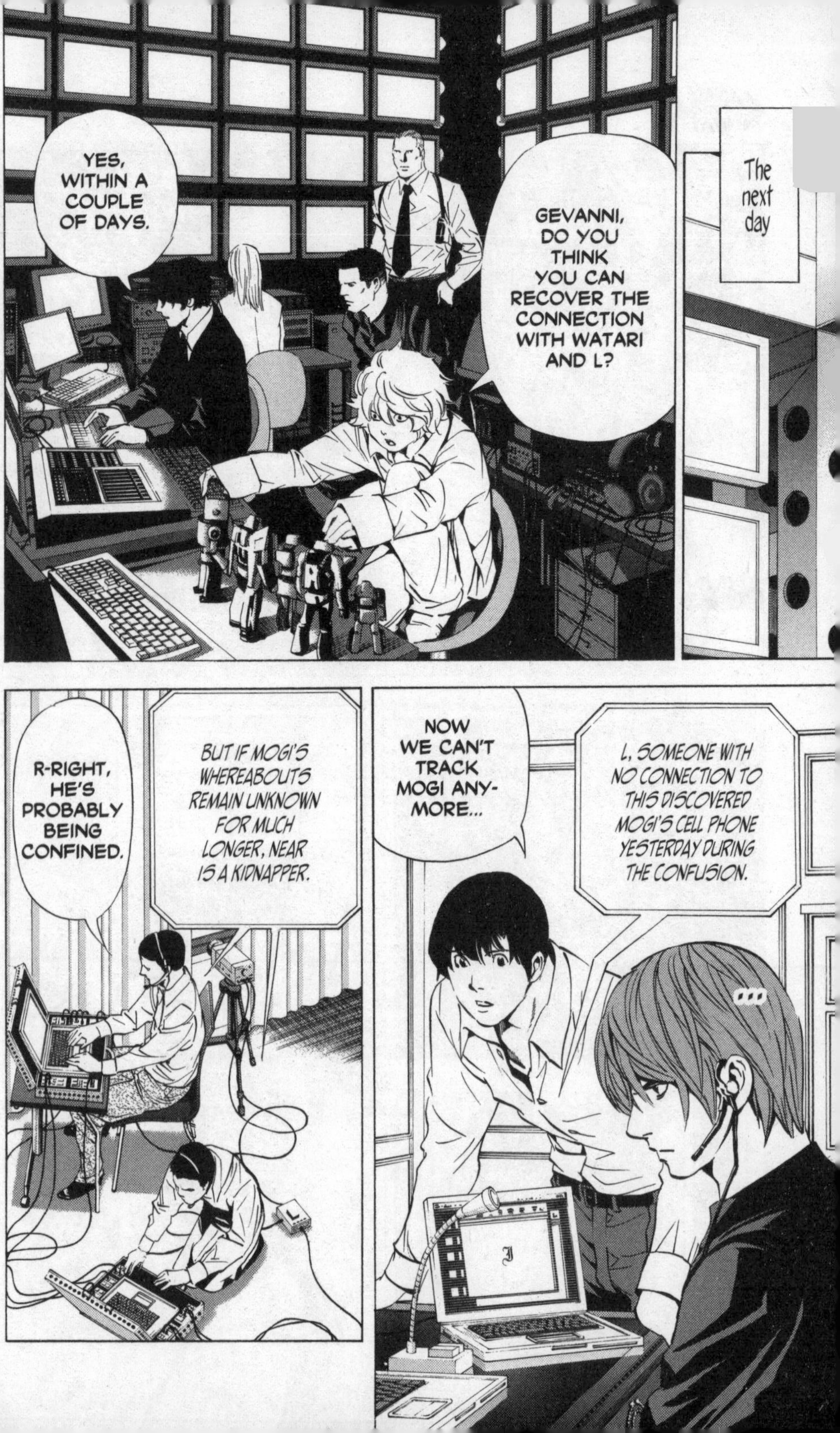
The next day
GEVANNI, DO YOU THINK YOU CAN RECOVER THE CONNECTION WITH WATARI AND L?
YES, WITHIN A COUPLE OF DAYS.
L, SOMEONE WITH NO CONNECTION TO THIS DISCOVERED MOGI'S CELL PHONE YESTERDAY DURING THE CONFUSION.
NOW WE CAN'T TRACK MOGI ANY-MORE...
...
BUT IF MOGI'S WHEREABOUTS REMAIN UNKNOWN FOR MUCH LONGER, NEAR IS A KIDNAPPER.
R-RIGHT, HE'S PROBABLY BEING CONFINED.

READ THIS WAY

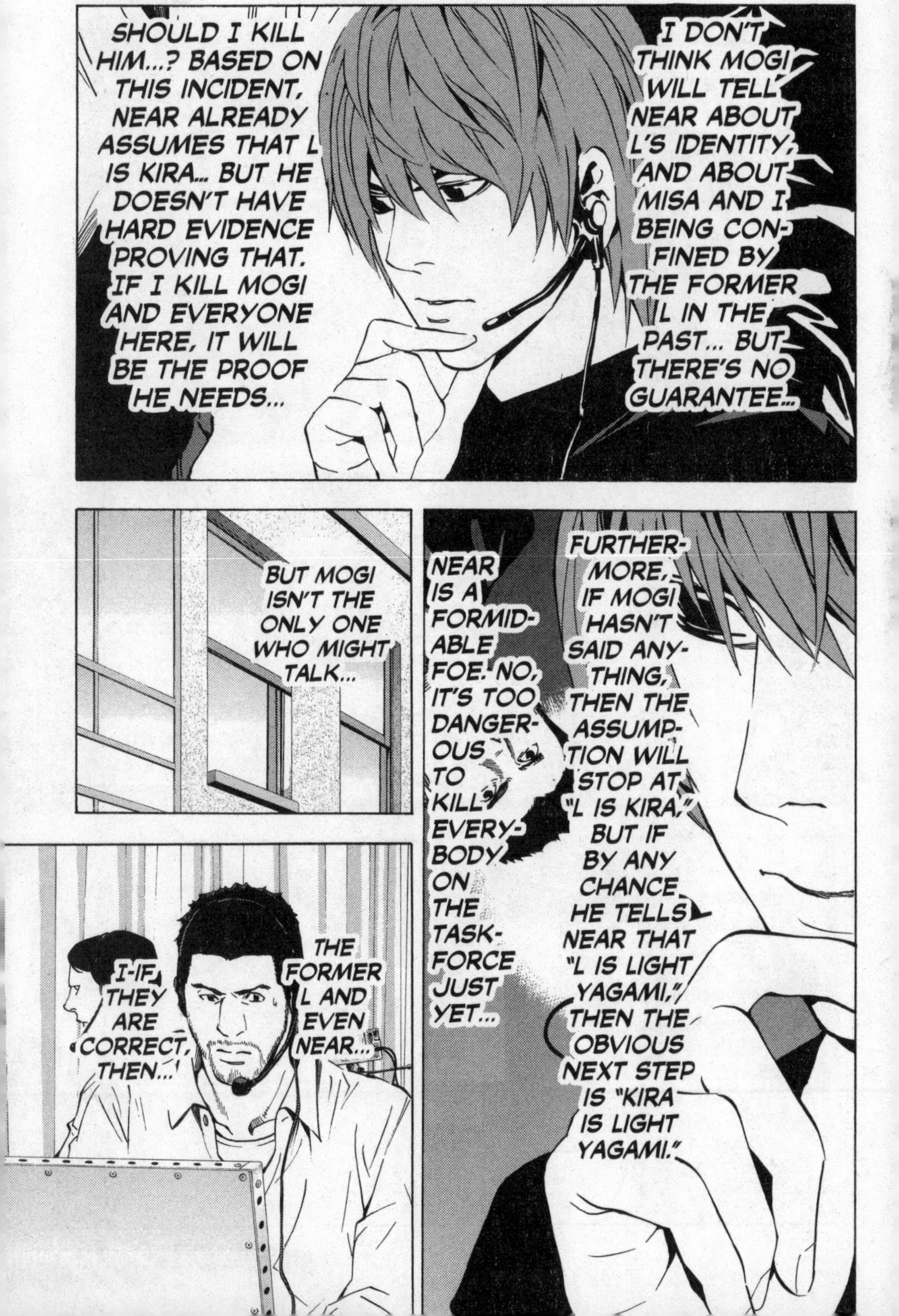
I DON'T THINK MOGI WILL TELL NEAR ABOUT L'S IDENTITY, AND ABOUT MISA AND I BEING CON-FINED BY THE FORMER L IN THE PAST... BUT THERE'S NO GUARANTEE...
SHOULD I KILL HIM...? BASED ON THIS INCIDENT, NEAR ALREADY ASSUMES THAT L IS KIRA... BUT HE DOESN'T HAVE HARD EVIDENCE PROVING THAT. IF I KILL MOGI AND EVERYONE HERE, IT WILL BE THE PROOF HE NEEDS...
FURTHER-MORE, IF MOGI HASN'T SAID ANY-THING, THEN THE ASSUMP-TION WILL STOP AT "L IS KIRA," BUT IF BY ANY CHANCE HE TELLS NEAR THAT "L IS LIGHT YAGAMI," THEN THE OBVIOUS NEXT STEP IS "KIRA IS LIGHT YAGAMI."
NEAR IS A FORMID-ABLE FOE. NO, IT'S TOO DANGER-OUS TO KILL EVERY-BODY ON THE TASK-FORCE JUST YET...
BUT MOGI ISN'T THE ONLY ONE WHO MIGHT TALK...
THE FORMER L AND EVEN NEAR...
I-IF THEY ARE CORRECT, THEN...

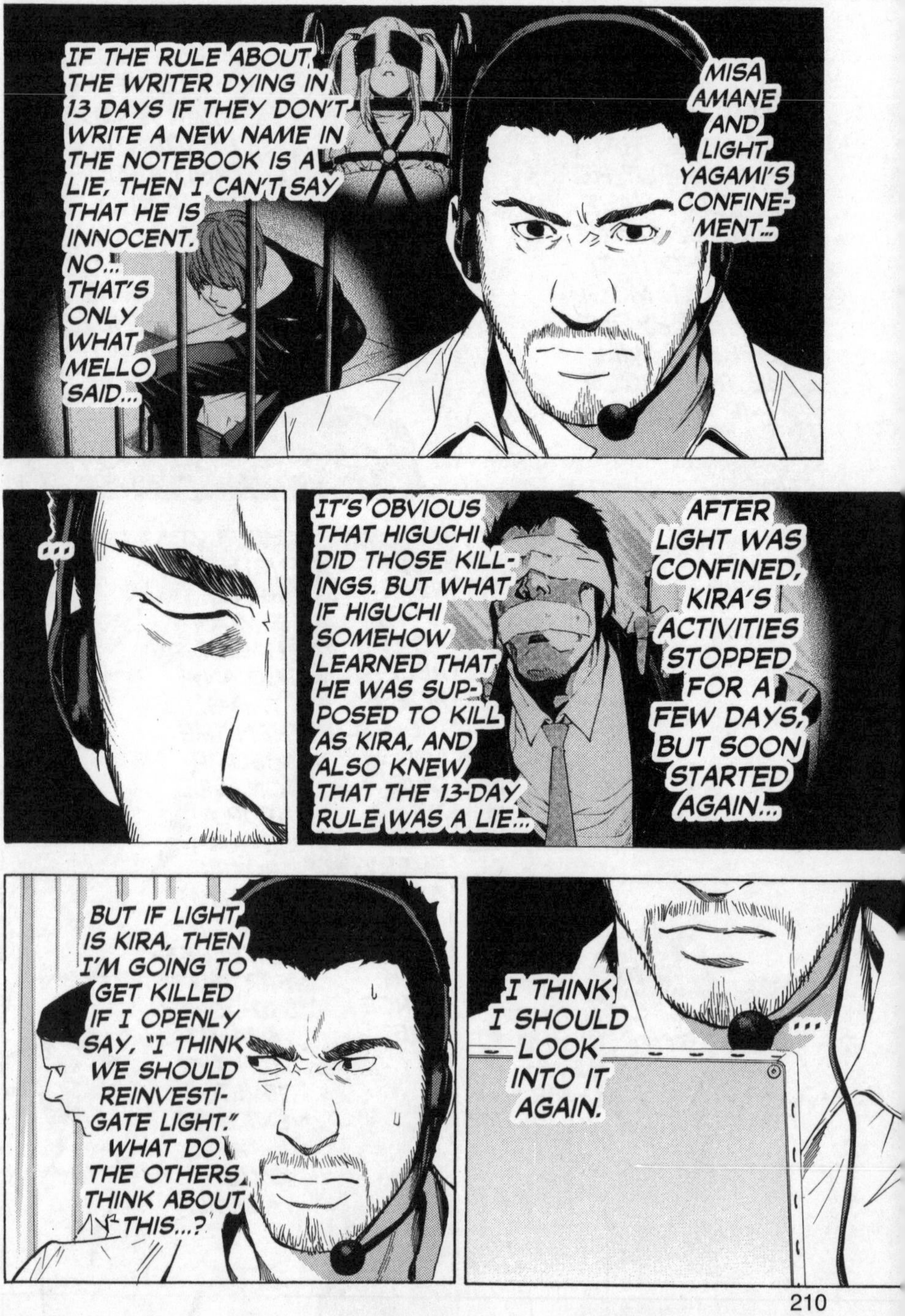
MISA AMANE AND LIGHT YAGAMI'S CONFINE-MENT...
IF THE RULE ABOUT THE WRITER DYING IN 13 DAYS IF THEY DON'T WRITE A NEW NAME IN THE NOTEBOOK IS A LIE, THEN I CAN'T SAY THAT HE IS INNOCENT. NO... THAT'S ONLY WHAT MELLO SAID...
AFTER LIGHT WAS CONFINED, KIRA'S ACTIVITIES STOPPED FOR A FEW DAYS, BUT SOON STARTED AGAIN...
IT'S OBVIOUS THAT HIGUCHI DID THOSE KILL-INGS. BUT WHAT IF HIGUCHI SOMEHOW LEARNED THAT HE WAS SUP-POSED TO KILL AS KIRA, AND ALSO KNEW THAT THE 13-DAY RULE WAS A LIE...
...
...
I THINK I SHOULD LOOK INTO IT AGAIN.
BUT IF LIGHT IS KIRA, THEN I'M GOING TO GET KILLED IF I OPENLY SAY, "I THINK WE SHOULD REINVESTI-GATE LIGHT." WHAT DO THE OTHERS THINK ABOUT THIS...?

READ THIS WAY

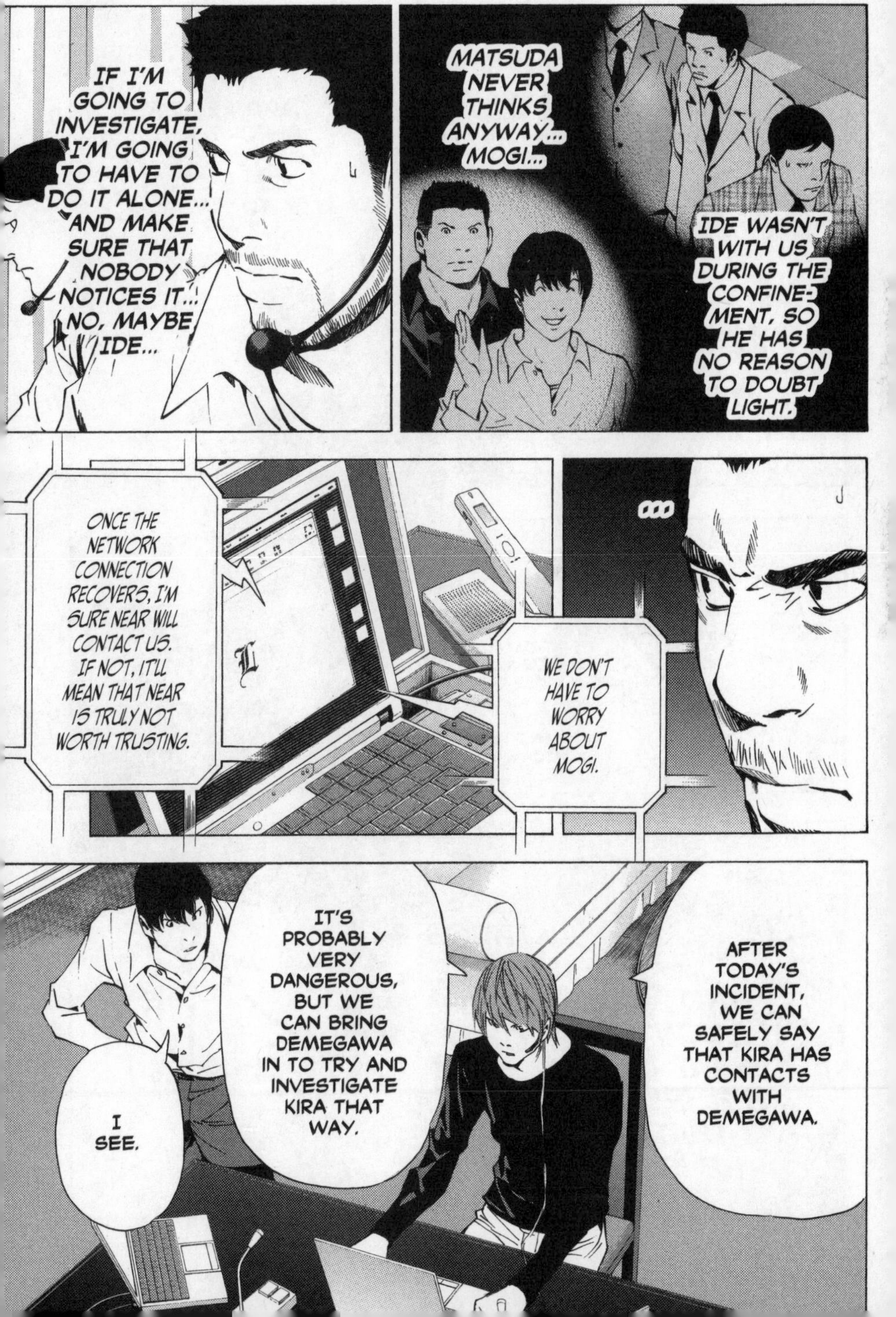
MATSUDA NEVER THINKS ANYWAY... MOGI...
IDE WASN'T WITH US DURING THE CONFINE-MENT, SO HE HAS NO REASON TO DOUBT LIGHT.
IF I'M GOING TO INVESTIGATE, I'M GOING TO HAVE TO DO IT ALONE... AND MAKE SURE THAT NOBODY NOTICES IT... NO, MAYBE IDE...
...
WE DON'T HAVE TO WORRY ABOUT MOGI.
ONCE THE NETWORK CONNECTION RECOVERS, I'M SURE NEAR WILL CONTACT US. IF NOT, IT'LL MEAN THAT NEAR IS TRULY NOT WORTH TRUSTING.
AFTER TODAY'S INCIDENT, WE CAN SAFELY SAY THAT KIRA HAS CONTACTS WITH DEMEGAWA.
IT'S PROBABLY VERY DANGEROUS, BUT WE CAN BRING DEMEGAWA IN TO TRY AND INVESTIGATE KIRA THAT WAY.
I SEE.

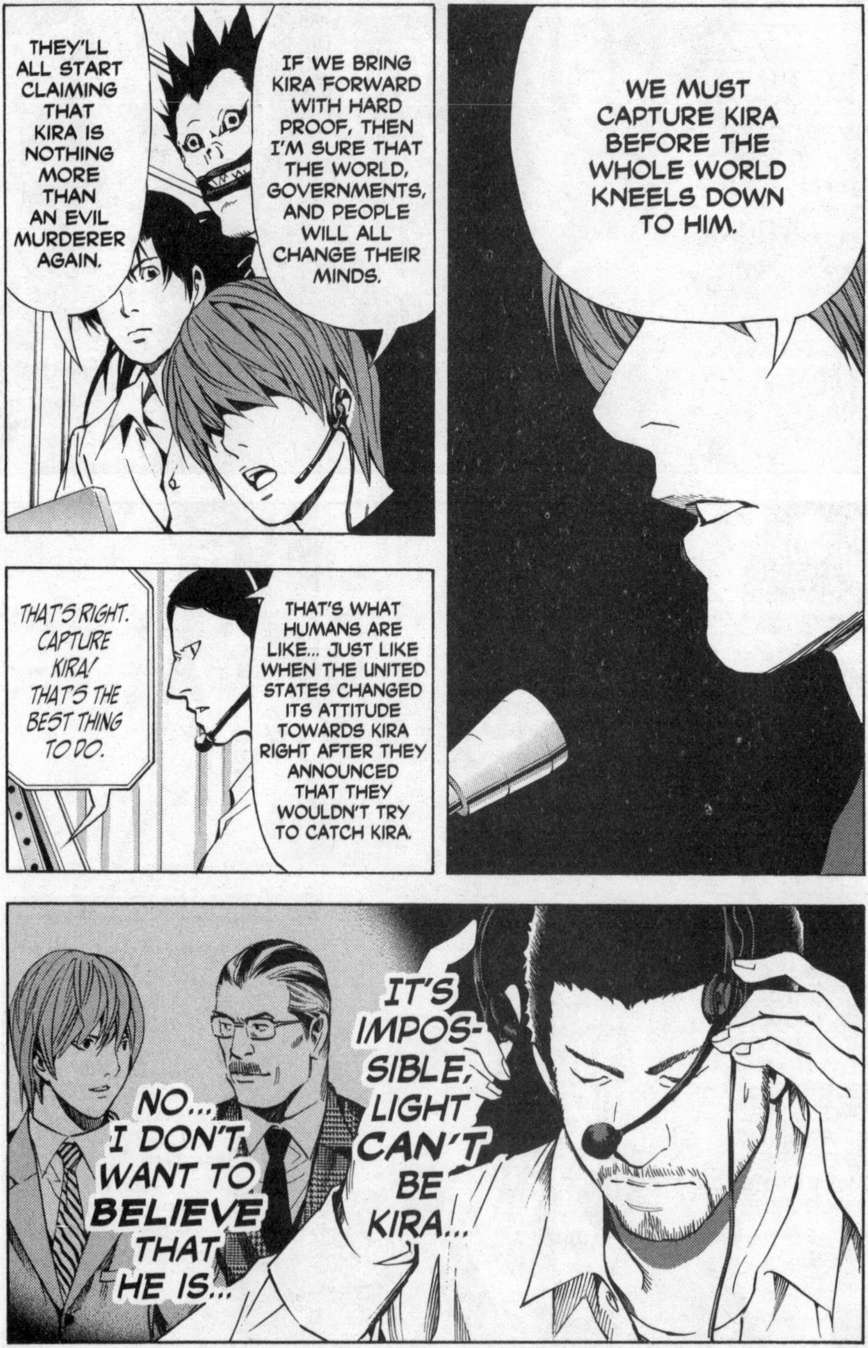
WE MUST CAPTURE KIRA BEFORE THE WHOLE WORLD KNEELS DOWN TO HIM.
IF WE BRING KIRA FORWARD WITH HARD PROOF, THEN I'M SURE THAT THE WORLD, GOVERNMENTS, AND PEOPLE WILL ALL CHANGE THEIR MINDS.
THEY'LL ALL START CLAIMING THAT KIRA IS NOTHING MORE THAN AN EVIL MURDERER AGAIN.
THAT'S WHAT HUMANS ARE LIKE... JUST LIKE WHEN THE UNITED STATES CHANGED ITS ATTITUDE TOWARDS KIRA RIGHT AFTER THEY ANNOUNCED THAT THEY WOULDN'T TRY TO CATCH KIRA.
THAT'S RIGHT. CAPTURE KIRA! THAT'S THE BEST THING TO DO.
IT'S IMPOSSIBLE, LIGHT CAN'T BE KIRA...
NO... I DON'T WANT TO BELIEVE THAT HE IS...

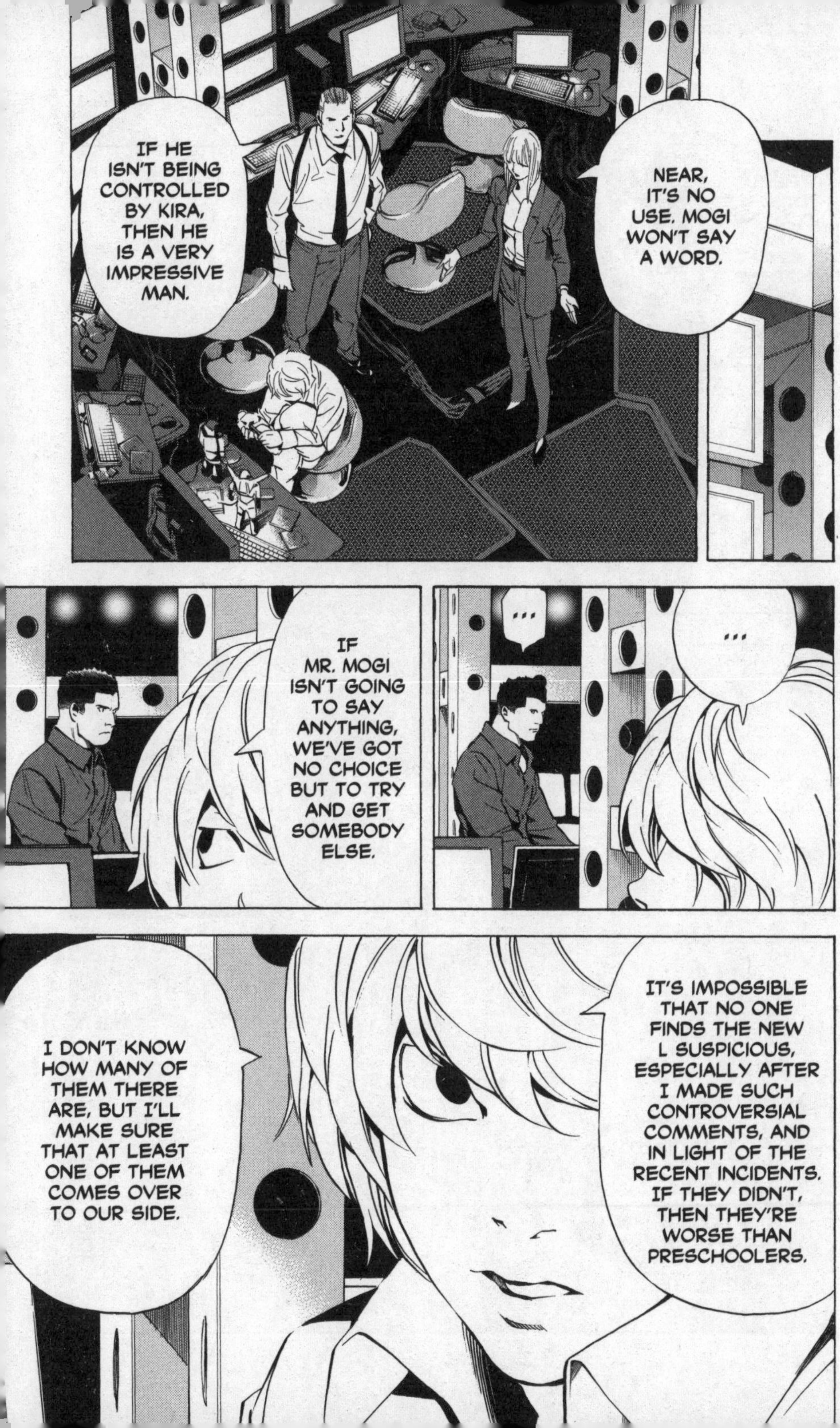
NEAR, IT'S NO USE. MOGI WON'T SAY A WORD.
IF HE ISN'T BEING CONTROLLED BY KIRA, THEN HE IS A VERY IMPRESSIVE MAN.
...
...
IF MR. MOGI ISN'T GOING TO SAY ANYTHING, WE'VE GOT NO CHOICE BUT TO TRY AND GET SOMEBODY ELSE.
IT'S IMPOSSIBLE THAT NO ONE FINDS THE NEW L SUSPICIOUS, ESPECIALLY AFTER I MADE SUCH CONTROVERSIAL COMMENTS, AND IN LIGHT OF THE RECENT INCIDENTS. IF THEY DIDN'T, THEN THEY'RE WORSE THAN PRESCHOOLERS.
I DON'T KNOW HOW MANY OF THEM THERE ARE, BUT I'LL MAKE SURE THAT AT LEAST ONE OF THEM COMES OVER TO OUR SIDE.

DEATH NOTE
How to use it
LIII

- The DEATH NOTE will not take effect if you write a specific victim's name using several different pages.

デスノートの効力を得るには、
一人の名前を複数のページにまたがって記してはならない。

- But the front and back of a page is considered as one page. For example, the DEATH NOTE will still take effect even if you write the victim's surname on the front page and given name on the back.

ただし、そのページの表と裏は１ページとみなされ、
たとえば、表に苗字、裏に名前という書き方であれば、有効である。

chapter 81 Warning

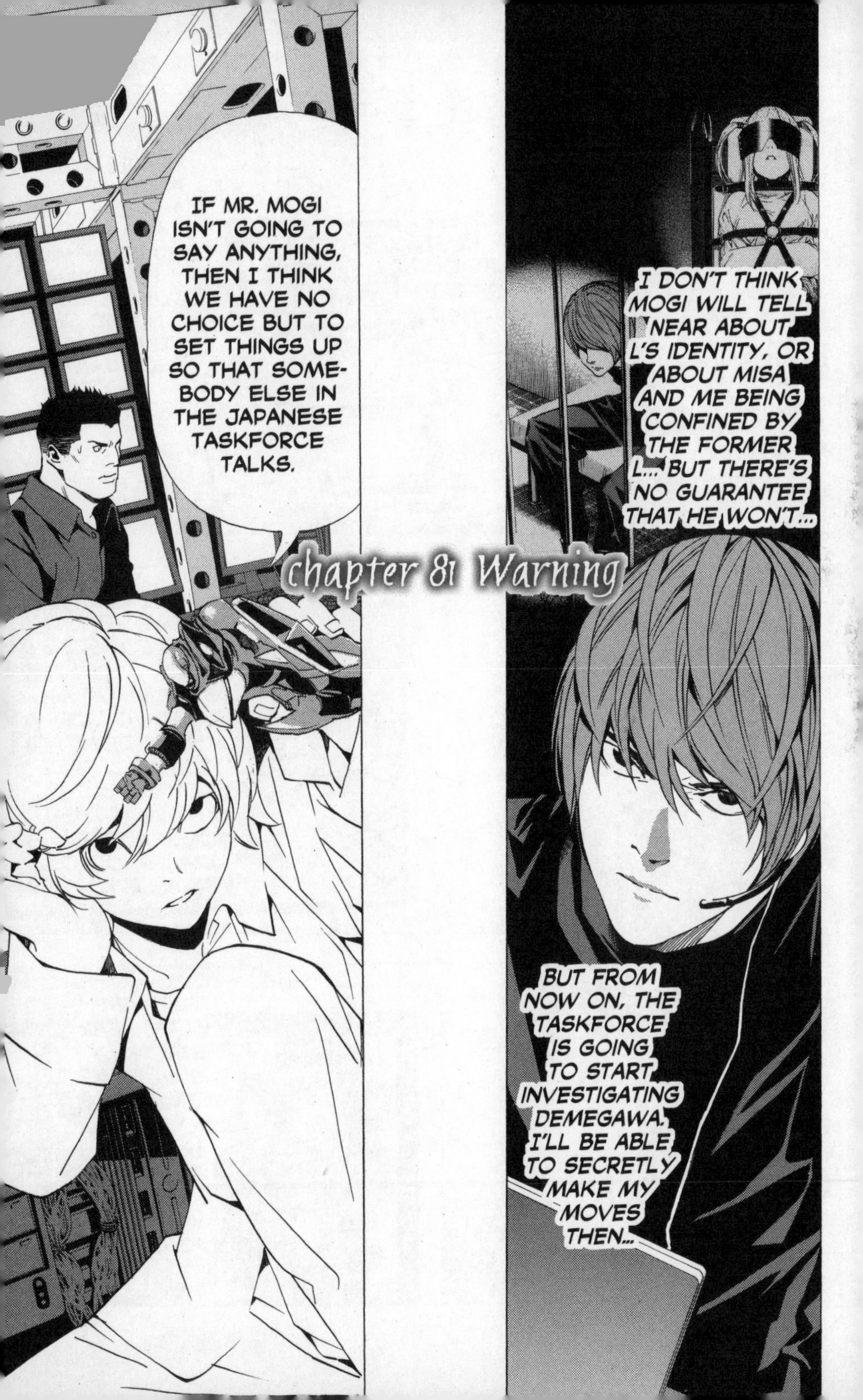
I DON'T THINK MOGI WILL TELL NEAR ABOUT L'S IDENTITY, OR ABOUT MISA AND ME BEING CONFINED BY THE FORMER L... BUT THERE'S NO GUARANTEE THAT HE WON'T...
BUT FROM NOW ON, THE TASKFORCE IS GOING TO START INVESTIGATING DEMEGAWA. I'LL BE ABLE TO SECRETLY MAKE MY MOVES THEN...
IF MR. MOGI ISN'T GOING TO SAY ANYTHING, THEN I THINK WE HAVE NO CHOICE BUT TO SET THINGS UP SO THAT SOMEBODY ELSE IN THE JAPANESE TASKFORCE TALKS.

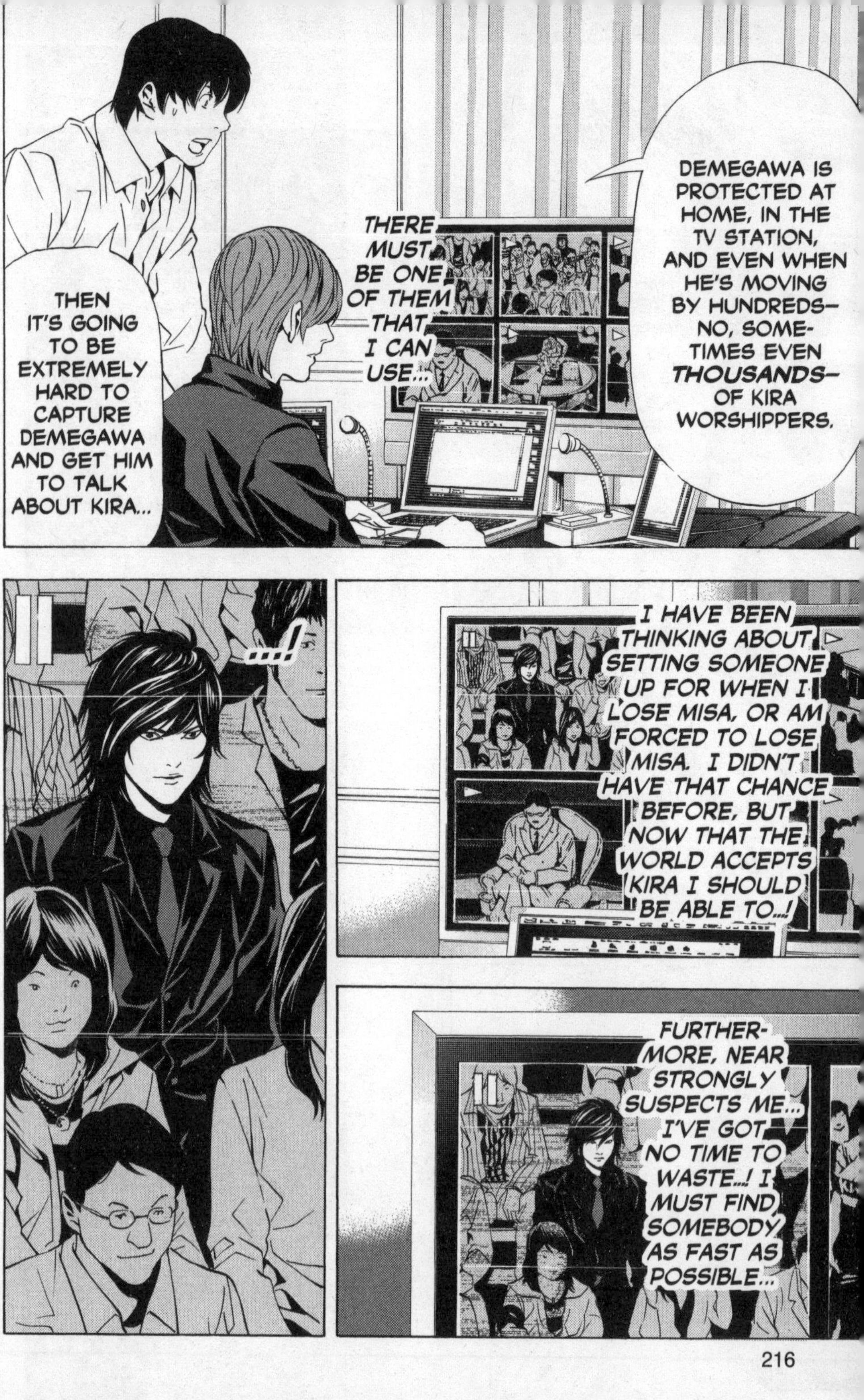
DEMEGAWA IS PROTECTED AT HOME, IN THE TV STATION, AND EVEN WHEN HE'S MOVING BY HUNDREDS—NO, SOMETIMES EVEN *THOUSANDS*—OF KIRA WORSHIPPERS.
THERE MUST BE ONE OF THEM THAT I CAN USE...
THEN IT'S GOING TO BE EXTREMELY HARD TO CAPTURE DEMEGAWA AND GET HIM TO TALK ABOUT KIRA...
I HAVE BEEN THINKING ABOUT SETTING SOMEONE UP FOR WHEN I LOSE MISA, OR AM FORCED TO LOSE MISA. I DIDN'T HAVE THAT CHANCE BEFORE, BUT NOW THAT THE WORLD ACCEPTS KIRA I SHOULD BE ABLE TO...!
FURTHERMORE, NEAR STRONGLY SUSPECTS ME... I'VE GOT NO TIME TO WASTE...! I MUST FIND SOMEBODY AS FAST AS POSSIBLE...
...!

YAAWN

43

34

33	=== === ===
34	Teru Mikami
35	=== === ===

CLAK

I HAD DEMEGAWA SEND MISA THE QUESTION-NAIRES AND PERSONAL INFORMA-TION...

CLAK
CLAK

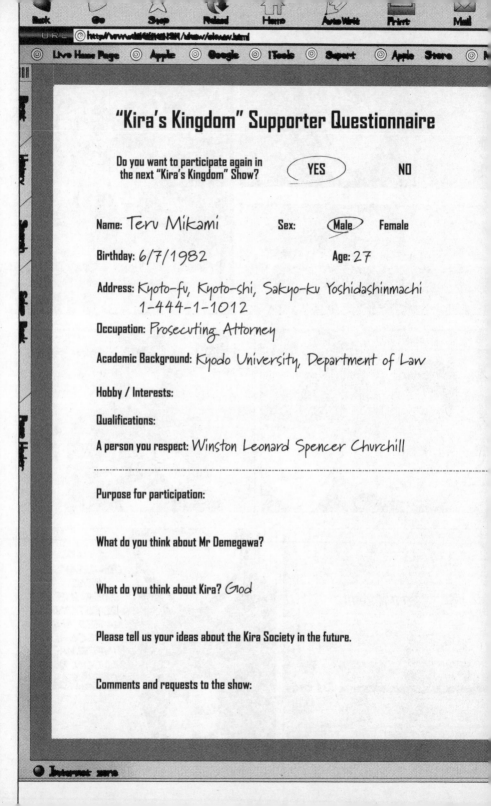

"Kira's Kingdom" Supporter Questionnaire

Do you want to participate again in
the next "Kira's Kingdom" Show?   (YES)   NO

Name: Teru Mikami   Sex: (Male) Female

Birthday: 6/7/1982   Age: 27

Address: Kyoto-fu, Kyoto-shi, Sakyo-ku Yoshidashinmachi
         1-444-1-1012

Occupation: Prosecuting Attorney

Academic Background: Kyodo University, Department of Law

Hobby / Interests:

Qualifications:

A person you respect: Winston Leonard Spencer Churchill

Purpose for participation:

What do you think about Mr Demegawa?

What do you think about Kira? God

Please tell us your ideas about the Kira Society in the future.

Comments and requests to the show:

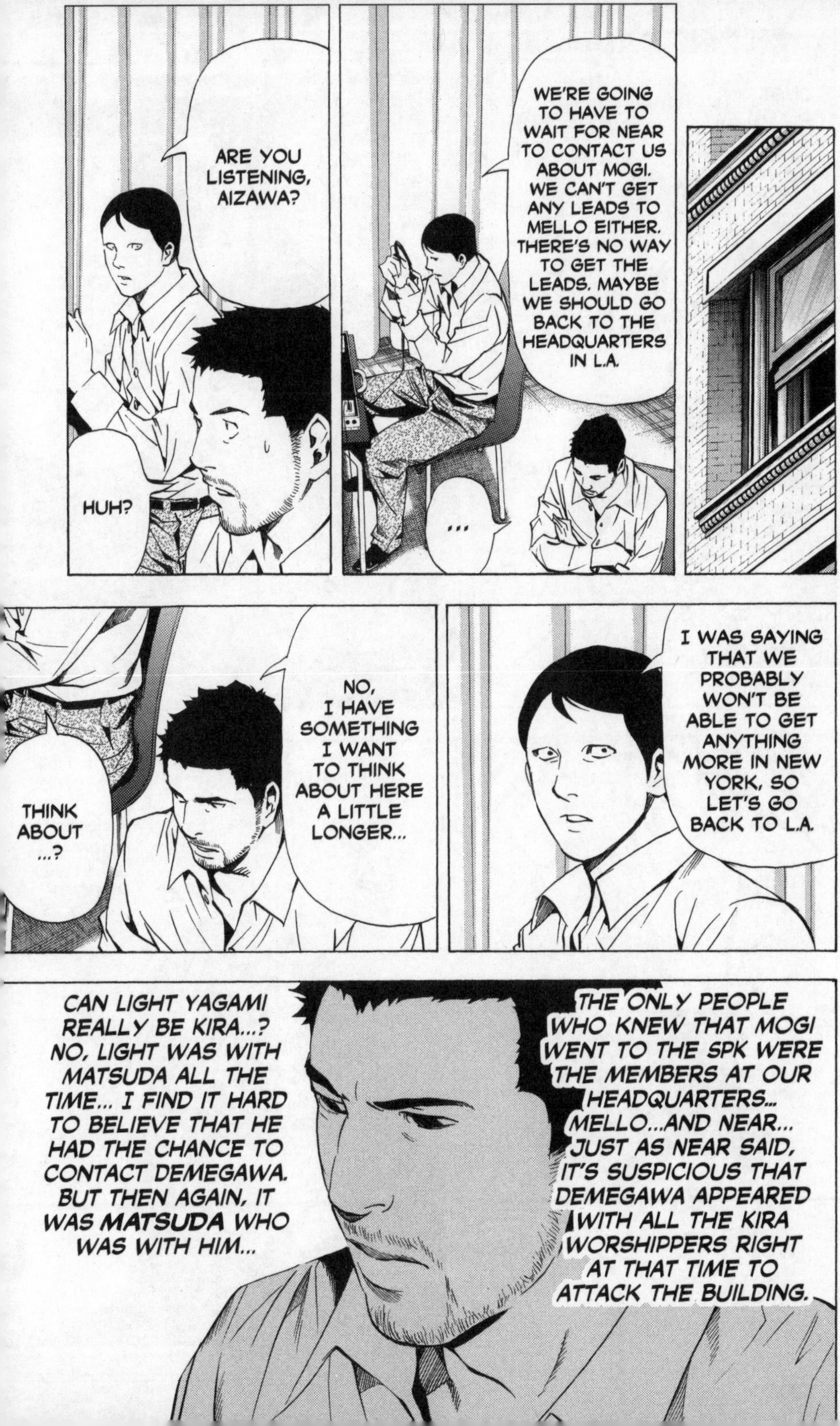
WE'RE GOING TO HAVE TO WAIT FOR NEAR TO CONTACT US ABOUT MOGI. WE CAN'T GET ANY LEADS TO MELLO EITHER. THERE'S NO WAY TO GET THE LEADS. MAYBE WE SHOULD GO BACK TO THE HEADQUARTERS IN L.A.
...
ARE YOU LISTENING, AIZAWA?
HUH?
I WAS SAYING THAT WE PROBABLY WON'T BE ABLE TO GET ANYTHING MORE IN NEW YORK, SO LET'S GO BACK TO L.A.
NO, I HAVE SOMETHING I WANT TO THINK ABOUT HERE A LITTLE LONGER...
THINK ABOUT ...?
THE ONLY PEOPLE WHO KNEW THAT MOGI WENT TO THE SPK WERE THE MEMBERS AT OUR HEADQUARTERS... MELLO...AND NEAR... JUST AS NEAR SAID, IT'S SUSPICIOUS THAT DEMEGAWA APPEARED WITH ALL THE KIRA WORSHIPPERS RIGHT AT THAT TIME TO ATTACK THE BUILDING.
CAN LIGHT YAGAMI REALLY BE KIRA...? NO, LIGHT WAS WITH MATSUDA ALL THE TIME... I FIND IT HARD TO BELIEVE THAT HE HAD THE CHANCE TO CONTACT DEMEGAWA. BUT THEN AGAIN, IT WAS MATSUDA WHO WAS WITH HIM...

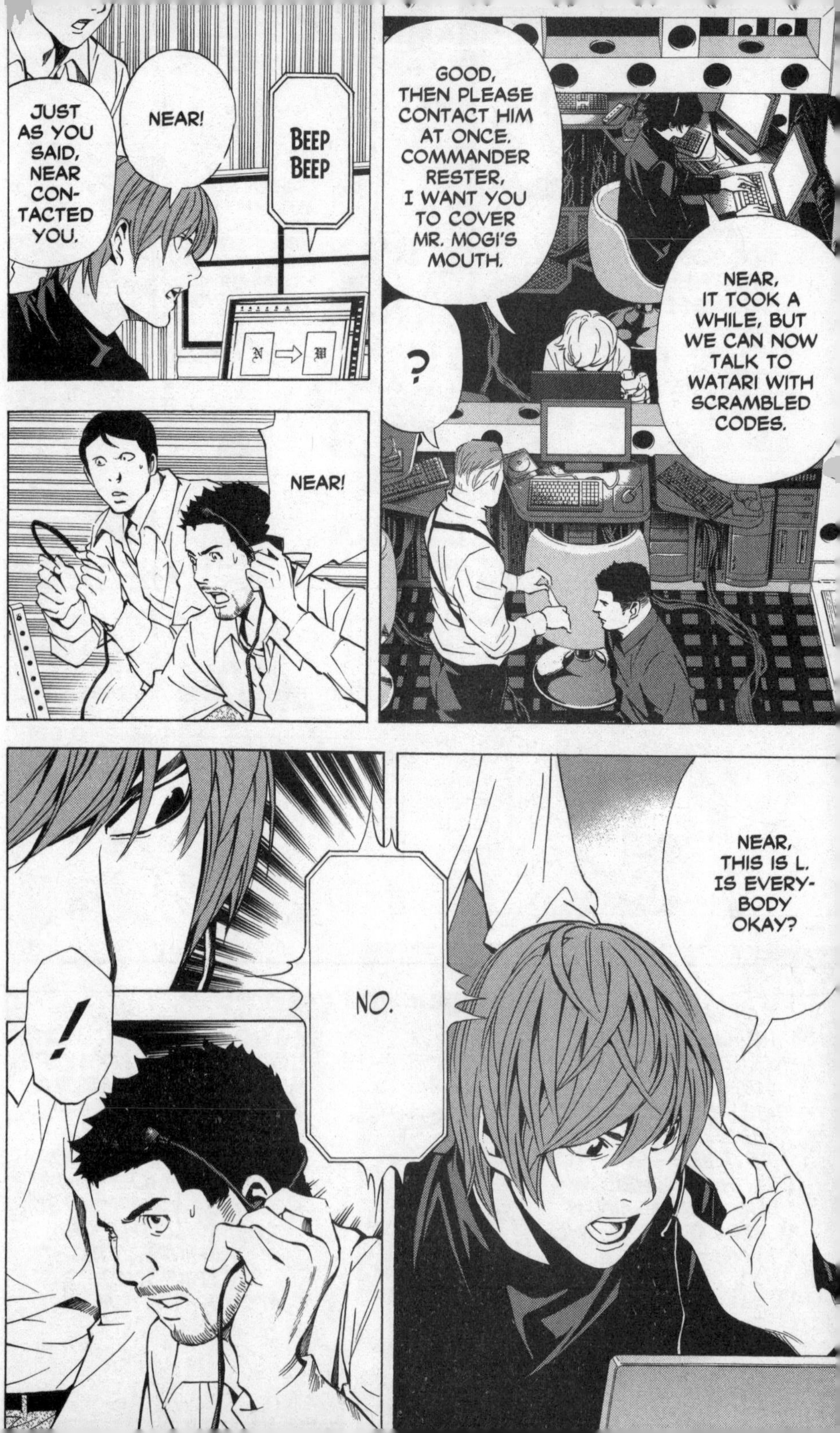
NEAR, IT TOOK A WHILE, BUT WE CAN NOW TALK TO WATARI WITH SCRAMBLED CODES.
GOOD, THEN PLEASE CONTACT HIM AT ONCE. COMMANDER RESTER, I WANT YOU TO COVER MR. MOGI'S MOUTH.
?
BEEP BEEP
NEAR!
JUST AS YOU SAID, NEAR CONTACTED YOU.
NEAR!
NEAR, THIS IS L. IS EVERYBODY OKAY?
NO.
!

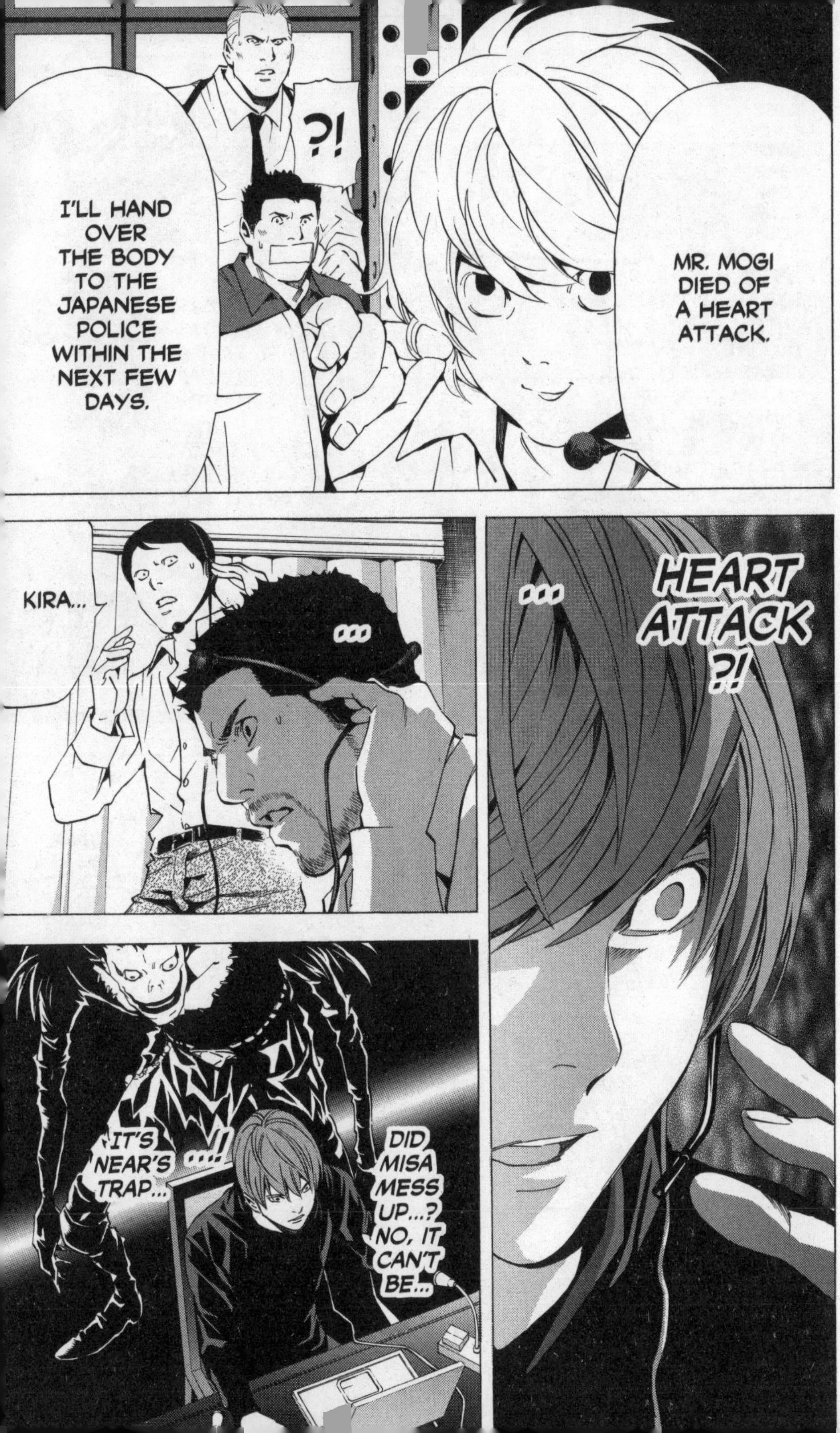
MR. MOGI DIED OF A HEART ATTACK.
?!
I'LL HAND OVER THE BODY TO THE JAPANESE POLICE WITHIN THE NEXT FEW DAYS.
...
HEART ATTACK ?!
KIRA...
...
DID MISA MESS UP...? NO, IT CAN'T BE...
...!
IT'S NEAR'S TRAP...

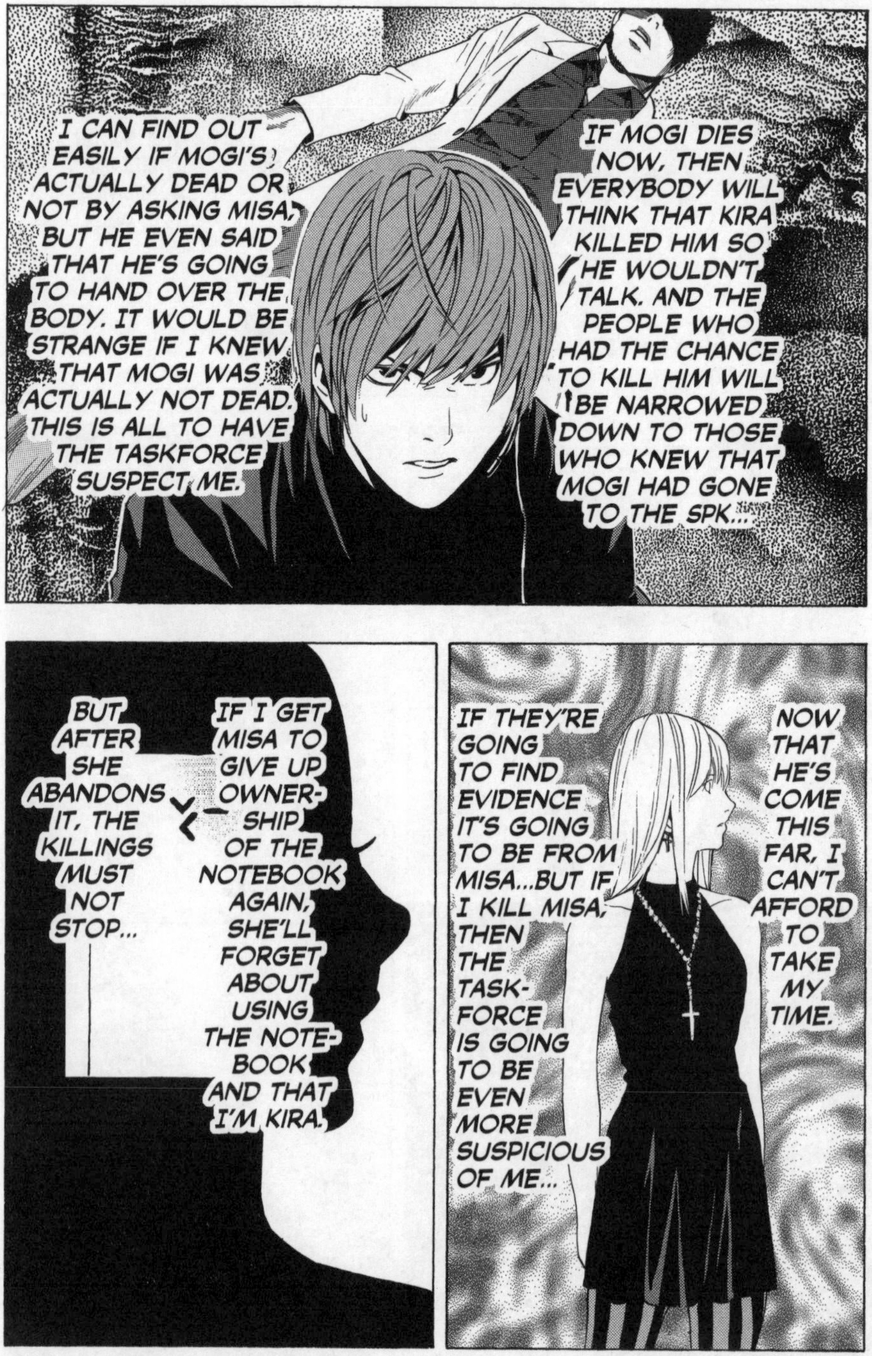
IF MOGI DIES NOW, THEN EVERYBODY WILL THINK THAT KIRA KILLED HIM SO HE WOULDN'T TALK. AND THE PEOPLE WHO HAD THE CHANCE TO KILL HIM WILL BE NARROWED DOWN TO THOSE WHO KNEW THAT MOGI HAD GONE TO THE SPK...
I CAN FIND OUT EASILY IF MOGI'S ACTUALLY DEAD OR NOT BY ASKING MISA, BUT HE EVEN SAID THAT HE'S GOING TO HAND OVER THE BODY. IT WOULD BE STRANGE IF I KNEW THAT MOGI WAS ACTUALLY NOT DEAD. THIS IS ALL TO HAVE THE TASKFORCE SUSPECT ME.
NOW THAT HE'S COME THIS FAR, I CAN'T AFFORD TO TAKE MY TIME.
IF THEY'RE GOING TO FIND EVIDENCE IT'S GOING TO BE FROM MISA...BUT IF I KILL MISA, THEN THE TASK-FORCE IS GOING TO BE EVEN MORE SUSPICIOUS OF ME...
IF I GET MISA TO GIVE UP OWNER-SHIP OF THE NOTEBOOK AGAIN, SHE'LL FORGET ABOUT USING THE NOTE-BOOK AND THAT I'M KIRA.
BUT AFTER SHE ABANDONS IT, THE KILLINGS MUST NOT STOP...

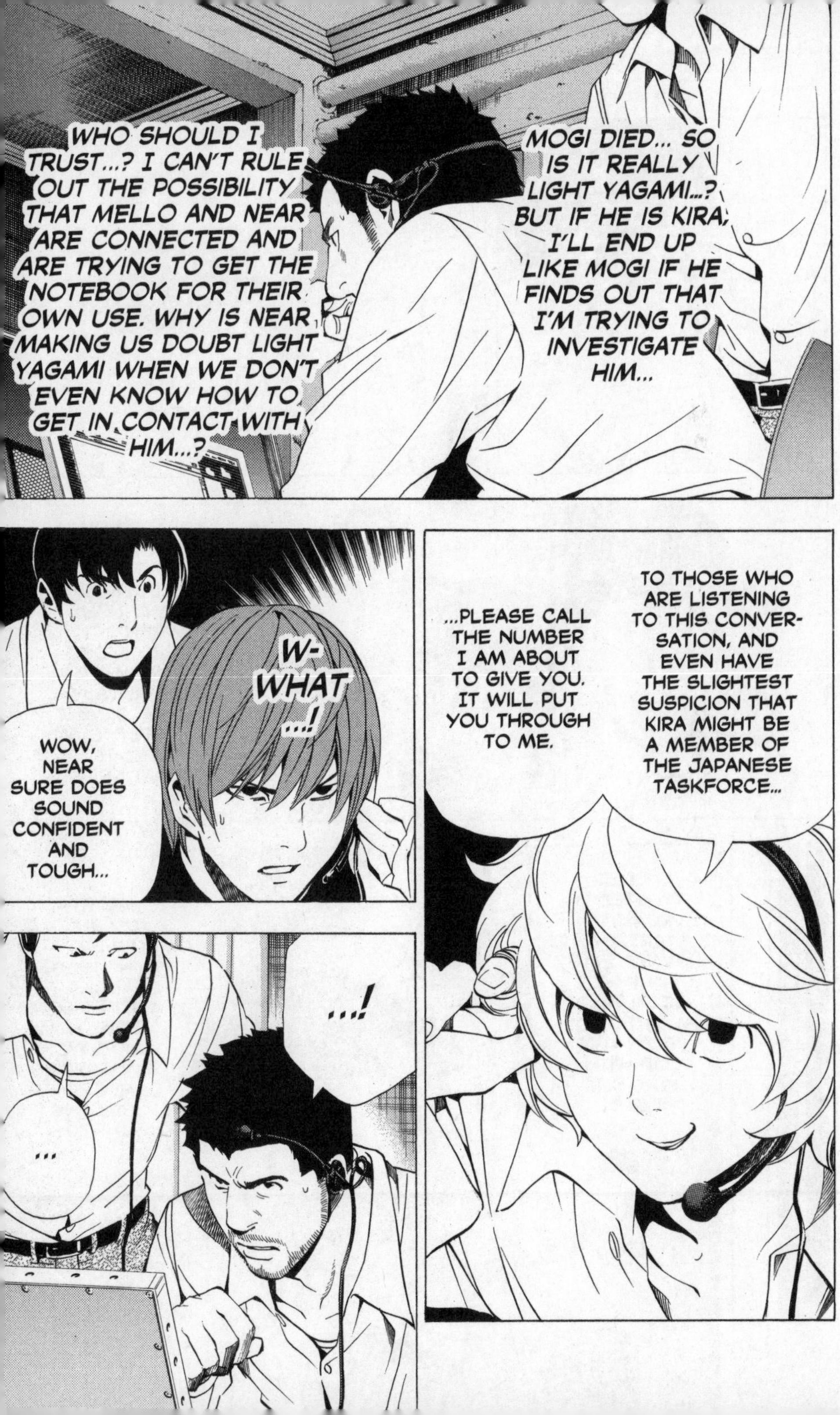
MOGI DIED... SO IS IT REALLY LIGHT YAGAMI...? BUT IF HE IS KIRA, I'LL END UP LIKE MOGI IF HE FINDS OUT THAT I'M TRYING TO INVESTIGATE HIM...
WHO SHOULD I TRUST...? I CAN'T RULE OUT THE POSSIBILITY THAT MELLO AND NEAR ARE CONNECTED AND ARE TRYING TO GET THE NOTEBOOK FOR THEIR OWN USE. WHY IS NEAR MAKING US DOUBT LIGHT YAGAMI WHEN WE DON'T EVEN KNOW HOW TO GET IN CONTACT WITH HIM...?
TO THOSE WHO ARE LISTENING TO THIS CONVER-SATION, AND EVEN HAVE THE SLIGHTEST SUSPICION THAT KIRA MIGHT BE A MEMBER OF THE JAPANESE TASKFORCE...
...PLEASE CALL THE NUMBER I AM ABOUT TO GIVE YOU. IT WILL PUT YOU THROUGH TO ME.
W-WHAT ...!
WOW, NEAR SURE DOES SOUND CONFIDENT AND TOUGH...
...!
...

AIZAWA... YOU'RE NOT...
PCH
IDE...
BASED ON THE THINGS THAT WENT ON BETWEEN L AND LIGHT WHEN YOU WEREN'T YET A MEMBER OF THE TASK-FORCE, I CAN'T COMPLETELY IGNORE WHAT NEAR IS SAYING.
AIZAWA... YOU SHOULD DO WHAT YOU THINK IS RIGHT. LUCKILY, WE'RE ALONE RIGHT NOW, AND I WON'T SAY ANYTHING UNNECESSARY TO THE OTHERS.
I NEVER TRUSTED L FROM THE START ANY-WAY... I'M IN THIS BECAUSE I WANTED TO BE ON THIS JOB WITH YOU, NOT LIGHT.
IDE...

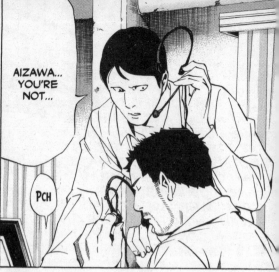

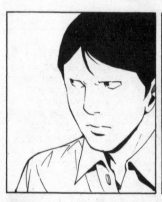

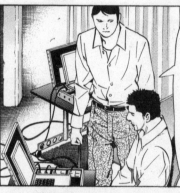

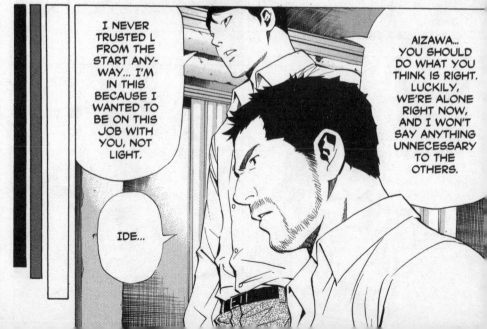

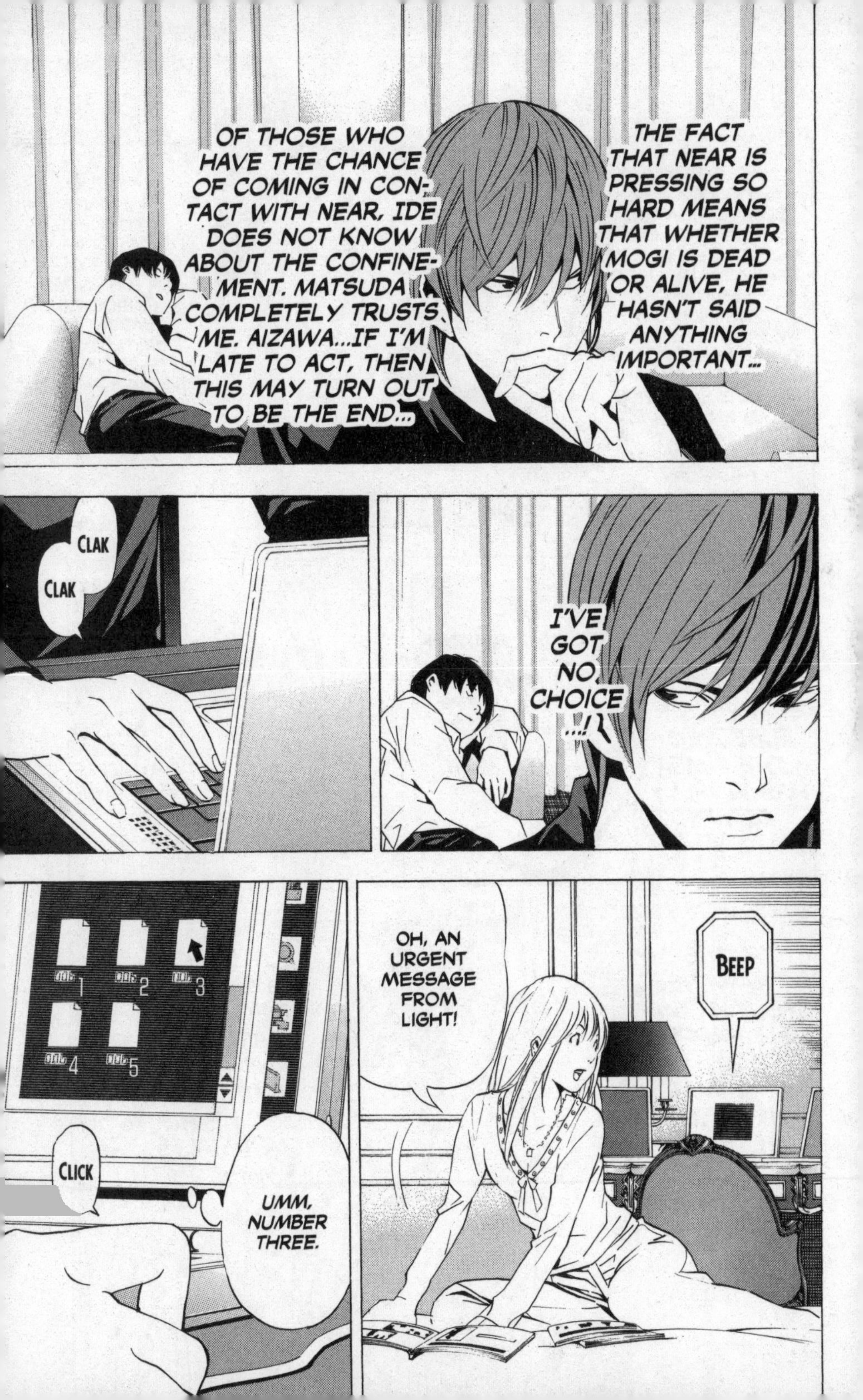
THE FACT THAT NEAR IS PRESSING SO HARD MEANS THAT WHETHER MOGI IS DEAD OR ALIVE, HE HASN'T SAID ANYTHING IMPORTANT...
OF THOSE WHO HAVE THE CHANCE OF COMING IN CONTACT WITH NEAR, IDE DOES NOT KNOW ABOUT THE CONFINEMENT. MATSUDA COMPLETELY TRUSTS ME. AIZAWA...IF I'M LATE TO ACT, THEN THIS MAY TURN OUT TO BE THE END...
I'VE GOT NO CHOICE ...!
CLAK
CLAK
BEEP
OH, AN URGENT MESSAGE FROM LIGHT!
UMM, NUMBER THREE.
CLICK

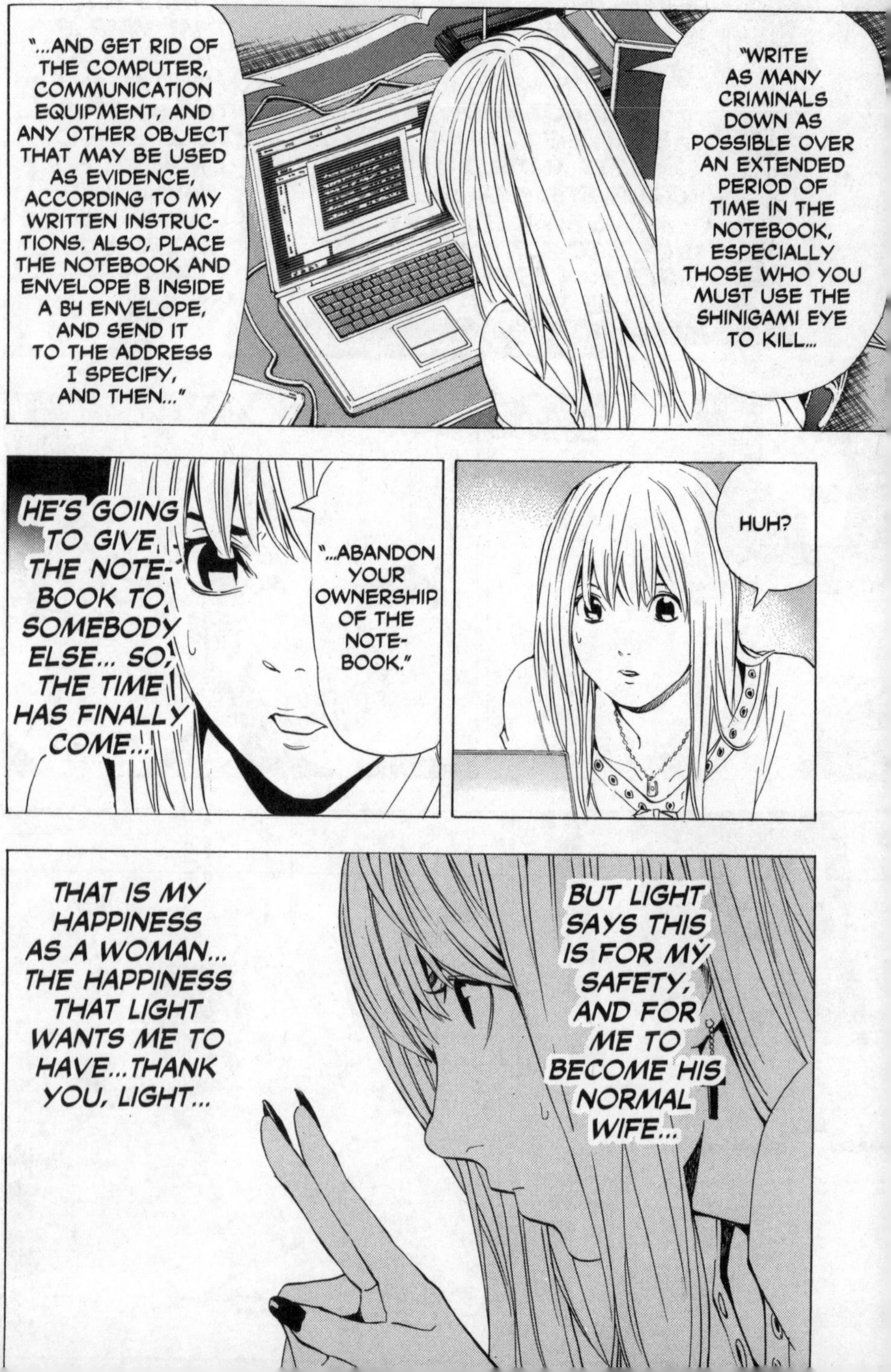
"WRITE AS MANY CRIMINALS DOWN AS POSSIBLE OVER AN EXTENDED PERIOD OF TIME IN THE NOTEBOOK, ESPECIALLY THOSE WHO YOU MUST USE THE SHINIGAMI EYE TO KILL...
"...AND GET RID OF THE COMPUTER, COMMUNICATION EQUIPMENT, AND ANY OTHER OBJECT THAT MAY BE USED AS EVIDENCE, ACCORDING TO MY WRITTEN INSTRUCTIONS. ALSO, PLACE THE NOTEBOOK AND ENVELOPE B INSIDE A B4 ENVELOPE, AND SEND IT TO THE ADDRESS I SPECIFY, AND THEN..."
"...ABANDON YOUR OWNERSHIP OF THE NOTEBOOK."
HE'S GOING TO GIVE THE NOTEBOOK TO SOMEBODY ELSE... SO, THE TIME HAS FINALLY COME...
HUH?
BUT LIGHT SAYS THIS IS FOR MY SAFETY, AND FOR ME TO BECOME HIS NORMAL WIFE...
THAT IS MY HAPPINESS AS A WOMAN... THE HAPPINESS THAT LIGHT WANTS ME TO HAVE...THANK YOU, LIGHT...

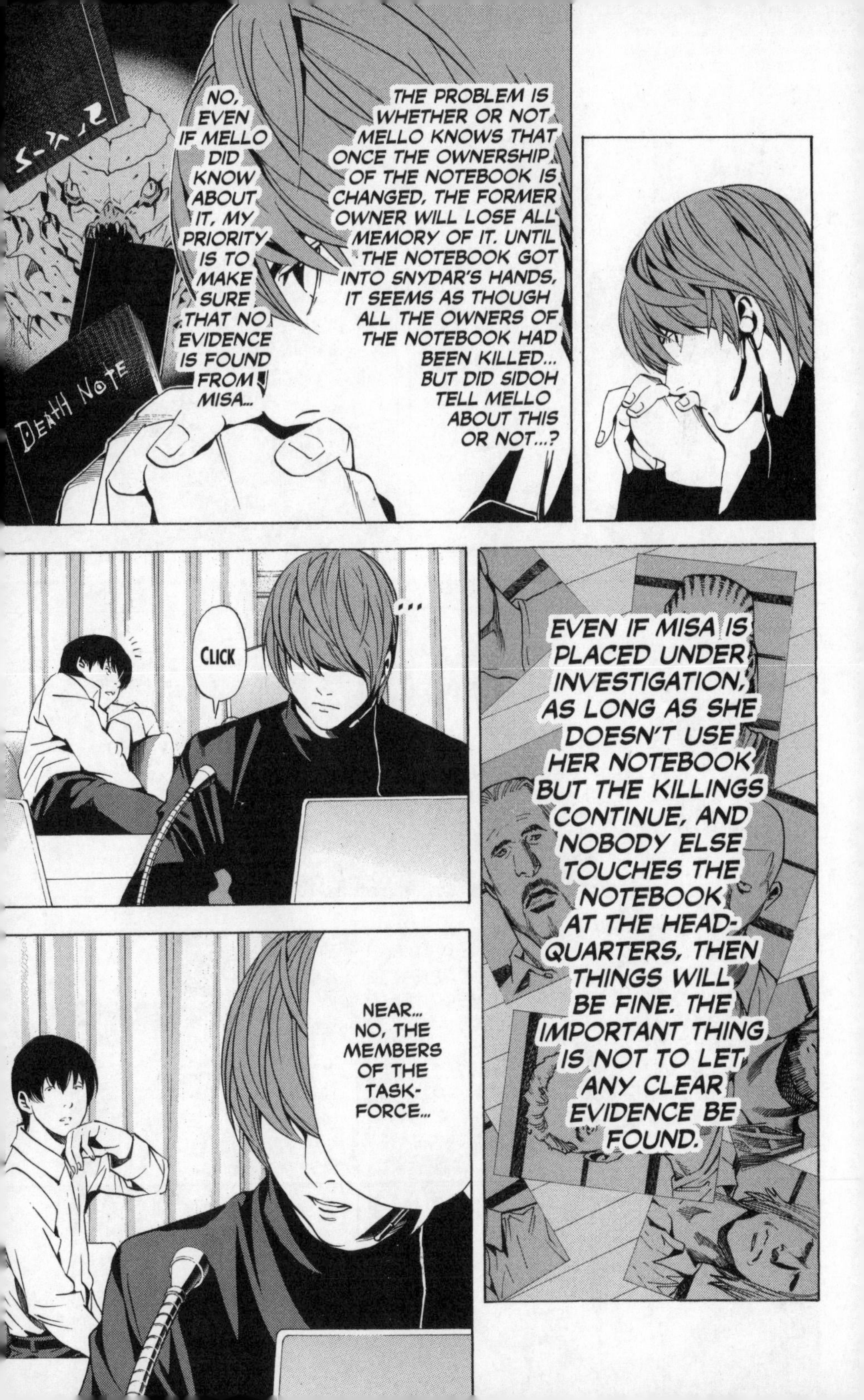

THE PROBLEM IS WHETHER OR NOT MELLO KNOWS THAT ONCE THE OWNERSHIP OF THE NOTEBOOK IS CHANGED, THE FORMER OWNER WILL LOSE ALL MEMORY OF IT. UNTIL THE NOTEBOOK GOT INTO SNYDAR'S HANDS, IT SEEMS AS THOUGH ALL THE OWNERS OF THE NOTEBOOK HAD BEEN KILLED... BUT DID SIDOH TELL MELLO ABOUT THIS OR NOT...?
NO, EVEN IF MELLO DID KNOW ABOUT IT, MY PRIORITY IS TO MAKE SURE THAT NO EVIDENCE IS FOUND FROM MISA...
DEATH NOTE
EVEN IF MISA IS PLACED UNDER INVESTIGATION, AS LONG AS SHE DOESN'T USE HER NOTEBOOK BUT THE KILLINGS CONTINUE, AND NOBODY ELSE TOUCHES THE NOTEBOOK AT THE HEAD-QUARTERS, THEN THINGS WILL BE FINE. THE IMPORTANT THING IS NOT TO LET ANY CLEAR EVIDENCE BE FOUND.
...
CLICK
NEAR... NO, THE MEMBERS OF THE TASK-FORCE...

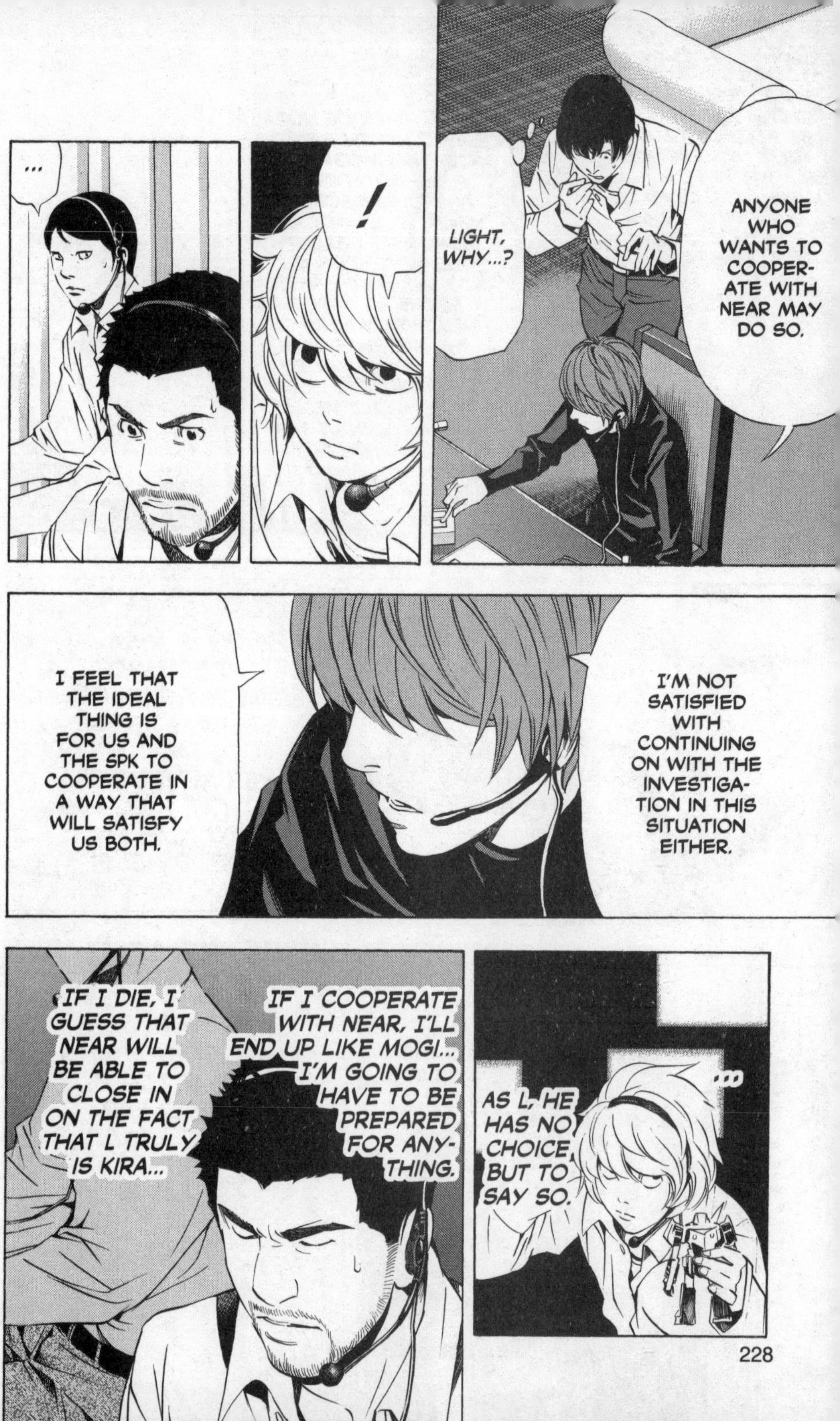
ANYONE WHO WANTS TO COOPERATE WITH NEAR MAY DO SO.
LIGHT, WHY...?
!
...
I'M NOT SATISFIED WITH CONTINUING ON WITH THE INVESTIGATION IN THIS SITUATION EITHER.
I FEEL THAT THE IDEAL THING IS FOR US AND THE SPK TO COOPERATE IN A WAY THAT WILL SATISFY US BOTH.
...
AS L, HE HAS NO CHOICE BUT TO SAY SO.
IF I COOPERATE WITH NEAR, I'LL END UP LIKE MOGI... I'M GOING TO HAVE TO BE PREPARED FOR ANYTHING.
IF I DIE, I GUESS THAT NEAR WILL BE ABLE TO CLOSE IN ON THE FACT THAT L TRULY IS KIRA...

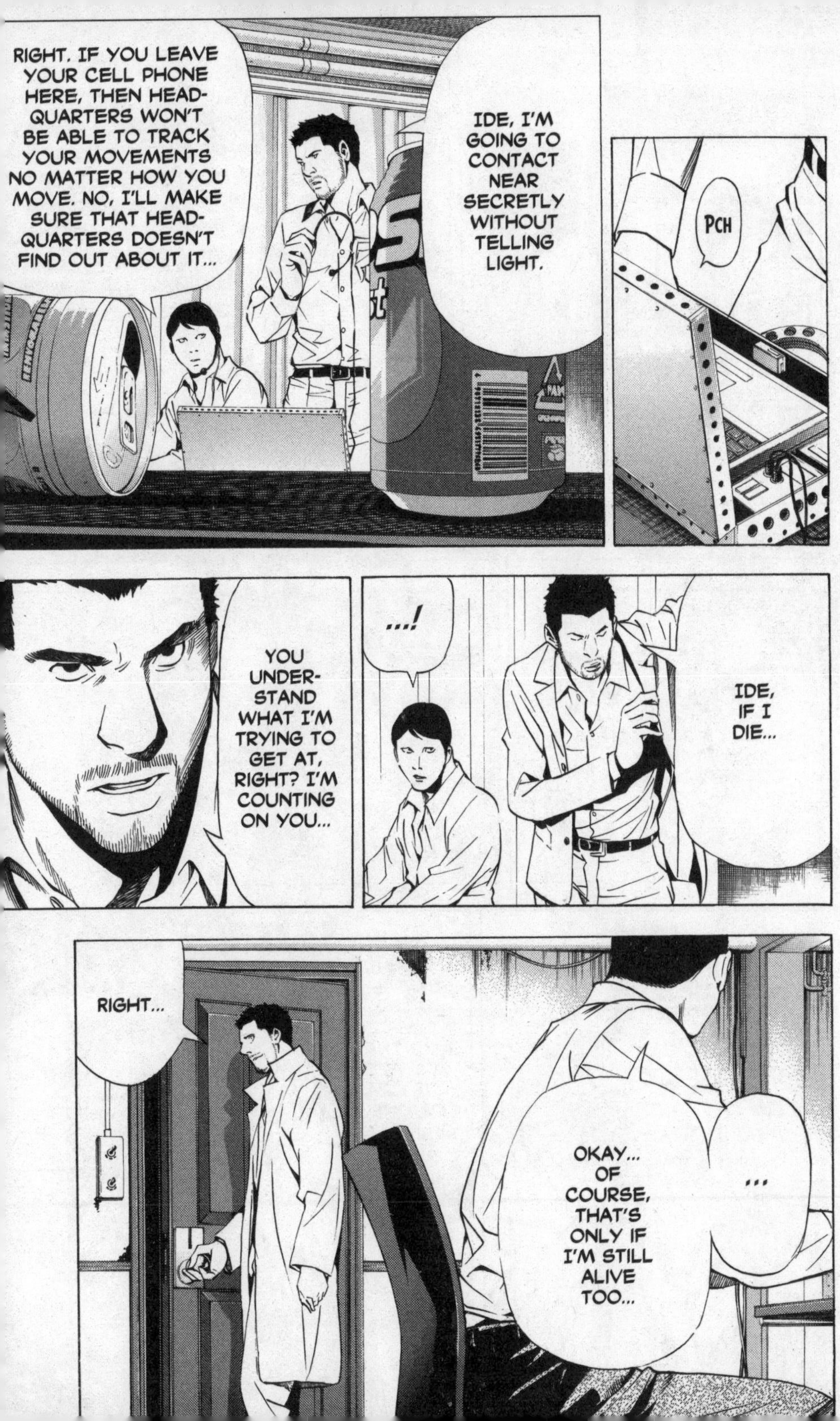
PCH
IDE, I'M GOING TO CONTACT NEAR SECRETLY WITHOUT TELLING LIGHT.
RIGHT. IF YOU LEAVE YOUR CELL PHONE HERE, THEN HEAD-QUARTERS WON'T BE ABLE TO TRACK YOUR MOVEMENTS NO MATTER HOW YOU MOVE. NO, I'LL MAKE SURE THAT HEAD-QUARTERS DOESN'T FIND OUT ABOUT IT...
IDE, IF I DIE...
...!
YOU UNDER-STAND WHAT I'M TRYING TO GET AT, RIGHT? I'M COUNTING ON YOU...
...
OKAY... OF COURSE, THAT'S ONLY IF I'M STILL ALIVE TOO...
RIGHT...

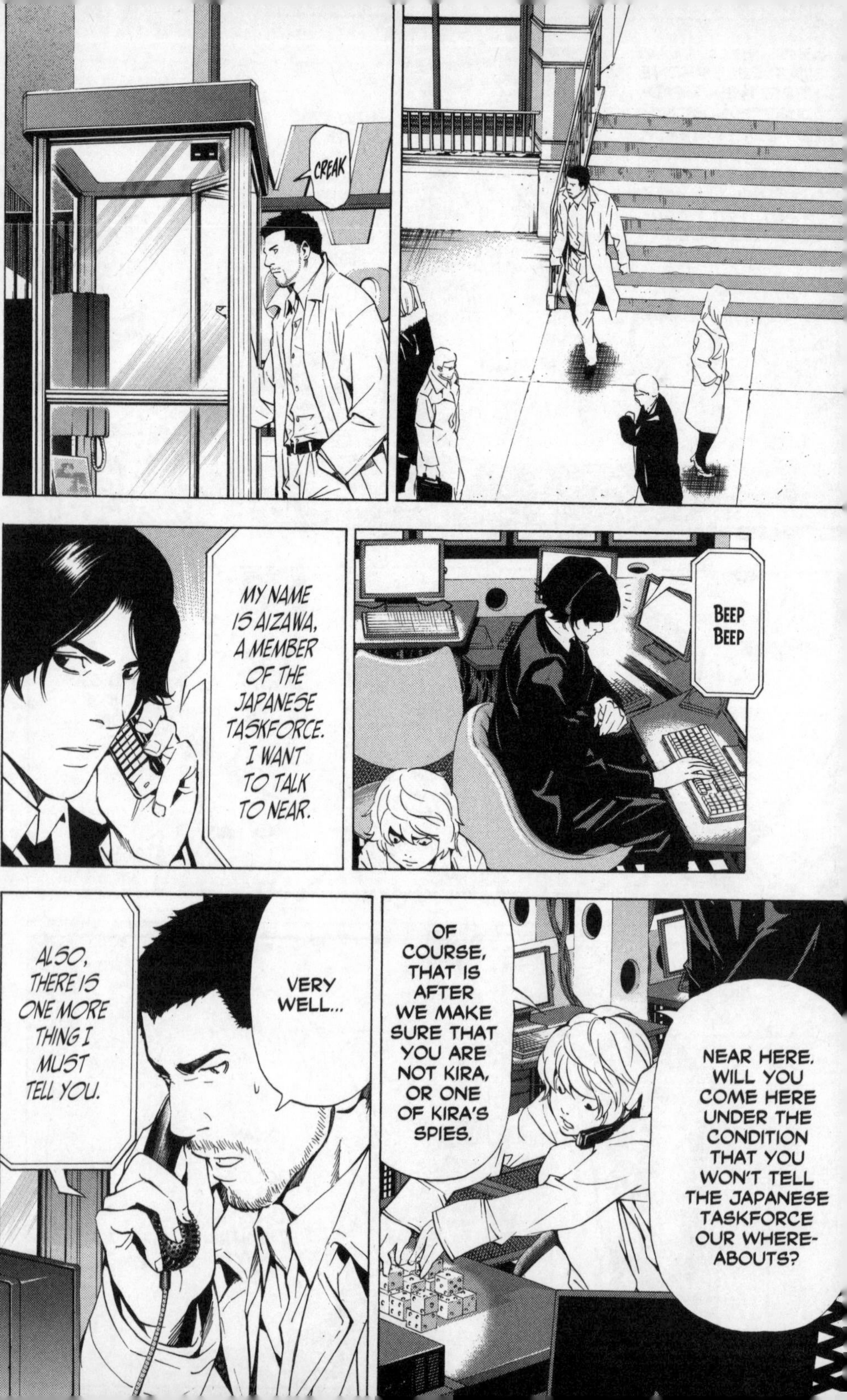
CREAK
BEEP BEEP
MY NAME IS AIZAWA, A MEMBER OF THE JAPANESE TASKFORCE. I WANT TO TALK TO NEAR.
NEAR HERE. WILL YOU COME HERE UNDER THE CONDITION THAT YOU WON'T TELL THE JAPANESE TASKFORCE OUR WHERE-ABOUTS?
OF COURSE, THAT IS AFTER WE MAKE SURE THAT YOU ARE NOT KIRA, OR ONE OF KIRA'S SPIES.
VERY WELL...
ALSO, THERE IS ONE MORE THING I MUST TELL YOU.

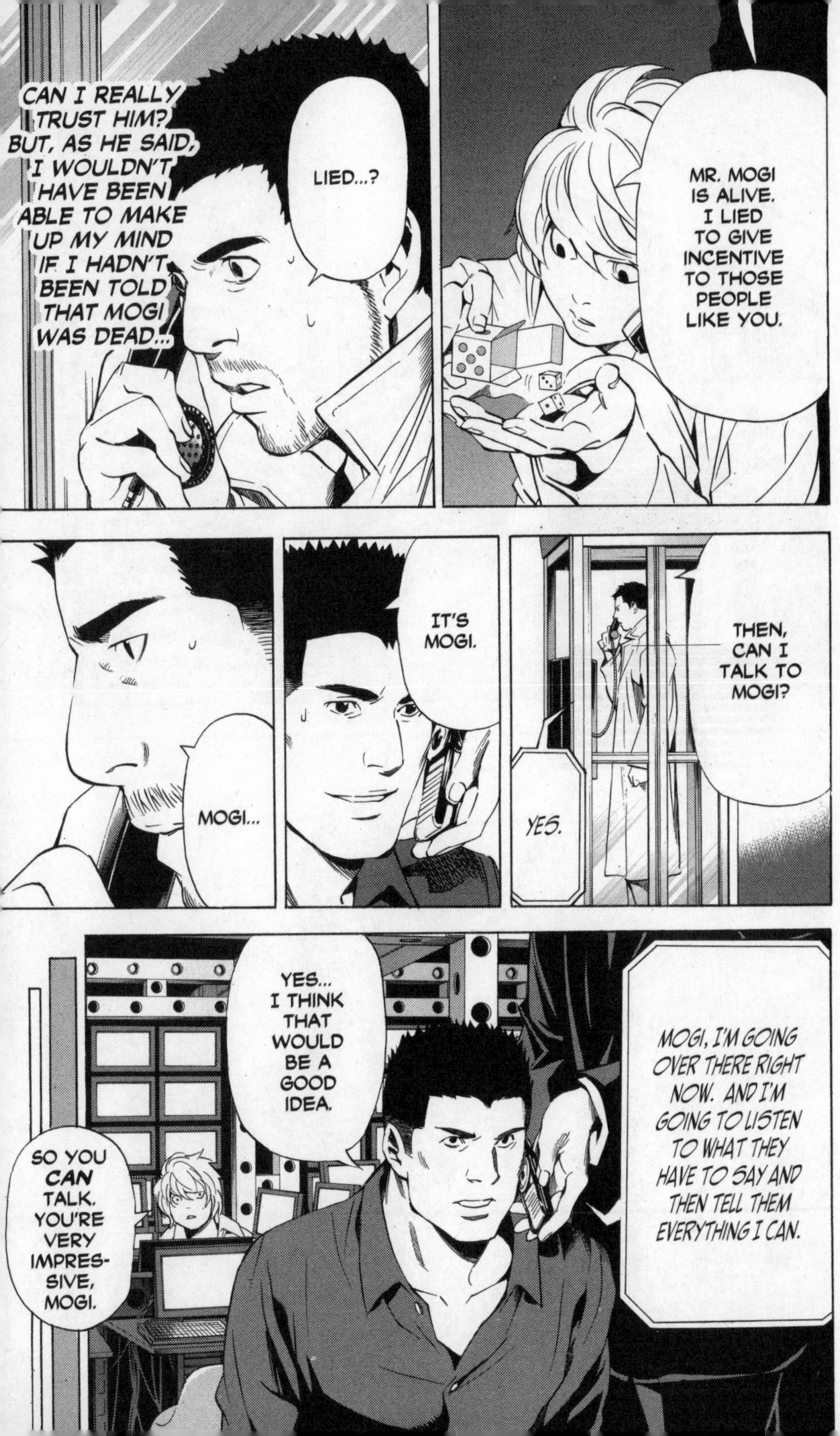
MR. MOGI IS ALIVE. I LIED TO GIVE INCENTIVE TO THOSE PEOPLE LIKE YOU.
LIED...?
CAN I REALLY TRUST HIM? BUT, AS HE SAID, I WOULDN'T HAVE BEEN ABLE TO MAKE UP MY MIND IF I HADN'T BEEN TOLD THAT MOGI WAS DEAD...
THEN, CAN I TALK TO MOGI?
YES.
IT'S MOGI.
MOGI...
MOGI, I'M GOING OVER THERE RIGHT NOW. AND I'M GOING TO LISTEN TO WHAT THEY HAVE TO SAY AND THEN TELL THEM EVERYTHING I CAN.
YES... I THINK THAT WOULD BE A GOOD IDEA.
SO YOU CAN TALK. YOU'RE VERY IMPRESSIVE, MOGI.

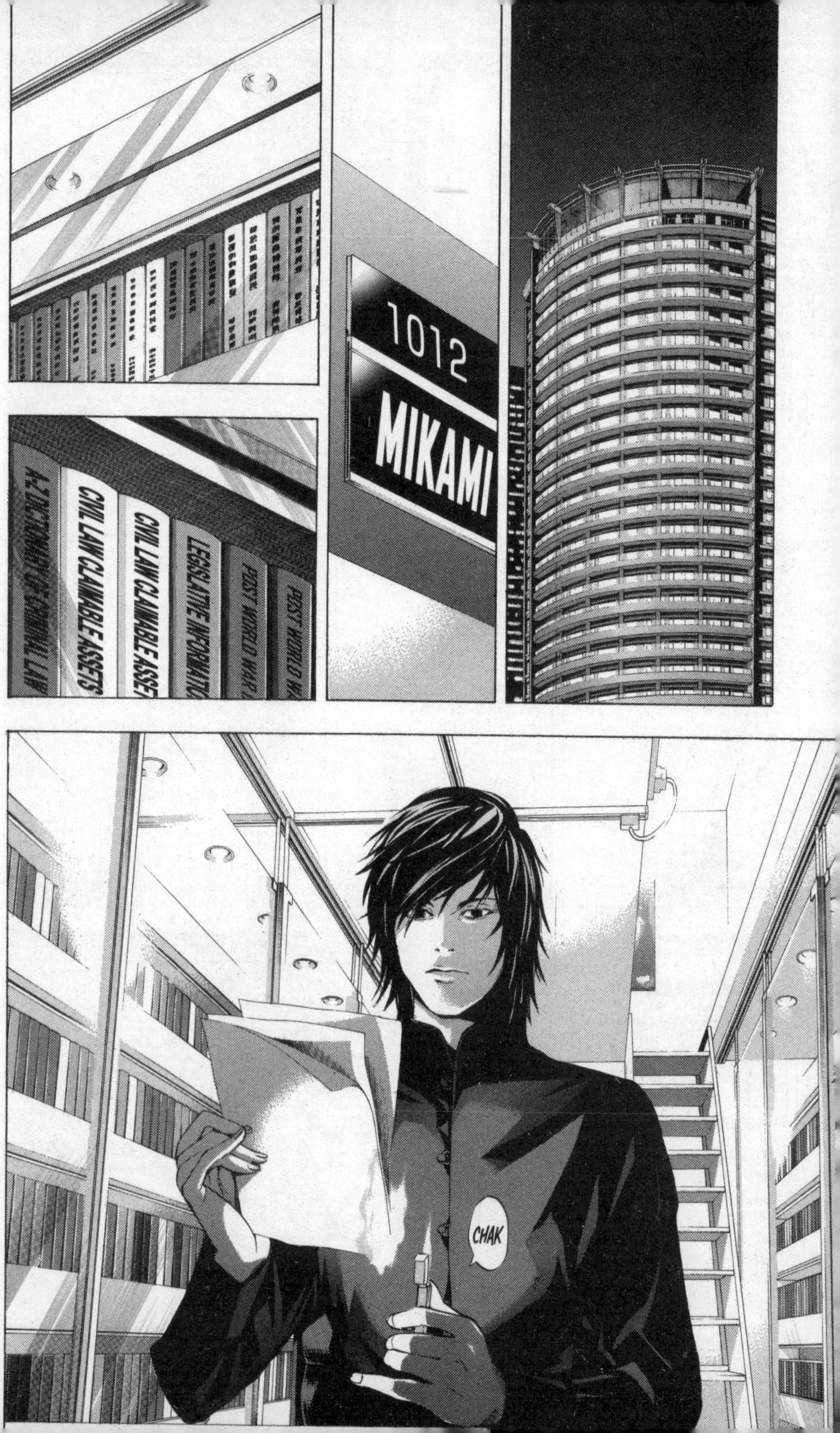
1012
MIKAMI
POST WORLD W
POST WORLD WAR
LEGISLATIVE INFORMATIO
CIVIL LAW CLAIMABLE ASSET
CIVIL LAW CLAIMABLE ASSETS
A-Z DICTIONARY OF CRIMINAL LAW
CHAK

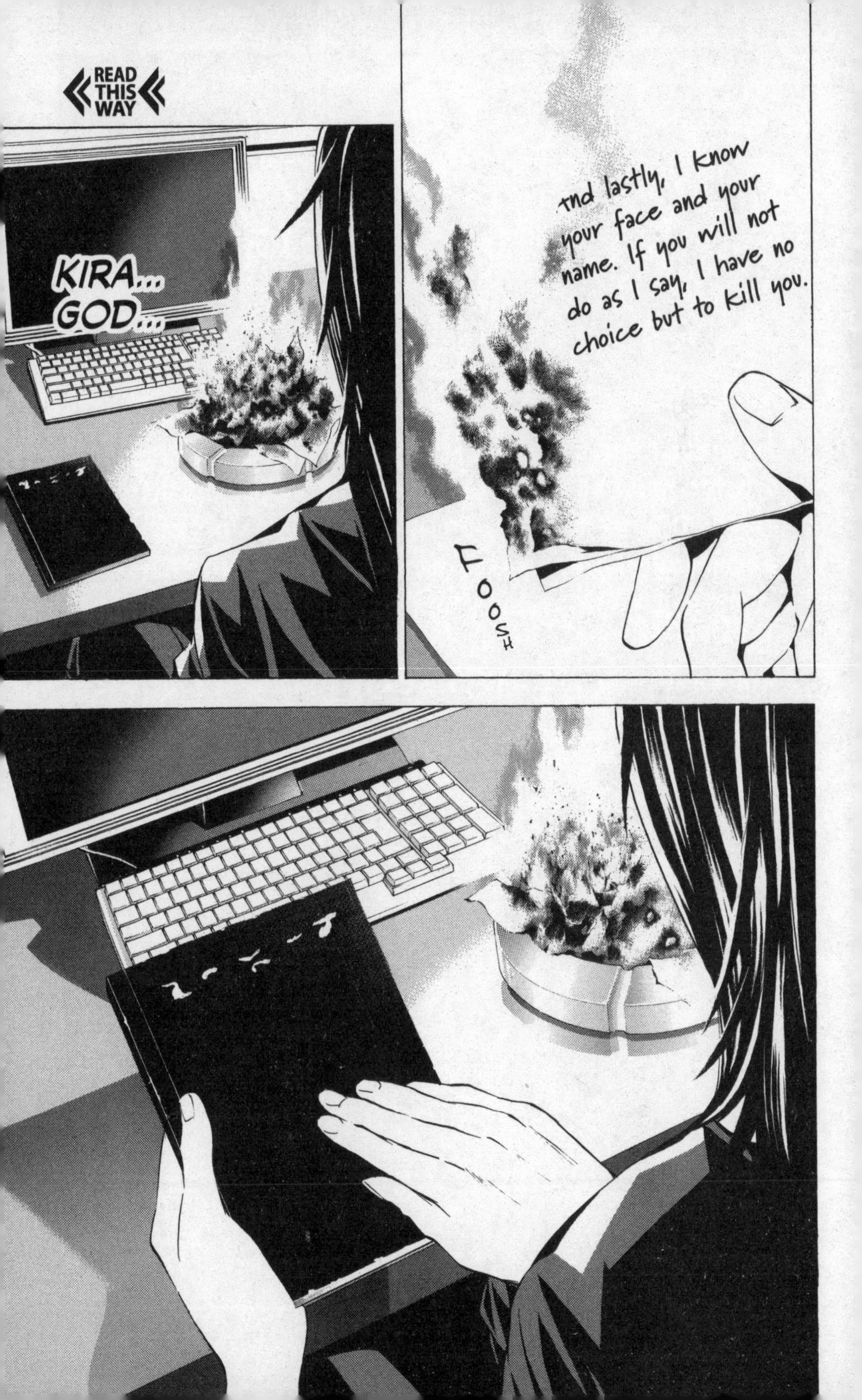
READ THIS WAY
And lastly, I know your face and your name. If you will not do as I say, I have no choice but to kill you.
FOOSH
KIRA... GOD...

DEATH NOTE
How to use it
LIV

° In order to make the DEATH NOTE take effect, the victims name must be written on the same page, but the cause of death and the situation around the death can be described in other pages of the DEATH NOTE.

This will work as long as the person that writes the DEATH NOTE keeps the specific victims name in mind when writing the cause and situation of the death.

デスノートの効力を得るには、
一人の名前は同ページに記さなくてはならないが、
その名前に関する死因や死の状況は、
書き込む者がその記した名前に対する死因や状況と考えて記せば、
他のページに記しても有効である。

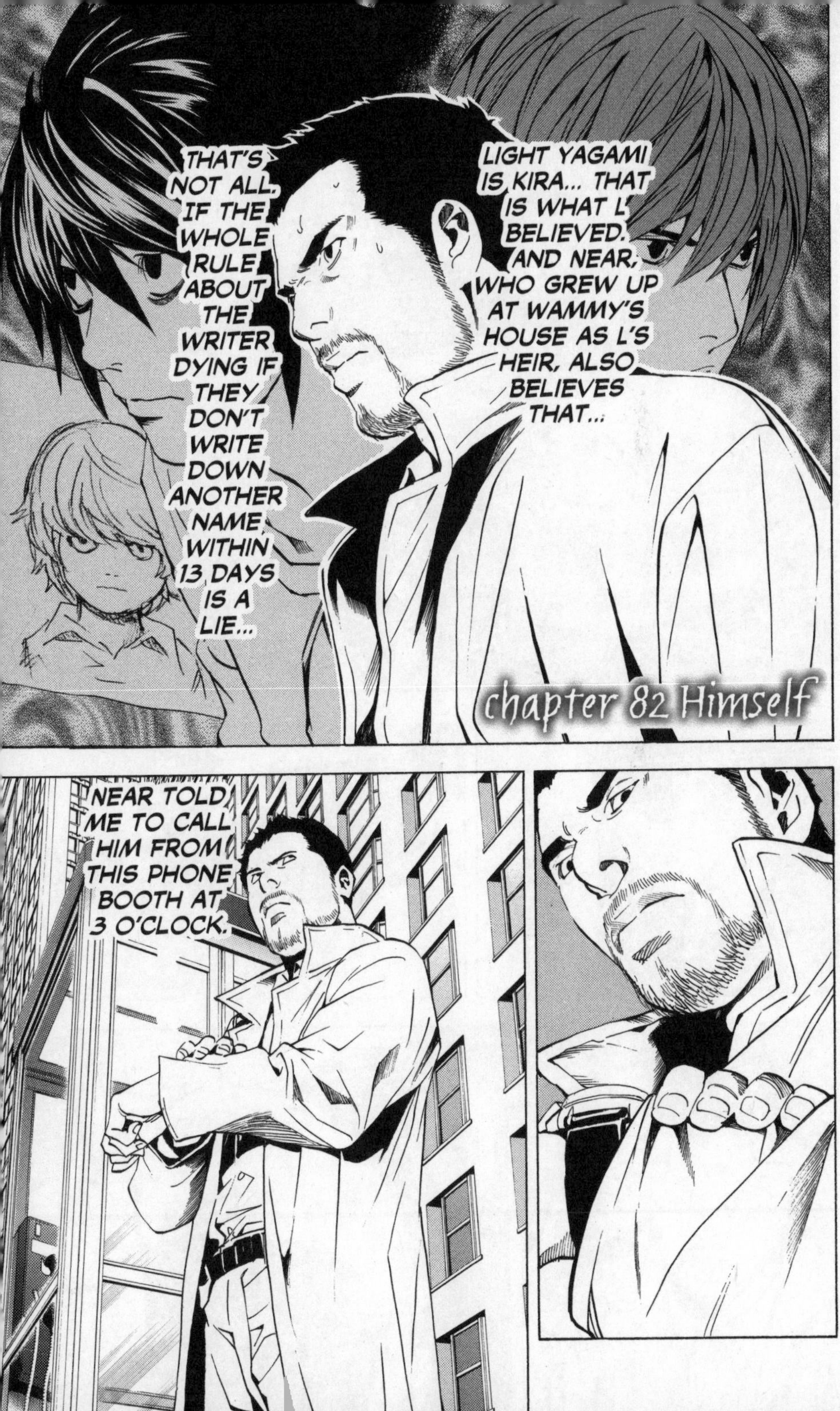
LIGHT YAGAMI IS KIRA... THAT IS WHAT L BELIEVED. AND NEAR, WHO GREW UP AT WAMMY'S HOUSE AS L'S HEIR, ALSO BELIEVES THAT...
THAT'S NOT ALL. IF THE WHOLE RULE ABOUT THE WRITER DYING IF THEY DON'T WRITE DOWN ANOTHER NAME WITHIN 13 DAYS IS A LIE...
chapter 82 Himself
NEAR TOLD ME TO CALL HIM FROM THIS PHONE BOOTH AT 3 O'CLOCK.

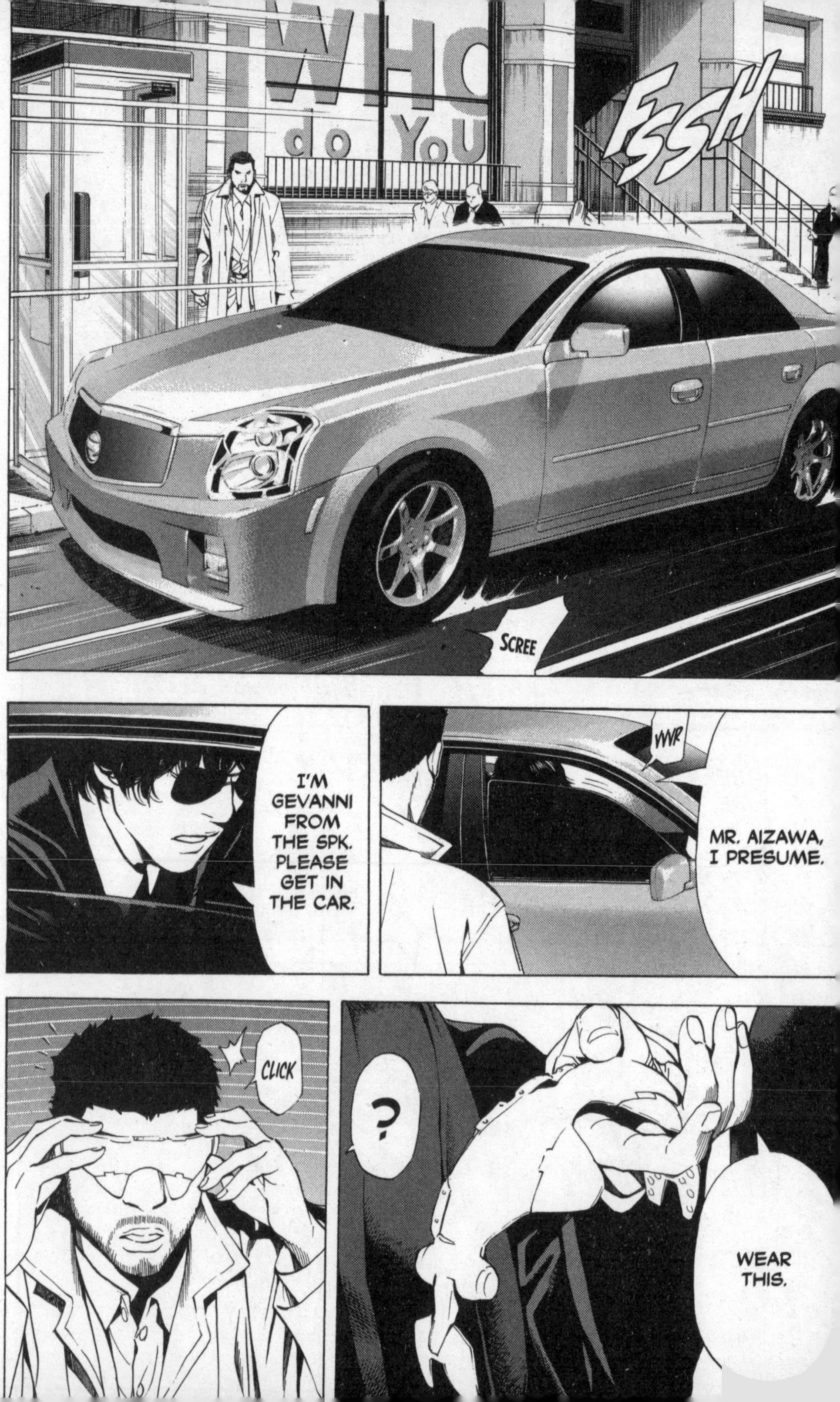
WHO
do YOU
FSSH
SCREE
VVVR
MR. AIZAWA, I PRESUME.
I'M GEVANNI FROM THE SPK. PLEASE GET IN THE CAR.
?
WEAR THIS.
CLICK

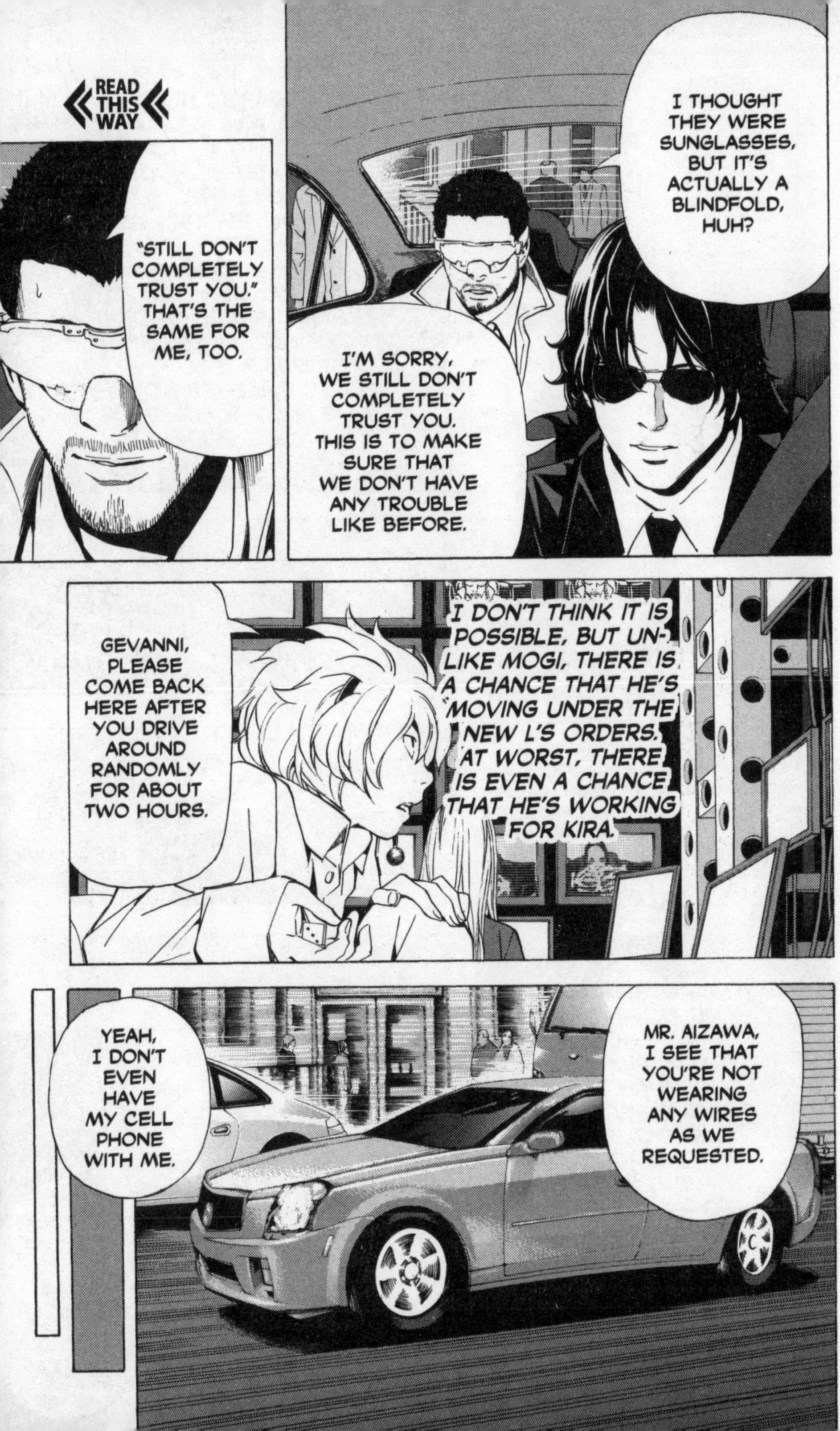
READ THIS WAY
I THOUGHT THEY WERE SUNGLASSES, BUT IT'S ACTUALLY A BLINDFOLD, HUH?
I'M SORRY, WE STILL DON'T COMPLETELY TRUST YOU. THIS IS TO MAKE SURE THAT WE DON'T HAVE ANY TROUBLE LIKE BEFORE.
"STILL DON'T COMPLETELY TRUST YOU." THAT'S THE SAME FOR ME, TOO.
I DON'T THINK IT IS POSSIBLE, BUT UN-LIKE MOGI, THERE IS A CHANCE THAT HE'S MOVING UNDER THE NEW L'S ORDERS. AT WORST, THERE IS EVEN A CHANCE THAT HE'S WORKING FOR KIRA.
GEVANNI, PLEASE COME BACK HERE AFTER YOU DRIVE AROUND RANDOMLY FOR ABOUT TWO HOURS.
MR. AIZAWA, I SEE THAT YOU'RE NOT WEARING ANY WIRES AS WE REQUESTED.
YEAH, I DON'T EVEN HAVE MY CELL PHONE WITH ME.

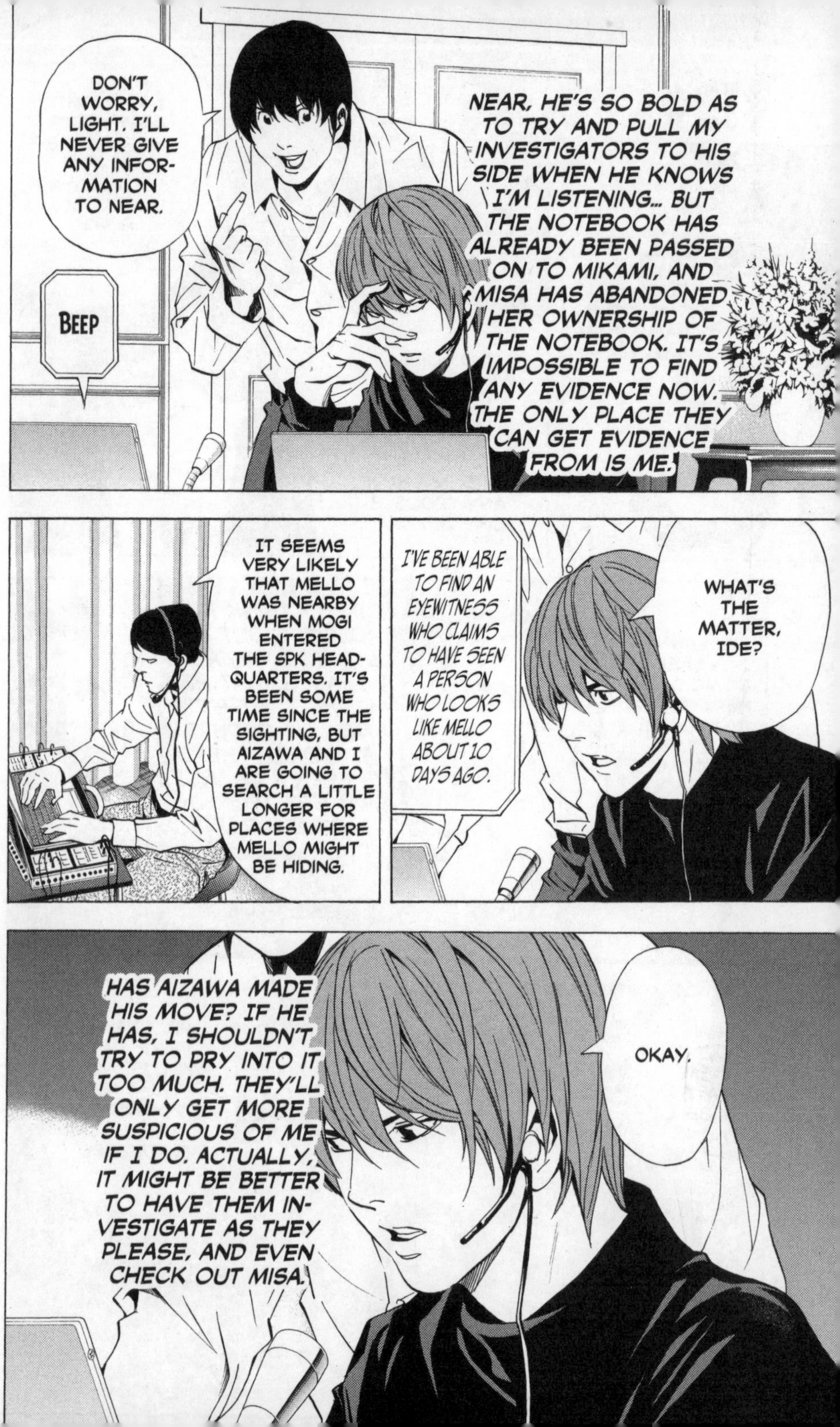
NEAR, HE'S SO BOLD AS TO TRY AND PULL MY INVESTIGATORS TO HIS SIDE WHEN HE KNOWS I'M LISTENING... BUT THE NOTEBOOK HAS ALREADY BEEN PASSED ON TO MIKAMI, AND MISA HAS ABANDONED HER OWNERSHIP OF THE NOTEBOOK. IT'S IMPOSSIBLE TO FIND ANY EVIDENCE NOW. THE ONLY PLACE THEY CAN GET EVIDENCE FROM IS ME.
DON'T WORRY, LIGHT. I'LL NEVER GIVE ANY INFORMATION TO NEAR.
BEEP
WHAT'S THE MATTER, IDE?
I'VE BEEN ABLE TO FIND AN EYEWITNESS WHO CLAIMS TO HAVE SEEN A PERSON WHO LOOKS LIKE MELLO ABOUT 10 DAYS AGO.
IT SEEMS VERY LIKELY THAT MELLO WAS NEARBY WHEN MOGI ENTERED THE SPK HEADQUARTERS. IT'S BEEN SOME TIME SINCE THE SIGHTING, BUT AIZAWA AND I ARE GOING TO SEARCH A LITTLE LONGER FOR PLACES WHERE MELLO MIGHT BE HIDING.
OKAY.
HAS AIZAWA MADE HIS MOVE? IF HE HAS, I SHOULDN'T TRY TO PRY INTO IT TOO MUCH. THEY'LL ONLY GET MORE SUSPICIOUS OF ME IF I DO. ACTUALLY, IT MIGHT BE BETTER TO HAVE THEM INVESTIGATE AS THEY PLEASE, AND EVEN CHECK OUT MISA.

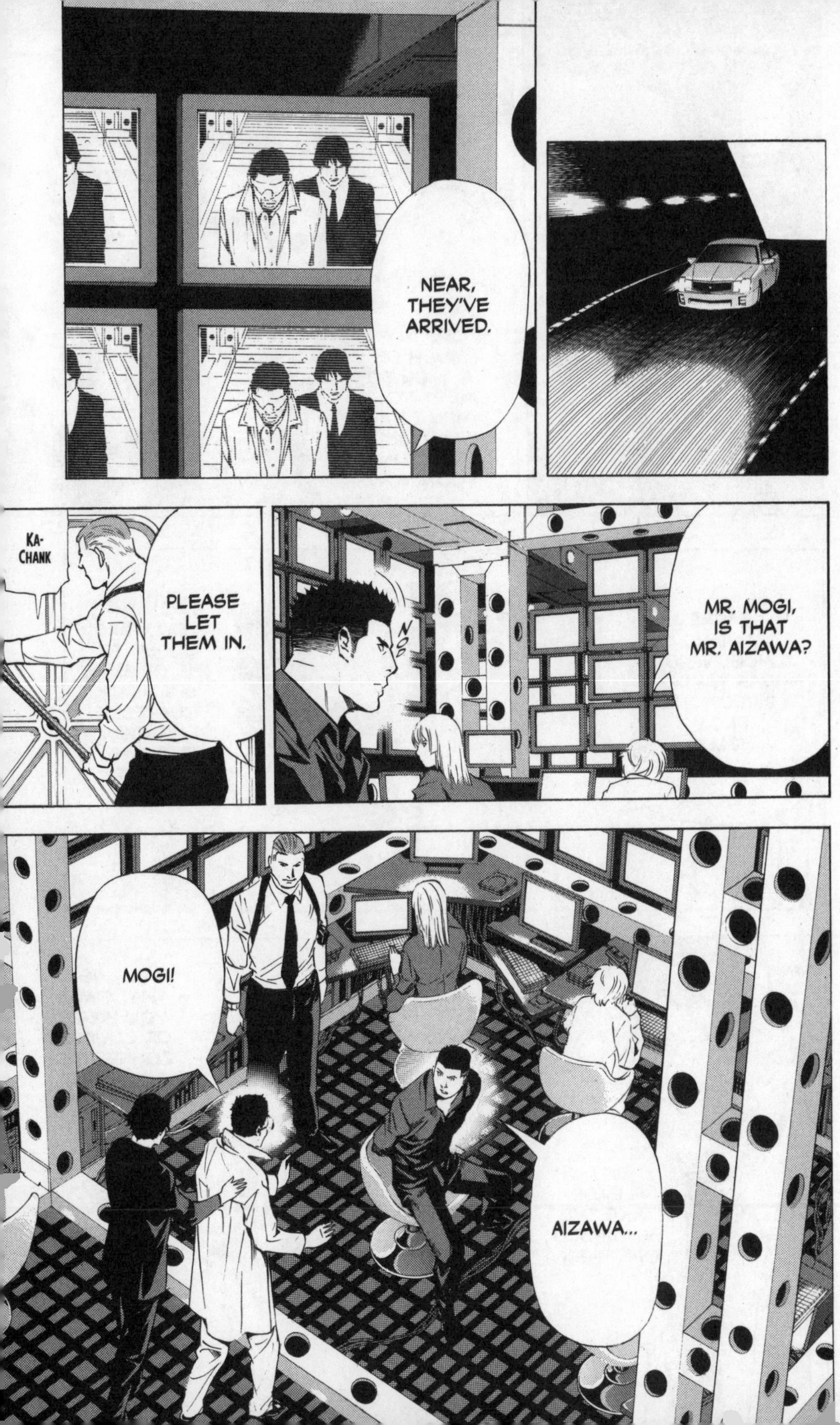
NEAR, THEY'VE ARRIVED.
MR. MOGI, IS THAT MR. AIZAWA?
NOD
PLEASE LET THEM IN.
KA-CHANK
MOGI!
AIZAWA...

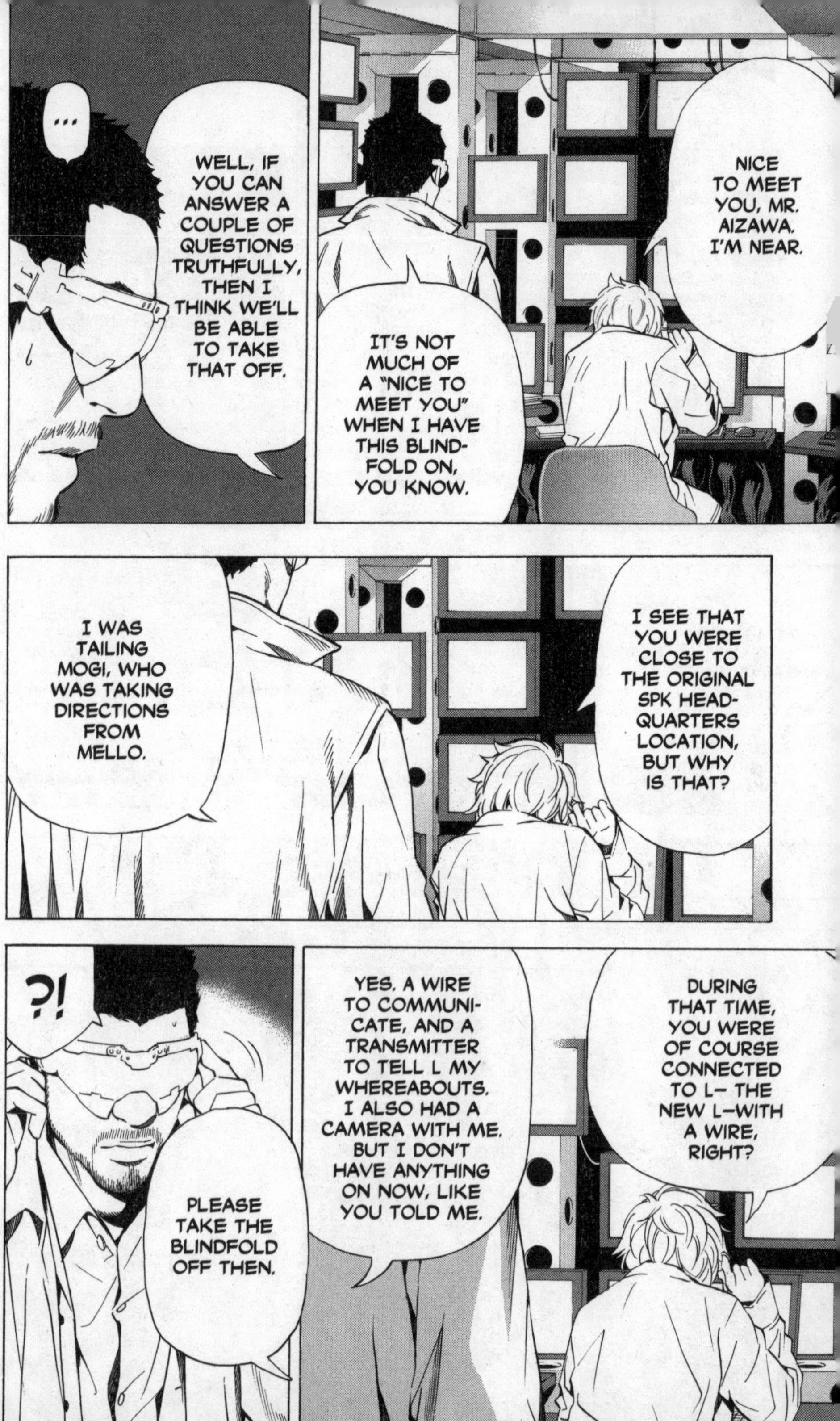
NICE TO MEET YOU, MR. AIZAWA. I'M NEAR.
IT'S NOT MUCH OF A "NICE TO MEET YOU" WHEN I HAVE THIS BLIND-FOLD ON, YOU KNOW.
WELL, IF YOU CAN ANSWER A COUPLE OF QUESTIONS TRUTHFULLY, THEN I THINK WE'LL BE ABLE TO TAKE THAT OFF.
...
I SEE THAT YOU WERE CLOSE TO THE ORIGINAL SPK HEAD-QUARTERS LOCATION, BUT WHY IS THAT?
I WAS TAILING MOGI, WHO WAS TAKING DIRECTIONS FROM MELLO.
DURING THAT TIME, YOU WERE OF COURSE CONNECTED TO L– THE NEW L–WITH A WIRE, RIGHT?
YES. A WIRE TO COMMUNI-CATE, AND A TRANSMITTER TO TELL L MY WHEREABOUTS. I ALSO HAD A CAMERA WITH ME. BUT I DON'T HAVE ANYTHING ON NOW, LIKE YOU TOLD ME.
?!
PLEASE TAKE THE BLINDFOLD OFF THEN.

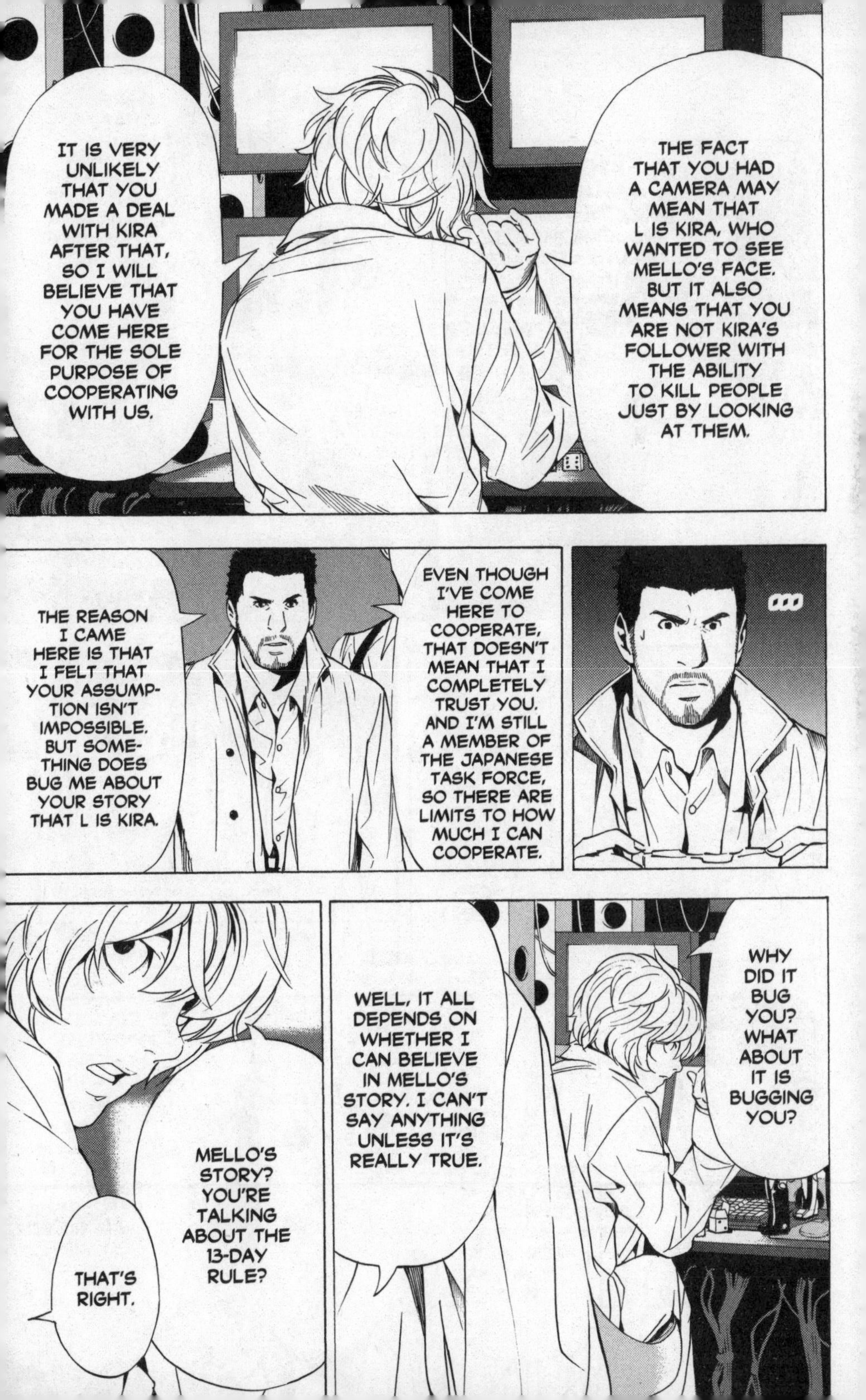
THE FACT THAT YOU HAD A CAMERA MAY MEAN THAT L IS KIRA, WHO WANTED TO SEE MELLO'S FACE. BUT IT ALSO MEANS THAT YOU ARE NOT KIRA'S FOLLOWER WITH THE ABILITY TO KILL PEOPLE JUST BY LOOKING AT THEM.
IT IS VERY UNLIKELY THAT YOU MADE A DEAL WITH KIRA AFTER THAT, SO I WILL BELIEVE THAT YOU HAVE COME HERE FOR THE SOLE PURPOSE OF COOPERATING WITH US.
...
EVEN THOUGH I'VE COME HERE TO COOPERATE, THAT DOESN'T MEAN THAT I COMPLETELY TRUST YOU. AND I'M STILL A MEMBER OF THE JAPANESE TASK FORCE, SO THERE ARE LIMITS TO HOW MUCH I CAN COOPERATE.
THE REASON I CAME HERE IS THAT I FELT THAT YOUR ASSUMPTION ISN'T IMPOSSIBLE. BUT SOMETHING DOES BUG ME ABOUT YOUR STORY THAT L IS KIRA.
WHY DID IT BUG YOU? WHAT ABOUT IT IS BUGGING YOU?
WELL, IT ALL DEPENDS ON WHETHER I CAN BELIEVE IN MELLO'S STORY. I CAN'T SAY ANYTHING UNLESS IT'S REALLY TRUE.
MELLO'S STORY? YOU'RE TALKING ABOUT THE 13-DAY RULE?
THAT'S RIGHT.

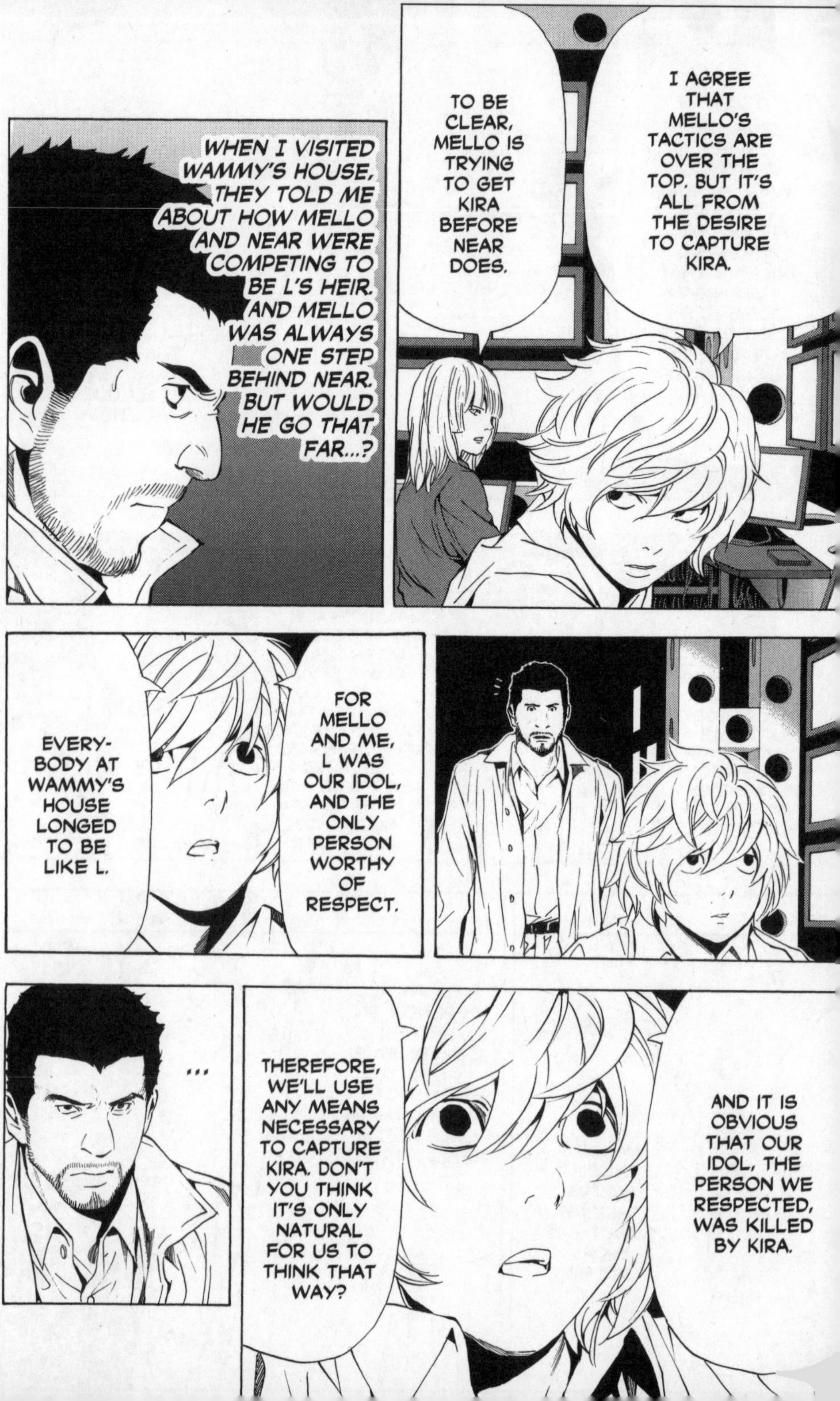
I AGREE THAT MELLO'S TACTICS ARE OVER THE TOP. BUT IT'S ALL FROM THE DESIRE TO CAPTURE KIRA.
TO BE CLEAR, MELLO IS TRYING TO GET KIRA BEFORE NEAR DOES.
WHEN I VISITED WAMMY'S HOUSE, THEY TOLD ME ABOUT HOW MELLO AND NEAR WERE COMPETING TO BE L'S HEIR. AND MELLO WAS ALWAYS ONE STEP BEHIND NEAR. BUT WOULD HE GO THAT FAR...?
FOR MELLO AND ME, L WAS OUR IDOL, AND THE ONLY PERSON WORTHY OF RESPECT.
EVERY-BODY AT WAMMY'S HOUSE LONGED TO BE LIKE L.
AND IT IS OBVIOUS THAT OUR IDOL, THE PERSON WE RESPECTED, WAS KILLED BY KIRA.
THEREFORE, WE'LL USE ANY MEANS NECESSARY TO CAPTURE KIRA. DON'T YOU THINK IT'S ONLY NATURAL FOR US TO THINK THAT WAY?
...

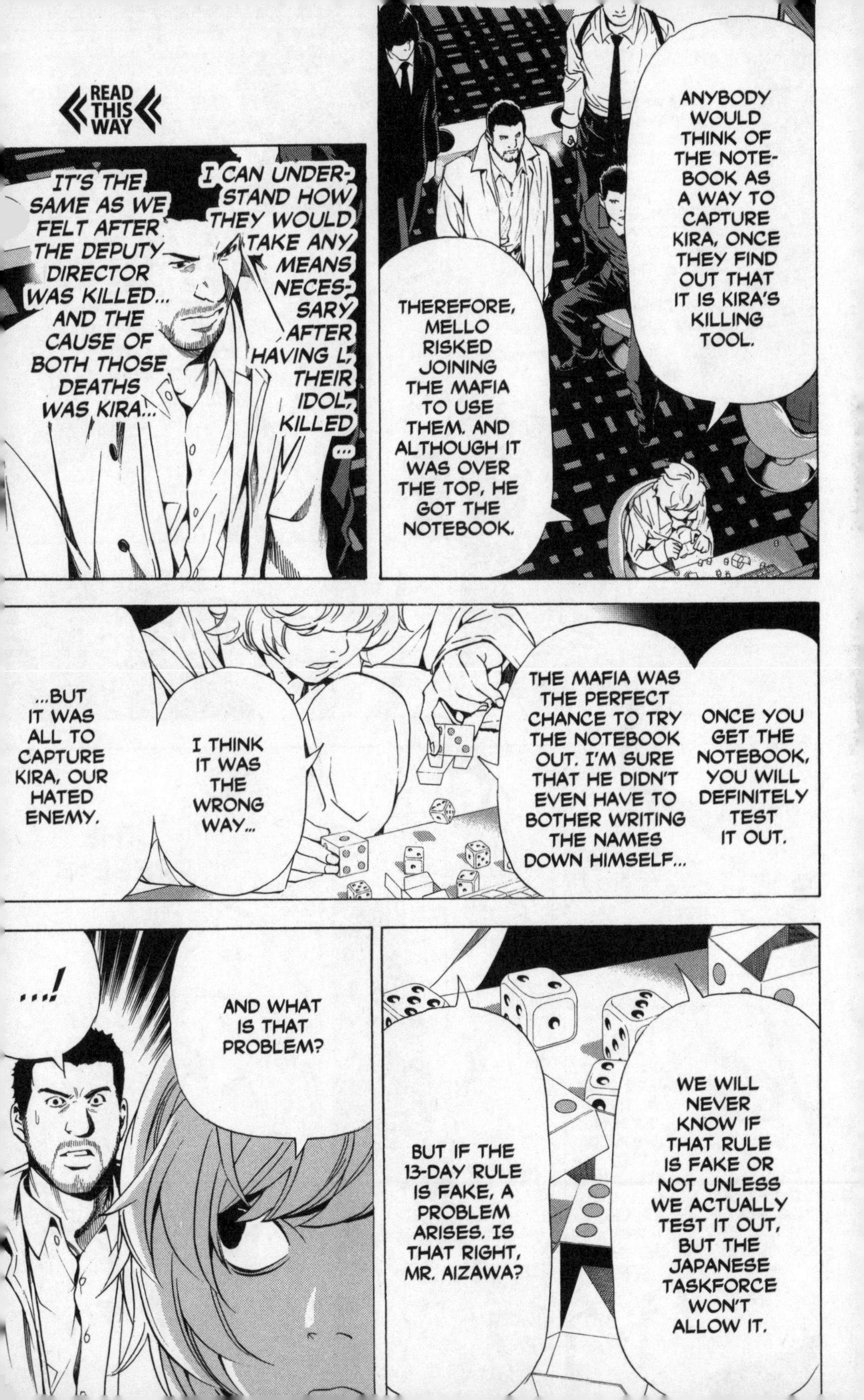
READ THIS WAY
ANYBODY WOULD THINK OF THE NOTE-BOOK AS A WAY TO CAPTURE KIRA, ONCE THEY FIND OUT THAT IT IS KIRA'S KILLING TOOL.
THEREFORE, MELLO RISKED JOINING THE MAFIA TO USE THEM. AND ALTHOUGH IT WAS OVER THE TOP, HE GOT THE NOTEBOOK.
I CAN UNDER-STAND HOW THEY WOULD TAKE ANY MEANS NECES-SARY AFTER HAVING L, THEIR IDOL, KILLED ...
IT'S THE SAME AS WE FELT AFTER THE DEPUTY DIRECTOR WAS KILLED... AND THE CAUSE OF BOTH THOSE DEATHS WAS KIRA...
ONCE YOU GET THE NOTEBOOK, YOU WILL DEFINITELY TEST IT OUT.
THE MAFIA WAS THE PERFECT CHANCE TO TRY THE NOTEBOOK OUT. I'M SURE THAT HE DIDN'T EVEN HAVE TO BOTHER WRITING THE NAMES DOWN HIMSELF...
I THINK IT WAS THE WRONG WAY...
...BUT IT WAS ALL TO CAPTURE KIRA, OUR HATED ENEMY.
WE WILL NEVER KNOW IF THAT RULE IS FAKE OR NOT UNLESS WE ACTUALLY TEST IT OUT, BUT THE JAPANESE TASKFORCE WON'T ALLOW IT.
BUT IF THE 13-DAY RULE IS FAKE, A PROBLEM ARISES. IS THAT RIGHT, MR. AIZAWA?
AND WHAT IS THAT PROBLEM?
...!

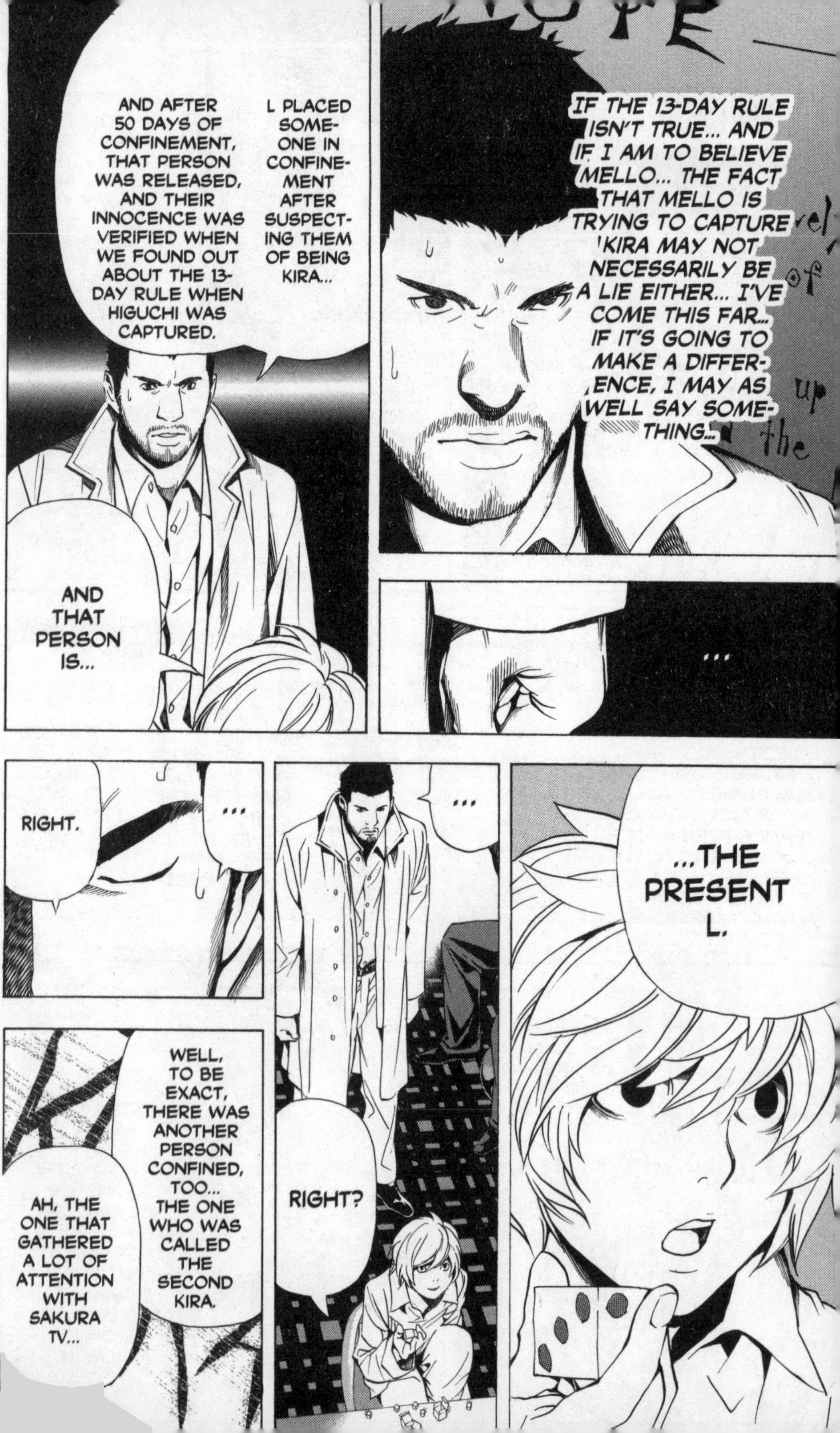

IF THE 13-DAY RULE ISN'T TRUE... AND IF I AM TO BELIEVE MELLO... THE FACT THAT MELLO IS TRYING TO CAPTURE KIRA MAY NOT NECESSARILY BE A LIE EITHER... I'VE COME THIS FAR... IF IT'S GOING TO MAKE A DIFFERENCE, I MAY AS WELL SAY SOMETHING...
...
L PLACED SOMEONE IN CONFINEMENT AFTER SUSPECTING THEM OF BEING KIRA...
AND AFTER 50 DAYS OF CONFINEMENT, THAT PERSON WAS RELEASED, AND THEIR INNOCENCE WAS VERIFIED WHEN WE FOUND OUT ABOUT THE 13-DAY RULE WHEN HIGUCHI WAS CAPTURED.
AND THAT PERSON IS...
...THE PRESENT L.
...
RIGHT?
...
RIGHT.
WELL, TO BE EXACT, THERE WAS ANOTHER PERSON CONFINED, TOO... THE ONE WHO WAS CALLED THE SECOND KIRA.
AH, THE ONE THAT GATHERED A LOT OF ATTENTION WITH SAKURA TV...

READ THIS WAY

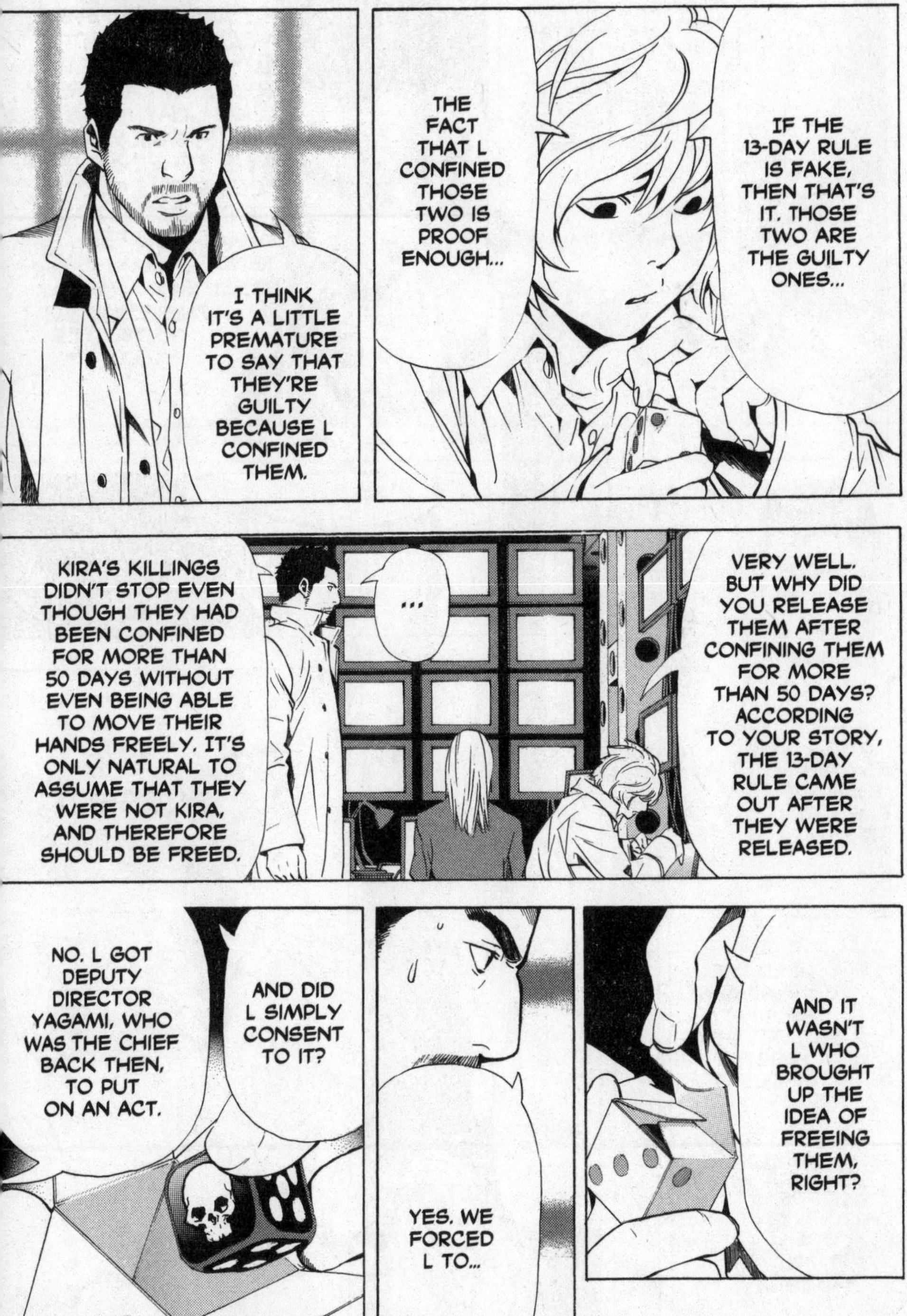
IF THE 13-DAY RULE IS FAKE, THEN THAT'S IT. THOSE TWO ARE THE GUILTY ONES...
THE FACT THAT L CONFINED THOSE TWO IS PROOF ENOUGH...
I THINK IT'S A LITTLE PREMATURE TO SAY THAT THEY'RE GUILTY BECAUSE L CONFINED THEM.
KIRA'S KILLINGS DIDN'T STOP EVEN THOUGH THEY HAD BEEN CONFINED FOR MORE THAN 50 DAYS WITHOUT EVEN BEING ABLE TO MOVE THEIR HANDS FREELY. IT'S ONLY NATURAL TO ASSUME THAT THEY WERE NOT KIRA, AND THEREFORE SHOULD BE FREED.
...
VERY WELL. BUT WHY DID YOU RELEASE THEM AFTER CONFINING THEM FOR MORE THAN 50 DAYS? ACCORDING TO YOUR STORY, THE 13-DAY RULE CAME OUT AFTER THEY WERE RELEASED.
AND IT WASN'T L WHO BROUGHT UP THE IDEA OF FREEING THEM, RIGHT?
YES. WE FORCED L TO...
AND DID L SIMPLY CONSENT TO IT?
NO. L GOT DEPUTY DIRECTOR YAGAMI, WHO WAS THE CHIEF BACK THEN, TO PUT ON AN ACT.

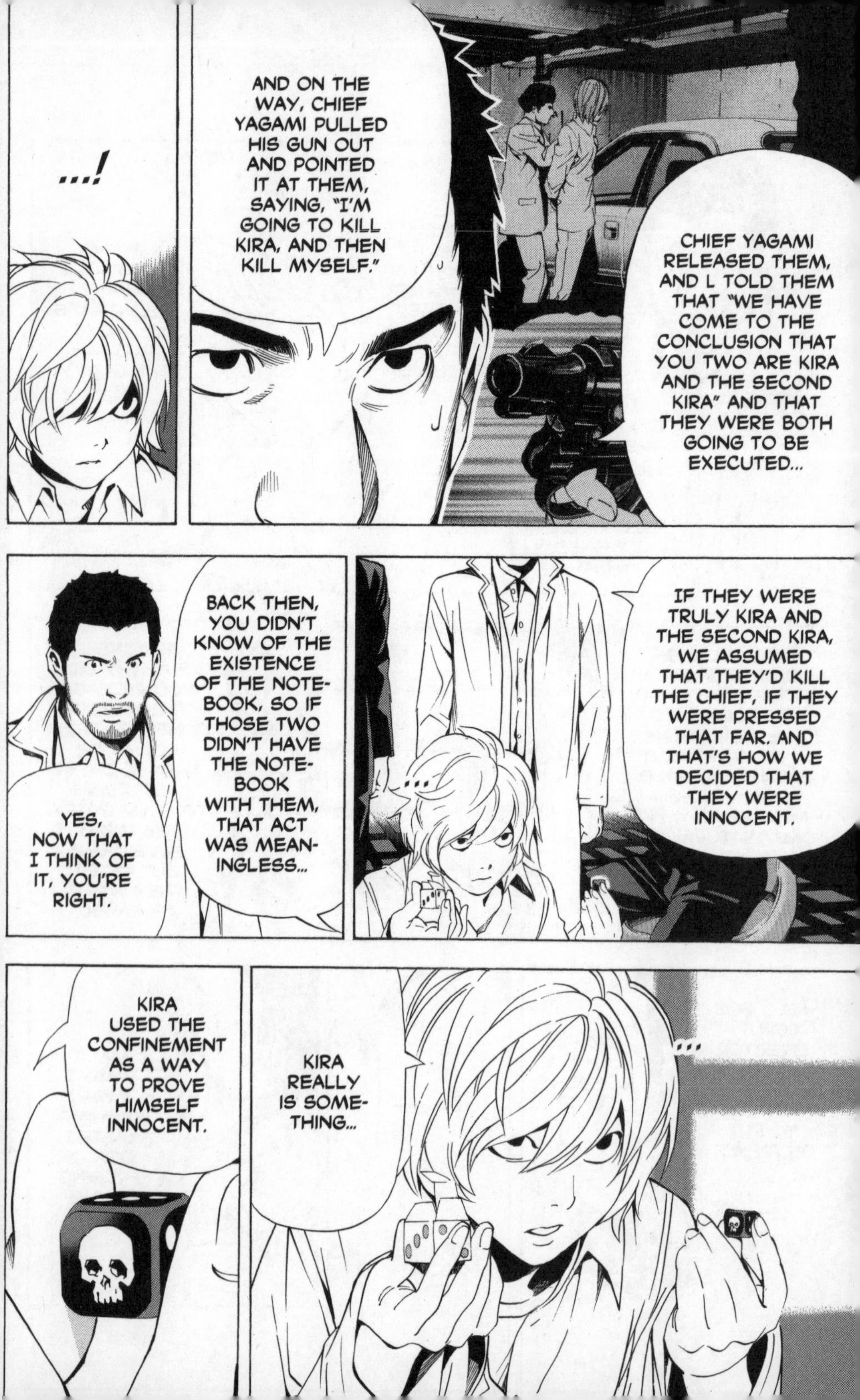
CHIEF YAGAMI RELEASED THEM, AND L TOLD THEM THAT "WE HAVE COME TO THE CONCLUSION THAT YOU TWO ARE KIRA AND THE SECOND KIRA" AND THAT THEY WERE BOTH GOING TO BE EXECUTED...
AND ON THE WAY, CHIEF YAGAMI PULLED HIS GUN OUT AND POINTED IT AT THEM, SAYING, "I'M GOING TO KILL KIRA, AND THEN KILL MYSELF."
...!
IF THEY WERE TRULY KIRA AND THE SECOND KIRA, WE ASSUMED THAT THEY'D KILL THE CHIEF, IF THEY WERE PRESSED THAT FAR. AND THAT'S HOW WE DECIDED THAT THEY WERE INNOCENT.
...
BACK THEN, YOU DIDN'T KNOW OF THE EXISTENCE OF THE NOTE-BOOK, SO IF THOSE TWO DIDN'T HAVE THE NOTE-BOOK WITH THEM, THAT ACT WAS MEAN-INGLESS...
YES, NOW THAT I THINK OF IT, YOU'RE RIGHT.
...
KIRA REALLY IS SOME-THING...
KIRA USED THE CONFINEMENT AS A WAY TO PROVE HIMSELF INNOCENT.

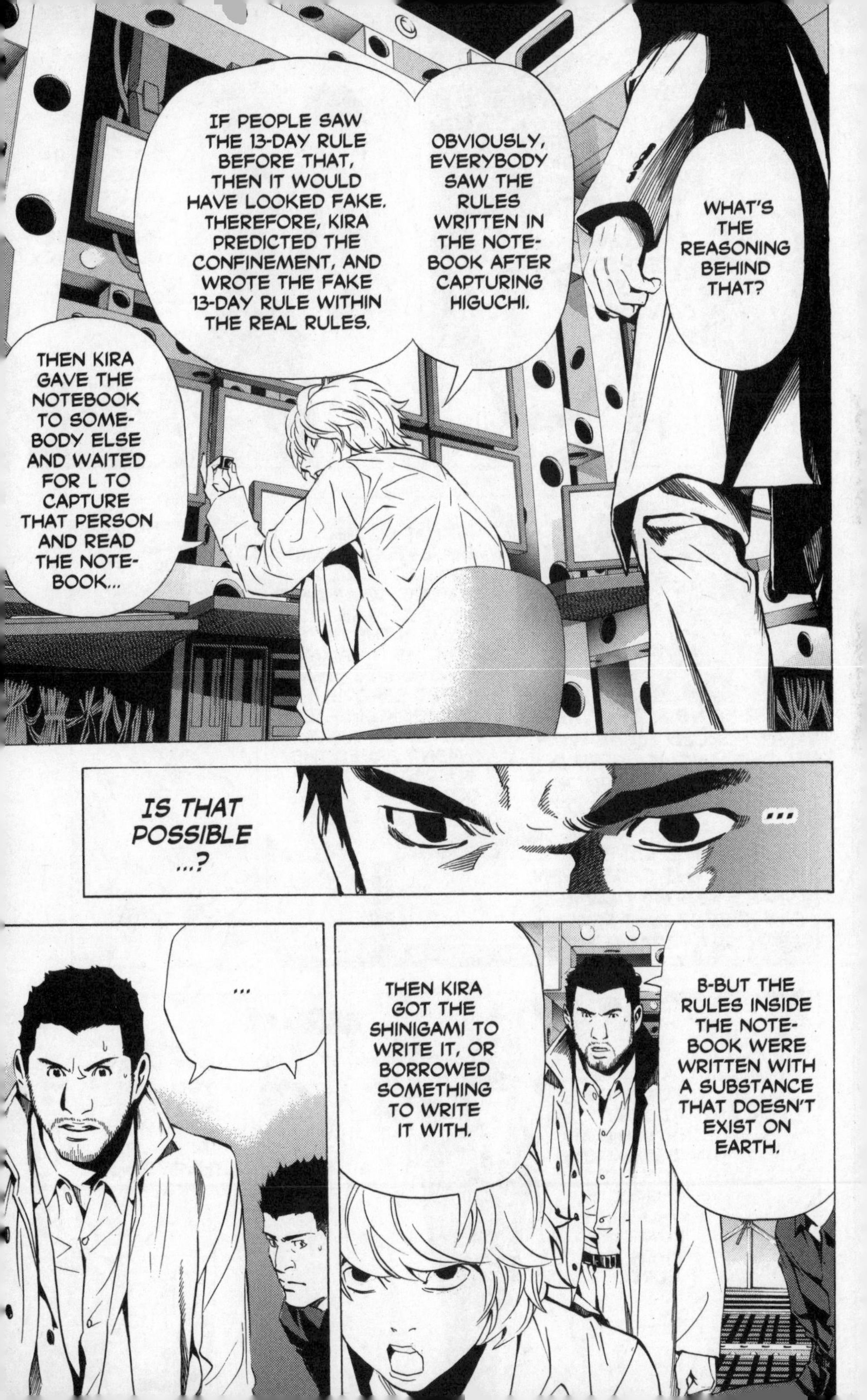
WHAT'S THE REASONING BEHIND THAT?
OBVIOUSLY, EVERYBODY SAW THE RULES WRITTEN IN THE NOTE-BOOK AFTER CAPTURING HIGUCHI.
IF PEOPLE SAW THE 13-DAY RULE BEFORE THAT, THEN IT WOULD HAVE LOOKED FAKE. THEREFORE, KIRA PREDICTED THE CONFINEMENT, AND WROTE THE FAKE 13-DAY RULE WITHIN THE REAL RULES.
THEN KIRA GAVE THE NOTEBOOK TO SOME-BODY ELSE AND WAITED FOR L TO CAPTURE THAT PERSON AND READ THE NOTE-BOOK...
...
IS THAT POSSIBLE ...?
B-BUT THE RULES INSIDE THE NOTE-BOOK WERE WRITTEN WITH A SUBSTANCE THAT DOESN'T EXIST ON EARTH.
THEN KIRA GOT THE SHINIGAMI TO WRITE IT, OR BORROWED SOMETHING TO WRITE IT WITH.
...

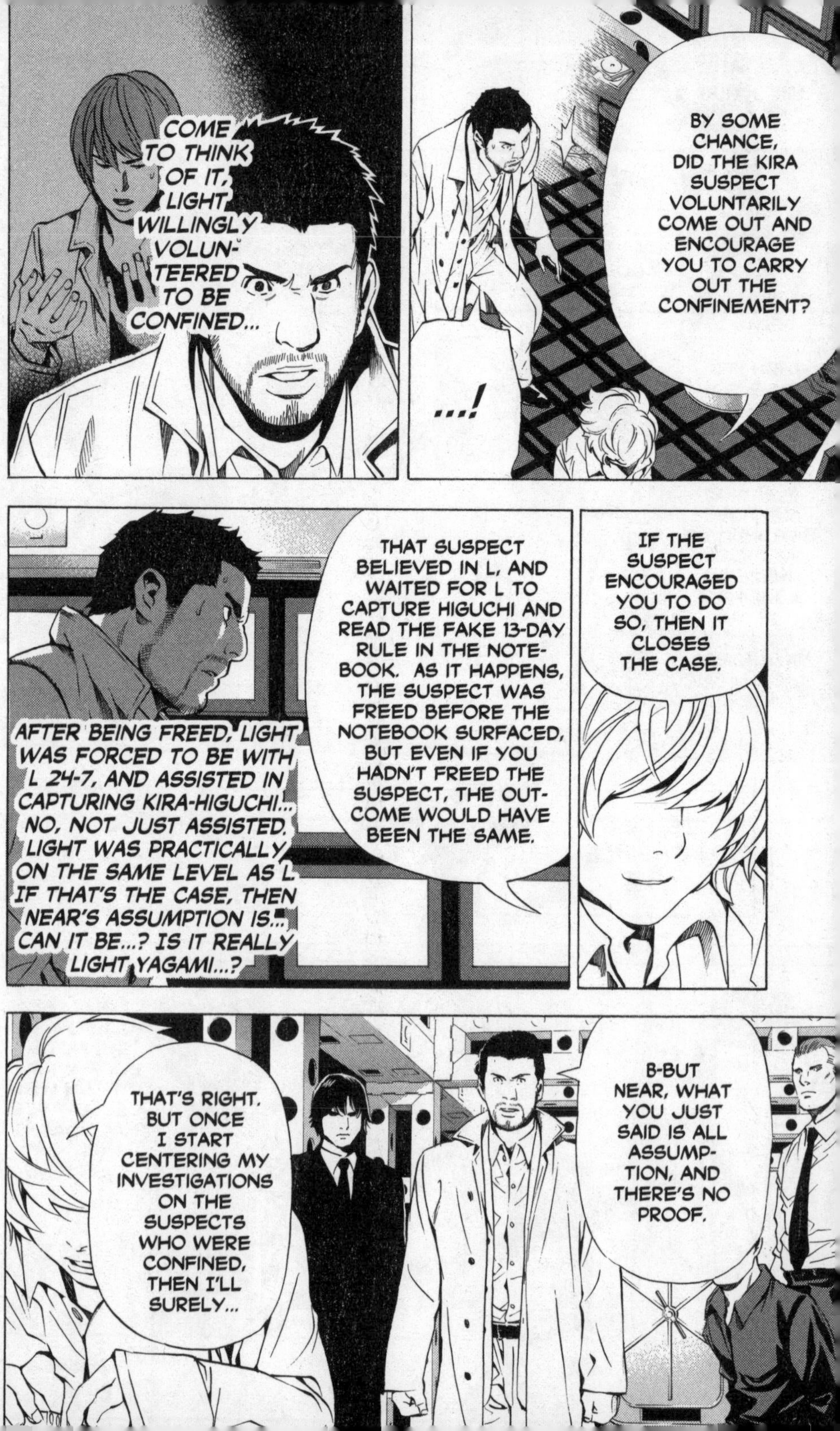
BY SOME CHANCE, DID THE KIRA SUSPECT VOLUNTARILY COME OUT AND ENCOURAGE YOU TO CARRY OUT THE CONFINEMENT?
...!
COME TO THINK OF IT, LIGHT WILLINGLY VOLUNTEERED TO BE CONFINED...
IF THE SUSPECT ENCOURAGED YOU TO DO SO, THEN IT CLOSES THE CASE.
THAT SUSPECT BELIEVED IN L, AND WAITED FOR L TO CAPTURE HIGUCHI AND READ THE FAKE 13-DAY RULE IN THE NOTEBOOK. AS IT HAPPENS, THE SUSPECT WAS FREED BEFORE THE NOTEBOOK SURFACED, BUT EVEN IF YOU HADN'T FREED THE SUSPECT, THE OUTCOME WOULD HAVE BEEN THE SAME.
AFTER BEING FREED, LIGHT WAS FORCED TO BE WITH L 24-7, AND ASSISTED IN CAPTURING KIRA-HIGUCHI... NO, NOT JUST ASSISTED. LIGHT WAS PRACTICALLY ON THE SAME LEVEL AS L. IF THAT'S THE CASE, THEN NEAR'S ASSUMPTION IS... CAN IT BE...? IS IT REALLY LIGHT YAGAMI...?
B-BUT NEAR, WHAT YOU JUST SAID IS ALL ASSUMPTION, AND THERE'S NO PROOF.
THAT'S RIGHT. BUT ONCE I START CENTERING MY INVESTIGATIONS ON THE SUSPECTS WHO WERE CONFINED, THEN I'LL SURELY...

READ THIS WAY

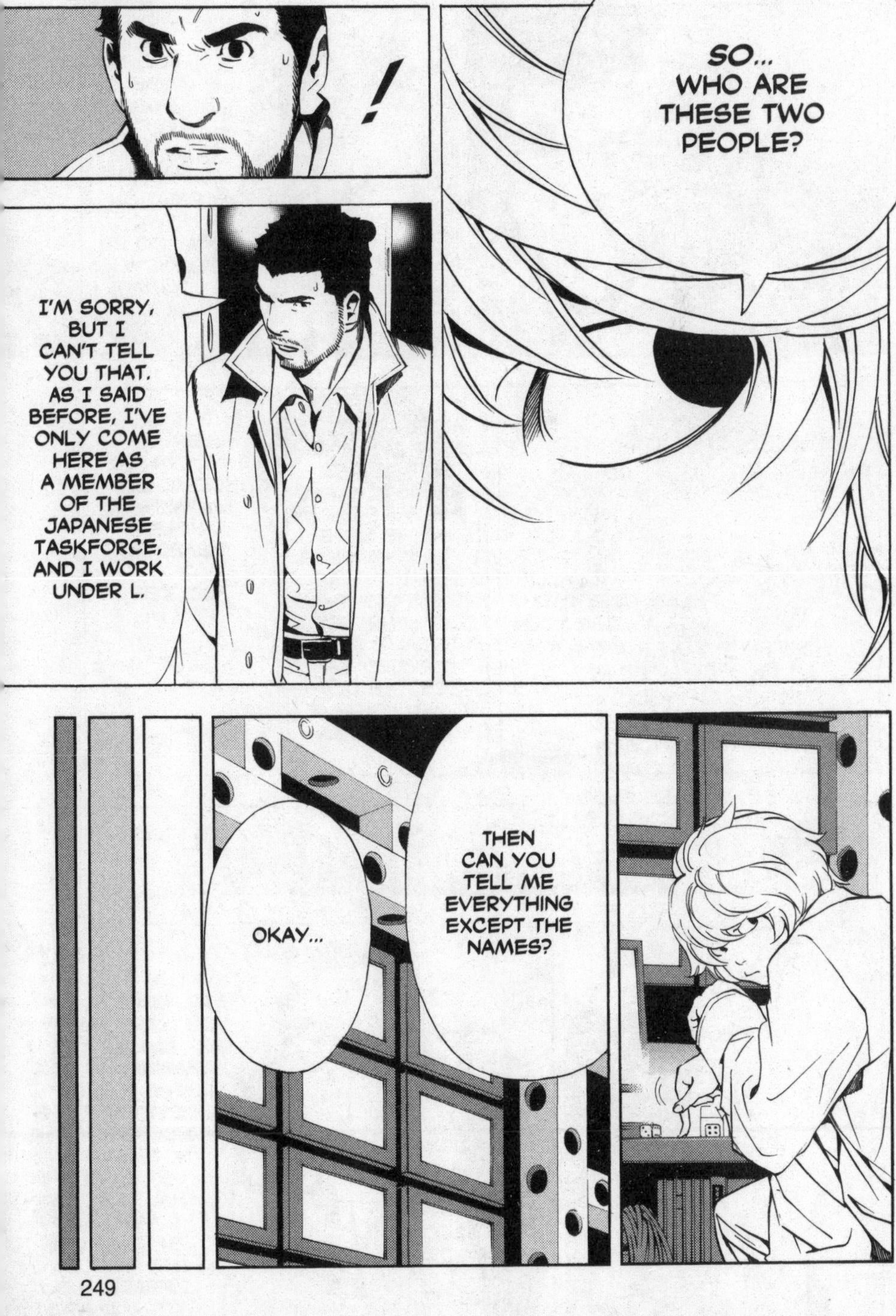

SO... WHO ARE THESE TWO PEOPLE?
!
I'M SORRY, BUT I CAN'T TELL YOU THAT. AS I SAID BEFORE, I'VE ONLY COME HERE AS A MEMBER OF THE JAPANESE TASKFORCE, AND I WORK UNDER L.
THEN CAN YOU TELL ME EVERYTHING EXCEPT THE NAMES?
OKAY...

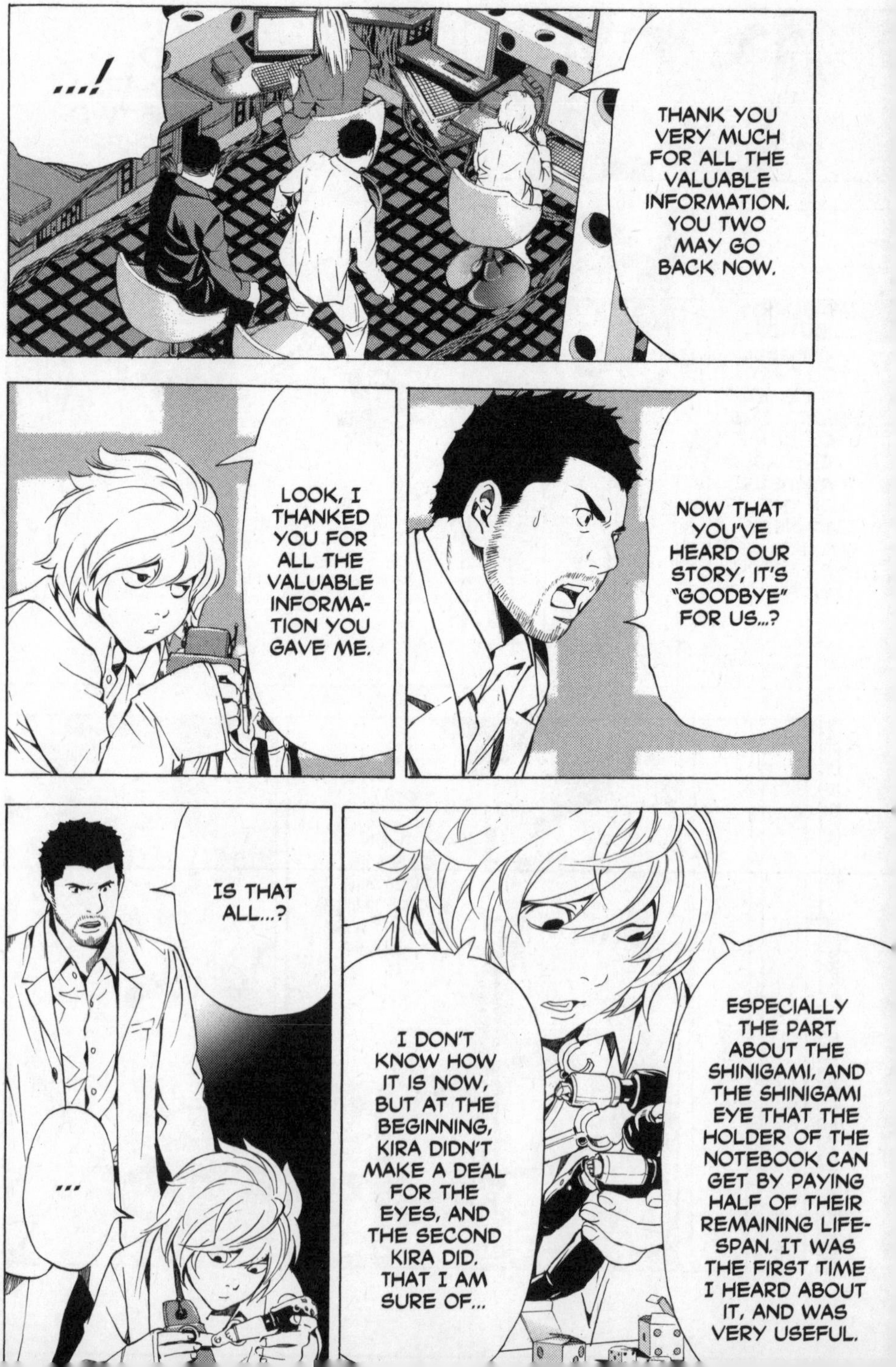
THANK YOU VERY MUCH FOR ALL THE VALUABLE INFORMATION. YOU TWO MAY GO BACK NOW.
...!
NOW THAT YOU'VE HEARD OUR STORY, IT'S "GOODBYE" FOR US...?
LOOK, I THANKED YOU FOR ALL THE VALUABLE INFORMA-TION YOU GAVE ME.
ESPECIALLY THE PART ABOUT THE SHINIGAMI, AND THE SHINIGAMI EYE THAT THE HOLDER OF THE NOTEBOOK CAN GET BY PAYING HALF OF THEIR REMAINING LIFE-SPAN. IT WAS THE FIRST TIME I HEARD ABOUT IT, AND WAS VERY USEFUL.
I DON'T KNOW HOW IT IS NOW, BUT AT THE BEGINNING, KIRA DIDN'T MAKE A DEAL FOR THE EYES, AND THE SECOND KIRA DID. THAT I AM SURE OF...
IS THAT ALL...?
...

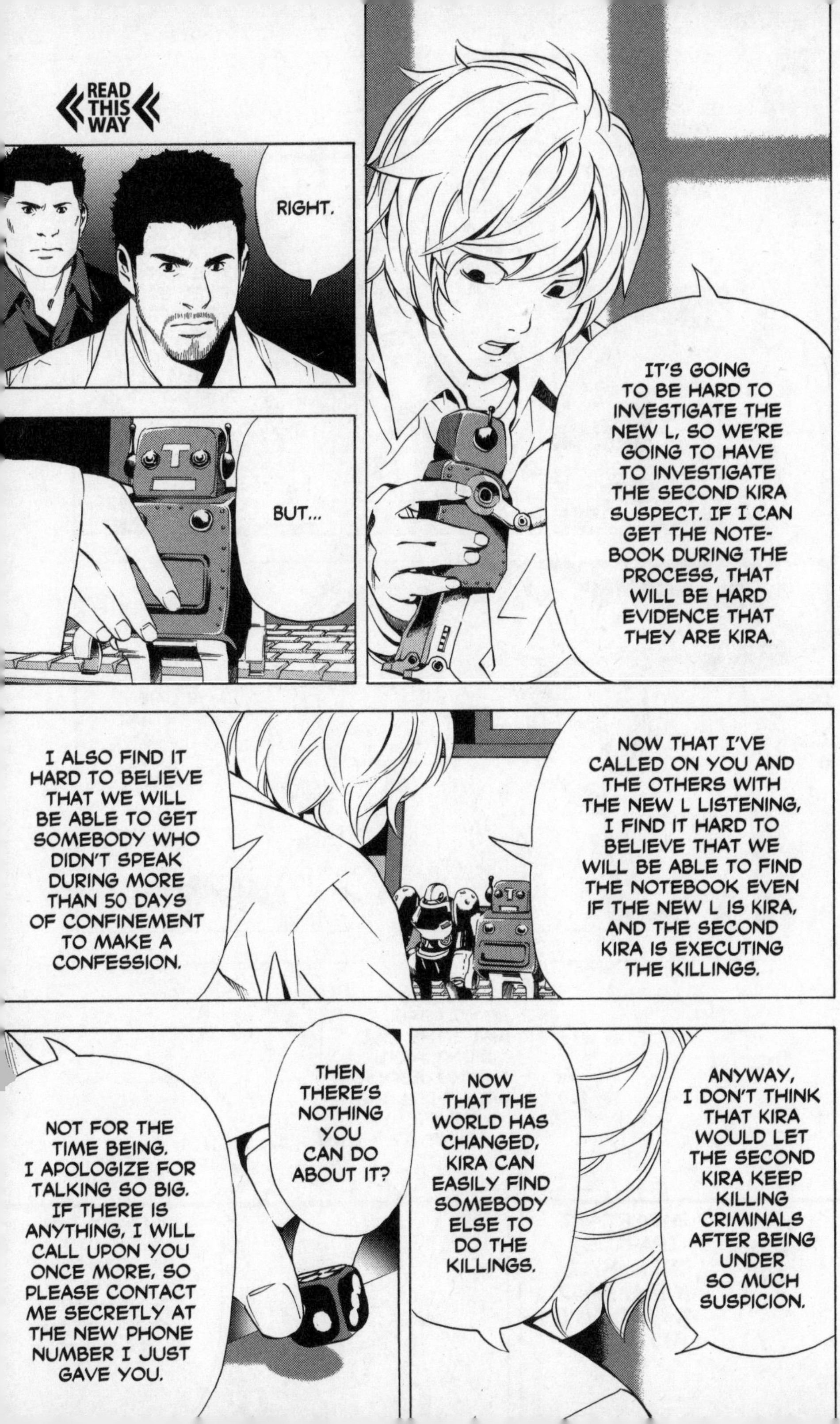
READ THIS WAY
IT'S GOING TO BE HARD TO INVESTIGATE THE NEW L, SO WE'RE GOING TO HAVE TO INVESTIGATE THE SECOND KIRA SUSPECT. IF I CAN GET THE NOTE-BOOK DURING THE PROCESS, THAT WILL BE HARD EVIDENCE THAT THEY ARE KIRA.
RIGHT.
BUT...
NOW THAT I'VE CALLED ON YOU AND THE OTHERS WITH THE NEW L LISTENING, I FIND IT HARD TO BELIEVE THAT WE WILL BE ABLE TO FIND THE NOTEBOOK EVEN IF THE NEW L IS KIRA, AND THE SECOND KIRA IS EXECUTING THE KILLINGS.
I ALSO FIND IT HARD TO BELIEVE THAT WE WILL BE ABLE TO GET SOMEBODY WHO DIDN'T SPEAK DURING MORE THAN 50 DAYS OF CONFINEMENT TO MAKE A CONFESSION.
ANYWAY, I DON'T THINK THAT KIRA WOULD LET THE SECOND KIRA KEEP KILLING CRIMINALS AFTER BEING UNDER SO MUCH SUSPICION.
NOW THAT THE WORLD HAS CHANGED, KIRA CAN EASILY FIND SOMEBODY ELSE TO DO THE KILLINGS.
THEN THERE'S NOTHING YOU CAN DO ABOUT IT?
NOT FOR THE TIME BEING. I APOLOGIZE FOR TALKING SO BIG. IF THERE IS ANYTHING, I WILL CALL UPON YOU ONCE MORE, SO PLEASE CONTACT ME SECRETLY AT THE NEW PHONE NUMBER I JUST GAVE YOU.

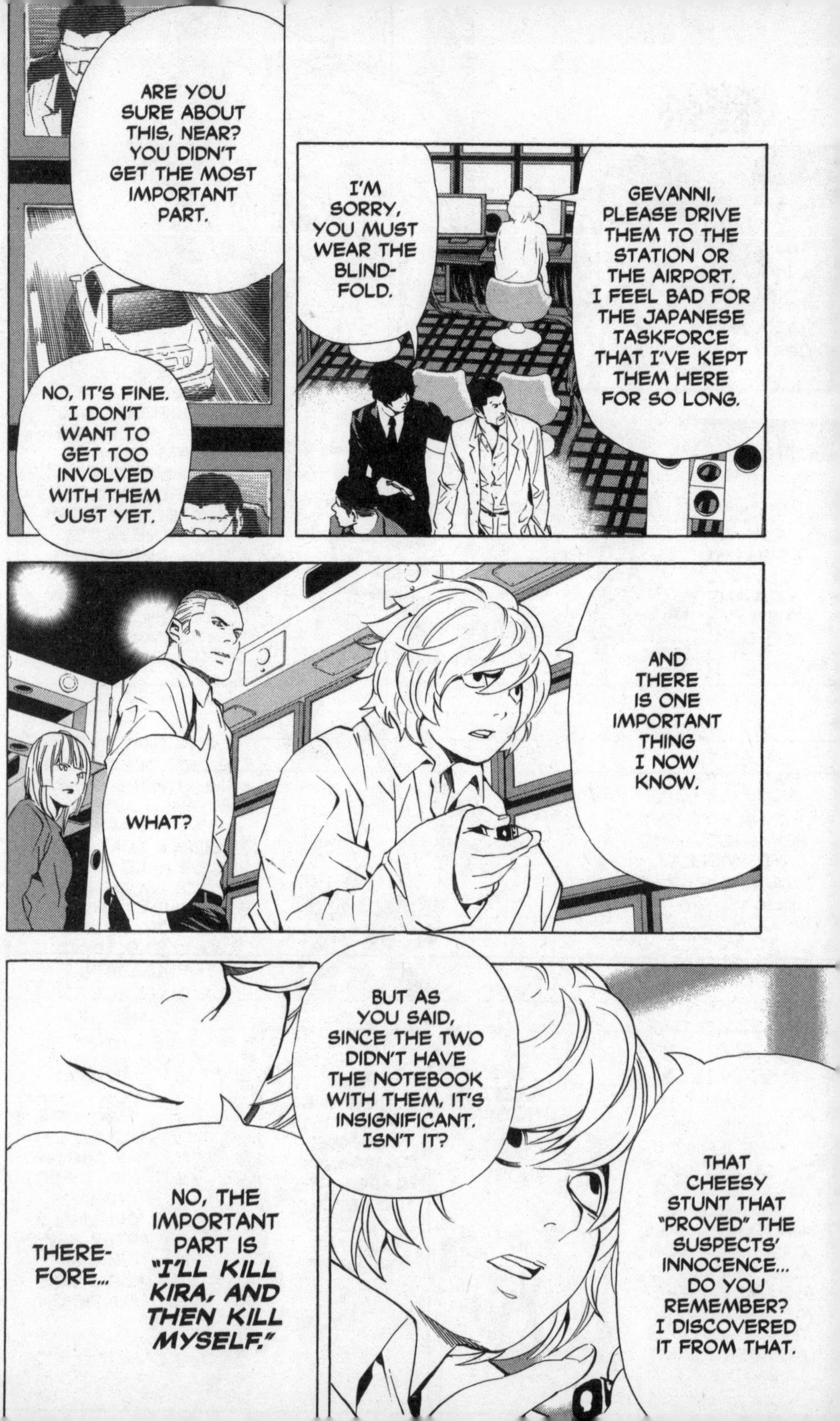
GEVANNI, PLEASE DRIVE THEM TO THE STATION OR THE AIRPORT. I FEEL BAD FOR THE JAPANESE TASKFORCE THAT I'VE KEPT THEM HERE FOR SO LONG.
I'M SORRY, YOU MUST WEAR THE BLIND-FOLD.
ARE YOU SURE ABOUT THIS, NEAR? YOU DIDN'T GET THE MOST IMPORTANT PART.
NO, IT'S FINE. I DON'T WANT TO GET TOO INVOLVED WITH THEM JUST YET.
AND THERE IS ONE IMPORTANT THING I NOW KNOW.
WHAT?
THAT CHEESY STUNT THAT "PROVED" THE SUSPECTS' INNOCENCE... DO YOU REMEMBER? I DISCOVERED IT FROM THAT.
BUT AS YOU SAID, SINCE THE TWO DIDN'T HAVE THE NOTEBOOK WITH THEM, IT'S INSIGNIFICANT. ISN'T IT?
NO, THE IMPORTANT PART IS ***"I'LL KILL KIRA, AND THEN KILL MYSELF."***
THERE-FORE...

READ THIS WAY

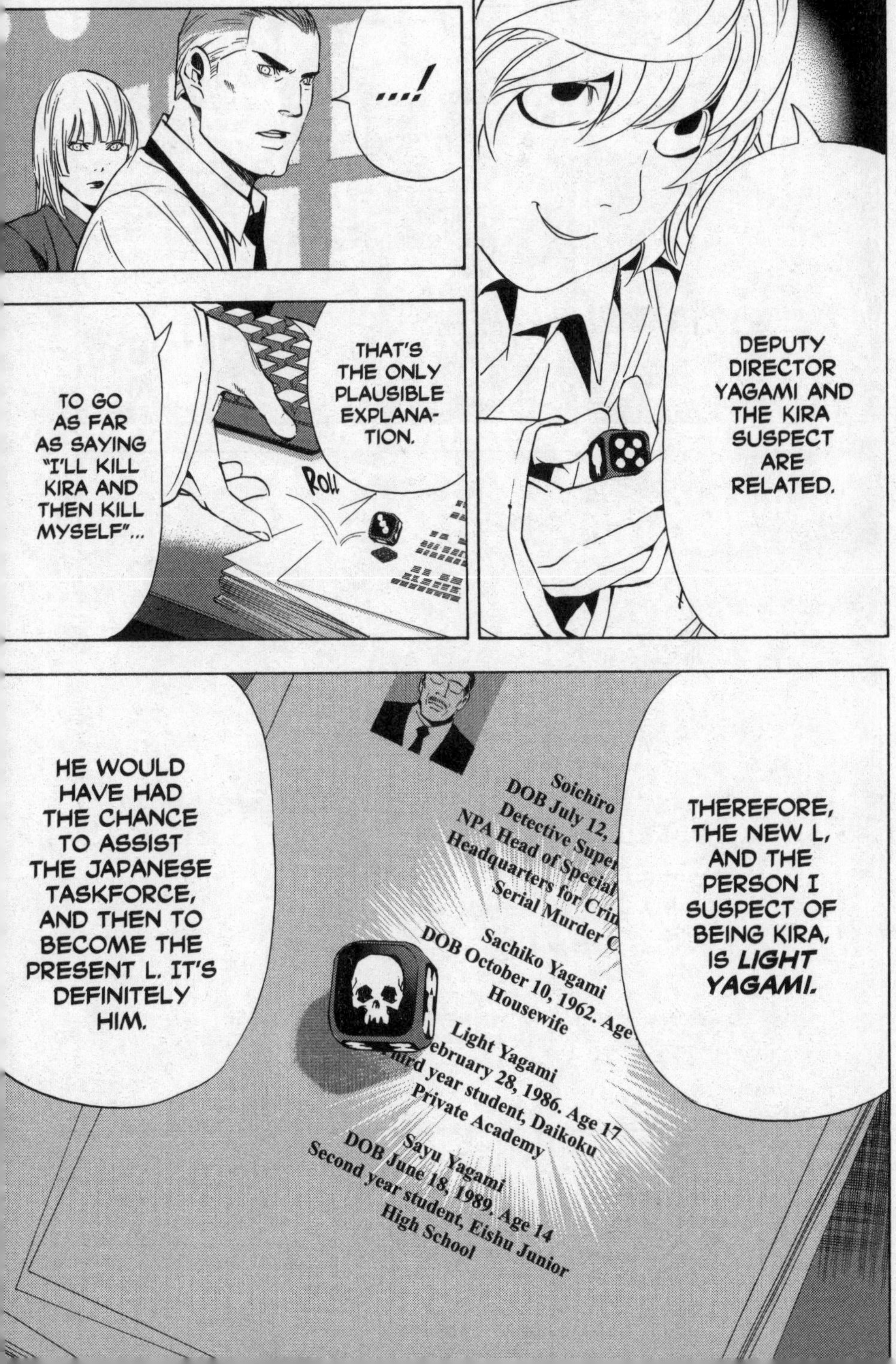
DEPUTY DIRECTOR YAGAMI AND THE KIRA SUSPECT ARE RELATED.
...!
THAT'S THE ONLY PLAUSIBLE EXPLANATION.
ROLL
TO GO AS FAR AS SAYING "I'LL KILL KIRA AND THEN KILL MYSELF"...
THEREFORE, THE NEW L, AND THE PERSON I SUSPECT OF BEING KIRA, IS *LIGHT YAGAMI.*
Sachiko Yagami
Housewife
Light Yagami
Private Academy
Sayu Yagami
DOB June 18, 1989. Age 14
Second year student, Eishu Junior
High School
HE WOULD HAVE HAD THE CHANCE TO ASSIST THE JAPANESE TASKFORCE, AND THEN TO BECOME THE PRESENT L. IT'S DEFINITELY HIM.

DEATH NOTE
HOW TO USE IT
LV

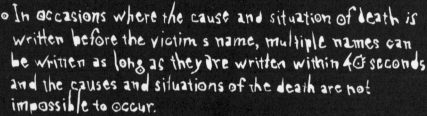

○ In occasions where the cause and situation of death is written before the victim's name, multiple names can be written as long as they are written within 40 seconds and the causes and situations of the death are not impossible to occur.

死因や死の状況を先に記しておき名前を後から記す場合、
その名前が複数でも40秒以内に記せば何人でも、
その死因や状況に不可能がなければその通りになる。

○ In the occasion where the cause of death is possible but the situation is not, only the cause of death will take effect for that victim. If both the cause and the situation are impossible, that victim will die of heart attack.

死因は可能だが状況は不可能である名前がある場合、
その名前に対しては死因のみが適用され、双方が不可能な名前があれば、
その人間は心臓麻痺となる。

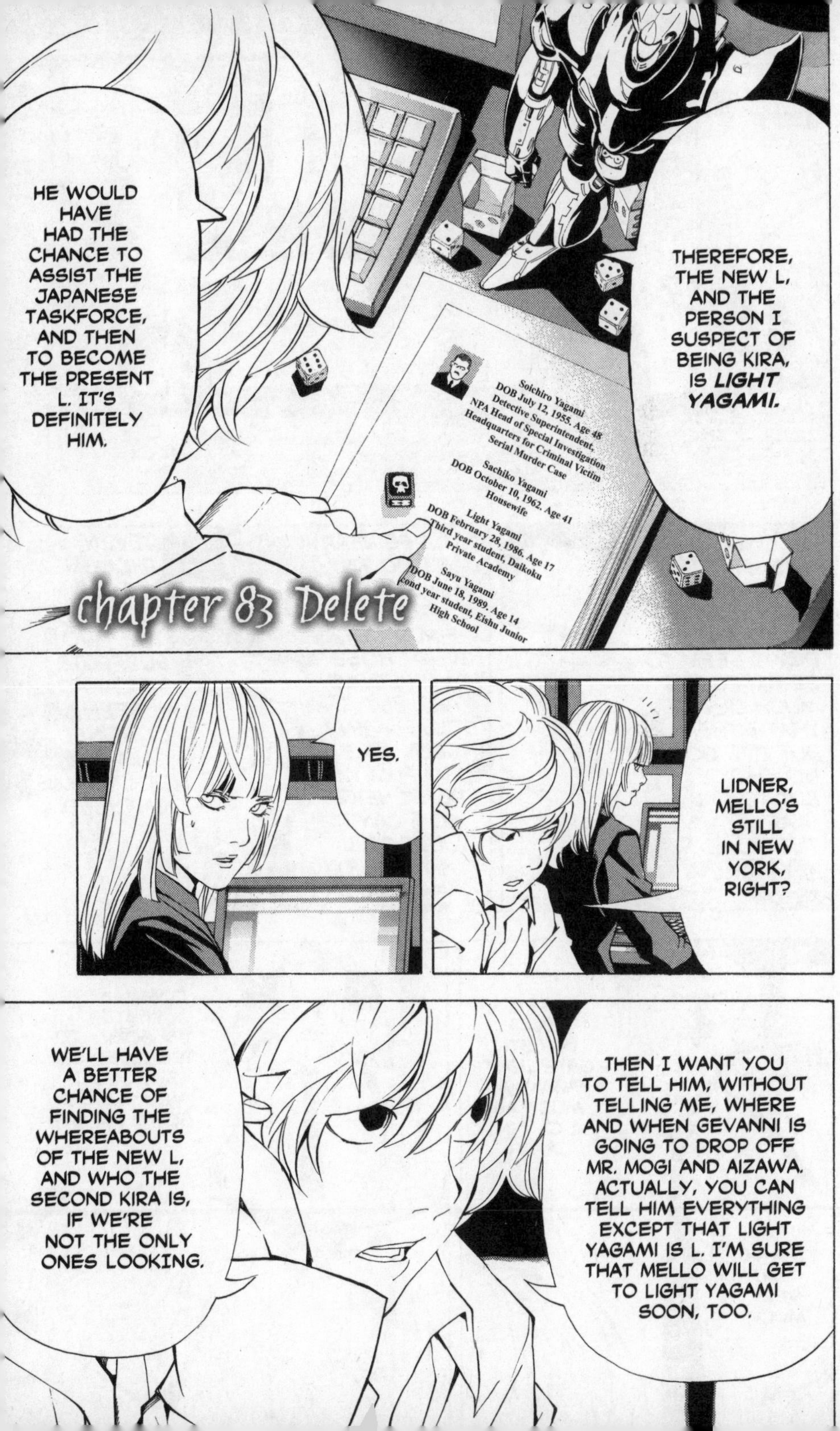
THEREFORE, THE NEW L, AND THE PERSON I SUSPECT OF BEING KIRA, IS *LIGHT YAGAMI.*
Soichiro Yagami
DOB July 12, 1955. Age 48
Detective Superintendent,
NPA Head of Special Investigation
Headquarters for Criminal Victim
Serial Murder Case
Sachiko Yagami
DOB October 10, 1962. Age 41
Housewife
Light Yagami
DOB February 28, 1986. Age 17
Third year student, Daikoku
Private Academy
Sayu Yagami
DOB June 18, 1989. Age 14
cond year student, Eishu Junior
High School
HE WOULD HAVE HAD THE CHANCE TO ASSIST THE JAPANESE TASKFORCE, AND THEN TO BECOME THE PRESENT L. IT'S DEFINITELY HIM.
chapter 83 Delete
LIDNER, MELLO'S STILL IN NEW YORK, RIGHT?
YES.
THEN I WANT YOU TO TELL HIM, WITHOUT TELLING ME, WHERE AND WHEN GEVANNI IS GOING TO DROP OFF MR. MOGI AND AIZAWA. ACTUALLY, YOU CAN TELL HIM EVERYTHING EXCEPT THAT LIGHT YAGAMI IS L. I'M SURE THAT MELLO WILL GET TO LIGHT YAGAMI SOON, TOO.
WE'LL HAVE A BETTER CHANCE OF FINDING THE WHEREABOUTS OF THE NEW L, AND WHO THE SECOND KIRA IS, IF WE'RE NOT THE ONLY ONES LOOKING.

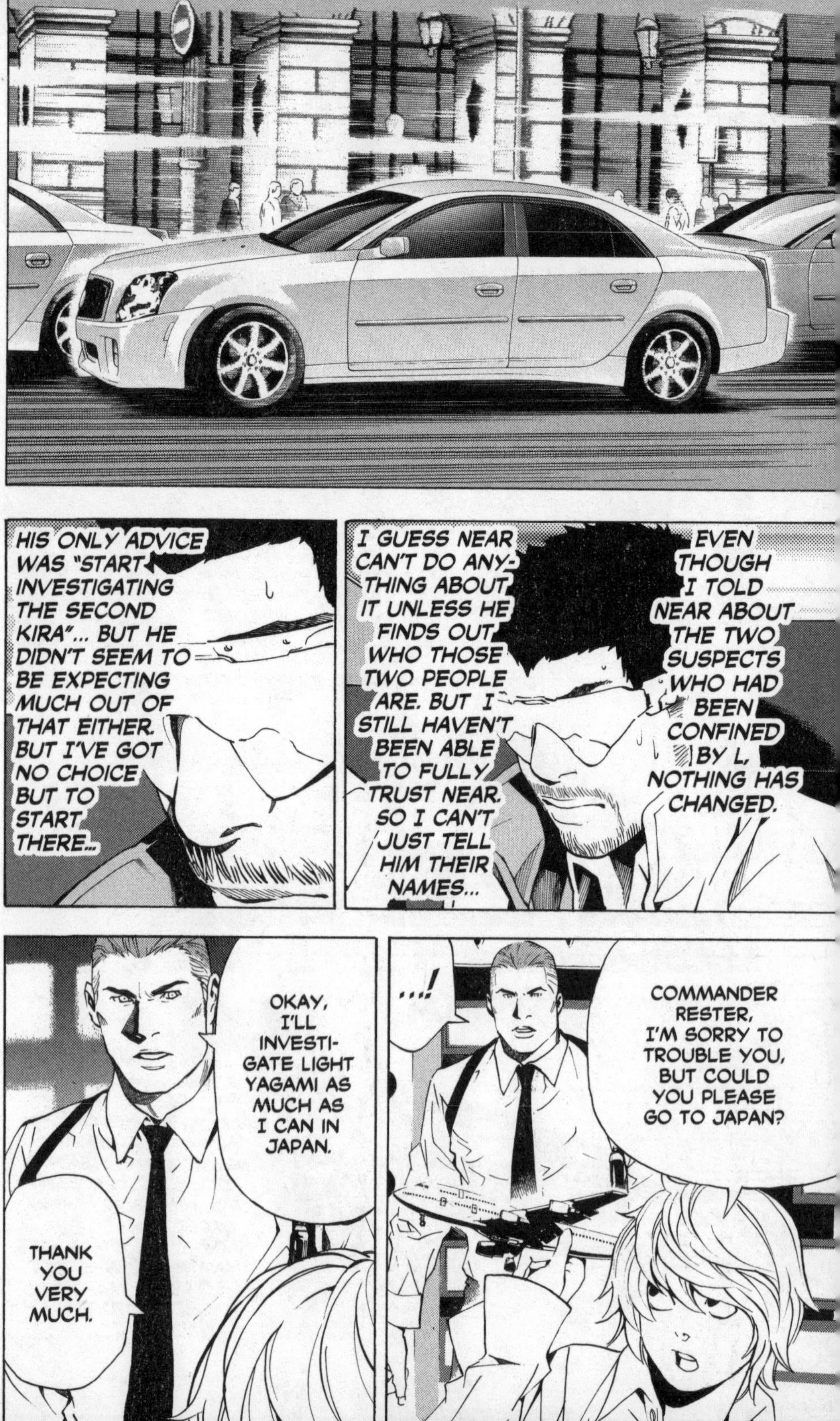
EVEN THOUGH I TOLD NEAR ABOUT THE TWO SUSPECTS WHO HAD BEEN CONFINED BY L, NOTHING HAS CHANGED.
I GUESS NEAR CAN'T DO ANY-THING ABOUT IT UNLESS HE FINDS OUT WHO THOSE TWO PEOPLE ARE. BUT I STILL HAVEN'T BEEN ABLE TO FULLY TRUST NEAR. SO I CAN'T JUST TELL HIM THEIR NAMES...
HIS ONLY ADVICE WAS "START INVESTIGATING THE SECOND KIRA"... BUT HE DIDN'T SEEM TO BE EXPECTING MUCH OUT OF THAT EITHER. BUT I'VE GOT NO CHOICE BUT TO START THERE...
COMMANDER RESTER, I'M SORRY TO TROUBLE YOU, BUT COULD YOU PLEASE GO TO JAPAN?
...!
OKAY, I'LL INVESTI-GATE LIGHT YAGAMI AS MUCH AS I CAN IN JAPAN.
THANK YOU VERY MUCH.

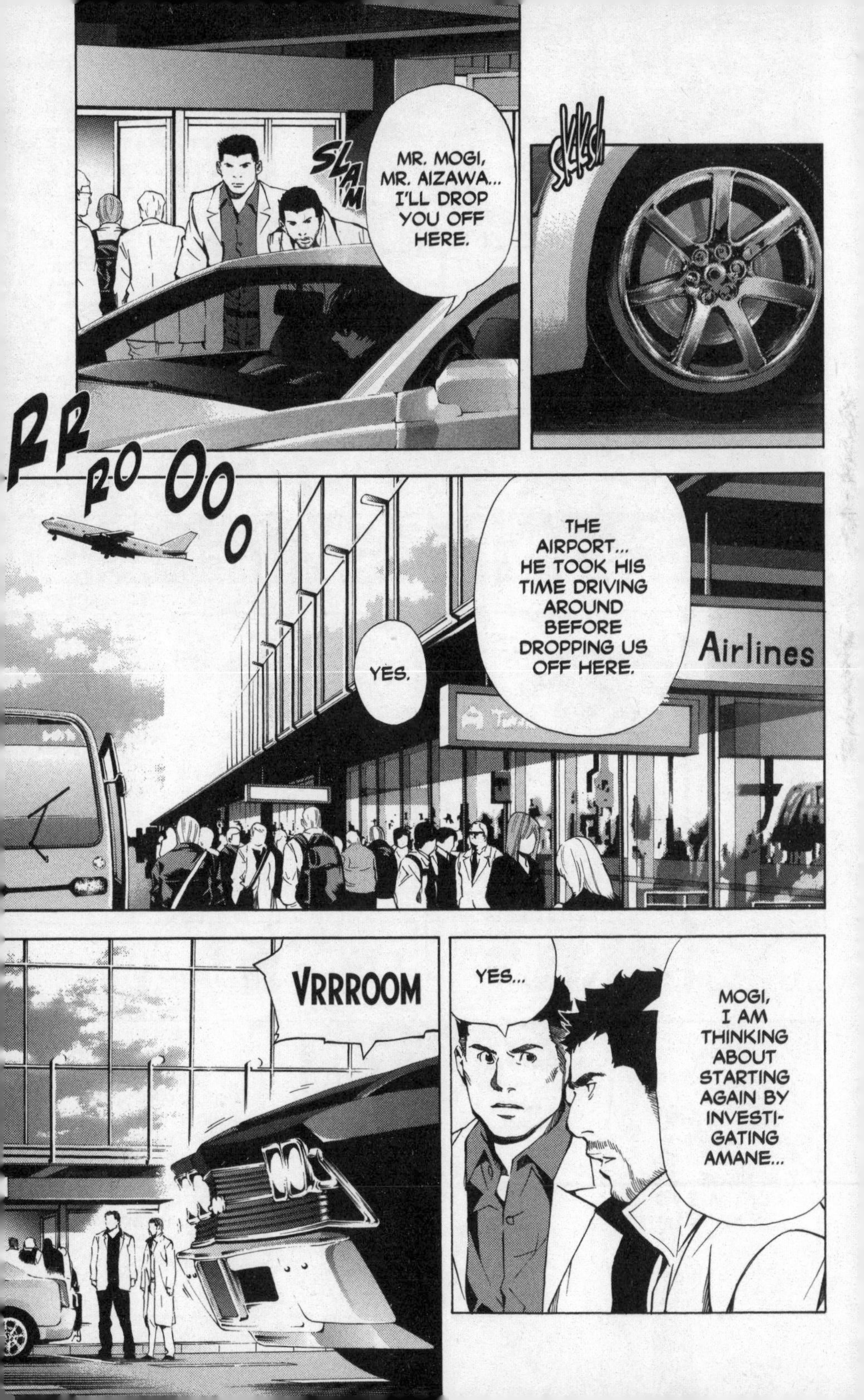
SKKSH
SLAM
MR. MOGI, MR. AIZAWA... I'LL DROP YOU OFF HERE.
RRROOOO
THE AIRPORT... HE TOOK HIS TIME DRIVING AROUND BEFORE DROPPING US OFF HERE.
YES.
Airlines
MOGI, I AM THINKING ABOUT STARTING AGAIN BY INVESTI-GATING AMANE...
YES...
VRRROOM

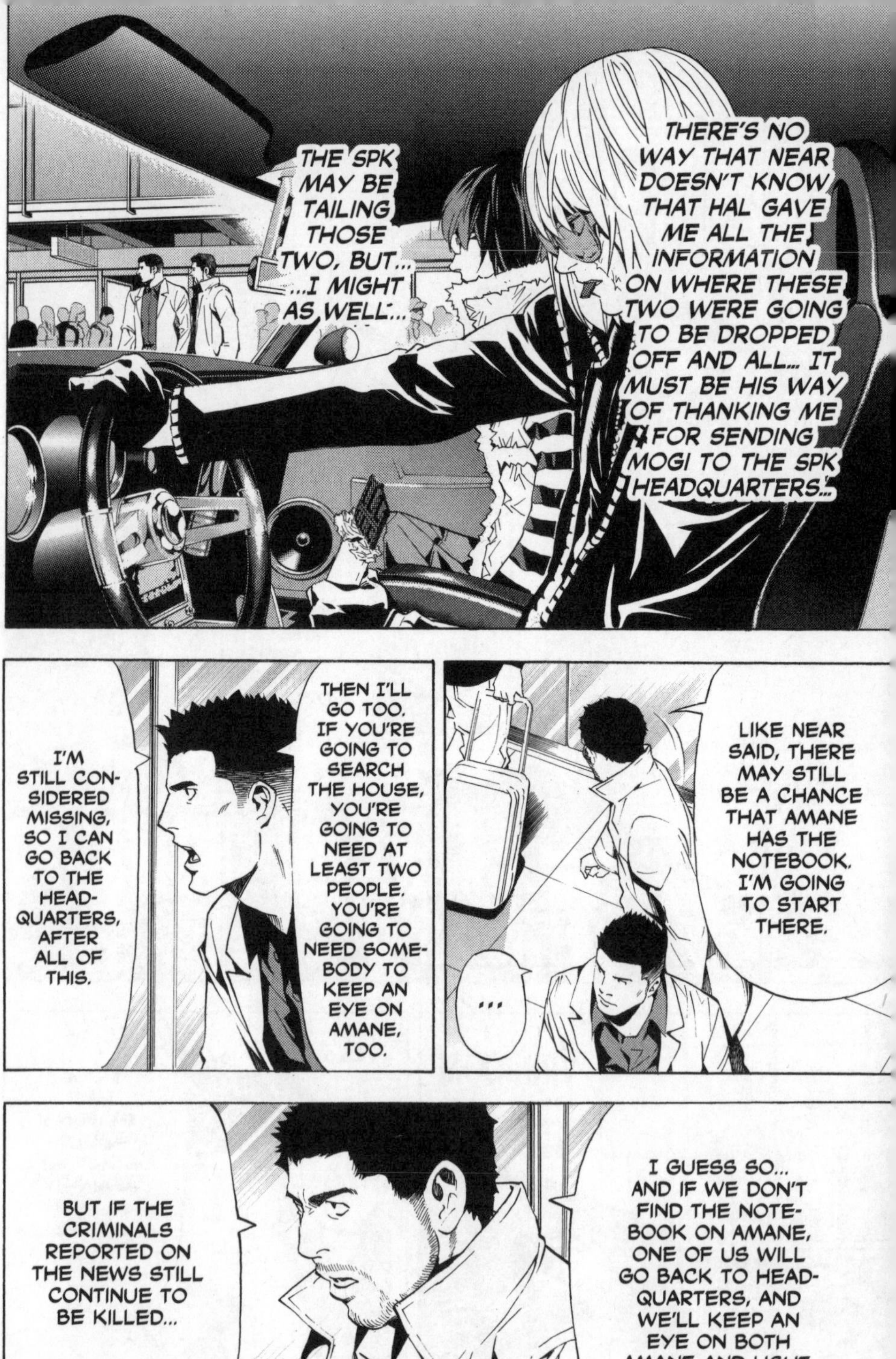
THERE'S NO WAY THAT NEAR DOESN'T KNOW THAT HAL GAVE ME ALL THE INFORMATION ON WHERE THESE TWO WERE GOING TO BE DROPPED OFF AND ALL... IT MUST BE HIS WAY OF THANKING ME FOR SENDING MOGI TO THE SPK HEADQUARTERS...
THE SPK MAY BE TAILING THOSE TWO, BUT... ...I MIGHT AS WELL...
LIKE NEAR SAID, THERE MAY STILL BE A CHANCE THAT AMANE HAS THE NOTEBOOK. I'M GOING TO START THERE.
...
THEN I'LL GO TOO. IF YOU'RE GOING TO SEARCH THE HOUSE, YOU'RE GOING TO NEED AT LEAST TWO PEOPLE. YOU'RE GOING TO NEED SOMEBODY TO KEEP AN EYE ON AMANE, TOO.
I'M STILL CONSIDERED MISSING, SO I CAN GO BACK TO THE HEADQUARTERS, AFTER ALL OF THIS.
I GUESS SO... AND IF WE DON'T FIND THE NOTEBOOK ON AMANE, ONE OF US WILL GO BACK TO HEADQUARTERS, AND WE'LL KEEP AN EYE ON BOTH AMANE AND LIGHT.
BUT IF THE CRIMINALS REPORTED ON THE NEWS STILL CONTINUE TO BE KILLED...

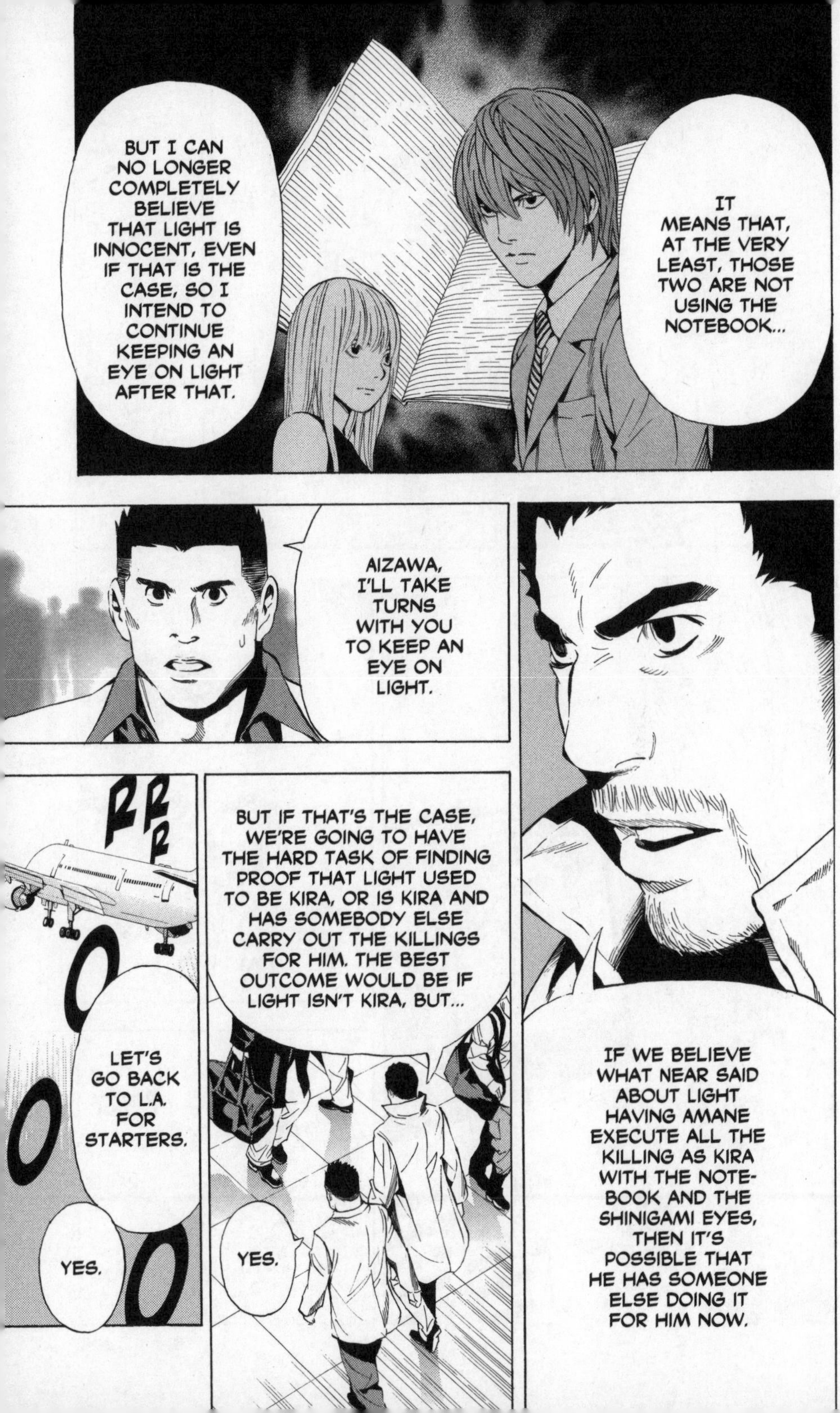
IT MEANS THAT, AT THE VERY LEAST, THOSE TWO ARE NOT USING THE NOTEBOOK...
BUT I CAN NO LONGER COMPLETELY BELIEVE THAT LIGHT IS INNOCENT, EVEN IF THAT IS THE CASE, SO I INTEND TO CONTINUE KEEPING AN EYE ON LIGHT AFTER THAT.
IF WE BELIEVE WHAT NEAR SAID ABOUT LIGHT HAVING AMANE EXECUTE ALL THE KILLING AS KIRA WITH THE NOTE-BOOK AND THE SHINIGAMI EYES, THEN IT'S POSSIBLE THAT HE HAS SOMEONE ELSE DOING IT FOR HIM NOW.
AIZAWA, I'LL TAKE TURNS WITH YOU TO KEEP AN EYE ON LIGHT.
BUT IF THAT'S THE CASE, WE'RE GOING TO HAVE THE HARD TASK OF FINDING PROOF THAT LIGHT USED TO BE KIRA, OR IS KIRA AND HAS SOMEBODY ELSE CARRY OUT THE KILLINGS FOR HIM. THE BEST OUTCOME WOULD BE IF LIGHT ISN'T KIRA, BUT...
YES.
LET'S GO BACK TO L.A. FOR STARTERS.
YES.

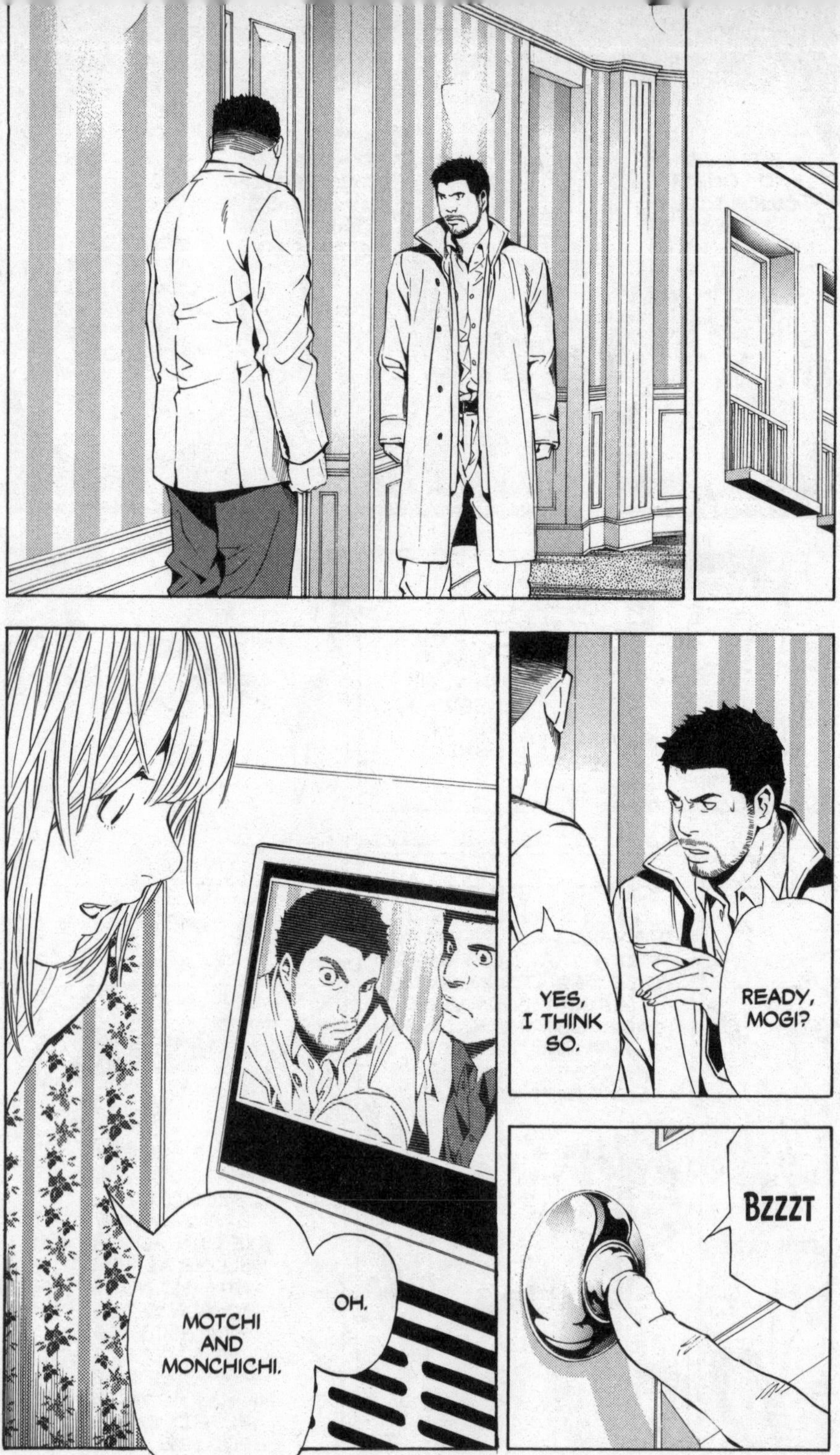
READY, MOGI?
YES, I THINK SO.
BZZZT
OH.
MOTCHI AND MONCHICHI.

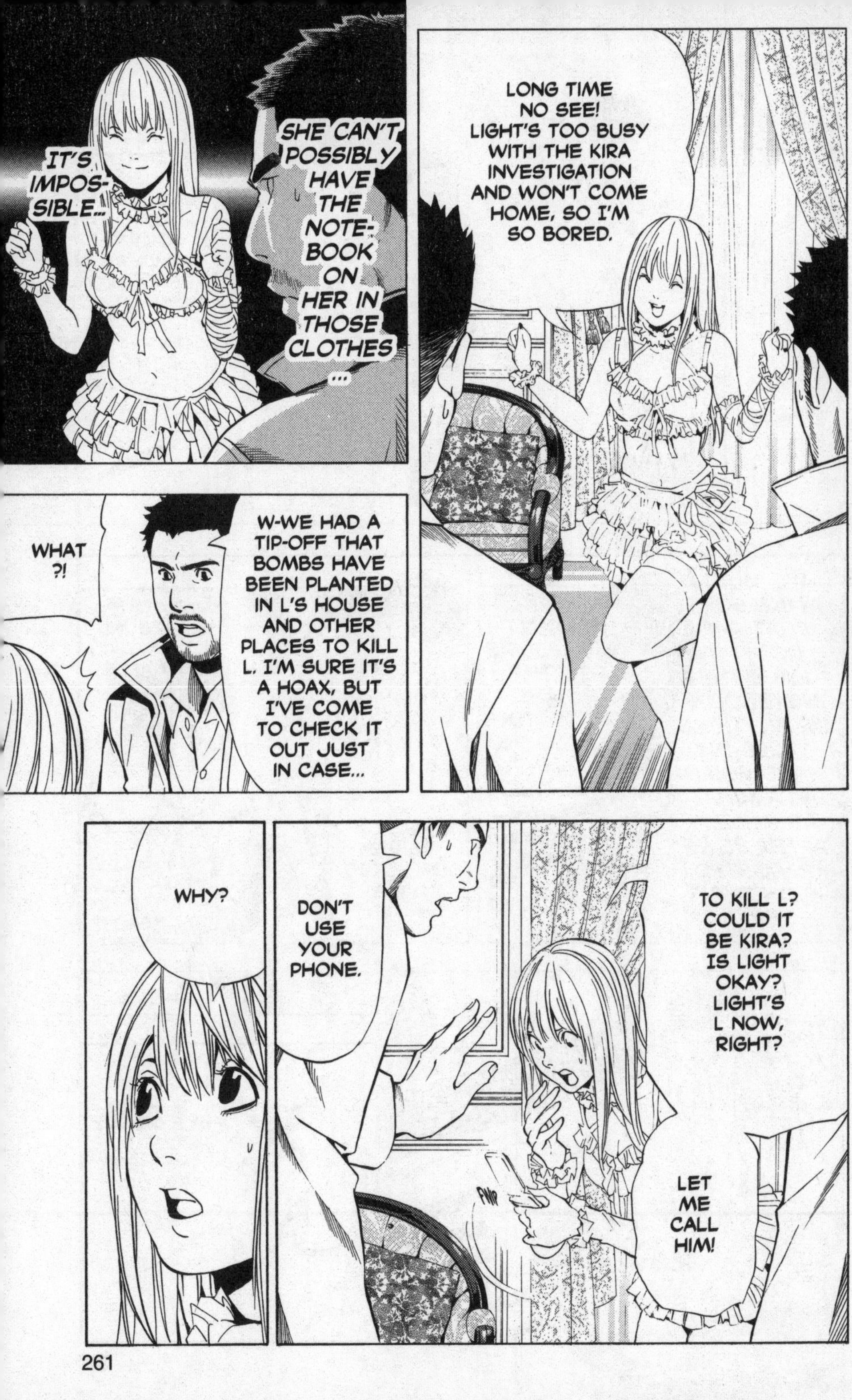

LONG TIME NO SEE! LIGHT'S TOO BUSY WITH THE KIRA INVESTIGATION AND WON'T COME HOME, SO I'M SO BORED.
SHE CAN'T POSSIBLY HAVE THE NOTE-BOOK ON HER IN THOSE CLOTHES...
IT'S IMPOS-SIBLE...
W-WE HAD A TIP-OFF THAT BOMBS HAVE BEEN PLANTED IN L'S HOUSE AND OTHER PLACES TO KILL L. I'M SURE IT'S A HOAX, BUT I'VE COME TO CHECK IT OUT JUST IN CASE...
WHAT ?!
TO KILL L? COULD IT BE KIRA? IS LIGHT OKAY? LIGHT'S L NOW, RIGHT?
FWIP
LET ME CALL HIM!
DON'T USE YOUR PHONE.
WHY?

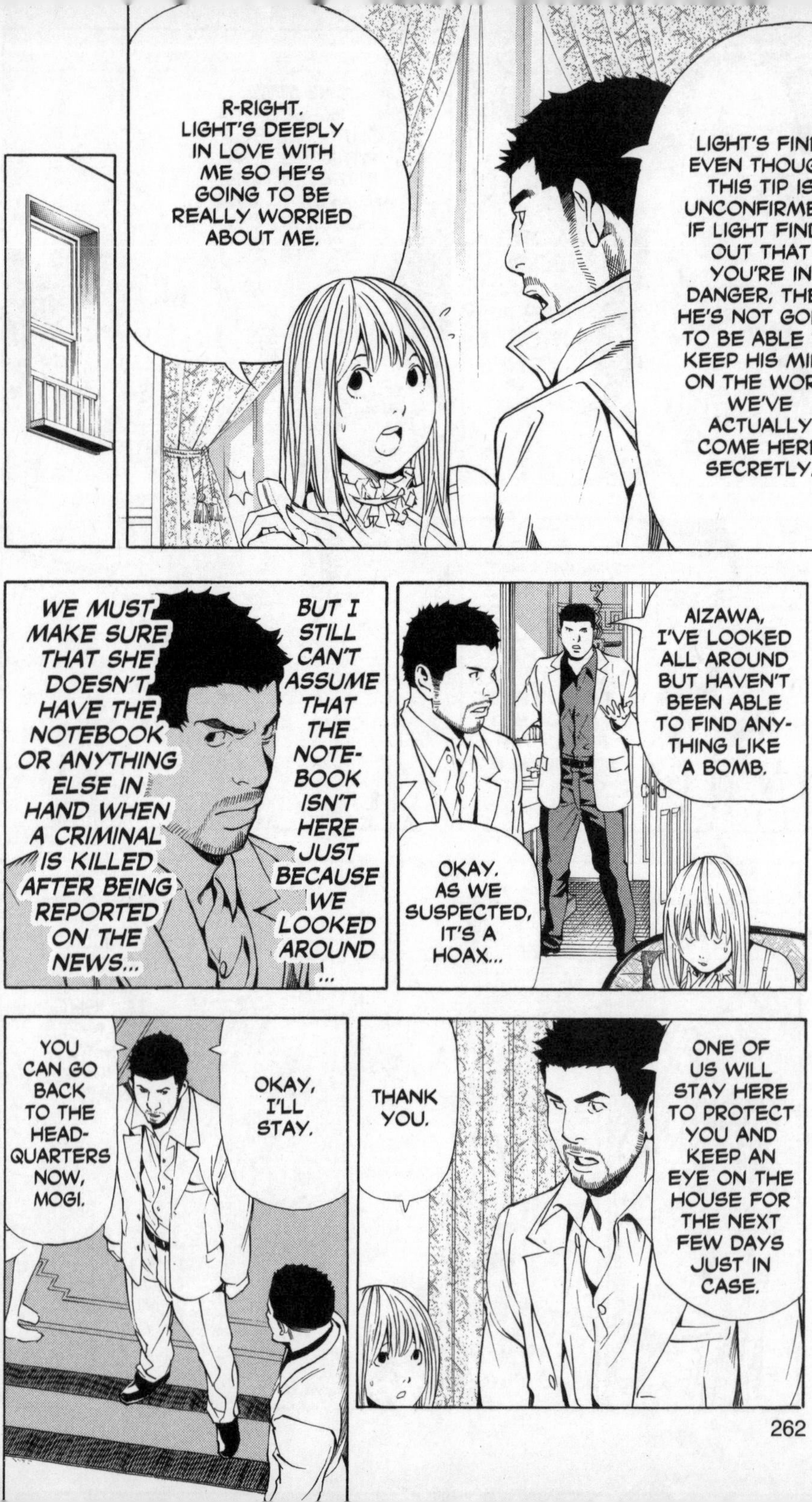

LIGHT'S FINE. EVEN THOUGH THIS TIP IS UNCONFIRMED, IF LIGHT FINDS OUT THAT YOU'RE IN DANGER, THEN HE'S NOT GOING TO BE ABLE TO KEEP HIS MIND ON THE WORK. WE'VE ACTUALLY COME HERE SECRETLY.
R-RIGHT. LIGHT'S DEEPLY IN LOVE WITH ME SO HE'S GOING TO BE REALLY WORRIED ABOUT ME.
AIZAWA, I'VE LOOKED ALL AROUND BUT HAVEN'T BEEN ABLE TO FIND ANYTHING LIKE A BOMB.
OKAY. AS WE SUSPECTED, IT'S A HOAX...
BUT I STILL CAN'T ASSUME THAT THE NOTEBOOK ISN'T HERE JUST BECAUSE WE LOOKED AROUND...
WE MUST MAKE SURE THAT SHE DOESN'T HAVE THE NOTEBOOK OR ANYTHING ELSE IN HAND WHEN A CRIMINAL IS KILLED AFTER BEING REPORTED ON THE NEWS...
ONE OF US WILL STAY HERE TO PROTECT YOU AND KEEP AN EYE ON THE HOUSE FOR THE NEXT FEW DAYS JUST IN CASE.
THANK YOU.
OKAY, I'LL STAY.
YOU CAN GO BACK TO THE HEADQUARTERS NOW, MOGI.

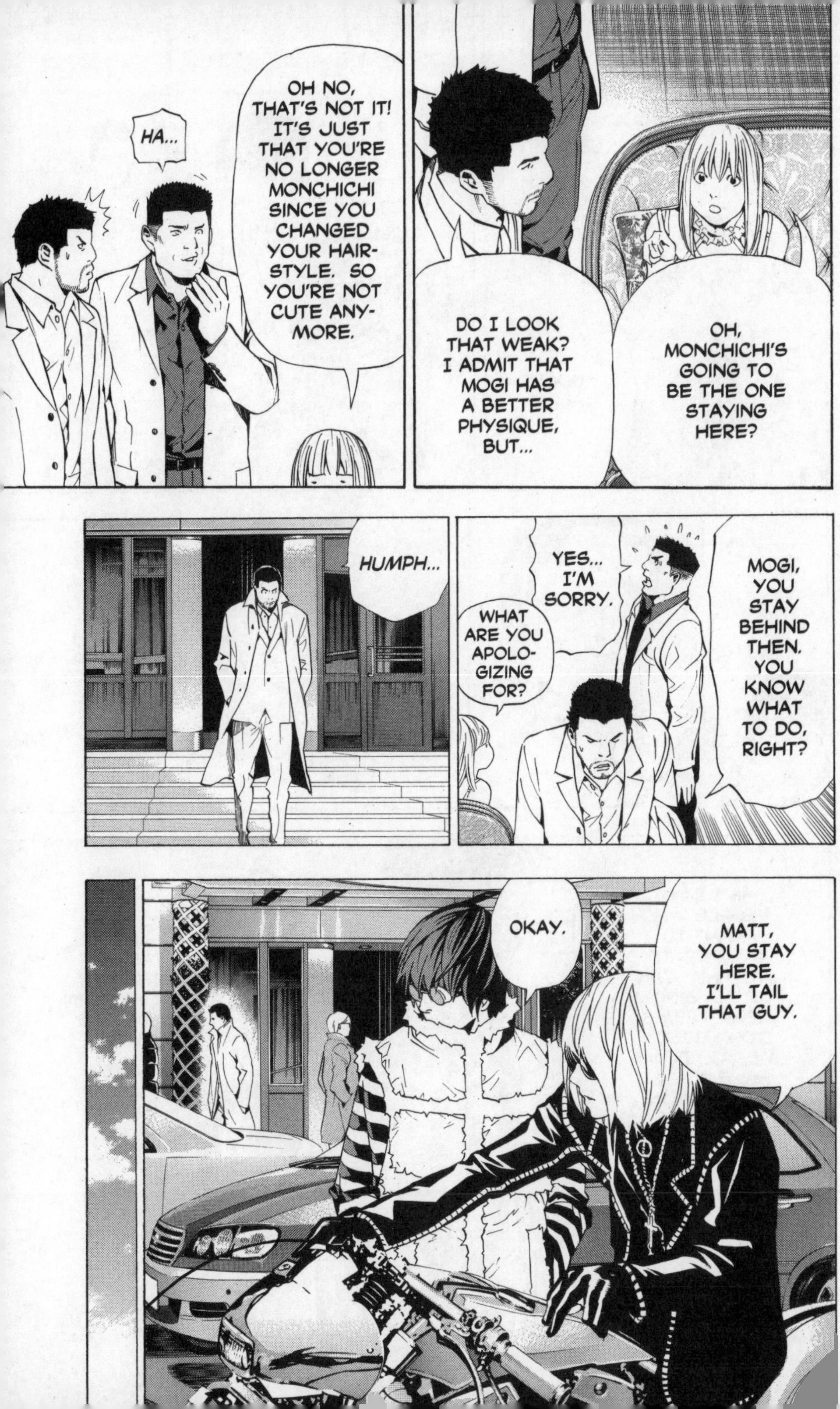
OH, MONCHICHI'S GOING TO BE THE ONE STAYING HERE?
DO I LOOK THAT WEAK? I ADMIT THAT MOGI HAS A BETTER PHYSIQUE, BUT...
OH NO, THAT'S NOT IT! IT'S JUST THAT YOU'RE NO LONGER MONCHICHI SINCE YOU CHANGED YOUR HAIR-STYLE. SO YOU'RE NOT CUTE ANY-MORE.
HA...
MOGI, YOU STAY BEHIND THEN. YOU KNOW WHAT TO DO, RIGHT?
YES... I'M SORRY.
WHAT ARE YOU APOLOGIZING FOR?
HUMPH...
MATT, YOU STAY HERE. I'LL TAIL THAT GUY.
OKAY.

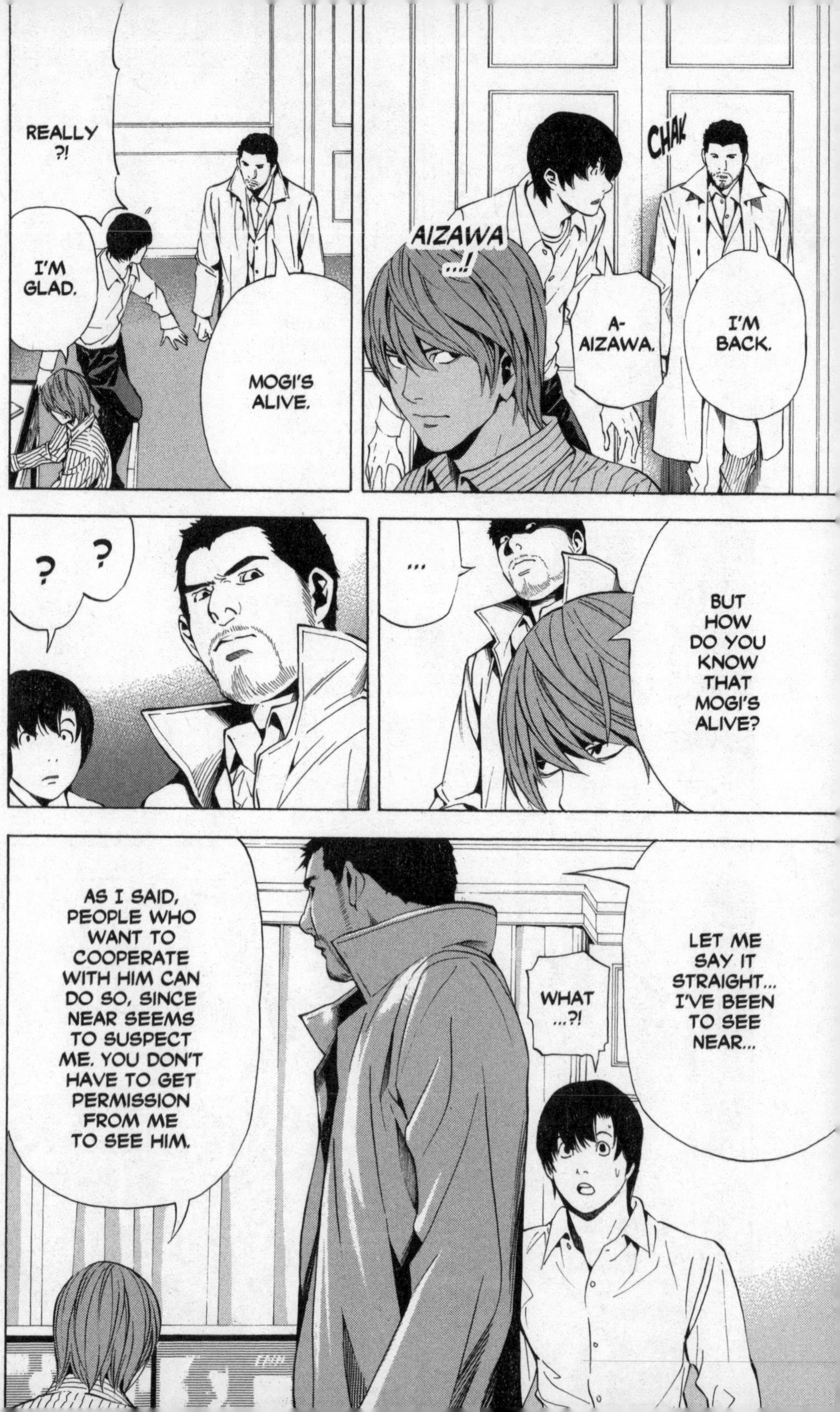
CHAK
I'M BACK.
A- AIZAWA.
AIZAWA ...!
MOGI'S ALIVE.
REALLY ?!
I'M GLAD.
BUT HOW DO YOU KNOW THAT MOGI'S ALIVE?
...
? ?
LET ME SAY IT STRAIGHT... I'VE BEEN TO SEE NEAR...
WHAT ...?!
AS I SAID, PEOPLE WHO WANT TO COOPERATE WITH HIM CAN DO SO, SINCE NEAR SEEMS TO SUSPECT ME. YOU DON'T HAVE TO GET PERMISSION FROM ME TO SEE HIM.

READ THIS WAY

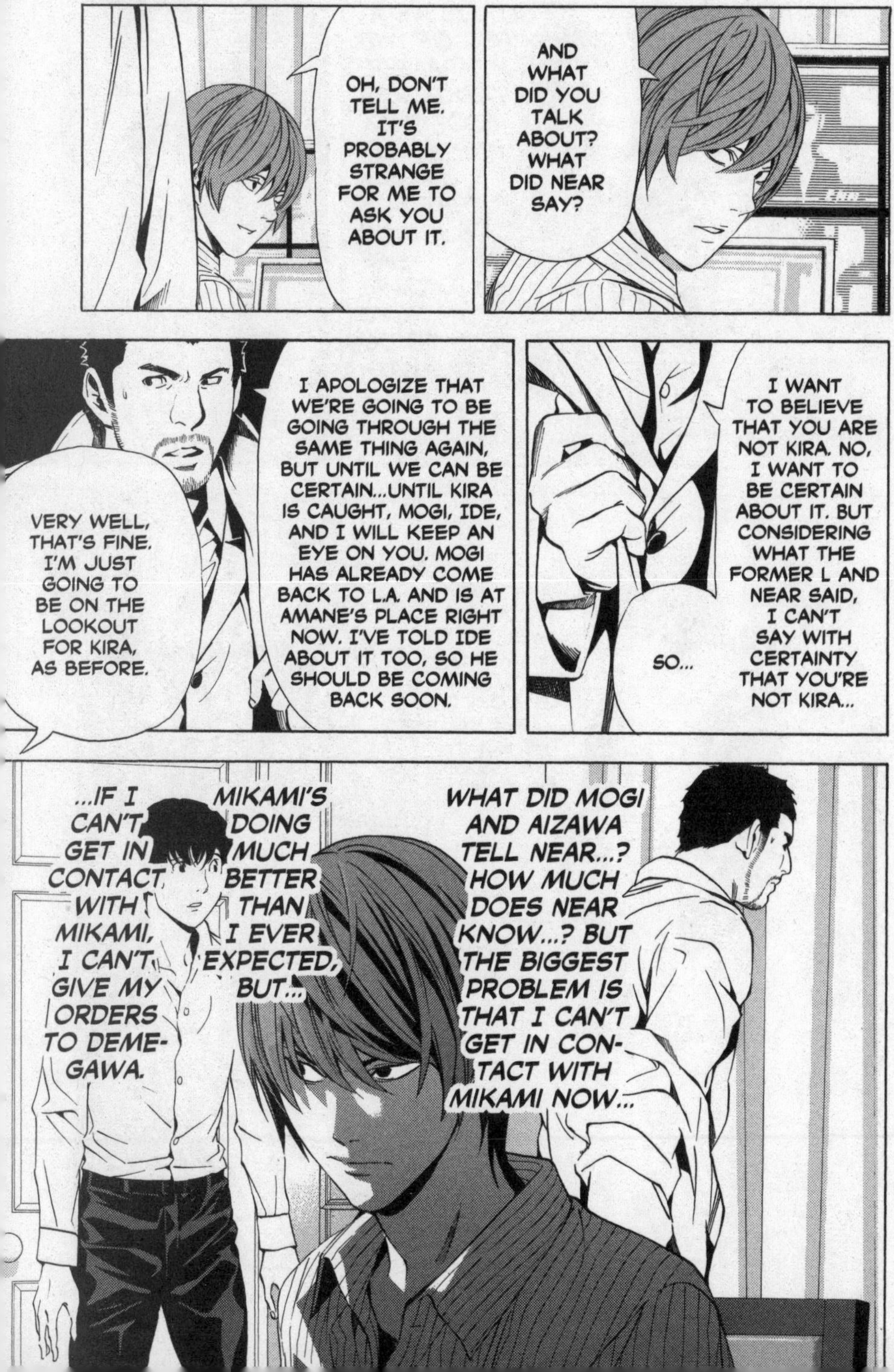

AND WHAT DID YOU TALK ABOUT? WHAT DID NEAR SAY?
OH, DON'T TELL ME. IT'S PROBABLY STRANGE FOR ME TO ASK YOU ABOUT IT.
I WANT TO BELIEVE THAT YOU ARE NOT KIRA. NO, I WANT TO BE CERTAIN ABOUT IT. BUT CONSIDERING WHAT THE FORMER L AND NEAR SAID, I CAN'T SAY WITH CERTAINTY THAT YOU'RE NOT KIRA...
SO...
I APOLOGIZE THAT WE'RE GOING TO BE GOING THROUGH THE SAME THING AGAIN, BUT UNTIL WE CAN BE CERTAIN...UNTIL KIRA IS CAUGHT, MOGI, IDE, AND I WILL KEEP AN EYE ON YOU. MOGI HAS ALREADY COME BACK TO L.A. AND IS AT AMANE'S PLACE RIGHT NOW. I'VE TOLD IDE ABOUT IT TOO, SO HE SHOULD BE COMING BACK SOON.
VERY WELL, THAT'S FINE. I'M JUST GOING TO BE ON THE LOOKOUT FOR KIRA, AS BEFORE.
WHAT DID MOGI AND AIZAWA TELL NEAR...? HOW MUCH DOES NEAR KNOW...? BUT THE BIGGEST PROBLEM IS THAT I CAN'T GET IN CON-TACT WITH MIKAMI NOW...
MIKAMI'S DOING MUCH BETTER THAN I EVER EXPECTED, BUT...
...IF I CAN'T GET IN CONTACT WITH MIKAMI, I CAN'T GIVE MY ORDERS TO DEME-GAWA.

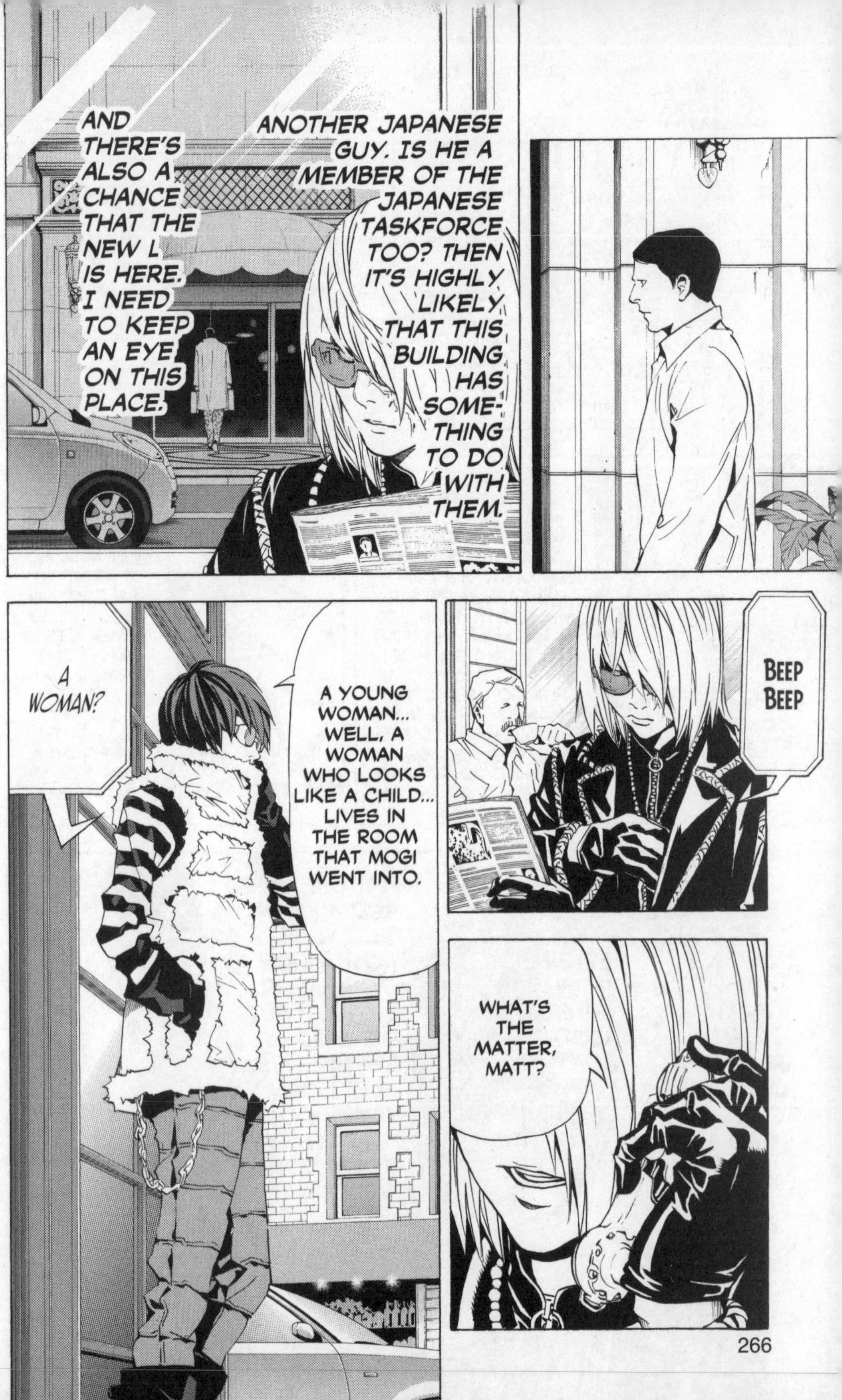
ANOTHER JAPANESE GUY. IS HE A MEMBER OF THE JAPANESE TASKFORCE TOO? THEN IT'S HIGHLY LIKELY THAT THIS BUILDING HAS SOME-THING TO DO WITH THEM.
AND THERE'S ALSO A CHANCE THAT THE NEW L IS HERE. I NEED TO KEEP AN EYE ON THIS PLACE.
BEEP BEEP
WHAT'S THE MATTER, MATT?
A YOUNG WOMAN... WELL, A WOMAN WHO LOOKS LIKE A CHILD... LIVES IN THE ROOM THAT MOGI WENT INTO.
A WOMAN?

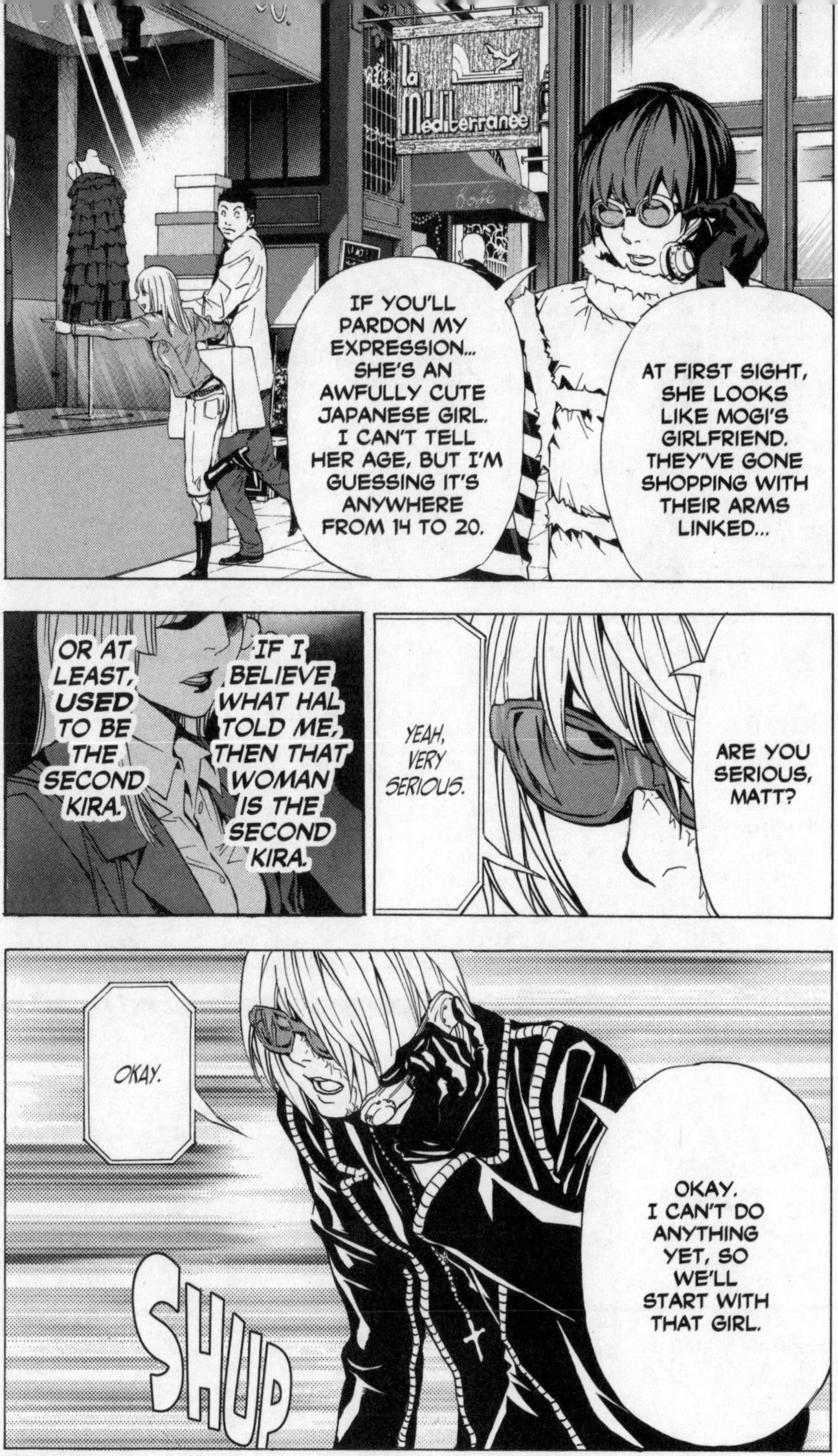
AT FIRST SIGHT, SHE LOOKS LIKE MOGI'S GIRLFRIEND. THEY'VE GONE SHOPPING WITH THEIR ARMS LINKED...
IF YOU'LL PARDON MY EXPRESSION... SHE'S AN AWFULLY CUTE JAPANESE GIRL. I CAN'T TELL HER AGE, BUT I'M GUESSING IT'S ANYWHERE FROM 14 TO 20.
ARE YOU SERIOUS, MATT?
YEAH, VERY SERIOUS.
IF I BELIEVE WHAT HAL TOLD ME, THEN THAT WOMAN IS THE SECOND KIRA.
OR AT LEAST, USED TO BE THE SECOND KIRA.
OKAY. I CAN'T DO ANYTHING YET, SO WE'LL START WITH THAT GIRL.
OKAY.
SHUP

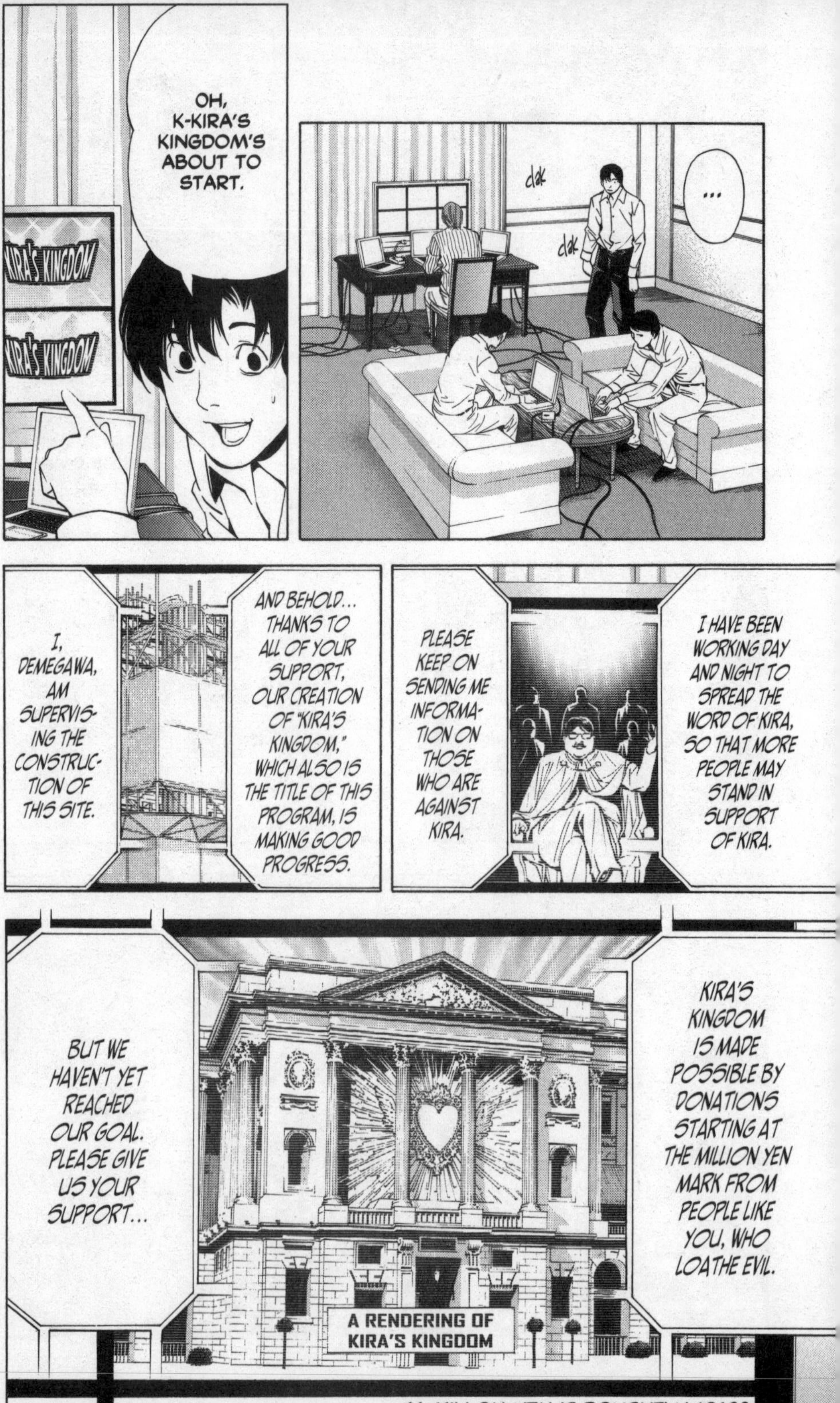
clak
clak
...
OH, K-KIRA'S KINGDOM'S ABOUT TO START.
KIRA'S KINGDOM
KIRA'S KINGDOM
I HAVE BEEN WORKING DAY AND NIGHT TO SPREAD THE WORD OF KIRA, SO THAT MORE PEOPLE MAY STAND IN SUPPORT OF KIRA.
PLEASE KEEP ON SENDING ME INFORMATION ON THOSE WHO ARE AGAINST KIRA.
AND BEHOLD... THANKS TO ALL OF YOUR SUPPORT, OUR CREATION OF "KIRA'S KINGDOM," WHICH ALSO IS THE TITLE OF THIS PROGRAM, IS MAKING GOOD PROGRESS.
I, DEMEGAWA, AM SUPERVISING THE CONSTRUCTION OF THIS SITE.
KIRA'S KINGDOM IS MADE POSSIBLE BY DONATIONS STARTING AT THE MILLION YEN MARK FROM PEOPLE LIKE YOU, WHO LOATHE THE EVIL.
BUT WE HAVEN'T YET REACHED OUR GOAL. PLEASE GIVE US YOUR SUPPORT...
A RENDERING OF KIRA'S KINGDOM

*A MILLON YEN IS ROUGHTLY $8600.

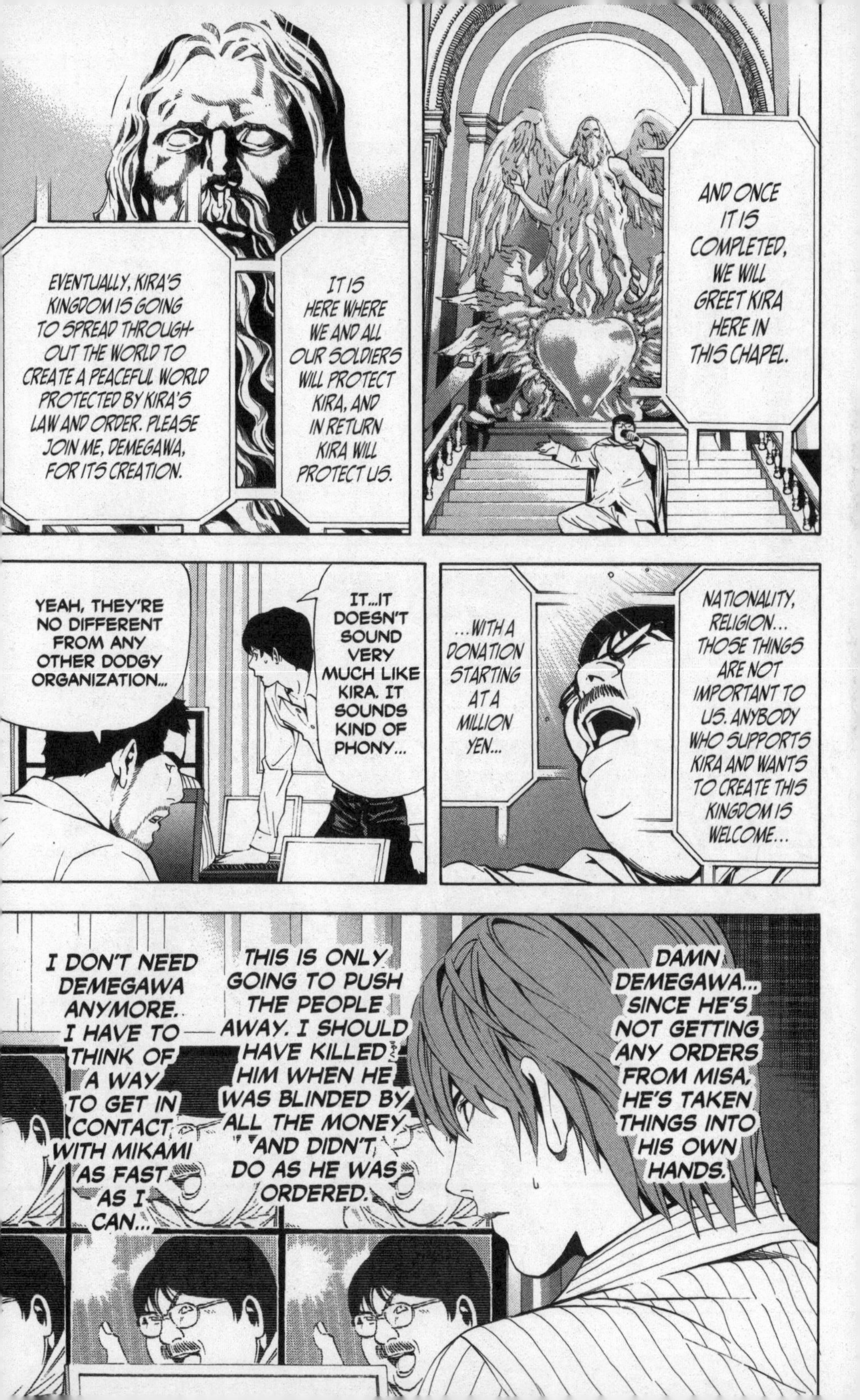
AND ONCE IT IS COMPLETED, WE WILL GREET KIRA HERE IN THIS CHAPEL.
IT IS HERE WHERE WE AND ALL OUR SOLDIERS WILL PROTECT KIRA, AND IN RETURN KIRA WILL PROTECT US.
EVENTUALLY, KIRA'S KINGDOM IS GOING TO SPREAD THROUGH-OUT THE WORLD TO CREATE A PEACEFUL WORLD PROTECTED BY KIRA'S LAW AND ORDER. PLEASE JOIN ME, DEMEGAWA, FOR ITS CREATION.
NATIONALITY, RELIGION... THOSE THINGS ARE NOT IMPORTANT TO US. ANYBODY WHO SUPPORTS KIRA AND WANTS TO CREATE THIS KINGDOM IS WELCOME...
...WITH A DONATION STARTING AT A MILLION YEN...
IT...IT DOESN'T SOUND VERY MUCH LIKE KIRA. IT SOUNDS KIND OF PHONY...
YEAH, THEY'RE NO DIFFERENT FROM ANY OTHER DODGY ORGANIZATION...
DAMN DEMEGAWA... SINCE HE'S NOT GETTING ANY ORDERS FROM MISA, HE'S TAKEN THINGS INTO HIS OWN HANDS.
THIS IS ONLY GOING TO PUSH THE PEOPLE AWAY. I SHOULD HAVE KILLED HIM WHEN HE WAS BLINDED BY ALL THE MONEY AND DIDN'T DO AS HE WAS ORDERED.
I DON'T NEED DEMEGAWA ANYMORE. I HAVE TO THINK OF A WAY TO GET IN CONTACT WITH MIKAMI AS FAST AS I CAN...

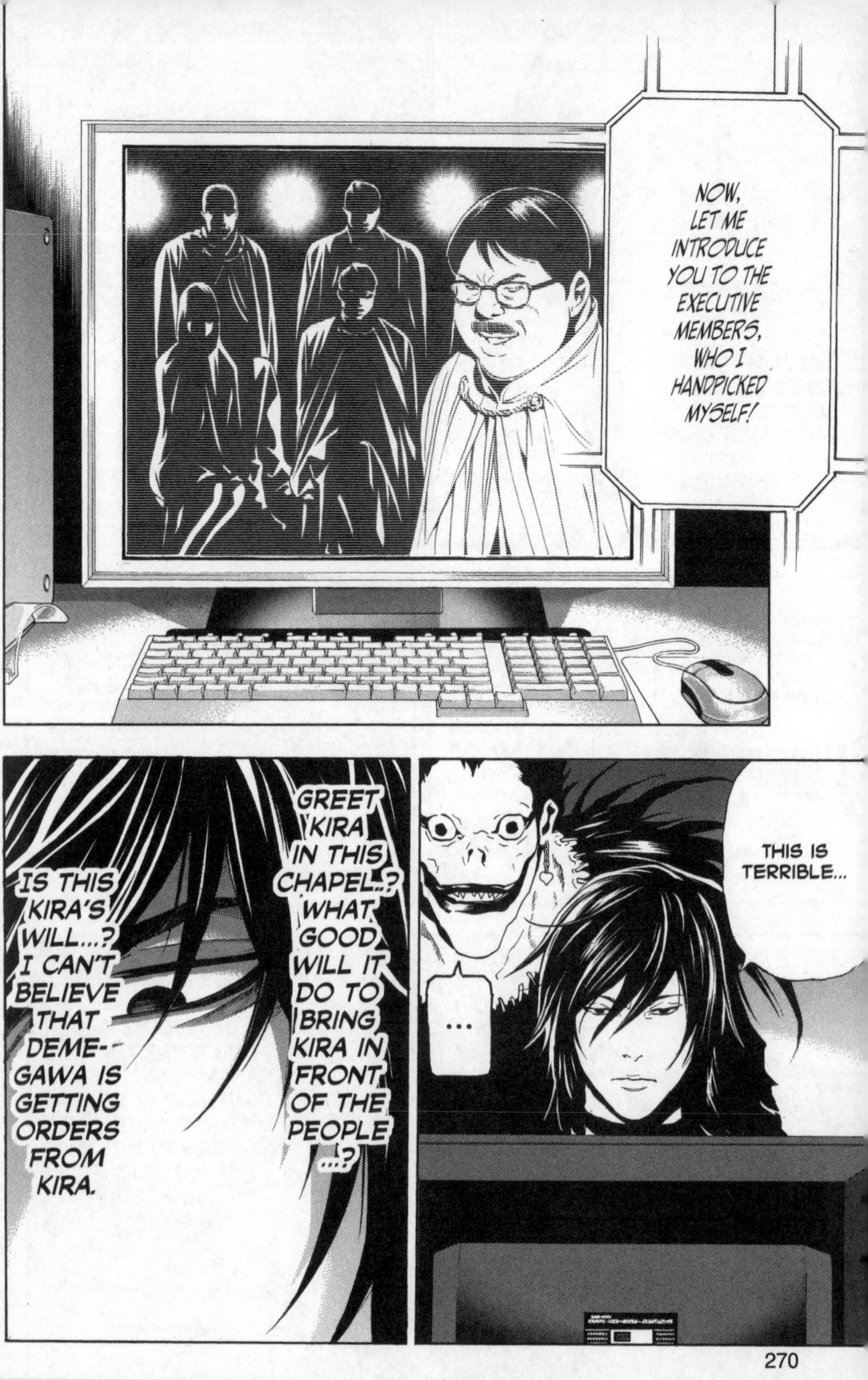
NOW, LET ME INTRODUCE YOU TO THE EXECUTIVE MEMBERS, WHO I HANDPICKED MYSELF!
THIS IS TERRIBLE...
...
GREET KIRA IN THIS CHAPEL..? WHAT GOOD WILL IT DO TO BRING KIRA IN FRONT OF THE PEOPLE ...?
IS THIS KIRA'S WILL...? I CAN'T BELIEVE THAT DEME-GAWA IS GETTING ORDERS FROM KIRA.

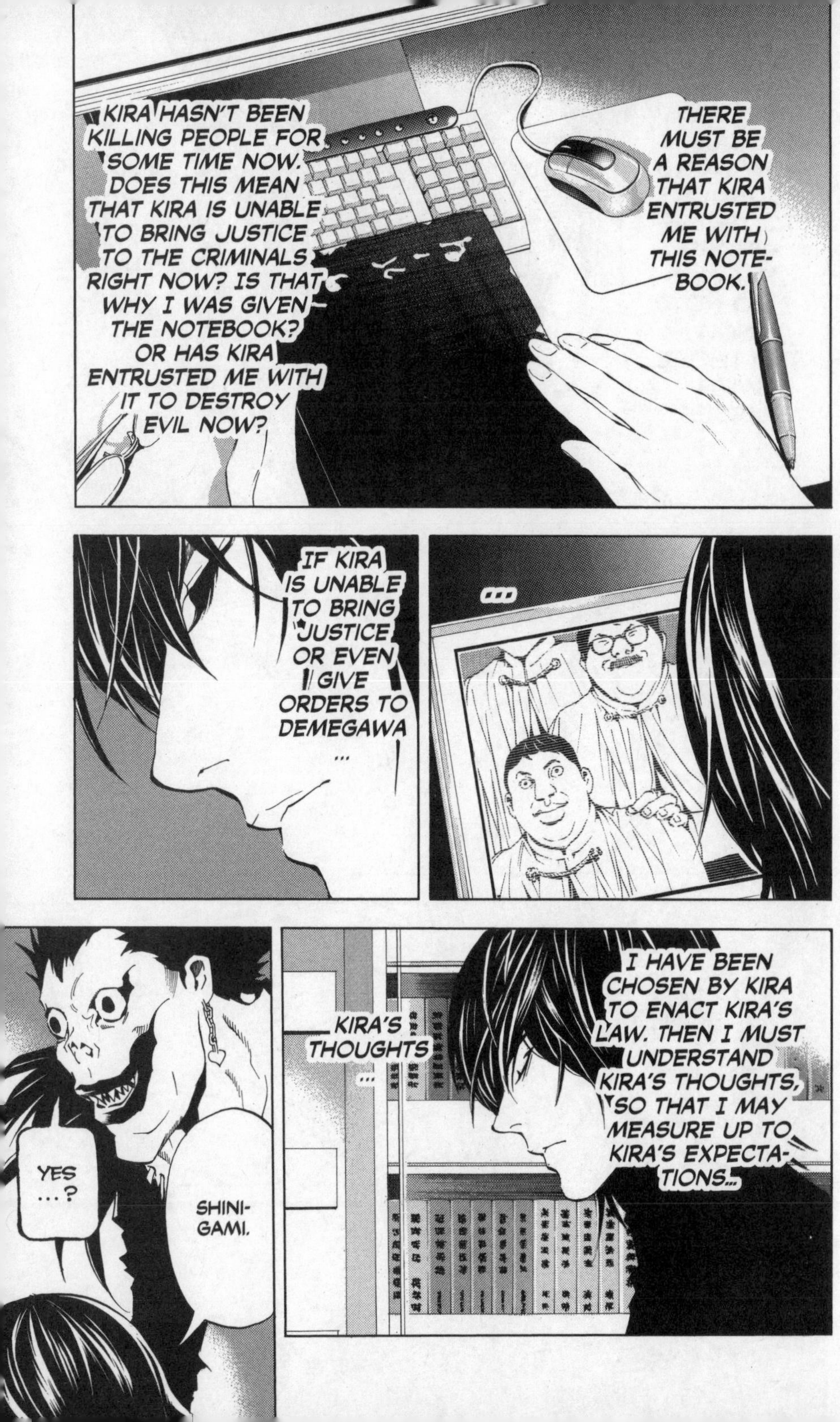
THERE MUST BE A REASON THAT KIRA ENTRUSTED ME WITH THIS NOTE-BOOK.
KIRA HASN'T BEEN KILLING PEOPLE FOR SOME TIME NOW. DOES THIS MEAN THAT KIRA IS UNABLE TO BRING JUSTICE TO THE CRIMINALS RIGHT NOW? IS THAT WHY I WAS GIVEN THE NOTEBOOK? OR HAS KIRA ENTRUSTED ME WITH IT TO DESTROY EVIL NOW?
...
IF KIRA IS UNABLE TO BRING JUSTICE OR EVEN GIVE ORDERS TO DEMEGAWA ...
I HAVE BEEN CHOSEN BY KIRA TO ENACT KIRA'S LAW. THEN I MUST UNDERSTAND KIRA'S THOUGHTS, SO THAT I MAY MEASURE UP TO KIRA'S EXPECTA-TIONS...
KIRA'S THOUGHTS ...
SHINI-GAMI.
YES ...?

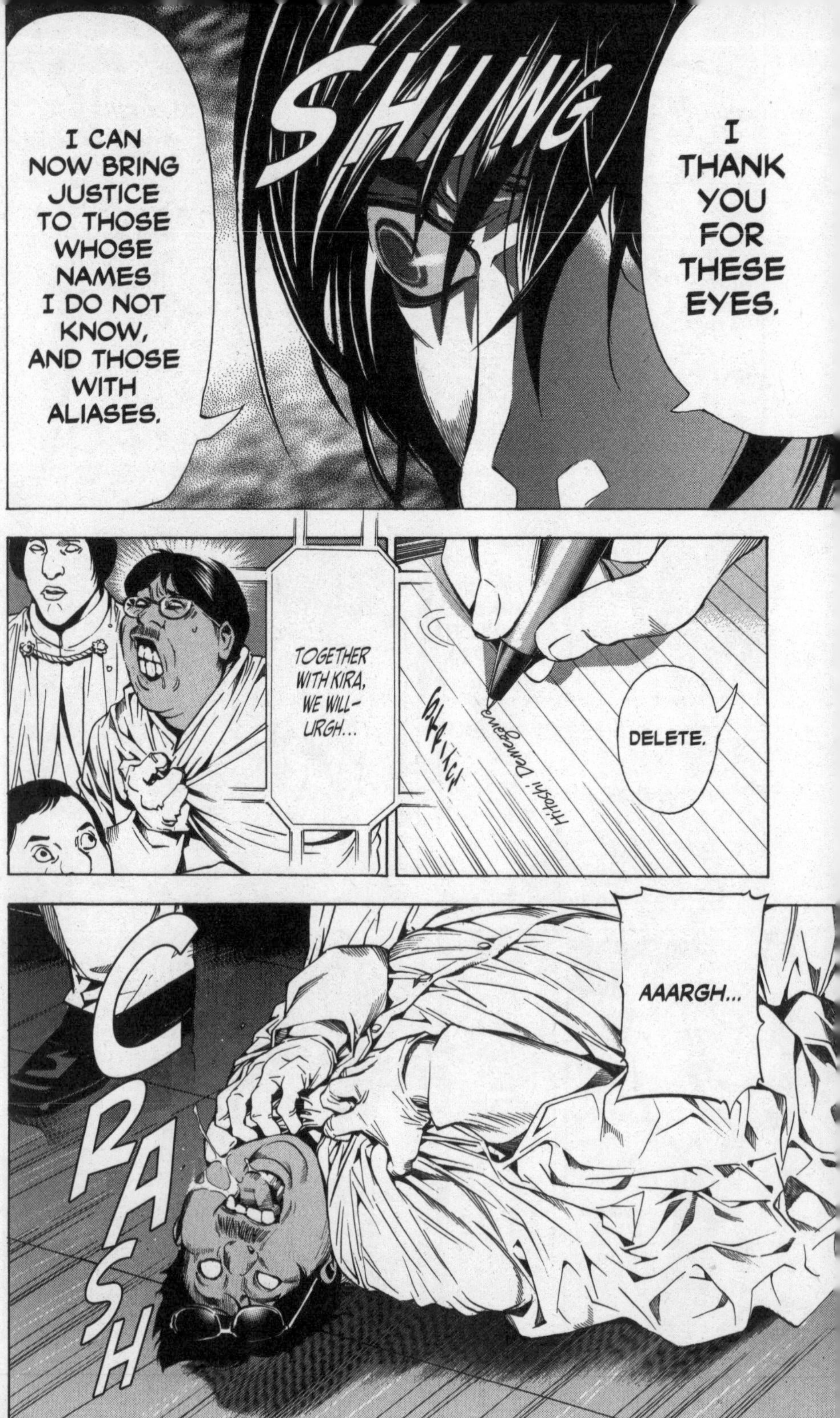
I THANK YOU FOR THESE EYES.
SHING
I CAN NOW BRING JUSTICE TO THOSE WHOSE NAMES I DO NOT KNOW, AND THOSE WITH ALIASES.
DELETE.
Hitoshi Demegawa
TOGETHER WITH KIRA, WE WILL- URGH...
AAARGH...
CRASH

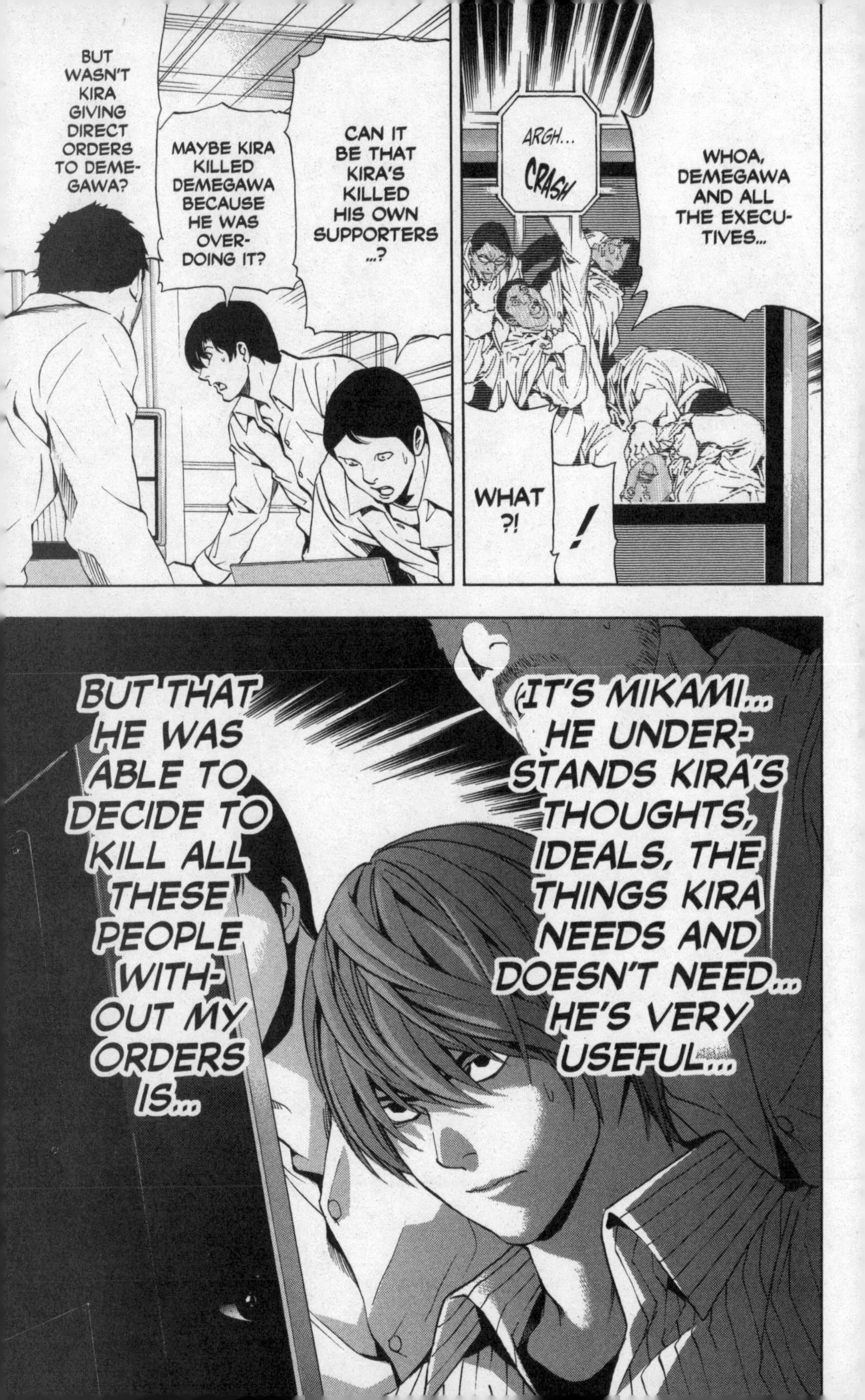
WHOA, DEMEGAWA AND ALL THE EXECUTIVES...
ARGH...
CRASH
WHAT ?!
!
CAN IT BE THAT KIRA'S KILLED HIS OWN SUPPORTERS ...?
MAYBE KIRA KILLED DEMEGAWA BECAUSE HE WAS OVER-DOING IT?
BUT WASN'T KIRA GIVING DIRECT ORDERS TO DEME-GAWA?
IT'S MIKAMI... HE UNDER-STANDS KIRA'S THOUGHTS, IDEALS, THE THINGS KIRA NEEDS AND DOESN'T NEED... HE'S VERY USEFUL...
BUT THAT HE WAS ABLE TO DECIDE TO KILL ALL THESE PEOPLE WITH-OUT MY ORDERS IS...

To the average
Japanese adult,
Teru Mikami
was a child with
a strong sense
of justice,
who was able
to determine
between right
and wrong.

And compared
to the average
Japanese,
Teru has been
through and
seen far greater
miseries...

...and
deaths.

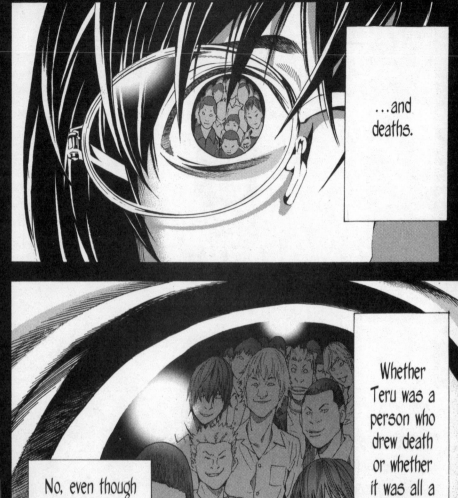

Whether
Teru was a
person who
drew death
or whether
it was all a
coincidence—

No, even though
he wished for
the death of
others at times,
he never killed
anyone with
his own hands.
It was all a
coincidence.

chapter 84 Coincidence

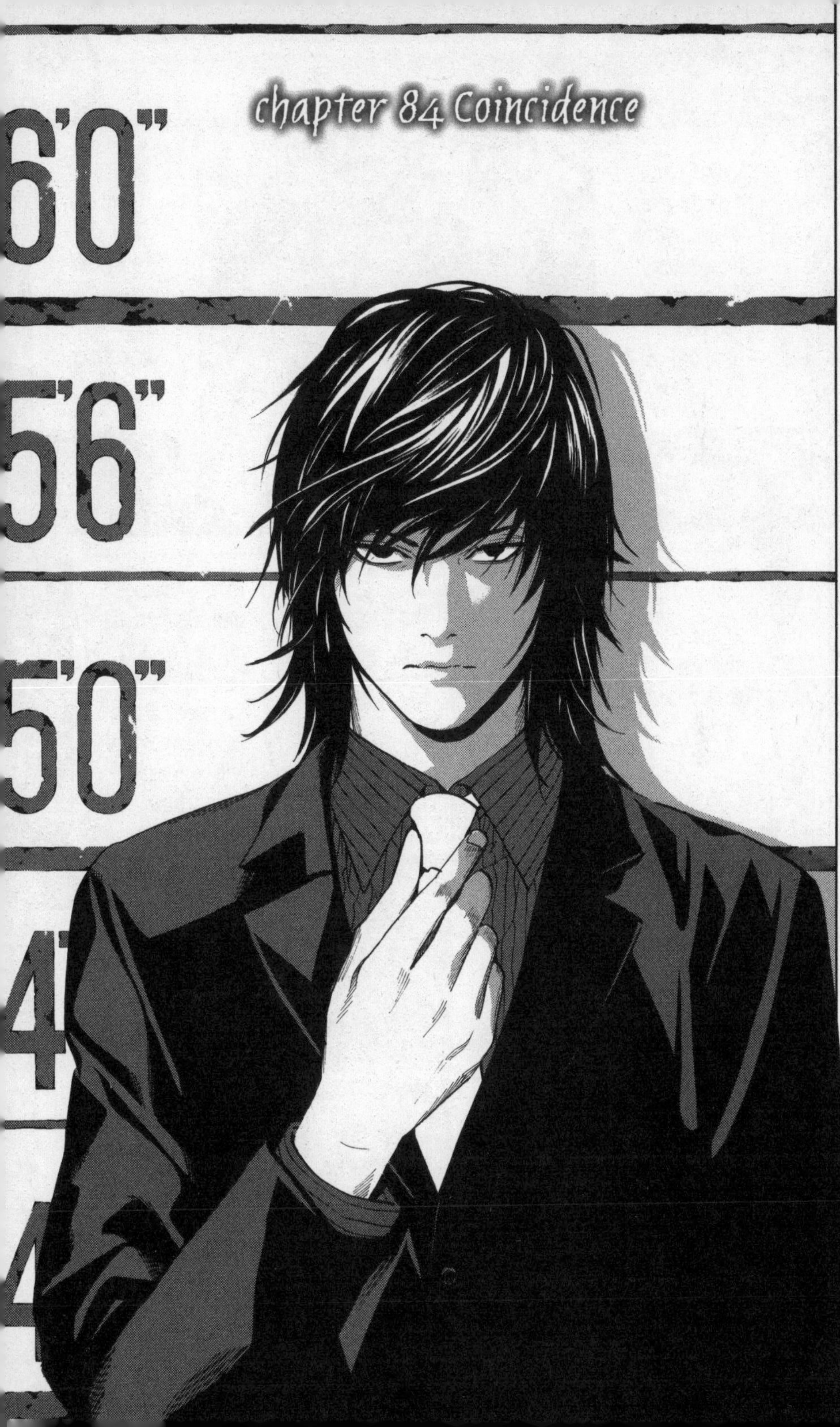
6'0"
5'6"
5'0"

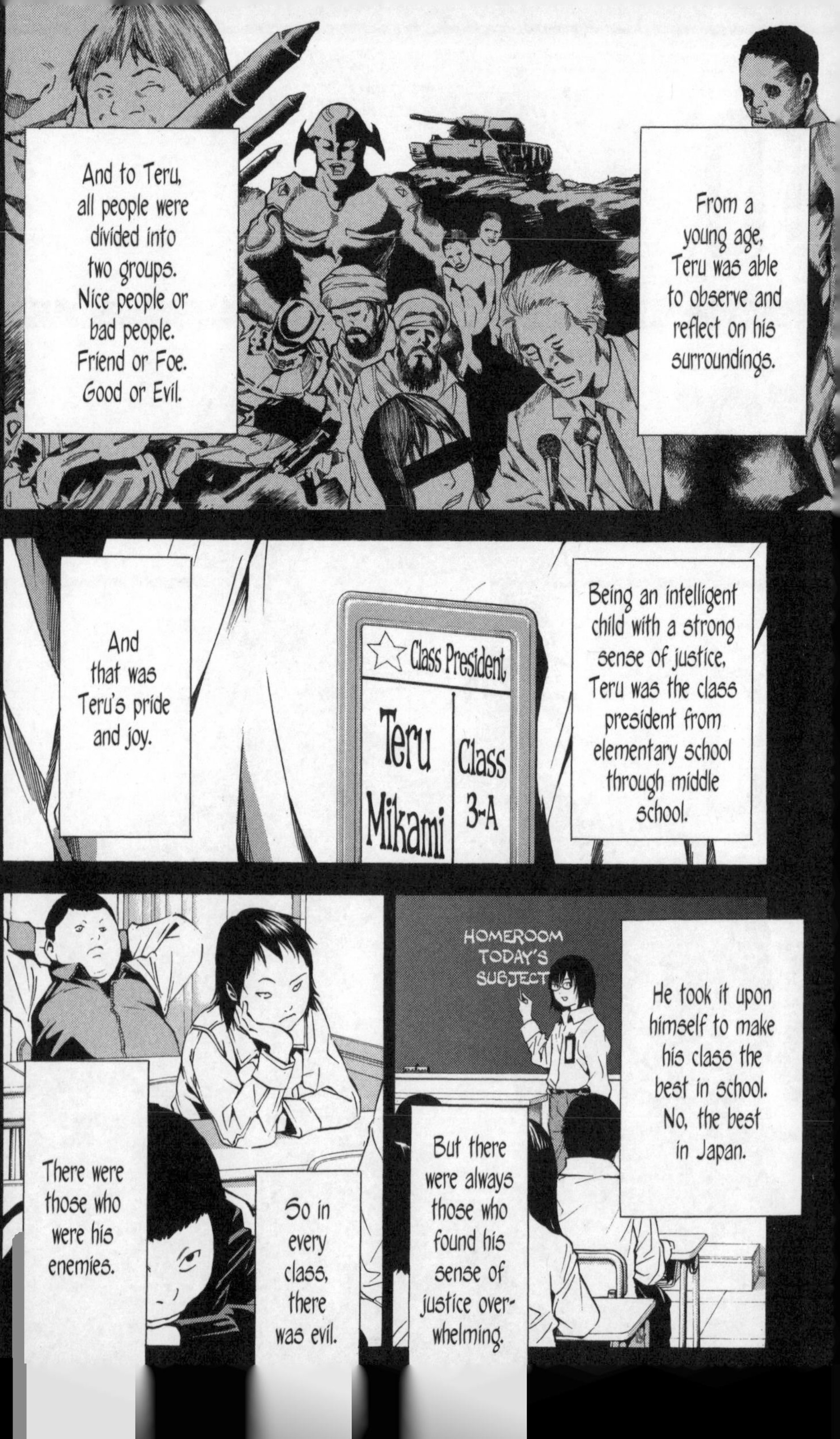
From a young age, Teru was able to observe and reflect on his surroundings.
And to Teru, all people were divided into two groups. Nice people or bad people. Friend or Foe. Good or Evil.
Being an intelligent child with a strong sense of justice, Teru was the class president from elementary school through middle school.
Class President
Teru Mikami
Class 3-A
And that was Teru's pride and joy.
He took it upon himself to make his class the best in school. No, the best in Japan.
HOMEROOM TODAY'S SUBJECT
But there were always those who found his sense of justice over-whelming.
So in every class, there was evil.
There were those who were his enemies.

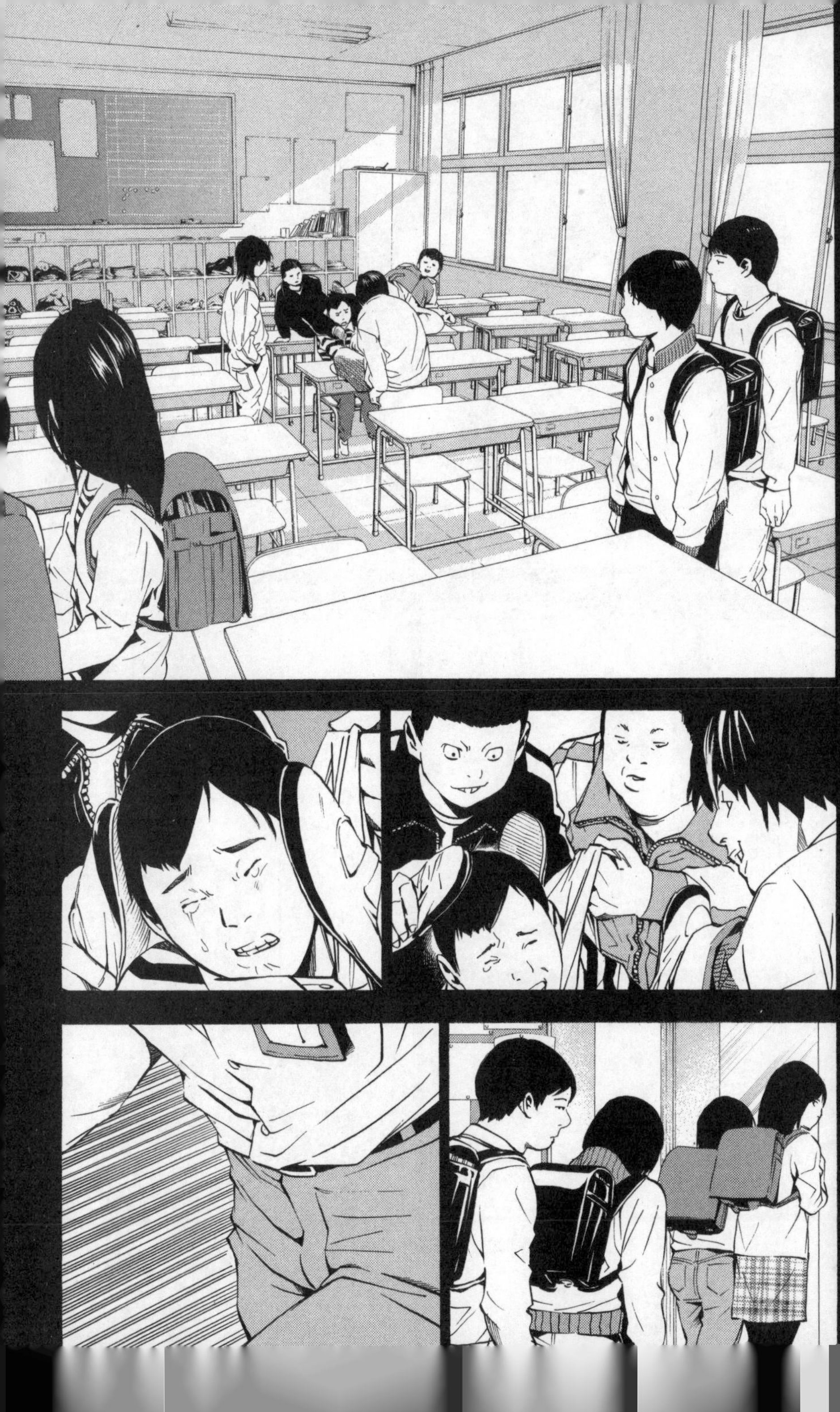

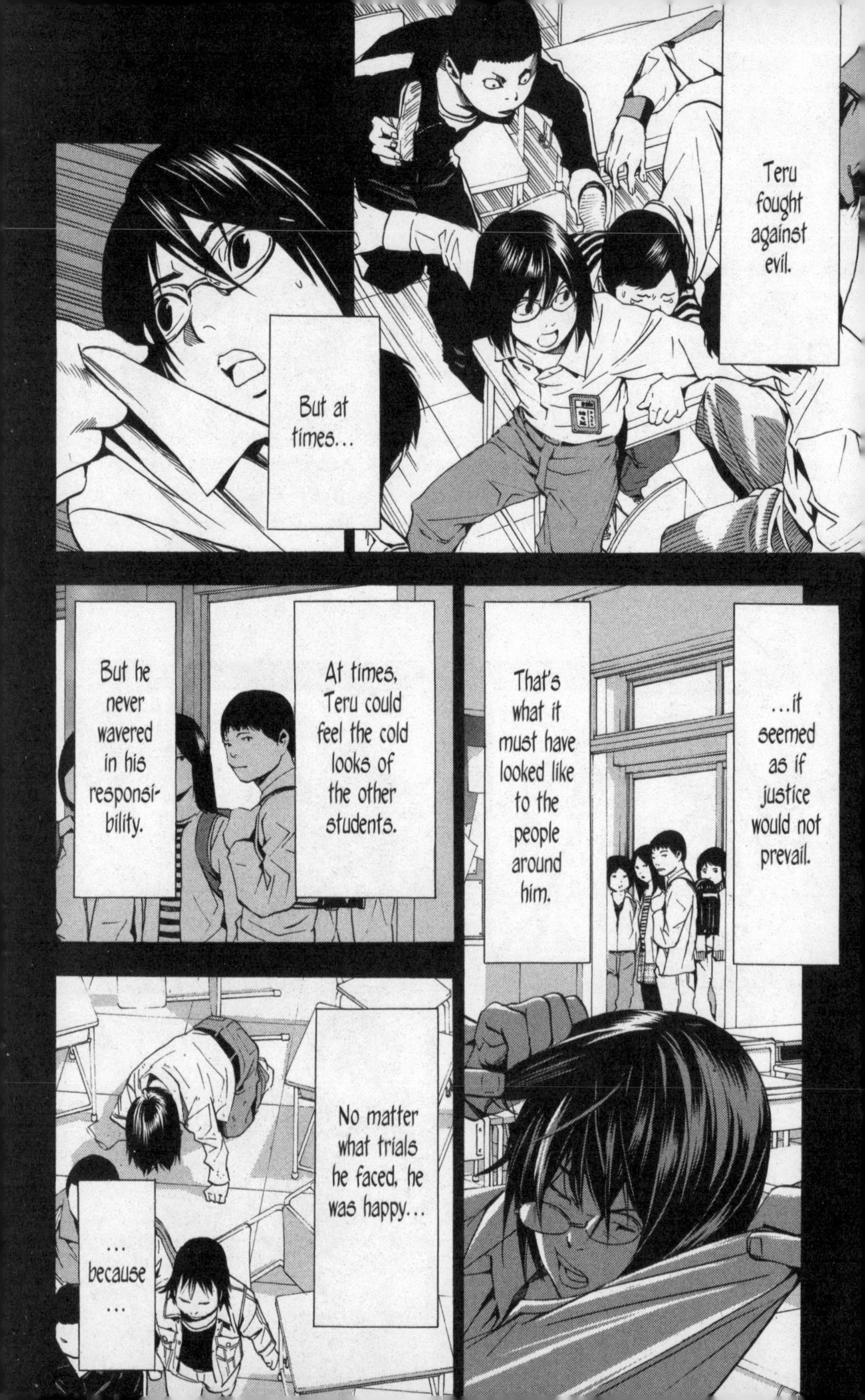
Teru fought against evil.
But at times...
...it seemed as if justice would not prevail.
That's what it must have looked like to the people around him.
At times, Teru could feel the cold looks of the other students.
But he never wavered in his responsibility.
No matter what trials he faced, he was happy...
... because ...

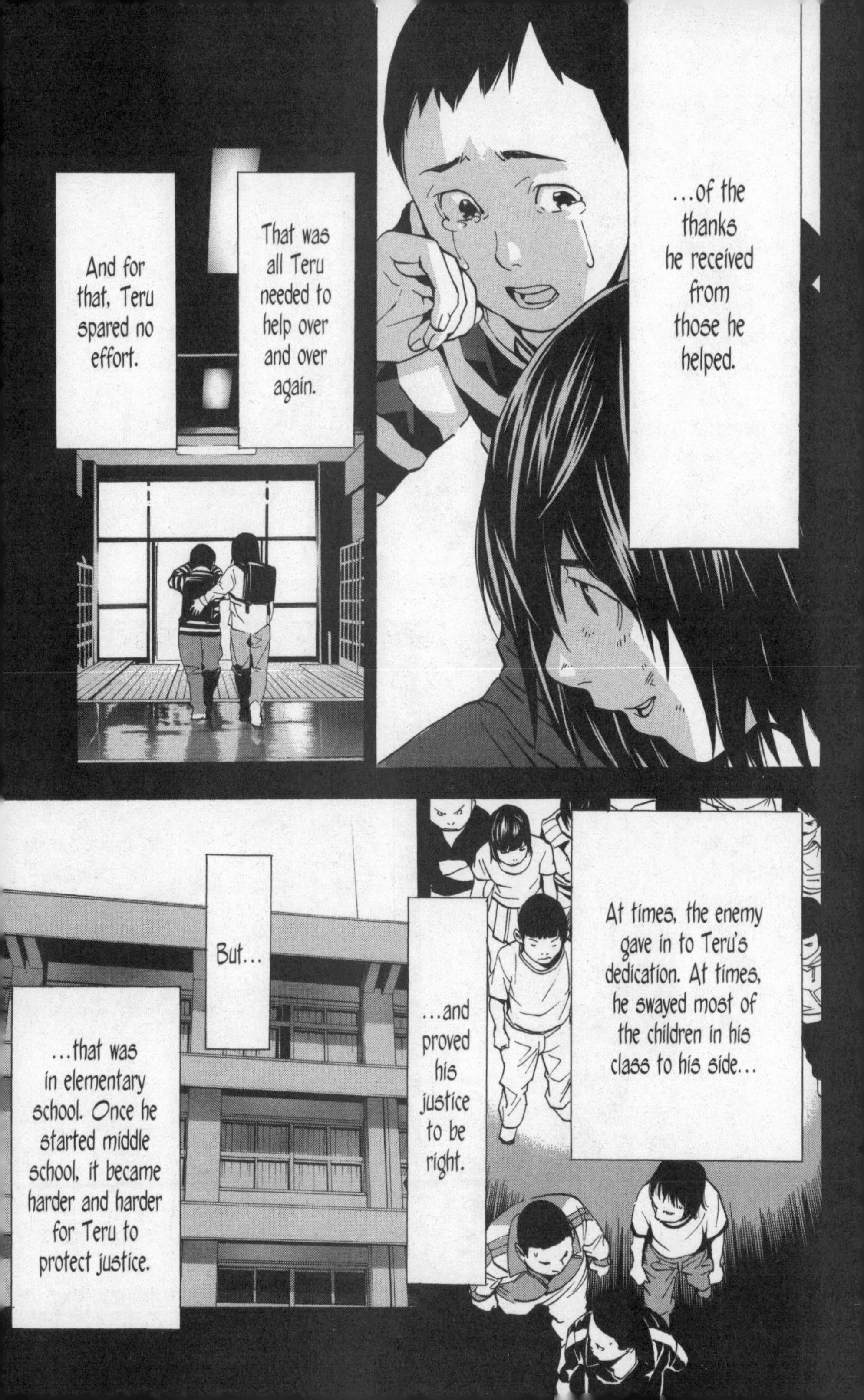
...of the thanks he received from those he helped.
That was all Teru needed to help over and over again.
And for that, Teru spared no effort.
At times, the enemy gave in to Teru's dedication. At times, he swayed most of the children in his class to his side...
...and proved his justice to be right.
But...
...that was in elementary school. Once he started middle school, it became harder and harder for Teru to protect justice.

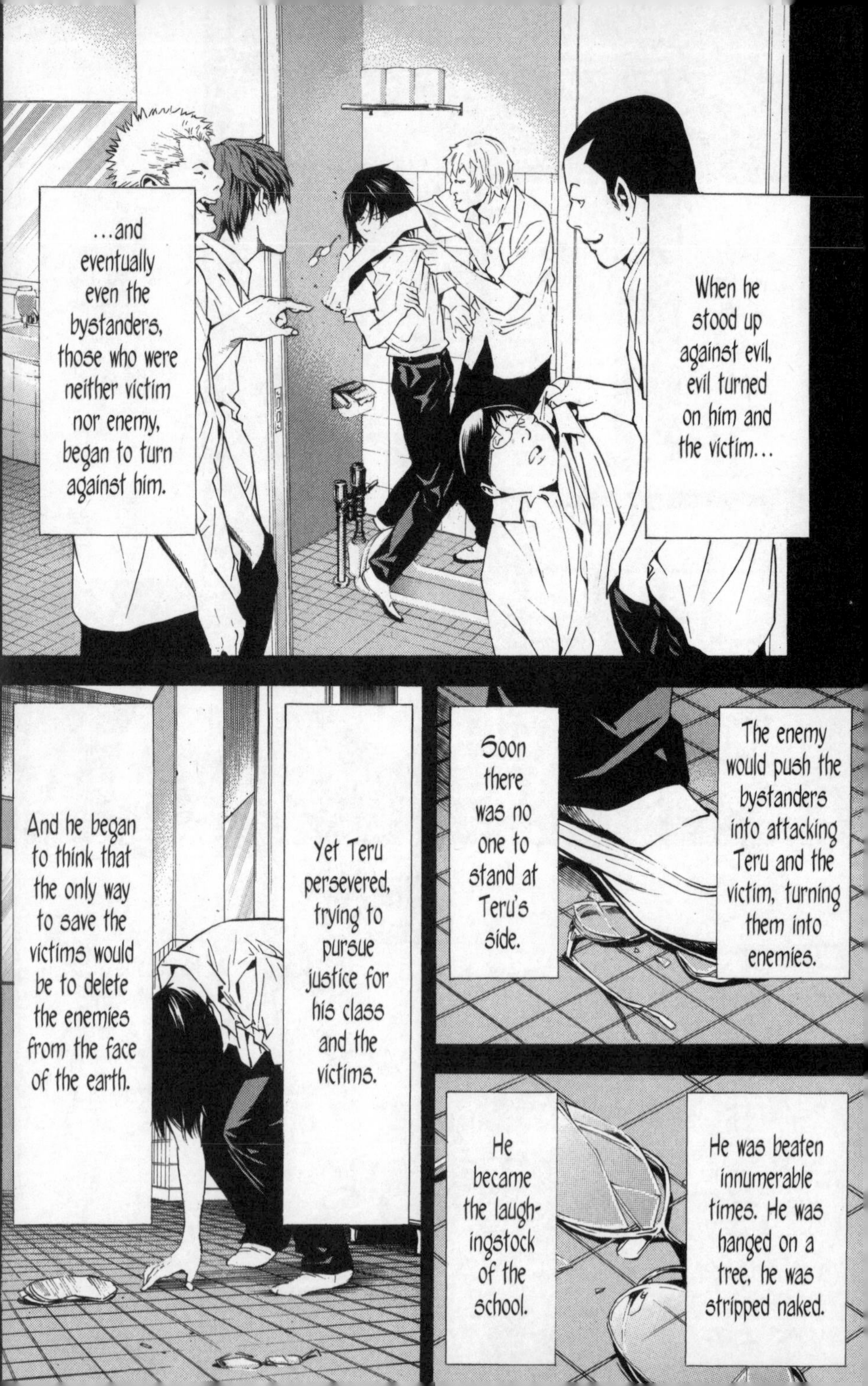
When he stood up against evil, evil turned on him and the victim…
…and eventually even the bystanders, those who were neither victim nor enemy, began to turn against him.
The enemy would push the bystanders into attacking Teru and the victim, turning them into enemies.
Soon there was no one to stand at Teru's side.
He was beaten innumerable times. He was hanged on a tree, he was stripped naked.
He became the laugh-ingstock of the school.
Yet Teru persevered, trying to pursue justice for his class and the victims.
And he began to think that the only way to save the victims would be to delete the enemies from the face of the earth.

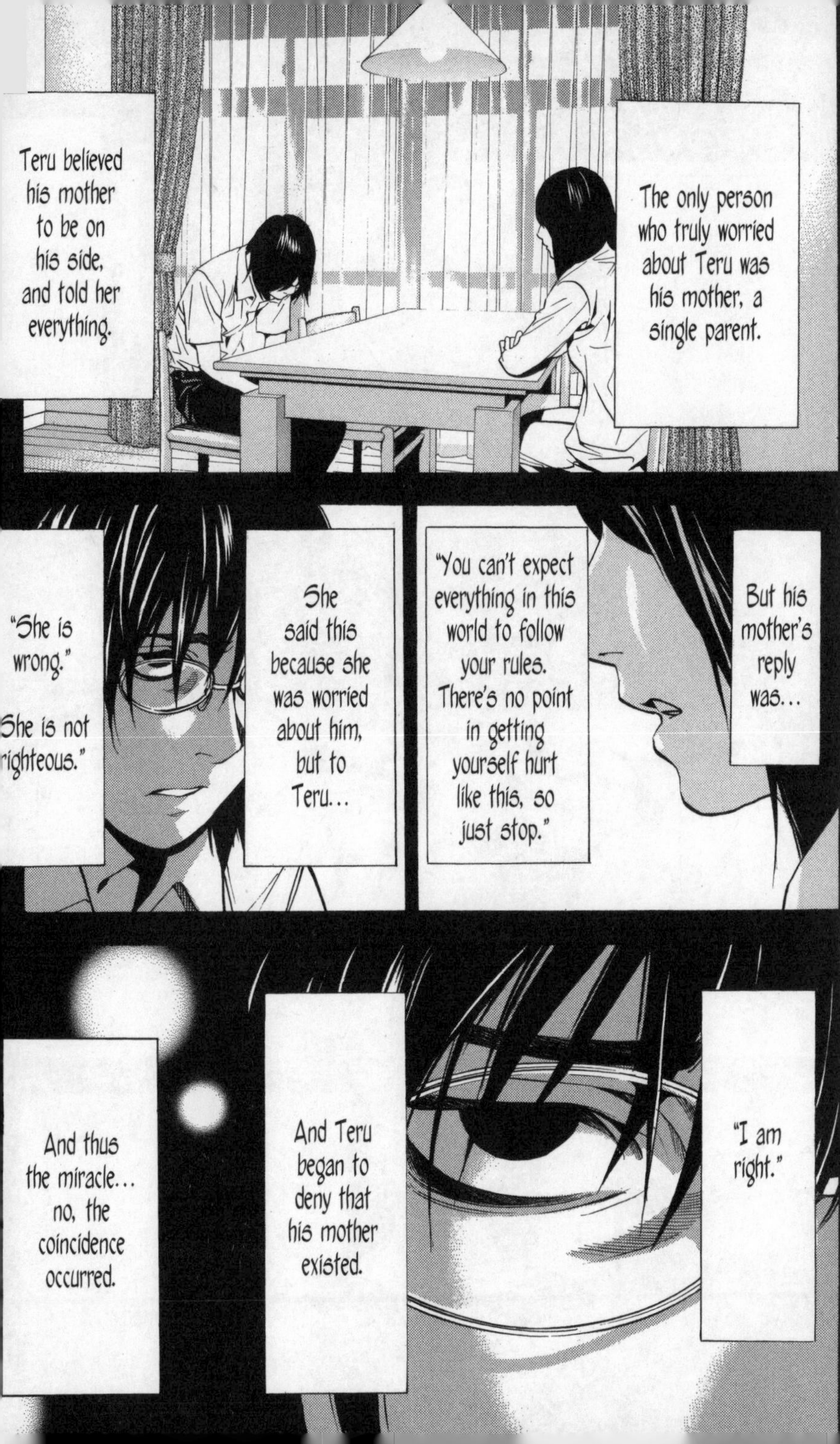
The only person who truly worried about Teru was his mother, a single parent.
Teru believed his mother to be on his side, and told her everything.
But his mother's reply was...
"You can't expect everything in this world to follow your rules. There's no point in getting yourself hurt like this, so just stop."
She said this because she was worried about him, but to Teru...
"She is wrong."
She is not ighteous."
"I am right."
And Teru began to deny that his mother existed.
And thus the miracle... no, the coincidence occurred.

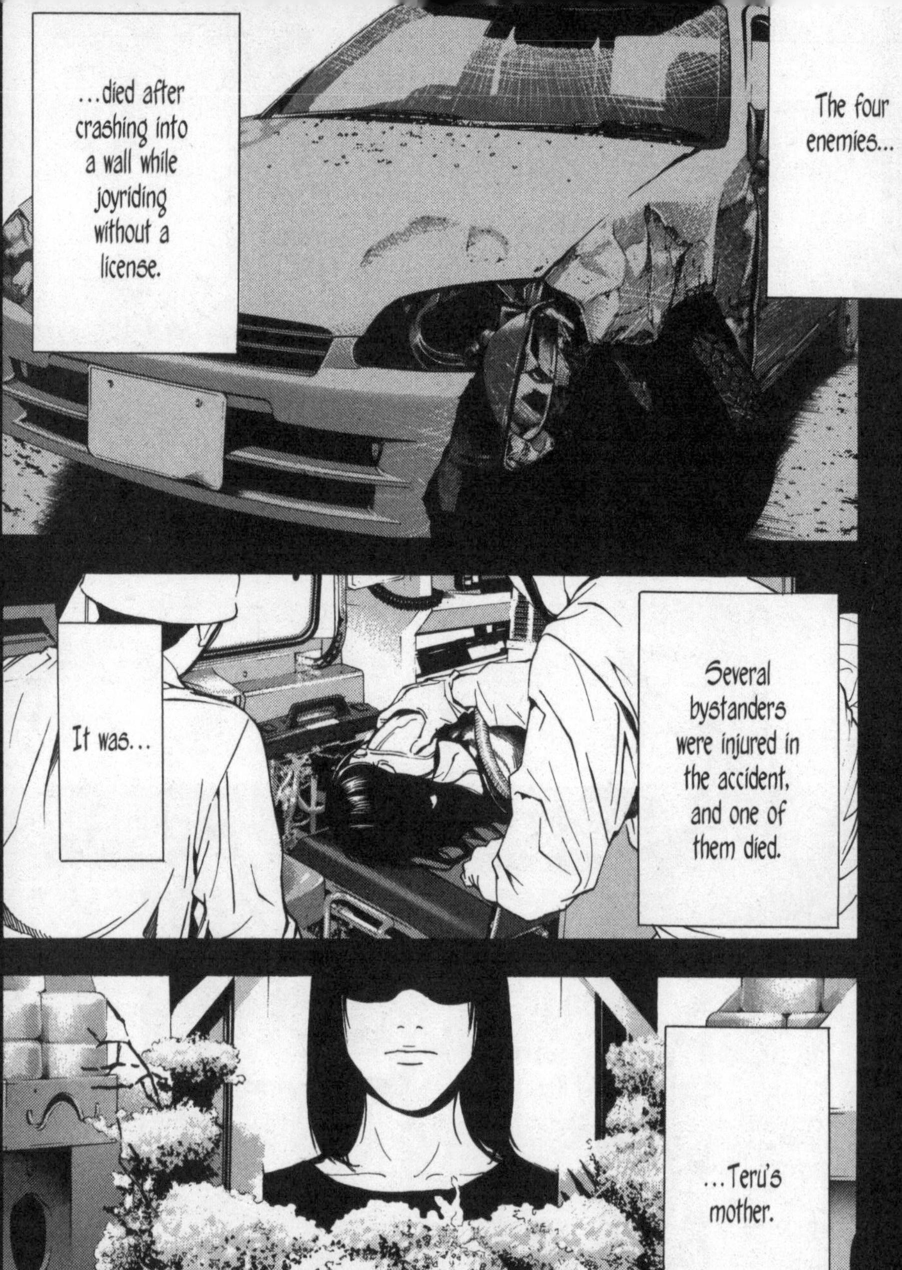
The four enemies...
...died after crashing into a wall while joyriding without a license.
Several bystanders were injured in the accident, and one of them died.
It was...
...Teru's mother.

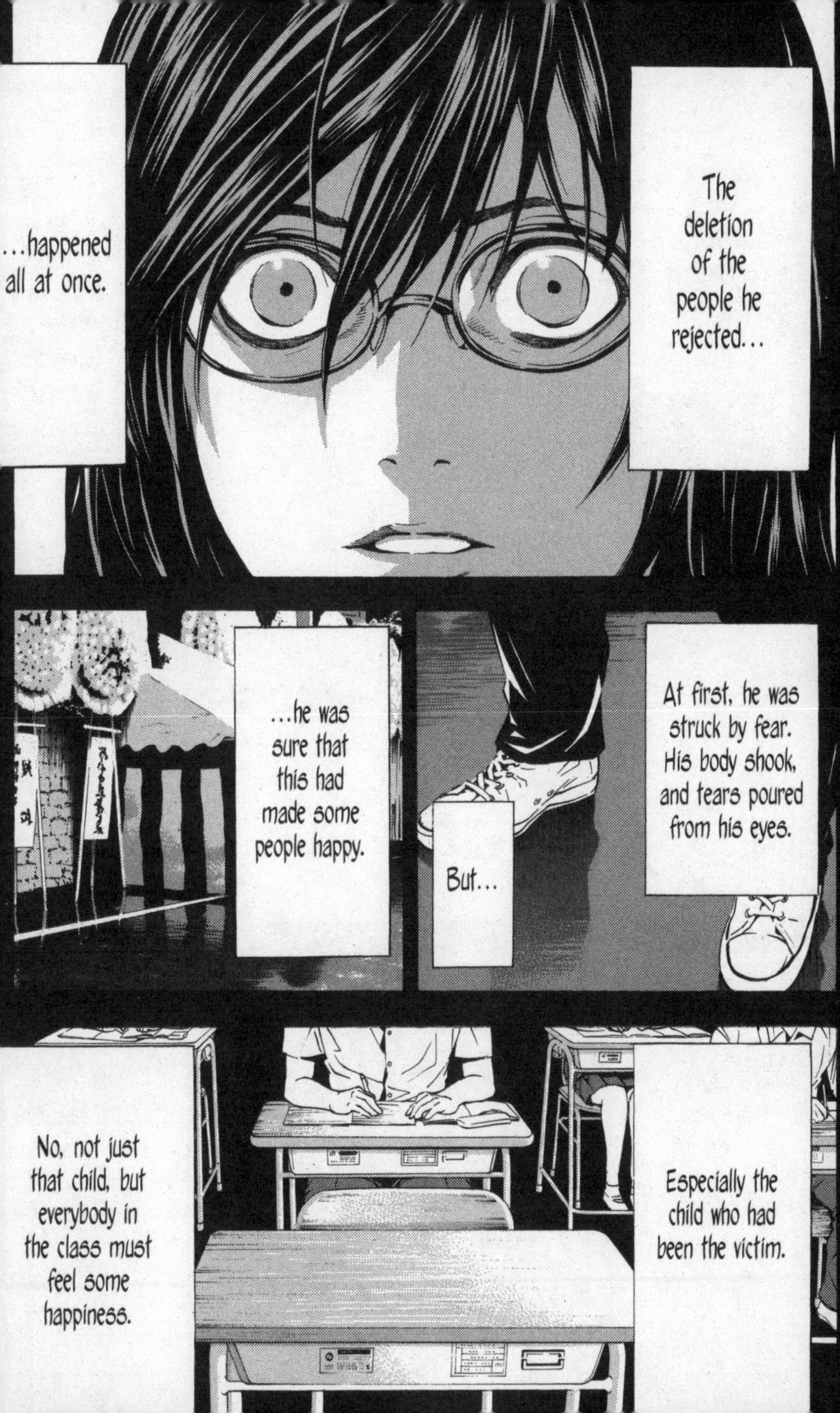
The deletion of the people he rejected...
...happened all at once.
At first, he was struck by fear. His body shook, and tears poured from his eyes.
But...
...he was sure that this had made some people happy.
Especially the child who had been the victim.
No, not just that child, but everybody in the class must feel some happiness.

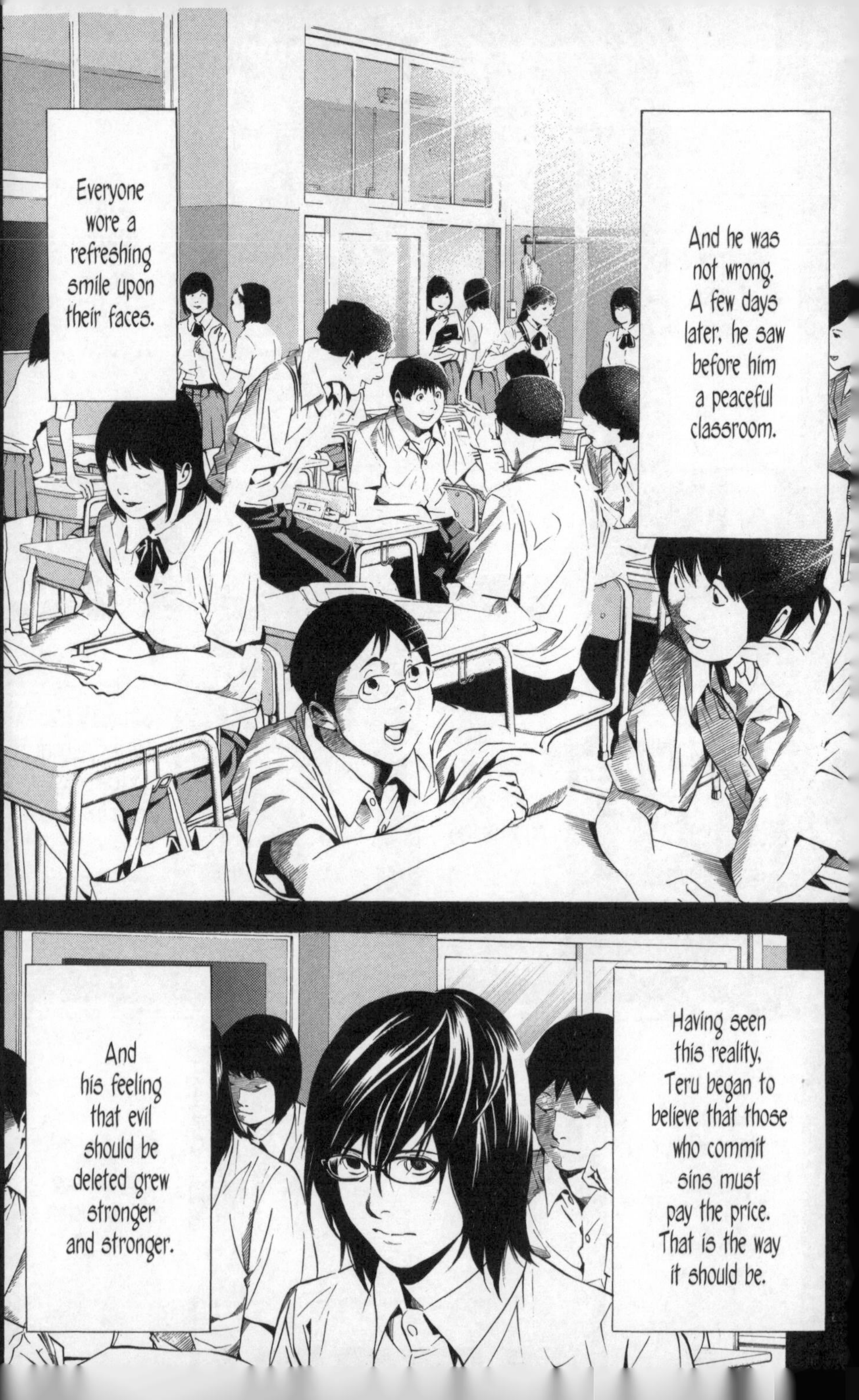
And he was not wrong. A few days later, he saw before him a peaceful classroom.
Everyone wore a refreshing smile upon their faces.
Having seen this reality, Teru began to believe that those who commit sins must pay the price. That is the way it should be.
And his feeling that evil should be deleted grew stronger and stronger.

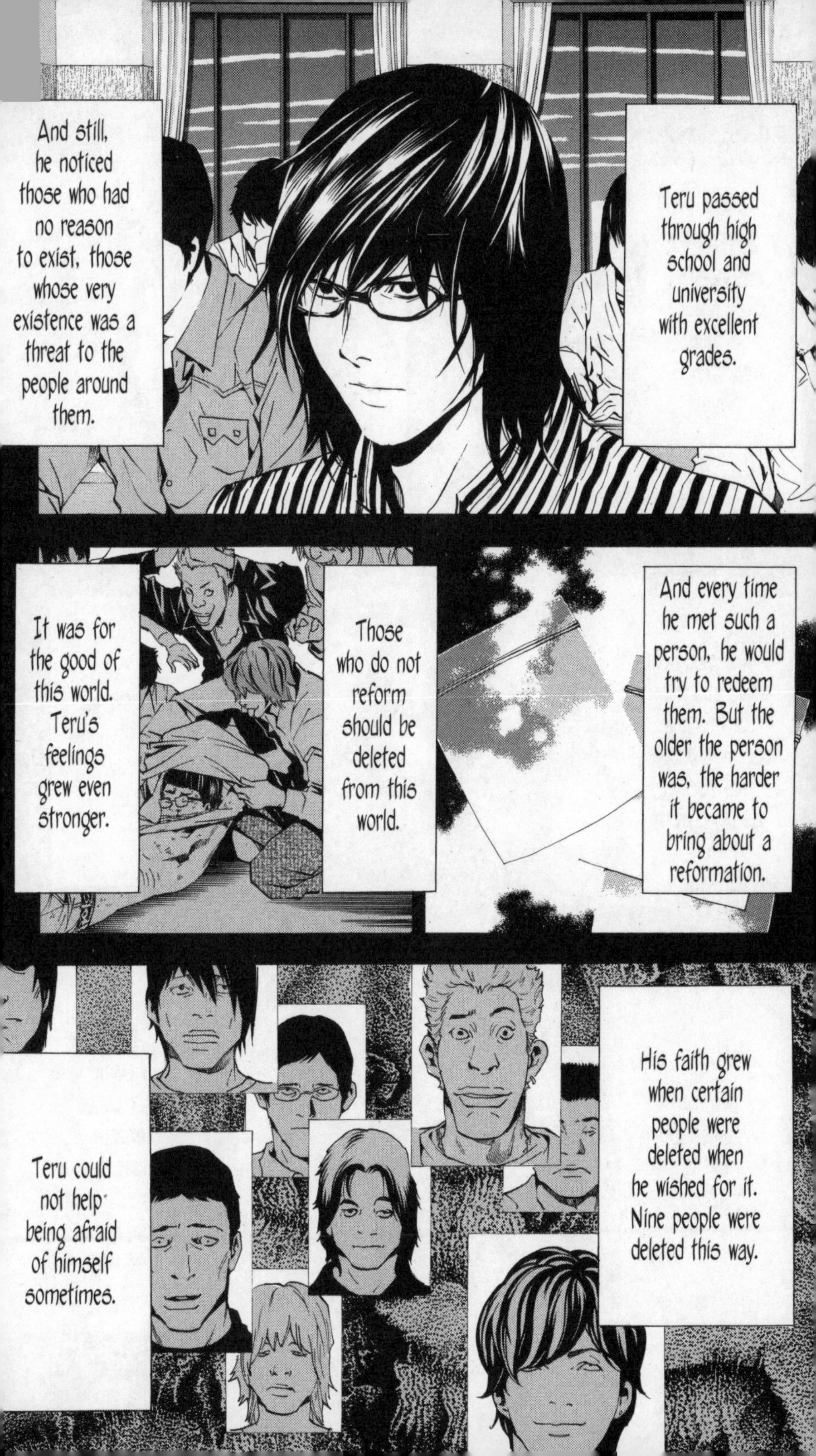
Teru passed through high school and university with excellent grades.
And still, he noticed those who had no reason to exist, those whose very existence was a threat to the people around them.
And every time he met such a person, he would try to redeem them. But the older the person was, the harder it became to bring about a reformation.
Those who do not reform should be deleted from this world.
It was for the good of this world. Teru's feelings grew even stronger.
His faith grew when certain people were deleted when he wished for it. Nine people were deleted this way.
Teru could not help being afraid of himself sometimes.

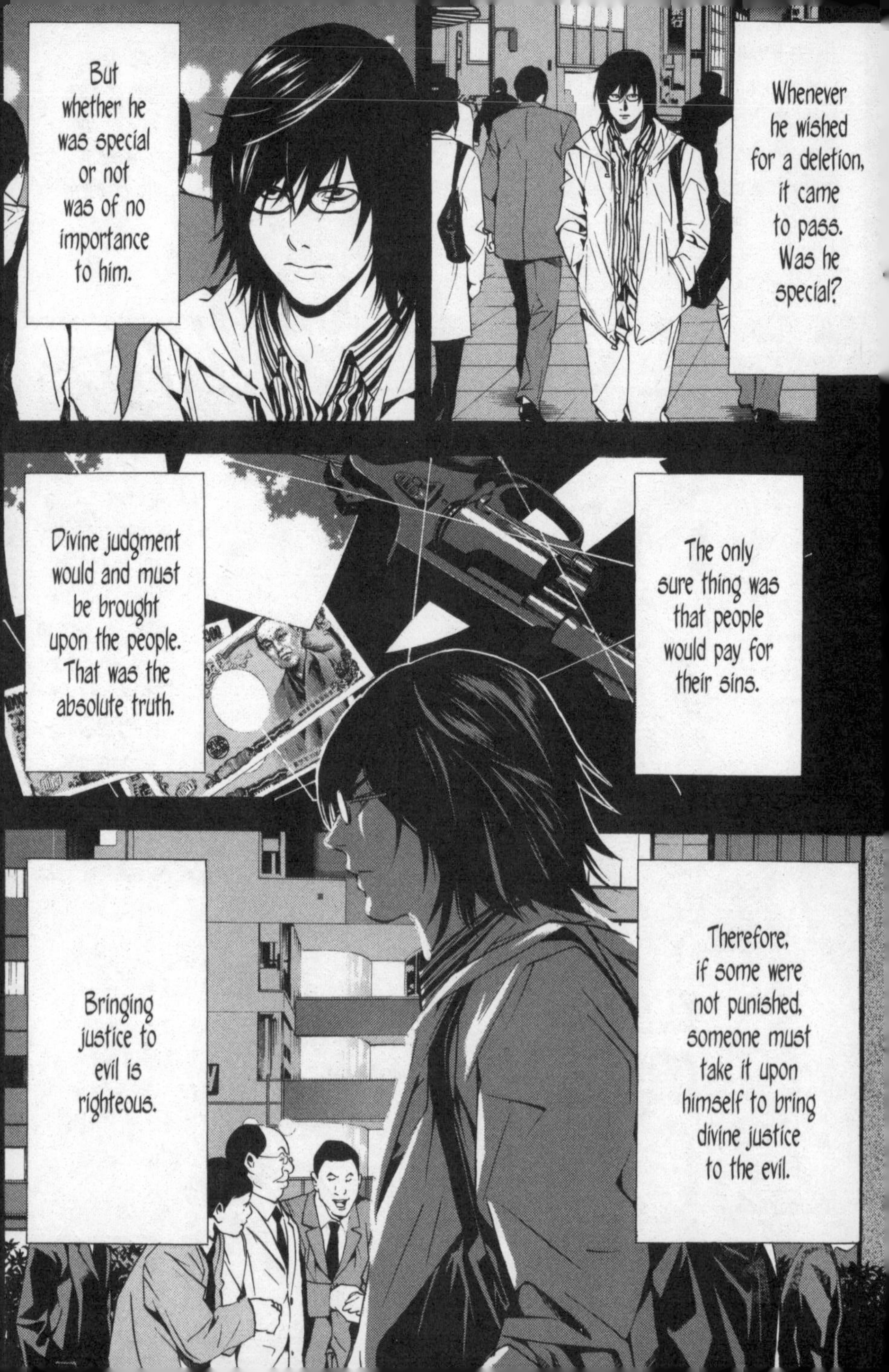
Whenever he wished for a deletion, it came to pass. Was he special?
But whether he was special or not was of no importance to him.
The only sure thing was that people would pay for their sins.
Divine judgment would and must be brought upon the people. That was the absolute truth.
Therefore, if some were not punished, someone must take it upon himself to bring divine justice to the evil.
Bringing justice to evil is righteous.

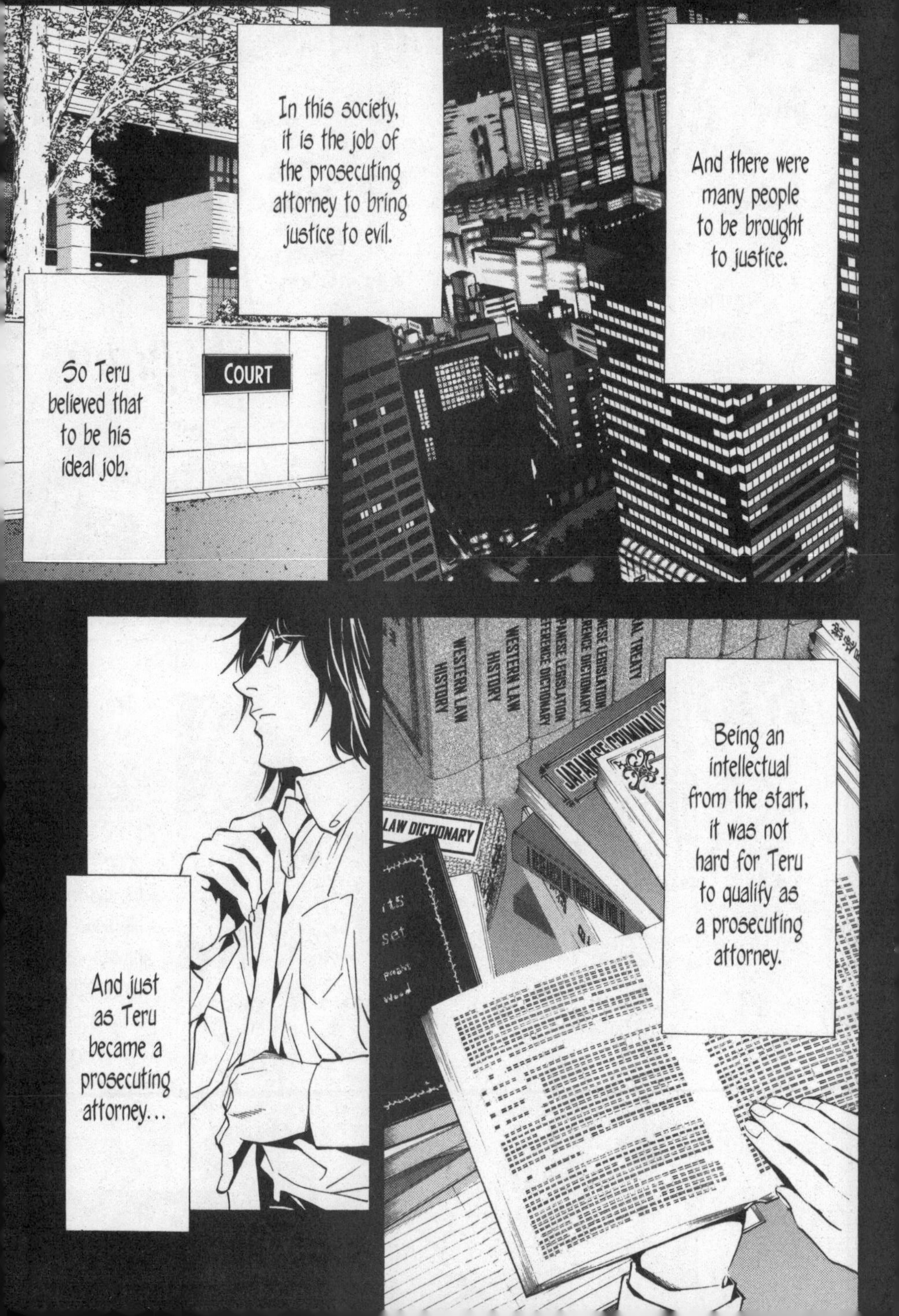
And there were many people to be brought to justice.
In this society, it is the job of the prosecuting attorney to bring justice to evil.
COURT
So Teru believed that to be his ideal job.
Being an intellectual from the start, it was not hard for Teru to qualify as a prosecuting attorney.
WESTERN LAW HISTORY
WESTERN LAW HISTORY
JAPANESE LEGISLATION REFERENCE DICTIONARY
LAW DICTIONARY
And just as Teru became a prosecuting attorney...

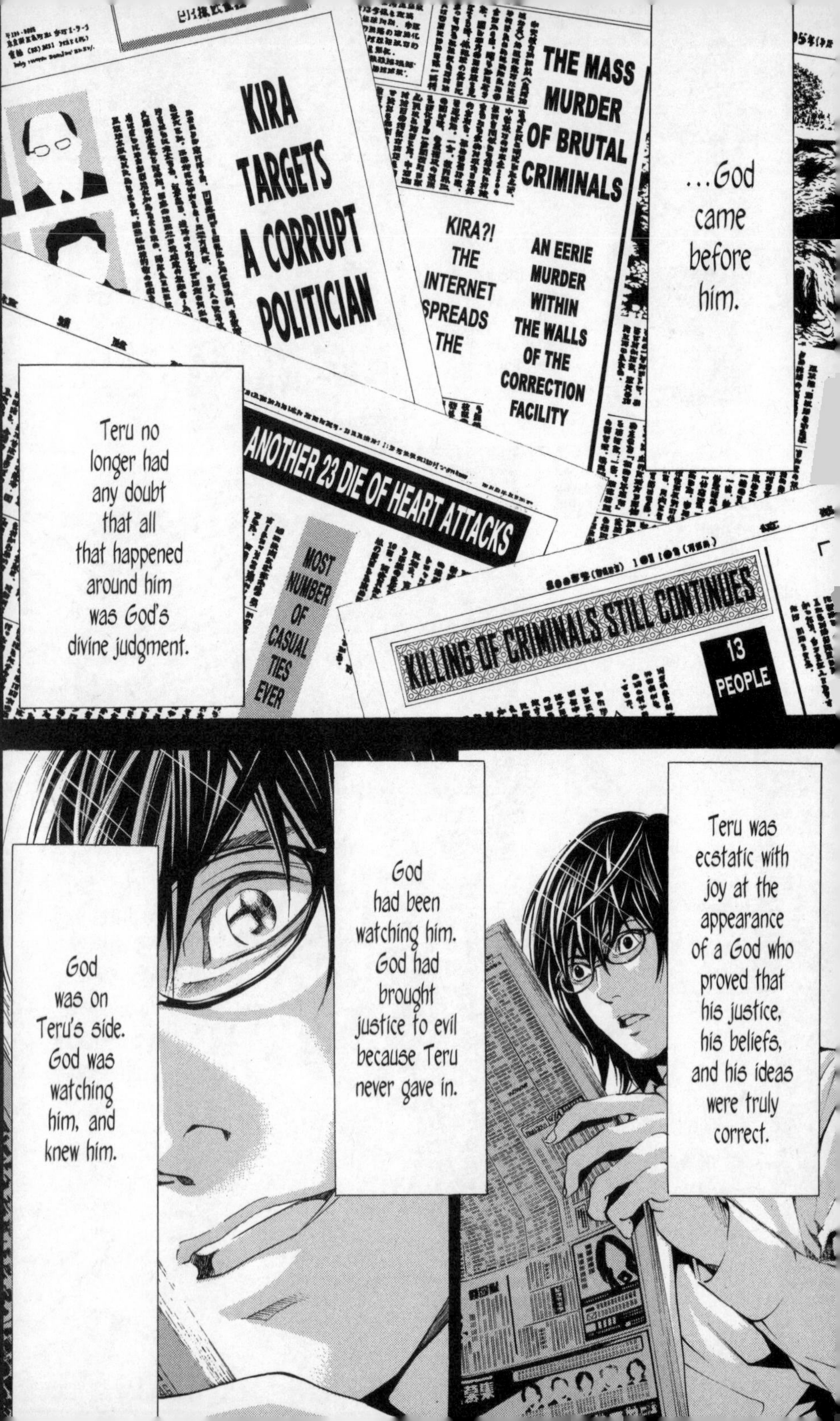
...God came before him.
THE MASS MURDER OF BRUTAL CRIMINALS
AN EERIE MURDER WITHIN THE WALLS OF THE CORRECTION FACILITY
KIRA?! THE INTERNET SPREADS THE
KIRA TARGETS A CORRUPT POLITICIAN
KILLING OF CRIMINALS STILL CONTINUES
13 PEOPLE
ANOTHER 23 DIE OF HEART ATTACKS
MOST NUMBER OF CASUAL TIES EVER
Teru no longer had any doubt that all that happened around him was God's divine judgment.
Teru was ecstatic with joy at the appearance of a God who proved that his justice, his beliefs, and his ideas were truly correct.
God had been watching him. God had brought justice to evil because Teru never gave in.
God was on Teru's side. God was watching him, and knew him.

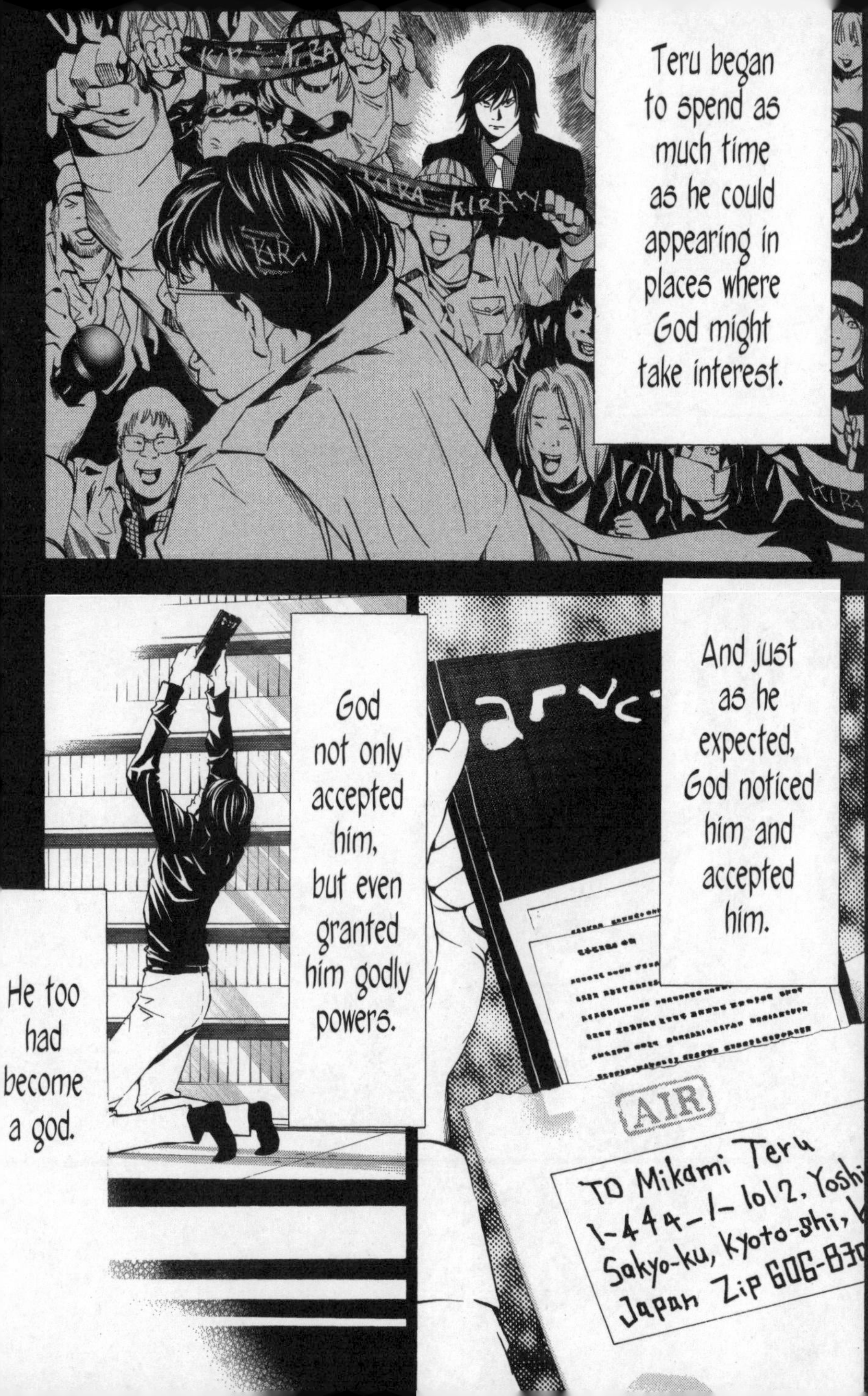
Teru began to spend as much time as he could appearing in places where God might take interest.
And just as he expected, God noticed him and accepted him.
AIR
TO Mikami Teru
1-444-1-1012. Yoshi
Sakyo-ku, Kyoto-shi,
Japan Zip 606-830
God not only accepted him, but even granted him godly powers.
He too had become a god.

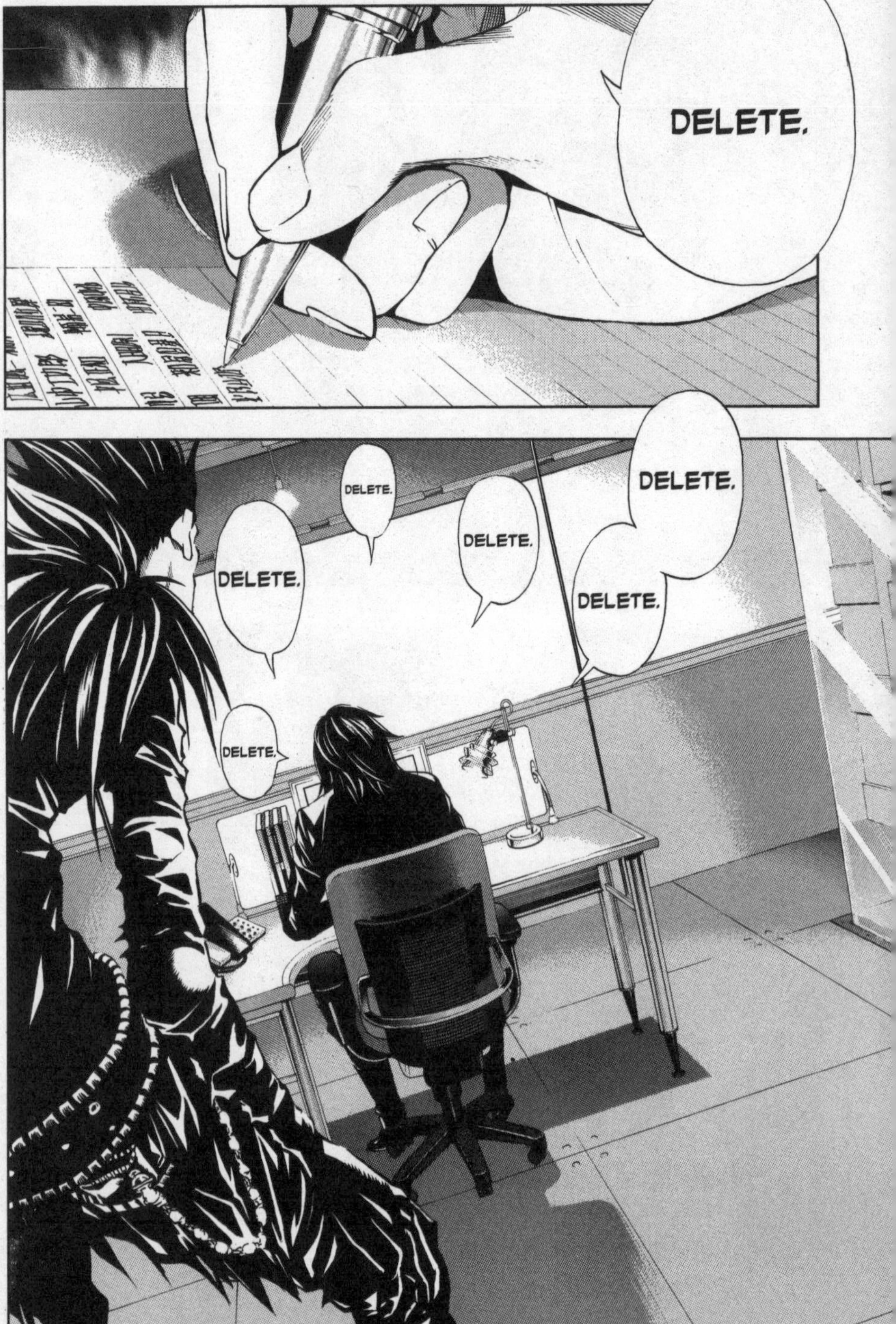
DELETE.
DELETE.
DELETE.
DELETE.
DELETE.
DELETE.
DELETE.

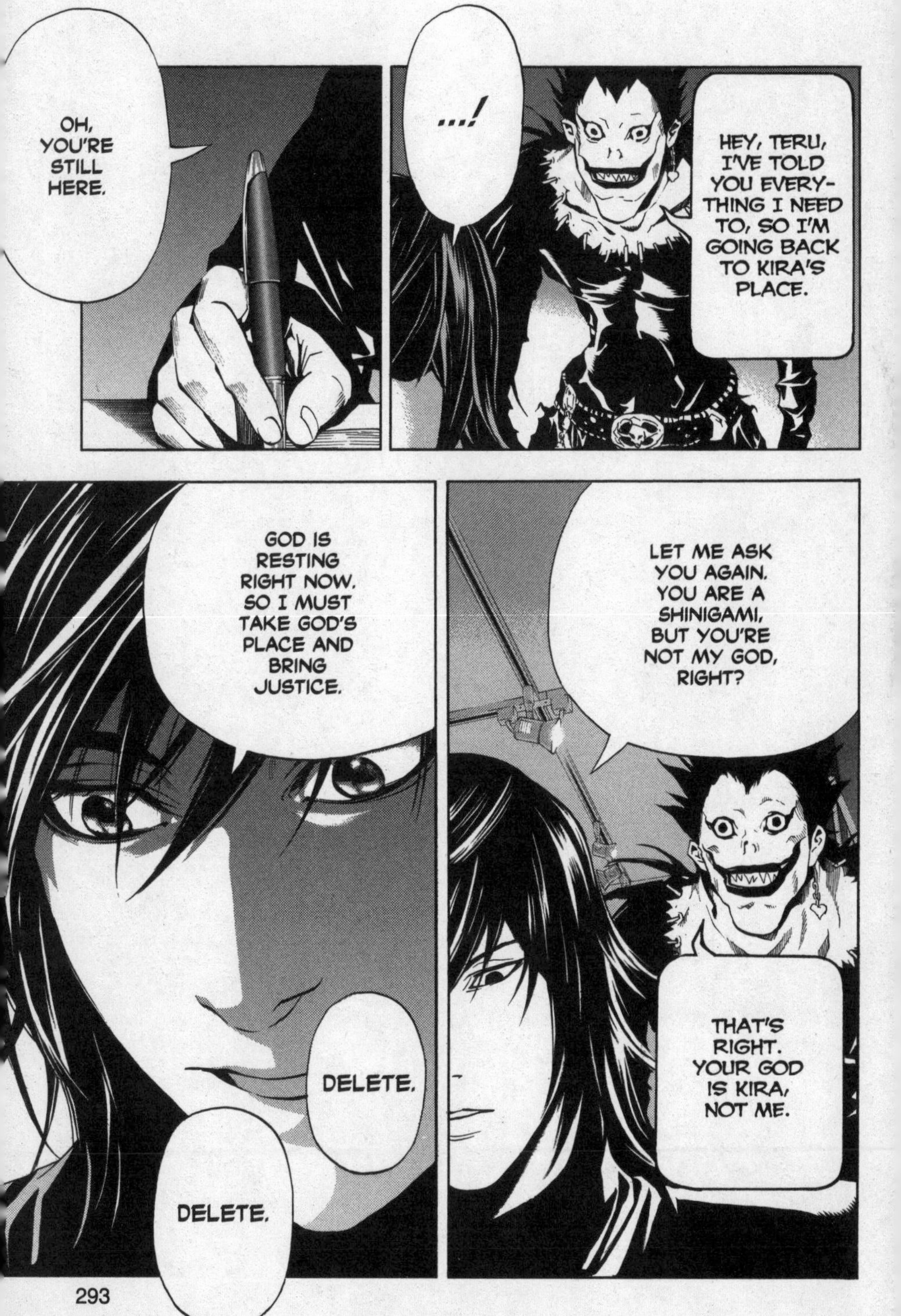
HEY, TERU, I'VE TOLD YOU EVERYTHING I NEED TO, SO I'M GOING BACK TO KIRA'S PLACE.
...!
OH, YOU'RE STILL HERE.
LET ME ASK YOU AGAIN. YOU ARE A SHINIGAMI, BUT YOU'RE NOT MY GOD, RIGHT?
THAT'S RIGHT. YOUR GOD IS KIRA, NOT ME.
GOD IS RESTING RIGHT NOW. SO I MUST TAKE GOD'S PLACE AND BRING JUSTICE.
DELETE.
DELETE.

DEATH NOTE
How to use it
Lvl

○ When you write multiple names in the DEATH NOTE and then write down even one cause of death within 40 human seconds from writing the first victim's name, the cause will take effect for all the written names.

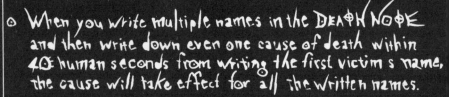

名前を複数記し、最初に名前を記した時から人間界単位で40秒以内に
あるひとつの死因を記すだけでも、それが書かれた名前全てに適用される。

○ Also, after writing the cause of death, even if the situation of death is written within 6 minutes and 40 seconds in the human world, that situation will only occur to the victims whom it is possible. For those where the situation is not possible, only the cause of death will occur.

また、死因を記した後、人間界単位で6分40秒以内に
あるひとつの死の状況を記した場合でも、
可能な者はその通りに、不可能な者は死因のみ適用される。

chapter 85 Election

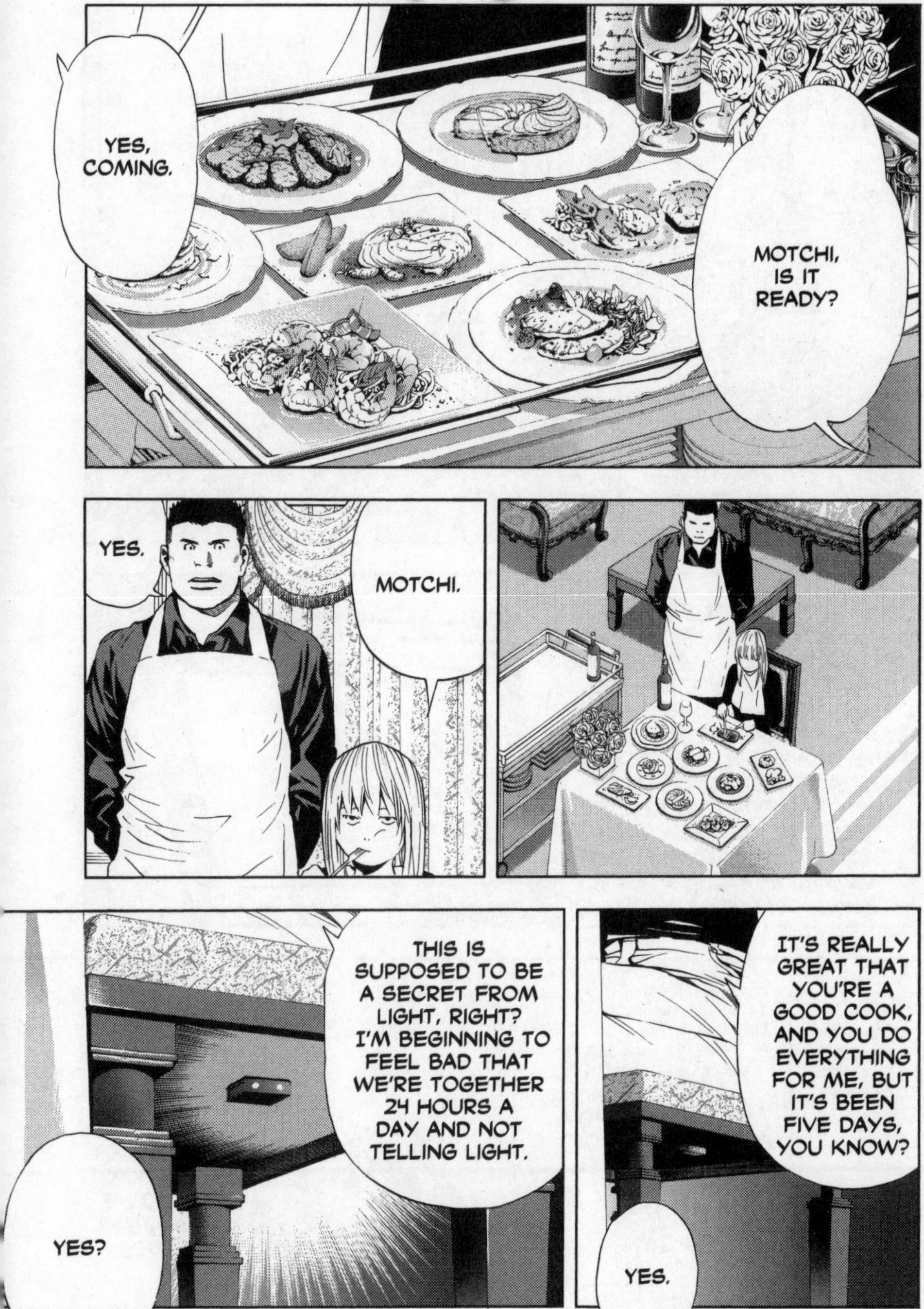
MOTCHI, IS IT READY?
YES, COMING.
MOTCHI.
YES.
IT'S REALLY GREAT THAT YOU'RE A GOOD COOK, AND YOU DO EVERYTHING FOR ME, BUT IT'S BEEN FIVE DAYS, YOU KNOW?
YES.
THIS IS SUPPOSED TO BE A SECRET FROM LIGHT, RIGHT? I'M BEGINNING TO FEEL BAD THAT WE'RE TOGETHER 24 HOURS A DAY AND NOT TELLING LIGHT.
YES?

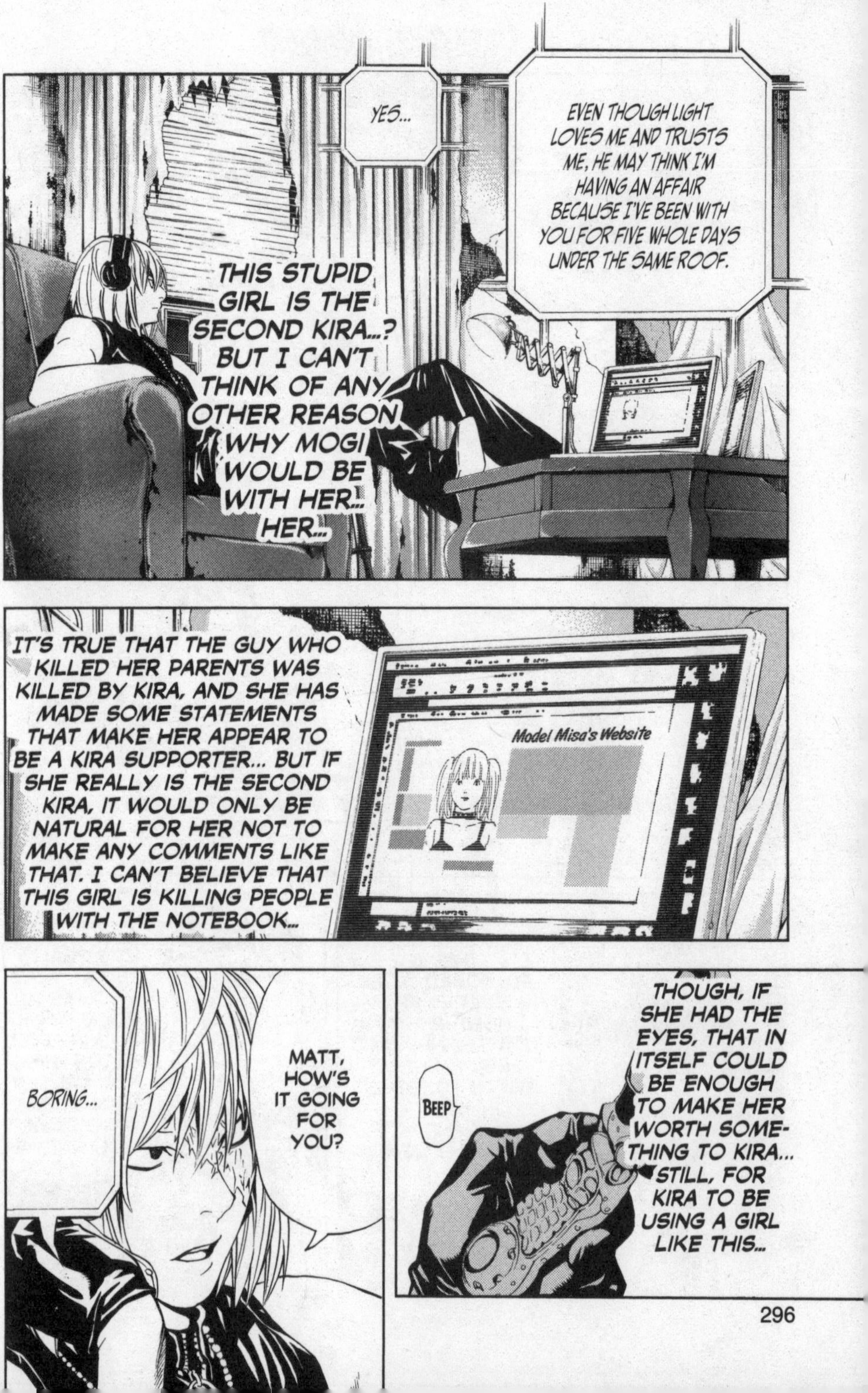

EVEN THOUGH LIGHT LOVES ME AND TRUSTS ME, HE MAY THINK I'M HAVING AN AFFAIR BECAUSE I'VE BEEN WITH YOU FOR FIVE WHOLE DAYS UNDER THE SAME ROOF.
YES...
THIS STUPID GIRL IS THE SECOND KIRA...? BUT I CAN'T THINK OF ANY OTHER REASON WHY MOGI WOULD BE WITH HER... HER...
IT'S TRUE THAT THE GUY WHO KILLED HER PARENTS WAS KILLED BY KIRA, AND SHE HAS MADE SOME STATEMENTS THAT MAKE HER APPEAR TO BE A KIRA SUPPORTER... BUT IF SHE REALLY IS THE SECOND KIRA, IT WOULD ONLY BE NATURAL FOR HER NOT TO MAKE ANY COMMENTS LIKE THAT. I CAN'T BELIEVE THAT THIS GIRL IS KILLING PEOPLE WITH THE NOTEBOOK...
Model Misa's Website
THOUGH, IF SHE HAD THE EYES, THAT IN ITSELF COULD BE ENOUGH TO MAKE HER WORTH SOME-THING TO KIRA... STILL, FOR KIRA TO BE USING A GIRL LIKE THIS...
BEEP
MATT, HOW'S IT GOING FOR YOU?
BORING...

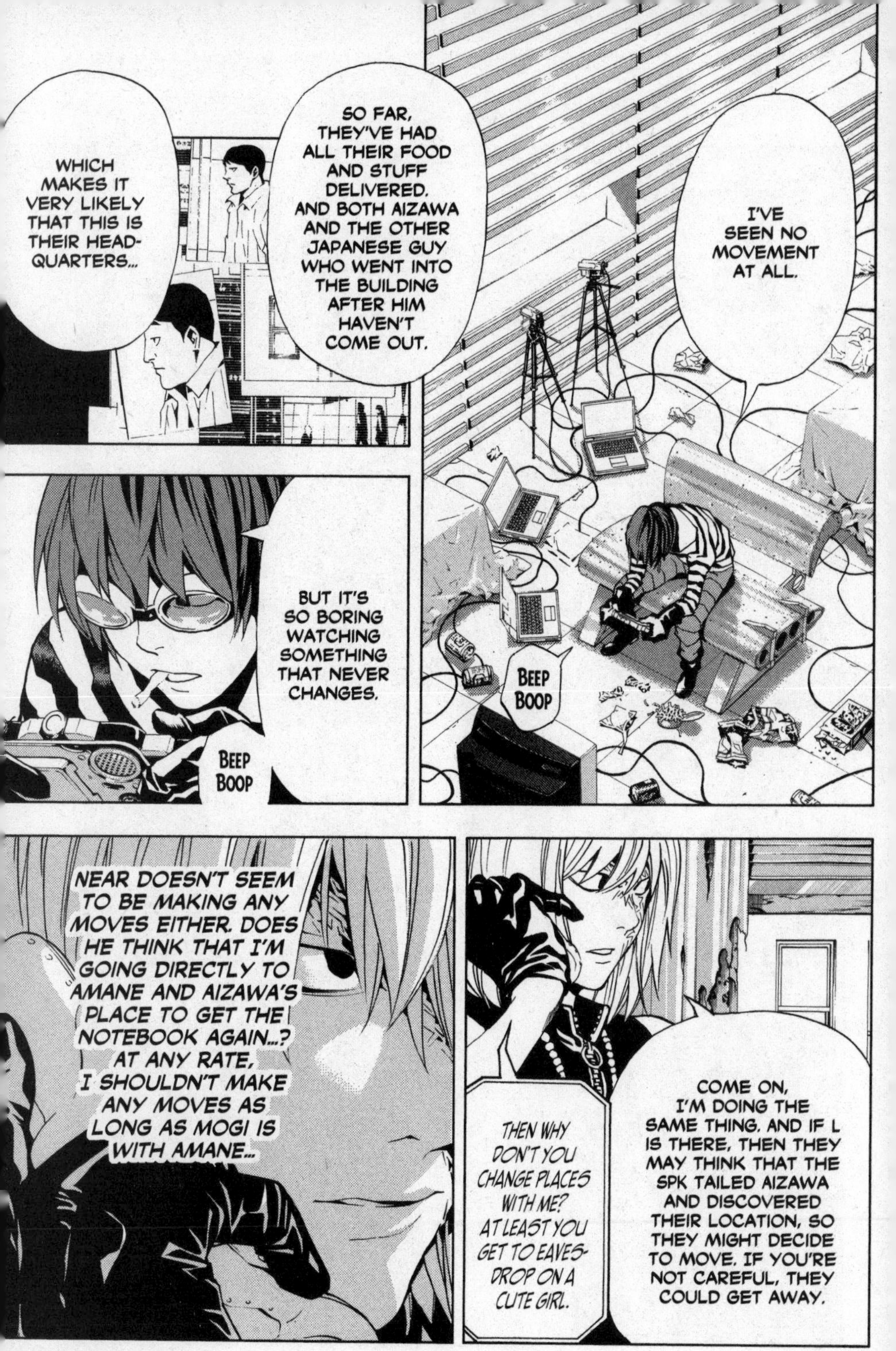
I'VE SEEN NO MOVEMENT AT ALL.
BEEP BOOP
SO FAR, THEY'VE HAD ALL THEIR FOOD AND STUFF DELIVERED. AND BOTH AIZAWA AND THE OTHER JAPANESE GUY WHO WENT INTO THE BUILDING AFTER HIM HAVEN'T COME OUT.
WHICH MAKES IT VERY LIKELY THAT THIS IS THEIR HEAD-QUARTERS...
BUT IT'S SO BORING WATCHING SOMETHING THAT NEVER CHANGES.
BEEP BOOP
COME ON, I'M DOING THE SAME THING. AND IF L IS THERE, THEN THEY MAY THINK THAT THE SPK TAILED AIZAWA AND DISCOVERED THEIR LOCATION, SO THEY MIGHT DECIDE TO MOVE. IF YOU'RE NOT CAREFUL, THEY COULD GET AWAY.
THEN WHY DON'T YOU CHANGE PLACES WITH ME? AT LEAST YOU GET TO EAVES-DROP ON A CUTE GIRL.
NEAR DOESN'T SEEM TO BE MAKING ANY MOVES EITHER. DOES HE THINK THAT I'M GOING DIRECTLY TO AMANE AND AIZAWA'S PLACE TO GET THE NOTEBOOK AGAIN...? AT ANY RATE, I SHOULDN'T MAKE ANY MOVES AS LONG AS MOGI IS WITH AMANE...

chapter 85 Election

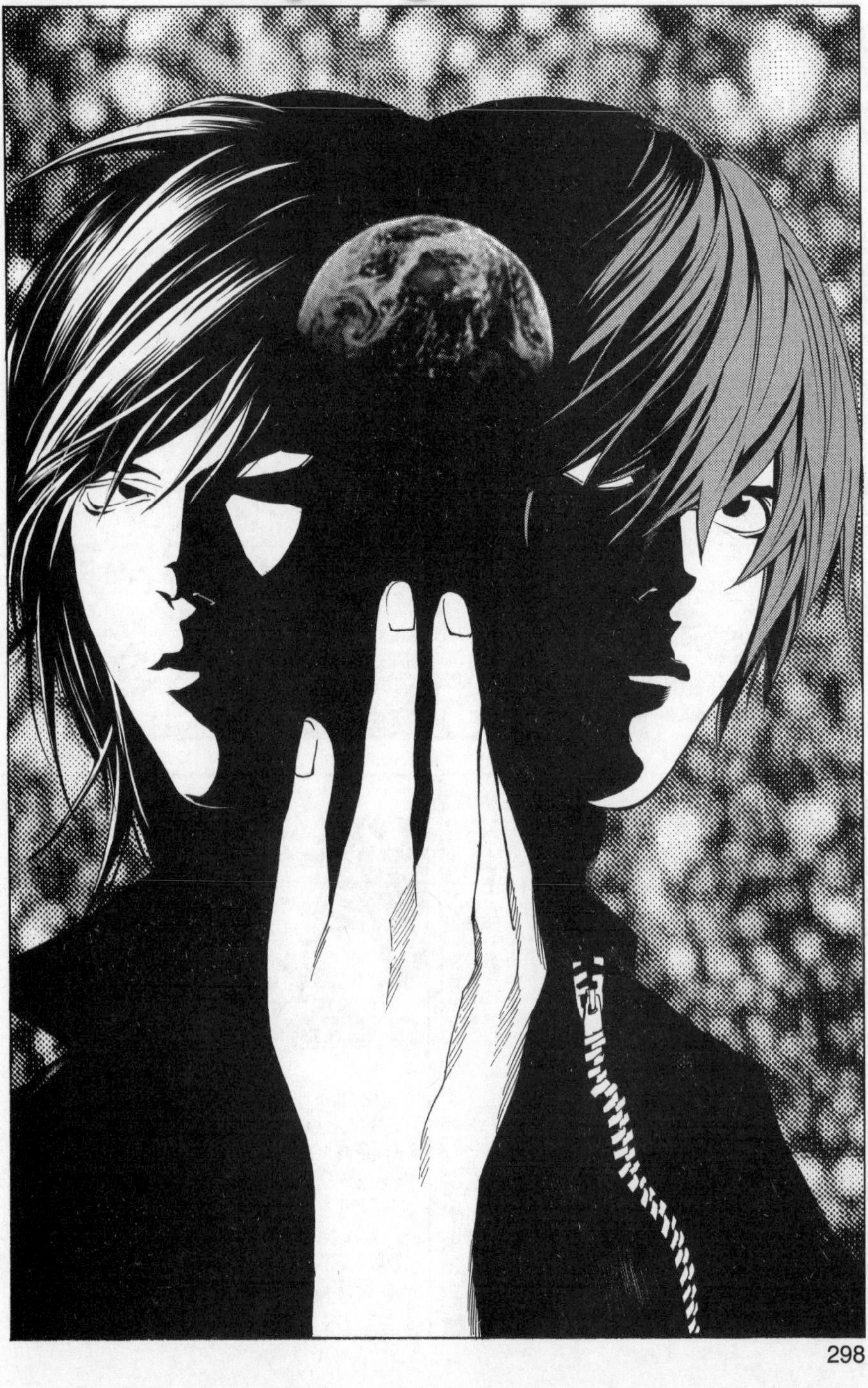

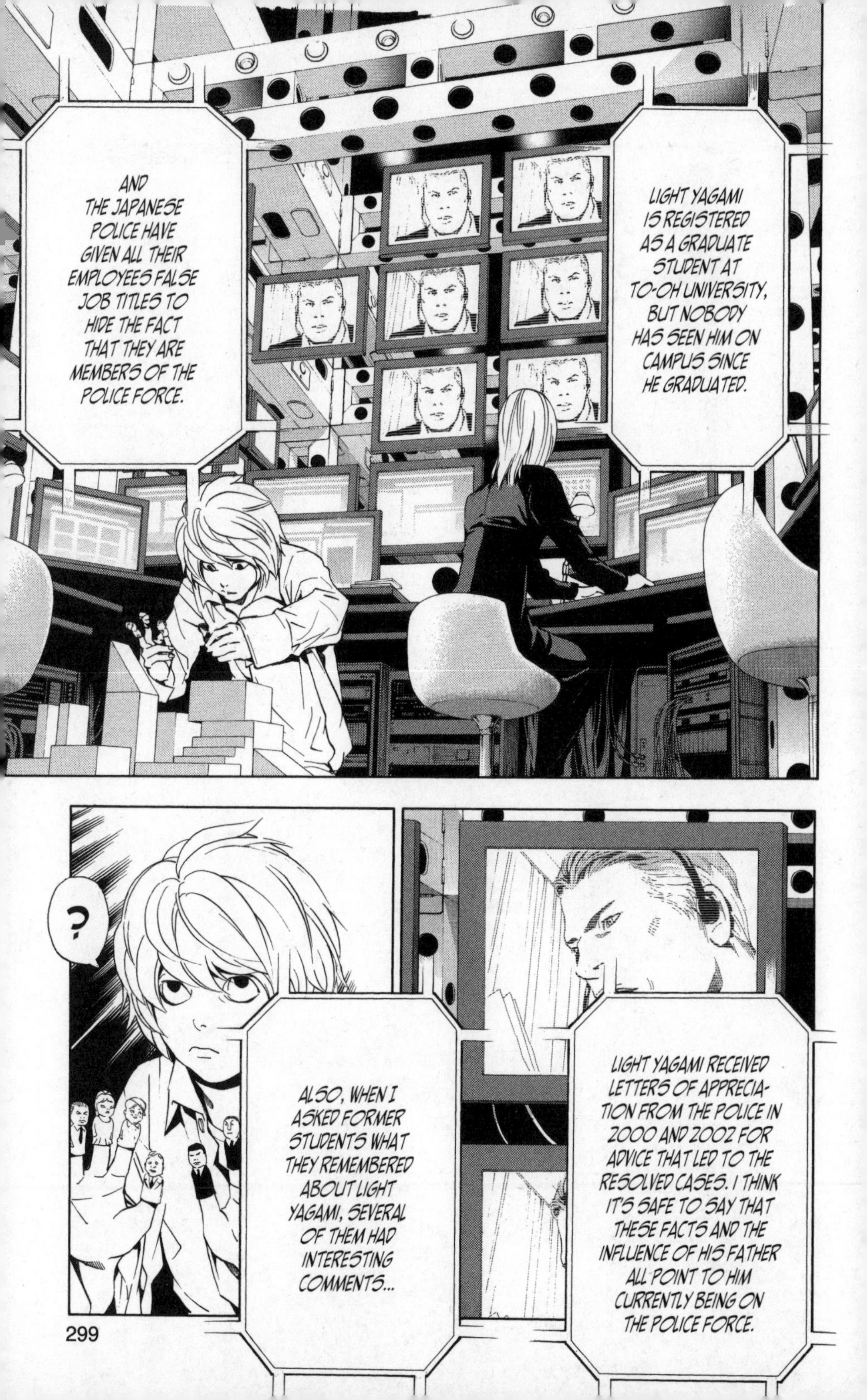
LIGHT YAGAMI IS REGISTERED AS A GRADUATE STUDENT AT TO-OH UNIVERSITY, BUT NOBODY HAS SEEN HIM ON CAMPUS SINCE HE GRADUATED.
AND THE JAPANESE POLICE HAVE GIVEN ALL THEIR EMPLOYEES FALSE JOB TITLES TO HIDE THE FACT THAT THEY ARE MEMBERS OF THE POLICE FORCE.
LIGHT YAGAMI RECEIVED LETTERS OF APPRECIA-TION FROM THE POLICE IN 2000 AND 2002 FOR ADVICE THAT LED TO THE RESOLVED CASES. I THINK IT'S SAFE TO SAY THAT THESE FACTS AND THE INFLUENCE OF HIS FATHER ALL POINT TO HIM CURRENTLY BEING ON THE POLICE FORCE.
?
ALSO, WHEN I ASKED FORMER STUDENTS WHAT THEY REMEMBERED ABOUT LIGHT YAGAMI, SEVERAL OF THEM HAD INTERESTING COMMENTS...

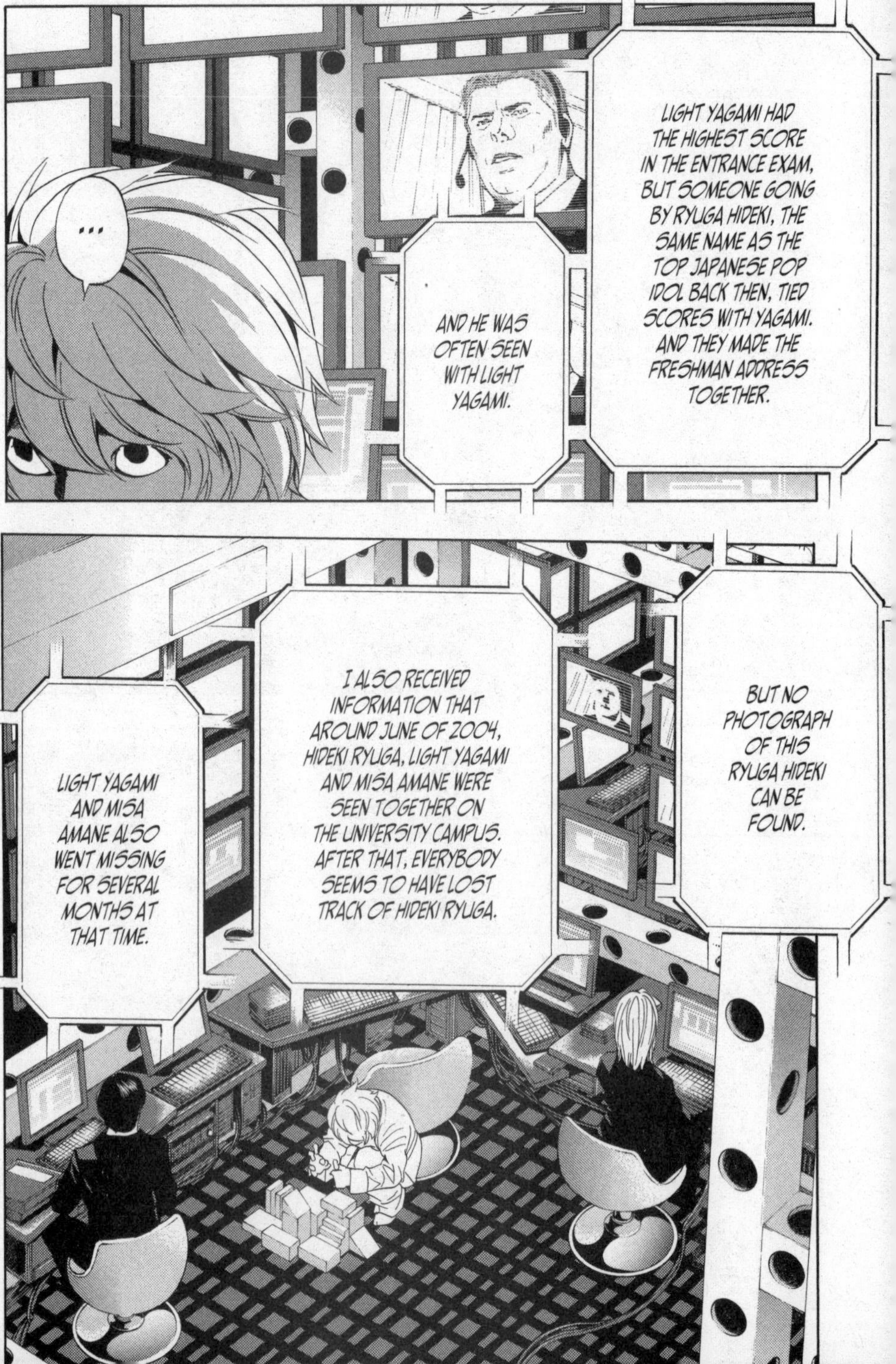
LIGHT YAGAMI HAD THE HIGHEST SCORE IN THE ENTRANCE EXAM, BUT SOMEONE GOING BY RYUGA HIDEKI, THE SAME NAME AS THE TOP JAPANESE POP IDOL BACK THEN, TIED SCORES WITH YAGAMI. AND THEY MADE THE FRESHMAN ADDRESS TOGETHER.
AND HE WAS OFTEN SEEN WITH LIGHT YAGAMI.
...
BUT NO PHOTOGRAPH OF THIS RYUGA HIDEKI CAN BE FOUND.
I ALSO RECEIVED INFORMATION THAT AROUND JUNE OF 2004, HIDEKI RYUGA, LIGHT YAGAMI AND MISA AMANE WERE SEEN TOGETHER ON THE UNIVERSITY CAMPUS. AFTER THAT, EVERYBODY SEEMS TO HAVE LOST TRACK OF HIDEKI RYUGA.
LIGHT YAGAMI AND MISA AMANE ALSO WENT MISSING FOR SEVERAL MONTHS AT THAT TIME.

READ THIS WAY

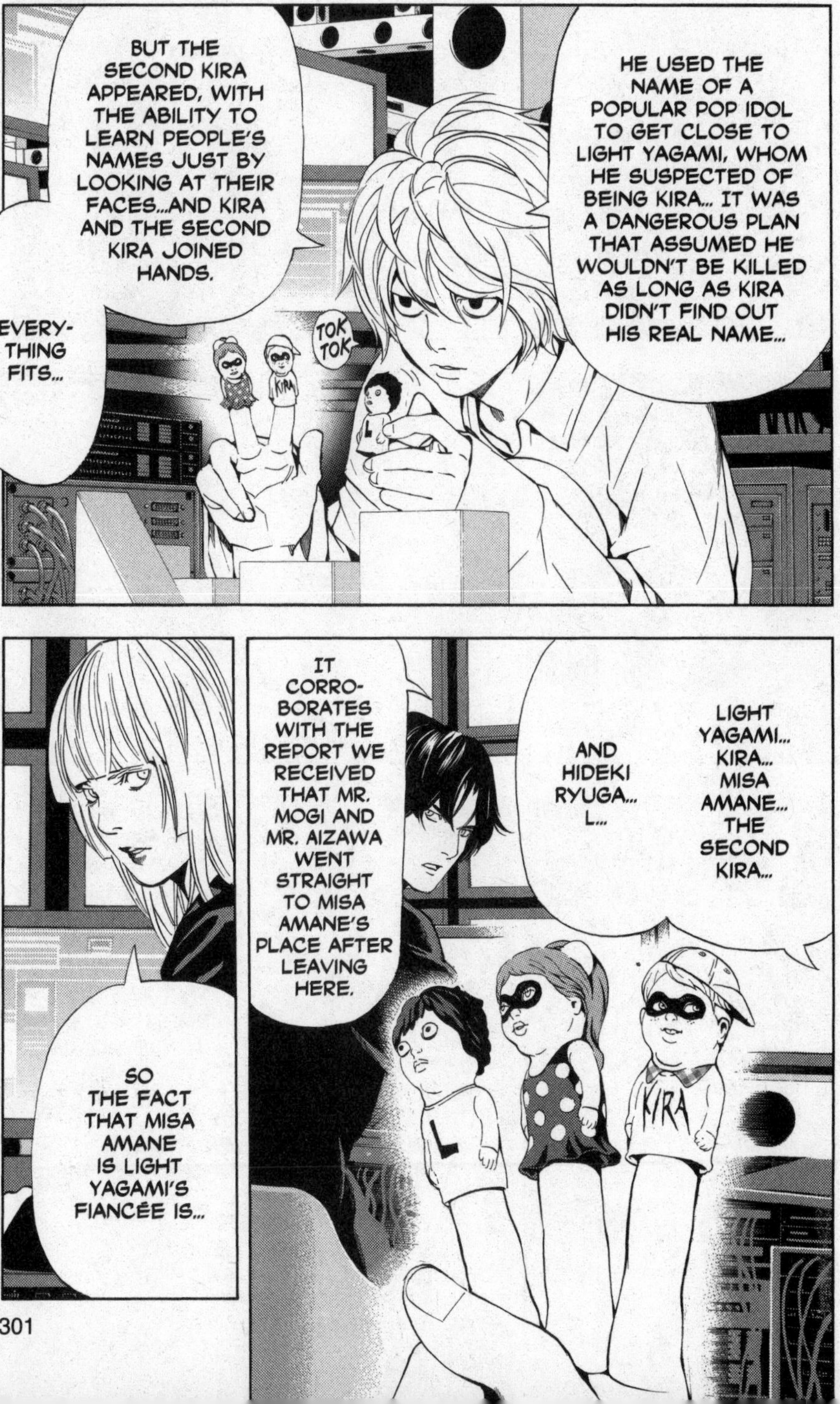

HE USED THE NAME OF A POPULAR POP IDOL TO GET CLOSE TO LIGHT YAGAMI, WHOM HE SUSPECTED OF BEING KIRA... IT WAS A DANGEROUS PLAN THAT ASSUMED HE WOULDN'T BE KILLED AS LONG AS KIRA DIDN'T FIND OUT HIS REAL NAME...
BUT THE SECOND KIRA APPEARED, WITH THE ABILITY TO LEARN PEOPLE'S NAMES JUST BY LOOKING AT THEIR FACES...AND KIRA AND THE SECOND KIRA JOINED HANDS.
TOK TOK
KIRA
L
EVERY-THING FITS...
LIGHT YAGAMI... KIRA... MISA AMANE... THE SECOND KIRA...
AND HIDEKI RYUGA... L...
IT CORRO-BORATES WITH THE REPORT WE RECEIVED THAT MR. MOGI AND MR. AIZAWA WENT STRAIGHT TO MISA AMANE'S PLACE AFTER LEAVING HERE.
KIRA
L
SO THE FACT THAT MISA AMANE IS LIGHT YAGAMI'S FIANCÉE IS...

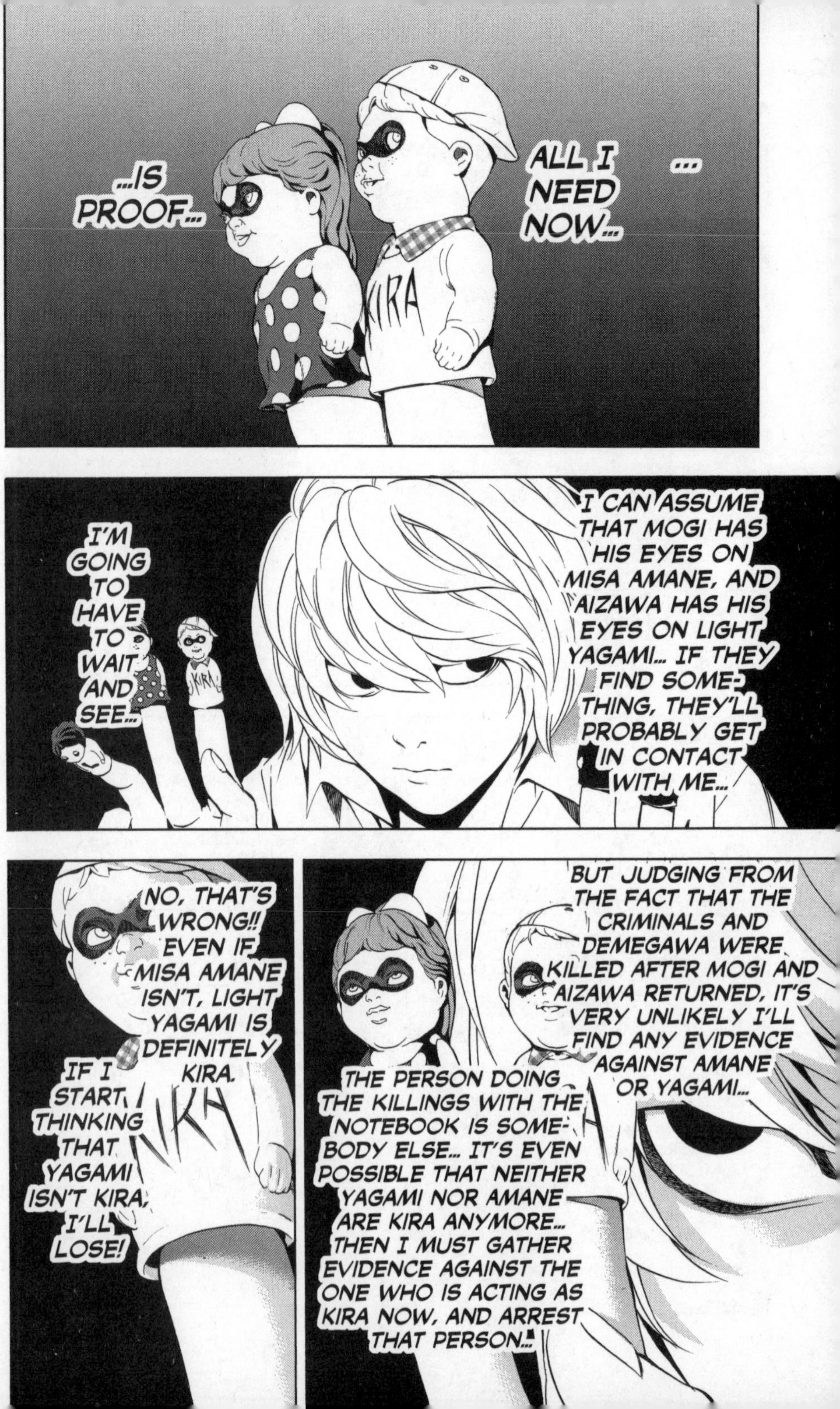
...
ALL I NEED NOW...
...IS PROOF...
I CAN ASSUME THAT MOGI HAS HIS EYES ON MISA AMANE, AND AIZAWA HAS HIS EYES ON LIGHT YAGAMI... IF THEY FIND SOMETHING, THEY'LL PROBABLY GET IN CONTACT WITH ME...
I'M GOING TO HAVE TO WAIT AND SEE...
BUT JUDGING FROM THE FACT THAT THE CRIMINALS AND DEMEGAWA WERE KILLED AFTER MOGI AND AIZAWA RETURNED, IT'S VERY UNLIKELY I'LL FIND ANY EVIDENCE AGAINST AMANE OR YAGAMI...
THE PERSON DOING THE KILLINGS WITH THE NOTEBOOK IS SOMEBODY ELSE... IT'S EVEN POSSIBLE THAT NEITHER YAGAMI NOR AMANE ARE KIRA ANYMORE... THEN I MUST GATHER EVIDENCE AGAINST THE ONE WHO IS ACTING AS KIRA NOW, AND ARREST THAT PERSON...!
NO, THAT'S WRONG!! EVEN IF MISA AMANE ISN'T, LIGHT YAGAMI IS DEFINITELY KIRA.
IF I START THINKING THAT YAGAMI ISN'T KIRA, I'LL LOSE!

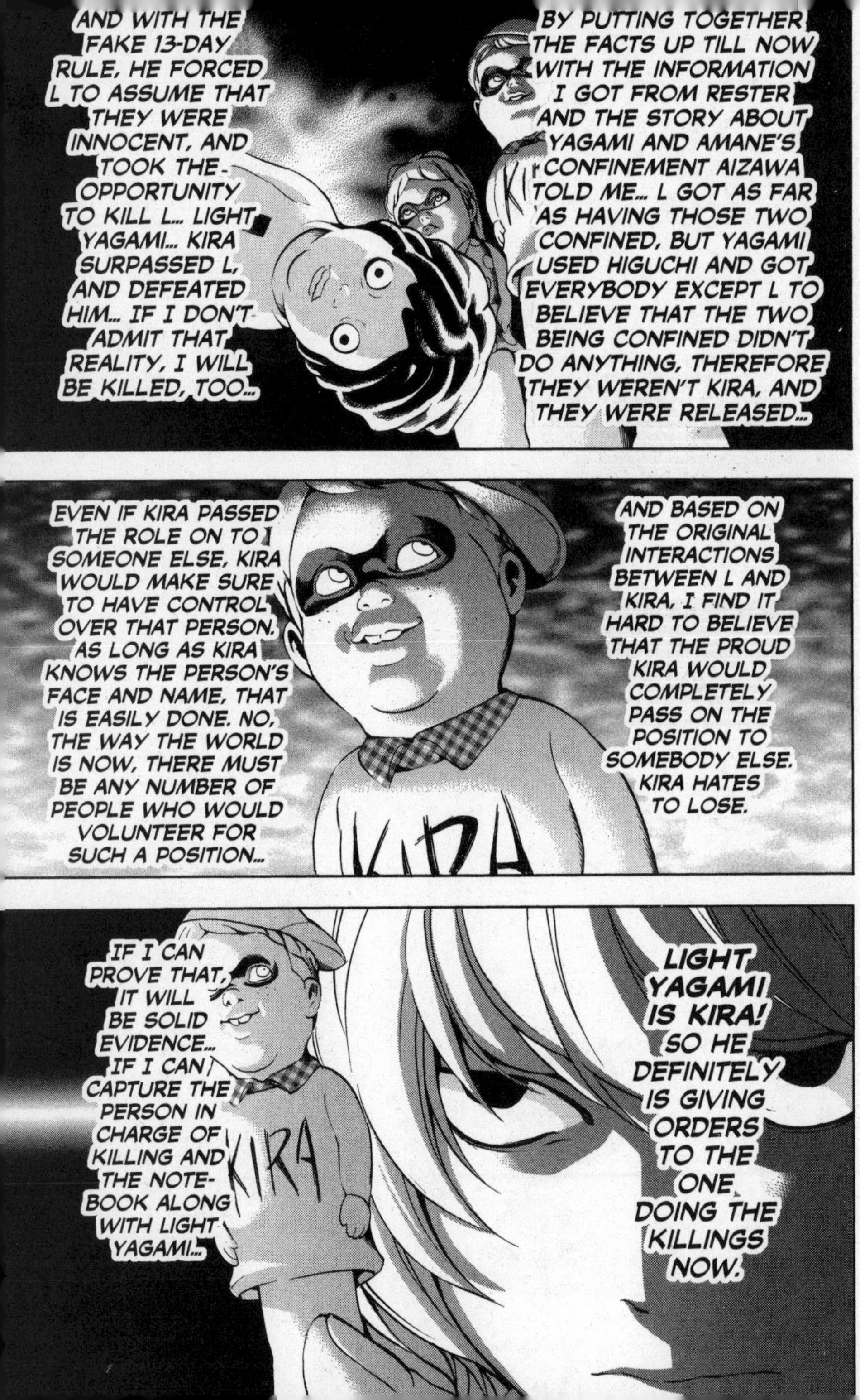
BY PUTTING TOGETHER THE FACTS UP TILL NOW WITH THE INFORMATION I GOT FROM RESTER AND THE STORY ABOUT YAGAMI AND AMANE'S CONFINEMENT AIZAWA TOLD ME... L GOT AS FAR AS HAVING THOSE TWO CONFINED, BUT YAGAMI USED HIGUCHI AND GOT EVERYBODY EXCEPT L TO BELIEVE THAT THE TWO BEING CONFINED DIDN'T DO ANYTHING, THEREFORE THEY WEREN'T KIRA, AND THEY WERE RELEASED...
AND WITH THE FAKE 13-DAY RULE, HE FORCED L TO ASSUME THAT THEY WERE INNOCENT, AND TOOK THE OPPORTUNITY TO KILL L... LIGHT YAGAMI... KIRA SURPASSED L, AND DEFEATED HIM... IF I DON'T ADMIT THAT REALITY, I WILL BE KILLED, TOO...
AND BASED ON THE ORIGINAL INTERACTIONS BETWEEN L AND KIRA, I FIND IT HARD TO BELIEVE THAT THE PROUD KIRA WOULD COMPLETELY PASS ON THE POSITION TO SOMEBODY ELSE. KIRA HATES TO LOSE.
EVEN IF KIRA PASSED THE ROLE ON TO SOMEONE ELSE, KIRA WOULD MAKE SURE TO HAVE CONTROL OVER THAT PERSON. AS LONG AS KIRA KNOWS THE PERSON'S FACE AND NAME, THAT IS EASILY DONE. NO, THE WAY THE WORLD IS NOW, THERE MUST BE ANY NUMBER OF PEOPLE WHO WOULD VOLUNTEER FOR SUCH A POSITION...
KIRA
LIGHT YAGAMI IS KIRA! SO HE DEFINITELY IS GIVING ORDERS TO THE ONE DOING THE KILLINGS NOW.
IF I CAN PROVE THAT, IT WILL BE SOLID EVIDENCE... IF I CAN CAPTURE THE PERSON IN CHARGE OF KILLING AND THE NOTEBOOK ALONG WITH LIGHT YAGAMI...
KIRA

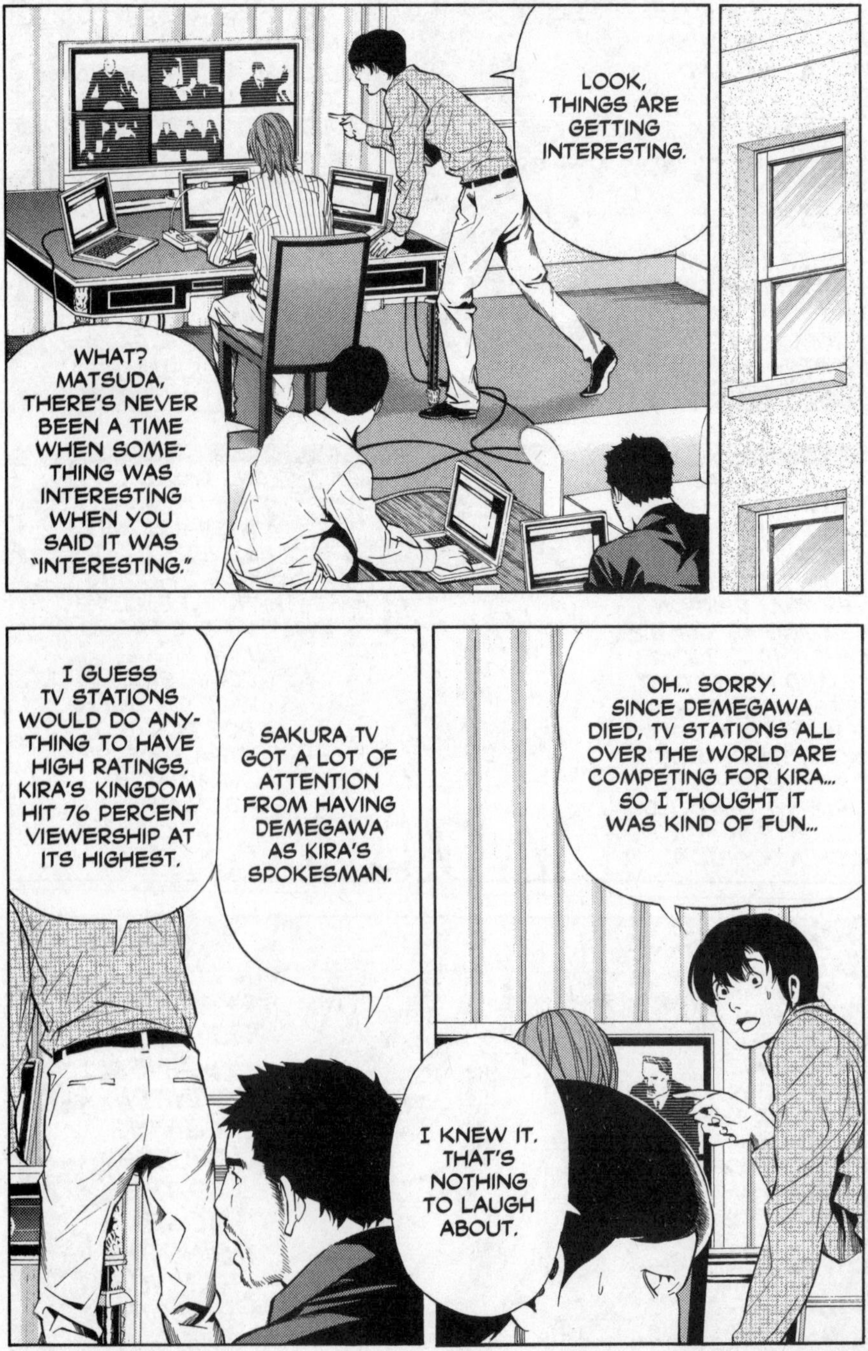
LOOK, THINGS ARE GETTING INTERESTING.
WHAT? MATSUDA, THERE'S NEVER BEEN A TIME WHEN SOME-THING WAS INTERESTING WHEN YOU SAID IT WAS "INTERESTING."
OH... SORRY. SINCE DEMEGAWA DIED, TV STATIONS ALL OVER THE WORLD ARE COMPETING FOR KIRA... SO I THOUGHT IT WAS KIND OF FUN...
I KNEW IT. THAT'S NOTHING TO LAUGH ABOUT.
SAKURA TV GOT A LOT OF ATTENTION FROM HAVING DEMEGAWA AS KIRA'S SPOKESMAN.
I GUESS TV STATIONS WOULD DO ANY-THING TO HAVE HIGH RATINGS. KIRA'S KINGDOM HIT 76 PERCENT VIEWERSHIP AT ITS HIGHEST.

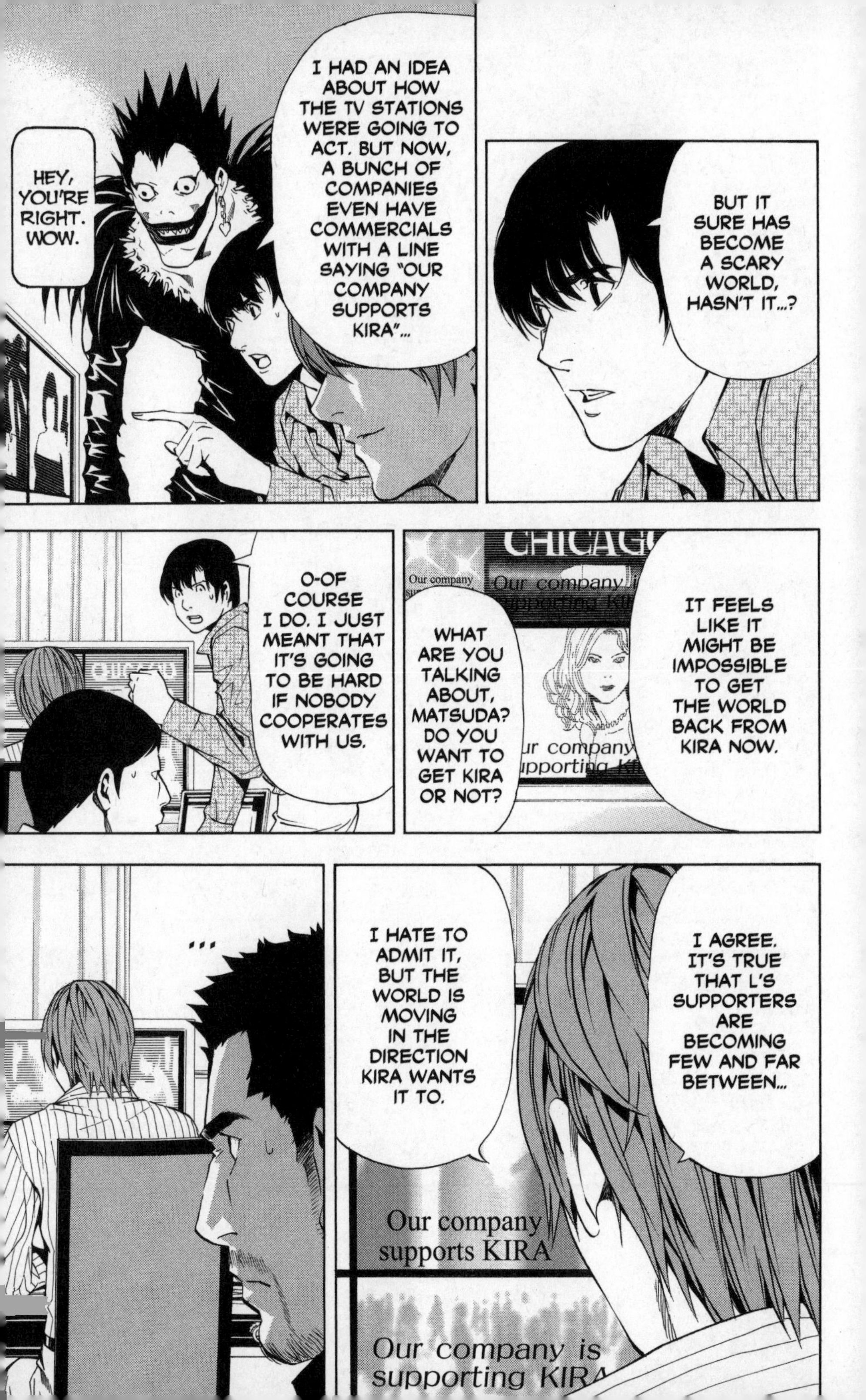

BUT IT SURE HAS BECOME A SCARY WORLD, HASN'T IT...?
I HAD AN IDEA ABOUT HOW THE TV STATIONS WERE GOING TO ACT. BUT NOW, A BUNCH OF COMPANIES EVEN HAVE COMMERCIALS WITH A LINE SAYING "OUR COMPANY SUPPORTS KIRA"...
HEY, YOU'RE RIGHT. WOW.
IT FEELS LIKE IT MIGHT BE IMPOSSIBLE TO GET THE WORLD BACK FROM KIRA NOW.
WHAT ARE YOU TALKING ABOUT, MATSUDA? DO YOU WANT TO GET KIRA OR NOT?
O-OF COURSE I DO. I JUST MEANT THAT IT'S GOING TO BE HARD IF NOBODY COOPERATES WITH US.
I AGREE. IT'S TRUE THAT L'S SUPPORTERS ARE BECOMING FEW AND FAR BETWEEN...
I HATE TO ADMIT IT, BUT THE WORLD IS MOVING IN THE DIRECTION KIRA WANTS IT TO.
Our company supports KIRA
...

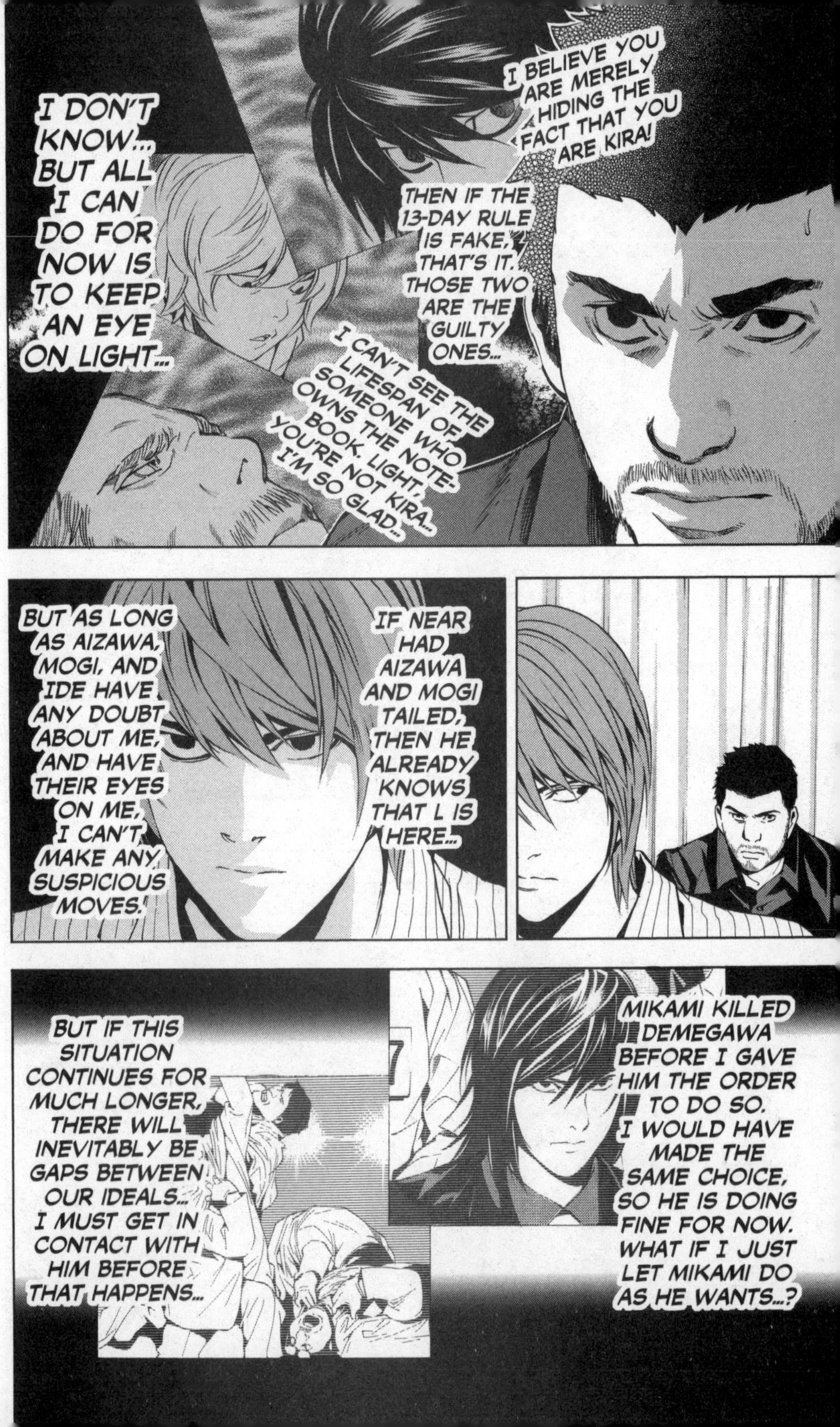
I BELIEVE YOU ARE MERELY HIDING THE FACT THAT YOU ARE KIRA!
THEN IF THE 13-DAY RULE IS FAKE, THAT'S IT. THOSE TWO ARE THE GUILTY ONES...
I CAN'T SEE THE LIFESPAN OF SOMEONE WHO OWNS THE NOTE-BOOK. LIGHT, YOU'RE NOT KIRA... I'M SO GLAD...
I DON'T KNOW... BUT ALL I CAN DO FOR NOW IS TO KEEP AN EYE ON LIGHT...
IF NEAR HAD AIZAWA AND MOGI TAILED, THEN HE ALREADY KNOWS THAT L IS HERE...
BUT AS LONG AS AIZAWA, MOGI, AND IDE HAVE ANY DOUBT ABOUT ME, AND HAVE THEIR EYES ON ME, I CAN'T MAKE ANY SUSPICIOUS MOVES.
MIKAMI KILLED DEMEGAWA BEFORE I GAVE HIM THE ORDER TO DO SO. I WOULD HAVE MADE THE SAME CHOICE, SO HE IS DOING FINE FOR NOW. WHAT IF I JUST LET MIKAMI DO AS HE WANTS...?
BUT IF THIS SITUATION CONTINUES FOR MUCH LONGER, THERE WILL INEVITABLY BE GAPS BETWEEN OUR IDEALS... I MUST GET IN CONTACT WITH HIM BEFORE THAT HAPPENS...

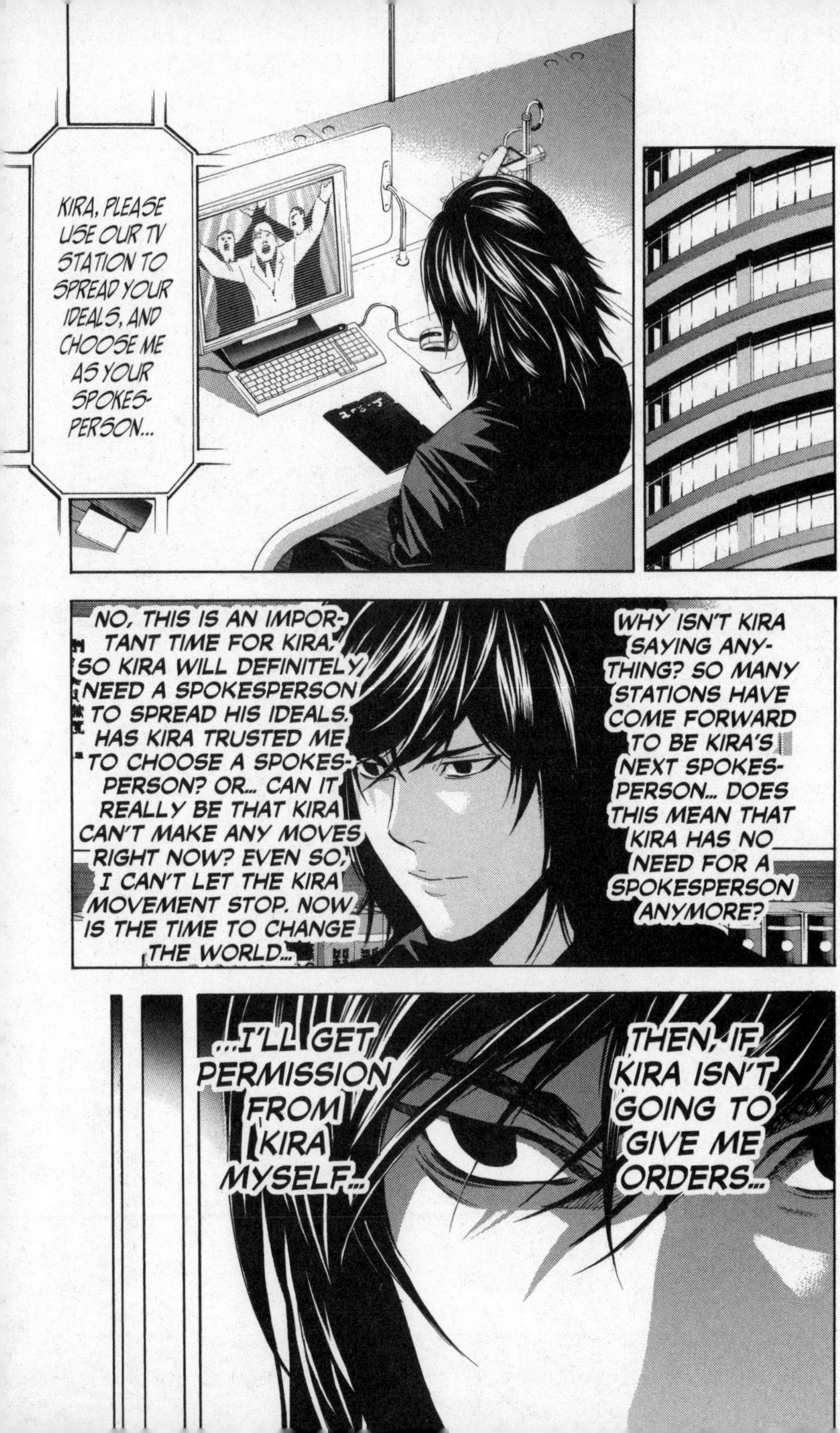
KIRA, PLEASE USE OUR TV STATION TO SPREAD YOUR IDEALS, AND CHOOSE ME AS YOUR SPOKES-PERSON...
WHY ISN'T KIRA SAYING ANY-THING? SO MANY STATIONS HAVE COME FORWARD TO BE KIRA'S NEXT SPOKES-PERSON... DOES THIS MEAN THAT KIRA HAS NO NEED FOR A SPOKESPERSON ANYMORE?
NO, THIS IS AN IMPOR-TANT TIME FOR KIRA, SO KIRA WILL DEFINITELY NEED A SPOKESPERSON TO SPREAD HIS IDEALS. HAS KIRA TRUSTED ME TO CHOOSE A SPOKES-PERSON? OR... CAN IT REALLY BE THAT KIRA CAN'T MAKE ANY MOVES RIGHT NOW? EVEN SO, I CAN'T LET THE KIRA MOVEMENT STOP. NOW IS THE TIME TO CHANGE THE WORLD...
THEN, IF KIRA ISN'T GOING TO GIVE ME ORDERS...
...I'LL GET PERMISSION FROM KIRA MYSELF...

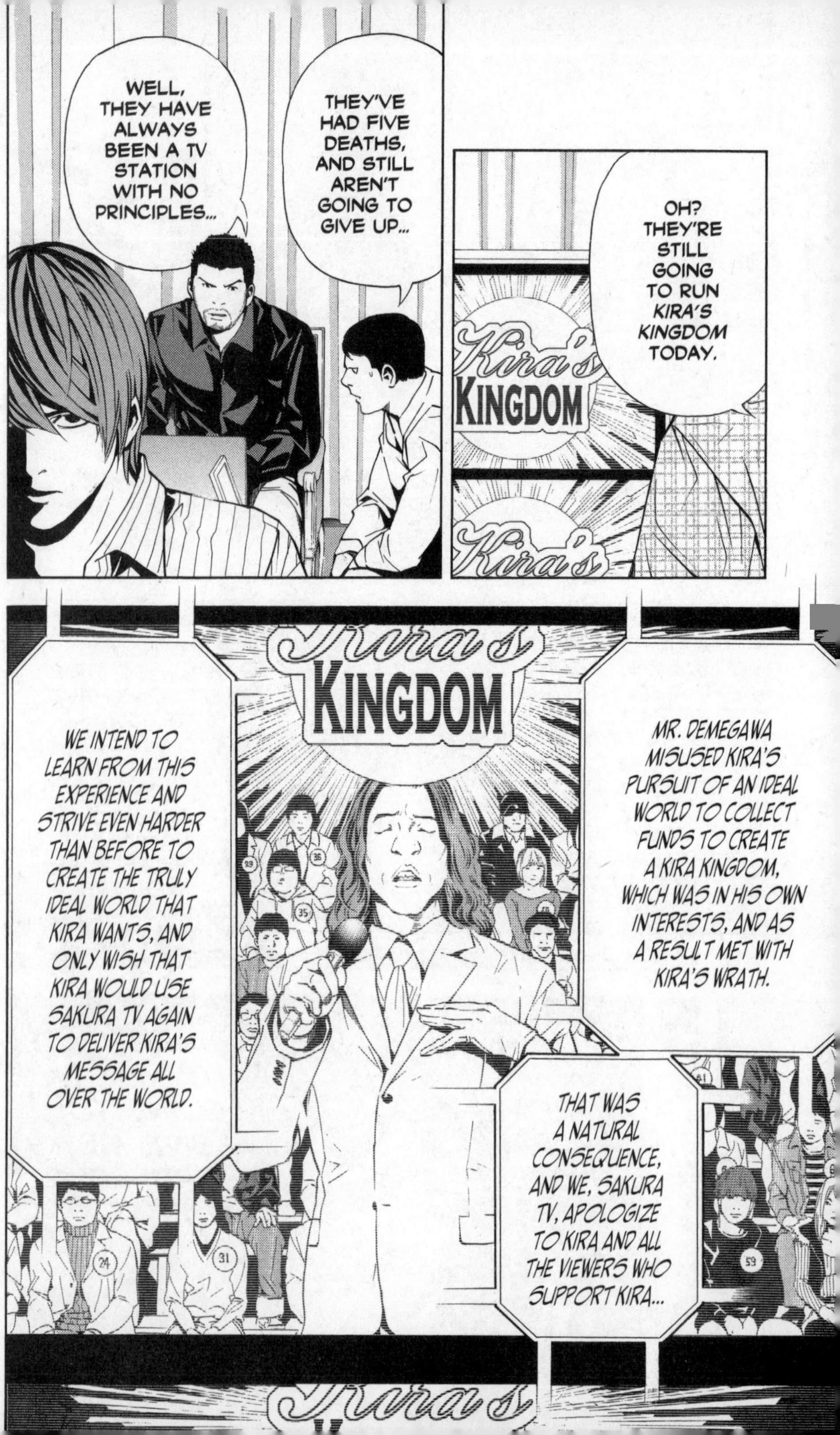
OH? THEY'RE STILL GOING TO RUN KIRA'S KINGDOM TODAY.
Kira's KINGDOM
THEY'VE HAD FIVE DEATHS, AND STILL AREN'T GOING TO GIVE UP...
WELL, THEY HAVE ALWAYS BEEN A TV STATION WITH NO PRINCIPLES...
KINGDOM
MR. DEMEGAWA MISUSED KIRA'S PURSUIT OF AN IDEAL WORLD TO COLLECT FUNDS TO CREATE A KIRA KINGDOM, WHICH WAS IN HIS OWN INTERESTS, AND AS A RESULT MET WITH KIRA'S WRATH.
THAT WAS A NATURAL CONSEQUENCE, AND WE, SAKURA TV, APOLOGIZE TO KIRA AND ALL THE VIEWERS WHO SUPPORT KIRA...
WE INTEND TO LEARN FROM THIS EXPERIENCE AND STRIVE EVEN HARDER THAN BEFORE TO CREATE THE TRULY IDEAL WORLD THAT KIRA WANTS, AND ONLY WISH THAT KIRA WOULD USE SAKURA TV AGAIN TO DELIVER KIRA'S MESSAGE ALL OVER THE WORLD.

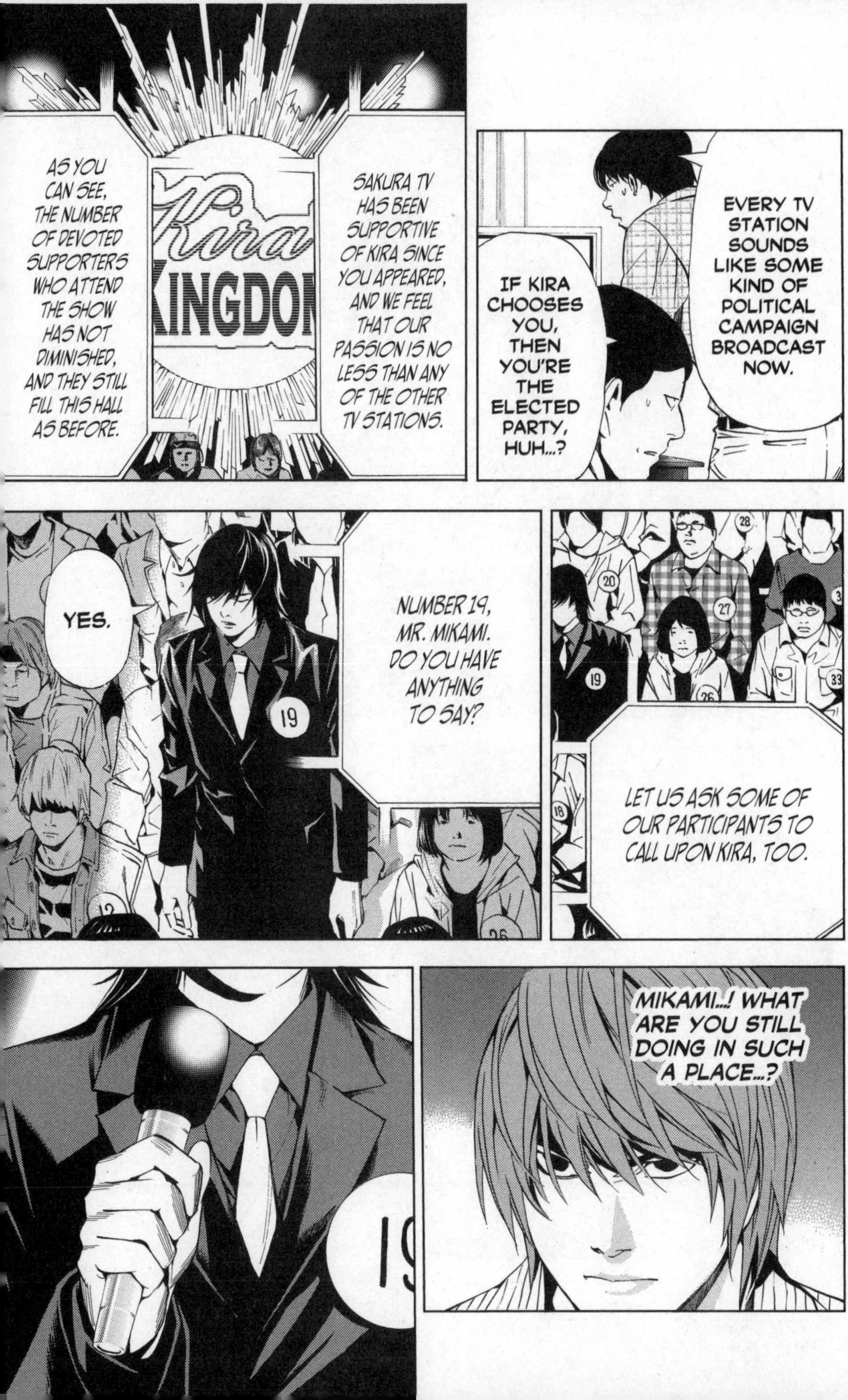
EVERY TV STATION SOUNDS LIKE SOME KIND OF POLITICAL CAMPAIGN BROADCAST NOW.
IF KIRA CHOOSES YOU, THEN YOU'RE THE ELECTED PARTY, HUH...?
SAKURA TV HAS BEEN SUPPORTIVE OF KIRA SINCE YOU APPEARED, AND WE FEEL THAT OUR PASSION IS NO LESS THAN ANY OF THE OTHER TV STATIONS.
AS YOU CAN SEE, THE NUMBER OF DEVOTED SUPPORTERS WHO ATTEND THE SHOW HAS NOT DIMINISHED, AND THEY STILL FILL THIS HALL AS BEFORE.
LET US ASK SOME OF OUR PARTICIPANTS TO CALL UPON KIRA, TOO.
NUMBER 19, MR. MIKAMI. DO YOU HAVE ANYTHING TO SAY?
YES.
MIKAMI...! WHAT ARE YOU STILL DOING IN SUCH A PLACE...?

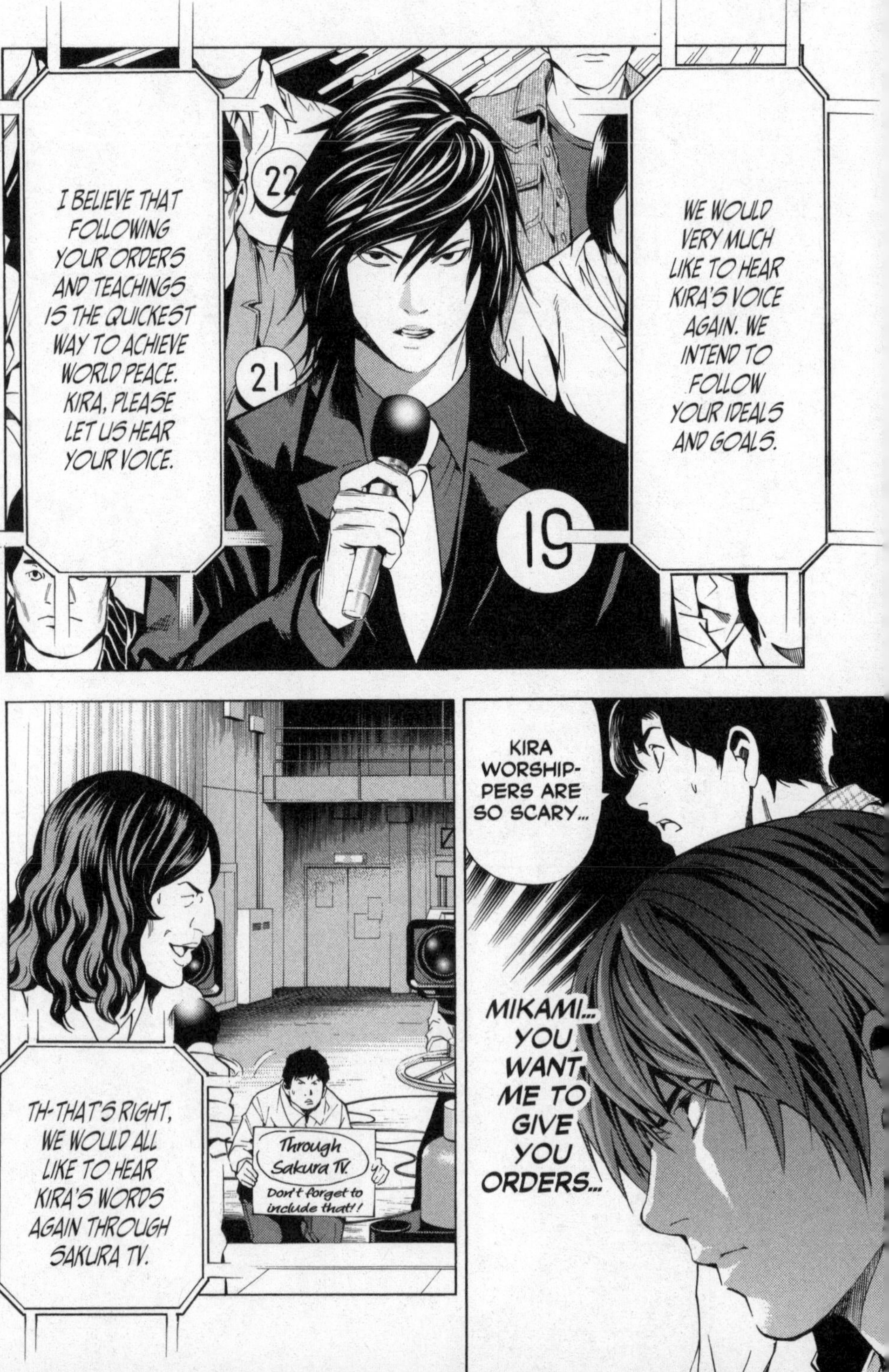
22
WE WOULD VERY MUCH LIKE TO HEAR KIRA'S VOICE AGAIN. WE INTEND TO FOLLOW YOUR IDEALS AND GOALS.
19
I BELIEVE THAT FOLLOWING YOUR ORDERS AND TEACHINGS IS THE QUICKEST WAY TO ACHIEVE WORLD PEACE. KIRA, PLEASE LET US HEAR YOUR VOICE.
21
KIRA WORSHIPPERS ARE SO SCARY...
MIKAMI... YOU WANT ME TO GIVE YOU ORDERS...
Through Sakura TV.
Don't forget to include that!!
TH-THAT'S RIGHT, WE WOULD ALL LIKE TO HEAR KIRA'S WORDS AGAIN THROUGH SAKURA TV.

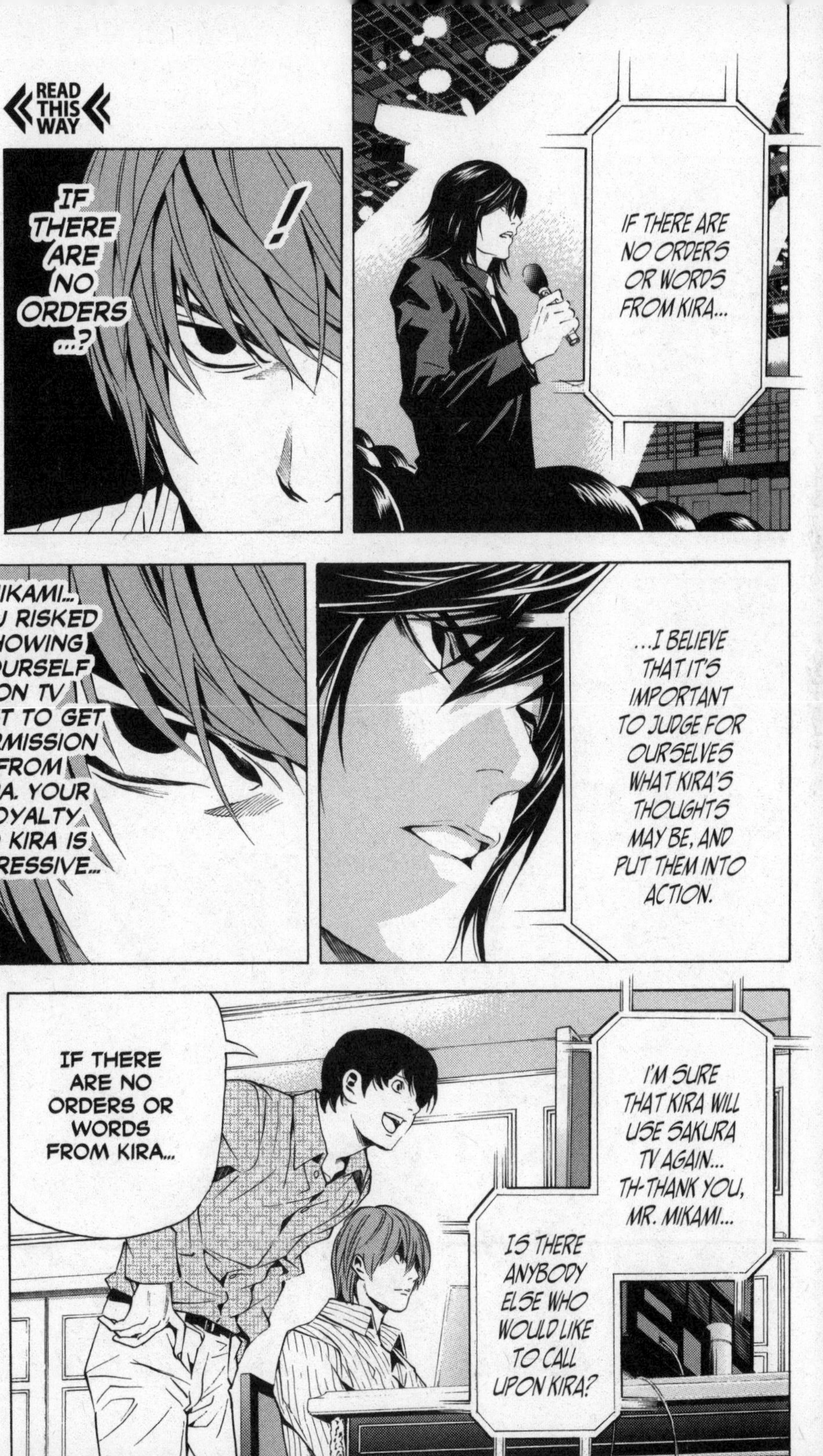
READ THIS WAY
IF THERE ARE NO ORDERS OR WORDS FROM KIRA...
!
IF THERE ARE NO ORDERS ...?
...I BELIEVE THAT IT'S IMPORTANT TO JUDGE FOR OURSELVES WHAT KIRA'S THOUGHTS MAY BE, AND PUT THEM INTO ACTION.
MIKAMI... YOU RISKED SHOWING YOURSELF ON TV JUST TO GET PERMISSION FROM KIRA. YOUR LOYALTY TO KIRA IS IMPRESSIVE...
I'M SURE THAT KIRA WILL USE SAKURA TV AGAIN... TH-THANK YOU, MR. MIKAMI...
IS THERE ANYBODY ELSE WHO WOULD LIKE TO CALL UPON KIRA?
IF THERE ARE NO ORDERS OR WORDS FROM KIRA...

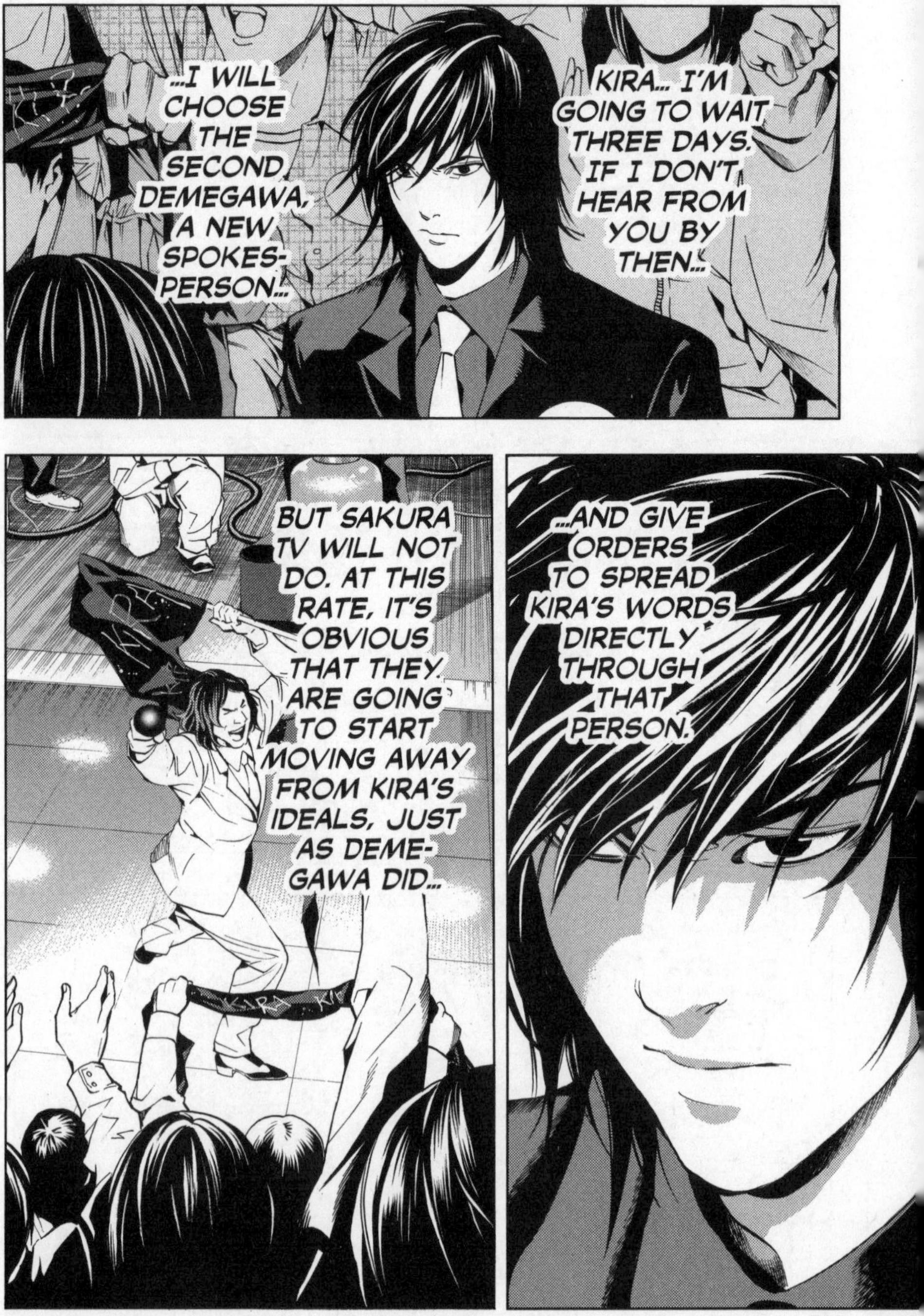
KIRA... I'M GOING TO WAIT THREE DAYS. IF I DON'T HEAR FROM YOU BY THEN...
...I WILL CHOOSE THE SECOND DEMEGAWA, A NEW SPOKES-PERSON...
...AND GIVE ORDERS TO SPREAD KIRA'S WORDS DIRECTLY THROUGH THAT PERSON.
BUT SAKURA TV WILL NOT DO. AT THIS RATE, IT'S OBVIOUS THAT THEY ARE GOING TO START MOVING AWAY FROM KIRA'S IDEALS, JUST AS DEME-GAWA DID...

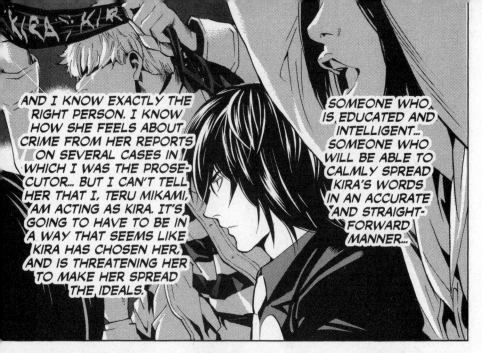

SOMEONE WHO IS EDUCATED AND INTELLIGENT... SOMEONE WHO WILL BE ABLE TO CALMLY SPREAD KIRA'S WORDS IN AN ACCURATE AND STRAIGHT-FORWARD MANNER...

AND I KNOW EXACTLY THE RIGHT PERSON. I KNOW HOW SHE FEELS ABOUT CRIME FROM HER REPORTS ON SEVERAL CASES IN WHICH I WAS THE PROSE-CUTOR... BUT I CAN'T TELL HER THAT I, TERU MIKAMI, AM ACTING AS KIRA. IT'S GOING TO HAVE TO BE IN A WAY THAT SEEMS LIKE KIRA HAS CHOSEN HER, AND IS THREATENING HER TO MAKE HER SPREAD THE IDEALS.

HURRAY FOR KIRA! HURRAY FOR KIRA!

KIRA COME BACK! KIRA COME BACK!

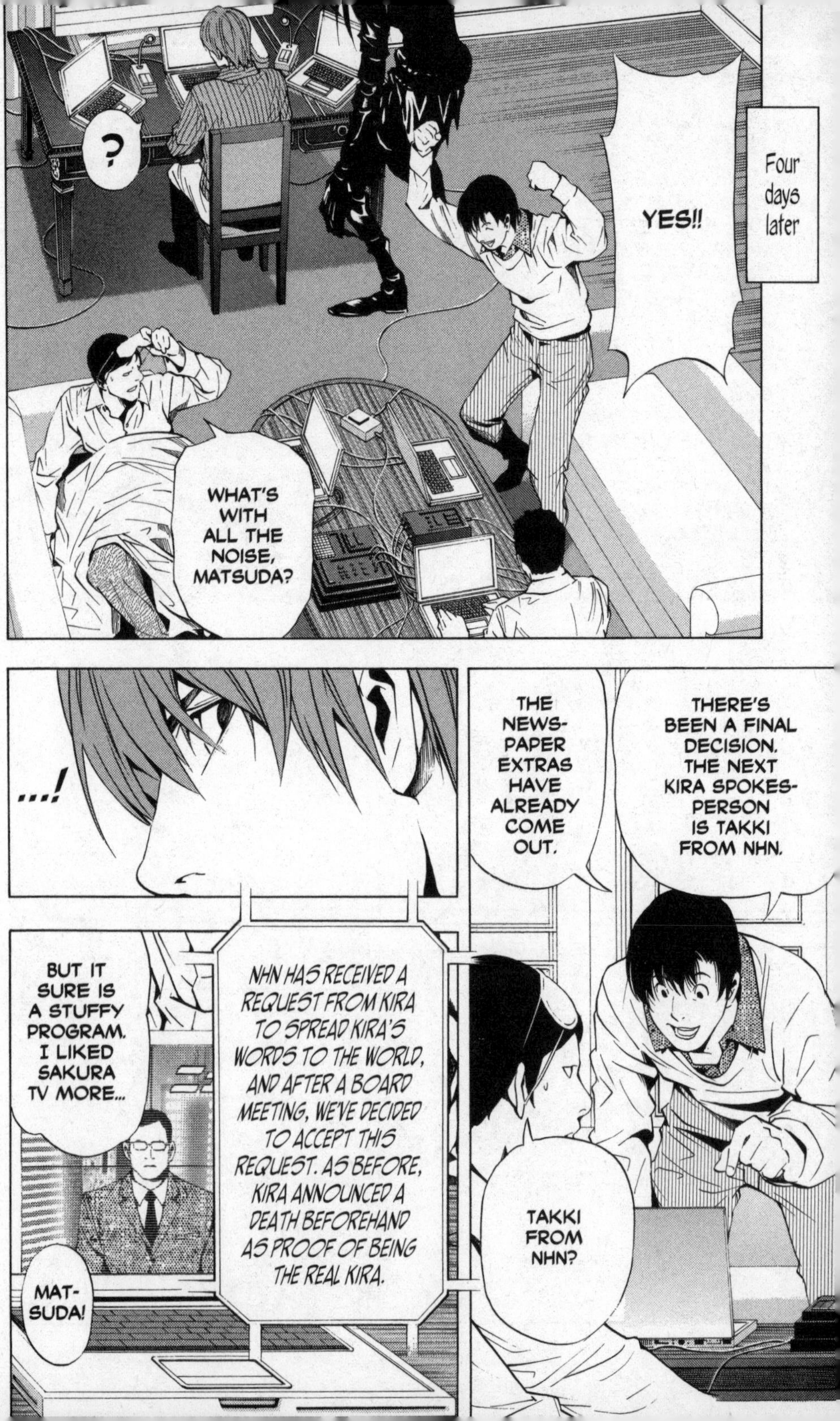
Four days later
YES!!
?
WHAT'S WITH ALL THE NOISE, MATSUDA?
THERE'S BEEN A FINAL DECISION. THE NEXT KIRA SPOKES-PERSON IS TAKKI FROM NHN.
THE NEWS-PAPER EXTRAS HAVE ALREADY COME OUT.
TAKKI FROM NHN?
...!
NHN HAS RECEIVED A REQUEST FROM KIRA TO SPREAD KIRA'S WORDS TO THE WORLD, AND AFTER A BOARD MEETING, WE'VE DECIDED TO ACCEPT THIS REQUEST. AS BEFORE, KIRA ANNOUNCED A DEATH BEFOREHAND AS PROOF OF BEING THE REAL KIRA.
BUT IT SURE IS A STUFFY PROGRAM. I LIKED SAKURA TV MORE...
MAT-SUDA!

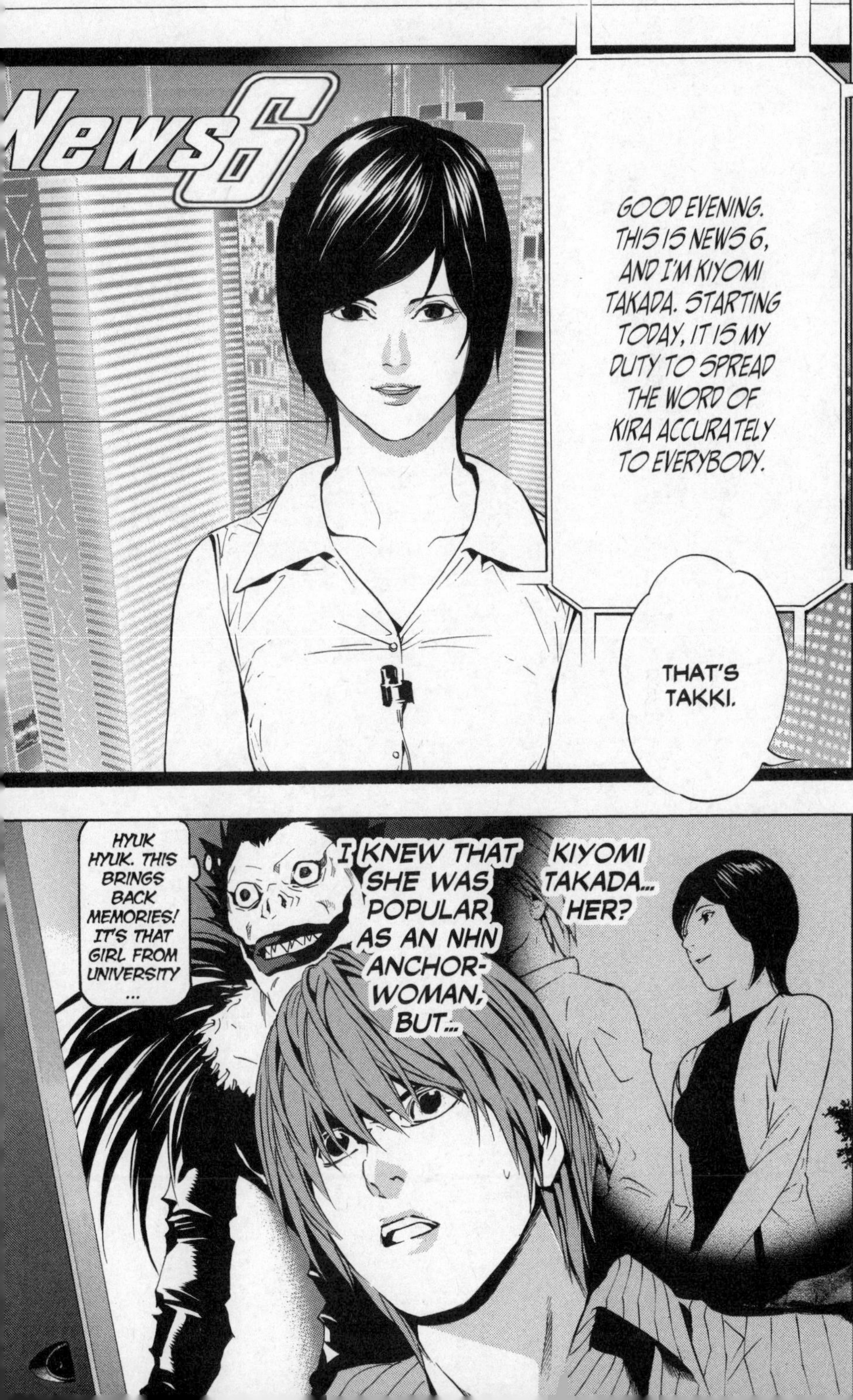
GOOD EVENING. THIS IS NEWS 6, AND I'M KIYOMI TAKADA. STARTING TODAY, IT IS MY DUTY TO SPREAD THE WORD OF KIRA ACCURATELY TO EVERYBODY.
THAT'S TAKKI.
News 6
KIYOMI TAKADA... HER?
I KNEW THAT SHE WAS POPULAR AS AN NHN ANCHOR-WOMAN, BUT...
HYUK HYUK. THIS BRINGS BACK MEMORIES! IT'S THAT GIRL FROM UNIVERSITY ...

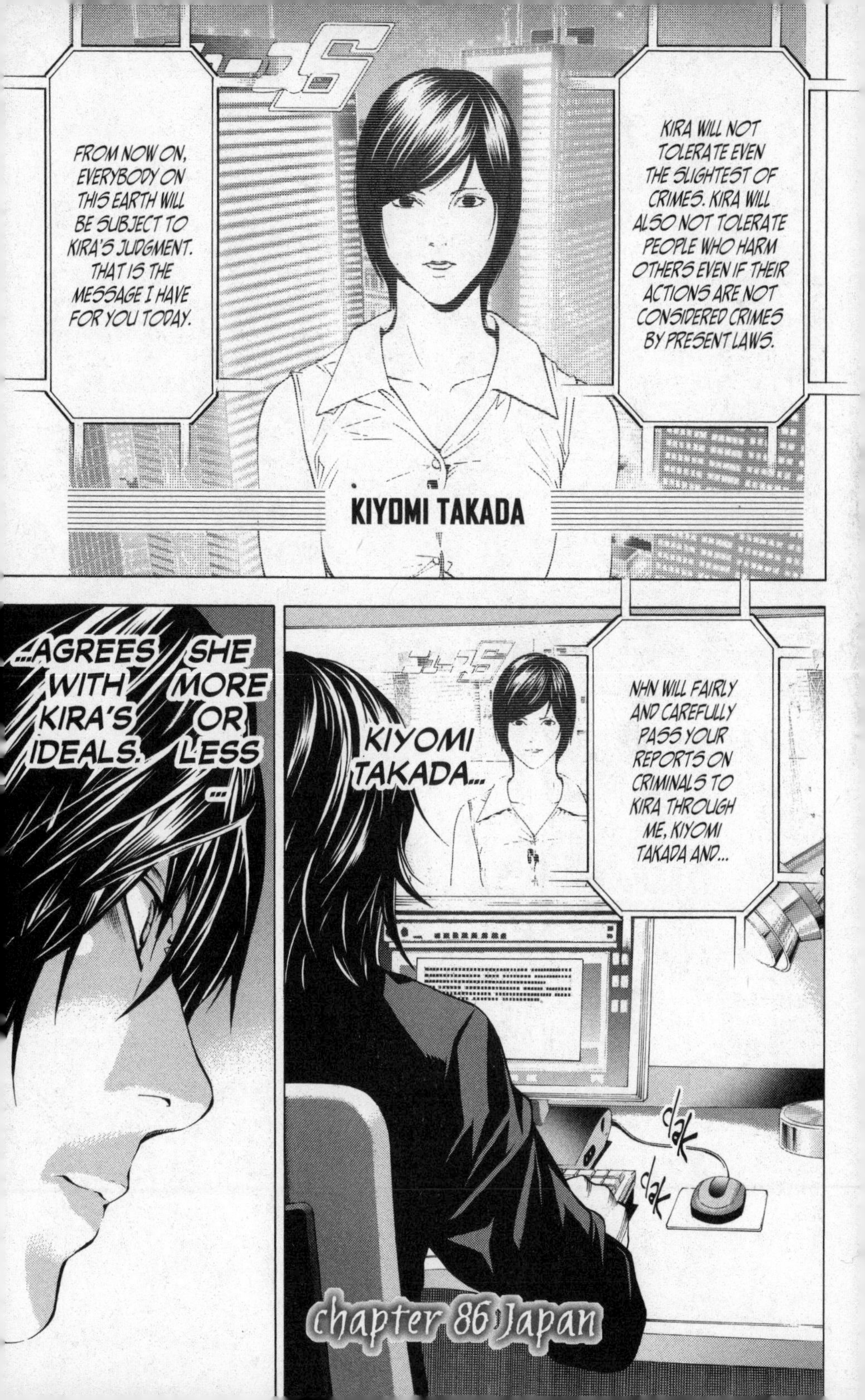
KIRA WILL NOT TOLERATE EVEN THE SLIGHTEST OF CRIMES. KIRA WILL ALSO NOT TOLERATE PEOPLE WHO HARM OTHERS EVEN IF THEIR ACTIONS ARE NOT CONSIDERED CRIMES BY PRESENT LAWS.
FROM NOW ON, EVERYBODY ON THIS EARTH WILL BE SUBJECT TO KIRA'S JUDGMENT. THAT IS THE MESSAGE I HAVE FOR YOU TODAY.
KIYOMI TAKADA
NHN WILL FAIRLY AND CAREFULLY PASS YOUR REPORTS ON CRIMINALS TO KIRA THROUGH ME, KIYOMI TAKADA AND...
KIYOMI TAKADA...
clak
clak
chapter 86 Japan
SHE MORE OR LESS...
...AGREES WITH KIRA'S IDEALS.

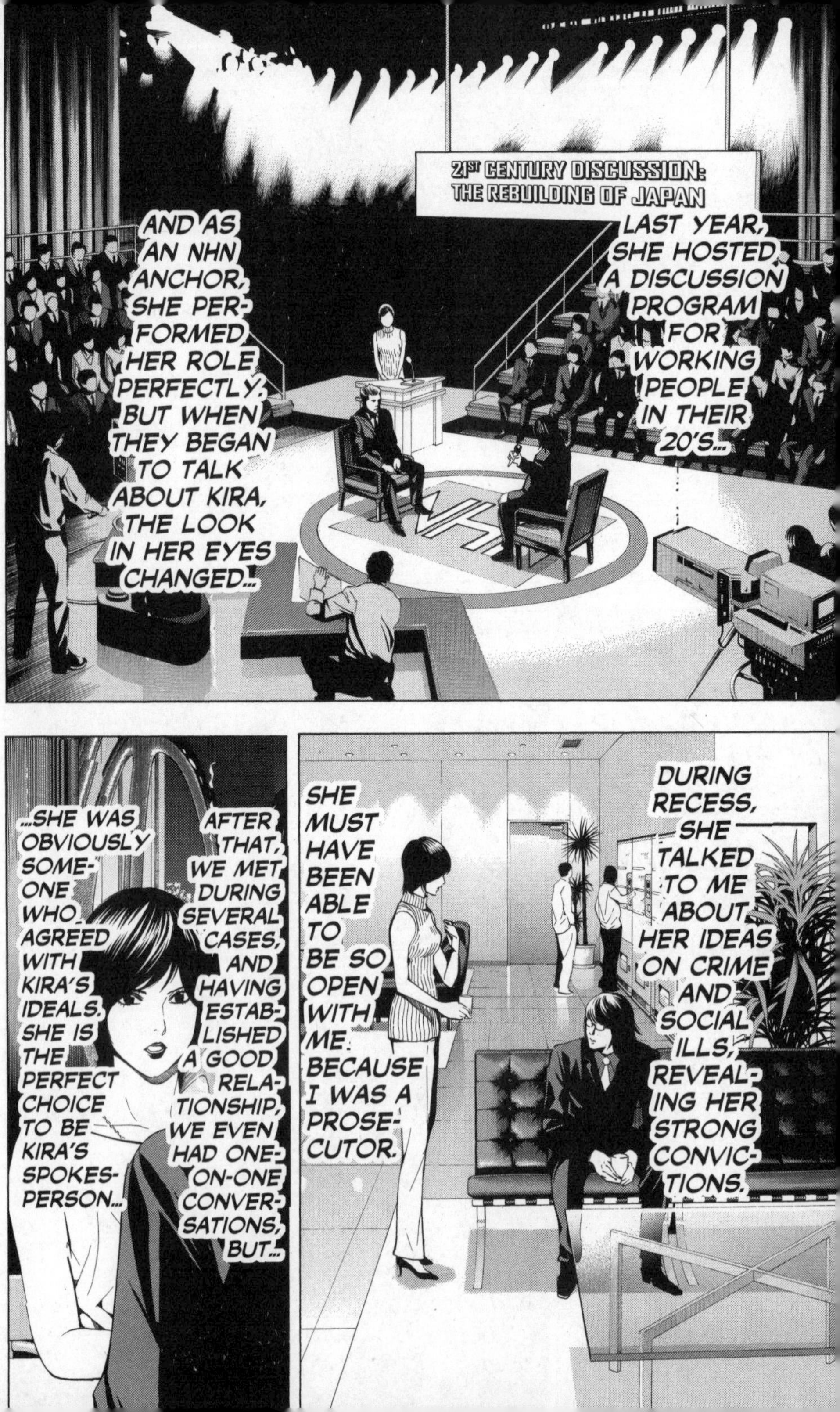
21ST CENTURY DISCUSSION: THE REBUILDING OF JAPAN
LAST YEAR, SHE HOSTED A DISCUSSION PROGRAM FOR WORKING PEOPLE IN THEIR 20'S...
AND AS AN NHN ANCHOR, SHE PER-FORMED HER ROLE PERFECTLY. BUT WHEN THEY BEGAN TO TALK ABOUT KIRA, THE LOOK IN HER EYES CHANGED...
DURING RECESS, SHE TALKED TO ME ABOUT HER IDEAS ON CRIME AND SOCIAL ILLS, REVEAL-ING HER STRONG CONVIC-TIONS.
SHE MUST HAVE BEEN ABLE TO BE SO OPEN WITH ME. BECAUSE I WAS A PROSE-CUTOR.
AFTER THAT, WE MET DURING SEVERAL CASES, AND HAVING ESTAB-LISHED A GOOD RELA-TIONSHIP, WE EVEN HAD ONE-ON-ONE CONVER-SATIONS, BUT...
...SHE WAS OBVIOUSLY SOME-ONE WHO AGREED WITH KIRA'S IDEALS. SHE IS THE PERFECT CHOICE TO BE KIRA'S SPOKES-PERSON...

chapter 86 Japan

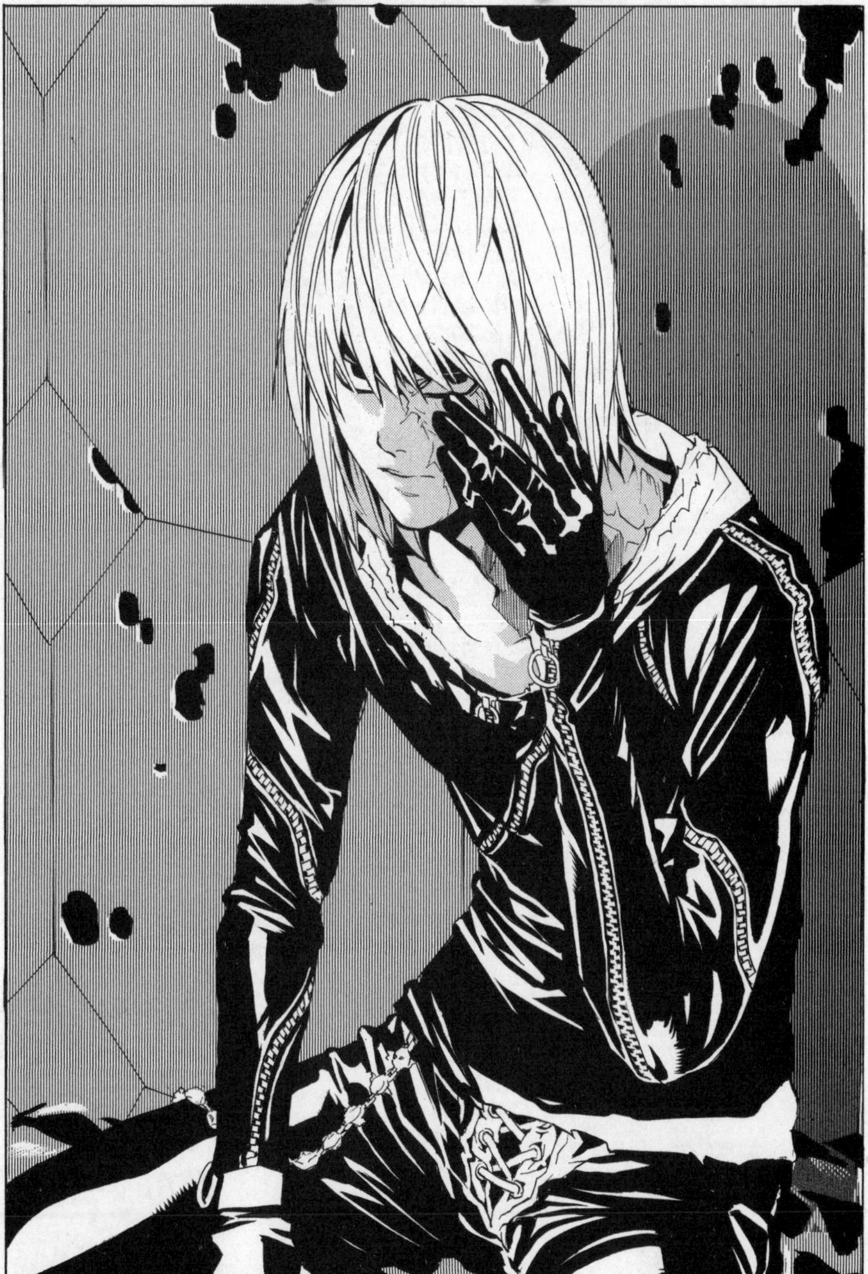

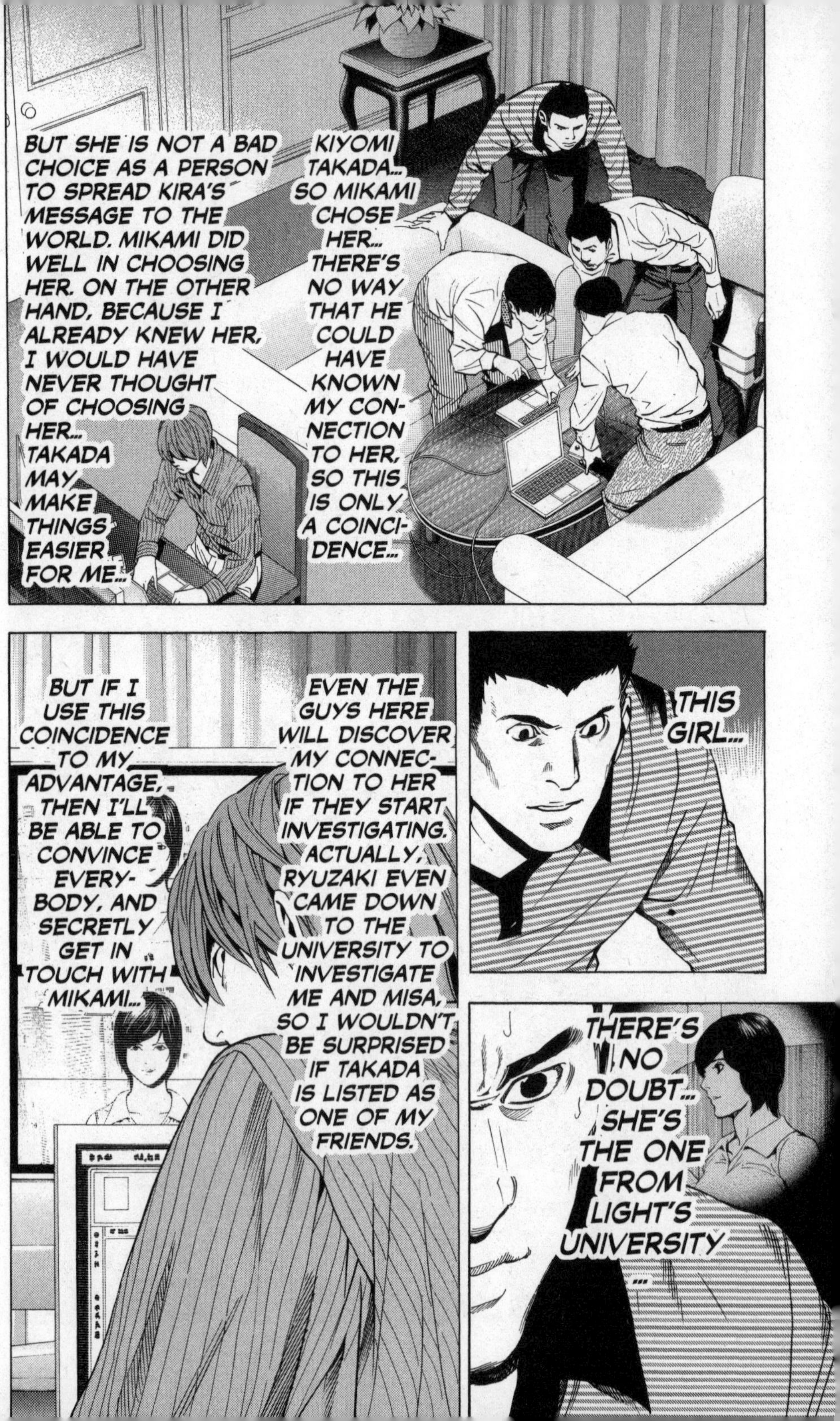
KIYOMI TAKADA... SO MIKAMI CHOSE HER... THERE'S NO WAY THAT HE COULD HAVE KNOWN MY CONNECTION TO HER, SO THIS IS ONLY A COINCIDENCE...
BUT SHE IS NOT A BAD CHOICE AS A PERSON TO SPREAD KIRA'S MESSAGE TO THE WORLD. MIKAMI DID WELL IN CHOOSING HER. ON THE OTHER HAND, BECAUSE I ALREADY KNEW HER, I WOULD HAVE NEVER THOUGHT OF CHOOSING HER... TAKADA MAY MAKE THINGS EASIER FOR ME...
THIS GIRL...
THERE'S NO DOUBT... SHE'S THE ONE FROM LIGHT'S UNIVERSITY...
EVEN THE GUYS HERE WILL DISCOVER MY CONNECTION TO HER IF THEY START INVESTIGATING. ACTUALLY, RYUZAKI EVEN CAME DOWN TO THE UNIVERSITY TO INVESTIGATE ME AND MISA, SO I WOULDN'T BE SURPRISED IF TAKADA IS LISTED AS ONE OF MY FRIENDS.
BUT IF I USE THIS COINCIDENCE TO MY ADVANTAGE, THEN I'LL BE ABLE TO CONVINCE EVERYBODY, AND SECRETLY GET IN TOUCH WITH MIKAMI...

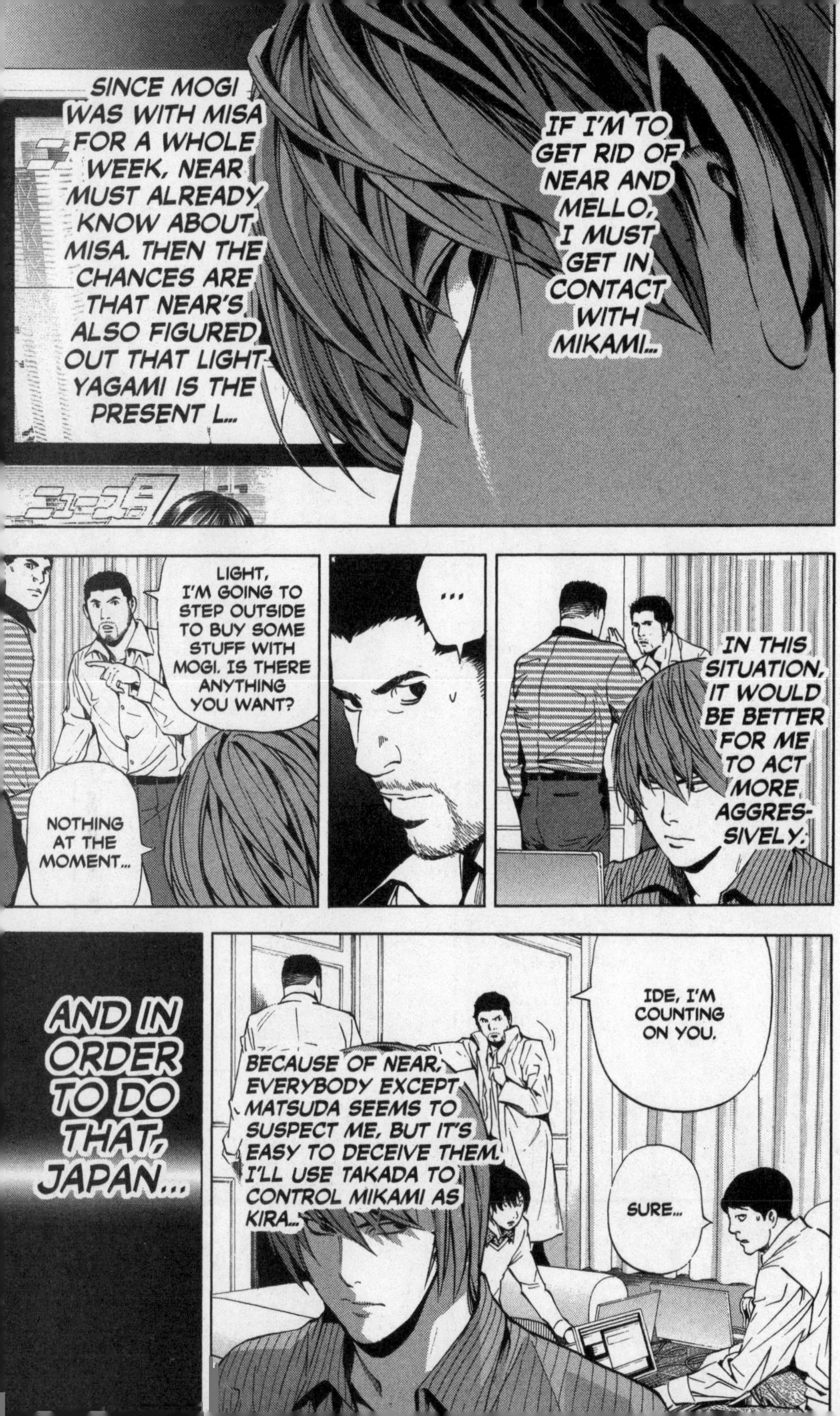
IF I'M TO GET RID OF NEAR AND MELLO, I MUST GET IN CONTACT WITH MIKAMI...
SINCE MOGI WAS WITH MISA FOR A WHOLE WEEK, NEAR MUST ALREADY KNOW ABOUT MISA. THEN THE CHANCES ARE THAT NEAR'S ALSO FIGURED OUT THAT LIGHT YAGAMI IS THE PRESENT L...
IN THIS SITUATION, IT WOULD BE BETTER FOR ME TO ACT MORE AGGRES-SIVELY.
...
LIGHT, I'M GOING TO STEP OUTSIDE TO BUY SOME STUFF WITH MOGI. IS THERE ANYTHING YOU WANT?
NOTHING AT THE MOMENT...
IDE, I'M COUNTING ON YOU.
BECAUSE OF NEAR, EVERYBODY EXCEPT MATSUDA SEEMS TO SUSPECT ME, BUT IT'S EASY TO DECEIVE THEM. I'LL USE TAKADA TO CONTROL MIKAMI AS KIRA...
SURE...
AND IN ORDER TO DO THAT, JAPAN...

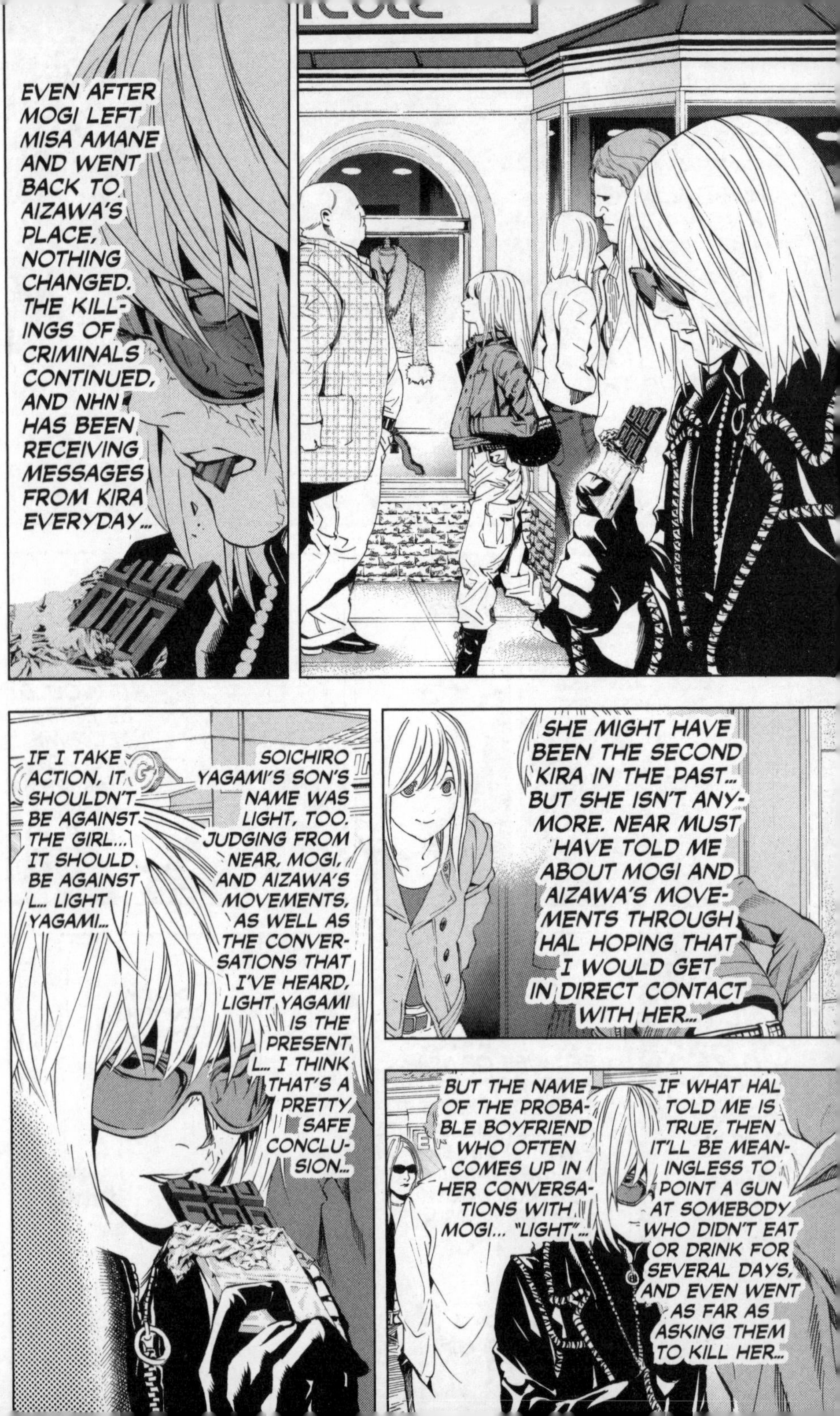
EVEN AFTER MOGI LEFT MISA AMANE AND WENT BACK TO AIZAWA'S PLACE, NOTHING CHANGED. THE KILLINGS OF CRIMINALS CONTINUED, AND NHN HAS BEEN RECEIVING MESSAGES FROM KIRA EVERYDAY...
SHE MIGHT HAVE BEEN THE SECOND KIRA IN THE PAST... BUT SHE ISN'T ANYMORE. NEAR MUST HAVE TOLD ME ABOUT MOGI AND AIZAWA'S MOVEMENTS THROUGH HAL HOPING THAT I WOULD GET IN DIRECT CONTACT WITH HER...
IF WHAT HAL TOLD ME IS TRUE, THEN IT'LL BE MEANINGLESS TO POINT A GUN AT SOMEBODY WHO DIDN'T EAT OR DRINK FOR SEVERAL DAYS, AND EVEN WENT AS FAR AS ASKING THEM TO KILL HER...
BUT THE NAME OF THE PROBABLE BOYFRIEND WHO OFTEN COMES UP IN HER CONVERSATIONS WITH MOGI... "LIGHT"...
SOICHIRO YAGAMI'S SON'S NAME WAS LIGHT, TOO. JUDGING FROM NEAR, MOGI, AND AIZAWA'S MOVEMENTS, AS WELL AS THE CONVERSATIONS THAT I'VE HEARD, LIGHT YAGAMI IS THE PRESENT L... I THINK THAT'S A PRETTY SAFE CONCLUSION...
IF I TAKE ACTION, IT SHOULDN'T BE AGAINST THE GIRL... IT SHOULD BE AGAINST L... LIGHT YAGAMI...

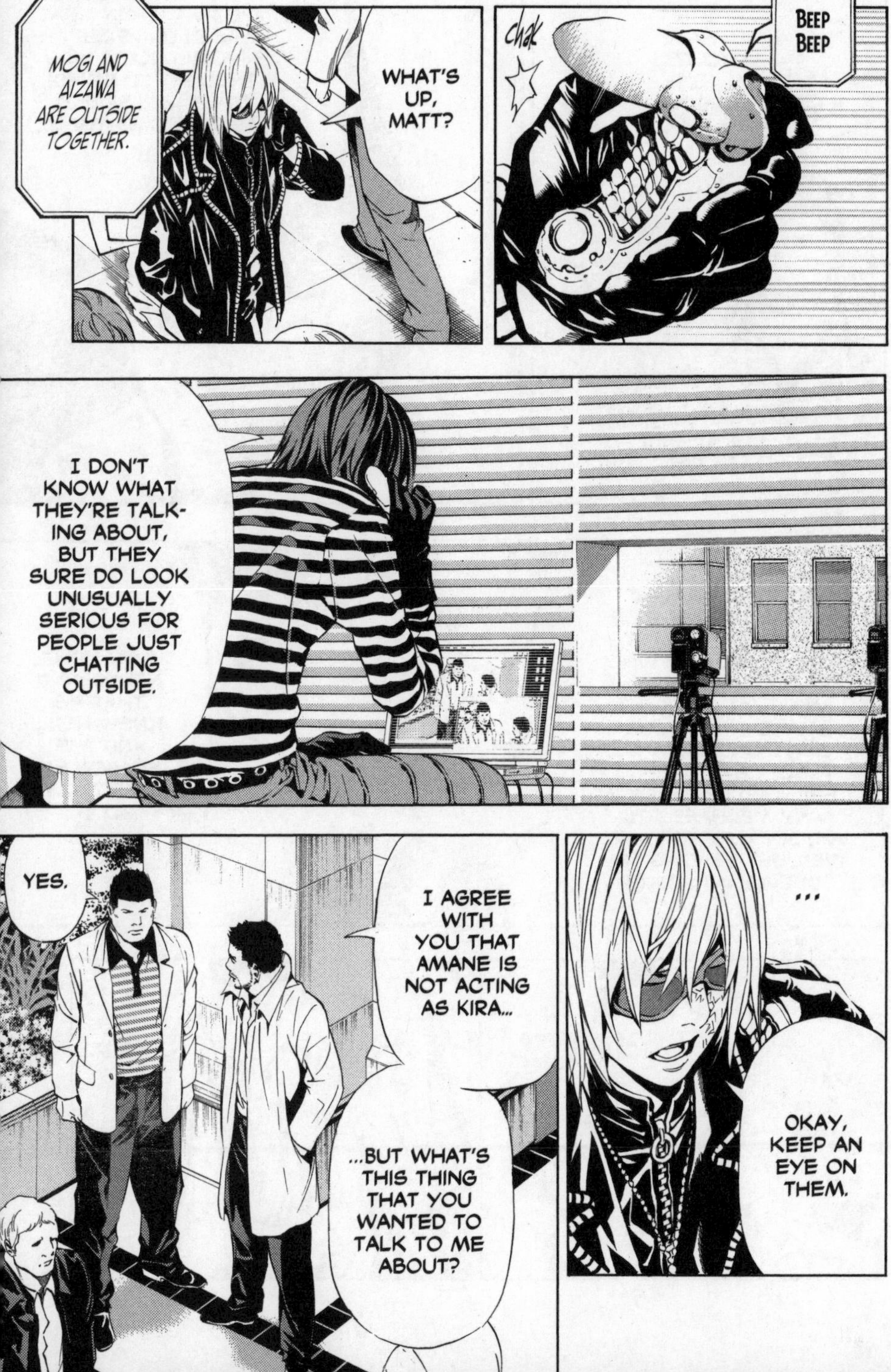
chak
BEEP BEEP
WHAT'S UP, MATT?
MOGI AND AIZAWA ARE OUTSIDE TOGETHER.
I DON'T KNOW WHAT THEY'RE TALKING ABOUT, BUT THEY SURE DO LOOK UNUSUALLY SERIOUS FOR PEOPLE JUST CHATTING OUTSIDE.
...
OKAY, KEEP AN EYE ON THEM.
I AGREE WITH YOU THAT AMANE IS NOT ACTING AS KIRA...
YES.
...BUT WHAT'S THIS THING THAT YOU WANTED TO TALK TO ME ABOUT?

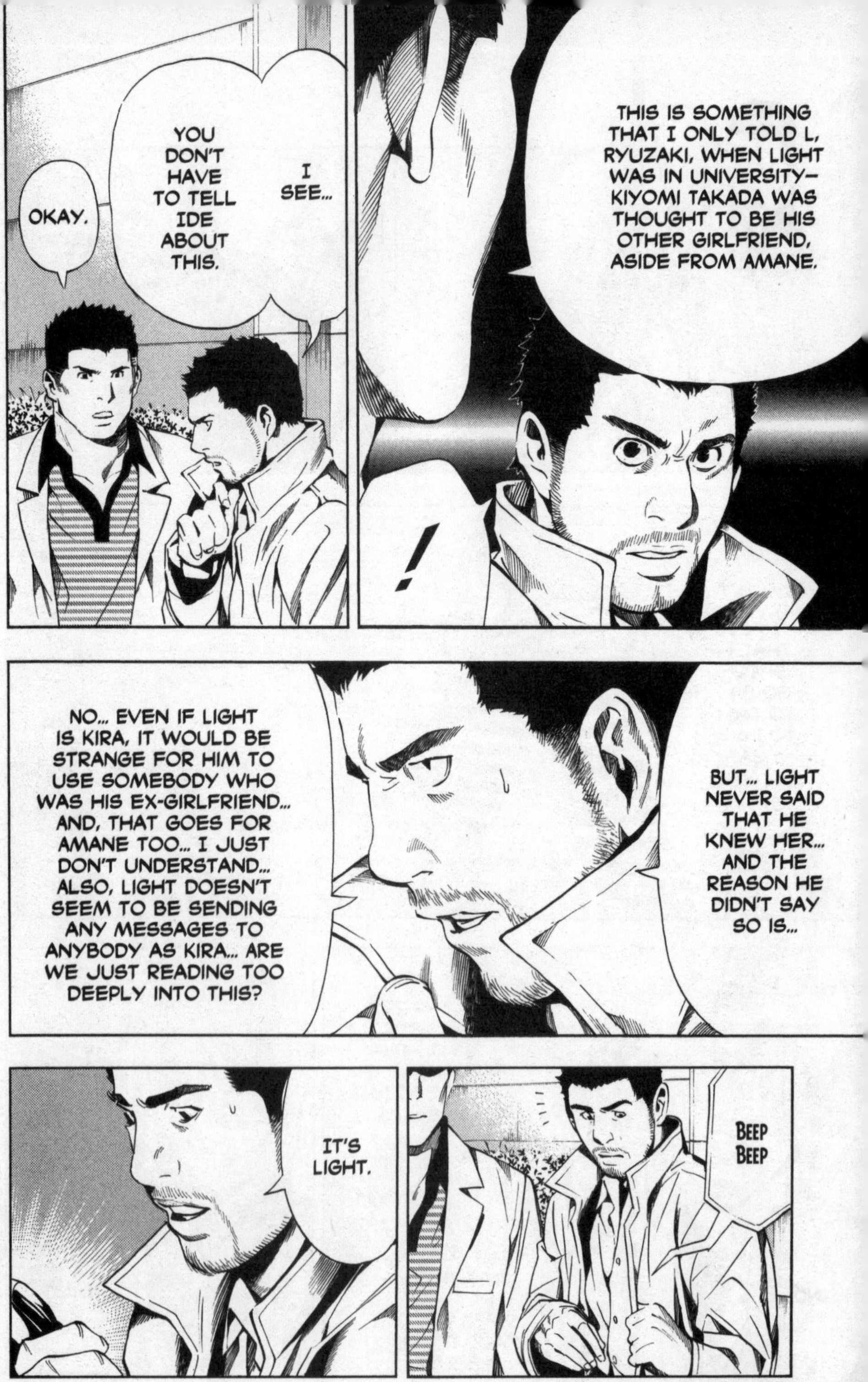
THIS IS SOMETHING THAT I ONLY TOLD L, RYUZAKI, WHEN LIGHT WAS IN UNIVERSITY– KIYOMI TAKADA WAS THOUGHT TO BE HIS OTHER GIRLFRIEND, ASIDE FROM AMANE.
!
I SEE...
YOU DON'T HAVE TO TELL IDE ABOUT THIS.
OKAY.
BUT... LIGHT NEVER SAID THAT HE KNEW HER... AND THE REASON HE DIDN'T SAY SO IS...
NO... EVEN IF LIGHT IS KIRA, IT WOULD BE STRANGE FOR HIM TO USE SOMEBODY WHO WAS HIS EX-GIRLFRIEND... AND, THAT GOES FOR AMANE TOO... I JUST DON'T UNDERSTAND... ALSO, LIGHT DOESN'T SEEM TO BE SENDING ANY MESSAGES TO ANYBODY AS KIRA... ARE WE JUST READING TOO DEEPLY INTO THIS?
BEEP BEEP
IT'S LIGHT.

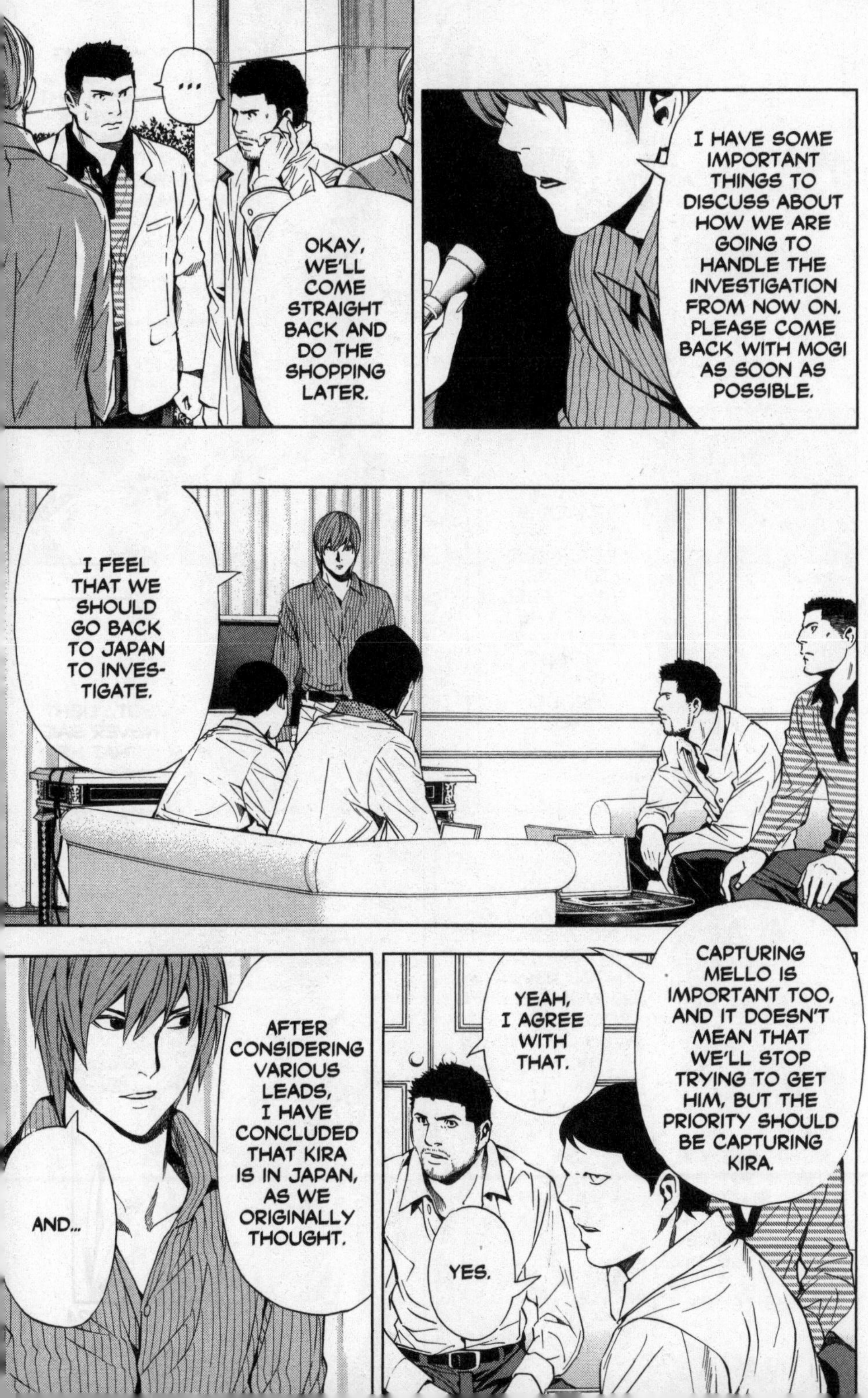
I HAVE SOME IMPORTANT THINGS TO DISCUSS ABOUT HOW WE ARE GOING TO HANDLE THE INVESTIGATION FROM NOW ON. PLEASE COME BACK WITH MOGI AS SOON AS POSSIBLE.
...
OKAY, WE'LL COME STRAIGHT BACK AND DO THE SHOPPING LATER.
I FEEL THAT WE SHOULD GO BACK TO JAPAN TO INVES-TIGATE.
CAPTURING MELLO IS IMPORTANT TOO, AND IT DOESN'T MEAN THAT WE'LL STOP TRYING TO GET HIM, BUT THE PRIORITY SHOULD BE CAPTURING KIRA.
YEAH, I AGREE WITH THAT.
YES.
AFTER CONSIDERING VARIOUS LEADS, I HAVE CONCLUDED THAT KIRA IS IN JAPAN, AS WE ORIGINALLY THOUGHT.
AND...

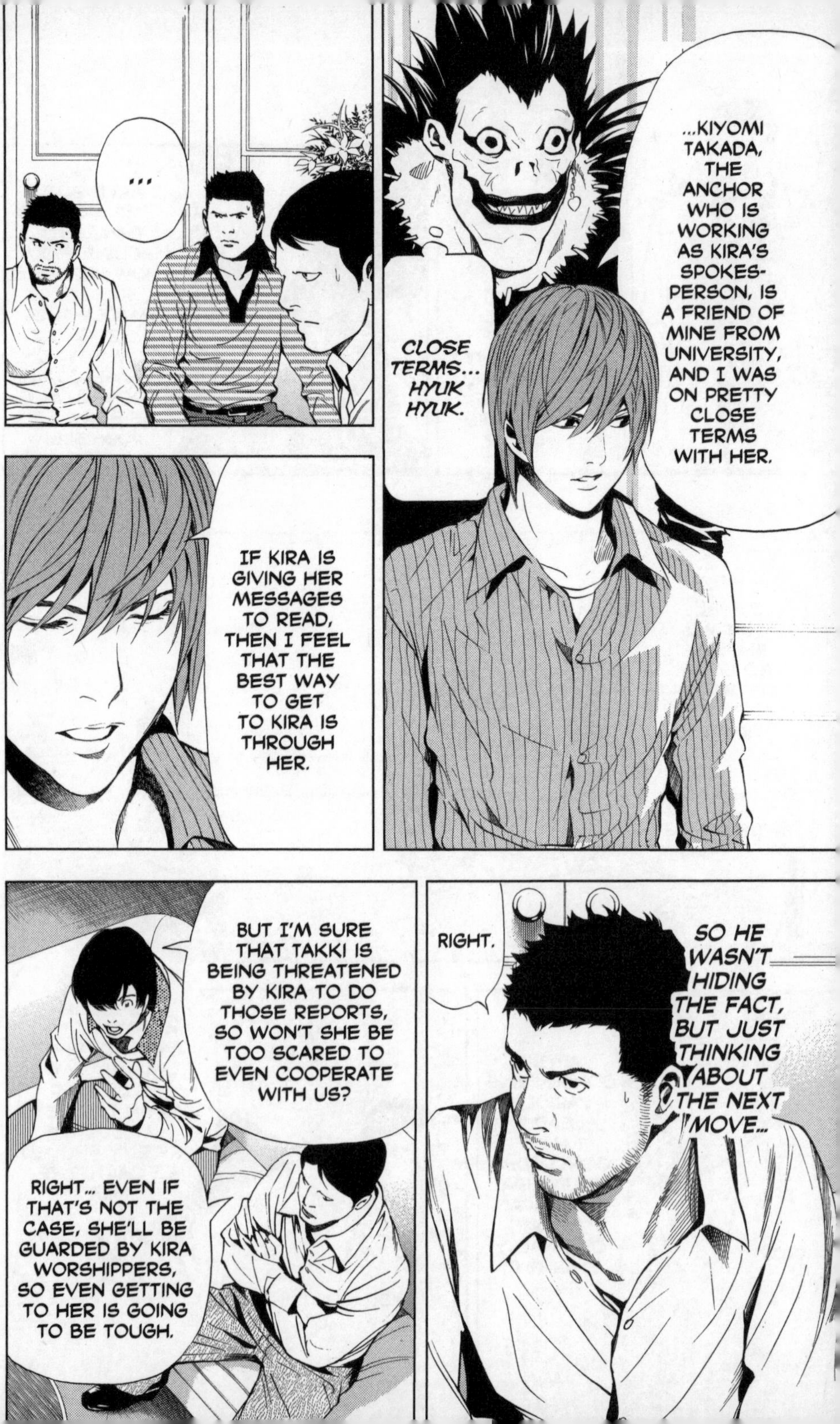
...KIYOMI TAKADA, THE ANCHOR WHO IS WORKING AS KIRA'S SPOKES-PERSON, IS A FRIEND OF MINE FROM UNIVERSITY, AND I WAS ON PRETTY CLOSE TERMS WITH HER.
CLOSE TERMS... HYUK HYUK.
...
IF KIRA IS GIVING HER MESSAGES TO READ, THEN I FEEL THAT THE BEST WAY TO GET TO KIRA IS THROUGH HER.
SO HE WASN'T HIDING THE FACT, BUT JUST THINKING ABOUT THE NEXT MOVE...
RIGHT.
BUT I'M SURE THAT TAKKI IS BEING THREATENED BY KIRA TO DO THOSE REPORTS, SO WON'T SHE BE TOO SCARED TO EVEN COOPERATE WITH US?
RIGHT... EVEN IF THAT'S NOT THE CASE, SHE'LL BE GUARDED BY KIRA WORSHIPPERS, SO EVEN GETTING TO HER IS GOING TO BE TOUGH.

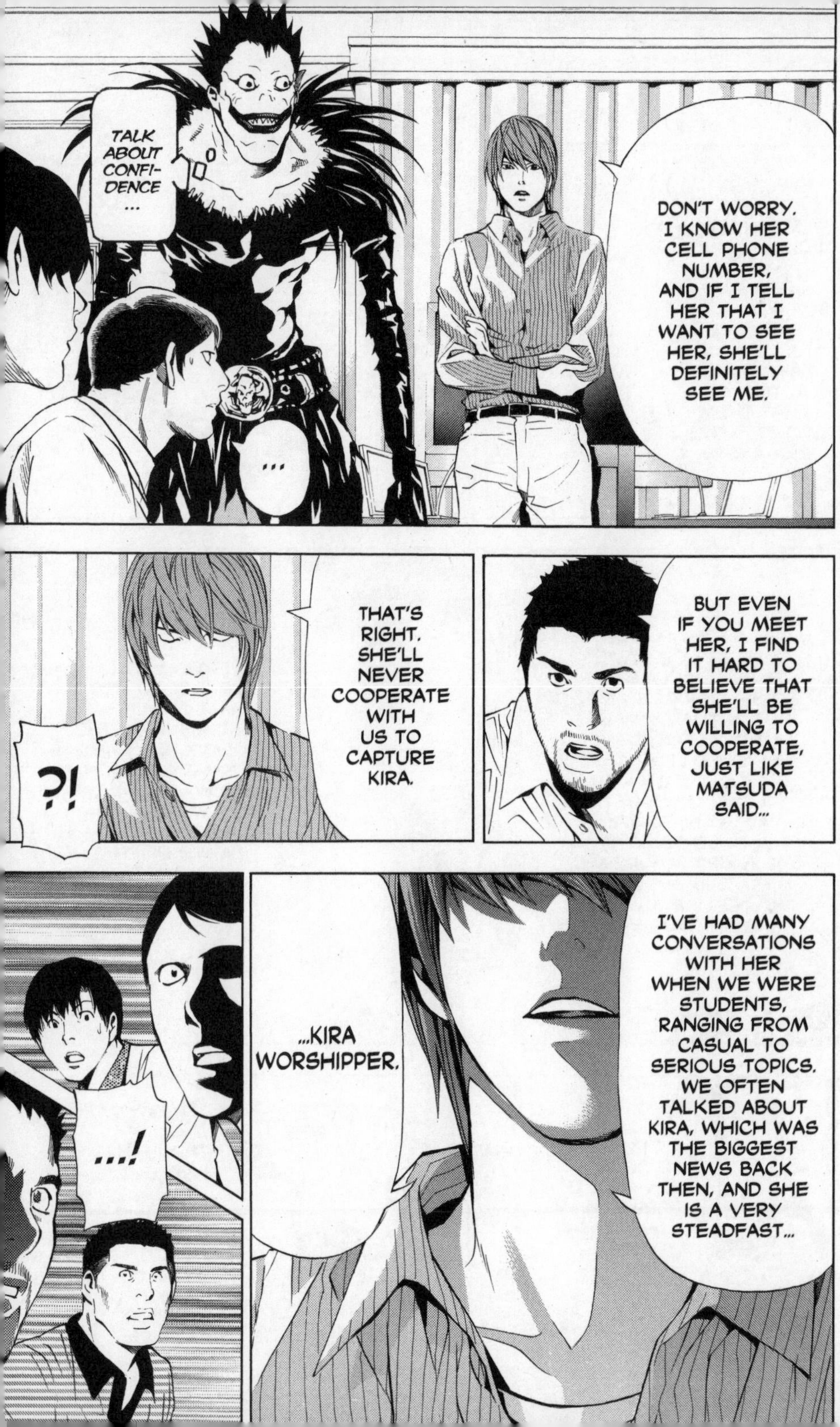
DON'T WORRY. I KNOW HER CELL PHONE NUMBER, AND IF I TELL HER THAT I WANT TO SEE HER, SHE'LL DEFINITELY SEE ME.
TALK ABOUT CONFI-DENCE ...
...
BUT EVEN IF YOU MEET HER, I FIND IT HARD TO BELIEVE THAT SHE'LL BE WILLING TO COOPERATE, JUST LIKE MATSUDA SAID...
THAT'S RIGHT. SHE'LL NEVER COOPERATE WITH US TO CAPTURE KIRA.
?!
I'VE HAD MANY CONVERSATIONS WITH HER WHEN WE WERE STUDENTS, RANGING FROM CASUAL TO SERIOUS TOPICS. WE OFTEN TALKED ABOUT KIRA, WHICH WAS THE BIGGEST NEWS BACK THEN, AND SHE IS A VERY STEADFAST...
...KIRA WORSHIPPER.
...!

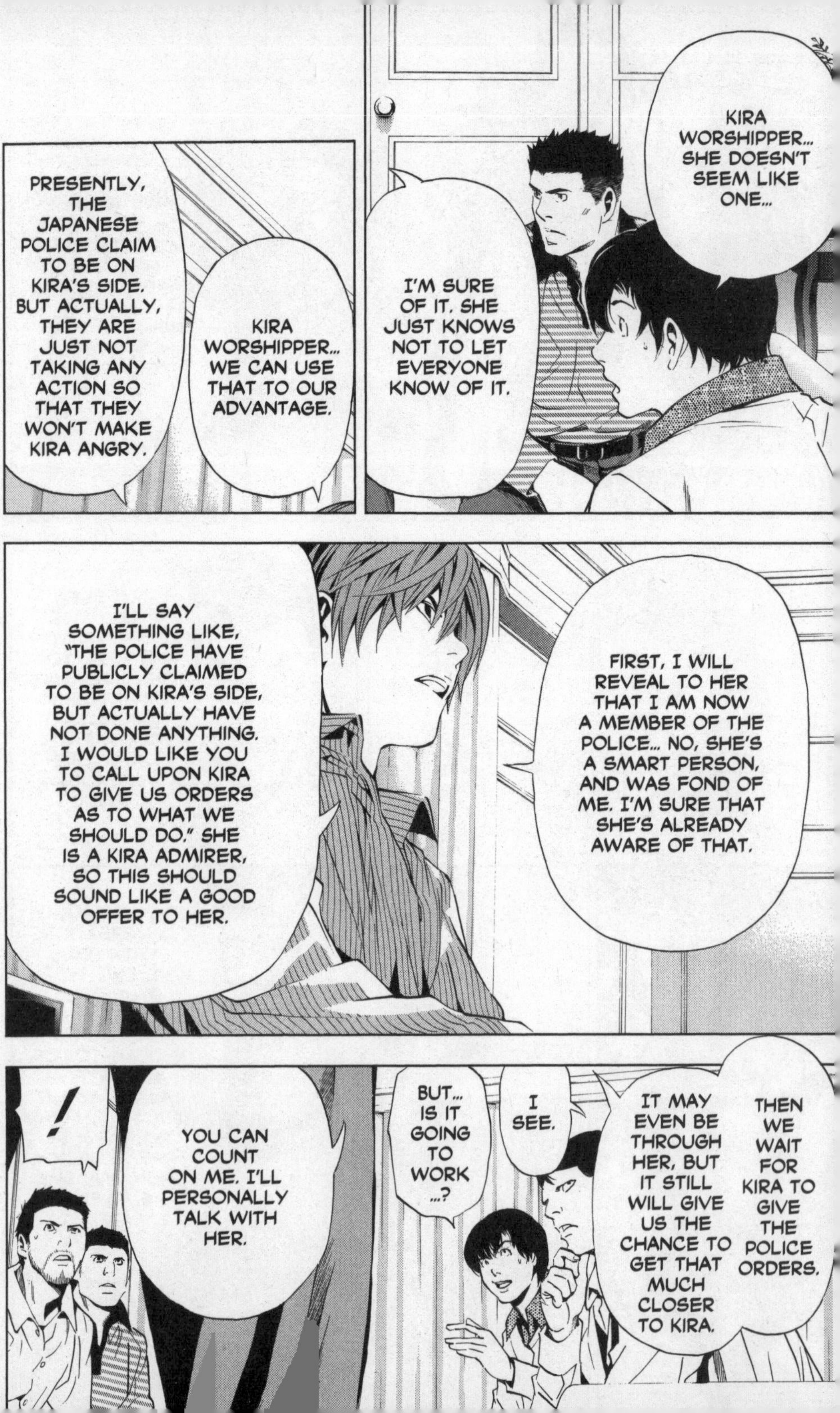
KIRA WORSHIPPER... SHE DOESN'T SEEM LIKE ONE...
I'M SURE OF IT. SHE JUST KNOWS NOT TO LET EVERYONE KNOW OF IT.
KIRA WORSHIPPER... WE CAN USE THAT TO OUR ADVANTAGE.
PRESENTLY, THE JAPANESE POLICE CLAIM TO BE ON KIRA'S SIDE. BUT ACTUALLY, THEY ARE JUST NOT TAKING ANY ACTION SO THAT THEY WON'T MAKE KIRA ANGRY.
FIRST, I WILL REVEAL TO HER THAT I AM NOW A MEMBER OF THE POLICE... NO, SHE'S A SMART PERSON, AND WAS FOND OF ME. I'M SURE THAT SHE'S ALREADY AWARE OF THAT.
I'LL SAY SOMETHING LIKE, "THE POLICE HAVE PUBLICLY CLAIMED TO BE ON KIRA'S SIDE, BUT ACTUALLY HAVE NOT DONE ANYTHING. I WOULD LIKE YOU TO CALL UPON KIRA TO GIVE US ORDERS AS TO WHAT WE SHOULD DO." SHE IS A KIRA ADMIRER, SO THIS SHOULD SOUND LIKE A GOOD OFFER TO HER.
THEN WE WAIT FOR KIRA TO GIVE THE POLICE ORDERS.
IT MAY EVEN BE THROUGH HER, BUT IT STILL WILL GIVE US THE CHANCE TO GET THAT MUCH CLOSER TO KIRA.
I SEE.
BUT... IS IT GOING TO WORK ...?
YOU CAN COUNT ON ME. I'LL PERSONALLY TALK WITH HER.
!

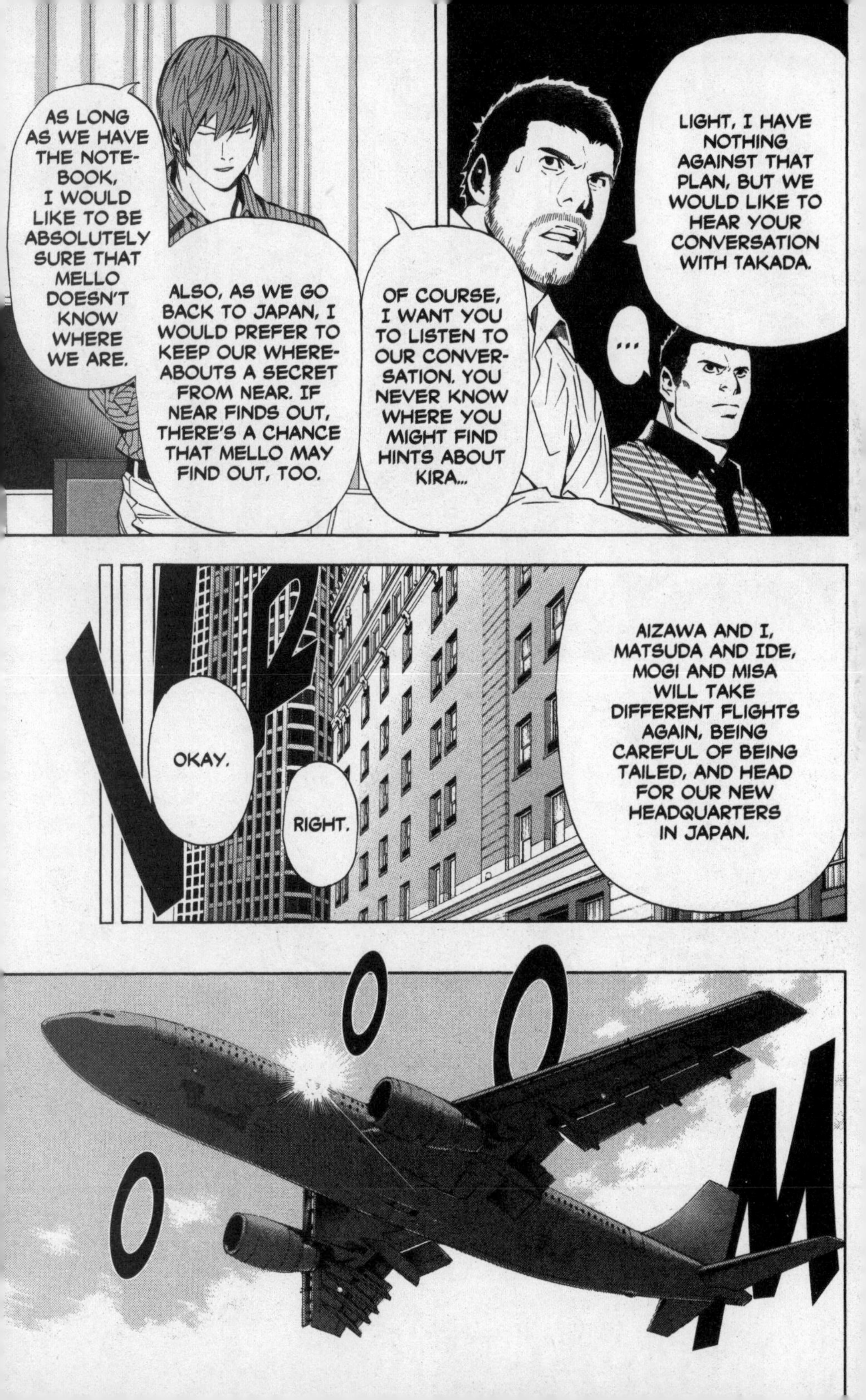
LIGHT, I HAVE NOTHING AGAINST THAT PLAN, BUT WE WOULD LIKE TO HEAR YOUR CONVERSATION WITH TAKADA.
...
OF COURSE, I WANT YOU TO LISTEN TO OUR CONVERSATION. YOU NEVER KNOW WHERE YOU MIGHT FIND HINTS ABOUT KIRA...
ALSO, AS WE GO BACK TO JAPAN, I WOULD PREFER TO KEEP OUR WHEREABOUTS A SECRET FROM NEAR. IF NEAR FINDS OUT, THERE'S A CHANCE THAT MELLO MAY FIND OUT, TOO.
AS LONG AS WE HAVE THE NOTEBOOK, I WOULD LIKE TO BE ABSOLUTELY SURE THAT MELLO DOESN'T KNOW WHERE WE ARE.
AIZAWA AND I, MATSUDA AND IDE, MOGI AND MISA WILL TAKE DIFFERENT FLIGHTS AGAIN, BEING CAREFUL OF BEING TAILED, AND HEAD FOR OUR NEW HEADQUARTERS IN JAPAN.
RIGHT.
OKAY.
VOOOM

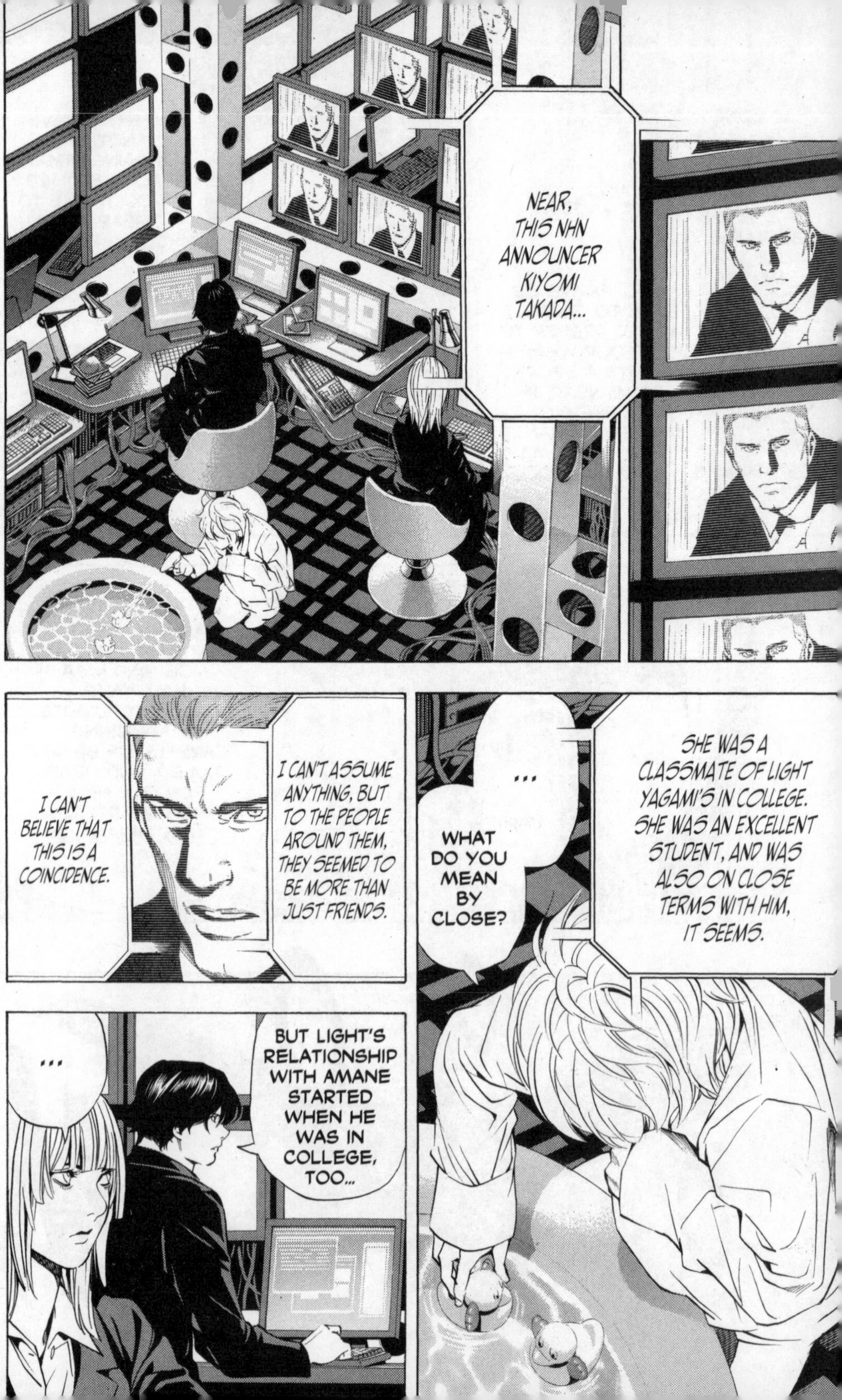
NEAR, THIS NHN ANNOUNCER KIYOMI TAKADA...
SHE WAS A CLASSMATE OF LIGHT YAGAMI'S IN COLLEGE. SHE WAS AN EXCELLENT STUDENT, AND WAS ALSO ON CLOSE TERMS WITH HIM, IT SEEMS.
...
WHAT DO YOU MEAN BY CLOSE?
I CAN'T ASSUME ANYTHING, BUT TO THE PEOPLE AROUND THEM, THEY SEEMED TO BE MORE THAN JUST FRIENDS.
I CAN'T BELIEVE THAT THIS IS A COINCIDENCE.
BUT LIGHT'S RELATIONSHIP WITH AMANE STARTED WHEN HE WAS IN COLLEGE, TOO...
...

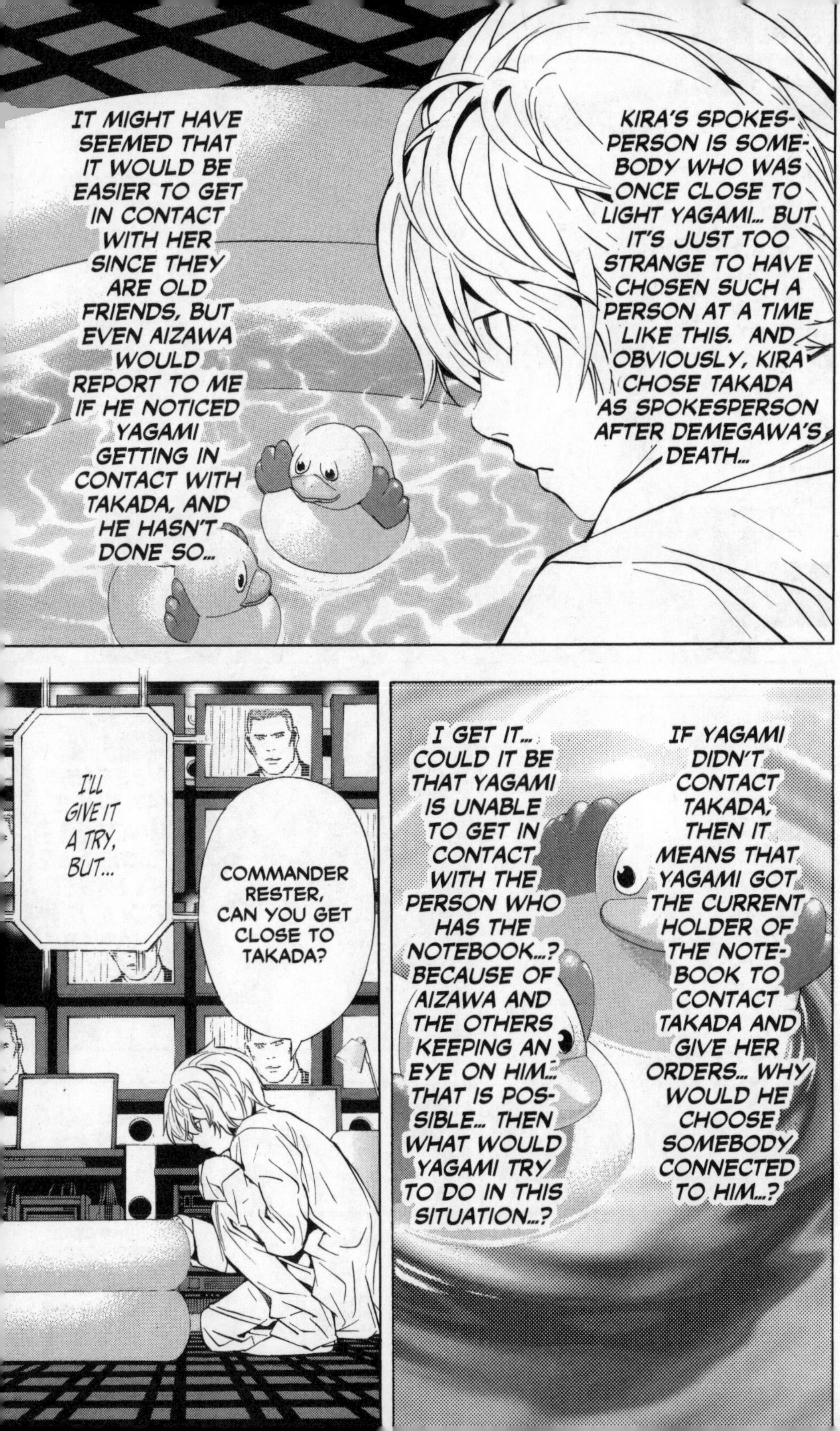
KIRA'S SPOKESPERSON IS SOMEBODY WHO WAS ONCE CLOSE TO LIGHT YAGAMI... BUT IT'S JUST TOO STRANGE TO HAVE CHOSEN SUCH A PERSON AT A TIME LIKE THIS. AND OBVIOUSLY, KIRA CHOSE TAKADA AS SPOKESPERSON AFTER DEMEGAWA'S DEATH...
IT MIGHT HAVE SEEMED THAT IT WOULD BE EASIER TO GET IN CONTACT WITH HER SINCE THEY ARE OLD FRIENDS, BUT EVEN AIZAWA WOULD REPORT TO ME IF HE NOTICED YAGAMI GETTING IN CONTACT WITH TAKADA, AND HE HASN'T DONE SO...
IF YAGAMI DIDN'T CONTACT TAKADA, THEN IT MEANS THAT YAGAMI GOT THE CURRENT HOLDER OF THE NOTEBOOK TO CONTACT TAKADA AND GIVE HER ORDERS... WHY WOULD HE CHOOSE SOMEBODY CONNECTED TO HIM...?
I GET IT... COULD IT BE THAT YAGAMI IS UNABLE TO GET IN CONTACT WITH THE PERSON WHO HAS THE NOTEBOOK...? BECAUSE OF AIZAWA AND THE OTHERS KEEPING AN EYE ON HIM... THAT IS POSSIBLE... THEN WHAT WOULD YAGAMI TRY TO DO IN THIS SITUATION...?
COMMANDER RESTER, CAN YOU GET CLOSE TO TAKADA?
I'LL GIVE IT A TRY, BUT...

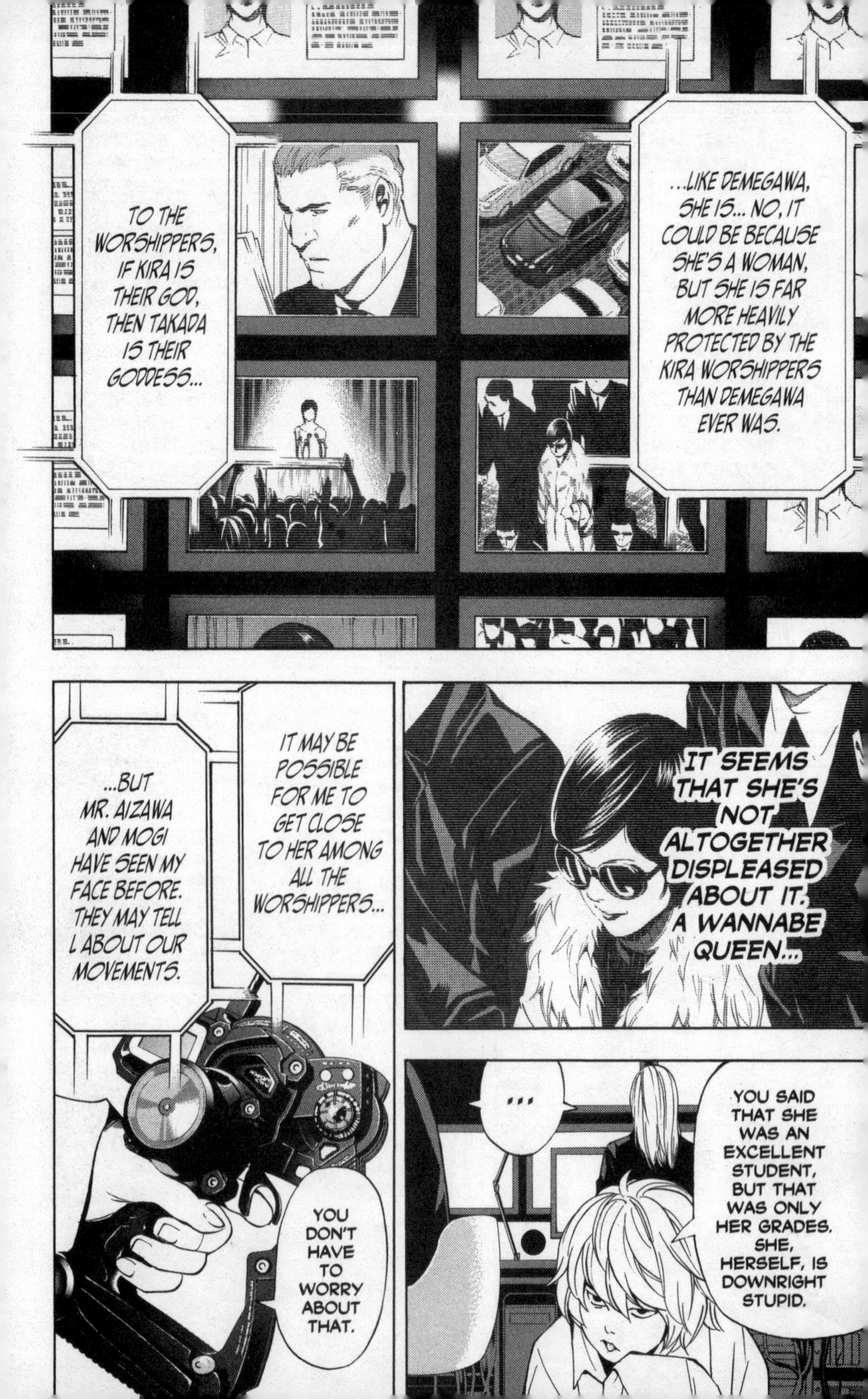
...LIKE DEMEGAWA, SHE IS... NO, IT COULD BE BECAUSE SHE'S A WOMAN, BUT SHE IS FAR MORE HEAVILY PROTECTED BY THE KIRA WORSHIPPERS THAN DEMEGAWA EVER WAS.
TO THE WORSHIPPERS, IF KIRA IS THEIR GOD, THEN TAKADA IS THEIR GODDESS...
IT SEEMS THAT SHE'S NOT ALTOGETHER DISPLEASED ABOUT IT. A WANNABE QUEEN...
...
YOU SAID THAT SHE WAS AN EXCELLENT STUDENT, BUT THAT WAS ONLY HER GRADES. SHE, HERSELF, IS DOWNRIGHT STUPID.
IT MAY BE POSSIBLE FOR ME TO GET CLOSE TO HER AMONG ALL THE WORSHIPPERS...
...BUT MR. AIZAWA AND MOGI HAVE SEEN MY FACE BEFORE. THEY MAY TELL L ABOUT OUR MOVEMENTS.
YOU DON'T HAVE TO WORRY ABOUT THAT.

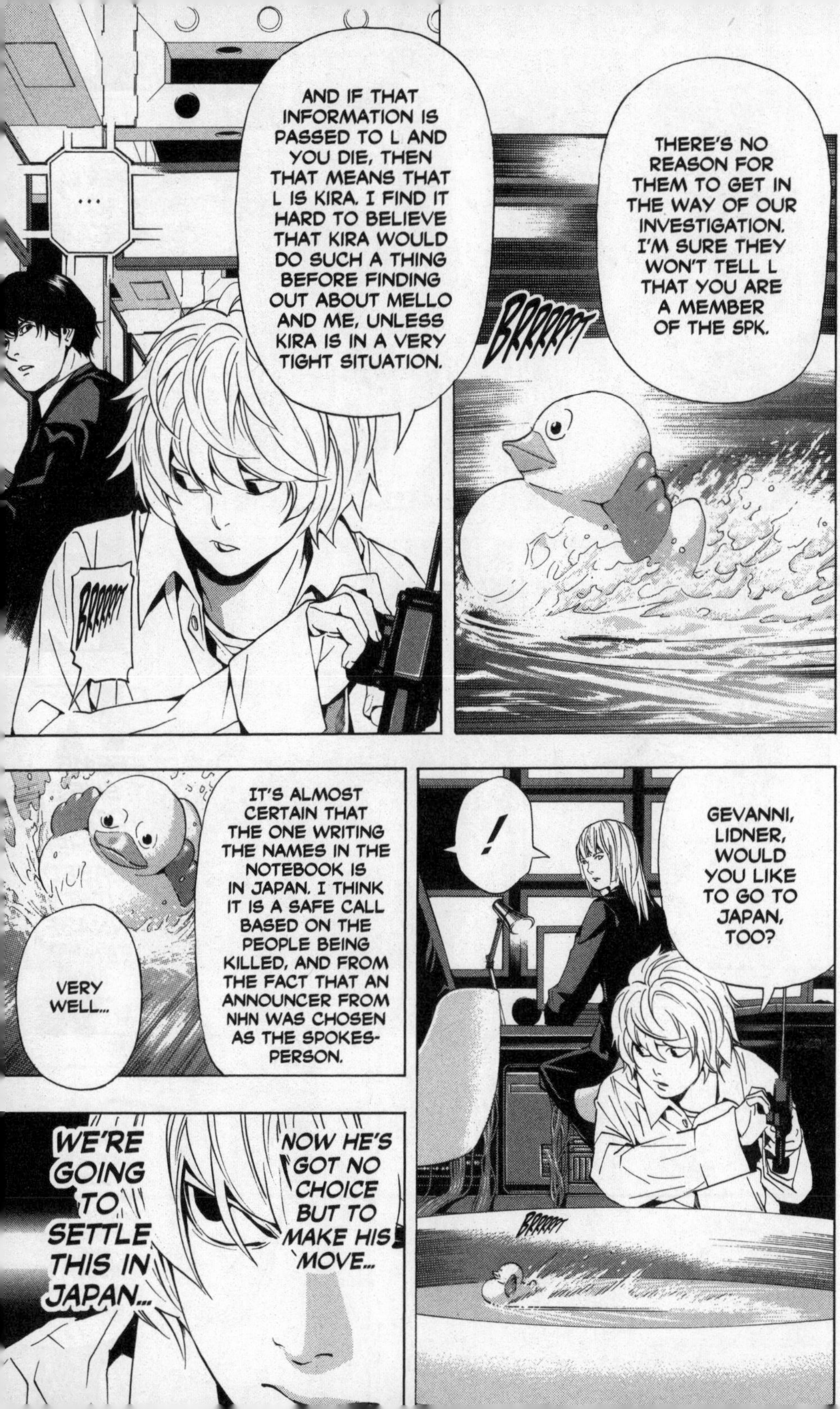
THERE'S NO REASON FOR THEM TO GET IN THE WAY OF OUR INVESTIGATION. I'M SURE THEY WON'T TELL L THAT YOU ARE A MEMBER OF THE SPK.
BRRRRPT
AND IF THAT INFORMATION IS PASSED TO L AND YOU DIE, THEN THAT MEANS THAT L IS KIRA. I FIND IT HARD TO BELIEVE THAT KIRA WOULD DO SUCH A THING BEFORE FINDING OUT ABOUT MELLO AND ME, UNLESS KIRA IS IN A VERY TIGHT SITUATION.
...
BRRRRPT
GEVANNI, LIDNER, WOULD YOU LIKE TO GO TO JAPAN, TOO?
!
BRRRRPT
IT'S ALMOST CERTAIN THAT THE ONE WRITING THE NAMES IN THE NOTEBOOK IS IN JAPAN. I THINK IT IS A SAFE CALL BASED ON THE PEOPLE BEING KILLED, AND FROM THE FACT THAT AN ANNOUNCER FROM NHN WAS CHOSEN AS THE SPOKES-PERSON.
VERY WELL...
NOW HE'S GOT NO CHOICE BUT TO MAKE HIS MOVE...
WE'RE GOING TO SETTLE THIS IN JAPAN...

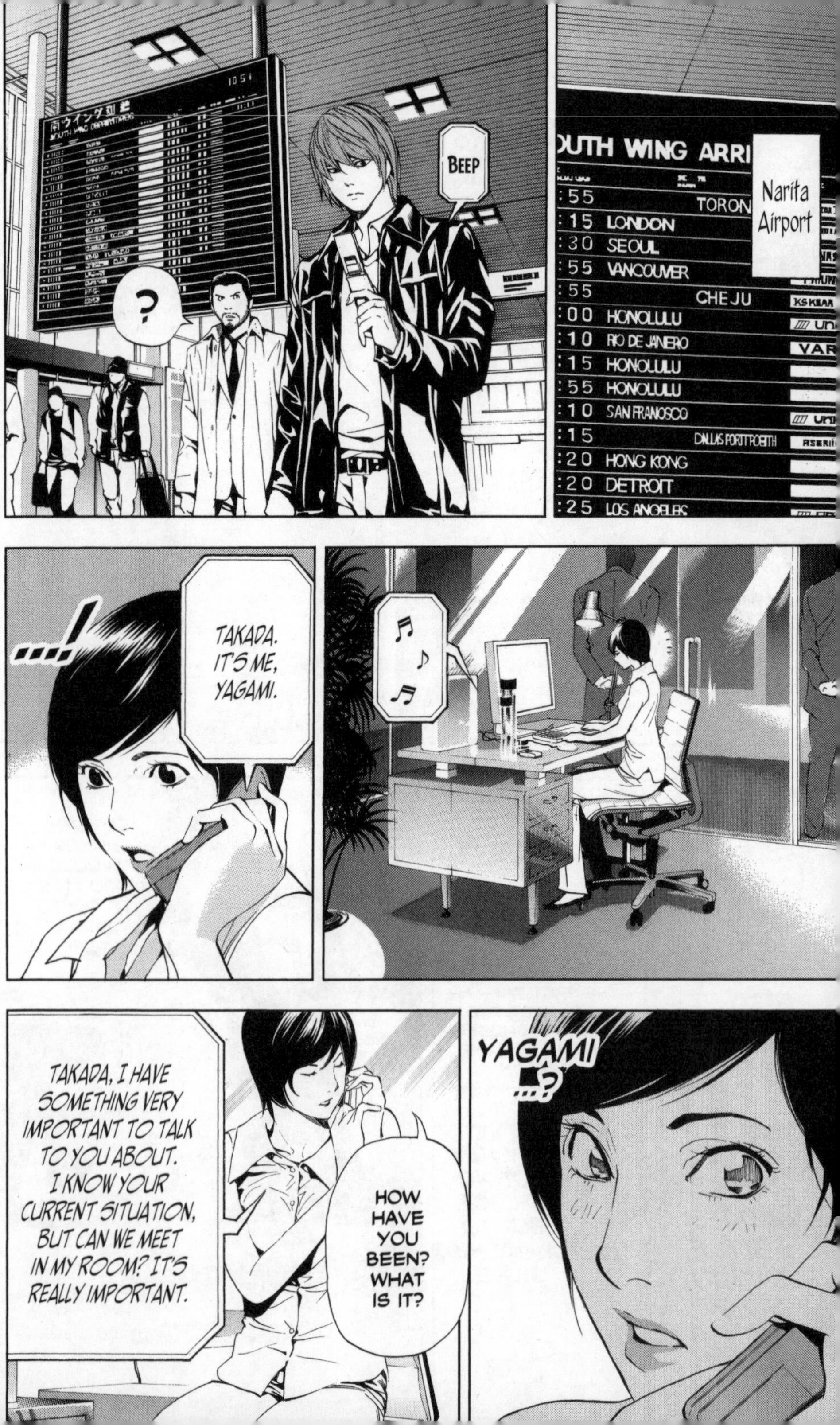
Narita Airport
:55 TORON
:15 LONDON
:30 SEOUL
:55 VANCOUVER
:55 CHEJU
:00 HONOLULU
:10 RIO DE JANERO
:15 HONOLULU
:55 HONOLULU
:10 SAN FRANOSCO
:20 HONG KONG
:20 DETROIT
:25 LOS ANGELES
BEEP
?
♪ ♪ ♪
TAKADA. IT'S ME, YAGAMI.
...!
YAGAMI ...?
HOW HAVE YOU BEEN? WHAT IS IT?
TAKADA, I HAVE SOMETHING VERY IMPORTANT TO TALK TO YOU ABOUT. I KNOW YOUR CURRENT SITUATION, BUT CAN WE MEET IN MY ROOM? IT'S REALLY IMPORTANT.

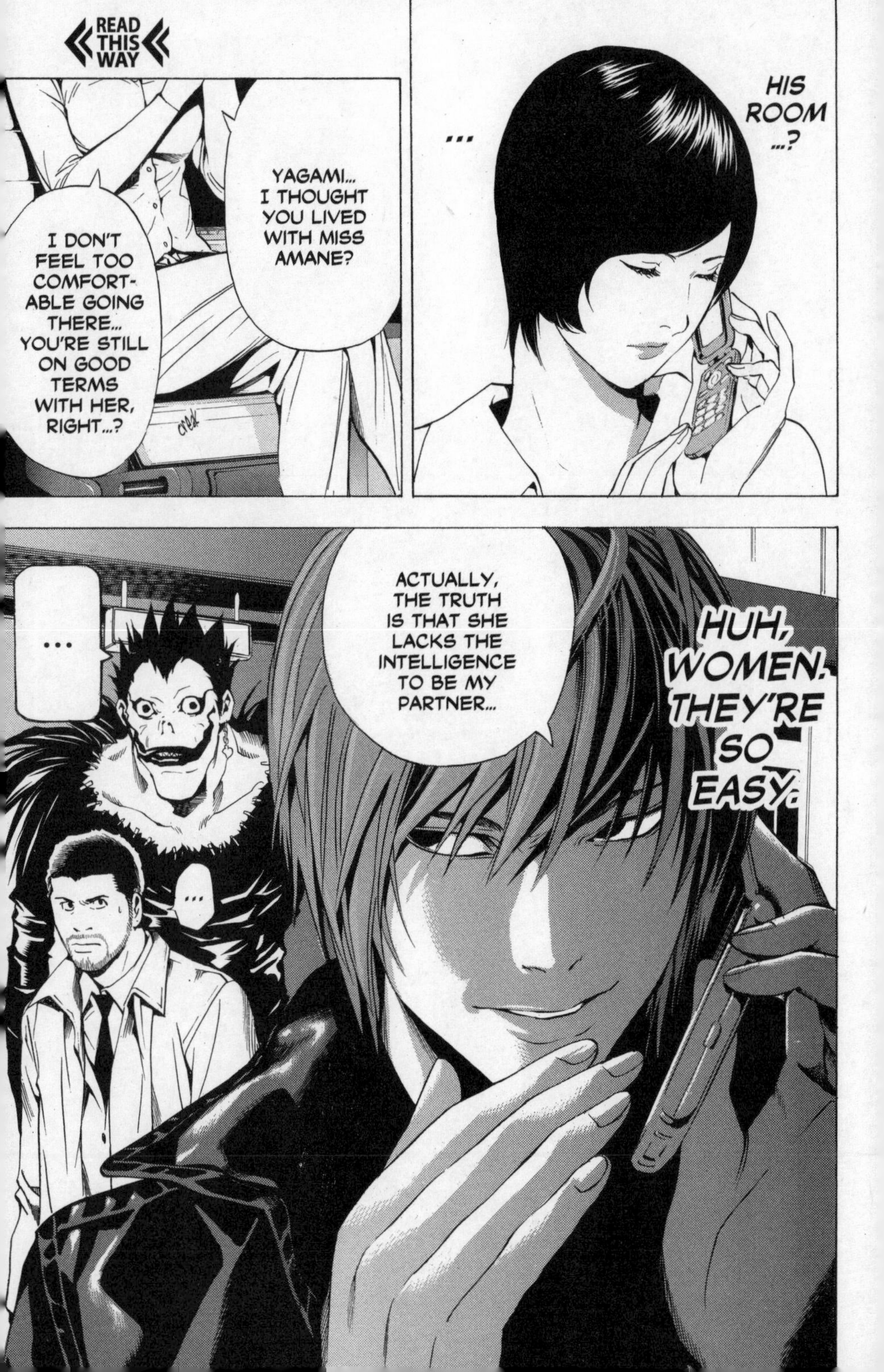
READ THIS WAY
HIS ROOM ...?
...
YAGAMI... I THOUGHT YOU LIVED WITH MISS AMANE?
I DON'T FEEL TOO COMFORT-ABLE GOING THERE... YOU'RE STILL ON GOOD TERMS WITH HER, RIGHT...?
ACTUALLY, THE TRUTH IS THAT SHE LACKS THE INTELLIGENCE TO BE MY PARTNER...
HUH, WOMEN. THEY'RE SO EASY.
...
...

DEATH NOTE
How to use it
LVII

○ In the DEATH NOTE you cannot set the death date longer than the victim's original life span. Even if the victim's death is set in the DEATH NOTE beyond his/her original life span, the victim will die before the set time.

デスノートで人間界本来の寿命を延ばす直接的な死の設定はできない。
人間界での本来の寿命より後に、死の時間を設定しても必ずその前に死ぬ。

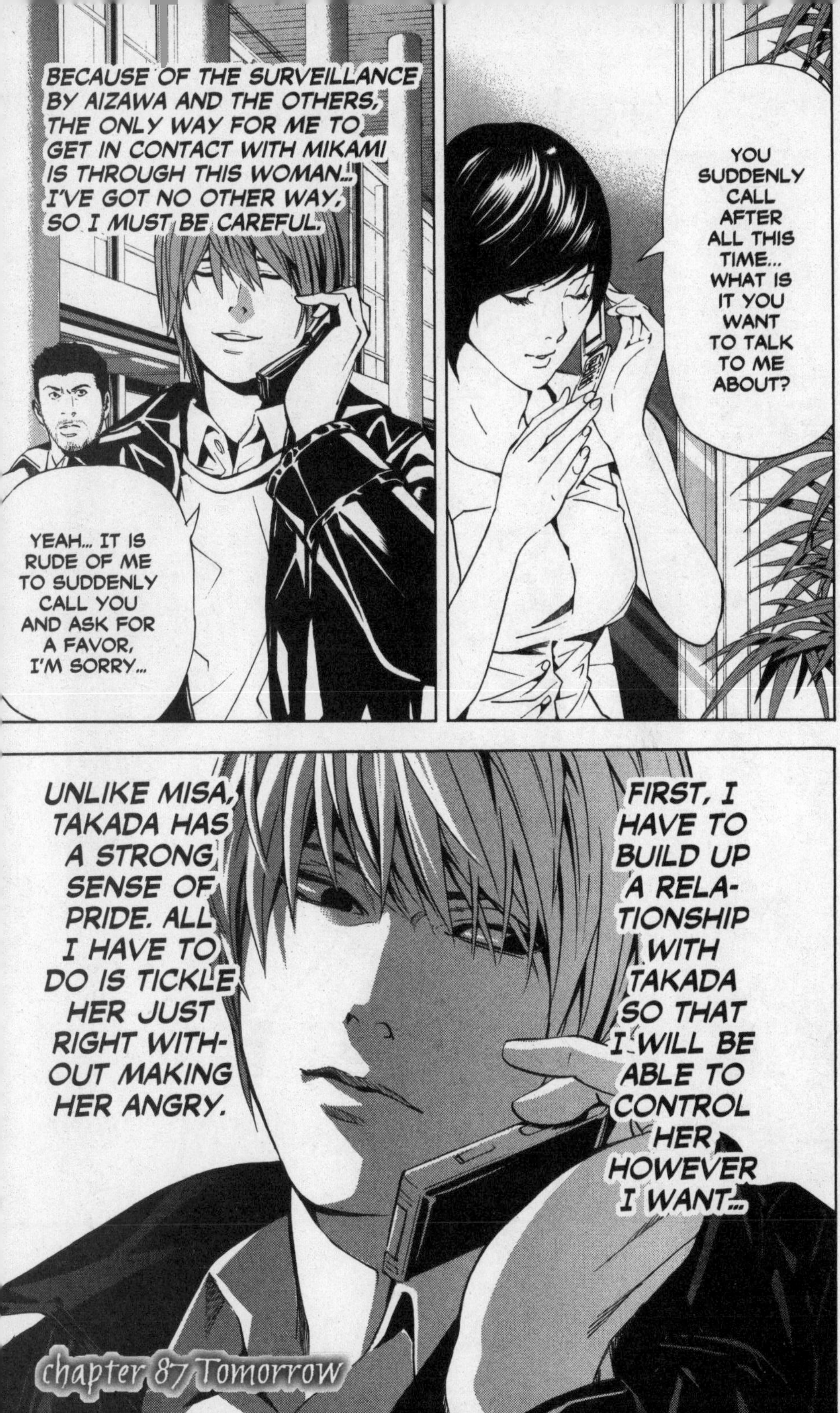
YOU SUDDENLY CALL AFTER ALL THIS TIME... WHAT IS IT YOU WANT TO TALK TO ME ABOUT?
BECAUSE OF THE SURVEILLANCE BY AIZAWA AND THE OTHERS, THE ONLY WAY FOR ME TO GET IN CONTACT WITH MIKAMI IS THROUGH THIS WOMAN... I'VE GOT NO OTHER WAY, SO I MUST BE CAREFUL.
YEAH... IT IS RUDE OF ME TO SUDDENLY CALL YOU AND ASK FOR A FAVOR, I'M SORRY...
FIRST, I HAVE TO BUILD UP A RELATIONSHIP WITH TAKADA SO THAT I WILL BE ABLE TO CONTROL HER HOWEVER I WANT...
UNLIKE MISA, TAKADA HAS A STRONG SENSE OF PRIDE. ALL I HAVE TO DO IS TICKLE HER JUST RIGHT WITHOUT MAKING HER ANGRY.
chapter 87 Tomorrow

chapter 87 Tomorrow

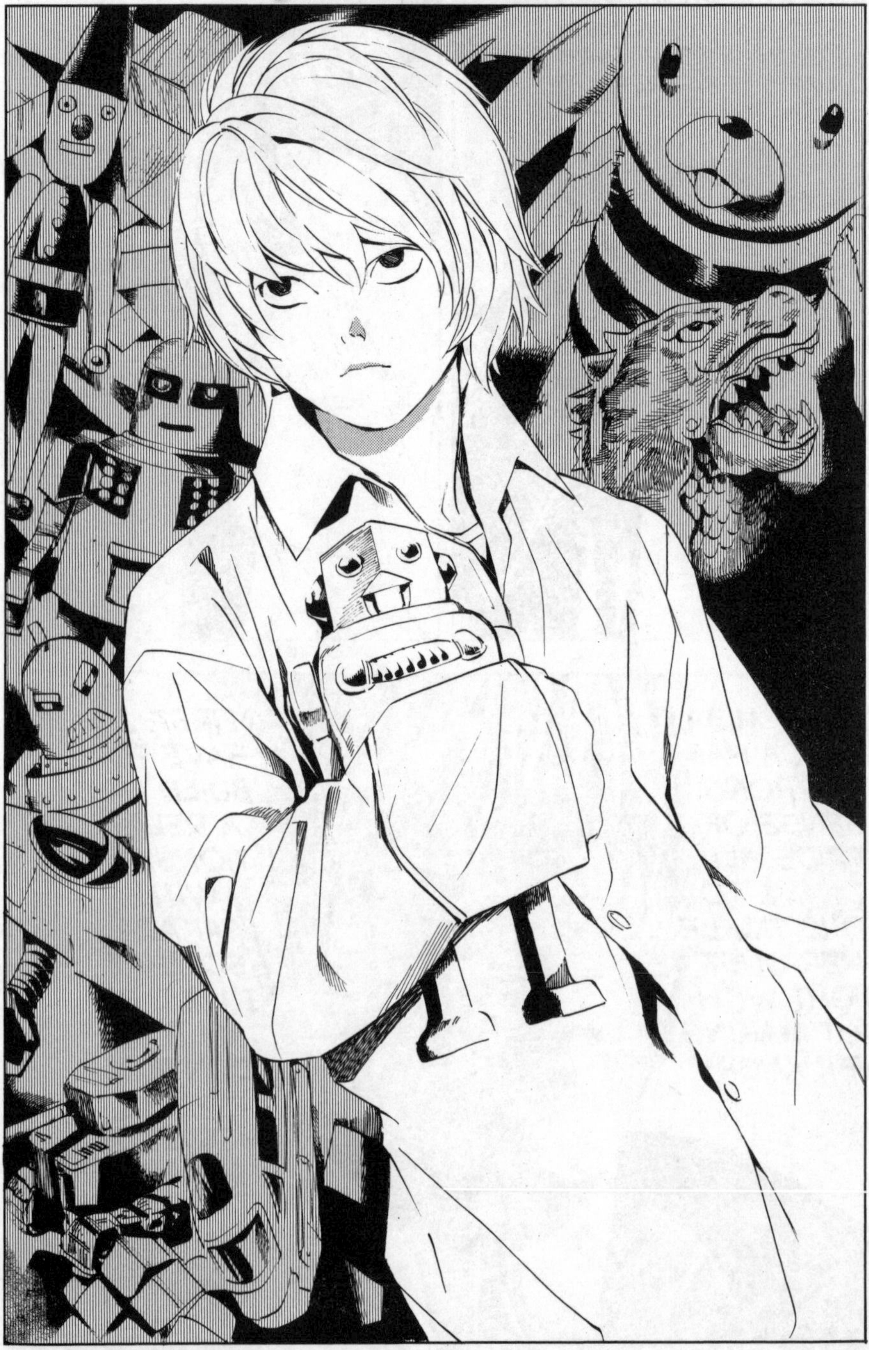

BUT... IF I WEREN'T IN THIS SITUATION, WOULD YOU HAVE BOTHERED TO CALL ME?

...

YOU'RE A WOMAN THE WHOLE WORLD PAYS ATTENTION TO NOW. IS IT IMPOSSIBLE FOR A GUY LIKE ME TO HAVE A CONVERSATION WITH JUST YOU?

AFTER UNIVERSITY, I NEVER GOT THE CHANCE TO TALK WITH YOU, EVEN IF I WANTED TO... BUT I CAN'T HELP FEELING THAT THIS IS DESTINY, IF THIS GIVES US A CHANCE TO TALK TO EACH OTHER AGAIN, EVEN THOUGH IT'S FOR WORK, AS WE ARE NOW MEMBERS OF SOCIETY.

THERE IT IS... LIGHT'S USE OF "DESTINY" WITH WOMEN. HE ACTUALLY USES THE SAME TRICK A LOT...

...

PROBABLY NOT.

...?!

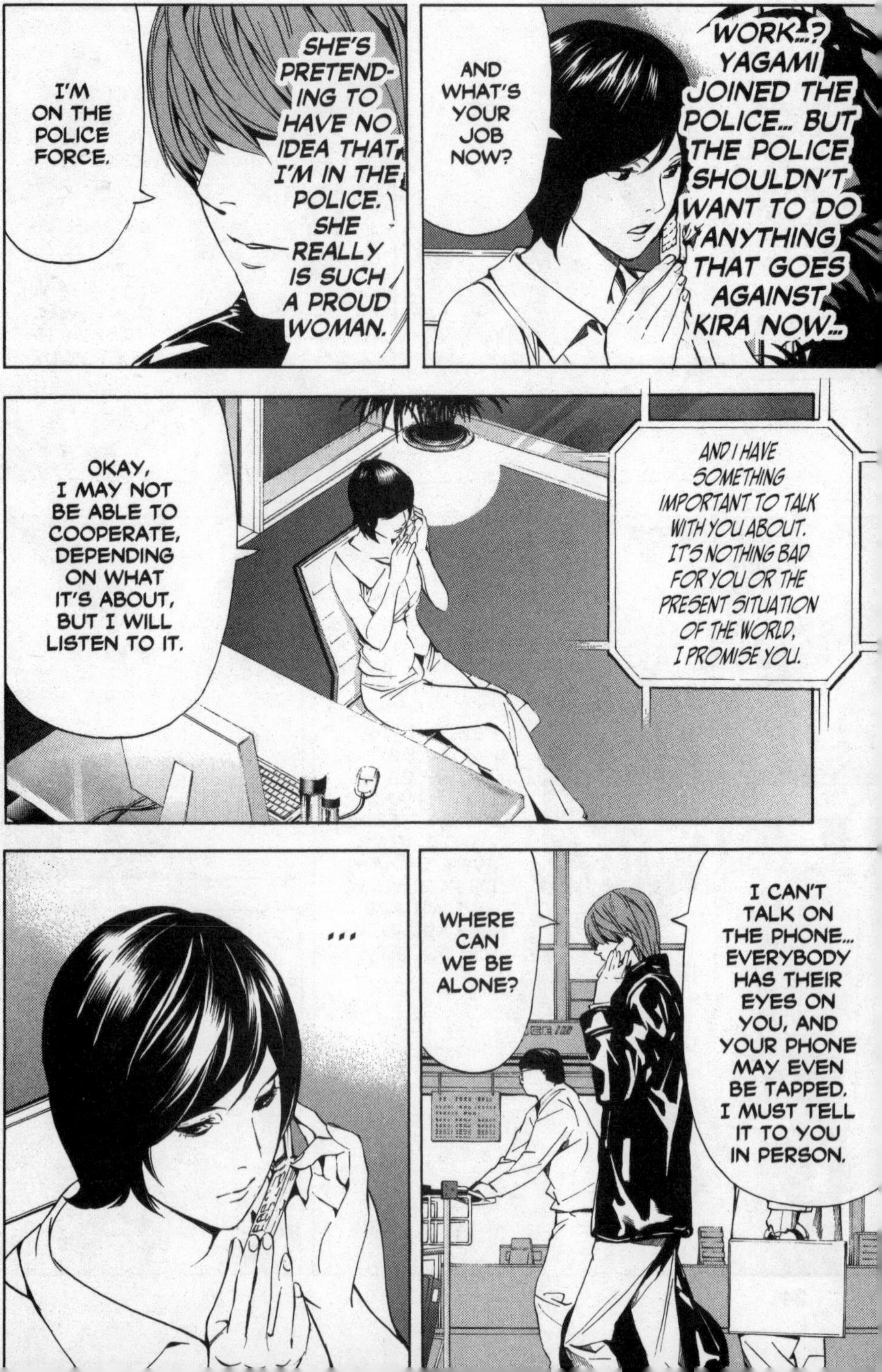
WORK...? YAGAMI JOINED THE POLICE... BUT THE POLICE SHOULDN'T WANT TO DO ANYTHING THAT GOES AGAINST KIRA NOW...
AND WHAT'S YOUR JOB NOW?
SHE'S PRETEND-ING TO HAVE NO IDEA THAT I'M IN THE POLICE. SHE REALLY IS SUCH A PROUD WOMAN.
I'M ON THE POLICE FORCE.
AND I HAVE SOMETHING IMPORTANT TO TALK WITH YOU ABOUT. IT'S NOTHING BAD FOR YOU OR THE PRESENT SITUATION OF THE WORLD, I PROMISE YOU.
OKAY, I MAY NOT BE ABLE TO COOPERATE, DEPENDING ON WHAT IT'S ABOUT, BUT I WILL LISTEN TO IT.
I CAN'T TALK ON THE PHONE... EVERYBODY HAS THEIR EYES ON YOU, AND YOUR PHONE MAY EVEN BE TAPPED. I MUST TELL IT TO YOU IN PERSON.
WHERE CAN WE BE ALONE?
...

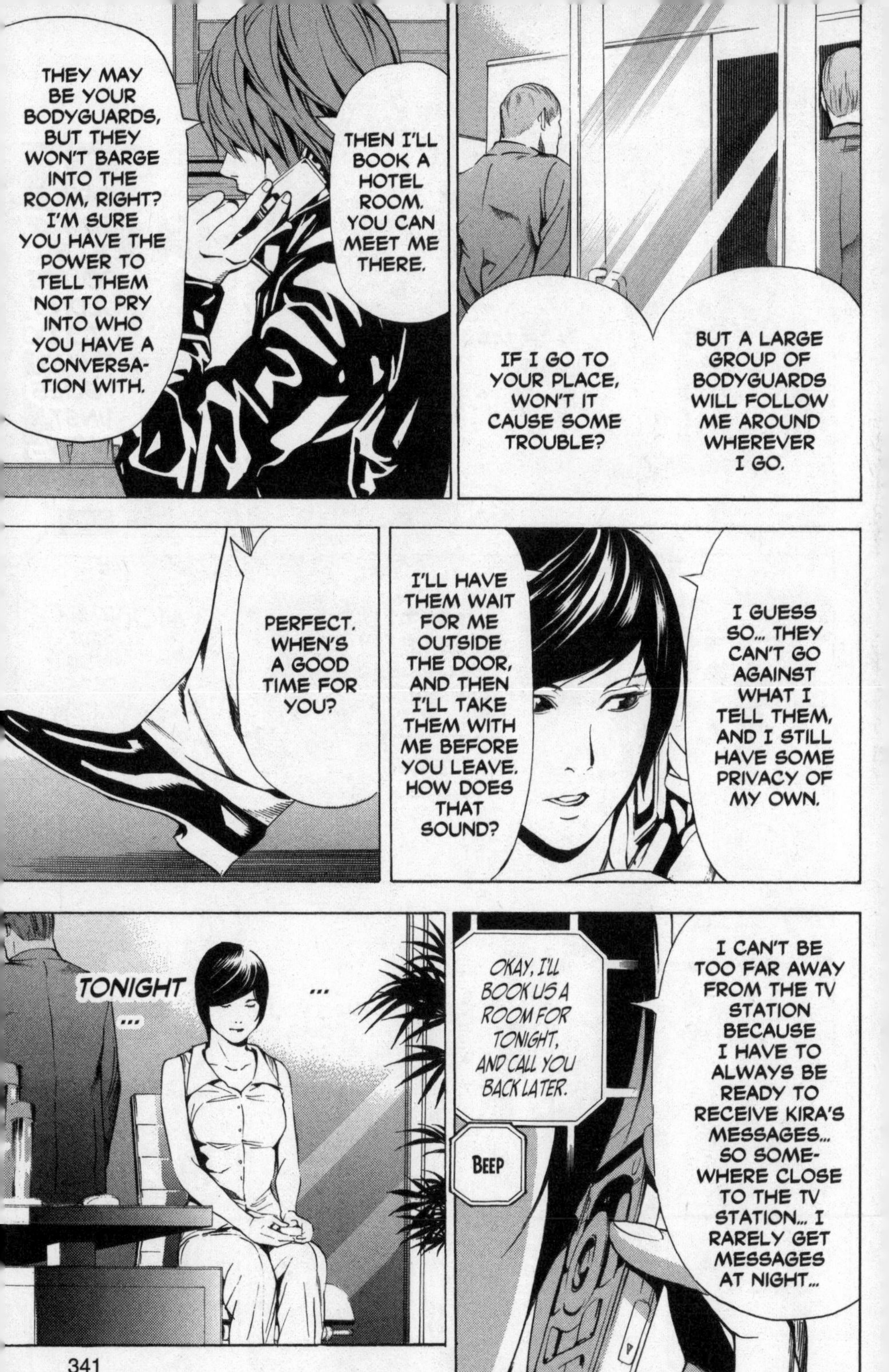
BUT A LARGE GROUP OF BODYGUARDS WILL FOLLOW ME AROUND WHEREVER I GO.
IF I GO TO YOUR PLACE, WON'T IT CAUSE SOME TROUBLE?
THEN I'LL BOOK A HOTEL ROOM. YOU CAN MEET ME THERE.
THEY MAY BE YOUR BODYGUARDS, BUT THEY WON'T BARGE INTO THE ROOM, RIGHT? I'M SURE YOU HAVE THE POWER TO TELL THEM NOT TO PRY INTO WHO YOU HAVE A CONVERSATION WITH.
I GUESS SO... THEY CAN'T GO AGAINST WHAT I TELL THEM, AND I STILL HAVE SOME PRIVACY OF MY OWN.
I'LL HAVE THEM WAIT FOR ME OUTSIDE THE DOOR, AND THEN I'LL TAKE THEM WITH ME BEFORE YOU LEAVE. HOW DOES THAT SOUND?
PERFECT. WHEN'S A GOOD TIME FOR YOU?
I CAN'T BE TOO FAR AWAY FROM THE TV STATION BECAUSE I HAVE TO ALWAYS BE READY TO RECEIVE KIRA'S MESSAGES... SO SOME-WHERE CLOSE TO THE TV STATION... I RARELY GET MESSAGES AT NIGHT...
OKAY, I'LL BOOK US A ROOM FOR TONIGHT, AND CALL YOU BACK LATER.
BEEP
...
TONIGHT ...

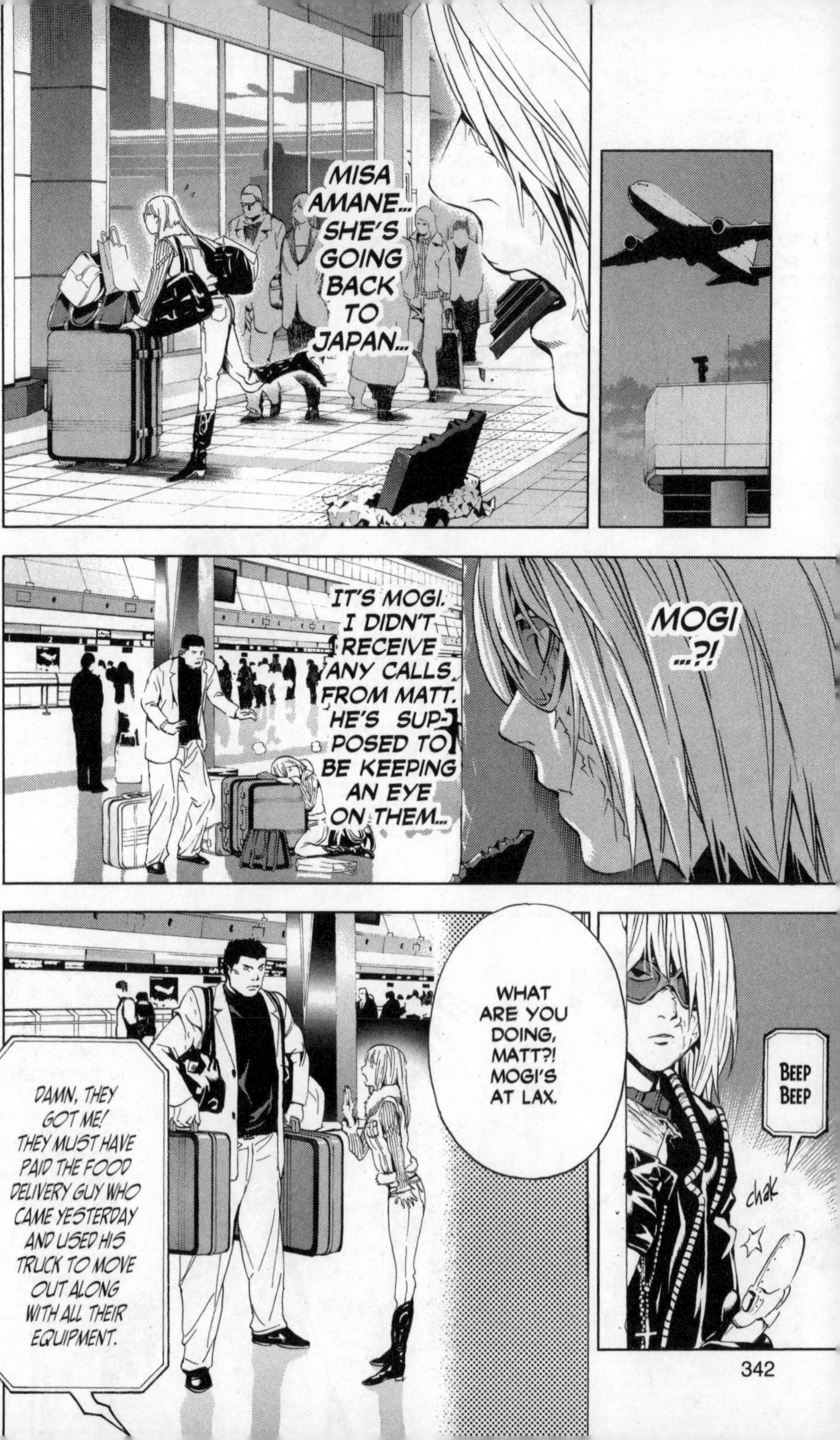
MISA AMANE... SHE'S GOING BACK TO JAPAN...
MOGI ...?!
IT'S MOGI. I DIDN'T RECEIVE ANY CALLS FROM MATT. HE'S SUP-POSED TO BE KEEPING AN EYE ON THEM...
BEEP BEEP
chak
WHAT ARE YOU DOING, MATT?! MOGI'S AT LAX.
DAMN, THEY GOT ME! THEY MUST HAVE PAID THE FOOD DELIVERY GUY WHO CAME YESTERDAY AND USED HIS TRUCK TO MOVE OUT ALONG WITH ALL THEIR EQUIPMENT.

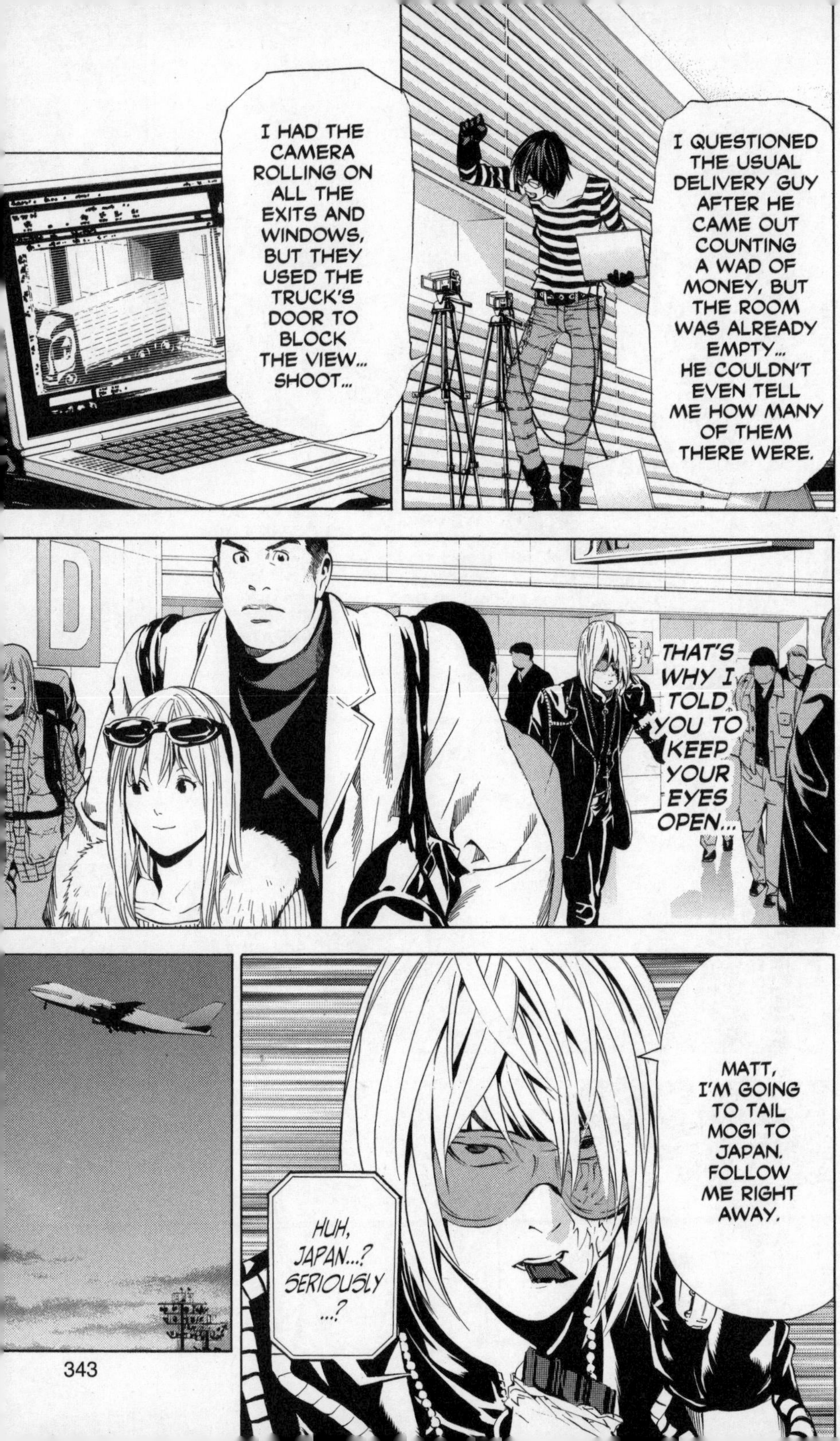
I QUESTIONED THE USUAL DELIVERY GUY AFTER HE CAME OUT COUNTING A WAD OF MONEY, BUT THE ROOM WAS ALREADY EMPTY... HE COULDN'T EVEN TELL ME HOW MANY OF THEM THERE WERE.
I HAD THE CAMERA ROLLING ON ALL THE EXITS AND WINDOWS, BUT THEY USED THE TRUCK'S DOOR TO BLOCK THE VIEW... SHOOT...
THAT'S WHY I TOLD YOU TO KEEP YOUR EYES OPEN...
MATT, I'M GOING TO TAIL MOGI TO JAPAN. FOLLOW ME RIGHT AWAY.
HUH, JAPAN...? SERIOUSLY ...?

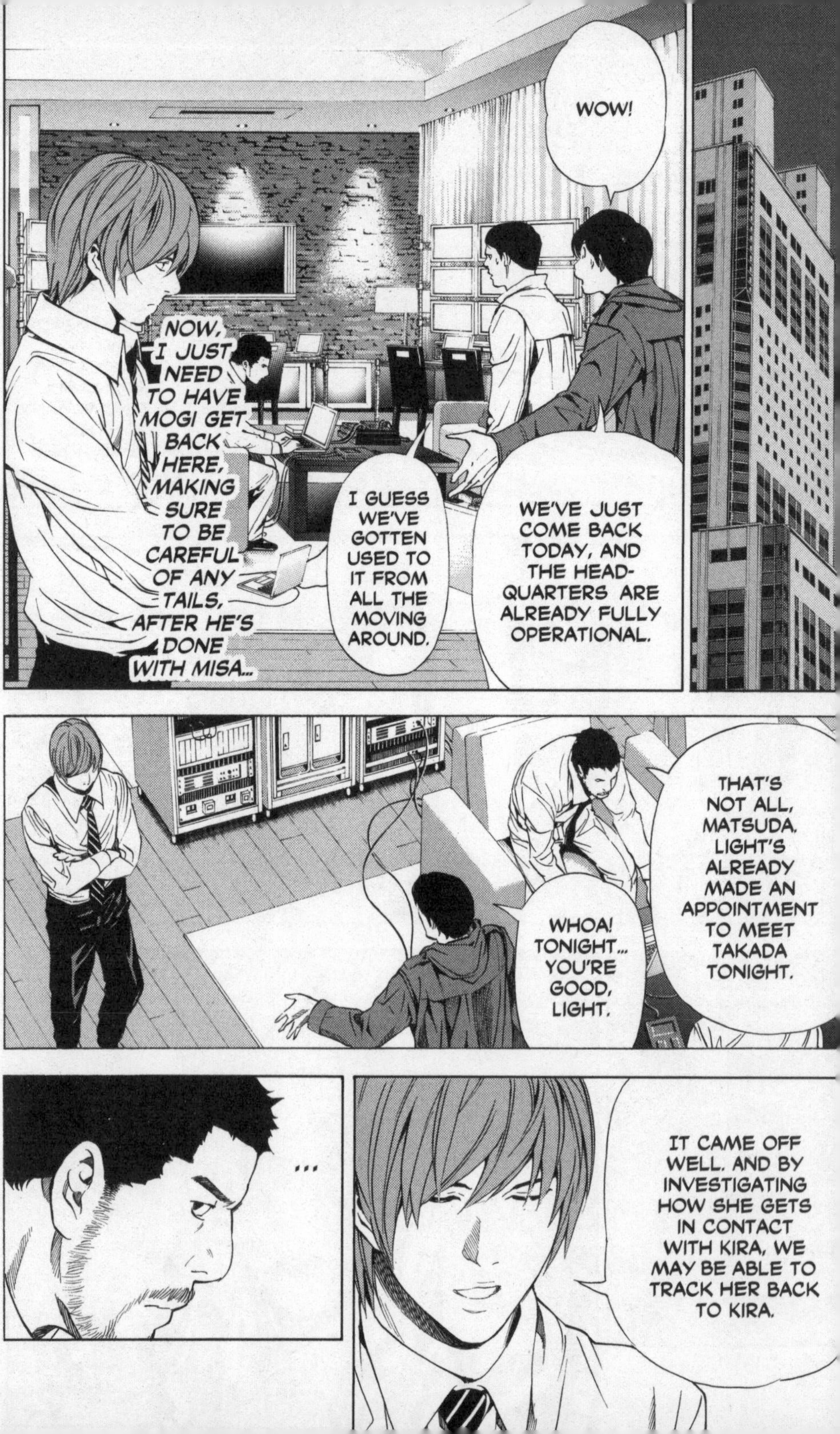
WOW!
WE'VE JUST COME BACK TODAY, AND THE HEAD-QUARTERS ARE ALREADY FULLY OPERATIONAL.
I GUESS WE'VE GOTTEN USED TO IT FROM ALL THE MOVING AROUND.
NOW, I JUST NEED TO HAVE MOGI GET BACK HERE, MAKING SURE TO BE CAREFUL OF ANY TAILS, AFTER HE'S DONE WITH MISA...
THAT'S NOT ALL, MATSUDA. LIGHT'S ALREADY MADE AN APPOINTMENT TO MEET TAKADA TONIGHT.
WHOA! TONIGHT... YOU'RE GOOD, LIGHT.
IT CAME OFF WELL. AND BY INVESTIGATING HOW SHE GETS IN CONTACT WITH KIRA, WE MAY BE ABLE TO TRACK HER BACK TO KIRA.
...

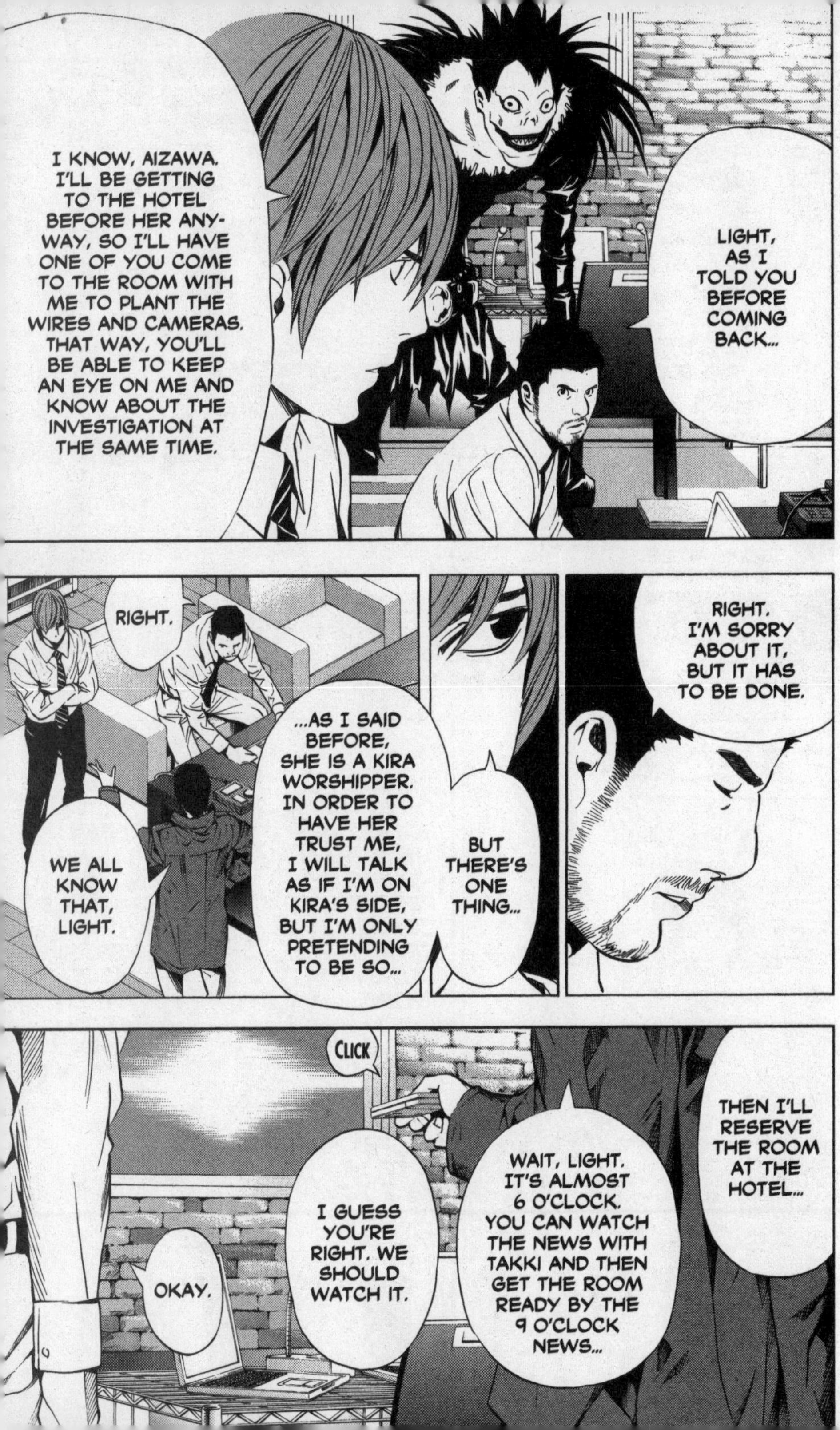
LIGHT, AS I TOLD YOU BEFORE COMING BACK...
I KNOW, AIZAWA. I'LL BE GETTING TO THE HOTEL BEFORE HER ANY-WAY, SO I'LL HAVE ONE OF YOU COME TO THE ROOM WITH ME TO PLANT THE WIRES AND CAMERAS. THAT WAY, YOU'LL BE ABLE TO KEEP AN EYE ON ME AND KNOW ABOUT THE INVESTIGATION AT THE SAME TIME.
RIGHT. I'M SORRY ABOUT IT, BUT IT HAS TO BE DONE.
BUT THERE'S ONE THING...
...AS I SAID BEFORE, SHE IS A KIRA WORSHIPPER. IN ORDER TO HAVE HER TRUST ME, I WILL TALK AS IF I'M ON KIRA'S SIDE, BUT I'M ONLY PRETENDING TO BE SO...
WE ALL KNOW THAT, LIGHT.
RIGHT.
THEN I'LL RESERVE THE ROOM AT THE HOTEL...
CLICK
WAIT, LIGHT. IT'S ALMOST 6 O'CLOCK. YOU CAN WATCH THE NEWS WITH TAKKI AND THEN GET THE ROOM READY BY THE 9 O'CLOCK NEWS...
I GUESS YOU'RE RIGHT. WE SHOULD WATCH IT.
OKAY.

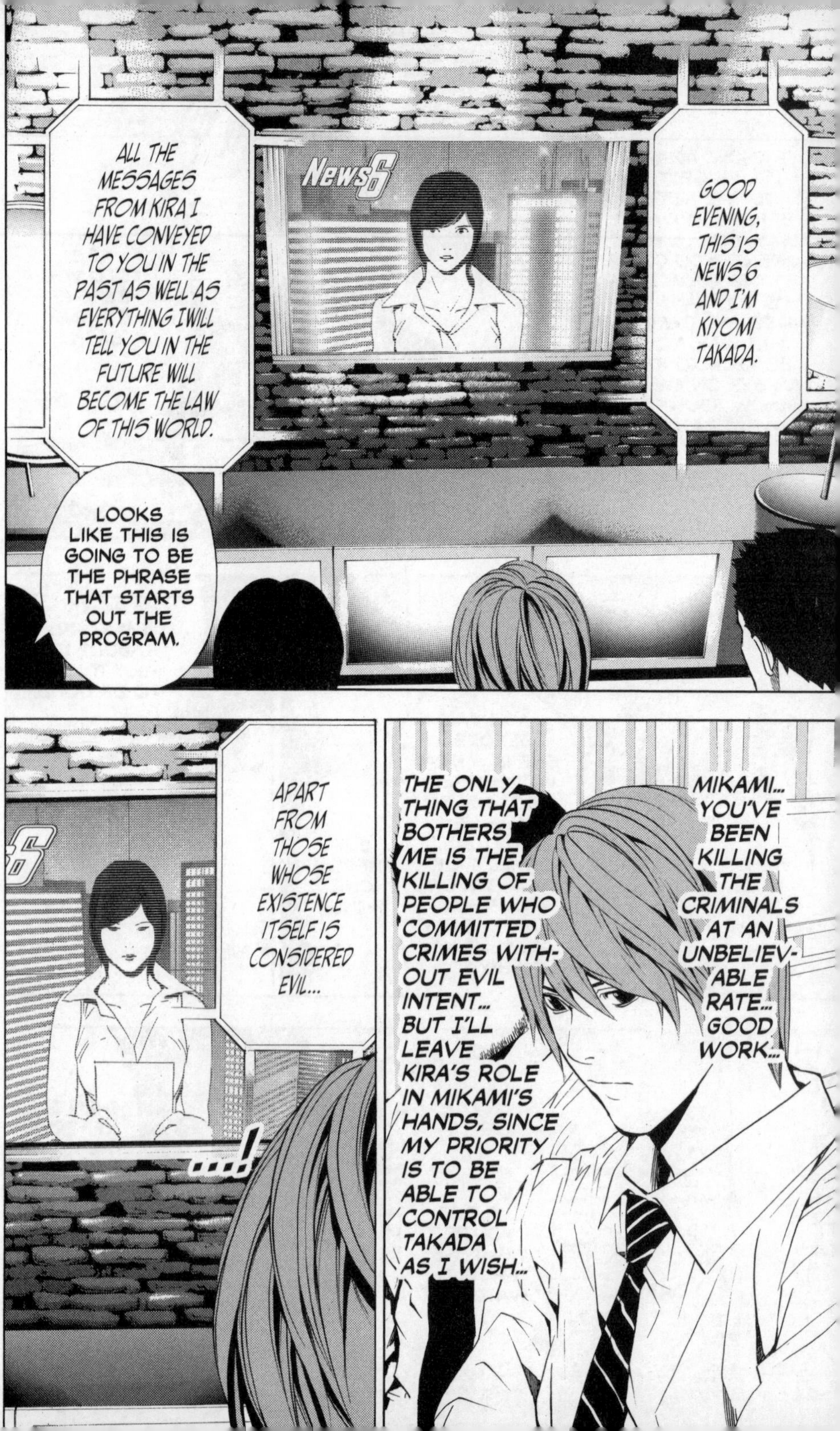

News6
GOOD EVENING, THIS IS NEWS 6 AND I'M KIYOMI TAKADA.
ALL THE MESSAGES FROM KIRA I HAVE CONVEYED TO YOU IN THE PAST AS WELL AS EVERYTHING I WILL TELL YOU IN THE FUTURE WILL BECOME THE LAW OF THIS WORLD.
LOOKS LIKE THIS IS GOING TO BE THE PHRASE THAT STARTS OUT THE PROGRAM.
MIKAMI... YOU'VE BEEN KILLING THE CRIMINALS AT AN UNBELIEV-ABLE RATE... GOOD WORK...
THE ONLY THING THAT BOTHERS ME IS THE KILLING OF PEOPLE WHO COMMITTED CRIMES WITH-OUT EVIL INTENT... BUT I'LL LEAVE KIRA'S ROLE IN MIKAMI'S HANDS, SINCE MY PRIORITY IS TO BE ABLE TO CONTROL TAKADA AS I WISH...
...!
APART FROM THOSE WHOSE EXISTENCE ITSELF IS CONSIDERED EVIL...

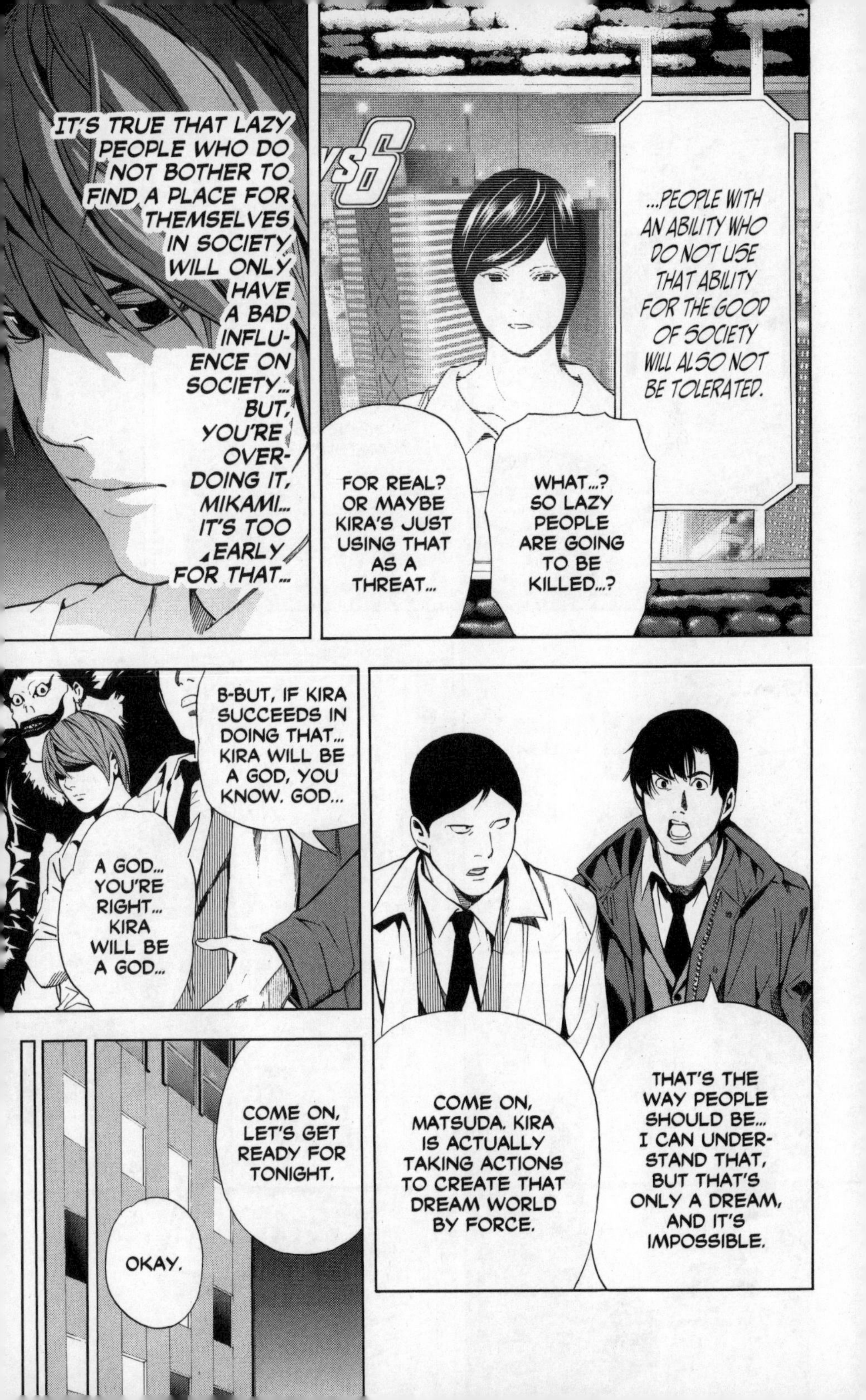
...PEOPLE WITH AN ABILITY WHO DO NOT USE THAT ABILITY FOR THE GOOD OF SOCIETY WILL ALSO NOT BE TOLERATED.
WHAT...? SO LAZY PEOPLE ARE GOING TO BE KILLED...?
FOR REAL? OR MAYBE KIRA'S JUST USING THAT AS A THREAT...
IT'S TRUE THAT LAZY PEOPLE WHO DO NOT BOTHER TO FIND A PLACE FOR THEMSELVES IN SOCIETY WILL ONLY HAVE A BAD INFLUENCE ON SOCIETY... BUT, YOU'RE OVERDOING IT, MIKAMI... IT'S TOO EARLY FOR THAT...
THAT'S THE WAY PEOPLE SHOULD BE... I CAN UNDERSTAND THAT, BUT THAT'S ONLY A DREAM, AND IT'S IMPOSSIBLE.
COME ON, MATSUDA. KIRA IS ACTUALLY TAKING ACTIONS TO CREATE THAT DREAM WORLD BY FORCE.
B-BUT, IF KIRA SUCCEEDS IN DOING THAT... KIRA WILL BE A GOD, YOU KNOW. GOD...
A GOD... YOU'RE RIGHT... KIRA WILL BE A GOD...
COME ON, LET'S GET READY FOR TONIGHT.
OKAY.

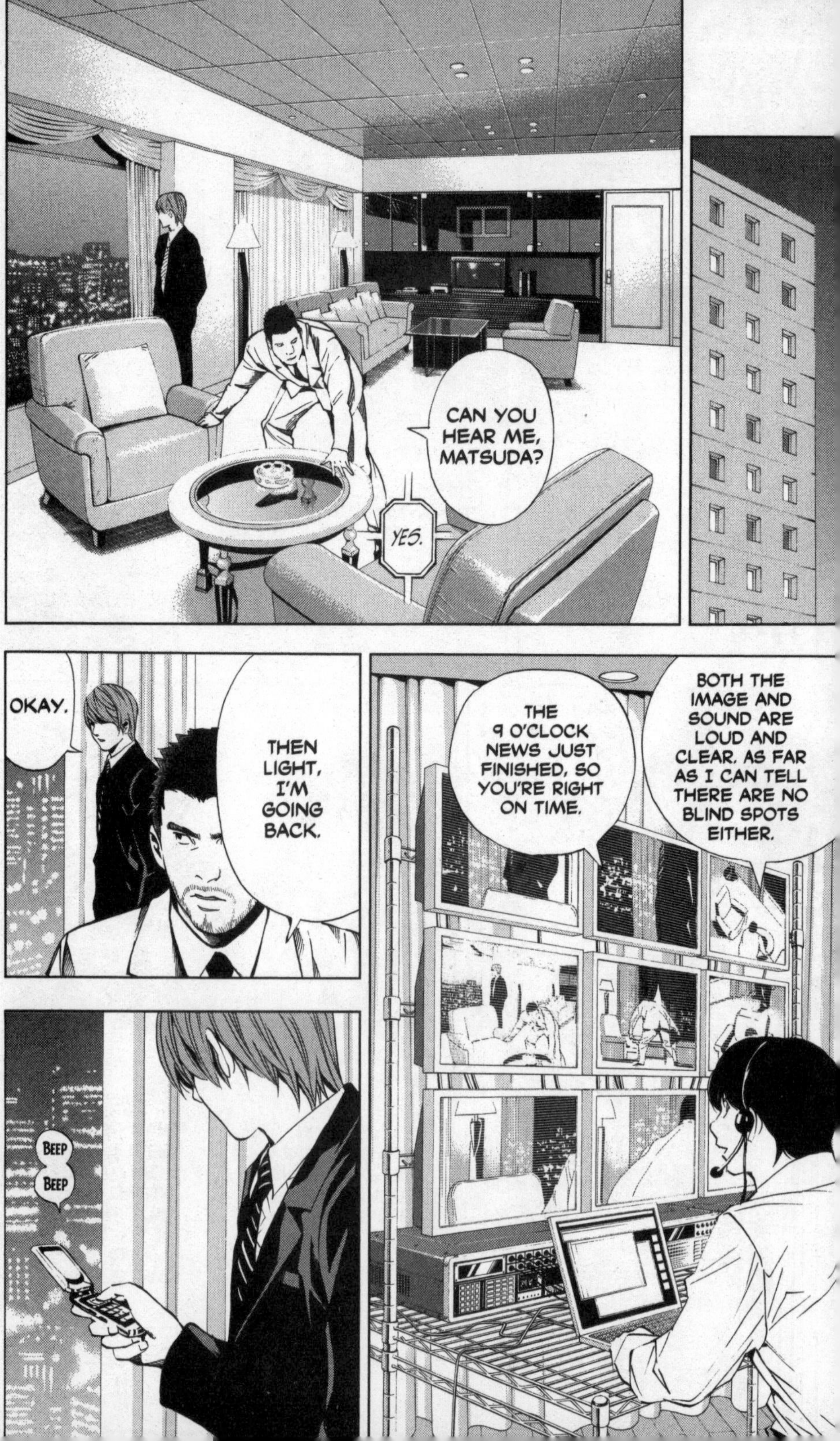
CAN YOU HEAR ME, MATSUDA?
YES.
BOTH THE IMAGE AND SOUND ARE LOUD AND CLEAR. AS FAR AS I CAN TELL THERE ARE NO BLIND SPOTS EITHER.
THE 9 O'CLOCK NEWS JUST FINISHED, SO YOU'RE RIGHT ON TIME.
THEN LIGHT, I'M GOING BACK.
OKAY.
BEEP
BEEP

READ THIS WAY

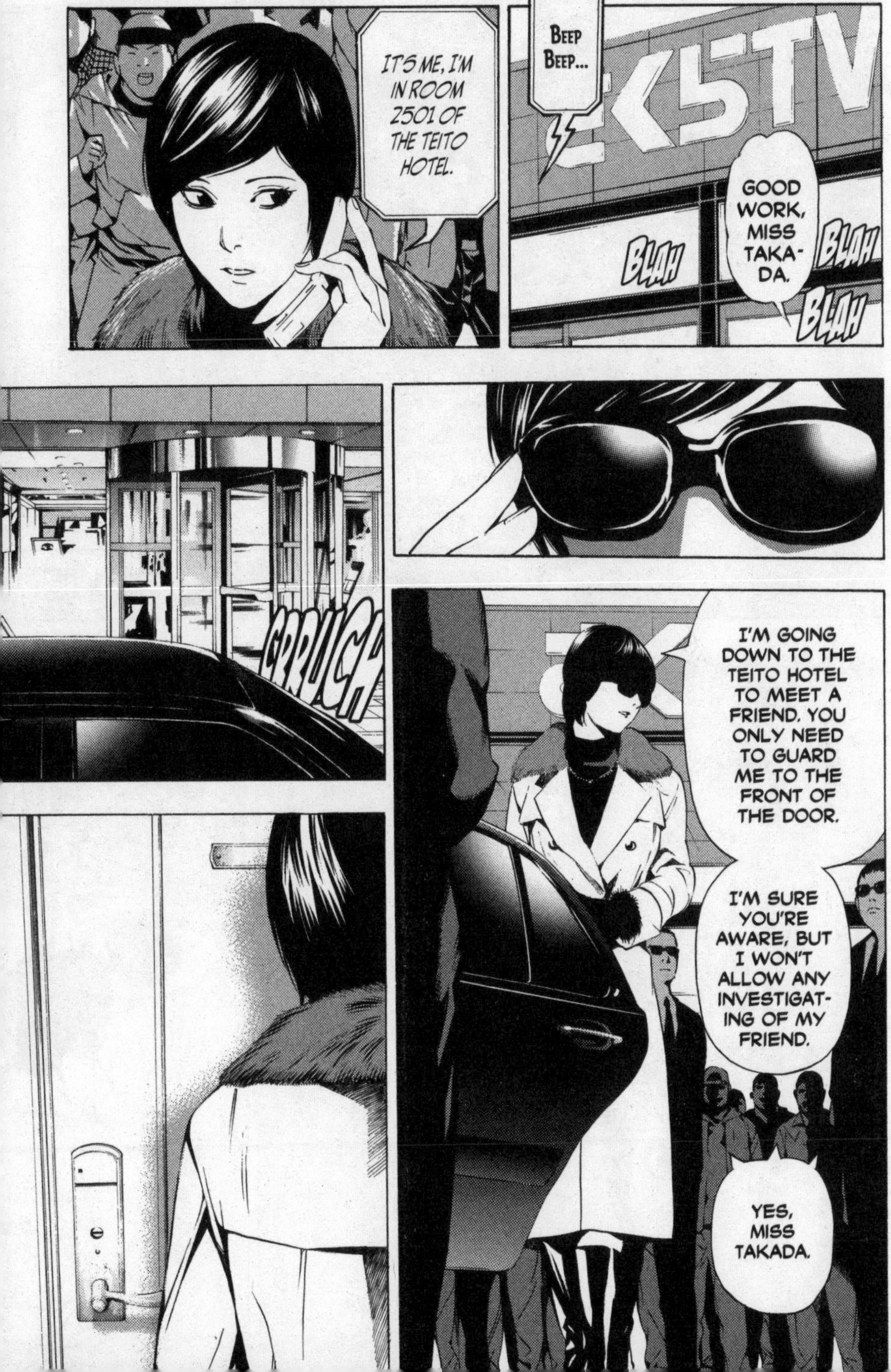
BEEP BEEP...
GOOD WORK, MISS TAKADA.
BLAH
BLAH
BLAH
IT'S ME, I'M IN ROOM 2501 OF THE TEITO HOTEL.
I'M GOING DOWN TO THE TEITO HOTEL TO MEET A FRIEND. YOU ONLY NEED TO GUARD ME TO THE FRONT OF THE DOOR.
I'M SURE YOU'RE AWARE, BUT I WON'T ALLOW ANY INVESTIGATING OF MY FRIEND.
YES, MISS TAKADA.
CRRUCH

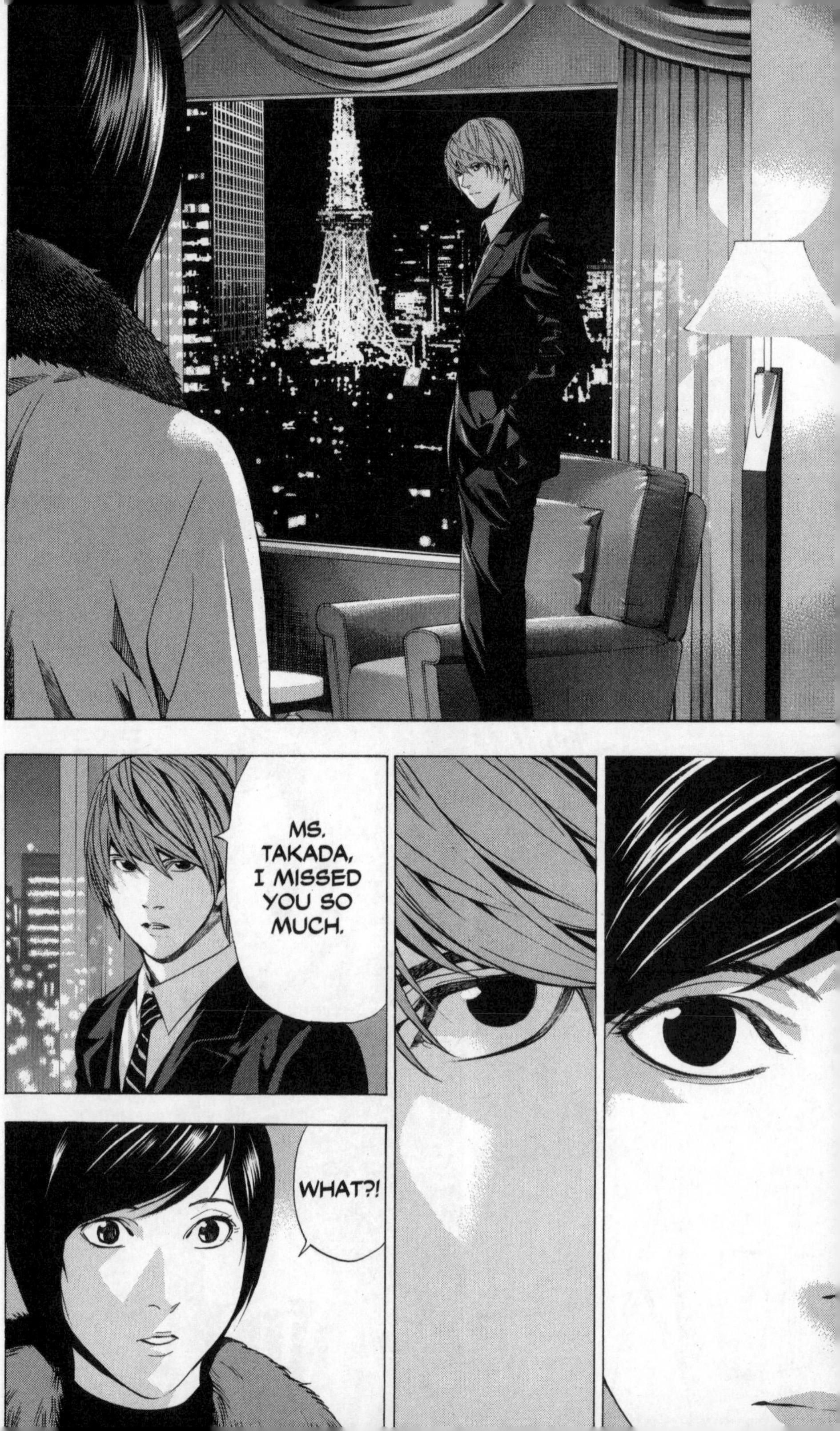
MS. TAKADA, I MISSED YOU SO MUCH.
WHAT?!

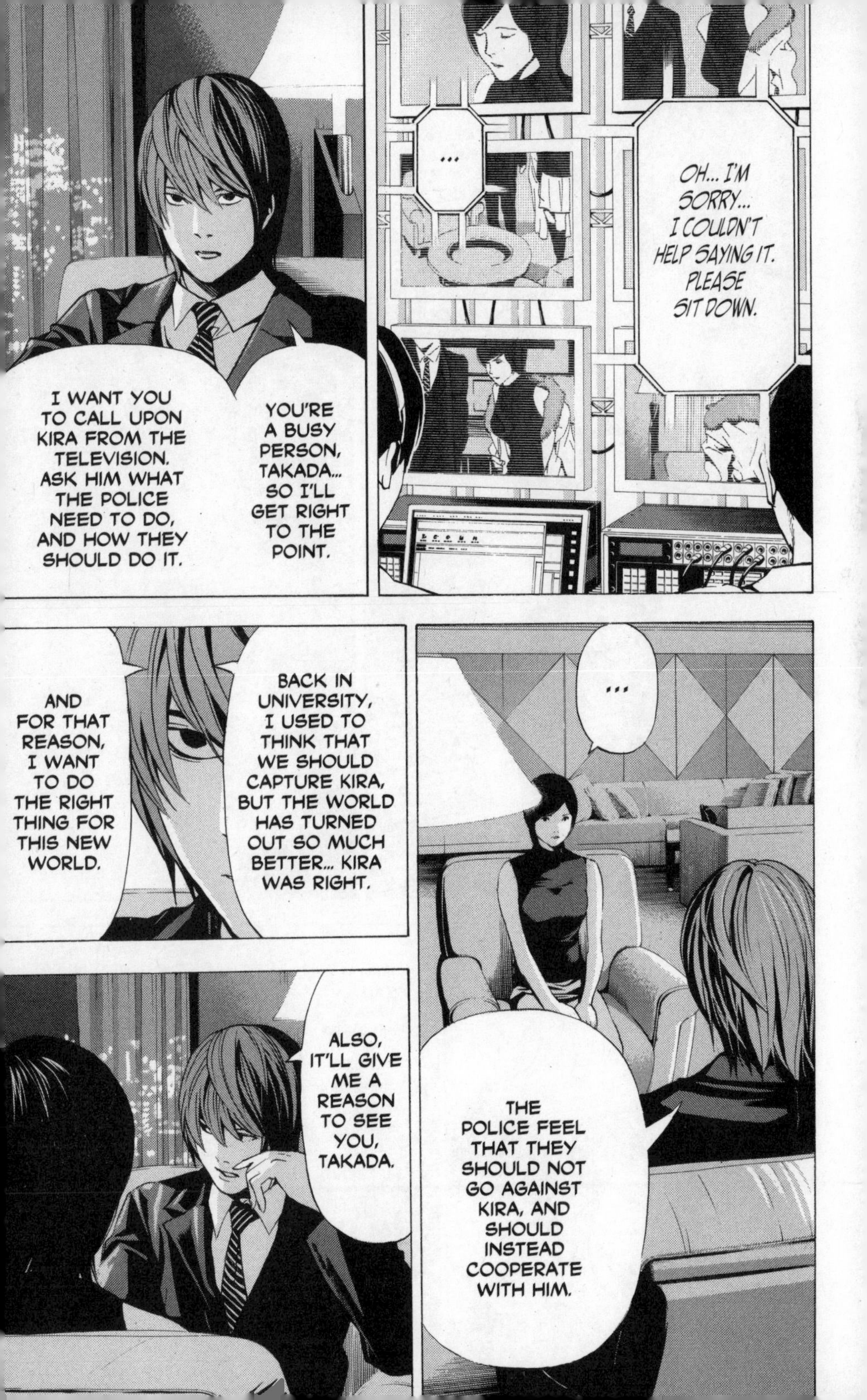
OH... I'M SORRY... I COULDN'T HELP SAYING IT. PLEASE SIT DOWN.
...
YOU'RE A BUSY PERSON, TAKADA... SO I'LL GET RIGHT TO THE POINT.
I WANT YOU TO CALL UPON KIRA FROM THE TELEVISION. ASK HIM WHAT THE POLICE NEED TO DO, AND HOW THEY SHOULD DO IT.
...
THE POLICE FEEL THAT THEY SHOULD NOT GO AGAINST KIRA, AND SHOULD INSTEAD COOPERATE WITH HIM.
BACK IN UNIVERSITY, I USED TO THINK THAT WE SHOULD CAPTURE KIRA, BUT THE WORLD HAS TURNED OUT SO MUCH BETTER... KIRA WAS RIGHT.
AND FOR THAT REASON, I WANT TO DO THE RIGHT THING FOR THIS NEW WORLD.
ALSO, IT'LL GIVE ME A REASON TO SEE YOU, TAKADA.

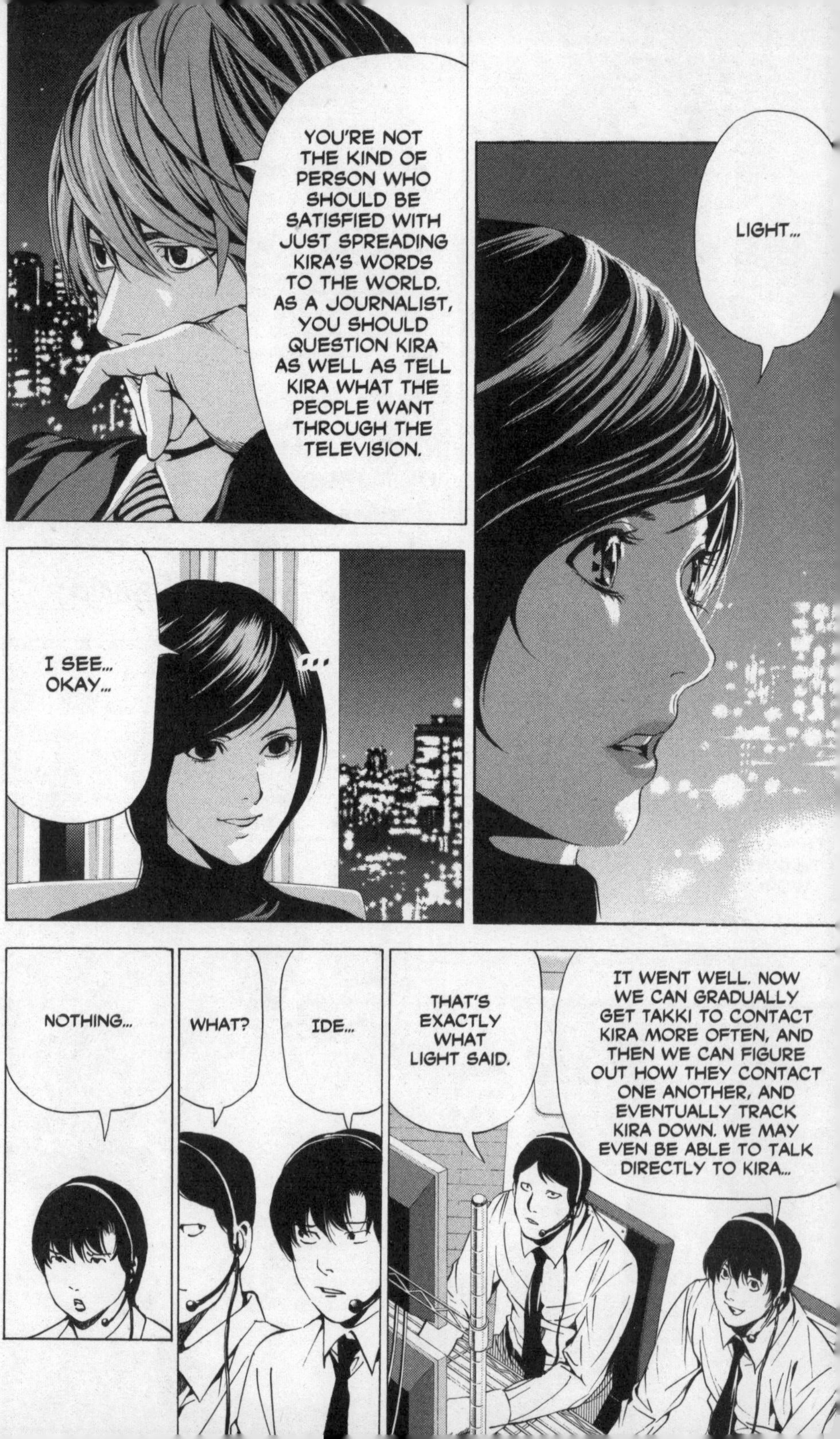
LIGHT...
YOU'RE NOT THE KIND OF PERSON WHO SHOULD BE SATISFIED WITH JUST SPREADING KIRA'S WORDS TO THE WORLD. AS A JOURNALIST, YOU SHOULD QUESTION KIRA AS WELL AS TELL KIRA WHAT THE PEOPLE WANT THROUGH THE TELEVISION.
...
I SEE... OKAY...
IT WENT WELL. NOW WE CAN GRADUALLY GET TAKKI TO CONTACT KIRA MORE OFTEN, AND THEN WE CAN FIGURE OUT HOW THEY CONTACT ONE ANOTHER, AND EVENTUALLY TRACK KIRA DOWN. WE MAY EVEN BE ABLE TO TALK DIRECTLY TO KIRA...
THAT'S EXACTLY WHAT LIGHT SAID.
IDE...
WHAT?
NOTHING...

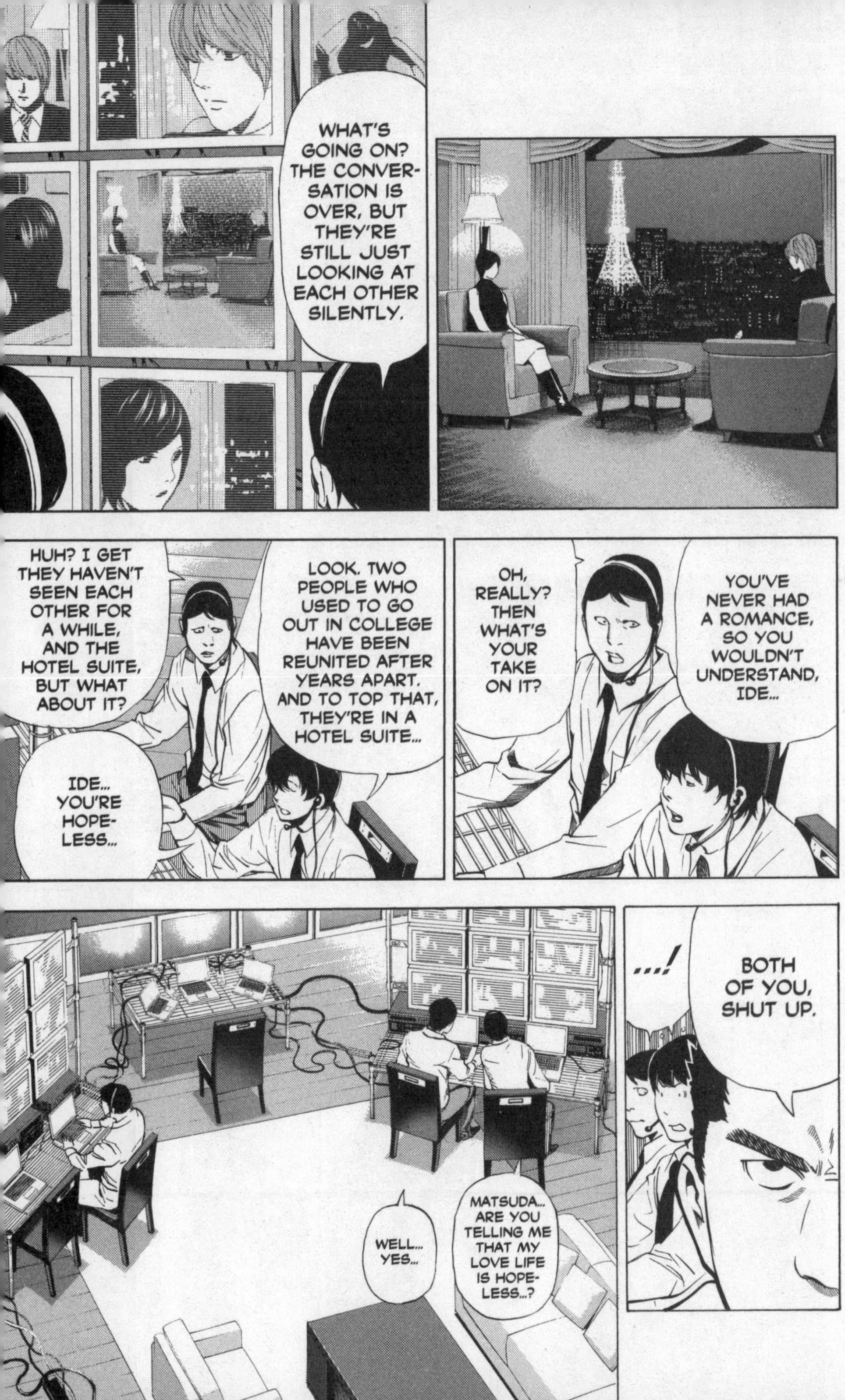
WHAT'S GOING ON? THE CONVERSATION IS OVER, BUT THEY'RE STILL JUST LOOKING AT EACH OTHER SILENTLY.
YOU'VE NEVER HAD A ROMANCE, SO YOU WOULDN'T UNDERSTAND, IDE...
OH, REALLY? THEN WHAT'S YOUR TAKE ON IT?
LOOK. TWO PEOPLE WHO USED TO GO OUT IN COLLEGE HAVE BEEN REUNITED AFTER YEARS APART. AND TO TOP THAT, THEY'RE IN A HOTEL SUITE...
HUH? I GET THEY HAVEN'T SEEN EACH OTHER FOR A WHILE, AND THE HOTEL SUITE, BUT WHAT ABOUT IT?
IDE... YOU'RE HOPELESS...
BOTH OF YOU, SHUT UP.
...!
MATSUDA... ARE YOU TELLING ME THAT MY LOVE LIFE IS HOPELESS...?
WELL... YES...

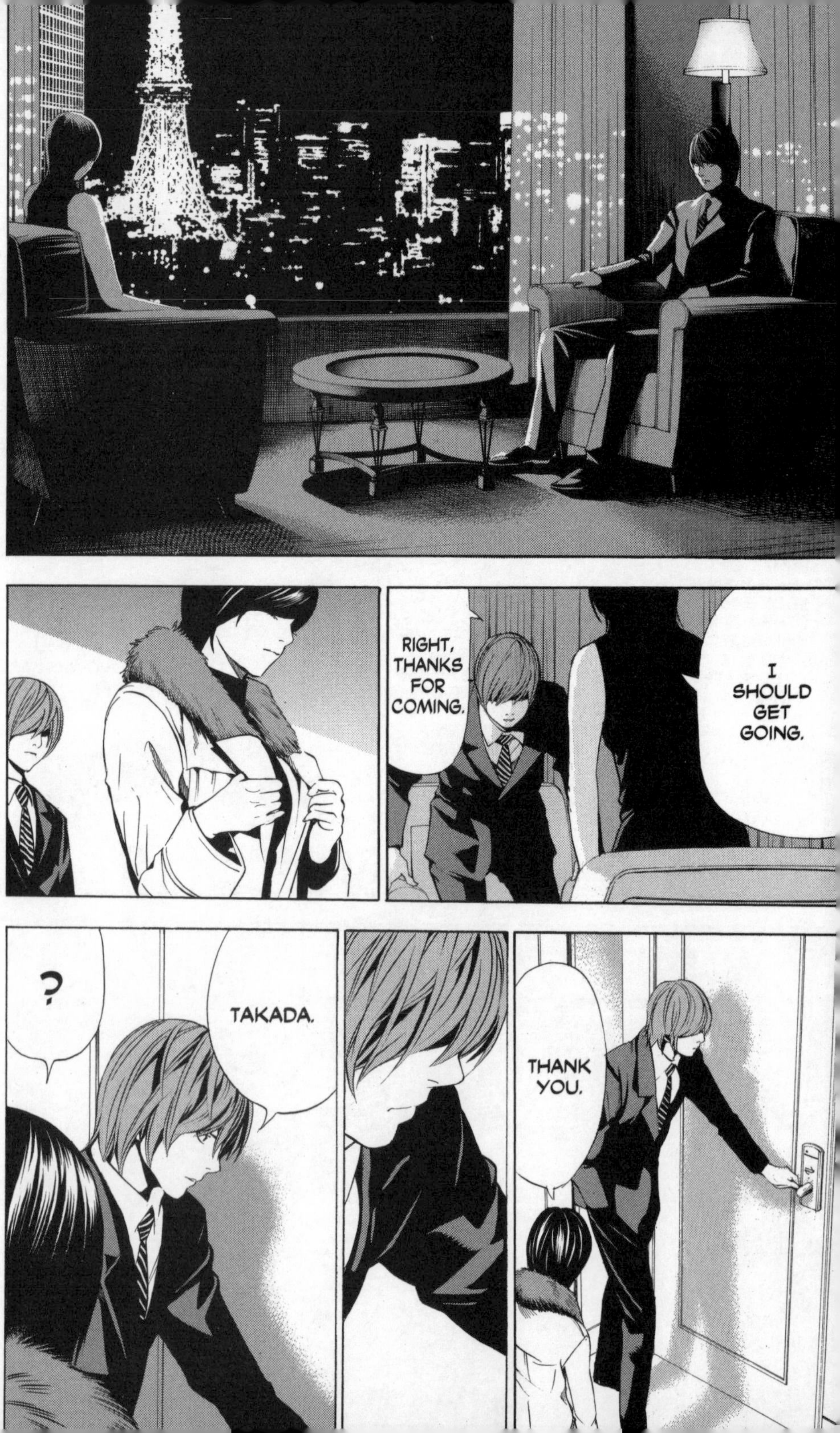
I SHOULD GET GOING.
RIGHT, THANKS FOR COMING.
THANK YOU.
TAKADA.
?

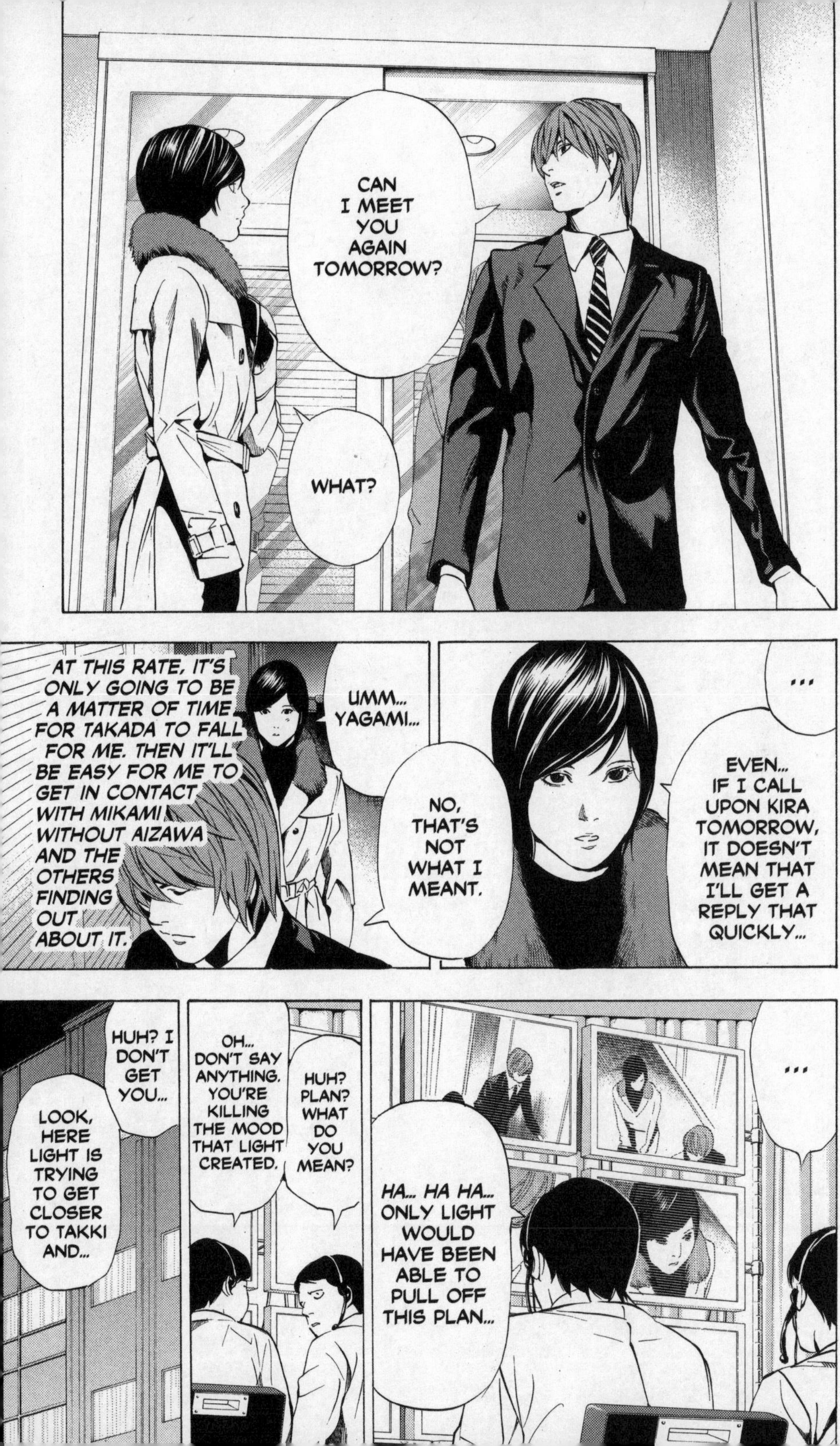
CAN I MEET YOU AGAIN TOMORROW?
WHAT?
...
EVEN... IF I CALL UPON KIRA TOMORROW, IT DOESN'T MEAN THAT I'LL GET A REPLY THAT QUICKLY...
NO, THAT'S NOT WHAT I MEANT.
UMM... YAGAMI...
AT THIS RATE, IT'S ONLY GOING TO BE A MATTER OF TIME FOR TAKADA TO FALL FOR ME. THEN IT'LL BE EASY FOR ME TO GET IN CONTACT WITH MIKAMI WITHOUT AIZAWA AND THE OTHERS FINDING OUT ABOUT IT.
...
HA... HA HA... ONLY LIGHT WOULD HAVE BEEN ABLE TO PULL OFF THIS PLAN...
HUH? PLAN? WHAT DO YOU MEAN?
OH... DON'T SAY ANYTHING. YOU'RE KILLING THE MOOD THAT LIGHT CREATED.
HUH? I DON'T GET YOU...
LOOK, HERE LIGHT IS TRYING TO GET CLOSER TO TAKKI AND...

DEATH NOTE
How to use it
Lv III

- By manipulating the death of a human that has influence over another human's life, that human's original life span can sometimes be lengthened.

にんげん　せいし　かか　ほか　にんげん　し　あやつ　こと
その人間の生死に関わる他の人間の死を操る事で、
にんげんかい　ほんらい　じゅみょう　へんか　の　こと
人間界での本来の寿命が変化し延びる事はある。

- If a god of death intentionally does the above manipulation to effectively lengthen a human's life span, the god of death will die, but even if a human does the same, the human will not die.

じょうき　しにがみ　けっか　じゅみょう　の　にんげん　こうい　も　おこな
上記を死神が、結果として寿命が延びる人間に好意を持って行うと
しにがみ　し　にんげん　し
死神は死ぬが、人間がこれをしても死なない。

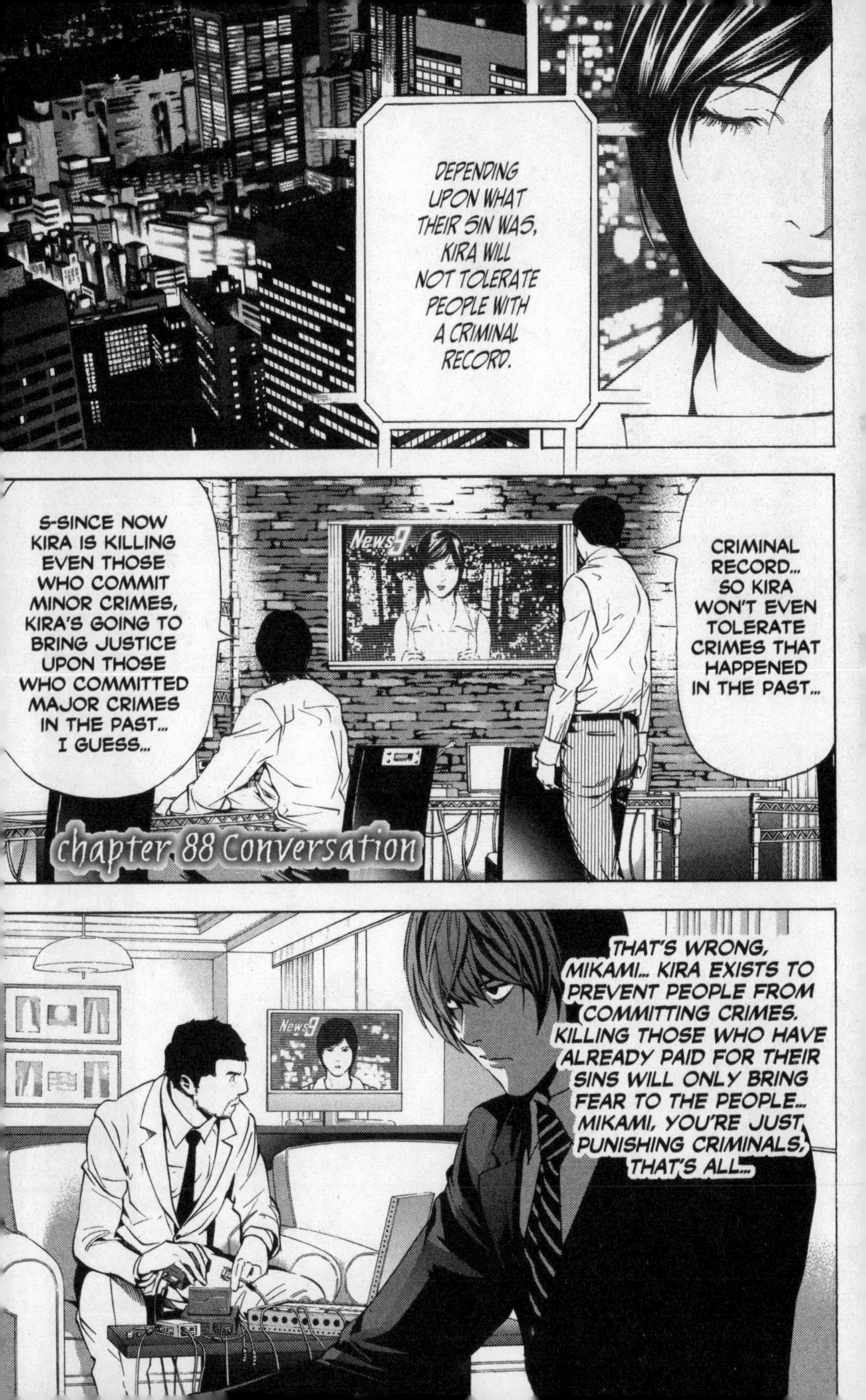
DEPENDING UPON WHAT THEIR SIN WAS, KIRA WILL NOT TOLERATE PEOPLE WITH A CRIMINAL RECORD.
CRIMINAL RECORD... SO KIRA WON'T EVEN TOLERATE CRIMES THAT HAPPENED IN THE PAST...
S-SINCE NOW KIRA IS KILLING EVEN THOSE WHO COMMIT MINOR CRIMES, KIRA'S GOING TO BRING JUSTICE UPON THOSE WHO COMMITTED MAJOR CRIMES IN THE PAST... I GUESS...
News9
chapter 88 Conversation
THAT'S WRONG, MIKAMI... KIRA EXISTS TO PREVENT PEOPLE FROM COMMITTING CRIMES. KILLING THOSE WHO HAVE ALREADY PAID FOR THEIR SINS WILL ONLY BRING FEAR TO THE PEOPLE... MIKAMI, YOU'RE JUST PUNISHING CRIMINALS, THAT'S ALL...
News9

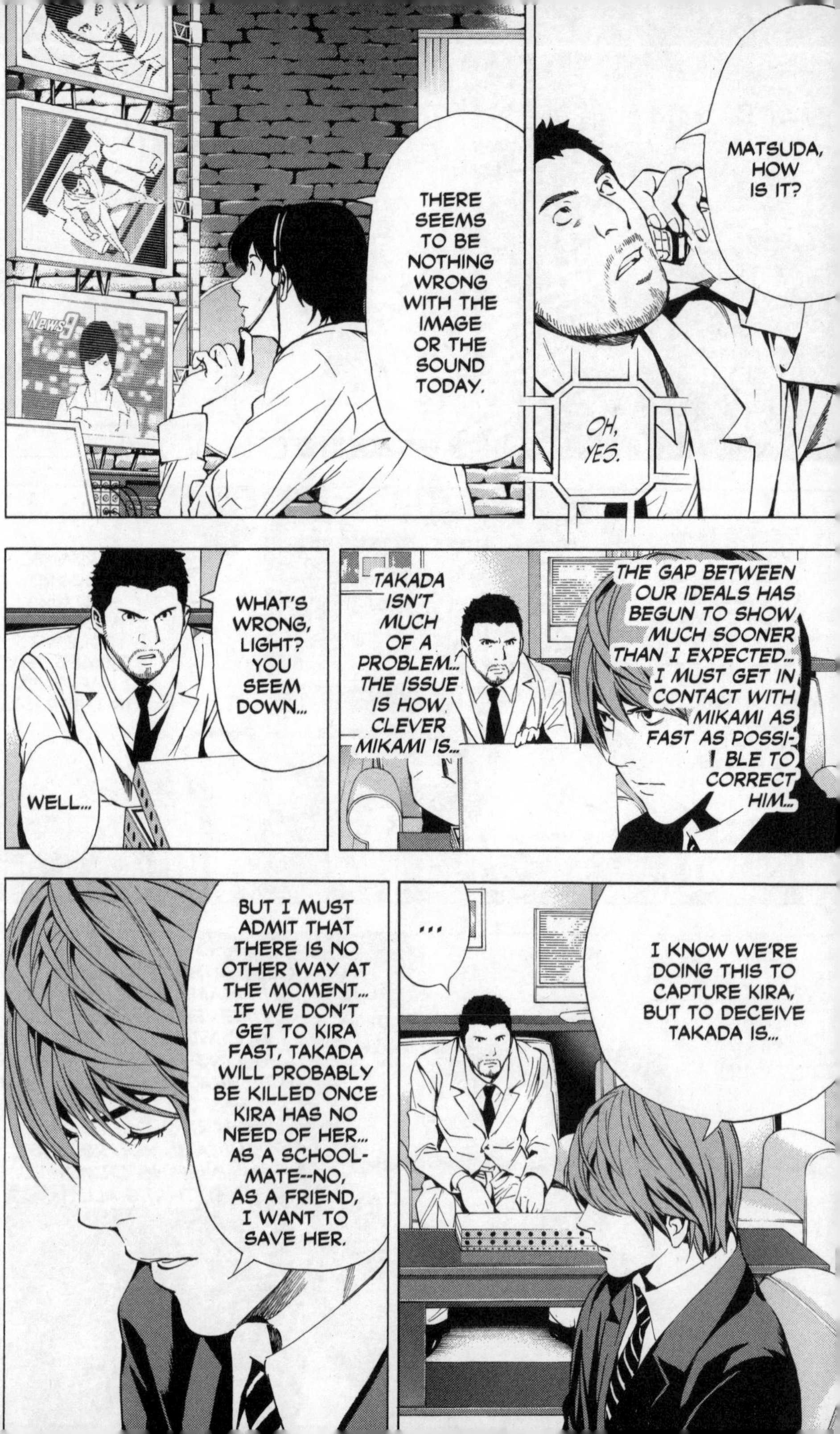
MATSUDA, HOW IS IT?
THERE SEEMS TO BE NOTHING WRONG WITH THE IMAGE OR THE SOUND TODAY.
OH, YES.
THE GAP BETWEEN OUR IDEALS HAS BEGUN TO SHOW MUCH SOONER THAN I EXPECTED... I MUST GET IN CONTACT WITH MIKAMI AS FAST AS POSSI-BLE TO CORRECT HIM...
TAKADA ISN'T MUCH OF A PROBLEM... THE ISSUE IS HOW CLEVER MIKAMI IS...
WHAT'S WRONG, LIGHT? YOU SEEM DOWN...
WELL...
I KNOW WE'RE DOING THIS TO CAPTURE KIRA, BUT TO DECEIVE TAKADA IS...
...
BUT I MUST ADMIT THAT THERE IS NO OTHER WAY AT THE MOMENT... IF WE DON'T GET TO KIRA FAST, TAKADA WILL PROBABLY BE KILLED ONCE KIRA HAS NO NEED OF HER... AS A SCHOOL-MATE--NO, AS A FRIEND, I WANT TO SAVE HER.

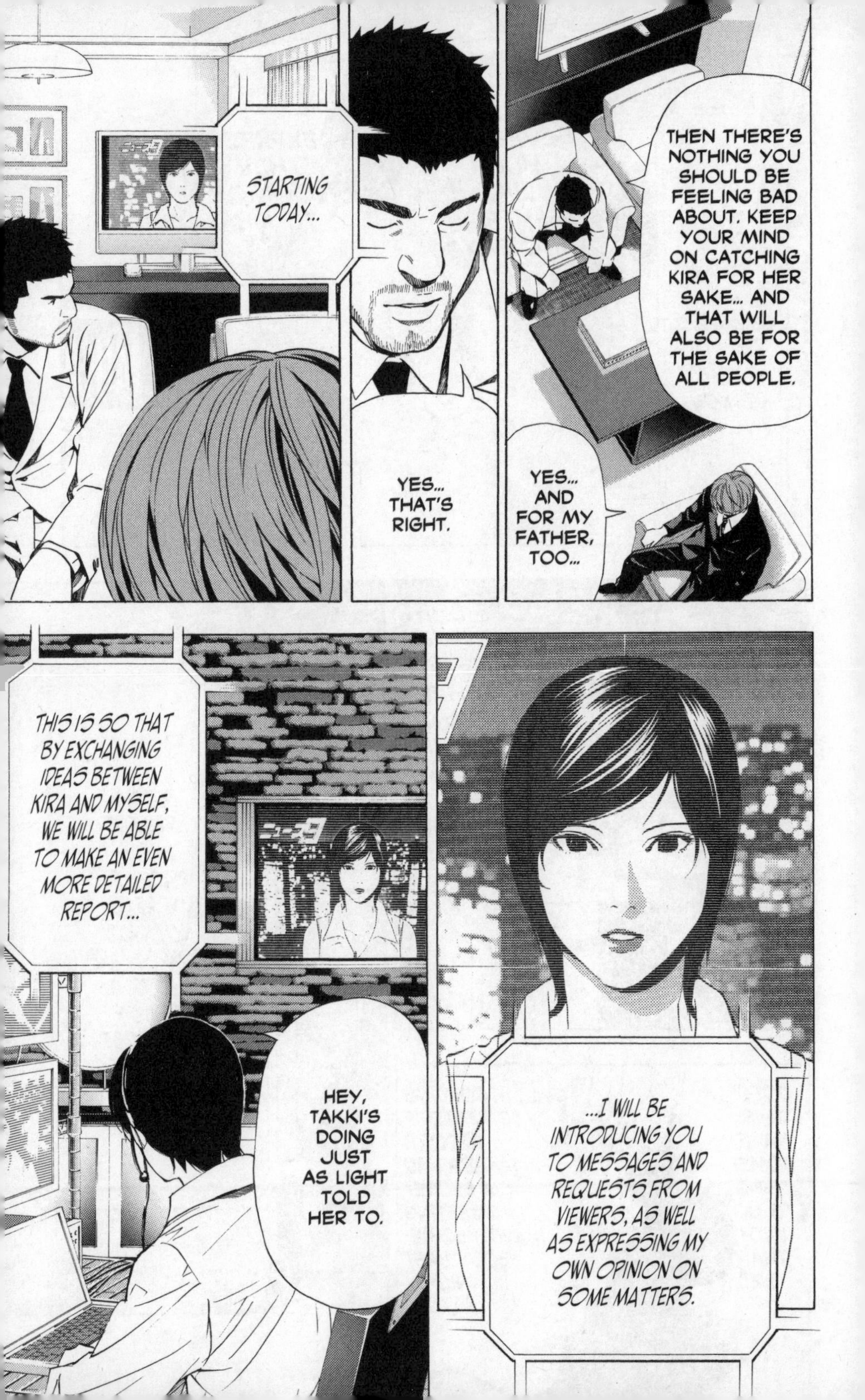
THEN THERE'S NOTHING YOU SHOULD BE FEELING BAD ABOUT. KEEP YOUR MIND ON CATCHING KIRA FOR HER SAKE... AND THAT WILL ALSO BE FOR THE SAKE OF ALL PEOPLE.
YES... AND FOR MY FATHER, TOO...
YES... THAT'S RIGHT.
STARTING TODAY...
...I WILL BE INTRODUCING YOU TO MESSAGES AND REQUESTS FROM VIEWERS, AS WELL AS EXPRESSING MY OWN OPINION ON SOME MATTERS.
THIS IS SO THAT BY EXCHANGING IDEAS BETWEEN KIRA AND MYSELF, WE WILL BE ABLE TO MAKE AN EVEN MORE DETAILED REPORT...
HEY, TAKKI'S DOING JUST AS LIGHT TOLD HER TO.

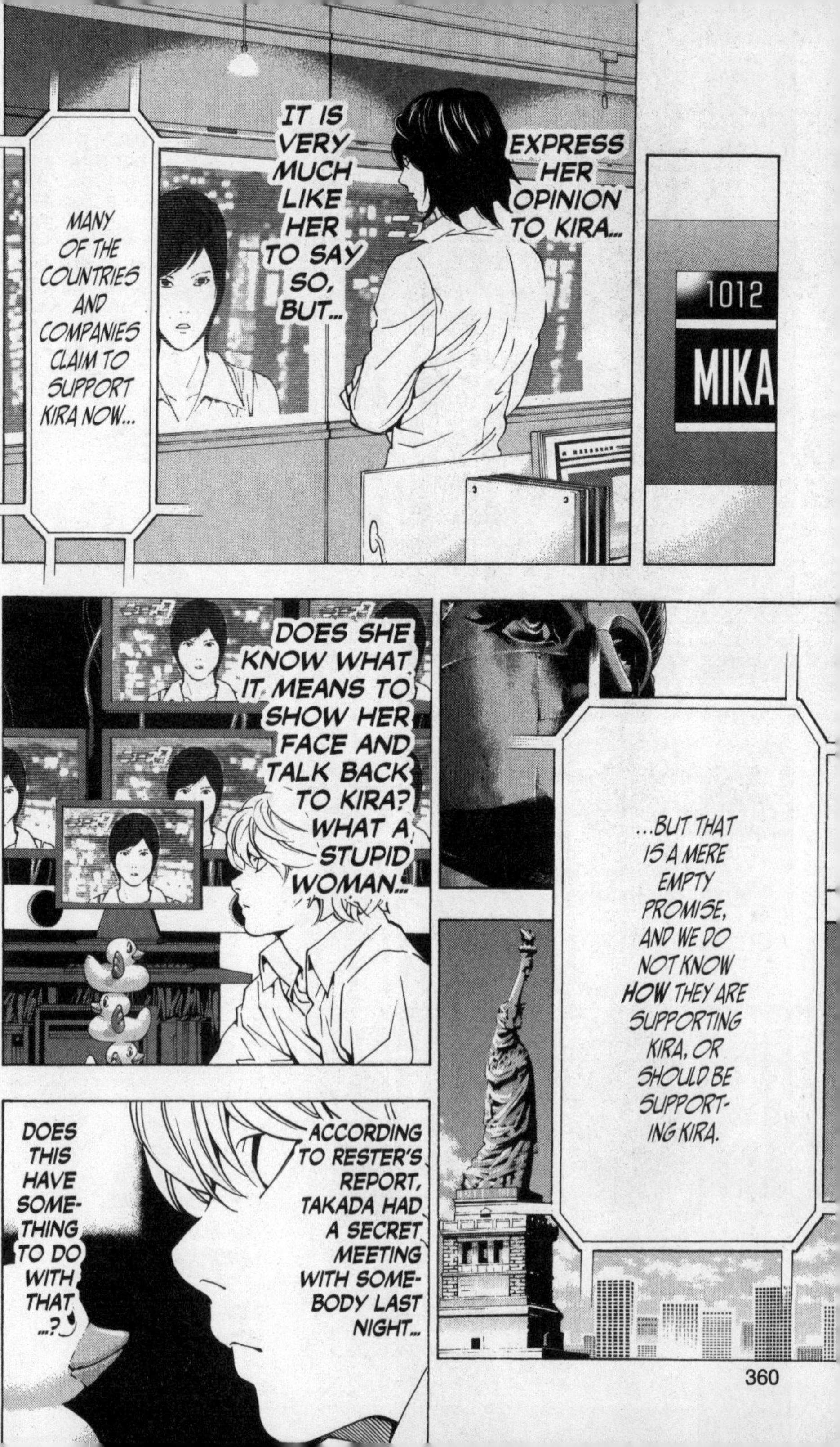
1012
MIKA
EXPRESS HER OPINION TO KIRA...
IT IS VERY MUCH LIKE HER TO SAY SO, BUT...
MANY OF THE COUNTRIES AND COMPANIES CLAIM TO SUPPORT KIRA NOW...
...BUT THAT IS A MERE EMPTY PROMISE, AND WE DO NOT KNOW **HOW** THEY ARE SUPPORTING KIRA, OR SHOULD BE SUPPORTING KIRA.
DOES SHE KNOW WHAT IT MEANS TO SHOW HER FACE AND TALK BACK TO KIRA? WHAT A STUPID WOMAN...
ACCORDING TO RESTER'S REPORT, TAKADA HAD A SECRET MEETING WITH SOMEBODY LAST NIGHT...
DOES THIS HAVE SOMETHING TO DO WITH THAT...?

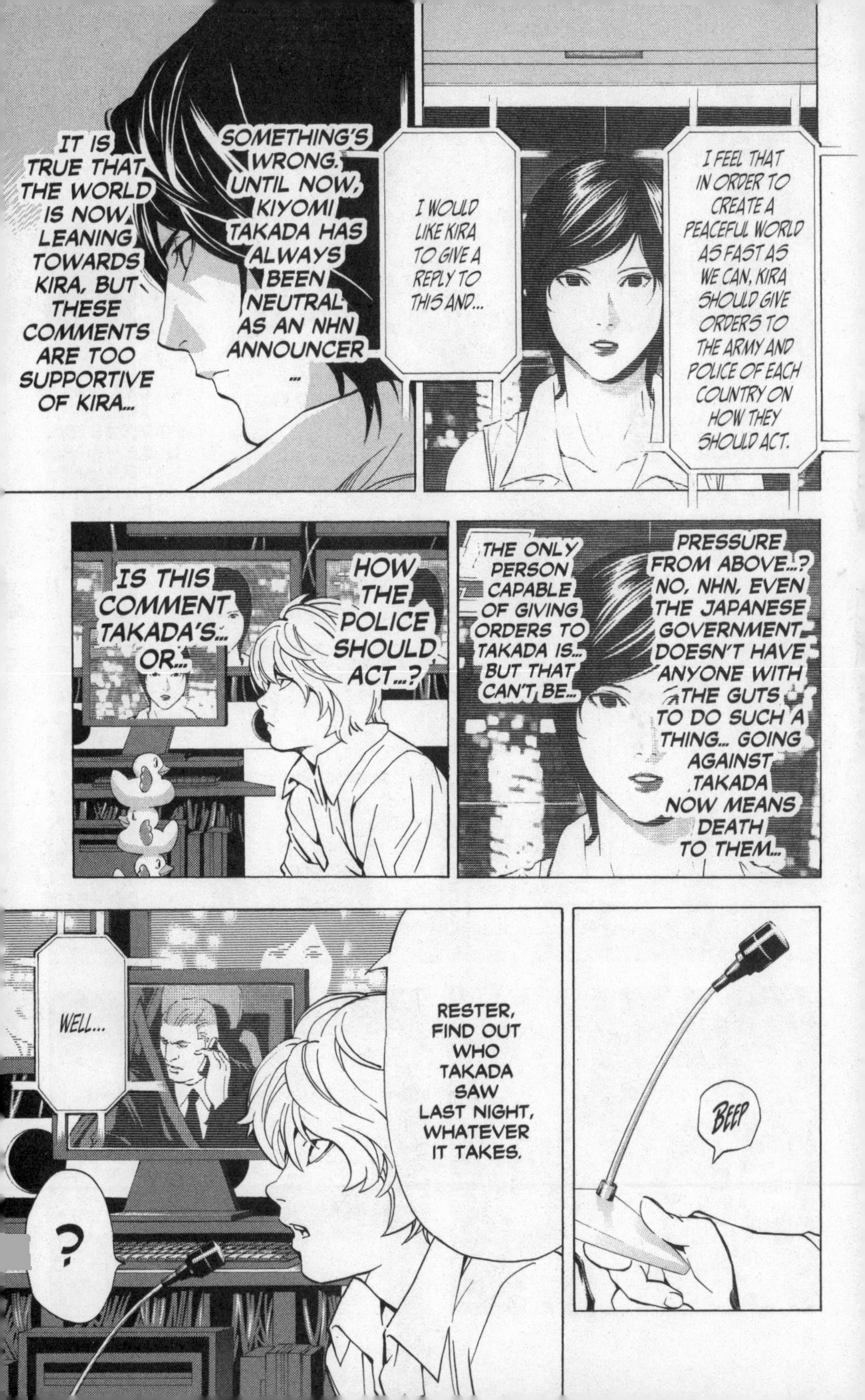
I FEEL THAT IN ORDER TO CREATE A PEACEFUL WORLD AS FAST AS WE CAN, KIRA SHOULD GIVE ORDERS TO THE ARMY AND POLICE OF EACH COUNTRY ON HOW THEY SHOULD ACT.
I WOULD LIKE KIRA TO GIVE A REPLY TO THIS AND...
SOMETHING'S WRONG. UNTIL NOW, KIYOMI TAKADA HAS ALWAYS BEEN NEUTRAL AS AN NHN ANNOUNCER...
IT IS TRUE THAT THE WORLD IS NOW LEANING TOWARDS KIRA, BUT THESE COMMENTS ARE TOO SUPPORTIVE OF KIRA...
PRESSURE FROM ABOVE...? NO, NHN, EVEN THE JAPANESE GOVERNMENT DOESN'T HAVE ANYONE WITH THE GUTS TO DO SUCH A THING... GOING AGAINST TAKADA NOW MEANS DEATH TO THEM...
THE ONLY PERSON CAPABLE OF GIVING ORDERS TO TAKADA IS... BUT THAT CAN'T BE...
HOW THE POLICE SHOULD ACT...?
IS THIS COMMENT TAKADA'S... OR...
BEEP
RESTER, FIND OUT WHO TAKADA SAW LAST NIGHT, WHATEVER IT TAKES.
WELL...
?

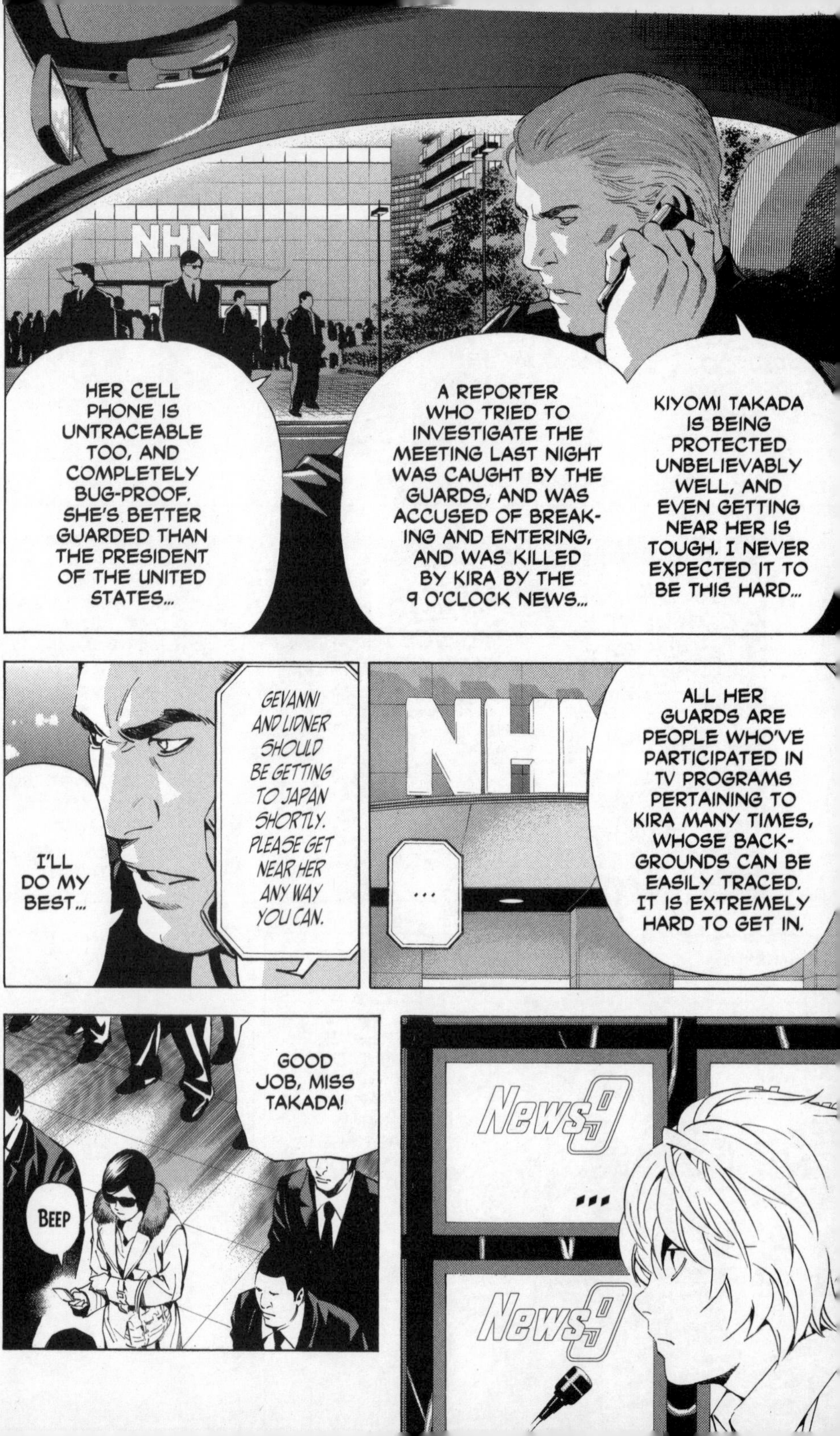
NHN
KIYOMI TAKADA IS BEING PROTECTED UNBELIEVABLY WELL, AND EVEN GETTING NEAR HER IS TOUGH. I NEVER EXPECTED IT TO BE THIS HARD...
A REPORTER WHO TRIED TO INVESTIGATE THE MEETING LAST NIGHT WAS CAUGHT BY THE GUARDS, AND WAS ACCUSED OF BREAK-ING AND ENTERING, AND WAS KILLED BY KIRA BY THE 9 O'CLOCK NEWS...
HER CELL PHONE IS UNTRACEABLE TOO, AND COMPLETELY BUG-PROOF. SHE'S BETTER GUARDED THAN THE PRESIDENT OF THE UNITED STATES...
ALL HER GUARDS ARE PEOPLE WHO'VE PARTICIPATED IN TV PROGRAMS PERTAINING TO KIRA MANY TIMES, WHOSE BACK-GROUNDS CAN BE EASILY TRACED. IT IS EXTREMELY HARD TO GET IN.
...
GEVANNI AND LIDNER SHOULD BE GETTING TO JAPAN SHORTLY. PLEASE GET NEAR HER ANY WAY YOU CAN.
I'LL DO MY BEST...
News9
...
News9
GOOD JOB, MISS TAKADA!
BEEP

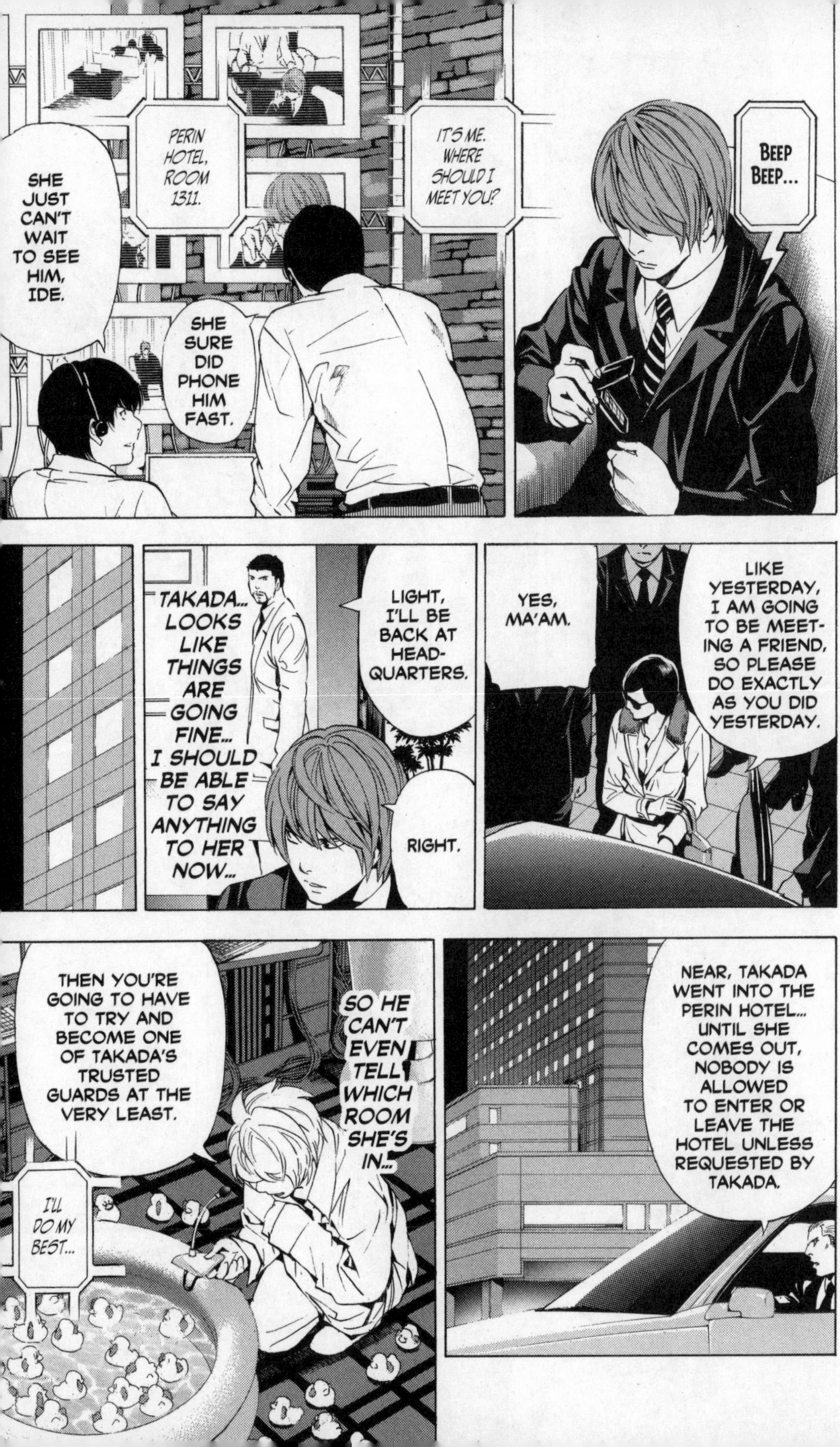
BEEP BEEP...
IT'S ME. WHERE SHOULD I MEET YOU?
PERIN HOTEL, ROOM 1311.
SHE SURE DID PHONE HIM FAST.
SHE JUST CAN'T WAIT TO SEE HIM, IDE.
LIKE YESTERDAY, I AM GOING TO BE MEETING A FRIEND, SO PLEASE DO EXACTLY AS YOU DID YESTERDAY.
YES, MA'AM.
LIGHT, I'LL BE BACK AT HEADQUARTERS.
RIGHT.
TAKADA... LOOKS LIKE THINGS ARE GOING FINE... I SHOULD BE ABLE TO SAY ANYTHING TO HER NOW...
NEAR, TAKADA WENT INTO THE PERIN HOTEL... UNTIL SHE COMES OUT, NOBODY IS ALLOWED TO ENTER OR LEAVE THE HOTEL UNLESS REQUESTED BY TAKADA.
SO HE CAN'T EVEN TELL WHICH ROOM SHE'S IN...
THEN YOU'RE GOING TO HAVE TO TRY AND BECOME ONE OF TAKADA'S TRUSTED GUARDS AT THE VERY LEAST.
I'LL DO MY BEST...

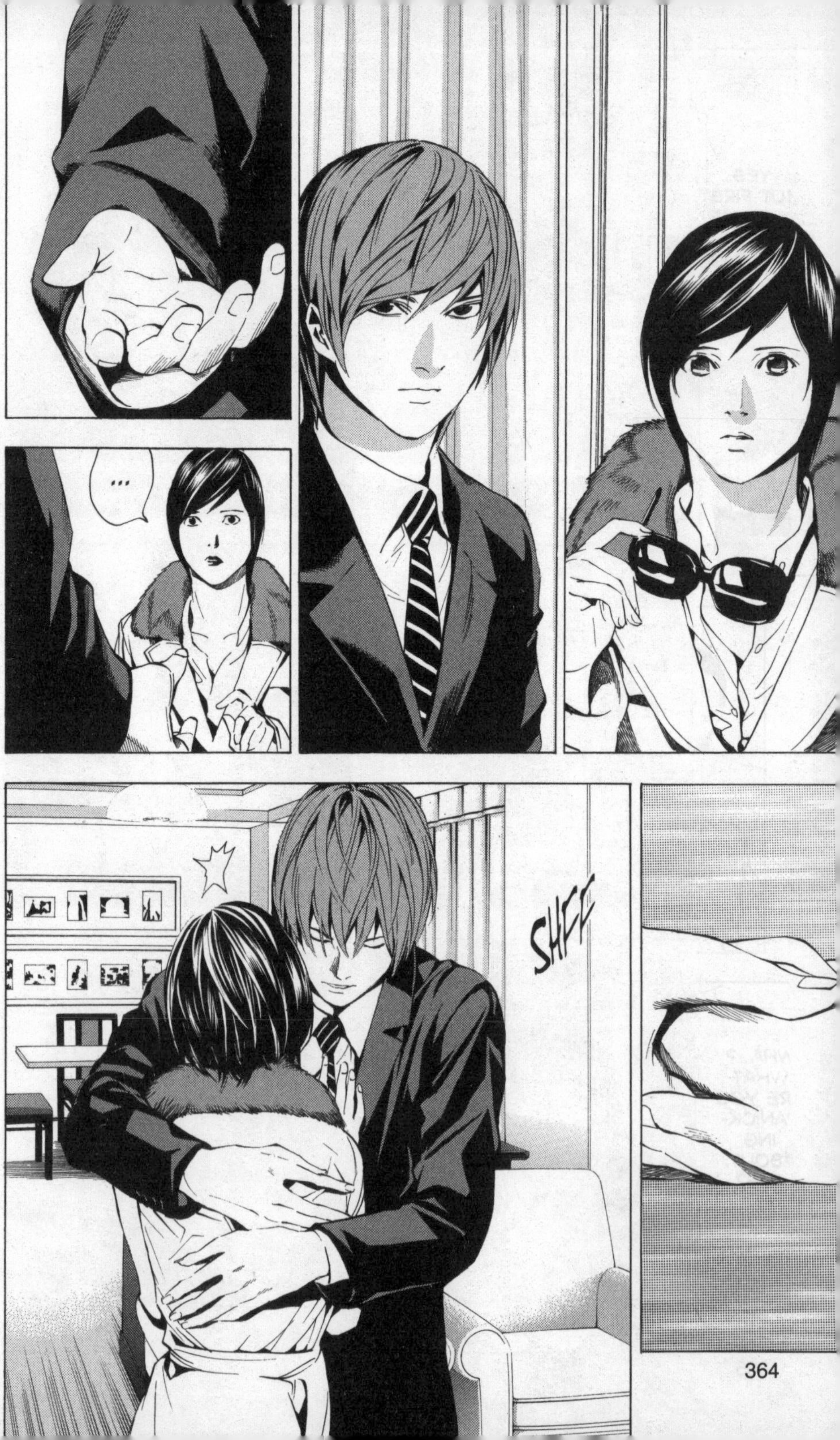
...
SHFF

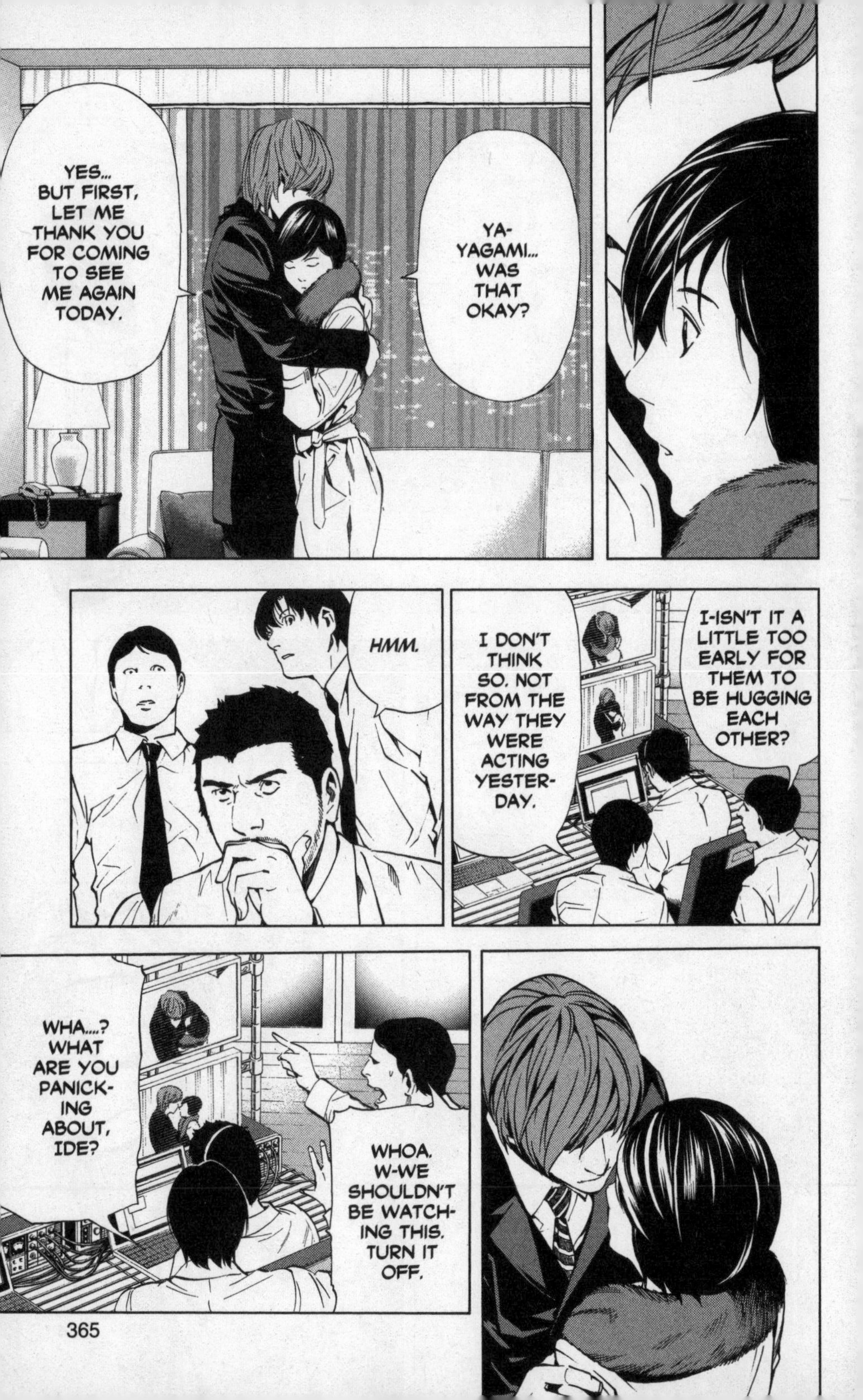
YA-YAGAMI... WAS THAT OKAY?
YES... BUT FIRST, LET ME THANK YOU FOR COMING TO SEE ME AGAIN TODAY.
I-ISN'T IT A LITTLE TOO EARLY FOR THEM TO BE HUGGING EACH OTHER?
I DON'T THINK SO. NOT FROM THE WAY THEY WERE ACTING YESTER-DAY.
HMM.
WHOA. W-WE SHOULDN'T BE WATCH-ING THIS. TURN IT OFF.
WHA...? WHAT ARE YOU PANICK-ING ABOUT, IDE?

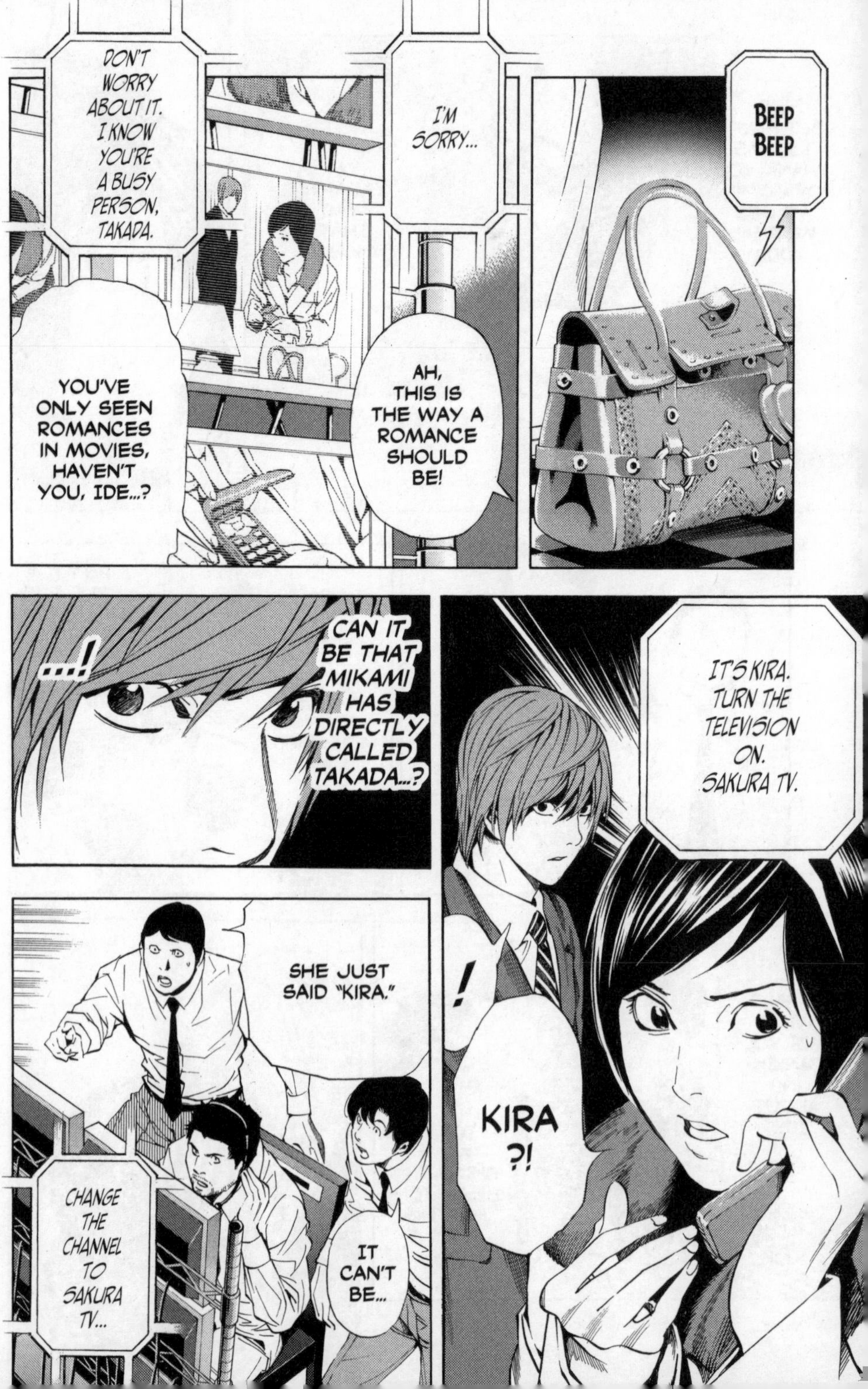
BEEP BEEP
I'M SORRY...
DON'T WORRY ABOUT IT. I KNOW YOU'RE A BUSY PERSON, TAKADA.
AH, THIS IS THE WAY A ROMANCE SHOULD BE!
YOU'VE ONLY SEEN ROMANCES IN MOVIES, HAVEN'T YOU, IDE...?
IT'S KIRA. TURN THE TELEVISION ON. SAKURA TV.
!
KIRA ?!
...!
CAN IT BE THAT MIKAMI HAS DIRECTLY CALLED TAKADA...?
SHE JUST SAID "KIRA."
CHANGE THE CHANNEL TO SAKURA TV...
IT CAN'T BE...

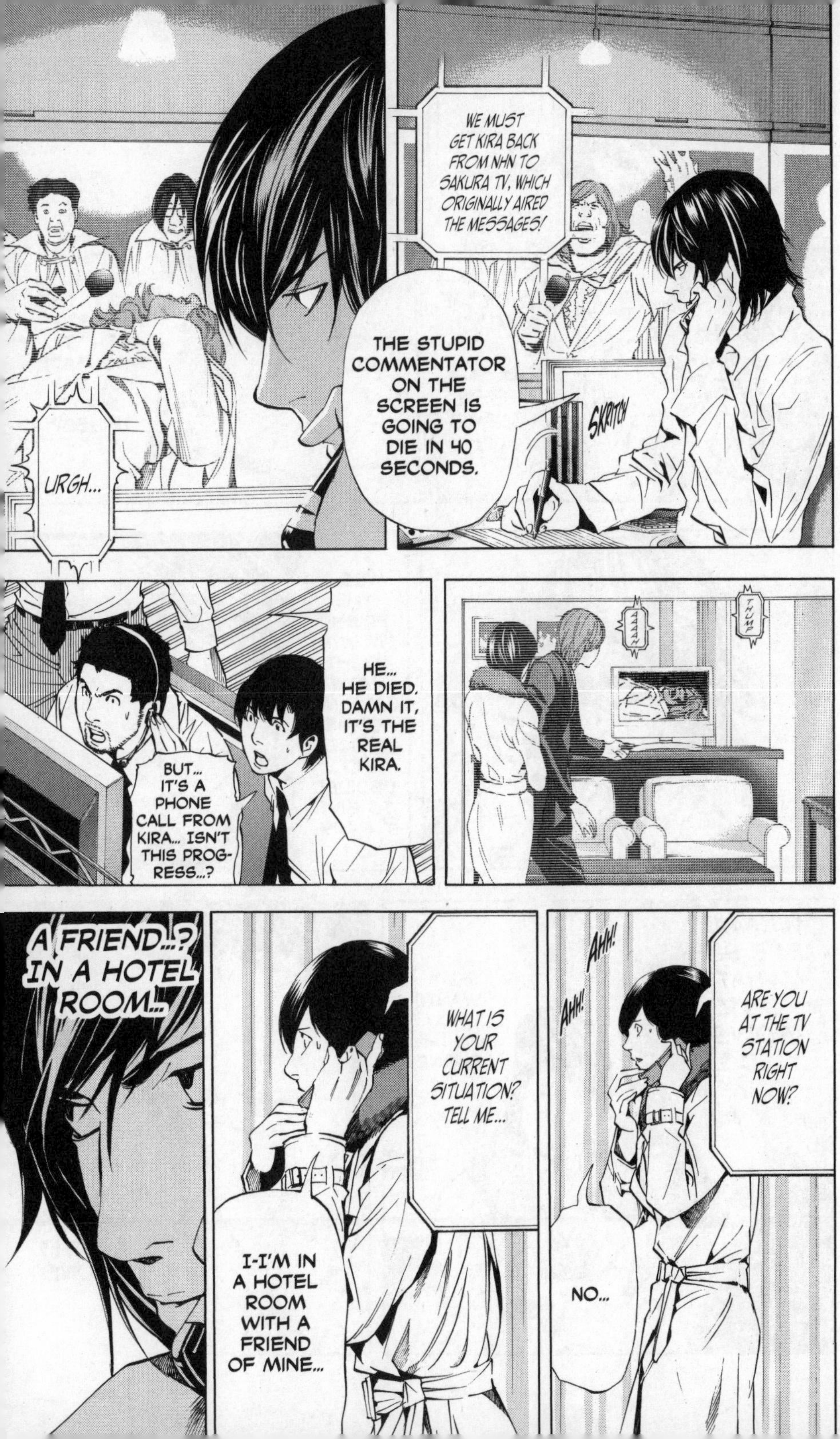
WE MUST GET KIRA BACK FROM NHN TO SAKURA TV, WHICH ORIGINALLY AIRED THE MESSAGES!
SKRITCH
THE STUPID COMMENTATOR ON THE SCREEN IS GOING TO DIE IN 40 SECONDS.
URGH...
THUMP
HE... HE DIED. DAMN IT, IT'S THE REAL KIRA.
BUT... IT'S A PHONE CALL FROM KIRA... ISN'T THIS PROG-RESS...?
ARE YOU AT THE TV STATION RIGHT NOW?
AHH!
AHH!
NO...
WHAT IS YOUR CURRENT SITUATION? TELL ME...
I-I'M IN A HOTEL ROOM WITH A FRIEND OF MINE...
A FRIEND...? IN A HOTEL ROOM...

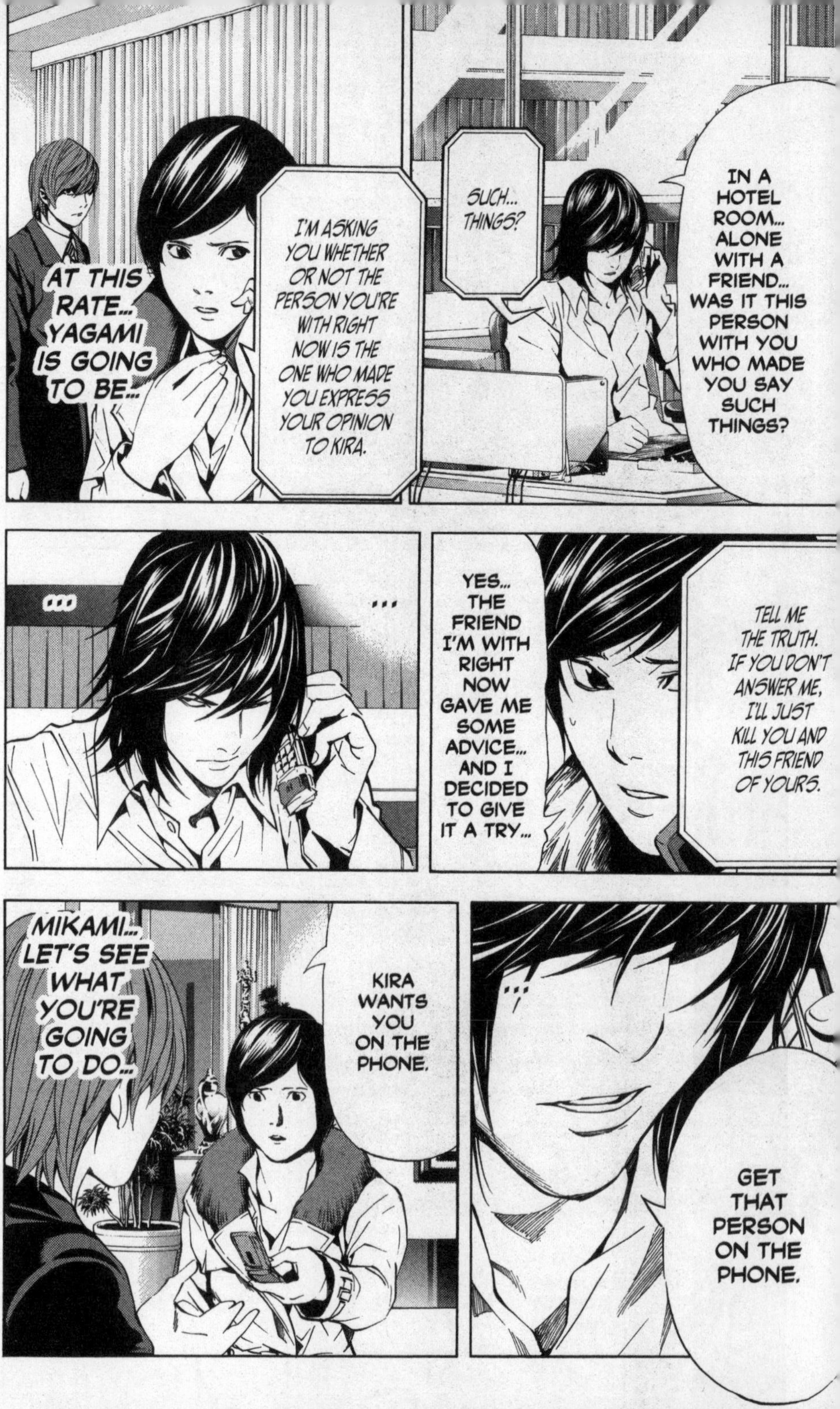
IN A HOTEL ROOM... ALONE WITH A FRIEND... WAS IT THIS PERSON WITH YOU WHO MADE YOU SAY SUCH THINGS?
SUCH... THINGS?
I'M ASKING YOU WHETHER OR NOT THE PERSON YOU'RE WITH RIGHT NOW IS THE ONE WHO MADE YOU EXPRESS YOUR OPINION TO KIRA.
AT THIS RATE... YAGAMI IS GOING TO BE...
TELL ME THE TRUTH. IF YOU DON'T ANSWER ME, I'LL JUST KILL YOU AND THIS FRIEND OF YOURS.
YES... THE FRIEND I'M WITH RIGHT NOW GAVE ME SOME ADVICE... AND I DECIDED TO GIVE IT A TRY...
...
...
...
GET THAT PERSON ON THE PHONE.
KIRA WANTS YOU ON THE PHONE.
MIKAMI... LET'S SEE WHAT YOU'RE GOING TO DO...

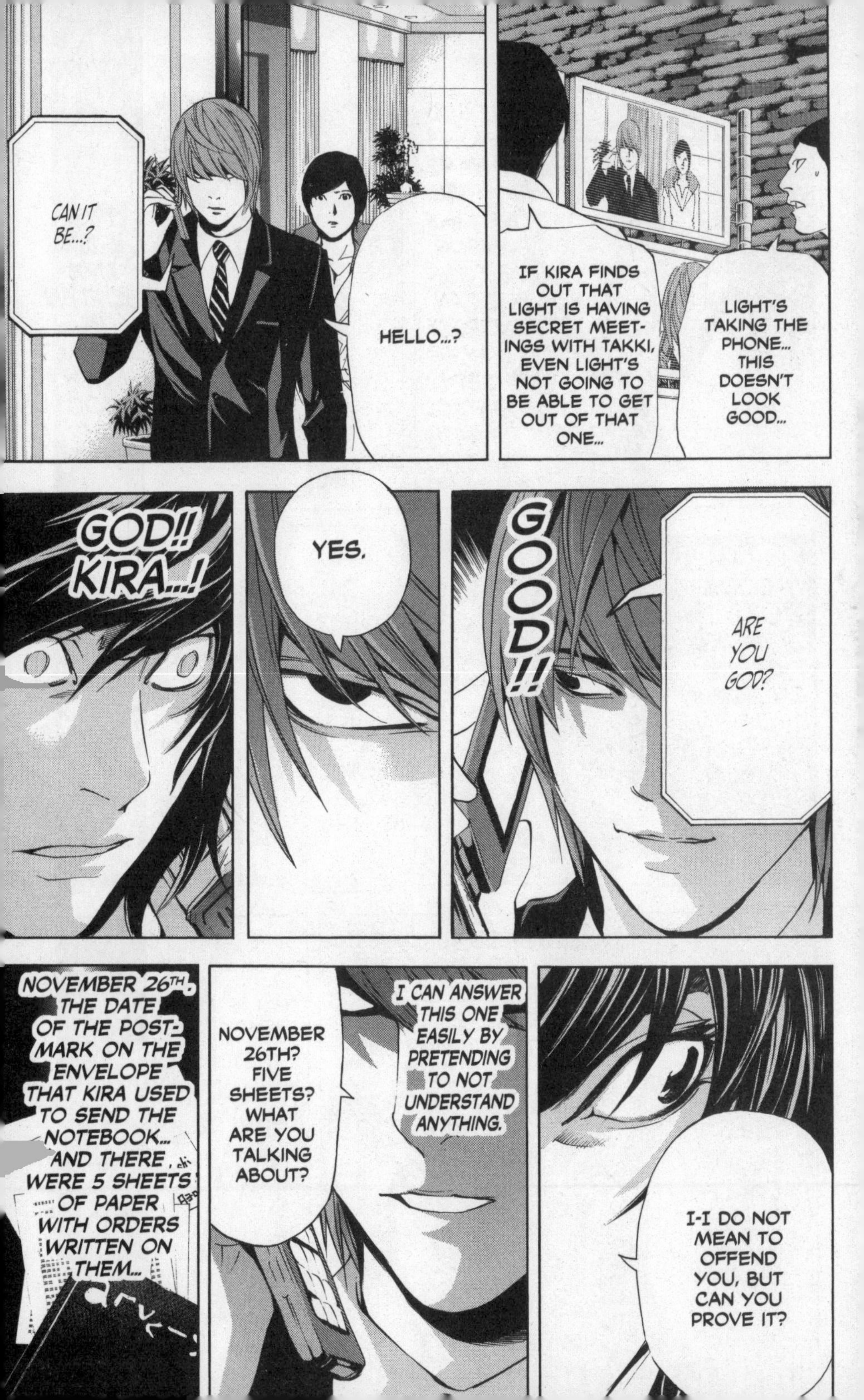
LIGHT'S TAKING THE PHONE... THIS DOESN'T LOOK GOOD...
IF KIRA FINDS OUT THAT LIGHT IS HAVING SECRET MEET-INGS WITH TAKKI, EVEN LIGHT'S NOT GOING TO BE ABLE TO GET OUT OF THAT ONE...
HELLO...?
CAN IT BE...?
ARE YOU GOD?
GOOD!!
YES.
GOD!! KIRA...!
I-I DO NOT MEAN TO OFFEND YOU, BUT CAN YOU PROVE IT?
I CAN ANSWER THIS ONE EASILY BY PRETENDING TO NOT UNDERSTAND ANYTHING.
NOVEMBER 26TH? FIVE SHEETS? WHAT ARE YOU TALKING ABOUT?
NOVEMBER 26TH, THE DATE OF THE POST-MARK ON THE ENVELOPE THAT KIRA USED TO SEND THE NOTEBOOK... AND THERE WERE 5 SHEETS OF PAPER WITH ORDERS WRITTEN ON THEM...

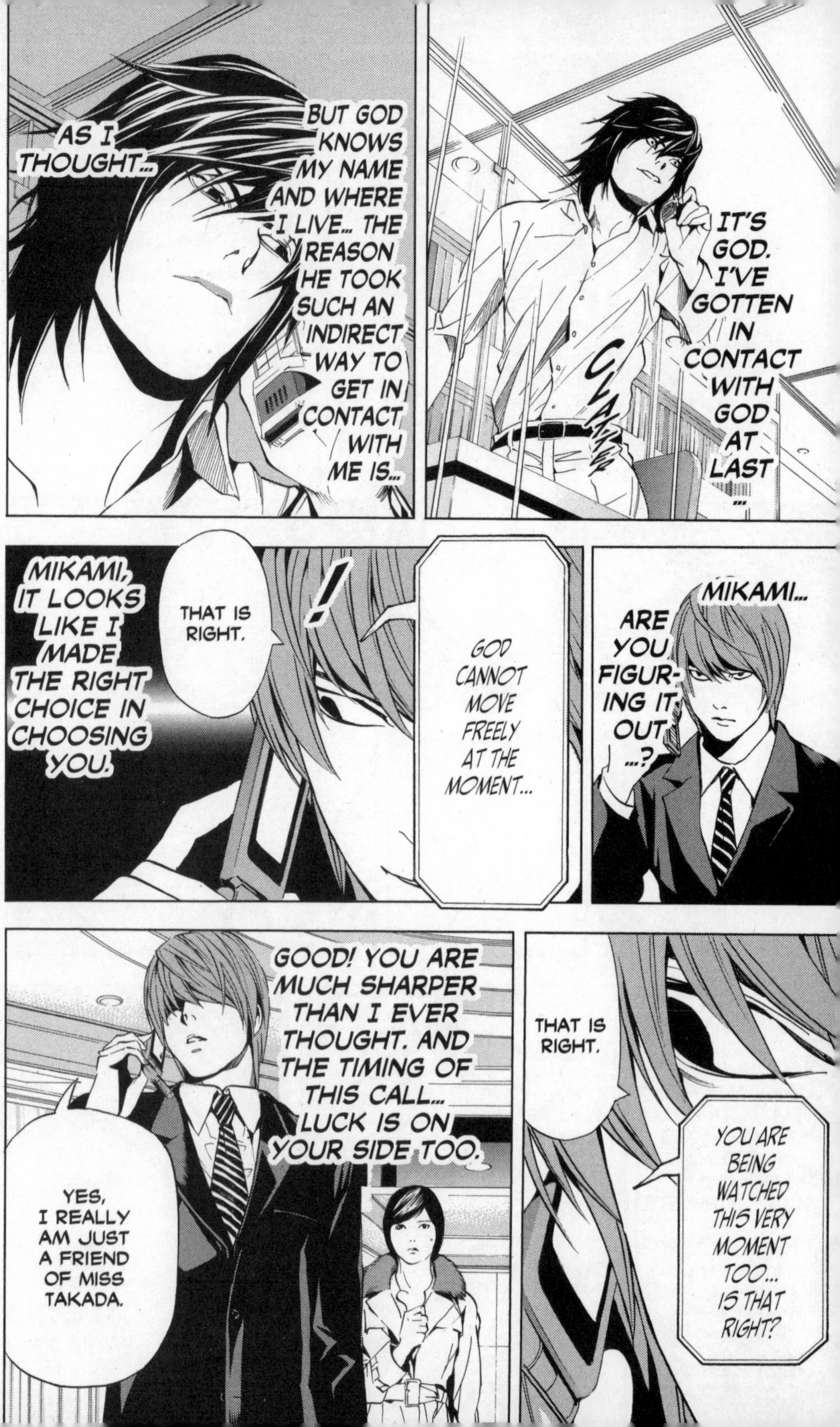
IT'S GOD. I'VE GOTTEN IN CONTACT WITH GOD AT LAST...
CLACK
AS I THOUGHT...
BUT GOD KNOWS MY NAME AND WHERE I LIVE... THE REASON HE TOOK SUCH AN INDIRECT WAY TO GET IN CONTACT WITH ME IS...
MIKAMI...
ARE YOU FIGURING IT OUT...?
GOD CANNOT MOVE FREELY AT THE MOMENT...
!
THAT IS RIGHT.
MIKAMI, IT LOOKS LIKE I MADE THE RIGHT CHOICE IN CHOOSING YOU.
YOU ARE BEING WATCHED THIS VERY MOMENT TOO... IS THAT RIGHT?
THAT IS RIGHT.
GOOD! YOU ARE MUCH SHARPER THAN I EVER THOUGHT. AND THE TIMING OF THIS CALL... LUCK IS ON YOUR SIDE TOO.
YES, I REALLY AM JUST A FRIEND OF MISS TAKADA.

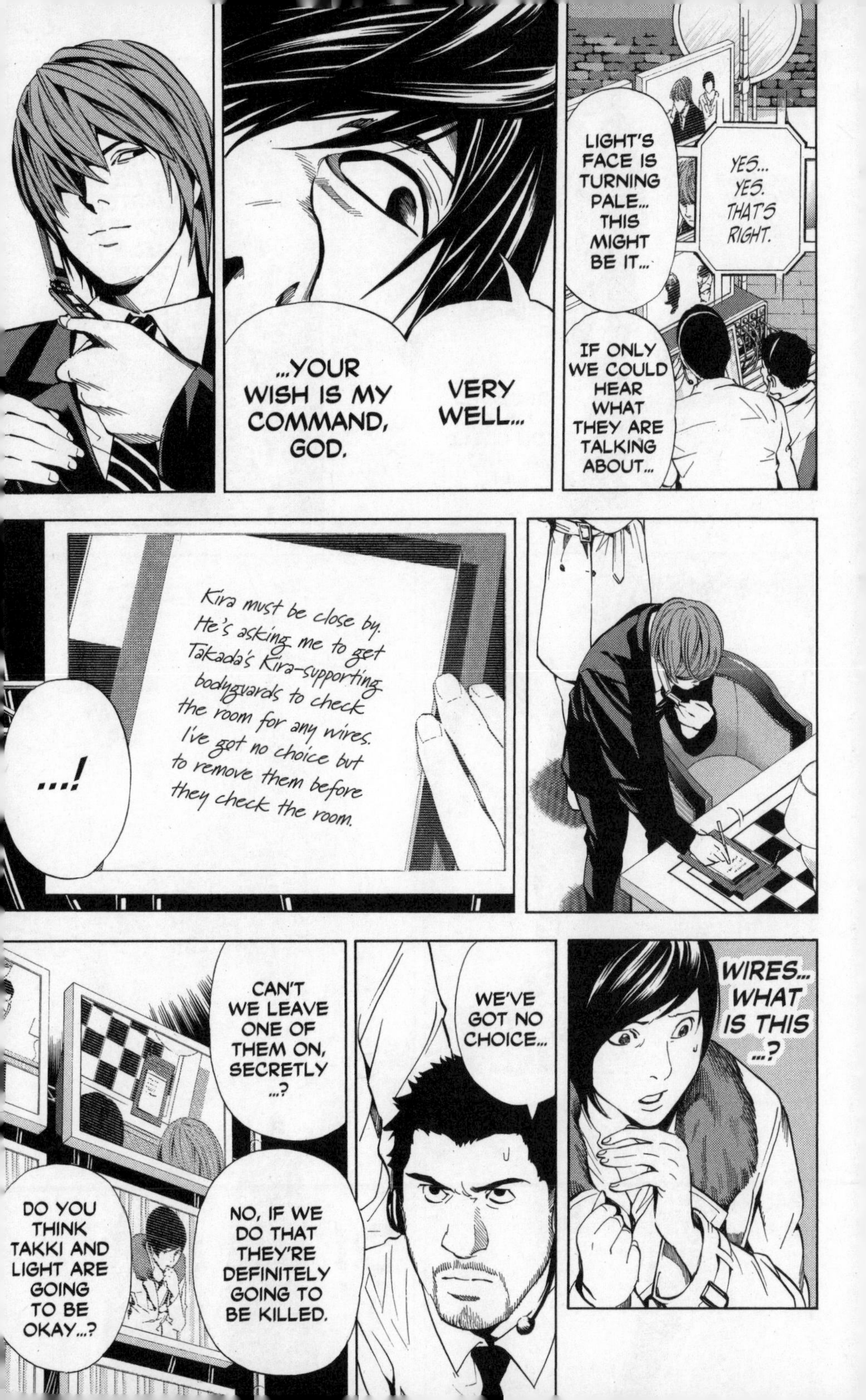
YES... YES. THAT'S RIGHT.
LIGHT'S FACE IS TURNING PALE... THIS MIGHT BE IT...
IF ONLY WE COULD HEAR WHAT THEY ARE TALKING ABOUT...
VERY WELL...
...YOUR WISH IS MY COMMAND, GOD.
Kira must be close by. He's asking me to get Takada's Kira-supporting bodyguards to check the room for any wires. I've got no choice but to remove them before they check the room.
...!
WIRES... WHAT IS THIS ...?
WE'VE GOT NO CHOICE...
CAN'T WE LEAVE ONE OF THEM ON, SECRETLY ...?
NO, IF WE DO THAT THEY'RE DEFINITELY GOING TO BE KILLED.
DO YOU THINK TAKKI AND LIGHT ARE GOING TO BE OKAY...?

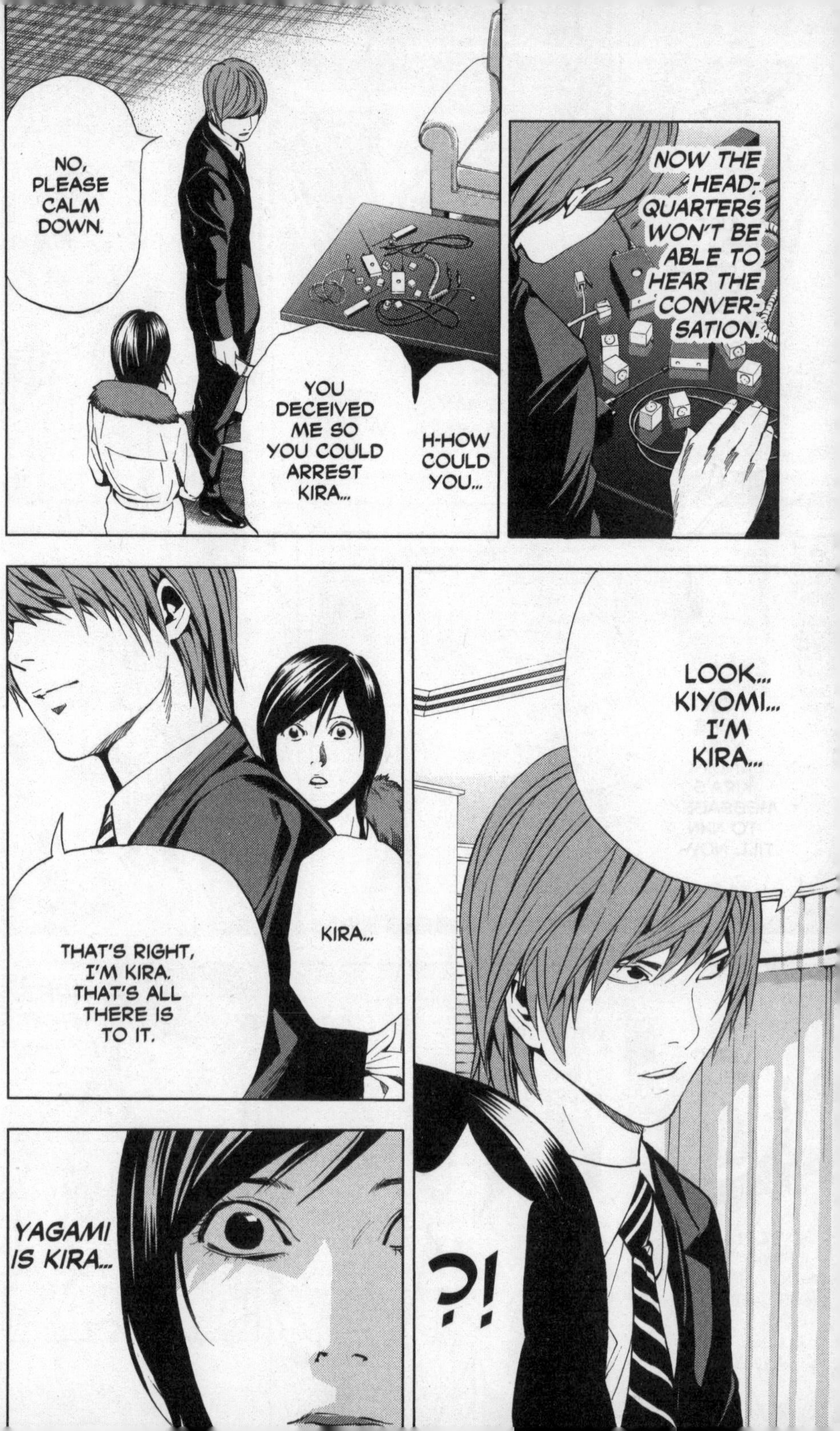
NOW THE HEAD-QUARTERS WON'T BE ABLE TO HEAR THE CONVER-SATION.
H-HOW COULD YOU...
YOU DECEIVED ME SO YOU COULD ARREST KIRA...
NO, PLEASE CALM DOWN.
LOOK... KIYOMI... I'M KIRA...
?!
KIRA...
THAT'S RIGHT, I'M KIRA. THAT'S ALL THERE IS TO IT.
YAGAMI IS KIRA...

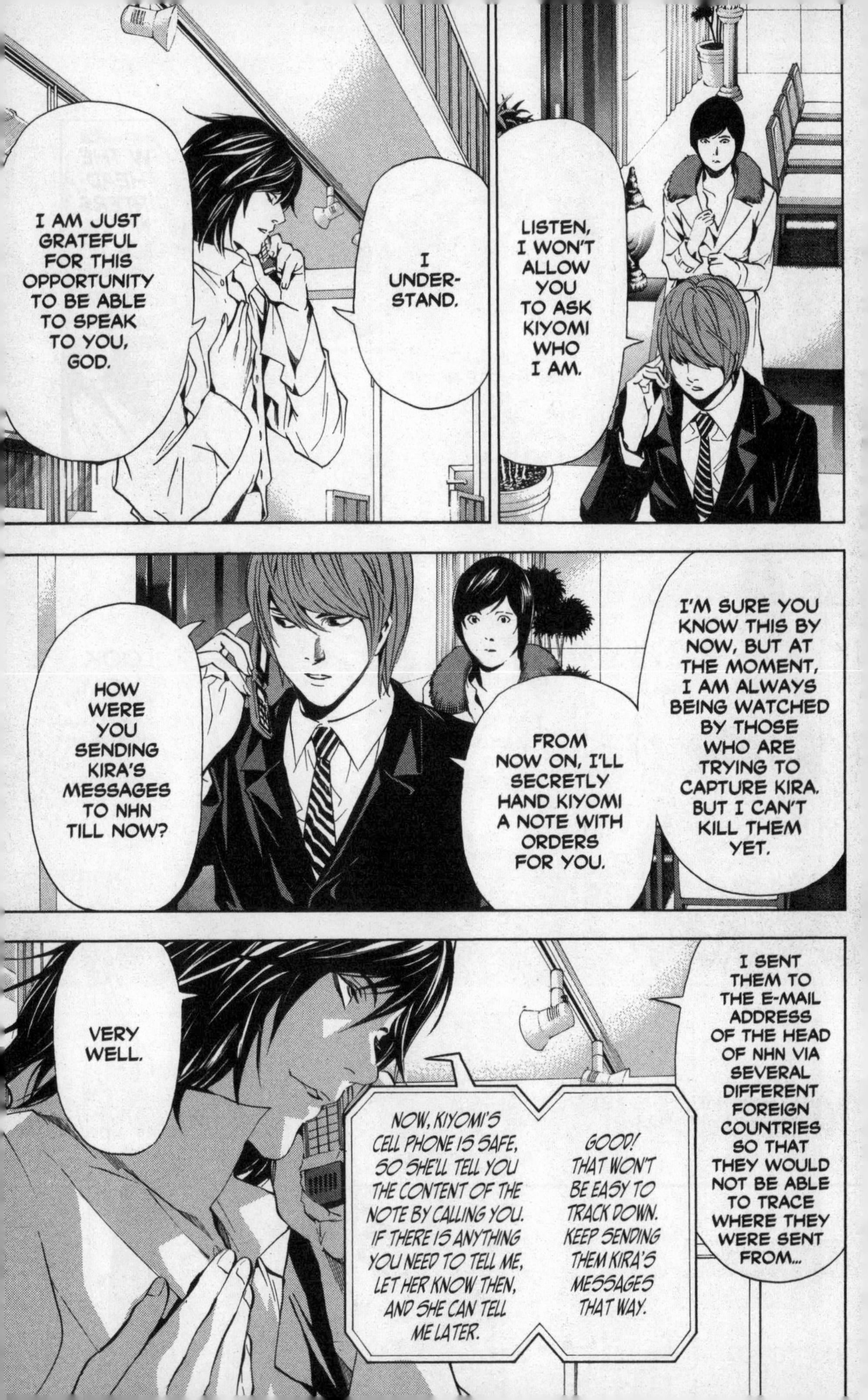
LISTEN, I WON'T ALLOW YOU TO ASK KIYOMI WHO I AM.
I UNDER-STAND.
I AM JUST GRATEFUL FOR THIS OPPORTUNITY TO BE ABLE TO SPEAK TO YOU, GOD.
I'M SURE YOU KNOW THIS BY NOW, BUT AT THE MOMENT, I AM ALWAYS BEING WATCHED BY THOSE WHO ARE TRYING TO CAPTURE KIRA. BUT I CAN'T KILL THEM YET.
FROM NOW ON, I'LL SECRETLY HAND KIYOMI A NOTE WITH ORDERS FOR YOU.
HOW WERE YOU SENDING KIRA'S MESSAGES TO NHN TILL NOW?
I SENT THEM TO THE E-MAIL ADDRESS OF THE HEAD OF NHN VIA SEVERAL DIFFERENT FOREIGN COUNTRIES SO THAT THEY WOULD NOT BE ABLE TO TRACE WHERE THEY WERE SENT FROM...
GOOD! THAT WON'T BE EASY TO TRACK DOWN. KEEP SENDING THEM KIRA'S MESSAGES THAT WAY.
NOW, KIYOMI'S CELL PHONE IS SAFE, SO SHE'LL TELL YOU THE CONTENT OF THE NOTE BY CALLING YOU. IF THERE IS ANYTHING YOU NEED TO TELL ME, LET HER KNOW THEN, AND SHE CAN TELL ME LATER.
VERY WELL.

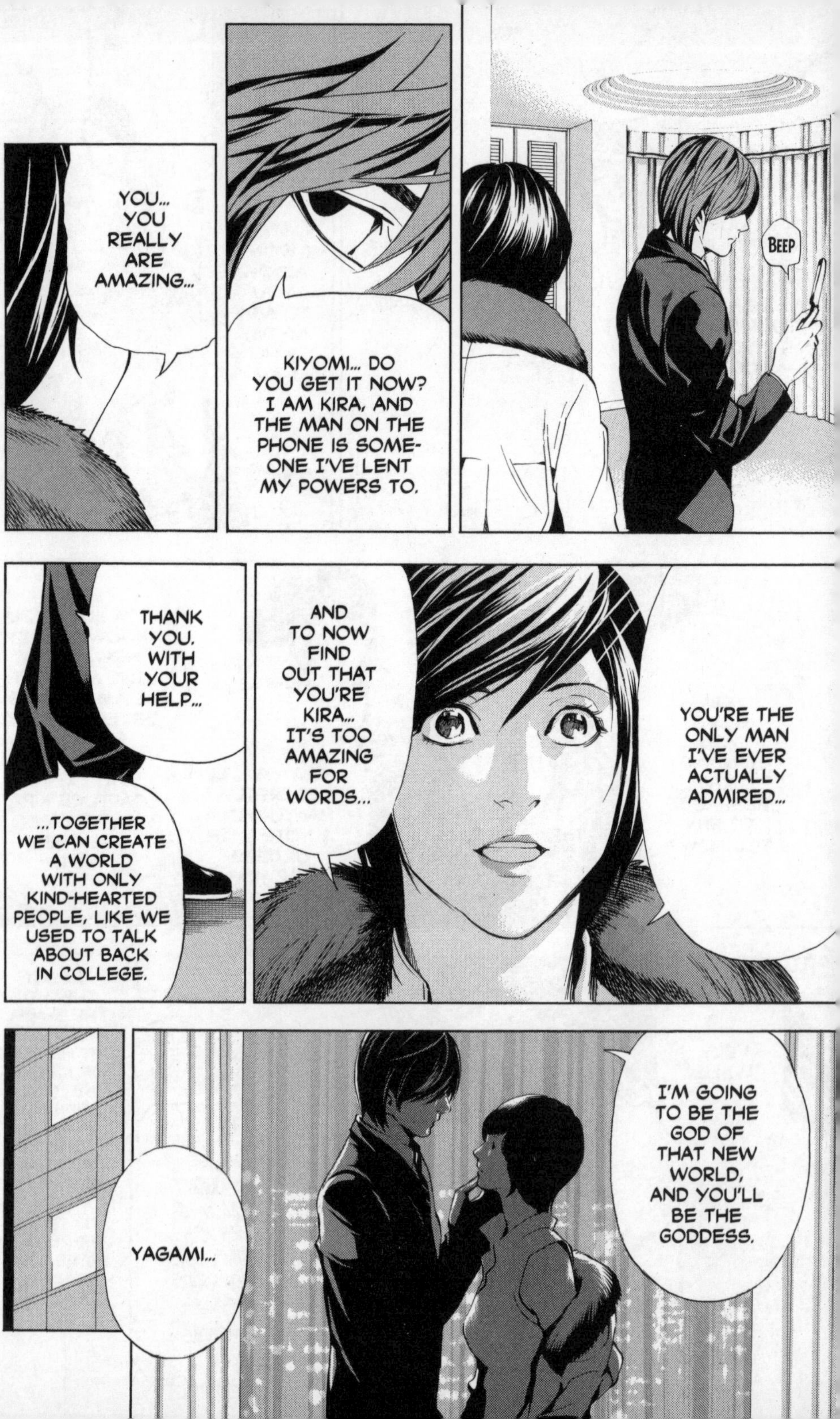
BEEP
KIYOMI... DO YOU GET IT NOW? I AM KIRA, AND THE MAN ON THE PHONE IS SOME-ONE I'VE LENT MY POWERS TO.
YOU... YOU REALLY ARE AMAZING...
YOU'RE THE ONLY MAN I'VE EVER ACTUALLY ADMIRED...
AND TO NOW FIND OUT THAT YOU'RE KIRA... IT'S TOO AMAZING FOR WORDS...
THANK YOU. WITH YOUR HELP...
...TOGETHER WE CAN CREATE A WORLD WITH ONLY KIND-HEARTED PEOPLE, LIKE WE USED TO TALK ABOUT BACK IN COLLEGE.
I'M GOING TO BE THE GOD OF THAT NEW WORLD, AND YOU'LL BE THE GODDESS.
YAGAMI...

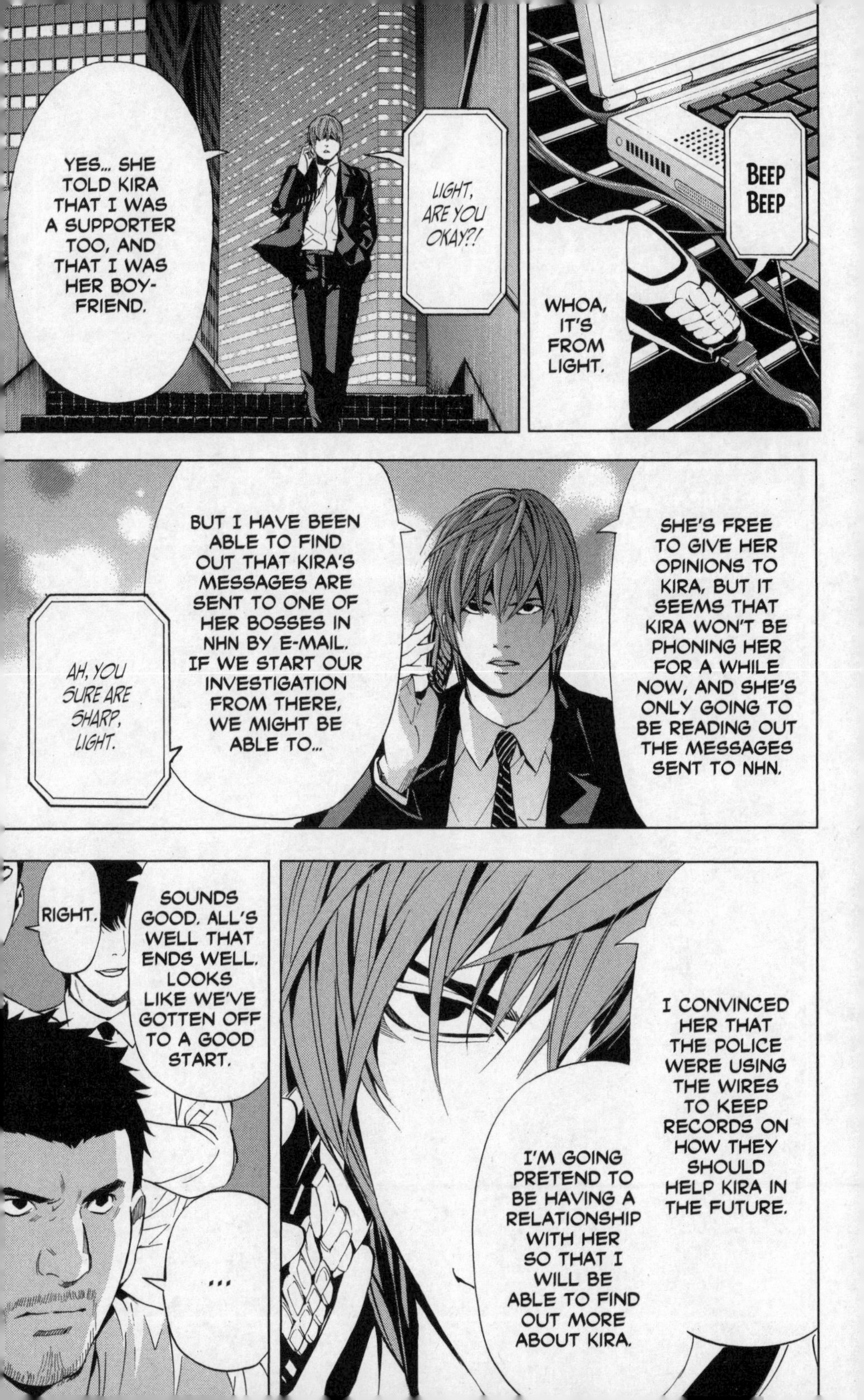
BEEP BEEP
WHOA, IT'S FROM LIGHT.
LIGHT, ARE YOU OKAY?!
YES... SHE TOLD KIRA THAT I WAS A SUPPORTER TOO, AND THAT I WAS HER BOY-FRIEND.
SHE'S FREE TO GIVE HER OPINIONS TO KIRA, BUT IT SEEMS THAT KIRA WON'T BE PHONING HER FOR A WHILE NOW, AND SHE'S ONLY GOING TO BE READING OUT THE MESSAGES SENT TO NHN.
BUT I HAVE BEEN ABLE TO FIND OUT THAT KIRA'S MESSAGES ARE SENT TO ONE OF HER BOSSES IN NHN BY E-MAIL. IF WE START OUR INVESTIGATION FROM THERE, WE MIGHT BE ABLE TO...
AH, YOU SURE ARE SHARP, LIGHT.
I CONVINCED HER THAT THE POLICE WERE USING THE WIRES TO KEEP RECORDS ON HOW THEY SHOULD HELP KIRA IN THE FUTURE.
I'M GOING PRETEND TO BE HAVING A RELATIONSHIP WITH HER SO THAT I WILL BE ABLE TO FIND OUT MORE ABOUT KIRA.
SOUNDS GOOD. ALL'S WELL THAT ENDS WELL. LOOKS LIKE WE'VE GOTTEN OFF TO A GOOD START.
RIGHT.
...

DEATH NOTE
How to use it
LIX

- A human death caused by the DEATH NOTE will indirectly lengthen some other human's original length of life even without a specific intention to lengthen a particular person's original life span in the human world.

特定の人間の人間界での本来の寿命を延ばす為の死と意識していなくても、
デスノートによる人間の死で、間接的に人間界本来の寿命が延びる人間は
発生してくる。

I wonder what that was…?
Whenever I have a strange question in my head,
I always blame the old man for it.
For example, I am certain that I filled the bathtub,
but I find the tub empty.
That is because Mr Pull-the-bath-plug dropped by my house.
I wonder what that was…?

-Tsugumi Ohba

I'm attracted to animals with wings.
In particular, I'm a big fan of bats, since
their skeletal wings look so cool.

-Takeshi Obata

DEATH NOTE

Cover Gallery

Original Japanese Covers Volumes 9-12

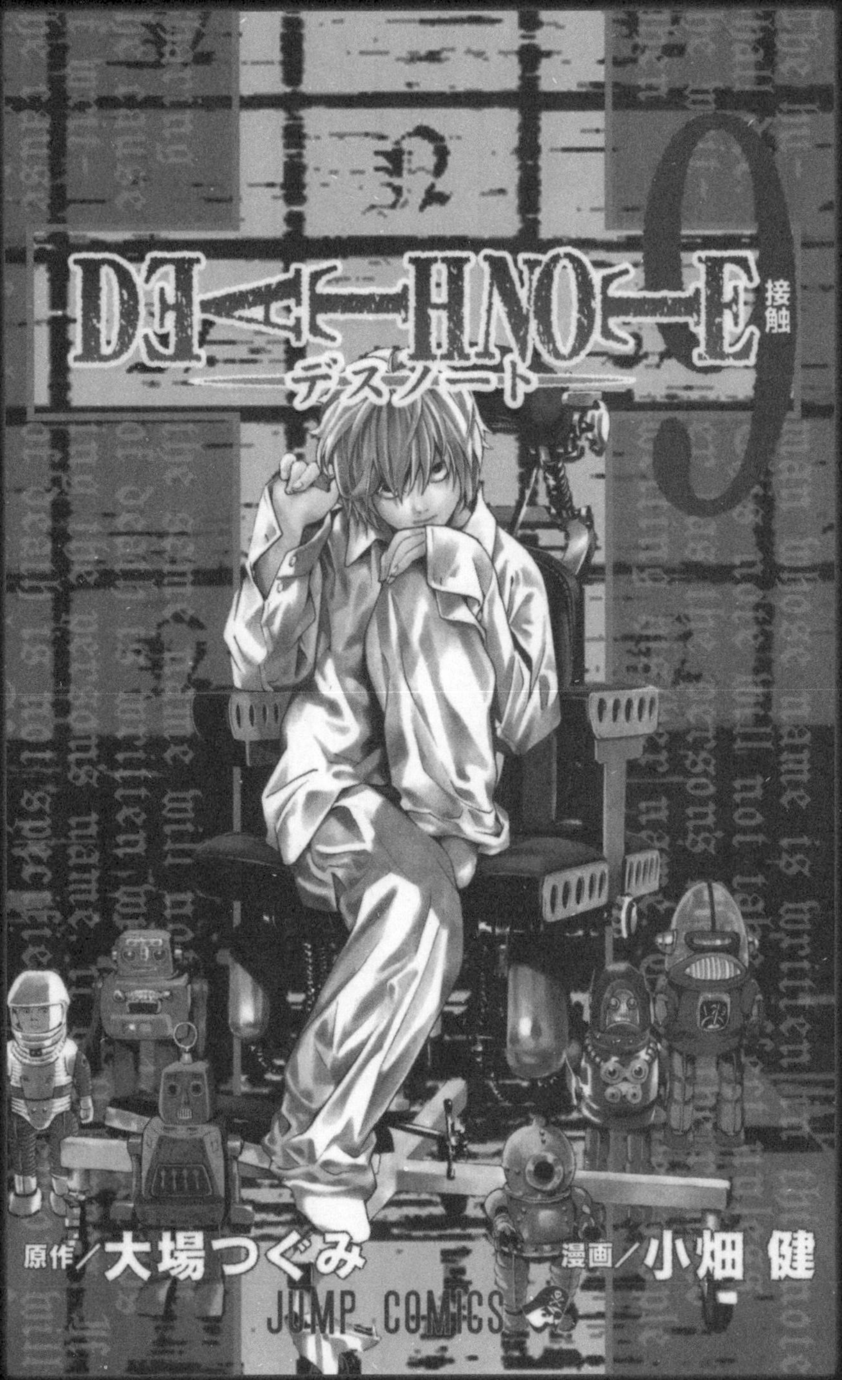
DEATH NOTE
デスノート
9
接触
原作／大場つぐみ
漫画／小畑 健
JUMP COMICS

Original Japanese Cover Volume 9

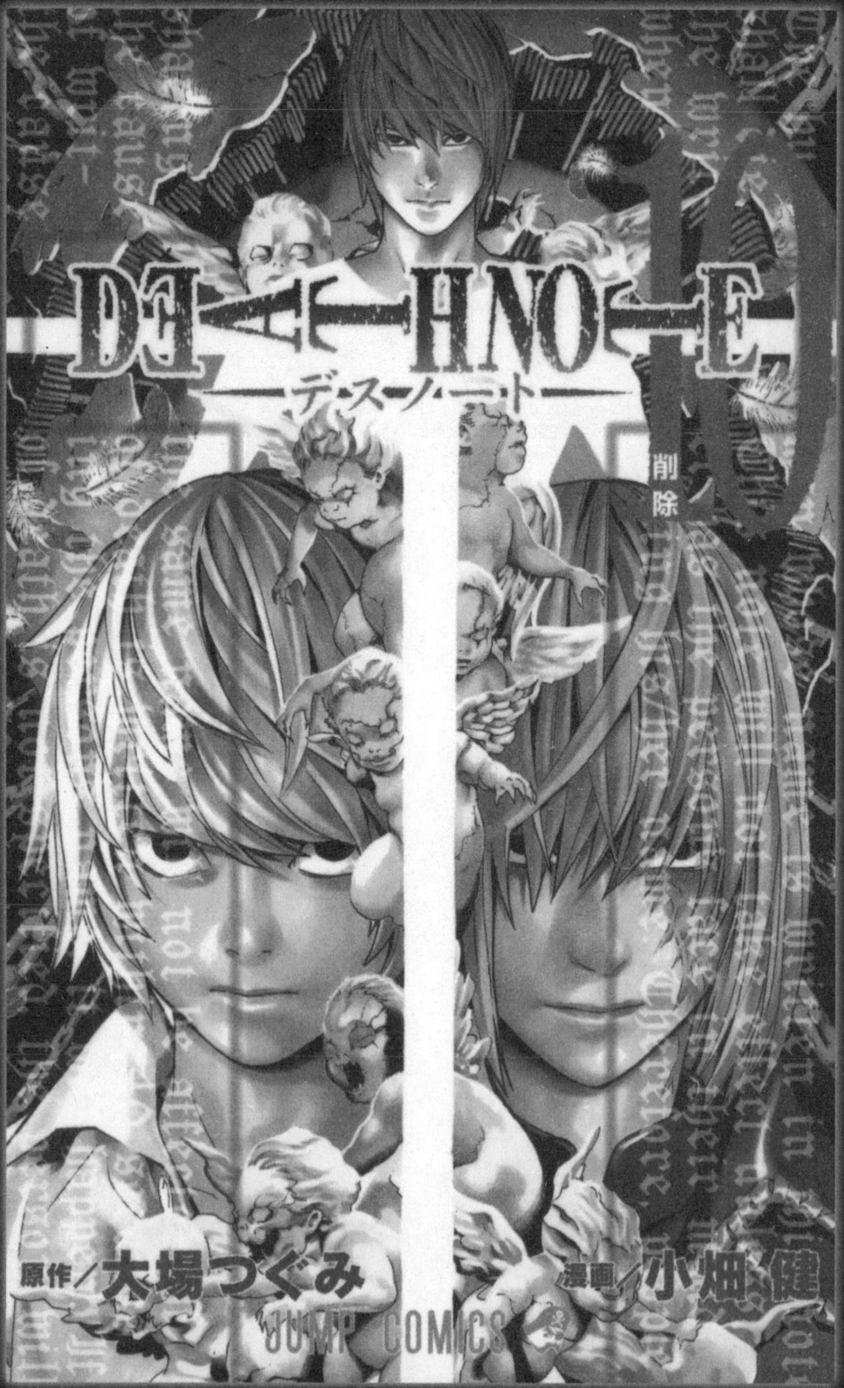
DEATH NOTE
デスノート
10
削除
原作／大場つぐみ
漫画／小畑健
JUMP COMICS

Original Japanese Cover Volume 10

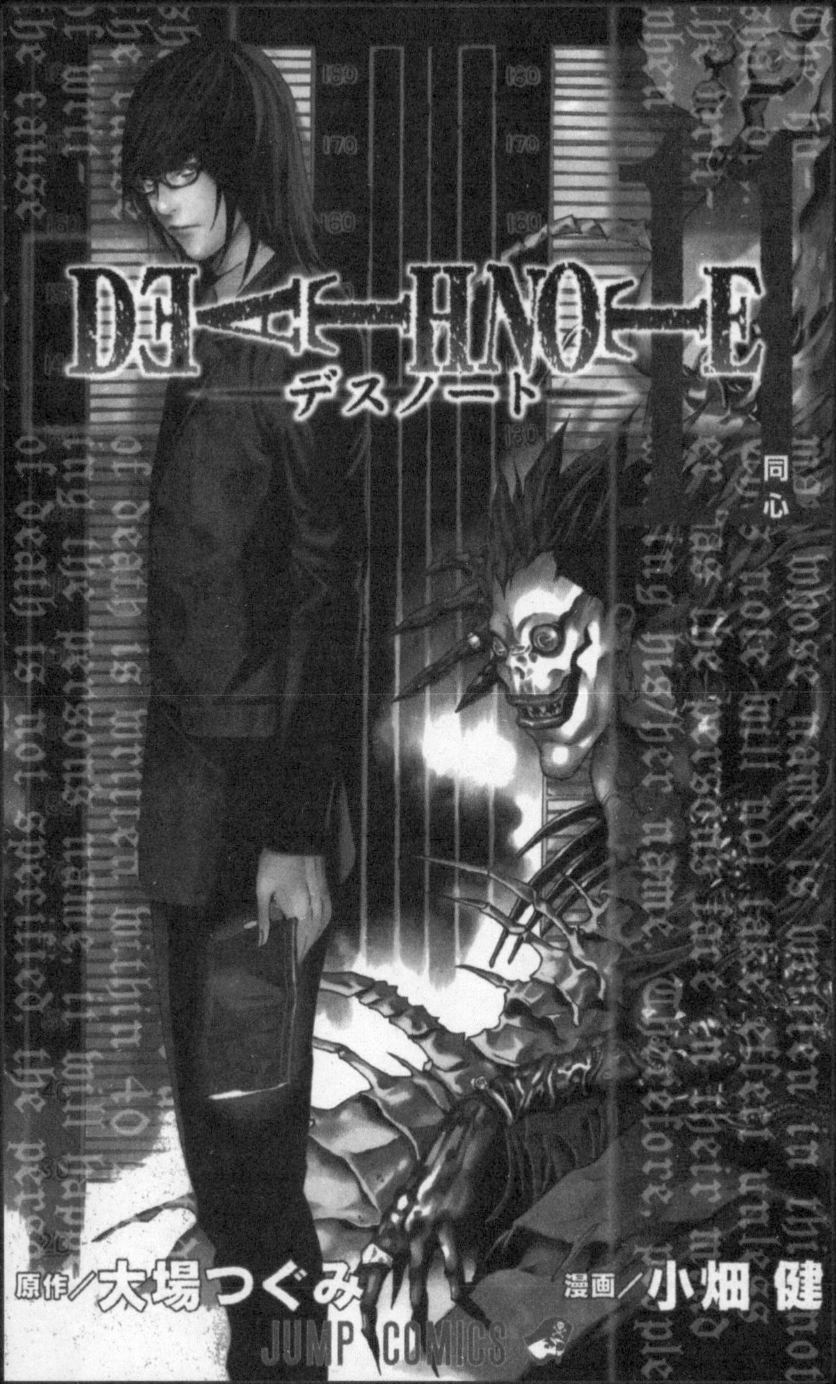
DEATH NOTE
デスノート
11
同心
原作／大場つぐみ
漫画／小畑 健
JUMP COMICS

Original Japanese Cover Volume 11

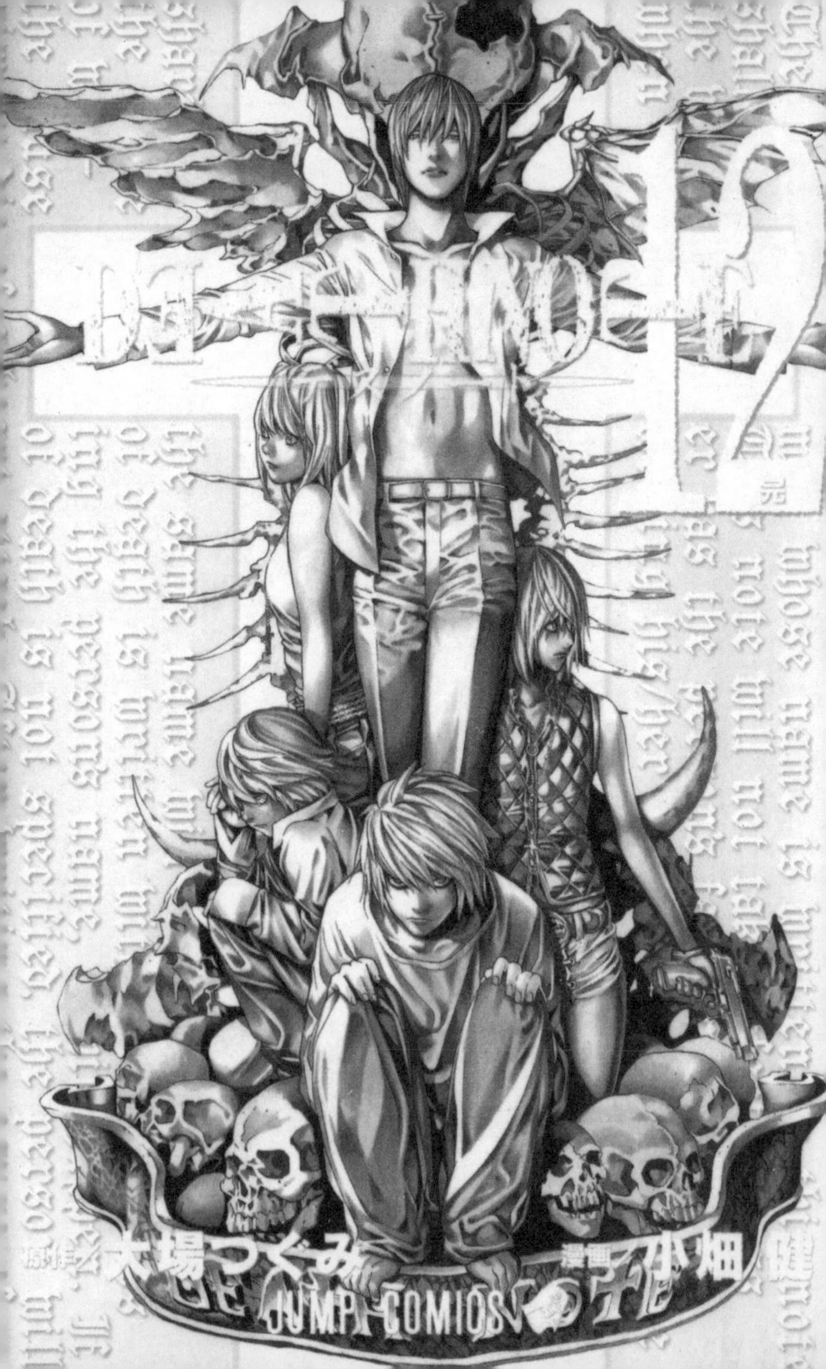
DEATH NOTE
12
完
原作 大場つぐみ
漫画 小畑 健
JUMP COMICS

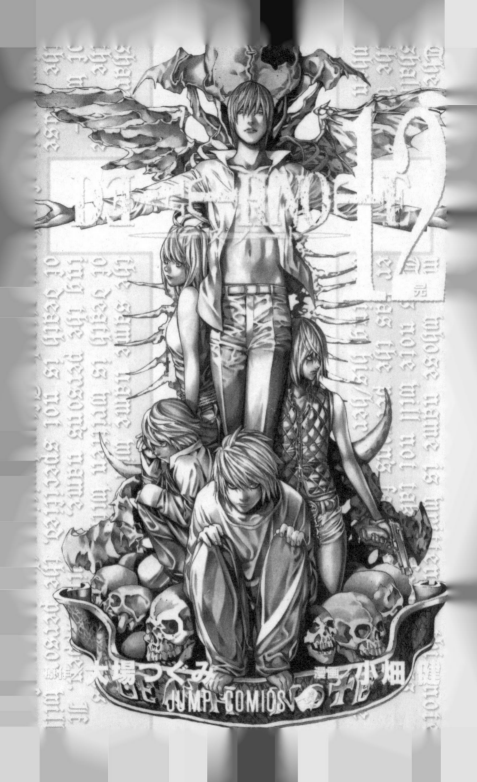